Writings of Nichiren Shōnin

Authors of *Nichiren Shōnin Zenshū, Volume 2*

Dr. Hōyō Watanabe
Former President, Risshō University

Rev. Gyōkai Sekido
Assistant Professor, Minobu-san College

EDITORIAL ADVISOR

Dr. Hōyō Watanabe
Former President, Risshō University

PROJECT INITIATOR

Rev. Bungyō Yoshida
President, NOPPA

ENGLISH TRANSLATION COMMITTEE

Dr. Kyōtsū Hori
Former Professor, Tokyo Risshō Junior College for Women

Rev. Zenchō Kitagawa
Professor, Risshō University

Rev. Taikyō Yajima
Kōkokuji Temple, Tokyo

Rev. Keiryū Shima
Jikōji Temple, Tokyo

Rev. Chikō Ichikawa
Myōanji Temple, Tokyo

Rev. Ryōkō Mochizuki
Daikyōji Temple, Tokyo

Rev. Hōyū Maruyama
Sempukuji Temple, Kanagawa-ken

Rev. Kenryū Asai
Jōsen'in Temple, Tokyo

Rev. Shinkai Oikawa
Secretary-General, NOPPA

Rev. Gen'ichi Oikawa
Honryūji Temple, Hachiōji-shi, Tokyo

Writings of Nichiren Shōnin
VOLUME TWO

DOCTRINE II

Compiled by Kyōtsū Hori
Edited by George Tanabe, Jr. and Shinkyo Warner

Twenty-three writings of Nichiren
included in the *Nichiren Shōnin Zenshū*
Complete Writings of Nichiren Shōnin
Volume II: Theology II
Tokyo, Shunjū-sha, 1996

Nichiren Shu Overseas Propagation Promotion Association
7–12–5 Nishishinjuku, Shinjuku-ku, Tokyo, Japan

Nichiren Shu

© Copyright 2002, 2021
Nichiren Shu Overseas Propagation Promotion Association.
All rights reserved.
Printed in the United States of America.

ISBN 978-1-7369557-0-3

Art Direction and Design by Alan Rowe

Contents

Compiler's Note	*vii*
1. Jisshō-shō (ST 81) A Treatise on the Ten Chapters of the Great Concentration and Insight	*1*
2. Teradomari Gosho (ST 92) A Letter from Teradomari	*7*
3. Hasshū Imoku-shō (ST 96) A Treatise on the Differences between the Lotus Sect and Eight Other Sects	*14*
4. Kaimoku-shō (ST 98) Open Your Eyes to the Lotus Teaching	*28*
5. Toki-dono Gohenji (ST 101) A Response to Lord Toki	*116*
6. Shingon Shoshū Imoku (ST 106) The Differences between the Lotus Sect and Other Sects such as the True Word Sect	*118*
7. Kanjin Honzon-shō (ST 118) A Treatise Revealing the Spiritual Contemplation and the Most Venerable One	*124*
8. Kanjin Honzon-shō Soejō (ST 119) The Cover Letter to the Kanjin Honzon-shō	*165*
9. Kembutsu Mirai-ki (ST 125) A Testimony to the Prediction of the Buddha	*167*
10. Toki-dono Gohenji (ST 126) A Response to Lord Toki	*177*
11. Hakii Saburō-dono Gohenji (ST 127) A Response to Lord Hakii Saburō	*179*
12. Shōjō Daijō Fumbetsu-shō (ST 136) The Differences between Hinayana and Mahayana Teachings	*187*

13. **Gochū Shujō Gosho (ST 139)** People in the World Letter	198
14. **Hokke Shuyō-shō (ST 145)** A Treatise on the Essence of the Lotus Sutra	201
15. **Risshō Kanjō (ST 158)** A Treatise on Establishing the Right Way of Meditation	215
16. **Risshō Kanjō Sōjō (ST 165)** The Cover Letter to the Treatise on Establishing the Right Way of Meditation	232
17. **Misawa-shō (ST 275)** A Letter to Lord Misawa of Suruga	236
18. **Shimon Butsujō-gi (ST 277)** Listening to the One Buddha Vehicle Teaching for the First Time	243
19. **Toki Nyūdō-dono Gohenji: Chibyō-shō (ST 294)** A Response to Lay Priest Lord Toki: Treatise on Healing Sickness	249
20. **Honzon Mondō Shō (ST 307)** Questions and Answers on the Honzon	256
21. **Toki Nyūdō-dono Gohenji: Hongon Shukkai-shō (ST 310)** A Response to Lay Priest Lord Toki: Treatise on Overcoming Illusions of the Triple World by Provisional Teachings	272
22. **Shokyō to Hokekyō to Nan'i no Koto (ST 367)** The Difficulty and Ease of Understanding the Lotus Sutra and Other Sutras	278
23. **Sandai Hihō Honjō-ji (ST 403)** The Transmission of the Three Great Secret Dharmas	283
Glossary	289
Japanese Equivalents	366

Compiler's Note

This volume, the ninth project of the English Translation Committee of the Nichiren Shu Overseas Propagation Promotion Association (NOPPA), constitutes all 23 writings of Nichiren Shōnin included in the *Nichiren Shōnin Zenshū, Complete Writings of Nichiren Shonin, Volume II: Theology II* (Tokyo, Shunjū-sha, 1996). The *Nichiren Shōnin Zenshū*, consisting of seven volumes, is a modern Japanese version of Nichiren's original writings, translated and edited, often with annotations, by modern scholars of Nichiren Buddhism. In this volume, where the translators chose to highlight these annotations, they are enclosed in brackets.

Despite its all-inclusive title, the *Zenshū* is highly selective in that it includes only writings considered in the light of modern scholarship to be bibliographically authentic: those verified by original manuscripts.

Among the printed texts, those included in the four volumes of the *Shōwa Teihon Nichiren Shōnin Ibun*, edited by Risshō Daigaku Nichiren Kyōgaku Kenkyū-jo. (Minobu-machi, Minobu Kuonji, 1952-59), abbreviated as ST, are considered most authoritative, and they provide the basic texts for the present work. In this collection of documents (ST), each writing is referred to by the title. However, occasionally two or more documents have exactly the same title (as are ST 101 and 126, and 294 and 310), making it necessary for us to use the document numbers to identify them.

The translators for this volume are either ministers or novice ministers of the Nichiren Order of Buddhism, Nichiren Shu, stationed either in Japan or abroad. Their names and the documents they translated are as follows:

Rev. Chishō Hirai: *Jisshō-shō (ST 81), A Treatise on the Ten Chapters of the Great Concentration and Insight; Toki-dono Gohenji (ST 101), A Response to Lord Toki;* and *Shingon Shoshū Imoku (ST 106), The Differences between the Lotus Sect and Other Sects such as the True Word Sect.*

Rev. Taikyō Yajima: *Teradomari Gosho (ST 92), A Letter from Teradomari;* and *Hasshū Imoku-shō (ST 96), A Treatise on the Differences between the Lotus Sect and Eight Other Sects.*

Dr. Kyōtsū Hori: *Kaimoku-shō (ST 98), Open Your Eyes to the Lotus Teaching; Kanjin Honzon-shō (ST 118), A Treatise Revealing the Spiritual Contemplation and the Most Venerable One; Kanjin Honzon-shō Soejō (ST 119), The Cover Letter to the Kanjin Honzon-shō; Kembutsu Mirai-ki (ST 125), A Testimony to the Prediction of the Buddha; Toki Nyūdō-dono Gohenji: Chibyō-shō (ST 294), A Response to Lay Priest Lord Toki: Treatise on Healing Sickness; Shokyō to Hokekyō to Nan'i no Koto (ST 367), The Difficulty and Ease of Understanding the Lotus Sutra and Other Sutras;* and *Sandai Hihō Honjō-ji (ST 403), The Transmission of the Three Great Secret Dharmas.*

Rev. Gakugyō Matsumoto: *Toki-dono Gohenji (ST 126), A Response to Lord Toki;* and *Gochū Shujō Gosho (ST 139), People in the World Letter.*

Rev. Eiyu Yoshiki: *Hakii Saburō-dono Gohenji (ST 127), A Response to Lord Hakii Saburō.*

Rev. Shōkai Kanai: *Shōjō Daijō Fumbetsu-shō (ST 136), The Differences Between Hinayana and Mahayana Teachings.*

Rev. Ryūken Akahoshi: *Hokke Shuyō-shō (ST 145), A Treatise on the Essence of the Lotus Sutra.*

Rev. Daiei Matsui: *Risshō Kanjō (ST 158), A Treatise on Establishing the Right Way of Meditation;* and *Risshō Kanjō Sōjō (ST 165), The Cover Letter to the Treatise on Establishing the Right Way of Meditation.*

Rev. Eisei Ikenaga: *Misawa-shō (ST 275), A Letter to Lord Misawa of Suruga; Shimon Butsujō-gi (ST 277), Listening to the One Buddha Vehicle Teaching for the First Time;* and *Toki Nyūdō-dono Gohenji: Hongon Shukkai-shō (ST 310), A Response to Lay Priest Lord Toki: Treatise on Overcoming Illusions of the Triple World by Provisional Teachings.*

Revs. Ryūshō Matsuda and Michael McCormick: *Honzon Mondō-shō (ST 307), Questions and Answers on the Honzon.*

Of those by Dr. Kyōtsū Hori, *Kaimoku-shō, Kanjin Honzon-shō, Kanjin Honzon-shō Soejō* and *Kembutsu Mirai-ki* had previously been translated and published by NOPPA, but they were extensively rewritten to conform to the interpretation of authors modern Japanese text in the *Zenshū*.

To provide a degree of uniformity in translation among different translators, the English Translation Committee of NOPPA made the following "Guidelines" for translators to follow:

(1) Translate more or less freely rather than word-by-word, making it easy for laymen to read.

(2) In transliterating foreign terms, the pronunciations of the language of its origin be used — those from Japan in Japanese pronunciation, those from China in Chinese pronunciation using the Wade-Giles System, and those from India in Sanskrit. Foreign terms not found in a collegiate dictionary are to be italicized and accompanied by macrons.

(3) Titles of sutras and names of Buddhas, bodhisattvas, etc. be translated into English as much as possible except those widely used.
(4) Footnotes be kept at a minimum.
(5) Mark words and phrases found in the glossary with asterisks.
(6) The introductory remarks for each writing be placed in front of each writing.
(7) Book titles, including titles of sutras be italicized.

We are grateful to have the help of Dr. George Tanabe, Chairman of the Department of Religion of the University of Hawaii, in editing and improving the English translation prepared by largely non-native translators. Finally but not least we are thankful to NOPPA members for continuing to support our project. We hope that this book will be helpful to those interested in Nichiren Buddhism.

> With *gasshō*,
> Kyōtsū Hori, compiler
> April 2001

Jisshō-shō (ST 81)

Introduction

This is believed to have been written in Kamakura in the fifth month of the eighth year in the Bun'ei Era (1271). The original manuscript is kept at the Nakayama Hokekyōji Temple in Chiba Prefecture. This is a letter to Nichiren's disciple Sammibō, who was then studying on Mt. Hiei. It is divided into two sections: the first section about the *Great Concentration and Insight*, and the second section about a lawsuit.

In the first section, Nichiren talks about T'ien-t'ai's main purpose for writing the *Great Concentration and Insight*, its organization, and the correct attitude towards the *Lotus Sutra*. It also discusses the doctrine of "3,000 existences contained in one thought," the relationships between the essential and theoretical sections of the *Lotus Sutra*, the *Odaimoku*, title of the sutra, and criticizes the *nembutsu* practice of the Tendai (T'ien-t'ai) and Shingon (True Word) schools. Interpreting the *Great Concentration and Insight* from the essential section of the *Lotus Sutra*, Nichiren points out several mistakes of the Tendai scholars and tells Sammibō to return soon after his study. As stated in another of his letters to Sammibō, *Hōmon Mōsarubekiyō no Koto*, Nichiren expresses his concern about Sammibō, who sometimes appeared to be overconfident of himself, and urged him not to lose sight of the true faith.

In the second section, Nichiren talks about a lawsuit. Although it seems difficult to solve the problem soon, he says, he does not care how long it would take because he knows that he is right.

A Treatise on the Ten Chapters of the Great Concentration and Insight

The Kegon (Flower Garland) sect* claims that both the *Flower Garland Sutra** and the *Lotus Sutra** preach the perfect teaching, but that what is preached in the *Flower Garland Sutra* is the main part of the perfect teaching whereas the *Lotus Sutra* is just a branch of it. The Hossō* (Dharma Characteristics) and the Sanron*

1

(Three Treatises) sects both claim the same. The Tendai (T'ien-t'ai) sect* does not need to be established if it agrees with other Buddhist schools in contending that the pre-Lotus* sutras preach the same perfect teaching as the *Lotus Sutra*. For example, they may contend that the *Lotus* and the *Nirvana Sutras** preach the same perfect teaching, but the *Nirvana Sutra* is regarded inferior because it was preached later. If the *Lotus Sutra* and the sutras preached before it were the same perfect teaching, we would have to say that the *Lotus Sutra* is inferior because it was preached later. It cannot be.

In short, their false views arose from misunderstanding such commentaries as the *Profound Meaning of the Lotus Sutra*, fascicle two, which states, "There is no difference in the meaning of wonderfulness *(myō)* of the perfect teaching in the *Lotus Sutra* and in other sutras expounded during the Kegon, Hōdō and Hannya periods of Śākyamuni's lifetime." From the *Words and Phrases of the Lotus Sutra*, fascicle one: "The perfect teaching in those sutras of the Kegon, Hōdō and Hannya periods must also be true." From the *Profound Meaning of the Lotus Sutra*, fascicle 10: "What was attained in the *Flower Garland Sutra* first and in the *Lotus Sutra* later are the same perfect and sudden wisdom of the Buddha." And in the first fascicle of the *Commentary on the Profound Meaning of the Lotus Sutra*: "The first three of the four doctrinal teachings, *piṭaka*, common and distinct teachings, are coarse whereas the last perfect teaching is supreme *(myō)*."

T'ien-t'ai quotes a passage from the *Flower Garland Sutra* in his *Great Concentration and Insight** to support *endon shikan*, the perfect and sudden way of stopping evil thoughts and meditating on the truth: "A mind creates many sorts of things as a skillful painter does. There is no difference between the mind, Buddha and people." The four ways of meditation* taught in the second fascicle of the *Great Concentration and Insight* are mostly the *nembutsu* practices. As it is said, "There is no pure stream from the dirty source of a river." If a man who considers that the perfect teaching of the *Lotus Sutra* and that of the pre-Lotus sutras are the same gives lectures on the *Great Concentration and Insight*, those who listen to him would all be like followers of Pure Land Buddhism.

However, there has been much discussion concerning whether the way of practicing meditation explained in the *Great Concentration and Insight* is based on the theoretical or the essential section of the *Lotus Sutra*. Some say that it is based on the theoretical section while others hold that it is on the essential section. Still others maintain that it is based on both sections. Putting this aside for now, it is stated in the *Annotations on the Great Concentration and Insight* that the book of the *Great Concentration and Insight* explains the way of practicing meditation based on the principle of the *Lotus Sutra* and that the pre-Lotus, provisional sutras are expedient means in preparation for preaching the True Dharma of the *Lotus Sutra*. This means that the whole of the *Great Concentration and Insight* is based on the doctrine of "replacing provisional teachings with the true teaching" of the *Lotus Sutra*. Therefore, although the *Great Concentration and Insight* quotes the pre-Lotus sutras and non-Buddhist writings, it does not accept what is preached in them. It just borrows their sentences without meanings.

The *Annotations on the Great Concentration and Insight* also explains the four ways of meditation: "The object of cognition is based on what is preached in the pre-Lotus sutras like the doctrine of twelve links of cause and effect. However, the wisdom of cognition is based on nothing but the Buddha wisdom of the *Lotus Sutra*." In other words, the true purpose of the *Great Concentration and Insight* is solely for the accomplishment of the way of meditation based on the *Lotus Sutra*, although it preaches the four ways of meditation by quoting from works such as the *Sutra of Mañjuśrī Asking Questions*, the Hōdō sutras, and the *Sutra of Beseeching Avalokiteśvara Bodhisattva for Protection Against Epidemics*. Therefore, it is said: "The *Great Concentration and Insight* seems to include all of the teachings of the Buddha as it quotes from many sources, but its real intention boils down to the *Lotus* and *Nirvana Sutras*."

The *Great Concentration and Insight** in 10 fascicles is divided into 10 chapters: the outline; meaning of the title, *chih-kuan*; appearances of the true entity; all phenomena contained in meditation; perfect and imperfect ways of meditation; expedients, [that is preparatory steps]; right way of meditation; rewards; preaching for others; and entering Nirvana. The first six chapters, from the outline to expedients, in the first four fascicles, restate the gist of the theoretical section of the *Lotus Sutra* as it is stated in the *Great Concentration and Insight* itself, that the first six chapters are the "wonderful understanding" gained through the theoretical section, the first half of the sutra. The seventh chapter, the right way of meditation, is the explanation of the 10 object, 10 stage meditation, which is the main doctrine of this writing that he claimed was established by the "wonderful understanding." This chapter describes the heart of the essential section, the latter half of the *Lotus Sutra*. The doctrine of "3,000 existences contained in one thought"* stems from this chapter.

It is not feasible to explain the true meaning of the doctrine of "3,000 existences contained in one thought" in the theoretical section of the *Lotus Sutra*. Needless to say, it is not mentioned at all in the pre-Lotus sutras. The doctrine stems from the passage describing the 10 aspects* of existence in the paragraph on the "brief replacement of the three vehicles with the one true vehicle," *ryaku kaisan-ken'ichi*, in the second chapter of the theoretical section of the *Lotus Sutra*. Nevertheless, the true meaning of the doctrine is based solely on the essential section of the sutra. The pre-Lotus sutras should be judged according to the meaning of the theoretical section, which in turn should be judged by the meaning of the essential section. Only the essential section of the *Lotus Sutra* can define its meaning as it preaches.

Therefore, there are many ways of practicing the perfect teaching. The *Flower Garland Sutra* preaches that even such acts of counting grains of sand and contemplating a great ocean are all practicing the perfect teaching. How much more so it is to chant the pre-Lotus sutras or invoke the name of Buddhas like the Buddha of Infinite Life.* However appropriate these practices are to their time, they are not the true practice of the perfect teaching. What we should chant all the time as the practice of the perfect teaching is *Namu Myōhō Renge-kyō*,* and what we should keep in mind is the way of meditation based on the truth of "3,000 existences contained in one thought." Only the wise practice both chanting *Namu Myōhō Renge-kyō* and meditating on the truth of "3,000 existences contained in one thought." Lay followers of Japan today should recite only *Namu Myōhō Renge-kyō*.* As the name has the virtue of reaching the body for which it stands, when one chants *Namu Myōhō Renge-kyō*, one will not fail to receive all the merit of the *Lotus Sutra*.

The *Lotus Sutra* has 17 alternate names. All Buddhas in the past, present and future, however, name it *Namu Myōhō Renge-kyō*. Various Buddhas such as Amida, the Buddha of Infinite Life, and Śākyamuni* meditated on the truth of "3,000 existences contained in one thought"* in mind and recited *Namu Myōhō Renge-kyō* by mouth while performing the bodhisattva practices until they became Enlightened Ones.

Those Tendai* and Shingon* monks who chant the *nembutsu* single-mindedly repeat *Namu Amida-butsu* like a hum without realizing that the basic practices for them should be the T'ien-t'ai way of meditation and *Odaimoku* chanting. So lay followers simply came to believe that the *nembutsu* was a practice of the Tendai (T'ien-t'ai) and Shingon (True Word) schools. Also followers of Shan-tao* and Hōnen* claim: "Look! Scholars of Tendai and Shingon Buddhism chant the *nembutsu* because they cannot attain enlightenment through their own teachings. Rather than studying complicated Tendai and Shingon Buddhism and reciting the *Lotus Sutra*, is it not better to chant the *nembutsu* wholeheartedly and gain enlightenment through the *Lotus Sutra* after being reborn in the Pure Land of the Buddha of Infinite Life?" As this idea of Pure Land Buddhism prevails over Japan today, scholars of the Tendai and Shingon schools are abandoned by the laity and their temples also are disappearing all over Japan.

The 96 non-Buddhist schools* in ancient India stemmed from misunderstanding the manner of a monk called Buddha-Wisdom. It is said that robbed by an evil hunter of his robes, Buddha-Wisdom smeared his body with mud and put on tree barks. Brahmans mistook him practicing a way of emancipation from the world of life and death, and they followed his manner, causing the rise of non-Buddhist heretic schools. Similarly, the sin of slandering the True Dharma in Japan arose from a false view that the perfect teaching of the pre-Lotus sutras is the same as that of the *Lotus Sutra*. What a shame!

Non-Buddhist religions in India claimed that this world was eternal, joyful, free and pure. On the contrary, to destroy their superficial views, the Buddha insisted that this world was impermanent, painful, empty and egoless. The Two Vehicles* [two kinds of Buddhists known as *śrāvaka* and *pratyekabuddha*] were stuck to the principle of emptiness preached by the Buddha and could not grasp the idea of eternity in Mahayana Buddhism. The Buddha, therefore, reproached them saying that even the five rebellious sins and evil passions* could be a cause of enlightenment, but that their inflexible belief in emptiness would never lead them to Buddhahood.

The use of the terms "eternity, joy, self and purity" by non-Buddhists in India were wrong in meaning, but they were so good as names that the Buddha used them later to name the four kinds of virtues of Nirvana in Mahayana Buddhism. However, the Buddha hated these terms at first in order to get rid of those non-Buddhist ideas. Even evil is the seed of Buddhahood, and so is virtue. Although the principle of emptiness to which *śrāvaka* and *pratyekabuddha* were stuck was virtuous, not evil at all, the Buddha reproached them in order to break their adherence to it. The *nembutsu* today destroys the *Lotus Sutra* in this country. Therefore, for the sake of the *Lotus Sutra*, the *nembutsu* must be denied and criticized even though it is good and not wrong in meaning. This is because in Buddhism there is a suitable Dharma for each country.

India is divided into many states, some of which believe in Hinayana Buddhism, others in Mahayana Buddhism, and still others in both Hinayana and Mahayana. The same can be said of China.* However, Japan is the country of Mahayana Buddhism alone, especially the *Lotus Sutra*, the teaching of the One Vehicle. She is not the country suitable even for such Mahayana teachings as those of the Flower Garland,* Dharma Characteristics,* and Three Treatises* schools, not to mention three Hinayana schools. The Pure Land* and Zen* schools, which are faddish today, are based on the triple Pure Land sutras and the *Heroic Valor Sutra* belonging to those preached during the Hōdō period.* Therefore, their doctrines are in the same category as the Dharma Characteristics, Three Treatises and Flower Garland schools.

The *nembutsu* chanting, invoking the name of the Buddha of Infinite Life, was the practice called for in the pre-Lotus sutras* for the purpose of being reborn in the Western Pure Land. However, it does not serve the purpose of the *Lotus Sutra*. Upon preaching the *Lotus Sutra*, it became clear that practices preached in other sutras were all preliminary steps for the practice of the *Lotus Sutra*. The *nembutsu* chanting then becomes a cause of attaining Buddhahood. The practice of chanting *Namu Myōhō Renge-kyō** has nothing to do with the pre-Lotus sutras, and it is related solely to the *Lotus Sutra* preached in the last eight years of the Buddha's lifetime of preaching. It is not the Dharma to be replaced by the *nembutsu*. The *Lotus Sutra* is the Dharma to replace the *nembutsu*. The *nembutsu* is the Dharma to be replaced by the *Lotus Sutra*. Therefore, one who practices the *Lotus Sutra* who believes in the *Lotus Sutra* and recites the *Odaimoku* has all the merit of the Buddha of Infinite Life and all other Buddhas throughout the universe without saying the *nembutsu* even once in his lifetime. It is like a wish-fulfilling gem* equipped with all the treasures such as gold and silver. On the contrary, we cannot have any merit of the *Lotus Sutra* even if we keep on chanting the *nembutsu* all our lives, just as gold and silver cannot produce all treasures like a crystal ball. It is just as we cannot exchange a crystal ball for all the gold and silver in the whole universe [triple-thousand worlds*].

And there is a difference between the provisional and true teachings even if we chant the *nembutsu*, realizing that it is a preliminary step to the *Lotus Sutra*. Practicing the *nembutsu*, a provisional teaching, cannot have merit equal to chanting the *Odaimoku*, the true teaching. Needless to say, very few wise men today practice the *nembutsu* with the understanding that it is a practice leading to the *Lotus Sutra*. Even if there is such a wise man, his disciples and followers would not be able to understand it the same way.

Seeing a wise man saying the *nembutsu*, ignorant people may think simply that he practices the *nembutsu*, not the *Lotus Sutra*.* However, if there is a man who recites *Namu Myōhō Renge-kyō*, everybody, no matter how stupid he is, thinks that such a man practices the *Lotus Sutra*.

Today, there are people more dreadful than those who kill their parents or rise in rebellion. They are those who are reputed as scholars of Tendai* and Shingon* Buddhism but recite the *Hymns of Praise Concerning Rebirth in the Pure Land* by Shan-tao, and chant the *nembutsu* advocated by Hōnen.

When the class for reading the *Great Concentration and Insight* is over, let its participants know about the content of this essay and then you should come back to Kamakura. You must come back right after the class.

Regarding the lawsuit, I suppose that it is difficult to reach the conclusion when my case is strong. It seems even more difficult to be finalized when people, who criticize our doctrine, all speak well of this lawsuit. I heard that Hei no Saemon Yoritsuna* had taken over the case from Lord Hōjō Naritoki. Remember that the longer it takes, the more advantageous will it be for us. At any rate it will be resolved someday. If it is not, people will think that I am right, so I am happy if it takes longer.

Recently, many people of the Tendai-Shingon schools have been in Kamakura. I shall stop writing here as various things keep me busy.

Teradomari Gosho (ST 92)

Introduction

This letter of Nichiren, written on the 22nd day of the 10th month in the eighth year of the Bun'ei Era (1271) at Teradomari, is addressed to Toki Jōnin of Shimōsa, about 30 kilometers east of the present city of Tokyo.

The original manuscript is preserved in the Shōgyōden Tower (Treasure House) at the Nakayama Hokekyōji Temple. Nichiren, who was arrested on the 12th day of the ninth month in Kamakura by the officials of the shogunal government and was sentenced to be exiled to Sado Island in the Sea of Japan, was about to be executed secretly at Tatsunokuchi Beach.

Narrowly escaping death, however, Nichiren was then sent to Sado Island for the exile to which he was originally sentenced. After leaving Tatsunokuchi he was kept about a month at Echi, a town to the north of Kamakura. Leaving Echi on the 10th day of the 10th month, he arrived 11 days later at Teradomari, Echigo Province (present-day Niigata Prefecture). He stayed there for about six days, waiting for favorable weather to sail for the island. In the meantime he wrote this letter just before setting out to cross the Sea of Japan.

Toki Jōnin, one of the most trusted devotees of Nichiren, was converted in Nichiren's early days of propagation. When Jōnin heard of Nichiren's exile to Sado, he seemed to have sent a *nyūdō*, a lay priest, to accompany Nichiren to Sado Island.

Cordially declining the offer, Nichiren sent the lay priest back and wrote this letter, in which he expressed his appreciation of Jōnin's kindness and stated his religious belief as well as the teachings of the *Lotus Sutra*.

In the beginning he describes the route from Echi to Teradomari, declaring that according to the *Lotus Sutra* those who spread the *Lotus Sutra* after the demise of the Buddha are bound to be persecuted and that therefore, it is nothing but proof of one's real practice of the *Lotus Sutra* for one to be persecuted.

Furthermore, refuting false views of various masters and sects, Nichiren expresses his firm belief that no one else but Nichiren is the one who practices the *Lotus Sutra* in the Latter Age of Degeneration and that he is "a deputy of the 800 thousands, millions, and *nayuta* of Bodhisattvas."

Lastly, he expressed his deep gratitude to Toki Jōnin for sending a *nyūdō* to accompany him all the way. He also expressed his words of concern over his disciples imprisoned in Kamakura while paying no attention to the danger to his own life.

A Letter from Teradomari

On the 10th day of this month, the 10th month in the eighth year of Bun'ei (1271), we left Homma Rokurōzaemon Shigetsura's residence, located in the village of Echi, Aikyō-gun, Sagami Province, and arrived at the post town of Kumegawa (present-day Higashi-murayamashi, Tokyo). Then traveling for twelve days, we reached the port of Teradomari, Echigo Province. We are to cross over the great Sea of Japan to get to Sado Island, but we do not know when we shall be able to leave because we do not have a favorable wind for sailing. While traveling from Echi to Teradomari, I had neither time to think about nor ability to describe the hardships of the journey. I have to ask you to imagine it. As I anticipated all these difficulties, I should stop writing about them and not lament .

In fascicle four, the 10th chapter of the *Lotus Sutra*,* The Teacher of the Dharma, it is said, "Many people hate the *Lotus Sutra* with jealousy even in My lifetime. Needless to say, more people will do so after My extinction." In fascicle five of the same sutra, the 14th chapter, Peaceful Practices, declares, "Many people in the world will hate it and few will believe it."

In its 38th fascicle, the *Nirvana Sutra** states: "At that time, all heretics there presented themselves in front of King Ajātaśatru proclaiming, 'Great King, there is the worst man in this world, who is Śākyamuni. Evil people in the world all come together to join his group for the sake of his own selfish gain, doing nothing better. Śākyamuni, with his magical power of words and spells, has converted Kāśyapa* (Kashō), Śāriputra* (Sharihotsu), Maudgalyāyana* (Mokkenren) and others to be his disciples.' "

This passage of the *Nirvana Sutra* is what non-Buddhist heretics all uttered when they spoke ill of the Buddha to the king because the Buddha thoroughly refuted their basic scriptures such as the Four Vedas preached by their principal teachers: two heavenly beings and three hermits.*

The term "hatred" in the *Lotus Sutra* does not mean considering the Buddha as an enemy by non-Buddhists as stated in the *Nirvana Sutra*. It means that "hatred" of the *Lotus Sutra* is found among devoted Buddhists and disciples of the Buddha. Grand Master Miao-lê defines in his *Annotations on the Words and Phrases of the Lotus Sutra, Fa-hua Wên-chü-chi*, that all the *śrāvaka* and *pratyekabuddha** who attached themselves to Hinayana enlightenment, and bodhisattvas* who believe in the Buddha's attaining enlightenment in this world, without believing in the eternal life of the Buddha, are those who hate the *Lotus Sutra*. He also declares that those who do not want to listen to, believe or accept the *Lotus Sutra* are "haters" of the *Lotus Sutra* even if they do not slander it publicly.

As I contemplate the state of affairs today after the death of the Buddha, compared to that during His lifetime, scholars of various sects today are all like heretics during the days of the Buddha. They called the Buddha the worst, and today this fits me, Nichiren. "Evil people in the world all coming together to join His group" fits Nichiren's disciples. Misunderstanding the teachings expounded by the past Buddhas in previous lives, heretics harbored evil thoughts, hated and persecuted Śākyamuni Buddha in this world. Scholars of various Buddhist sects today are acting similarly to those heretics in the past. In a word, they misunderstand what the Buddha preached and this misunderstanding leads them to hold wicked ideas. It is like a dizzy man seeing a great mountain turning around.

Eight or 10 Buddhist sects exist side by side in Japan today. Their disputes are continuous. The *Nirvana Sutra*, fascicle 18, preaches a simile of "atoning for life with a priceless treasure." Grand Master T'ien-t'ai* explains this simile: "Life refers to the *Lotus Sutra*. The treasure which atones for life means the first three of the Four Teachings: *tripiṭaka (zō)*, common *(tsū)*, distinct *(betsu)*, and perfect *(en)* teachings as preached in the *Nirvana Sutra*." Regarding the perfect *(en)* teaching referred to in the *Nirvana Sutra*, it is the restatement of the "permanent existence of Buddha-nature"* doctrine expounded in the *Lotus Sutra* in order to clarify the truth of the *Lotus Sutra* and to store it in the *Lotus Sutra*. When the doctrine of "permanent existence of Buddha-nature," the perfect teaching of the *Nirvana Sutra*, was returned to the *Lotus Sutra*, what is left in the *Nirvana Sutra* is limited to the first three of the Four Teachings.

In the third fascicle of the *Profound Meaning of the Lotus Sutra,* Fa-hua Hsüan-i*, by T'ien-t'ai, it is said, "The *Nirvana Sutra* is the priceless treasure to atone for the life of the *Lotus Sutra*. It is just a clap of hands to express its agreement in order to save the life of the *Lotus Sutra*." In *A Commentary on the Profound Meaning of the Lotus Sutra, Fa-hua Hsüan-i Shih-chien,** fascicle three, Grand Master Miao-lê states on this point, "To the followers of T'ien-t'ai the simile of atoning for life with priceless treasure means that the *Nirvana Sutra* is the priceless treasure and the *Lotus Sutra* is the life." Grand Master T'ien-t'ai declares in his *Four Types of Meditation, Ssu-nien-ch'u*, that as the *Lotus Sutra*, Chapter Two, affirms its use of expedient means to be for the purpose of inducing people into the teaching of the *Lotus Sutra*, various sutras expounded before the *Lotus Sutra*, sutras with the first four of the Five Flavors [preached in the Kegon, Agon, Hōdō, and Hannya periods], are the priceless treasure to atone for the life of the *Lotus Sutra*. If so, various sutras preached both before and after the *Lotus Sutra* are all the treasure for atonement of the life of the *Lotus Sutra*.

Scholars of other sects contradict this, claiming that such an idea is limited to the Tendai sect alone and is unacceptable to other sects.

I, Nichiren, believe that since eight or 10 sects of Buddhism were all established by respective founders after the Buddha's extinction, we should not dispute the content of the sutras expounded by the Buddha from the viewpoint based on the principle of the sects founded after the death of the Buddha. What Grand Master T'ien-t'ai insisted concerning the comparative superiority of Buddhist scriptures agrees with the true intent of all the scriptures of Buddhism* and is universal. It must not be rejected as a sectarian view of the Tendai sect alone. Adhering to the false views of their respective founders, sectarian scholars today maintain that the ability of the people to understand is immature or that what was preached by the predecessors of these scholars is correct. Catering to the whim of a smart king, they in the end came to harbor evil designs, start fights and indulge in watching innocent people being persecuted or exiled.

Among the various sects, the Shingon sect is especially slanted in view. Śubhākarasiṃha* and Vajrabodhi* believed that "3,000 existences contained in one thought" was the supreme doctrine of T'ien-t'ai and was the most important of all doctrines preached by Śākyamuni during His lifetime. However, putting aside for awhile this "3,000 existences contained in one thought" doctrine, which seems to be the essence of both the exoteric and esoteric teachings, Śubhākarasiṃha and Vajrabodhi insisted that besides the "3,000 existences contained in one thought" doctrine, the finger signs,* that is *mudrā,* and mantra were the most important in Buddhism.

Shingon scholars thereafter slighted sutras without *mudrā* and mantra to be as coarse as non-Buddhist scriptures, based on the authority of Śubhākarasiṃha and Vajrabodhi. Some of them insisted that the *Great Sun Buddha Sutra** was not expounded by Śākyamuni Buddha but by the Dharma-bodied Great Sun Buddha. Others said that the *Great Sun Buddha Sutra* was the prime sutra expounded by Śākyamuni Buddha. Still others maintained that the Great Sun Buddha* sometimes appeared as Śākyamuni Buddha preaching exoteric sutras with neither *mudrā* nor mantra, but at other times appeared as the Great Sun Buddha and preached the esoteric sutras with both *mudrā* and mantra.

Thus they keep on embracing numerous wrong views without holding to the proper reason of Buddhism. It is like a person who does not know the color of milk trying in vain to find the correct color by guessing various colors. It also resembles the parable of a blind man trying to tell what an elephant is like. Shingon masters should know this: if Shingon sutras such as the *Great Sun Buddha Sutra* were preached before the *Lotus Sutra,* they are equal to the *Flower Garland Sutra.* And if they are preached after the *Lotus Sutra,* they are equal to the *Nirvana Sutra*. Anyway they should know that they cannot compete with the *Lotus Sutra*.

It is conceivable that the original text of the *Lotus Sutra* in India contained finger signs, that is *mudrā*, and mantra, that is *dhāraṇī*, which were omitted by translators. It could be that Kumārajīva's* translation without them was named the *Lotus Sutra* while Śubhākarasiṃha's translation including them was named the *Great Sun Buddha Sutra.* For example, the *Lotus Sutra* itself is known by several names such as *Shō-Hokekyō, Tembon-Hokekyō, Hokke-sammaikyō* and *Satsuun-fundarikyō*.

After the extinction of the Buddha Śākyamuni, those who understood correctly that the *Lotus Sutra* is the most superior of all sutras were Bodhisattva Nāgārjuna in India and Chih-i or Grand Master T'ien-t'ai in China. Those such as Śubhākarasiṃha of the True Word (Shingon) sect, Ch'eng-kuan* of the Flower Garland (Kegon) sect, Chia-hsiang* of the Three Treatises (Sanron) sect and Tz'ŭ-ên* of the Dharma Characteristics (Hossō) sect established respective sects in name, but they submitted to the Tendai sect in heart. Their disciples who do not know this adhere to their respective sects. How can they escape the grave sin of slandering the True Dharma?*

Someone accusingly says that I, Nichiren, established a coarse doctrine high-handedly without considering the capacity of people to understand, and that this has led to my persecutions.

Others say that what is preached in the 13th chapter of the *Lotus Sutra,* Encouragement for Keeping This Sutra,* about those who practice the *Lotus Sutra* encountering difficulties without fail is applicable to bodhisattvas on a high grade. One with a low grade practice like Nichiren, they maintain, ought to practice the tolerant way preached in the 14th chapter of the *Lotus Sutra,* Peaceful Practices, but he fails to follow it.

Still others say that I know the Dharma in principle but they dare not speak out.

Some people say that Nichiren stresses only the theoretical study, neglecting the practice of meditation, and I have been fully aware of their criticisms.

Pien-ch'u, a loyal subject of King Wu in ancient China, had both his legs amputated. In Japan, Wake no Kiyomaro, who blocked Priest Dōkyō's usurpation attempt, was renamed Kegaremaro (Defiled-man) and was about to be executed. Those who laughed at them were all forgotten while Pien-ch'u and Kiyomaro are still remembered by the people. Those who condemn me, Nichiren, will be the same as those who laughed at Pien-ch'u and Kiyomaro.

The 13th chapter of the *Lotus Sutra,* Encouragement for Keeping This Sutra, declares, "Ignorant people will speak ill of us [we who practice the True Dharma] and abuse us." I, Nichiren, have been as utterly despised as mentioned in the sutra. Are not those who slander me the "ignorant people" referred to in the sutra? The same chapter continues, "They [ignorant people] threaten us [we who practice the True Dharma] with swords and sticks." I, Nichiren, have experienced what the sutra preaches with my own body. Why don't you, slanderers and persecutors, understand what the sutra preaches?

It is also said in the same chapter: "They always try to slander us in the midst of the great multitude;" "they speak ill of us to kings, ministers, Brahmans, and householders;" or "they speak ill of us, frown at us, or drive us often out of our monasteries." "Often" here means not a few times. I, Nichiren, was driven out of my dwelling several times and exiled twice.

According to the second chapter of the *Lotus Sutra*, Expedients, Buddhas in the past, present and future are to preach provisional teachings first in order to lead people to the *Lotus Sutra*, which is to be preached last. Accordingly, the order of preaching or the method of propagation are the same among Buddhas. The method of preaching should be thoroughly similar to that of the *Lotus Sutra*. This is why the teaching of the 20th chapter of the *Lotus Sutra*, Never-Despising Bodhisattva,* preached in the days of Powerful Voice King Buddha is expounded by the present Śākyamuni Buddha in the 13th chapter, Encouragement for Keeping This Sutra. Likewise, the teaching of the present Śākyamuni Buddha in the 13th chapter will be preached in the days of future Buddhas as the 20th chapter expounded in the past, Buddhas demonstrating the example of propagating the True Dharma. Never-Despising Bodhisattva,* mentioned in the 20th chapter of the *Lotus Sutra*, gave guidance to devotees as well as slanderers without discrimination. He was sometimes struck with swords and sticks, or pieces of tiles and pebbles were thrown at him. When this chapter, Encouragement for Keeping This Sutra, is preached in the future and respected as the Never-Despising Bodhisattva chapter in the past, Nichiren will be looked up to as the exemplary propagator of the True Dharma: Never-Despising Bodhisattva in the past.

The *Lotus Sutra* consists of 28 chapters in eight fascicles, and I heard that in the original form in India this sutra has as much volume as to cover 40 *ri* of the earth, approximately 156 km. I am sure it has more chapters, too. The sutra with 28 chapters transmitted to China and Japan today is the simplified essence of the original. Each of the first half and second half of the *Lotus Sutra* is divided into three parts: preface, main discourse and epilogue. Putting aside the preface and the main discourse for now, let me say that the epilogue part of the first half of the sutra, the Three Pronouncements* exhorting for the spread of the *Lotus Sutra* in the 11th chapter, Beholding the Stupa of Treasures,* were given to all listeners at the assemblies on Mt. Sacred Eagle* and in the sky above the mountain, where the assembly was moved later. The 13th chapter, Encouragement for Keeping This Sutra, describes the great bodhisattvas gathering in groups of 20,000, 80,000 or 80 trillion in response to the Three Pronouncements, swearing to propagate the sutra after the Buddha's demise. Nichiren's shallow wisdom does not have enough ability to know how they did it in reality. Nevertheless, I am sure that the reference to "in the horrible evil world" in the sutra means today, the beginning of the Latter Age of Degeneration.*

Following the 13th chapter, Encouragement for Keeping This Sutra, which talks about "the horrible evil world," the 14th chapter, Peaceful Practices, speaks of "in the latter days." In the *Shō-Hokekyō*, which was translated from the same original manuscript as the *Lotus Sutra*, "latter days" or "coming latter days" are mentioned, and in the *Tembon Hokekyō*, "in the horrible evil world."

Looking at the present world, we see the three sorts of resentful enemies* of the *Lotus Sutra* in front of our own eyes, but none of the 800 thousands, millions, and *nayuta* of bodhisattvas who made the vow to spread the *Lotus Sutra* in front of the Buddha Śākyamuni can be seen. This is a situation in which we feel something amiss like the ebb tide that does not rise or the waned moon which does not wax. When the water becomes clear and tranquil, the moon naturally reflects upon it. When trees are planted, birds come to live. Nichiren, who preaches on the *Lotus Sutra* in place of the 800 thousands, millions and *nayuta* of bodhisattvas, is under the protective wings of those bodhisattvas.

This lay priest, whom you sent to me, says that he wants to accompany me to Sado Province as you ordered him, but thinking of expenses, his hardship, and many other troubles, I have told him to return. Needless to say, I feel greatly obliged for your thoughtfulness. Please give my best regards to everyone. I only worry about Nichirō and other disciples of mine being imprisoned. If you have a chance, please tell me as soon as possible how they are getting along.

Around six p.m., 22nd day of the 10th month
Nichiren (signature)
To Lord Toki

Hasshū Imoku-shō (ST 96)

Introduction

This treatise is believed to have been written in the ninth year of the Bun'ei Era (1272) although some scholars insist that it was written in the 10th year of the same era. It is a letter addressed to Toki Jōnin, or all disciples of Nichiren Shōnin. It reveals the differences, in the question and answer style, between the Lotus sect and eight other Buddhist schools: Kusha, Jōjitsu, Ritsu, Kegon, Sanron, Hossō, Shingon, and Pure Land (Jōdo), regarding the Most Venerable One *(honzon)* and the "3,000 existences contained in one thought" doctrine.

First, regarding the *honzon*, Nichiren declares that the Buddha possesses the permanent three bodies while all living beings are equipped with three kinds of Buddha-nature inherently, and that other schools or sects have not preached Śākyamuni Buddha possessing the three virtues of the lord, master and parents since the eternal past.

Pointing out that the three schools of Kusha, Jōjitsu and Ritsu uphold the Buddha Śākyamuni with Accommodative Body *(ōjin)* as their honzon, that each of the Kegon, Sanron and Hossō sects worships the Buddha Śākyamuni with three different bodies, and that the *honzon* for the Shingon sect is the Great Sun Buddha and that of the Jōdo sect is the Buddha of Infinite Life, Nichiren Shōnin criticizes them for not respecting the Eternal Buddha Śākyamuni with three bodies in one as their father.

As for the "3,000 existences contained in one thought" doctrine, Nichiren declares that although the Kegon and Shingon sects utilize it in their theologies, the truth of *ichinen sanzen* is not found in the *Flower Garland Sutra*. Only the *Lotus Sutra* clearly preaches the doctrines of *jikkai gogu*, characteristics of each of the 10 realms of beings contained in the other nine realms, and *ichinen sanzen*, 3,000 existences contained in one thought.

Finally, Nichiren proves that practice of *shikan*, introspection into the mind, is in accordance with the *Lotus Sutra* by citing from the *Great Concentration and Insight*, fascicle five, and the *Annotations on the Great Concentration and Insight*, fascicle five. Nichiren's thoughts about contemplation of mind, specifically the

"3,000 existences contained in one thought" doctrine, and the Most Venerable One, *honzon*, expressed in this essay came to bear fruit in his *Kanjin Honzon-shō, A Treatise Revealing the Spiritual Contemplation and the Most Venerable One.*

A Treatise on the Differences between the Lotus Sect and Eight Other Sects

In the ninth fascicle of his *Annotations on the Words and Phrases of the Lotus Sutra** Grand Master Miao-lê declares: "Before the eternal life of the Buddha Śākyamuni was revealed in the Duration of the Life of the Tathāgata chapter, the permanence of the three bodies of the Buddha had not been revealed. When the permanence of the Buddha's lifetime was revealed* in this chapter of the *Lotus Sutra*, the unified threefold body* in both the essential and theoretical sections of this sutra was clarified." In his *Words and Phrases of the Lotus Sutra,** fascicle nine, Grand Master T'ien-t'ai preaches: "The three bodies of the Buddha have always been fused into one throughout the past, present and future lives.* However, this was kept in secrecy and not revealed in the pre-Lotus sutras."

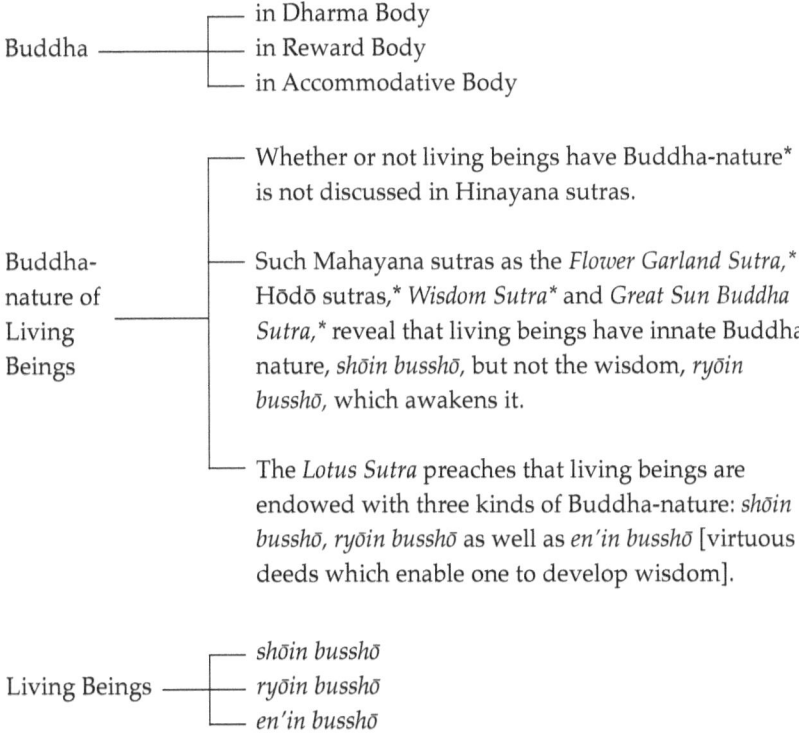

Buddha
— in Dharma Body
— in Reward Body
— in Accommodative Body

Buddha-nature of Living Beings
— Whether or not living beings have Buddha-nature* is not discussed in Hinayana sutras.
— Such Mahayana sutras as the *Flower Garland Sutra,** Hōdō sutras,* *Wisdom Sutra** and *Great Sun Buddha Sutra,** reveal that living beings have innate Buddha-nature, *shōin busshō,* but not the wisdom, *ryōin busshō,* which awakens it.
— The *Lotus Sutra* preaches that living beings are endowed with three kinds of Buddha-nature: *shōin busshō, ryōin busshō* as well as *en'in busshō* [virtuous deeds which enable one to develop wisdom].

Living Beings
— *shōin busshō*
— *ryōin busshō*
— *en'in busshō*

The *Words and Phrases of the Lotus Sutra,** fascicle 10, preaches: "The *shōin busshō* is possessed by the Dharma-bodied Buddha, and it is innately possessed by all people throughout past, present and future lives. By nature they are endowed also with seeds of *en'in busshō* and *ryōin busshō*. These Buddha-natures are not acquired as a result of practicing Buddhism."

Śākyamuni Buddha is quoted to have declared in fascicle two of the *Lotus Sutra*, Chapter Three, A Parable, "This triple world is My domain." This means that the Buddha Śākyamuni has the virtue of being our master, the king and the most respectable in the world. His words, "All living beings therein are My children," means that the Buddha has the virtue of our parent. And "There are many sufferings in this world. Only I can save all living beings" points out His virtue of being our teacher. In the 16th chapter of the *Lotus Sutra*, The Duration of the Life of the Tathāgata, the Buddha is quoted to have declared, "I am the father of the world."

```
┌---- Lord ----- King ----- Buddha in the Reward Body
├---- Teacher ------------- Buddha in the Accommodative Body
└---- Parent -------------- Buddha in the Dharma Body
```

Grand Master Miao-lê declares in his F*ive Hundred Questions and Answers, Wu-pai Wên-lun:* "A man who does not know the long life of his father is like a man who wanders around in the country governed by his father. Such a man cannot be a son of a man no matter how talented he is." And "Even though his talent is as great as that of all the people in the country put together, he is nothing but a fool if he does not know how old his parents are." Precept Master Tao-hsüan (Dōsen) of the Fen-te-ssŭ Temple at Chung-nan-shan in T'ang China mentions in his *Ancient and Modern Disputes between Buddhism and Taoism, Ku-chin Fu-tao Lun-hêng*, "In ancient China, before the time of the Three Emperors [Fu Hsi, Shen Nung and the Yellow Emperor], they had no characters for writing. They knew who their mother was but did not know their father. They acted as if they were birds and beasts." These are words that Priest Hui-yüan (Eon) of Sui China uttered when he admonished Emperor Wu of Northern Chou for persecuting Buddhists.

```
Kusha sect* ─────┐  These three sects solely worship the Buddha
Jōjitsu sect* ───┤  Śākyamuni as the honzon but only with
Ritsu sect* ─────┘  Accommodative Body.
```

Hasshū Imoku-shō (ST 96) 17

Kegon sect* Sanron sect* Hossō sect*	These three sects worship Śākyamuni Buddha as the Most Venerable One* *(honzon)*, but they consider the three bodies of the Buddha to be separate entities: the Dharma Body having no beginning and no ending, the Reward Body having beginning but no ending, and the Accommodative Body having both beginning and ending.
Shingon sect*	This sect solely worships the Great Sun Buddha (Mahāvairocana).* Their Most Venerable One,* however, has two different meanings. The first group holds that the Great Sun Buddha is the Buddha Śākyamuni in the Dharma Body while the second believes that the Great Sun Buddha is not the Dharma-bodied Śākyamuni Buddha but is the Dharma Body of an entirely different Buddha. However, as the *Great Sun Buddha Sutra* states that the Great Sun Buddha stands for the Buddha Śākyamuni, disputes on it are merely the prejudices of scholars.
Pure Land sect*	This sect solely worships the Buddha of Infinite Life* as the *honzon*.

The seven sects of Buddhism such as the Shingon sect, other than the Hokke sect, as well as the Pure Land sect do not know that the Buddha Śākyamuni is their father. They are like those in ancient China before the time of the Three Emperors,* who acted as though they were birds and beasts. No birds, from a *misosazai* to a Chinese phoenix, know their father. Beasts, from lions to rabbits, do not know their father either. Prior to the appearance of the Three Emperors neither great kings nor their subjects knew their father. Among Buddhist schools such as the Shingon sect, other than the Tendai sect, those based on Mahayana teachings are similar to lions or a Chinese phoenix, and those based on Hinayana teachings are like *misosazai* or rabbits. Neither of them are aware that the Buddha Śākyamuni is their true father who provides guidance for them.

Regarding the Kegon doctrines of *jikkai gogu,** mutual possession of the 10 Realms: each of the 10 realms containing characteristics of other nine realms, and *ichinen sanzen*, 3,000 existences contained in one thought,* Ch'eng-kuan* refers to them in his *Commentary on the Flower Garland Sutra*. The Shingon sect, too, claims to have these two doctrines as stated in their *Commentary on the Great Sun Buddha*

Sutra, which is said to have been orally transmitted from Śubhākarasiṃha to Zen Master I-hsing. Is there any difference between theirs and those of the T'ien-t'ai sect? Was there anyone who established these two doctrines before the T'ien-t'ai sect?

The *Annotations on the Words and Phrases of the Lotus Sutra,** fascicle three, states: "Comparing various viewpoints, I see that both One Vehicle and Three Vehicle doctrines state that all living beings are endowed with '10 aspects' such as nature and form referred to in the second chapter of the *Lotus Sutra*. How could they not recognize that even the six realms of illusions are equipped with the 10 aspects?" This leads me to an assumption that those scholars who had appeared during the same 500-year period prior to Grand Master T'ien-t'ai set up the "3,000 existences contained in one thought" doctrine without the basis of the *Lotus Sutra*.

Question: Does the Kegon sect established during the reign of Empress Wu in T'ang China adopt the doctrine of "3,000 existences contained in one thought"?

Answer: A *Commentary on the Flower Garland Sutra* was written by State Master Ch'ing-liang (Ch'eng-kuan), the fourth patriarch of the Kegon sect. The 33rd fascicle states: "Grand Master T'ien-t'ai's *Great Concentration and Insight,** fascicle five, reveals the 10 ways of contemplation for completeness, *Shih-fa Ch'eng-ch'eng*, second of which is the true and pure aspiration for enlightenment. The meaning of aspiration for both upper and lower in the *Flower Garland Sutra* is profound, but it explains the gist of the 10 ways of contemplation for completeness quite well. Grand Master T'ien-t'ai, therefore, cited it for verification." The commentary also says in the 29th fascicle: "The second chapter of the *Lotus Sutra,** Expedients, states that only Buddhas can see all things as they really are. The Tendai sect considers the doctrines of mutual possession of 10 realms,* *jikkai gogu*, and 3,000 existences contained in one thought, *ichinen sanzen*, to be fundamental. So does the Kegon sect."

The *Flower Garland Sutra** was expounded by Bodhisattva Kung-te-lin according to the old translation, by Chüen-lin according to the new translation, and by Bodhisattva Ju-lai-lin according to the *Annotations on the Great Concentration and Insight, Mo-ho Chih-kuan Fu-shing-chuan Hung-chüeh*. This *Flower Garland Sutra* declares: "Our mind produces everything consisting of five aggregates* just as a painter with a brush draws all things. Mind, living beings and the Buddha all work in the same way, and they are in unison and cannot be found separately. If one wants to know about Buddhas in past, present and future lives, one should realize that those Buddhas are in one's mind and that no Buddha is found outside one's mind." The statement of the so-called *ryaku-kaisan ken'ichi*, briefly revealing the One Vehicle teaching replacing the Three Vehicle

Hasshū Imoku-shō (ST 96)

teaching, found in the second chapter of the *Lotus Sutra,* Expedients, reads: "All things have appearances, natures, entities, power, activities, primary causes, environmental causes, effects, rewards and retributions, which are equal despite differences. When these 10 suchnesses* (aspects) are fused into one and are equal, this is the reality of all things."

It is also stated in the same chapter: "Only the Buddhas know the Dharma because Buddhas appear in the world only for one great purpose.* What is their great purpose? They appear in the world in order to cause all living beings to obtain the wisdom of the Buddha, with which He is able to see through everything." The *Lotus Samādhi Sutra, Lien-hua Sammei-ching* or *Renge Sammai-kyō,* says:

> Homage to the Original, Everlasting Myō-hō Renge Buddha residing in our hearts! On the platform of lotus flowers in His mind dwell the 37 honorables of the Diamond Realm, who are innately equipped with the virtue of the three bodies of a Buddha. The King of Mind, the substance of mind, is the All-shining Great Sun Buddha, and various functions of the mind are uncountable Buddhas. This mind inherently possesses the virtue of *samādhi,* which saves all living beings equally, regardless of the quantity of their merit of practicing Buddhism and power obtained by it. Contented with the unlimited expanse of the sea of virtue, one pays respect to one's Buddhas in his mind.

The *Sutra of Buddhist Repository, Fu-tsang-ching,* says: "The Buddha beholds a Buddha sitting in meditation in the mind of each living being."

Question: Does the Shingon sect* adopt the "3,000 existences contained in one thought" doctrine?

Answer: The *Commentary on the Great Sun Buddha Sutra* preached by Śubhākarasiṃha for Vajrabodhi, Pu-k'ung, and I-hsing of T'ang China and written by I-hsing has five versions. Neither Dengyō nor Kōbō saw it in 10 fascicles. It was transmitted later to Japan by Grand Master Chishō. It states:

> This *Great Sun Buddha Sutra* is the secret treasure of the King of the Dharma [Great Sun Buddha] and is seldom shown to base persons. It is like Śākyamuni Buddha who preached the *Sutra of the Lotus Flower of the Wonderful Dharma* summarizing what He had preached in over 40 years after three earnest requests of Śāriputra* and others. The substance of this Great Sun Buddha is the most profound and secret of the *Lotus*

Sutra. Therefore, what is meant by the 16th chapter of the *Lotus Sutra*, The Duration of the Life of the Tathāgata,* when it states: "I, the Buddha, live on Mt. Sacred Eagle* and everywhere.... My Pure Land is indestructible, but people consider it burnt up" must be the same as enlightenment in Shingon Buddhism. Also, as the most profound secret of the *Lotus Sutra* is the substance of the Great Sun Buddha, Śākyamuni Buddha at the earnest request of Bodhisattva Maitreya, His successor, three times decided to reveal the eternal life of the Buddha.

The *Commentary on the Great Sun Buddha Sutra* also states:

> The idea of the *Great Sun Buddha Sutra* includes all the Buddhist doctrines horizontally. Its Jūshin chapter states: "Various things in the world are egoless and consist of five elements in combination according to the rule of cause and effect. Based on this unworldly idea, people dare not seek the Mahayana principle of emptiness." It shows that this sutra is inclusive of all Hinayana sutras, precepts and discourses. It teaches that by contemplating the store-consciousness *(ālaya-vijñana)*, which is the substance of all existence, we see that mind is by nature nonproducing *(fushō)*. That is to say, the *Great Sun Buddha Sutra* is inclusive of such doctrines as eight consciousnesses *(hasshiki)*, three kinds of existence *(sanshō)*, and sentient beings without Buddha-nature *(mushō)*."
>
> The sutra preaches also that there is no self in various things in the world, which comes to existence according to the rule of cause and effect, and that the whole Dharma is perfect and interfused. It means that the various realms of wonder described in such sutras as the *Flower Garland* and *Wisdom* are all put into the Dharma world of the Great Sun Buddha. "One knows oneself as one is" refers to the Buddha's wisdom, in which included are the Nirvana doctrine of Buddha-nature possessed by every living being, One Vehicle doctrine of the *Lotus Sutra* inclusive of all the teachings of the Buddha, and the esoteric store of the *Great Sun Buddha Sutra*. Thus the essences of various sacred words and sutras are all stored in this *Great Sun Buddha Sutra*.

The latter part of the seventh fascicle of the *Commentary on the Great Sun Buddha Sutra*, which both Grand Masters Kōbō* and Dengyō* saw, reads: "It is needless to say that reciting sutras earnestly in the Tendai sect is namely the perfect and sudden way of breathing meditation." This reveals the Tendai doctrine of "3,000 existences contained in one thought, *ichinen sanzen*" being adopted by the Shingon sect.

The biography of Han-kuang in the *Biographies of Eminent Buddhist Masters of Sung China*, fascicle 27, says:

> Shingon Buddhism was transmitted to China during the reigns of Emperor Hsüan-tsung and Tai-tsung. Tai-tsung respected Han-kuang (Gankō) as he respected his teacher, Tripiṭaka Master Pu-k'ung.* By an imperial order Han-kuang went to Mt. Wu-t'ai for training, achieving splendid merit. Just then the sixth patriarch of the Tendai sect, Miao-lê,* who mastered the "Zen meditation for dispelling illusions" conceived by Grand Master T'ien-t'ai, entered the quiet and peaceful Mt. Wu-t'ai together with some 40 monks in the area of the Yangtze and Huai Rivers. Meeting with Han-kuang, Miao-lê inquired about the propagation of Buddhism in the area west of China.
>
> Han-kuang then told Miao-lê that a monk from a certain country who had mastered the Mahayana principle of emptiness *(śunyatā)* asked Grand Master T'ien-t'ai questions about the doctrine. Han-kuang also quoted a monk from India who had told him: "I heard that the doctrine of T'ien-t'ai discriminating between right and wrong, clarifying partial views from the complete view, and revealing the method of *chih-kuan* [contemplation to dispel illusions] is the most meritorious. I hope you will bring works of T'ien-t'ai translated into Sanskrit, if you have a chance to come to India again." The Indian monk repeated his request several times, grasping the hands of Han-kuang, who related the incident to Grand Master Miao-lê.

The reason why incidents such as this happened was that there were many who followed the theory of Nāgārjuna in Southern India and hoped to spread the T'ien-t'ai doctrine, which had transmitted the teaching of Nāgārjuna* correctly. It is stated in the *Meanings of the Aspiration for Buddhahood, P'u-ti Hsin-i*, fascicle three:

> Master I-hsing* was a Zen master who had trained himself in the I-hsing *samādhi* of the Tendai sect. He practiced it so seriously that what he preached tended to be the same as that of T'ien-t'ai in expression and rhetoric. When Han-kuang, disciple of Tripiṭaka Master Pu-k'ung, returned to India, an Indian monk told him, "I heard of the teaching of T'ien-t'ai in China. How about translating and transmitting it into India?" The thinking of Tripiṭaka Master Pu-k'ung is, in some parts, similar to that of T'ien-t'ai. Now a certain Buddhist master is said to have made his disciples all angry when he said, "If one wants to study Shingon Buddhism, in the first place he should study Tendai theology at the same time."

This shows that Shingon Buddhism is also mixed with Tendai theology.

Tripiṭaka teaching (Hinayana Āgama sutras)	Preaches that the six realms of hell, hungry beings, beasts, *asura*, human beings and heavenly beings all stem from the mind without saying that they are innate.
Common teaching (Mahayana Buddhism)	Preaches the same as *tripiṭaka,* teaching that the six realms stem from the mind but does not preach that they are innate in mind.
Distinct teaching	Preaches that the 10 realms are in the mind without saying that they are innate. Therefore the 10 realms it preaches are called the "10 realms in thinking." The "perfect teaching" in the pre-Lotus sutras such as the *Kegon* does not say that the mind is equipped with 10 realms, so their 10 realms are also the "10 realms in thinking."
Perfect teaching	As the "perfect teaching" of the *Lotus Sutra* preaches that each of the 10 realms contains the characteristics of the other nine realms and they are innate in mind, the 10 realms it preaches is called the "ten realms beyond thinking."

Question: Does the *Flower Garland Sutra** speak of the "3,000 existences contained in one thought, ichinen sanzen" doctrine?

Answer: The *Flower Garland Sutra* preaches, "The three: mind, Buddha and living beings, are fused in one...," and the *Great Concentration and Insight, Mo-ho Chih-kuan,** fascicle one, says:

> This one moment of mind consists of the void, impermanence and the middle, which are all related to one another, inseparable in any direction and existing in the same place at the same time. How wonderful it is! Besides, not only a mind is this way but a Buddha and living beings are also

this way. Therefore, it is preached in the *Flower Garland Sutra* that a mind, a Buddha and living beings are one and inseparable. It shows that a mind is equipped with all things.

The *Annotations on the Great Concentration and Insight,** fascicle one, explains this:

> The reason why Grand Master T'ien-t'ai quoted the passage from the *Flower Garland Sutra* is because he intended to verify that the *Lotus Sutra* and the *Flower Garland Sutra* are the same in claiming that a mind, a Buddha and living beings are one and inseparable. For this reason, praising the mind of a bodhisattva in the initial stage, the *Flower Garland Sutra* preaches: "The mind, the Buddha and living beings are one and inseparable. Buddhas know well that everything stems from the mind. If one understands this, one can truly meet the Buddha. A body is not a mind, nor is a mind a body. They are separate entities, but are able to render all sorts of Buddhist functions, which none but a body and a mind have been able to achieve. If one wants to know all the Buddhas in the past, present and future lives, one should contemplate that a mind makes those Buddhas." If not for the "3,000 existences contained in one thought," doctrine of T'ien-t'ai, it would be impossible to make out the meaning of this passage cited from the *Flower Garland Sutra*.

The *Great Concentration and Insight, Mo-ho Chih-kuan,* fascicle five, states: "It is stated in the *Flower Garland Sutra* that just as a talented painter with a paintbrush draws every phenomenon as it really is, a mind produces every thing and phenomenon in existence. The five aggregates* which constitute all existences are matter, perception, conception, volition and consciousness, which are derived from the body and mind of every living being in 10 realms." It also states: "Each of the 10 kinds of five aggregates in 10 realms have 10 Dharmas in them. These 10 Dharmas refer to 10 aspects:* appearances, natures, entities, power, activities, primary causes, environmental causes, effects, rewards and retributions of all things and phenomena, and the ultimate equality of these nine aspects [despite their differences]." It further preaches: "One mind contains 10 Dharma worlds [realms]. Each of the 10 realms contains 10 realms in it, making 100 Dharma worlds to exist. As each of the 10 realms, moreover, contains 30 modes of existence, there are altogether 3,000 modes of existence in 100 Dharma worlds. That is to say, these 3,000 modes of existence are contained in an instance of our thought."

It is stated in the fifth fascicle of the *Annotations on the Great Concentration and Insight:**

Grand Master T'ien-t'ai explained all sorts of ways of contemplation such as *kakui-sammai, kanjin-jikihō, jukyōhō* and *shōshikan,* showing the way of deliberating three-impermanences [Dharma-impermanence, receiving-impermanence and nominal impermanence] by means of individual contemplation. However, he revealed neither the term of "3,000 existences contained in one thought" nor the method of contemplation based on it. In his *Treatise on the Contemplation of Mind,* T'ien-t'ai paid much attention to the four-minds [self, others, cooperation and nothing] through 36 questions, but he did not go so far as to reveal the "3,000 existences contained in one thought" doctrine. He only briefly touched upon 10 realms of contemplation in his *Four Types of Meditation, Ssu-nien-ch'u.* Describing the method of contemplation clearly in fascicle five of the *Great Concentration and Insight,* in the seventh chapter, Right Contemplation, T'ien-t'ai for the first time showed the doctrine of "3,000 existences contained in one thought" as the guiding principle for contemplation.

This fact that Grand Master T'ien-t'ai did not mention even the name of the "3,000 existences contained in one thought" doctrine in his various works tells us that it was the most treasured and ultimate doctrine to him. Therefore it is understandable that Chang-an, who recorded the *Great Concentration and Insight* as T'ien-t'ai preached it, stated in his preface that the teaching of the *Mo-ho Chih-kuan* was nothing but what Grand Master T'ien-t'ai practiced deep in his mind. Those who wish to read and understand the *Great Concentration and Insight* should never think that there are any other secret doctrines of Grand Master T'ien-t'ai.

The *Great Concentration and Insight,** fascicle five, also reads:

> The Ten Modes of Contemplation are a subtle and exquisite synthesis of wisdoms and virtues put together both horizontally and vertically. At the beginning, those who practice can correctly judge the spot, which is the object of contemplation. In the midway, the main and auxiliary practices can work together well. And in the end, those who practice can get rid of all attachments completely.
>
> When one takes the way of these Ten Modes of Contemplation, his intent is refined and his method of contemplation skillfully equipped with all sorts of wisdom, virtue and practice. Beginners in practice can follow his example to proceed into the stage of *shojū* [first stage]. Such monks who practice Zen meditation only without any knowledge of doctrines or those

who busy themselves with doctrines without practicing meditation cannot know this at all.

What the Buddha sought by piling up His merit for a long time, what He attained at the Hall of Enlightenment, what the Buddha expounded in the second chapter of the *Lotus Sutra*, Expedients, after three earnest requests of Śāriputra, and what He preached in three circles [direct, simile, and cause and effect preachings] are all aimed at having all living beings gain the same insight as the Buddha through practicing these Ten Modes of Contemplation.

The *Annotations on the Great Concentration and Insight, Hung-chüeh,** fascicle five, explains this:

> The Buddha's preachings in His lifetime are classified as 16 gates in four teachings:* or eight teachings in five periods. All these are clarified, bundled together and stored in the One Vehicle of the *Lotus Sutra*, and various sutras are preserved in the truth of the *Lotus Sutra*. Therefore the intent of the Ten Modes of Contemplation cannot be grasped even by the lords of sutras preached before the *Lotus Sutra*, much less those Zen masters who practiced only meditation without knowing anything about Buddhism.
>
> The part in the *Mo-ho Chih-kuan* following the phrase "what the Buddha pursued by practicing and training for a long time," praises the tranquility and meditation of the Ten Modes of Contemplation. Since the Ten Modes of Contemplation are the way of attaining enlightenment in the *Lotus Sutra*, it was praised with the words of the *Lotus Sutra*. What the Buddha sought for a long time means, according to the theoretical section, the duration of time since the days of the Daitsūchishō, Great Universal Wisdom Buddha. What He gained at the Hall of Enlightenment* means attaining enlightenment under the pipal tree at Buddhagayā. According to the essential section of the *Lotus Sutra*, it has been innumerable *kalpa* since He practiced the way of bodhisattvas, and His attainment of Buddhahood "500 dust particle *kalpa* ago" [in the inconceivably remote past] is called the enlightenment at the hall of practice. Both the essential and theoretical teachings preach the seeking of the Ten Modes of Contemplation and the enlightenment gained through them.
>
> What Śāriputra begged the Buddha three times to expound refers to what the Buddha intended to preach at the Hall of Enlightenment in Gayā after attaining enlightenment. Since the people's ability to understand was not ripe, the Buddha was afraid that they would both not believe in Him and also rebel against Him, and thus fall into hell. The Buddha, therefore,

for more than 40 years preached expedient teachings to nurture gradually the ability of the people to understand, until at the assembly of the *Lotus Sutra*, He for the first time showed the true teaching that replaced the expedient teachings. The people who had long listened to the provisional teachings* then wondered with doubt, and cordially requested the Buddha three times to expound the most important teaching. At that moment, those five thousand self-conceited monks left the assembly, leaving behind those who were pure and mature. Those who remained were all induced into the one-Buddha teaching without discrimination in teachings, practices, persons, and principles.

This shows the order of preaching adopted by five Buddhas: provisional teachings first, followed by the true teaching. The way of preaching the principle of Dharma directly for people with greater capability is the Preaching by Dharma Circle, and preaching with similes for people with mediocre ability is called the Preaching by Simile Circle, while preaching with cause and effect stories for those with low caliber is the Preaching by Cause and Effect Circle. The Buddha definitely intends to cause living beings to awaken themselves through these Ten Modes of Contemplation. Grand Master T'ien-t'ai therefore, after showing the meditation methods, likens them to the Great White Bullock Cart in the simile of three carts and the burning house. Contemplating this, we may say that what Grand Master T'ien-t'ai wanted to state in his *Great Concentration and Insight* was to establish the perfect and sudden practice, based on the intent of the *Lotus Sutra* to reveal the truth replacing the expedient, in order for us all to attain the Buddha wisdom preached in the *Lotus Sutra*.

However, those who were bewildered went astray in other Buddhist teachings. Ch'eng-kuan of the Flower Garland sect, for instance, misunderstood that the *Flower Garland Sutra* was perfect and sudden in teachings without realizing that the sutra preaches the perfect and One Vehicle teaching mixed with distinct, provisional, and expedient teachings. He lost sight of the intention of the *Lotus Sutra* revealing the true teaching to replace the expedient, and looked down upon the profound and wonderful teaching expounded only in the *Lotus Sutra*. If we understand both the essential and theoretical teachings correctly, thoroughly examining the teachings of the Buddha preached in the five periods of His lifetime, there will be no doubt that the most perfect and sudden teaching is none other than the *Lotus Sutra*. Grand Master T'ien-t'ai, therefore, states in conclusion, "The teaching which the Buddha had long practiced... and preached in three circles is nothing but the Ten Modes of Contemplation" on the perfect and sudden teaching of the *Lotus Sutra*.

The *Annotations on the Great Concentration and Insight* continues:

> Quoting a passage from the *Flower Garland Sutra* in the beginning is to reintroduce the appearance of the world *(kyō)* on which to contemplate. As for the statement in the *Flower Garland Sutra* which says that "Mind produces everything," it is exactly what is meant by "mind is equipped with everything" in the *Great Concentration and Insight*. Therefore, the "Mind produces" passage is cited from the *Flower Garland Sutra* to prove what the "mind is equipped with" passage means. In the *Flower Garland Sutra*, fascicle 18, Bodhisattva Kung-te-lin utters in verse, "Just as a skillful painter draws every phenomenon freely, a mind can produce every kind of phenomenon and existence in the world. Since the mind, the Buddha and living beings are united in one without discrimination, one who wants to know all Buddhas in past, present and future lives should contemplate that one's mind produces every Buddha." Unless one understands the meaning of "3,000 existences contained in one thought" as stated in the *Great Concentration and Insight*, how can one comprehend what is meant by the scriptural statement that there is no discrimination among the three: minds, Buddhas and living beings?
>
> Sincerely,

In considering the superiority between the Tendai-Lotus sect and various other sects, it is recommended that you investigate them with such as this "3,000 existences contained in one thought" doctrine discussed herein.

> On the 18th day of the second month
> Nichiren (signature)

Kaimoku-shō (ST 98)

Introduction

The *Kaimoku-shō* was written in the snow-covered Sammaidō Hall at Tsukahara on Sado Island in the second month of the ninth year of the Bun'ei Period (1272), when Nichiren Shōnin was 50 years old. Commencing the life of a propagator at Kamakura in the fifth year of the Kenchō Period (1253) at the age of 31, Nichiren began encountering successive persecutions in 1260 after he admonished the Kamakura Shogunate in his *Risshō Ankoku-ron, Spreading Peace Throughout the Country by Establishing the True Dharma*. On the 12th day of the ninth month in the eighth year of the Bun'ei Period (1271), he was arrested, ostensibly to be banished to Sado Island. However, late at night he was taken to be beheaded at Tatsunokuchi, a beach outside Kamakura, but narrowly escaped death. Nichiren was then sent to Sado, arriving at the Sammaidō Hall in the 11th month. Immediately he began to write this lengthy treatise in order to tell his followers, as his last will, that the *Lotus Sutra* is the very teaching for the salvation of people in the Latter Age of Degeneration *(mappō)*.

The title of this treatise, *Kaimoku*, meaning eye-opening, signifies its purpose: exhorting people to open their eyes wide to perceive that the *Lotus Sutra* is the teaching for the salvation of those living in the Latter Age as a revelation of the True Dharma. Its purpose is also to show that Nichiren himself is the very teacher predicted in the sutra to appear in the Latter Age to guide the people with the True Dharma, making it the revelation of the true teacher.

Generally speaking, this writing can be divided into three parts. Part I, Prologue (chapters 1-3), stresses the importance of Buddhism, especially the *Lotus Sutra*, as the core of spiritual civilization including Confucianism and non-Buddhist teachings. Part II, Main Discourse (chapters 4-16), maintains that the *Lotus Sutra* is the clear mirror showing and predicting what the evil world in the Latter Age of Degeneration would be and that its prediction has proven to be true through the personal practice of the *Lotus Sutra* by Nichiren and the resulting persecutions that he encountered. Finally in Part III, Epilogue (chapters 17-18), he covers dissemination of the Lotus teaching in the future.

Open Your Eyes to the Lotus Teaching

CHAPTER 1
Confucianism, Non-Buddhist Teachings and Buddhism

A man should respect these three: his ruler, his teacher, and his parents.* Everyone should study these three disciplines: Confucianism, non-Buddhist teachings and Buddhism.

First of all, in Confucianism the Three Emperors* [Fu Hsi, Shen Nung, and the Yellow Emperor], Five Rulers* [Shan-hao, Chuan-hsu, Ti-hung, Yao, and Shun], and the Three Kings* [Yu, T'ang, and Wen or Wu,] of ancient China are called the most respected under heaven. They are regarded as the leaders of the people and the bridge for them to cross the river of illusions. Until the time of the Three Emperors, people were like birds and beasts who had no idea who their fathers were. However, since the time of the Five Rulers, people became aware of who their parents were and acted dutifully toward them. King Shun, for instance, treated his stubborn and ignorant father respectfully despite his father plotting to have him killed in favor of his younger half-brother. Han Kao-tze, the founder of the Former Han dynasty, continued to revere his father even after he became the emperor. King Wu, the founder of the Chou dynasty, had a wooden statue carved of his late father, King Wen, and carried it in battle against the last, evil king of Yin [Shang]. A man called Ting-lan of Later Han in China is said to have had a statue of his late mother made and treated it respectfully as though it were alive. These are examples of filial devotion.

It is said that Pi-kan of the Yin [Shang] dynasty, worrying about the downfall of the dynasty, dared to speak up against King Chieh, who was his nephew, and was beheaded by the king. Returning from a political mission, a man named Hung-yen of Wei found that his ruler, the Duke of I [Yee], had been killed. The northern barbarians had cannibalized the duke leaving only his liver on the road. Hung-yen picked the liver up, cut open his own stomach to insert it, and died. These are examples of loyal subjects.

I-shou was the teacher of Yao, Wu-shih was that of Shun, T'ai-kung-wang was the teacher of King Wen of Chou, and Lao-tzu was that of Confucius. They were called the Four Sages. Even the kings and rulers, who were most respected under heaven, bowed low and all the people respectfully held their hands together in front of them.

These sages wrote some 3,000 scrolls including the *San-fen, Records of the Three Emperors, Wu-tien, Records of the Five Rulers,* and *San-shih, Records of the*

Three Dynasties. Explained in them, however, was nothing more than the "Three Mysteries." The "Three Mysteries" mean, first of all, the "mystery of being" which is the philosophy established by such as the Duke of Chou. The second is the "mystery of non-being," set forth by such sages as Lao-tzu. Finally the "mystery of being and non-being" is the philosophy of Chuang-tzu.

Mystery can mean profundity, but it also can mean darkness. In explaining the origin of life, some of these sages state that life is created from an original substance called *t'ai-chi*, while others maintain that positions in society, happiness and sorrow, right and wrong, or gains and losses, are merely spontaneous. Exquisite though their philosophies may appear, they actually know nothing of life in the past or in the future. As they are in darkness, their philosophies are mysterious. Knowing only the present, they insist that in this present world we have to protect ourselves and maintain peace in our country by establishing benevolence and righteousness to avoid bringing ruin upon our families and our country.

These wise and holy men are sages, but they are ignorant of the past, just as ordinary men* cannot see their backs, and they cannot see into the future just as blind men cannot see in front. They merely maintain that if one manages his house well, performs filial devotions, and practices the Five Virtues [benevolence, righteousness, politeness, wisdom and fidelity] in this world, people will revere him, and his fame will spread so widely in the land that a wise king will invite him to be his minister or teacher, or even put him on the throne. Even heaven will come to defend and serve him! For instance, they say, King Wu of Chou had five elders who served him, and 28 constellations* came to assist Emperor Kuang-wu of the Later Han as his 28 generals.

Ignorant of the past and future, however, these sages cannot help the future lives of their parents, rulers or teachers. Not knowing what they owe to them in the past, they cannot be considered truly holy and wise. This is why Confucius said, "Truly wise and holy men do not exist in China, but in the land to the west, there is a man called Buddha. He is a true sage."

Confucius thus designated Confucianism, which is non-Buddhist *(geten)*,* to be the first step toward Buddhism. It would be easier, Confucius knew, for people to understand the fundamental Buddhist teachings of precepts, meditation, and wisdom if they first learned the fundamental Confucian concepts of rituals and music. He therefore taught the kings' subjects to be loyal to their rulers, children to be devoted to their parents, and students to respect their teachers. Grand Master Miao-lê* therefore declared in his *Annotations on the Great Concentration and Insight:** "The dissemination of Buddhism in China indeed depended on Confucianism. Buddhism found its way by following on the heels of the rituals and music of Confucianism."

Grand Master T'ien-t'ai states in his *Mo-ho Chih-kuan, Great Concentration and Insight:* "The *Konkōmyō-kyō, Sutra of the Golden Splendor* preaches that since all the right teachings in the world are based on this sutra, those who truly know the worldly teachings know the teachings of the Buddha." He also states: "The Buddha sent three sages to convert the people in China." Miao-lê's commentary on this in his *Annotations on the Great Concentration and Insight* is: "According to the *Shōjō Hōgyō-kyō, Practicing the Pure Dharma Sutra,* Bodhisattva Moon Light reincarnated as Yen-hui in China, Bodhisattva Light Purity, as Confucius, and Bodhisattva Kāśyapa, as Lao-tzu."

Next, in non-Buddhist teachings in India *(gedō),** the three-eyed and eight-armed god and goddess, Maheśvara and Viṣṇu, are considered to be the compassionate parents and supreme lords of all the people. The masters named Kapila, Ulūka, and Ṛṣabha, who lived about 800 years before the time of Śākyamuni Buddha, are called the Three Hermits. The teachings of these Three Hermits, 60,000 in number, are entitled the Four Vedas. Thus at the time of Śākyamuni's birth, six powerful non-Buddhist masters who had studied these non-Buddhist scriptures had become teachers of kings all over India. Their branch schools numbered in the 90s.

Each of these schools was divided into many sub-branches. They all took pride in themselves, each claiming to be higher than the top of heaven *(Hisōten)*, and sticking to their own rock-like contentions. Their teachings are incomparably more profound and exquisite than those of the Confucian masters. They see through not only two, three, or seven lives in the past and future but also 80,000 *kalpa*[1] past and future.

Their teachings may be summed up in three categories: (1) Some maintain that all phenomena arise from causes, (2) while others claim that all phenomena are spontaneous without any relationship between cause and effect. (3) Still others insist that such relationship may or may not exist between cause and effect.

Among these non-Buddhist schools, better ones observe the five precepts or 10 precepts, practice preliminary meditation, looking at the Realms of Form *(shikikai)* and non-Form *(mushiki-kai)*, and work their way up gradually like a measuring worm to the summit of heaven *(Hisōten)*. They take it for the world of Nirvana but as soon as they reach their heaven, they all plunge into the Three Evil Realms* [hell, realm of hungry spirits, and that of beasts] at the bottom. None remain in their heaven although they believe that those who reach *Hisōten* remain there forever enjoying complete freedom from the cycle of life and death.

Still they are less objectionable compared to other non-Buddhist schools, which stubbornly insist on following what they inherited from their masters. Some of them bathe in the Ganges River three times a day in the midst of winter, while others pull out hairs, throw themselves against rocks, roast themselves in fire, burn their limbs and heads, or stay naked. They sacrifice a number of horses, burn grass and trees, or worship every tree, hoping to gain happiness. These evil teachings are vast in number, and their teachers are revered as highly as Indra* by the gods and as an emperor by his subjects.

Nevertheless, followers of the 95 non-Buddhist schools (gedō),* whether they are better or worse, are unable to leave the cycle of life and death. Those who follow better masters will fall into evil realms in two or three lives, while those who follow worse masters are bound to fall there in the next life.

Still, the most important thing for non-Buddhist teachings, like Confucianism, is to prepare the way to Buddhism. This is why some non-Buddhists maintain that the Buddha will be born 1,000 years later, while others insist on 100 years later. It is said, therefore, in the *Nirvana Sutra** that what is written in all the non-Buddhist scriptures is nothing but the teaching of the Buddha. Again, it is said in the *Lotus Sutra*,* chapter eight, Assurance of Future Buddhahood, that disciples of the Buddha sometimes pretend to be contaminated with the Three Poisons* of greed, anger, and ignorance or show the heretic view denying the law of cause and effect as an expedient means to save people.

In the third place, Śākyamuni Buddha is the supreme leader and excellent eyes for all the people. He is the bridge that enables them to cross the river of evil passions. He is the captain who guides them over the sea of life and death. And He is the fertile field in which they plant the seed of merits. The so-called Four Sages of Confucianism and Three Hermits of Brahmanism, despite their worthy names, are actually unenlightened ordinary men unable to rid themselves of the Three Delusions [all delusions and evil passions]. Although their names suggest that they are wise, in reality they are as ignorant as infants, who know nothing of the principle of cause and effect. How can we cross the sea of life and death aboard a ship steered by such men? How can we pass through the winding street of the Six Realms[2] over to the world of Nirvana by means of a bridge constructed by such men? Our Śākyamuni has already crossed the sea of life and death for *arhats*, not to mention that for the unenlightened. He has already extinguished fundamental darkness,* not to mention delusions in view and thought arising from it.

Throughout His life, 50 years since attaining enlightenment at the age of 30 to His death at the age of 80, Śākyamuni Buddha preached His holy teachings. Each of His writings and words represents the truth. Not a sentence or line does not ring true. Not even those sages and wise men of Confucianism (geten)* and non-Buddhist teachings in India (gedō)* ever spoke falsely in presenting their thoughts. They spoke the truth. How much more so with Śākyamuni Buddha, who was a man of truth since innumerable *kalpa* in the past?

Therefore what He preached during His life of 50 years is Mahayana* [greater vehicle] as a teaching of salvation when compared to *geten* and *gedō*. From His attainment of Buddhahood until the eve of His entering Nirvana,* He preached only the truth.

Considering the 80,000 teachings preached by the Buddha in various sutras for 50 years, we do see differences among them, such as those between Hinayana* and Mahayana Buddhism, provisional and ultimate sutras, exoteric and esoteric teachings,* gentle and rough expressions, genuine and expedient words or true and false opinions.

The *Lotus Sutra* alone among them represents the true words of our Lord Śākyamuni Buddha and various Buddhas residing in the world throughout the universe in the past, present, and future.

Śākyamuni Buddha declared that, although the scriptures preached during the first 40 years or so* were as numerous as sands of the Ganges River, they did not reveal the truth, which would be explained in the *Lotus Sutra* during the following eight years. At that moment the Buddha of Many Treasures* emerged from the earth and verified it all to be the truth. Then various Buddhas in manifestation *(funjin)** came crowding together from various worlds in the universe verifying it to be true and rejoicing by touching the Brahma Heaven* with their long, wide tongues.* The meaning of these words in the *Lotus Sutra* shines clear: brighter than the sun in the blue sky and the full moon at midnight. Look up and put your faith in it. Prostrate yourself before it and think hard about it.

CHAPTER 2
"3,000 Existences Contained in One Thought," the Cardinal Doctrine of the Lotus Sutra

Twenty important doctrines are in this *Lotus Sutra*. Such sects as Kusha,* Jōjitsu,* Ritsu,* Hossō,* and Sanron* do not know even their names while two sects of Kegon* and Shingon* plagiarized them to build their own fundamental structure. The "3,000 existences contained in one thought" doctrine* is hidden between the lines of the 16th chapter, The Duration of the Life of the Tathāgata,* in the essential *(hommon)* section of the *Lotus Sutra.** Although Nāgārjuna* and Vasubandhu* were aware of it, they did not speak of it. It is only our Grand Master T'ien-t'ai who embraced it.

The teaching of "3,000 existences contained in one thought"* is based on the "mutually-possessed characteristics of the Ten Realms,"*[3] meaning that each of the Ten Realms has the characteristics of the other nine. Ignorant of the Ten Realms, the Hossō* and Sanron* sects established the Eight Realm theology, missing the realm of bodhisattvas and that of Buddhas. How can they know of the mutually-possessed characteristics of the Ten Realms? The Kusha,* Jōjitsu,* and Ritsu* sects, based on the Āgama sutras,* preach only Six Realms, ignoring the top four of the ten. They insist on the existence of the one and only Buddha in the worlds throughout the universe, denying the existence of His manifestations in each of these worlds. It is only natural that they leave out the concept of every living being having Buddha-nature.* They do not recognize the possession of Buddha-nature* by humans. Nevertheless, the Ritsu and Jōjitsu sects today speak of the existence of Buddhas in various worlds throughout the universe or of Buddha-nature in humans. It must have been that scholars after the death of the Buddha plagiarized the Mahayana* doctrines to the advantage of their own schools.

For instance, non-Buddhist teachings in India *(gedō),** before the time of the Buddha, were shallow in theology. After the Buddha, however, they seemed to realize their own shortcomings as they learned from Buddhism and cunningly stole Buddhist concepts to make their own heretical teaching more sophisticated. They are the so-called Buddhists assisting heretics and heretics stealing Buddhism.

The same can be said of those in China *(geten).** Before Buddhism was introduced to China, Confucian and Taoist scholars were as simple and immature as infants. However, in the Later Han dynasty, when Buddhism came to China and gradually spread after initial controversies, some Buddhist monks returned home because they could not keep Buddhist precepts or chose to return to secular life. Some Buddhist monks simply adopted Buddhist teachings into Confucianism and Taoism in collaboration with secular men. Therefore, Grand Master T'ien-t'ai states in his *Mo-ho Chih-kuan, Great Concentration and Insight,*" fascicle five: "Nowadays there are many evil monks who, having abandoned the Buddhist precepts, go back to secular life and, being afraid of punishment, become Taoist teachers. Again contrary to the Taoist teaching, they would seek fame and profit by boastfully talking about Chuang-tzu and Lao-tzu. They would utilize Buddhist concepts in their interpretation of Taoism, forcibly taking the high for the low, crushing the honorable to mix it with the humble, and leveling Buddhism to Taoism."

Grand Master Miao-lê elaborates on this in his *Annotations on the Great Concentration and Insight:**

> Some Buddhist monks destroy Buddhism. Men like Wei Yüan-sung abandon Buddhist precepts, secularize themselves, and wreak havoc upon Buddhism as laymen. They plagiarize Buddhism to bolster Taoism. "Forcibly taking the high for the low" means that these men with the hearts

of Taoist masters forcibly equate Buddhism and Taoism, mixing up the right and evil. With their shallow background in Buddhist ministry, they plagiarize the true teaching of Buddhism to back up the false teaching of Taoism, and forcibly cram the 80,000 teachings of the Buddha in twelve kinds of scriptures into the base teaching of Taoism with 5,000 words in two rolls in order to support their false and base teaching. This is what is meant by "crushing the honorable to mix with the humble."

You had best look at these interpretations by T'ien-t'ai and Miao-lê. They are in agreement with what I stated above.

The same thing was happening within Buddhism itself. Introduced in the Yung-p'ing era of the Later Han period, Buddhism showed supremacy over the evil teaching of Taoism, establishing itself in China. Three Southern and seven Northern masters* of Chinese Buddhism competed with each other for supremacy as though orchids and chrysanthemums bloomed at the same time. They were all refuted, however, by Grand Master T'ien-t'ai* of Ch'en-Sui China, and Buddhism was revived by him for the salvation of all living beings.

CHAPTER 3
Why Should Various Sects Be Criticized?

Afterward the Hossō* and Shingon* sects were transmitted from India and the Kegon sect* was revived in China. The Hossō sect among them was against the T'ien-t'ai sect* in theology, both opposing each other like water and fire. Although the Tripiṭaka Master Hsüan-chuang* and his disciple, Grand Master Tz'ŭ-ên* of the Hossō sect did not go so far as to abandon their own schools, they seem to have surrendered to T'ien-t'ai in heart as they read his interpretations carefully and realized their own fallacies.

Next, the Kegon* and Shingon sects* were originally provisional sects based on provisional sutras.* Tripiṭaka Masters Śubhākarasiṃha (Shan-wu-wei)* and Vajrabodhi (Chin-kang-chih)* stole the "3,000 existences contained in one thought"* concept from T'ien-t'ai and used it as the basis for their own school. To appear superior to others, they added to it the symbolic finger signs, that is *mudrā*, and mantra.* Those scholars who do not know this believe that the *Great Sun Buddha Sutra** had the "3,000 existences contained in one thought" doctrine from its beginning in India. At the time of Ch'eng-kuan,* the Kegon sect stole the doctrine and read it into the words of the *Flower Garland Sutra* asserting, "Mind is like a skillful painter." People do not realize this.

The six sects of Nara such as Kegon were brought over to Japan before the Tendai and Shingon sects. The Kegon, Sanron, and Hossō sects continued to disagree like water and fire. Then, Grand Master Dengyō* appeared in Japan and not only refuted the fallacies of the six sects in the southern capital* of Nara but also decisively proved that the Shingon sect had stolen the T'ien-t'ai interpretation of the *Lotus Sutra** in order to establish its own foundation.

Grand Master Dengyō cast aside opinions of various teachers in various sects and based his argument solely on Buddhist scriptures. He thus won debates against high priests of the six sects, eight, 12, 14, and some 300 in number, including Grand Master Kōbō.* Everyone in Japan without exception surrendered to the Tendai sect, as temples in Nara, the Tōji Temple* in Kyoto, and all the temples in the entire land of Japan came under the spell of Mt. Hiei. It also became clear that founders of various Buddhist sects in China had surrendered to T'ien-t'ai, which made it possible for them to escape the charge of slandering the True Dharma.*

Afterwards, as the world degenerated and the understanding of the people deteriorated, the fine theology of T'ien-t'ai was no longer studied. As other sects grew stronger in devotion, the Tendai sect* was reduced gradually by the six sects of Nara and Shingon until it was no longer equal even to them. It was further reduced by the unworthy Zen* and Pure Land* sects with lay members moving over to those false sects. The movement was gradual at first, but in the end even revered high priests all left Tendai to strengthen those sects of Zen and Pure Land. Meanwhile, the farms and fiefs of the six Nara sects as well as those of the Tendai and Shingon sects were all destroyed and the True Dharma of the *Lotus* disappeared. Not having tasted the delicacy of the True Dharma, such great righteous guardian deities as Goddess Amaterasu, Shōhachiman and Sannō left the land, leaving room for demons to grow in power, and this country about to crumble.

CHAPTER 4
Obtaining Buddhahood by the Two Vehicles

Now in my humble opinion, there are many differences between those scriptures preached by the Buddha during the first 40 years or so* and the *Lotus Sutra*, which was preached during the last eight years. However, what scholars consider to be most important, with which I certainly agree, are the concepts of "Obtaining Buddhahood by the Two Vehicles *(nijō sabutsu)*"* and "Attaining Enlightenment in the Eternal Past *(kuon jitsujō)*."*

First, as for *nijō sabutsu*, it is revealed in the *Lotus Sutra** that Śāriputra* is the future Flower Light Buddha [in Chapter Three] while Kāśyapa* will be Light Buddha in the future; Subhūti,* Beautiful Form Buddha; Kātyāyana,* Jāmbūnada Golden Light Buddha; Maudgalyāyana,* Tamālapattracandana

Fragrance Buddha [Chapter Six]; Pūrṇa,* Dharma Brightness Buddha [Chapter Eight]; Ānanda,* Mountain Sea Wisdom Buddha; Rāhula,* Stepping On Flowers of Seven Treasures Buddha; two groups of *arhats,* 500 and 700 in number respectively, Universal Brightness Buddhas; 2,000 of those who have obtained the stage of *arhats* and those who have not, Treasure Form Buddhas [Chapter Nine]; and female disciples of Mahā Prajāpatī* and Yaśodharā* will be Gladly Seen by All Beings Buddha and Emitting Ten Million Rays of Light Buddha respectively in the future [Chapter 13].

These people of the Two Vehicles appear to be respected as future Buddhas in the *Lotus Sutra,** but are often disappointing in scriptures preached before it, where it is considered that they are unable to ever obtain Buddhahood. The Buddha is a man of true words. That is why He is called a holy or great man. Wise men, sages, or non-Buddhist *(geten* and *gedō)** hermits must have been so named because they were men of true words. The Buddha is called a great man because He is superior to all these people. This great man, the Buddha, declares in the second chapter of the *Lotus Sutra,* Expedients: "Buddhas have come to this world for the sole purpose of carrying out one important task." He also declares in the *Muryōgi-kyō, Sutra of Infinite Meaning:* "The true teaching has not been revealed for some 40 years since My enlightenment." It is further stated in the second chapter of the *Lotus Sutra:* "The truth will be revealed at long last, after preaching for a long time," and "He will reveal it by casting aside all expedient means." These words of the Buddha were verified to be true by the Buddha of Many Treasures in the Beholding the Stupa of Treasures chapter of the *Lotus Sutra,* and various Buddhas in manifestation *(funjin)* also stuck out their long and broad tongues confirming the truth of these words in the Supernatural Powers of the Tathāgata chapter of the *Lotus Sutra.* Under the circumstances who could cast doubt on the words in the *Lotus Sutra* assuring that such Hinayana sages of the Two Vehicles such as Śāriputra and Kāśyapa would be the future Flower Light Buddha and Light Buddha?

It is also true, however, that pre-Lotus sutras* are the true words of the Buddha. Among those scriptures

(1) the *Flower Garland Sutra** states: "There are just two places where the Great Medicine King Tree, representing the wisdom of the Buddha, is unable to grow: a large chasm where Hinayana sages of the Two Vehicles *(nijō)** have fallen into believing they have attained the stage of *arhats* and a great body of poisonous water, contaminated with greed and attachment, where those who have destroyed goodness in mind and are unable to listen to Buddhism are drowned."

This means that in the Himalaya Mountains there is a huge tree named the "Limitless Root" or "Great Medicine King Tree." It is the supreme king of all trees in the entire world *(Jambudvīpa),** measuring 168,000 *yojana*[4] in height. All trees and grasses in the whole world have roots in it, bearing flowers and fruits in accordance with the condition of the branches, leaves, flowers and fruits of this giant tree. In this sutra, the giant tree stands for Buddha-nature* while all the trees and grasses represent all the people. However, this giant tree cannot grow in a burning pit and in poisonous water. The state of mind of the people referred to in the Two Vehicles is likened to a burning pit, and the hearts of *icchantika,** those who do not listen to Buddhism, are likened to this poisonous body of water. It means that these two kinds of people will never become Buddhas.

(2) The *Daijik-kyō, Sutra of the Great Assembly,* expresses: "Two categories of people, *śrāvaka** and *pratyekabuddha,** will never be born after death, and therefore they will never be able to repay what they owe to their parents even if they appreciate them. They are like a man who has fallen into a chasm, unable to help himself and others. Having fallen into a pit of liberation from delusions and evil passions, they are unable to help others as well as themselves."

The 3,000 scrolls of Confucian writings *(geten)** can be boiled down to two: filial devotion and loyalty to the ruler. Loyalty also stems from filial devotion. To be filial means to be high. Heaven is high but not at all higher than being filial. To be filial also means to be deep. The earth is deep but not any deeper than being filial.[5] Both sages and wise men also come from filial devotion. How much more should students of Buddhism realize the favors they receive and repay them? Disciples of the Buddha should not fail to feel grateful for the Four Favors [received from parents, people, sovereign, and Buddhism] and repay them.

Moreover, such men of the Two Vehicles* as Śāriputra* and Kāśyapa* kept 250 Buddhist precepts, lived a life of dignity in accordance with 3,000 rules, progressively mastered the three steps of meditation, completely studied the Āgama sutras* and won liberty from all delusions and evil passions in the triple world [the realm of desire, the realm of form, and the formless realm]. They should be examples of people who know the Four Favors and repay them. In spite of all this, the Buddha condemned them for not realizing what they had owed. The reason for this is that it is for the purpose of saving parents that man leaves his parents' house and takes a Buddhist vow, but those men of the Two Vehicles, who free themselves from delusions and evil passions, do not save others. Even if they help others to a certain degree, they are still to be blamed for not repaying what they owe their parents so long as their parents are left wandering on the path with no possibility whatsoever of obtaining Buddhahood.

(3) It is said in the *Yuima Sutra, Vimalakīrti Sutra:**

Vimalakīrti also asked Mañjuśrī:* "What is the seed of Buddhahood?"
Mañjuśrī replied, "All the delusions and evil passions of men are the seed

of Buddhahood. Even those who have committed the Five Rebellious Sins* such as murdering their own parents, and are bound to go to the bottom of hell can have an aspiration for Buddhahood.... Good men! Just as the beautiful and fragrant blue lotus flowers bloom in a muddy field and do not bloom on a dry plateau, the seed of Buddhahood does not germinate in the heart of the Two Vehicles.... Those who have already achieved complete freedom from all cravings and obtained the stage of *arhats* are unable to aspire for Buddhahood and obtain it. It is just like those whose five sensory organs are damaged, and cannot enjoy five desires of form, sound, smell, taste and touch."

This means that even if the Three Poisons of greed, anger, and ignorance become the seed of Buddhahood, even if the Five Rebellious Sins* such as murdering one's father become the seed of Buddhahood, and even if the blue lotus plants would grow on a dry plateau, the men of the Two Vehicles* will never become Buddhas. That is to say, in comparing good deeds by the men of the Two Vehicles with evil acts of the ignorant and ordinary,* although the latter deserve to be Buddhas, the former do not. While Hinayana* sutras chastise the evil and praise the virtuous, this *Vimalakīrti Sutra* slanders the virtuous acts of the men of the Two Vehicles and praises the evil deeds of ordinary men. This sounds like a heretic teaching (*gedō*)* rather than a Buddhist sutra. It needed to be said, however, to stress the impossibility of ever obtaining Buddhahood by the men of the Two Vehicles.

(4) Again it is stated in the *Hōdō-darani-kyō, Sutra of Mahayana Dhāranī*: "Bodhisattva Mañjuśrī* asked Śāriputra,* 'Would you say that dead trees would bloom, rivers would go back to mountains, pieces of a broken rock would become whole, and toasted seeds would ever germinate?' Śāriputra answered, 'No, that would be impossible.' The bodhisattva then retorted, 'If these cannot happen, why do you, a man of the Two Vehicles, feel happy in asking about obtaining Buddhahood in the future?' "

This means that just as dead trees will not bloom, river water will never flow back to the original mountain, broken rocks will never become whole, and toasted seeds will never germinate, the men of the Two Vehicles like Śāriputra will never obtain Buddhahood as their seed of Buddhahood has been burned.

(5) The *Daibon-hannya-kyō, Larger Wisdom Sutra*, expresses: "Those in the realm of heaven, who have not yet aspired to Buddhahood, should do so now. Having reached the realm of *śrāvaka*, they will never have aspiration for Buddhahood. Why will they not? It is because it will present an obstacle for a man of *śrāvaka* to terminate the cycle of life and death."

This means that we should not admire those in the realms of the Two Vehicles because they will never aspire to Buddhahood. We should admire those in heaven because they will.

(6) Again in the *Shuryō-gon-gyō, Heroic Valor Sutra:** "Even those who committed Five Rebellious Sins* will be able to obtain Buddhahood if they aspire to it upon hearing about this Heroic Valor Meditation. Oh, World Honored One, those *arhats* who have gotten rid of all delusions and evil passions are like a broken utensil. They will never deserve this meditation and obtain Buddhahood."

(7) Finally, it is stated again in the *Yuima Sutra, Vimalakīrti Sutra,* "Those who give alms to you, men of the Two Vehicles, cannot sow in a rich field, where seeds of Buddhahood can grow. Those who give offerings to the Two Vehicles will plunge into the Three Evil Realms."*

This means that those men and gods who support such saintly monks as Śāriputra and Kāśyapa will never fail to plunge into the Three Evil Realms of hell, the realm of hungry spirits and that of birds and beasts. With the exception of the Buddha Himself, these saintly monks were considered no less than the eyes for men and gods, and the leaders of all the people. It was therefore hard to understand why it was repeatedly stated before a great crowd of men and gods that those saintly Hinayana men would never obtain Buddhahood. Was the Buddha simply trying to punish His own disciples with death?

In addition, the Buddha cited numerous parables such as "cow's milk and donkey's milk," "ceramics and golden utensils," and "fireflies under the sun" to compare bodhisattvas and men of the Two Vehicles,* harshly condemning the latter. Not in a few words, not for a few days or months or years, and not in a few scriptures, the Buddha relentlessly condemned them for some 40 years,* before the *Lotus Sutra* was preached, in numerous scriptures, and before crowds of great assemblies.

Everyone knows, you and I and heaven and earth, that the Buddha is a man of truth. It is not one or two persons but hundreds, thousands, and tens of thousands of people who know this. Gods, dragons, and *asura* demons in the triple world of illusion [the realm of desire, realm of form and the formless realm] know it. All the people, gods, men of the Two Vehicles* and great bodhisattvas who have gathered together from all over India, four continents of the world, six heavens in the realm of desire, the realm of form, the formless realm and from all the worlds in the universe know this. They all heard the Buddha condemn the men of the Two Vehicles. Upon returning to their own lands, they told everyone what they had heard from Śākyamuni Buddha* in the Sahā World. Therefore, everyone in the entire universe without exception knew that such men of the Two Vehicles as Kāśyapa and Śāriputra would never achieve Buddhahood and that therefore no one should give offerings to them.

Nevertheless, the Buddha suddenly retracted His words and stated in the *Lotus Sutra*, preached in the last eight years, that the men of the Two Vehicles could obtain Buddhahood.* How could a large assembly of men and gods believe this? Not only did they find it hard to believe, they began finding contradictions between the *Lotus* and earlier sutras. As a result His preachings over 50 years were about to be judged false. While they were wondering whether the Buddha had revealed the truth during the first 40 years or so* of His preaching and if a demon from heaven now appearing to be the Buddha preached the *Lotus Sutra* in the last eight years, the Buddha earnestly proceeded to define the times, places and names of those men of the Two Vehicles as future Buddhas. That is to say, the Buddha declared in which lands and when they would attain Buddhahood and what disciples they would have then.

Lord Śākyamuni Buddha* seemed in effect to have contradicted Himself. It was not without reason that non-Buddhist heretics *(gedō)** laughed at Him as a great liar. Accused of contradiction in His own words by the dumbfounded crowd of men and gods, Lord Śākyamuni Buddha tried in vain to dispel their doubts by explaining the contradictions away one way or another. Just when the Buddha was having a difficult time quieting them, the Buddha of Many Treasures* of the Treasure Purity (Hōjō) World to the east emerged from the earth in front of Him aboard the great stupa of seven treasures, 500 *yojana* high and 250 *yojana* wide, and ascended up high in the sky. It was as though the full moon appeared over a mountain range in the midst of a pitch-dark night. From this great stupa of seven treasures, hanging in the sky without touching the earth or sky, sounded the crisp voice of the Buddha of Many Treasures verifying that Śākyamuni Buddha spoke truly. It is declared in the *Lotus Sutra*, Chapter 11, Beholding the Stupa of Treasures:

> Just then resounded the loud voice of the Buddha of Many Treasures in the stupa of treasures praising Śākyamuni Buddha, "Excellent, excellent! You, Śākyamuni Buddha, have preached to this large crowd the *Sutra of the Lotus Flower of the Wonderful Dharma*, representing the great wisdom of the Buddha, who perceives the absolute truth in every phenomenon and who makes no distinction among all living beings. It teaches the way of bodhisattvas, and is recognized and upheld by various Buddhas. You are right. You are correct. What You, Śākyamuni Buddha, have preached is all true."

Then Lord Śākyamuni and His *funjin* Buddhas manifested in various worlds all over the universe also verified the truth of the *Lotus Sutra* as stated in its 21st chapter, The Supernatural Powers of the Tathāgata:

At this point, Śākyamuni Buddha displayed a great supernatural power in the presence of a large crowd, including not only the countless bodhisattvas,* such as Mañjuśrī,* who had long lived in this Sahā World,* but also other human and non-human beings. He stretched out His broad, long tongue* upward until its tip reached the Brahma Heaven and emitted rays of light from all of His pores to shine through the entire universe. All Buddhas sitting on the lion-shaped thrones under the jeweled trees in their respective worlds in the whole universe also stretched out their broad, long tongues and emitted countless rays of light.

"Then Śākyamuni Buddha," says the 22nd chapter of the *Lotus Sutra,* Transmission, "sent back to their home worlds those *funjin* Buddhas who had come from all over the universe, and said to the Buddha of Many Treasures, 'May this stupa of the Buddha of Many Treasures be where it was.' "

When Śākyamuni Buddha* obtained Buddhahood under the bodhi tree and began preaching the *Flower Garland Sutra,* various Buddhas came from all over the universe to comfort Him. In addition, those Buddhas sent great bodhisattvas* to hear Him preach. At the time of preaching the *Hannya-kyō, Wisdom Sutra*,* the broad, long tongue* of Śākyamuni Buddha covered his entire domain consisting of one billion worlds,"⁶ verifying the truth, while 1,000 Buddhas appeared from all directions. When the *Sutra of the Golden Splendor*,* was preached, four Buddhas appeared in four directions. At the time of the *Pure Land Sutra,*,* Buddhas appeared in six directions, each covering their one-billion-world domain with their tongue to testify to its truth. In case of the *Daijik-kyō, Sutra of the Great Assembly,** various Buddhas and bodhisattvas* gathered together in a courtyard called Dai-hōbō.

Considering these testimonies of Buddhas and bodhisattvas in various sutras with those in the *Lotus Sutra,** they are like yellow rocks against gold nuggets, white clouds against white mountains, white pieces of ice against mirrors of silver, and black color against blue color. Even such a clear difference may not be distinguished by those poor-sighted, crooked-eyed, one-eyed, or evil-eyed.

As the *Kegon, Flower Garland Sutra** was preached first, it had no preceding sutras to compare with. The words of the Buddha could not be contradictory. How could there be any serious doubt about the sutra? As for such sutras as the *Daijik-kyō, Sutra of the Great Assembly,** Hannya-kyō, Wisdom Sutra,** Konkōmyō-kyō, Sutra of the Golden Splendor,* and *Pure Land Sutra,** it was for the purpose of chastising men of the Two Vehicles,* who attached themselves to the Hinayana sutras, that the existence of the Pure Land in each of all the worlds in the universe was preached. It was to encourage the ordinary* and bodhisattvas* to aspire to the Pure Land and men of the Two Vehicles to realize what was wrong with themselves.

Because these Mahayana* sutras were a little different from the Hinayana* sutras, such things were mentioned as Buddhas appearing all over the universe, bodhisattvas dispatched from all over the universe, the same Mahayana sutras preached in all the worlds in the universe and Buddhas coming together from all over the universe. It was also said that Śākyamuni Buddha* covered His entire domain of one billion worlds with His huge tongue or the various Buddhas did the same. This must have been just to tear apart what was preached in the Hinayana sutras: the existence of the sole Buddha in the entire universe. The *Lotus Sutra,** which revealed the fundamental differences from other Mahayana sutras preached before and after it, caused *śrāvaka** men such as Śāriputra,* great bodhisattvas, and men and gods to wonder whether it was a devil pretending to be the Buddha who preached the sutra. It was not as serious a matter as that. Nevertheless, those poor-sighted followers of the Kegon,* Hossō,* Sanron,* Shingon,* and Nembutsu (Pure Land) sects saw no difference between their canons and the *Lotus Sutra*. Their eyes must have been poor indeed.

During the lifetime of Śākyamuni Buddha there might have been some who cast aside the sutras preached during the first 40 years or so* of His preaching and sided, though with difficulty, with the *Lotus Sutra*. After His death, however, it must have been very difficult to open, read and put faith in this sutra. For one, while those sutras preached before the *Lotus (nizen)** consist of many words, the *Lotus Sutra* itself consists of just a few words. While the former consist of many sutras, the latter consists of just one. While the former are preachings of many years, the latter is of just eight years. To many, the Buddha is a great liar who cannot be trusted. If they believe in Him at all, they might believe in those sutras preached before the *Lotus Sutra*, never in the *Lotus Sutra* itself. Also it appears today that everyone seems to put faith in the *Lotus Sutra*, but their faith is superficial, not with heart. They willingly put faith in those who do not see any difference between the *Lotus Sutra* on one hand and the *Great Sun Buddha Sutra,** the *Flower Garland Sutra,** or the *Pure Land Sutra** on the other, without believing those who see differences between them. Even if they believe the latter, they do so reluctantly.

Nobody believes me, Nichiren, who is saying that it was Grand Master Dengyō* alone who read the *Lotus Sutra* correctly some 700 years after the introduction of Buddhism to Japan. It is stated, however, in the *Lotus Sutra:* "It is not difficult to grab Mt. Sumeru, the highest peak in the world, and throw it over to any of those numerous Buddha lands, but is difficult to preach this *Lotus Sutra* in this decadent world after the death of the Buddha." My stubborn insistence is matched by the sutra.

It is said in the *Nirvana Sutra*,* an amplification *(rutsū)** of the *Lotus Sutra*: "The slanderers of the True Dharma in the latter age of decay are countless in number just as the soil of all the entire in the universe is immeasurable. Those who keep the True Dharma are few in number just like a bit of soil on a fingernail."* What should we think of this? Please think hard whether or not the people in Japan represent a bit of soil on a fingernail, and Nichiren represents the soil in the entire universe.

Reason wins under the rule of a wise king, and foolishness gets the upper hand under the rule of an unwise sovereign. So remember it is in the world of saintly people that the true teachings of the *Lotus Sutra* are revealed. Regarding this theology concerning whether it is possible for men of the Two Vehicles to become Buddhas, those sutras preached before the *Lotus Sutra* appear more powerful than the theoretical section *(shakumon)* of the *Lotus*. If the former, which insist that it is impossible, win over the latter, which maintains that it is possible that such men of the Two Vehicles* as Śāriputra* will never be able to attain Buddhahood. How regrettable it would be for them!

CHAPTER 5
Attaining Enlightenment in the Eternal Past

In the second place, let us discuss the concept of *kuon jitsujō*, attaining Enlightenment by Śākyamuni Buddha in the eternal past, revealed in the essential section *(hommon)* of the *Lotus Sutra* .

Lord Śākyamuni, grandson of King Siṃhahanu and the first son of King Śuddhodana, was born during the ninth small *kalpa* within the Kalpa of Continuance, when the human life span was gradually decreasing to 100 years.[7] As a child He was called Prince Siddhārtha, namely Bodhisattva Goal Achieved. Śākyamuni Buddha, who had left home at the age of 19 and obtained enlightenment at the age of 30, immediately began preaching the *Flower Garland Sutra* at the Hall of Enlightenment (Jakumetsu Dōjō).* Appearing as Vairocana Buddha in the Lotus Repository World, He preached the great Dharma based on an extremely refined theology of "ten mysteries," "six characteristics," and "interdependency of all phenomena."[8] Various Buddhas in the universe appeared, and all the bodhisattvas gathered to listen to Him. In view of the place, intelligence of the audience, and number of Buddhas gathered there, as well as the fact that it was the first sermon of Śākyamuni Buddha, there did not seem to be any reason why any great Dharma should have been concealed in the *Flower Garland Sutra.**

Therefore, it is stated in the *Flower Garland Sutra* that the Buddha showed His unrestricted power in expounding the sutra of perfection. According to this statement, the 60-fascicled *Flower Garland Sutra,* each word or letter in it without exception, should be flawless and perfect. For instance a single wish-fulfilling gem,* which could produce as much treasure as you wished, is as good as a countless number of them. One gem would pour out as much treasure as 10,000 gems. So one word in the *Flower Garland Sutra* should have been as valuable as 10,000 words. An assertion in the sutra that "there is no distinction between the mind, the Buddha, and the unenlightened" is said to be the theoretical foundation of not only the Kegon* but also the Hossō,* Sanron,* Shingon* and Tendai* sects. What should be concealed in such a great sutra as this? Nevertheless, it is asserted in this sutra that men of the Two Vehicles* as well as those who do not listen to Buddhism *(icchantika)** will never attain Buddhahood. This seems like a flaw in the gem. In addition, it is repeated three times that Śākyamuni Buddha achieved enlightenment for the first time* under the bodhi tree,* concealing His enlightenment in the eternal past* as expounded in the 16th chapter of the *Lotus Sutra,* The Duration of the Life of the Tathāgata.* This seems to be like a cracked gem, the moon hidden by clouds, or the sun eclipsed. This is indeed inexplicable.

Compared to the *Flower Garland Sutra,* such scriptures as the Āgama sutras,* Hōdō sutras,* *Wisdom Sutra** and *Great Sun Buddha Sutra** are not worth mentioning, although they too embody the honorable teachings of the Buddha. No reason seems to be given why what is not revealed in the former should be revealed in the latter. Consequently, the Āgama sutras say, "When He achieved enlightenment for the first time...." The *Daijik-kyō, Sutra of the Great Assembly,** speaks of "the first 16 years after the Buddha achieved enlightenment." It is said in the *Yuima Sutra, Vimalakīrti Sutra,** that He at first sat under the bodhi tree, striving to expel demons. The *Great Sun Buddha Sutra* says, "I once sat under the bodhi tree to obtain enlightenment," while the *Ninnō-kyō, Sutra of the Benevolent King,** speaks of 29 years since His enlightenment.

These provisional sutras are not worthy of discussion. What surprises me is that even the *Muryōgi-kyō, Sutra of Infinite Meaning,* the preliminary to the *Lotus Sutra,* agrees with the *Flower Garland Sutra* when it says, "Having sat in meditation under the bodhi tree for six years, I finally obtained perfect enlightenment." This is strange because the sutra looks down on such profound doctrines as the "mind as ultimate reality"[9] of the *Flower Garland Sutra,* the "ocean-imprint meditation"[10] of the *Sutra of the Great Assembly,* and the "indistinguishableness of phenomena"[11] of the *Wisdom Sutra* as "not yet revealing the truth," or "a roundabout way to Buddhahood." However, since this *Sutra of Infinite Meaning* is merely the introduction to the *Lotus Sutra,* perhaps the main discourse* has not been given yet.

In the *Lotus Sutra* proper, however, the Buddha revealed the single path to Enlightenment, having synthesized three kinds of teaching *(kaisan ken'itsu).** He declared in the theoretical *(shakumon)* section of the *Lotus Sutra:* "Only Buddhas wholly perceive the reality of all phenomena,"* "truth will be revealed after preaching provisional teachings for more than 40 years," and "He will discard provisional teachings and will concentrate only on the supreme way." The Buddha of Many Treasures* then declared that those words of the Buddha in the eight [from the second to ninth] chapters in the theoretical section *(shakumon)** of the *Lotus Sutra* were all true. What then should have been left unrevealed? Nevertheless, the eternal life of the Buddha was not revealed. Instead it is said, "At first, He sat at the place of enlightenment, gazed on the tree, and walked around it meditating." This is the greatest wonder of all.

Then the 15th chapter of the *Lotus Sutra,* Appearance of Bodhisattvas from Underground,* states that Bodhisattva Maitreya* wondered why the Buddha claimed to have taught the great bodhisattvas, who had never been seen before in the last 40 years or so,* and caused them to aspire for enlightenment. So he asked: "When You, the Buddha, were the crown prince, You left the palace of the Śākya clan, sat in meditation under the bodhi tree not far from the city of Gayā and obtained perfect enlightenment. It has only been some 40 years since then. How could You, World Honored One, have achieved so much in a short period of time?"

It was at this point that Lord Śākyamuni Buddha decided to preach The Duration of the Life of the Tathāgata* chapter to dispel such doubts. Referring to what has been said in the pre-Lotus sutras* and in the theoretical section* of the *Lotus Sutra,* He said, "Gods, men and *asura* demons in all the worlds think that I, Śākyamuni Buddha, left the palace of the Śākya clan, sat under the bodhi tree not far from the city of Gayā, and attained perfect enlightenment." Then He answered the question squarely by declaring, "To tell the truth, however, it has been innumerable and incalculable *kalpa* since I attained Buddhahood."

Such sutras as *Flower Garland, Wisdom,* and *Great Sun Buddha* conceal not only the possibility of the men of the Two Vehicles attaining Buddhahood* but also Śākyamuni Buddha attaining perfect enlightenment in the eternal past. Those sutras have two faults. In the first place, as they make a clear distinction among ranks and divisions, they fail to outgrow the provisional teachings and to reveal the doctrine of "3,000 existences contained in one thought" preached in the theoretical section of the *Lotus Sutra.* In the second place, by stating that Śākyamuni Buddha attained Buddhahood for the first time in this life, they have not yet outgrown the theoretical section of the *Lotus Sutra,* failing to reveal the Eternal Buddha expounded in the essential section* of the *Lotus Sutra.* These two great doctrines, "Obtaining Buddhahood by the Two Vehicles" and "Attaining Enlightenment in the Eternal Past," are the backbone of the teaching of the Buddha throughout His life and the essence of all the Buddhist scriptures.

The second chapter, Expedients, in the theoretical section of the *Lotus Sutra*, makes up for one of the two faults of the pre-Lotus sutras by revealing the teachings of "3,000 existences contained in one thought"* and "Obtaining Buddhahood by the Two Vehicles."* Yet, since the chapter has not yet revealed the Original and Eternal Buddha by "outgrowing the provisional and revealing the essential,"* it does not show the real concept of the "3,000 existences contained in one thought." Nor does it establish the true meaning of "Obtaining Buddhahood by the Two Vehicles." They are like the reflections of the moon in the water, or rootless grass floating on waves.

In the essential section* of the *Lotus Sutra*, it was revealed that the Buddha had attained perfect enlightenment in the eternal past, making it untenable to assert that He attained Buddhahood for the first time in this world.* Thus the Eternal Buddha doctrine destroyed the Buddhahood resulting from the Four Teachings* [all Buddhist scriptures other than the essential section of the *Lotus Sutra*]. As the Buddhahood resulting from the Four Teachings became untenable, the way leading to Buddhahood shown in those Four Teachings proved to be invalid. Thus, in the essential section of the *Lotus Sutra*, the Ten Realm doctrine preached both in the pre-Lotus and in the theoretical section of the *Lotus Sutra* was destroyed, and the doctrine of causal relationship among the eternal Ten Realms was established. This is the doctrine of the "true cause and true result."* In this relationship the Nine Realms are all included in the realm of the Eternal Buddha, and the realm of the Buddha is in each of the eternal Nine Realms. This is truly the "mutually-possessed characteristics of the Ten Realms,"* "100 realms and 1,000 aspects of existence"* and "3,000 existences contained in one thought."

Seen in this light, Vairocana Buddha on the lotus platform and various Buddhas around Him who came from all over the universe as described in the *Flower Garland Sutra*,* Śākyamuni Buddha of the Hinayana Āgama sutras,* as well as the provisional Buddhas of all the pre-Lotus sutras [such as Hōdō sutras,* *Wisdom Sutra*,* *Sutra of the Golden Splendor*,* *Pure Land Sutra*,* and *Great Sun Buddha Sutra**] are all mere manifestations of this Eternal Buddha. They are like shadows of the moon in the sky reflected in large or small containers of water. Sectarian students, confused with doctrines of their own schools or not knowing the 16th chapter of the *Lotus Sutra*, The Duration of the Life of the Tathāgata, mistake the moon in the water for the real one. They try to go into the water to grasp this illusion or tie it up with a rope. In T'ien-t'ai's* words "they look at only the moon in the pond, without knowing the moon in the sky."

I, Nichiren, believe that even with the doctrine of "Obtaining Buddhahood by the Two Vehicles,"* the pre-Lotus sutras seem to have the upper hand. Concerning the doctrine of "Attaining Enlightenment in the Eternal Past"* expounded in the essential section of the *Lotus Sutra*, the pre-Lotus sutras,* which maintain that Śākyamuni's attainment of Buddhahood occurred in this world, are incomparably stronger. For not only are they stronger, the first 14 chapters *(shakumon)** of the *Lotus Sutra,* too, solely side with them and do not mention the eternal life of the Buddha. With the exception of the 15th and 16th chapters, [Appearance of Bodhisattvas from Underground* and The Duration of the Life of the Tathāgata,*] the first 14 chapters of the *Lotus Sutra* all describe Śākyamuni's attainment of Buddhahood for the first time in this world."

In the 40-fascicled *Nirvana Sutra,* Śākyamuni's last preaching under the twin *śāla* trees, as well as in various Mahayana sutras preached before and after the *Lotus Sutra,* not a single word is said of the Eternal Buddha. Although the Dharma Body* of the Buddha has been explained to be "without beginning and without end," the eternity of Buddhas in Buddha lands (Reward Body)* or in this world (Accommodative Body)* has not been revealed. How can anyone side with only the two chapters in the Lotus and discard the wide range of Mahayana sutras: pre-Lotus, most of the *Lotus,* and *Nirvana?*

Now, the Hossō sect of Buddhism originated with Bodhisattva Asaṅga, a great commentator appearing in India 900 years after the death of the Buddha. At night he went up to the inner palace of Bodhisattva Maitreya* in the Tuṣita Heaven and asked him questions concerning all the holy teachings of the Buddha's lifetime.* During the day he spread the Hossō doctrine in the state of Ayodhyā. His disciples included such great commentators as Vasubandhu,* Dharmapāla, Ānanda, and Śīlabhadra. Even King Harṣavardhana bowed before him and all the people in India pulled down their banners and followed him. Tripiṭaka Master Hsüan-chuang* of China spent 17 years in India visiting some 130 states and studying Buddhism. Rejecting all other schools, he chose the Hossō sect to transmit to China and passed it on to the sage king, Emperor T'ai-tsung of T'ang. He had such disciples as Shen-fang, Chia-shang, P'u-kuang and K'uei-chi, and he resided at the great Tz'ŭ-ên Temple, spreading the teaching in more than 360 states in China.

In Japan, during the reign of Emperor Kōtoku, the 37th ruler, such monks as Dōji and Dōshō transmitted this school from China and practiced it at the Kōfukuji Temple at Yamashina. Thus this sect must have been the prime school of Buddhism in the three countries of India, China, and Japan. The gist of this Hossō is as follows:

> According to all Buddhist scriptures, beginning with the *Flower Garland Sutra* and ending with *Lotus* and *Nirvana Sutras,* those who do not have Buddha-nature *(mushō)** and those whose nature is fixed *(ketsujō-shō)** as men of the Two Vehicles *(śrāvaka* and *pratyekabuddha)* will never become Buddhas. The Buddha is never two-faced. Once He decides that Buddhahood is

unattainable, He will never change His mind even if the sun and moon should fall and the great earth should tumble. Therefore, not even in the *Lotus Sutra* and *Nirvana Sutra* is it definitely stated that the two categories of people who had been rejected in the pre-Lotus sutras, those without Buddha-nature and men of the Two Vehicles, will attain Buddhahood.

Close your eyes and think hard. If it is stated in the *Lotus Sutra* and *Nirvana Sutra** that those two categories of men, who are hated in the pre-Lotus sutras,* will obtain Buddhahood, why is it that such great commentators in India as Asaṅga* and Vasubandhu,* and such Tripiṭaka masters of China as Hsüan-chuang* and Tz'ŭ-ên* did not find this? Why is it that they did not write about it, believe it and transmit it, or ask Bodhisattva Maitreya* about it? Although you appear to rely on the words of the *Lotus Sutra*, actually you believe the slanted view of T'ien-t'ai,* Miao-lê,* and Dengyō* and read Buddhist scriptures through their prejudices. This may be the reason why you consider the *Lotus Sutra* and those sutras preached before it incompatible to each other like fire and water.

The Kegon* and Shingon* sects, which claim to be incomparably superior to the Hossō* and Sanron* sects, maintain:

> Concepts of "Obtaining Buddhahood by the Two Vehicles" and "Attaining Enlightenment in the Eternal Past"* are not limited to the *Lotus Sutra*. They are clearly mentioned in the *Flower Garland Sutra** and the *Great Sun Buddha Sutra*.* Tu-shun,* Chih-yen,* Fa-tsang,* Ch'eng-kuan" of the Kegon sect and Śubhākarasiṃha (Shan-wu-wei),* Vajrabodhi,* and Amoghavajra (Pu-k'ung)* of the Shingon sect are incomparably higher in rank than T'ien-t'ai* and Dengyō.* Furthermore, Śubhākarasiṃha and others are in the direct line of the Great Sun Buddha. How could these people, temporary manifestations of Buddhas and bodhisattvas, make mistakes? Accordingly, it is said in the *Flower Garland Sutra*, "It has been immeasurable *kalpa* since Śākyamuni attained Buddhahood." The *Great Sun Buddha Sutra* states, "I am the origin of everything." How could you say that the doctrine of "Attaining Enlightenment in the Eternal Past" is limited to the 16th chapter of the *Lotus Sutra*, The Duration of the Life of the Tathāgata? It is speaking like a frog in a well who has never seen an ocean, or a mountain woodcutter who has never visited the capital. Isn't it that you have seen only one chapter of the Lotus without knowing such sutras as the *Flower Garland* and the *Great Sun Buddha*? Moreover, do all those in India, China, Silla, and Paekche except T'ien-t'ai, Miao-lê, and Dengyō say that the teachings of "Obtaining Buddhahood by the Two Vehicles" and "Attaining Enlightenment in the Eternal Past" are revealed only in the *Lotus Sutra*?

According to these opinions, although the *Lotus Sutra* expounded in the last eight years is superior to those other sutras expounded in the previous 40 years or so, and although it is the rule that when there is a discrepancy between older and newer legal judgements, the newer one takes precedence over the old, the pre-Lotus sutras seem more influential than the Lotus. Things might have been as they should be while Śākyamuni Buddha was alive, but after His death many commentators in India* and teachers in China and Japan* have been leaning toward the pre-Lotus sutras.*

Thus, it is difficult to have faith in the *Lotus Sutra*. Moreover, we gradually approach the Latter Age of Degeneration. Sages and wise men gradually disappear while the confused grow in number. These people easily fall into error even in dealing with trivial matters of the world, not to mention understanding the exquisite Dharma, transcending worldly matters. Men like Vātsīputriya and Vaipulya in India were wise people, yet they were unable to distinguish between Mahayana and Hinayana sutras. Wu-kou and Mo-t'a, also in India, were clever but unable to differentiate the true teaching from the provisional one.* It was within the first 1,000 years after the death of Śākyamuni Buddha, not far from His time, and within the land of India that errors like this had already occurred. How much more so in countries such as China and Japan, which are far away from the land of the Buddha, where different languages are spoken, where people are slow to understand the teaching of the Buddha, where the life span is shorter, and where greed, anger, and stupidity are twice as strong!

It has been many years since the Buddha passed away. Buddhist sutras are misunderstood. Does anyone understand them correctly? The Buddha predicts in the *Nirvana Sutra:** "Those who uphold the True Dharma in the Latter Age of Degeneration* are as few as a bit of soil on a fingernail* while slanderers of the True Dharma* are as plentiful as the soil of the entire universe."

It is said in the *Hōmetsujin-kyō, Sutra on the Decline of the Dharma:** "Slanderers of Buddhism are as numerous as sands of the Ganges River, while those who uphold the True Dharma are just a pebble or two." It would be difficult to find even one person upholding the True Dharma in a period of 500 or 1,000 years. Those who fall into the evil realms, because of their worldly crimes, are as few as a bit of soil on a fingernail, while those who fall there because of crimes against Buddhism are as plentiful as the soil of the entire worlds in the universe. More monks than laymen, more nuns than laywomen fall into the evil realms.

CHAPTER 6
Unbending Aspiration to Buddhahood

Now I, Nichiren, believe it has already been more than 200 years since the arrival of the Latter Age of Degeneration. I was born in a remote country place. Moreover, I am a poor monk without social status. While having traversed the Six Realms in my past lives, I must have sometimes been born a great king in the human or celestial realm, making everyone obey me just as a strong wind sways the twigs of small trees. Still, I could not obtain Buddhahood then. At other times, I must have studied the teachings of Mahayana* and Hinayana* sutras, going step by step up the initial and advanced stages of practicing Buddhism, the way of a great bodhisattva.* Having practiced the way of a bodhisattva for as long as one, two, and innumerable *kalpa,* I was about to reach the state of non-retrogression. However, a powerful, evil karma prevented me from obtaining Buddhahood.

According to the Parable of a Magic City chapter of the *Lotus Sutra*, there were three categories of people who had an opportunity to listen to the sutra and sow the seed of Buddhahood during the time of Daitsūchishō (Great Universal Wisdom) Buddha* in the past. They were all to obtain Buddhahood eventually with the third and last group being guaranteed to be future Buddhas upon listening to Śākyamuni Buddha preach the *Lotus Sutra*. I wonder whether or not I was excluded from the third category of people. Or, am I one of those who, while having listened to the *Lotus Sutra* and sowed the seed of Buddhahood 500 dust-particle *kalpa (gohyaku-jindengō)** in the past, have until today kept falling back without eventually getting it?

While practicing the *Lotus Sutra** in this present life and overcoming bad worldly karma, royal persecutions, and accusations by heretics and Hinayana schools, I was able to discern that people have been fooled by such men as Tao-ch'o,* Shan-tao,* and Hōnen,* who were possessed by devils and gave the appearance of having mastered provisional and true Mahayana sutras. Speaking highly of the *Lotus Sutra* and slighting the intelligence of the people, they fooled the people by saying that the doctrine of the Lotus was "too exquisite *(rijin mige)** to understand, that there never had been anyone who obtained Buddhahood through the sutra, or that "not even one out of 1,000"* persons had obtained Buddhahood through it. During an innumerable number of past lives, people have been fooled this way as many times as the number of the sands in the Ganges River into believing provisional sutras. From provisional sutras they fell into non-Buddhist scriptures and finally to evil realms.

I, Nichiren, am the only one who knows this in Japan. If I speak out with even one word of this, royal persecutions will never fail to befall my parents, brothers, and teachers. If I do not speak out, however, it would seem that I did not have compassion. Wondering whether or not I should speak out in the light of the *Lotus, Nirvana* and other sutras, I came to realize that if I did not speak out, I would fall without fail into the Hell of Incessant Suffering in future lives even if nothing happened to me in this life. If I spoke out, I realized, the Three Hindrances and Four Devils* would overtake me.

Vacillating between the two, whether I should speak out or I should not, were I to back down in the face of royal persecutions, I hit upon the "six difficult and nine easier actions"* mentioned in the 11th chapter of the *Lotus Sutra*, Beholding the Stupa of Treasures. It says that even a man as powerless as me can throw Mt. Sumeru,* even a man with as little superhuman power as me can carry a stack of hay on his back and survive the disastrous conflagration at the end of the world, and even a man as ignorant as me can memorize various sutras as numerous as the sands of the Ganges River. Even more so, it is not easy to uphold even a word or a phrase of the *Lotus Sutra* in the Latter Age of Degeneration. This must be it! I have made a vow that this time I will have an unbending aspiration to Buddhahood and never fall back!

CHAPTER 7
Proving the Buddha's Prediction in the Lotus Sutra

It has already been more than 20 years since I began speaking for this sutra, and my troubles have been increasing day by day, month by month, and year by year. Small troubles are incalculable while severe ones are four in number. Not speaking of two of them, I have already been twice the target of royal persecution, and my life now is in jeopardy. Moreover, my disciples and lay supporters, including those laymen who had just come to hear me speak, were punished severely as though they had been rebels.

It is said in the *Lotus Sutra*, fascicle four [Chapter 10, The Teacher of the Dharma]: "This sutra was the target of much hatred and jealousy even during the lifetime of the Buddha, not to mention after His death." It says in the second fascicle [Chapter Three, A Parable]: "Seeing a person who reads, recites, copies, or keeps this sutra, some will despise and hate him, look at him with jealousy, and harbor enmity against him." And in the fifth fascicle [Chapter 14, Peaceful Practices]: "Many people in the world will hate it and very few believe it." In the 13th chapter, Encouragement for Keeping This Sutra: "Ignorant people will speak ill of him and abuse him," "In order to speak ill of him and to slander him, they will say to kings, ministers, Brahmans, and influential householders that he has heretical views," and "He will sometimes be driven out of his monastery." It is also said in the seventh fascicle [Chapter 20, Never-Despising Bodhisattva]:

"They will strike him with sticks, pieces of wood and tile or stones." The *Nirvana Sutra* states:

> Thereupon numerous non-Buddhists gathered together and went to see King Ajātaśatru* of the Magadha kingdom saying, "Now, there is a most wicked man, a wanderer, who is Gautama. For the purpose of making a profit, all wicked men in the world are gathering around him and becoming his followers, doing nothing good. With his occult power Gautama converted such men as Kāśyapa,* Śāriputra,* and Maudgalyāyana."*

Explaining the hatred and jealousy towards the *Lotus Sutra* during the Buddha's lifetime referred to in the fourth fascicle, T'ien-t'ai said in his *Words and Phrases of the Lotus Sutra*, fascicle eight: "Even during the lifetime of the Buddha it was difficult to spread the *Lotus Sutra*. How much more so after His death? It is because people do not listen to the True Dharma that it is difficult to teach and guide them." Commenting on this, Miao-lê said in his *Annotations on the Words and Phrases of the Lotus Sutra*, fascicle eight: "Hatred means slavery to delusions, and evil passions and jealousy mean unwillingness to listen to the *Lotus Sutra*."

Just as the Buddha was confronted with hatred and jealousy when He tried to preach the *Lotus Sutra*, so it is with those who tried to do so after His death. Numerous scholars in China, including three Southern masters and seven Northern masters,* considered T'ien-t'ai their hated enemy. A Japanese Hossō monk, Tokuitsu,* had this to say: "What's the matter with you, Master T'ien-t'ai? Whose disciple are you? With your less than eight centimeter long tongue, you have slandered the Hossō doctrine preached by the Buddha with His long and wide tongue."

It is stated in the *Tendai Interpretation of the Meaning of the Lotus Sutra* by Chih-tu of Tung-ch'un:*

> A question was asked: "Much hatred and jealousy existed even during the Buddha's lifetime. Why is it that those who expound this *Lotus Sutra* after His death encounter so many difficulties?" He answered: "As a popular saying goes, a good medicine tastes bitter. This sutra tears down the barriers among the Five Realms [of human beings, gods, *śrāvaka*, *pratyekabuddha* and bodhisattvas] and establishes the one ultimate teaching. Therefore, it rejects common men and scolds holy men, refuses the Mahayana and breaks down the Hinayana, calls celestial demons poisonous insects, regards non-Buddhists as vicious devils, disparagingly calls men of the Two Vehicles who stick to the Hinayana the poor and lowly, and discourages bodhisattvas

by calling them novices. This is the reason why celestial demons hate to listen to it: it grates upon non-Buddhist ears, Hinayana sages of the Two Vehicles are alarmed, and bodhisattvas are discouraged. All of these fellows make trouble for those who spread the *Lotus Sutra*. How can we say that much hatred and jealousy is merely an empty expression?"

Grand Master Dengyō stated in his *Kenkai-ron, Clarification of the Precepts:**

Superintendents of Buddhist priests in Nara defamed Dengyō in their petition to the Imperial Court, "There was a Brahman wizard in the land of Hsia to the west of China, while there is a bald-headed Buddhist monk with a honey tongue in the land to the East. They are in a secret league to fool the world." Dengyō refuted this, "We hear of Hui-kuang who was defeated in debate and tried to poison Grand Master Bodhidharma in the past in Ch'i China. Now we see six superintendents of Nara in Japan who, defeated in debate, are trying to persecute Dengyō. How true is it of the *Lotus Sutra* prediction: 'How much more hatred and jealousy after the death of the Buddha!'"

Grand Master Dengyō also stated in the *Hokke Shūku, Outstanding Principles of the Lotus Sutra:**

As for the time, it is toward the end of the Age of the Semblance Dharma* and in the beginning of the Latter Age of Degeneration. As for the land, it is to the east of T'ang China and west of Katsu.[12] And as for the people, they live in the evil world filled with five defilements* and engage in constant warfare. It is said in the *Lotus Sutra*, "There is much hatred and jealousy even during the Buddha's lifetime, not to mention after His death." How true this is!

Now if a child is given moxa treatment by his mother, he inevitably resents his mother. Given precious medicine, a seriously sick person may grumble at its bitter taste. So it was with the *Lotus Sutra* even during the lifetime of the Buddha. How much more so after the death of the Buddha and in a remote corner of the land! Just like mountains placed on tops of mountains and waves on tops of waves, difficulties on top of difficulties and abuses on top of abuses will occur.

It was T'ien-t'ai alone who correctly read the *Lotus Sutra* and all the Buddhist scriptures during the Age of the Semblance Dharma.* Various masters in Northern and Southern China hated him. However, as sagacious rulers of the Chen and Sui dynasties in China clarified through debates in front of their own eyes who was right, his enemies eventually disappeared. Toward the end of the Age of the Semblance Dharma, Dengyō* alone in Japan correctly read the *Lotus Sutra* and all the Buddhist scriptures. Although seven great temples of Nara, the Southern Capital,* rose against him, nothing happened to him because Emperors Kammu and Saga themselves clarified who was right.

But now, it has been over 200 years since the beginning of the Latter Age of Degeneration.* I have not been allowed to meet opponents in debate. Instead I have been banished and my life put in jeopardy. It proves that the warning in the *Lotus Sutra* about much hatred and jealousy after the death of the Buddha is not an empty threat. It also proves that we are in the beginning of endless warfare and in a decadent world of corruption where foolishness takes precedence over reason.

Therefore, although my comprehension of the *Lotus Sutra* is not worth even one ten millionth of that of T'ien-t'ai and Dengyō, I dare say that my endurance on its behalf and compassion for the people are beyond these masters. I am sure that I deserve to receive heavenly protection, but there is not even a shred of it. Instead I have been condemned to heavier and heavier penalties. Looking back in this light, I wonder whether or not I am one who practices the *Lotus Sutra* and whether or not various gods and deities have left this land.

However, had not I, Nichiren, been born in this country, the 20-line verse of the 13th chapter, Encouragement for Keeping This Sutra,* in the fifth fascicle of the *Lotus Sutra* would be empty words and the Buddha would almost be a great liar. Those uncountable number of bodhisattvas,* who made the vow to uphold the *Lotus Sutra*, would be accused of committing the same sin of lying as Devadatta.* The verse says, "Ignorant people will speak ill of us, abuse us, and threaten us with swords or sticks."

In the world today, is there any Buddhist priest other than me, Nichiren, who is spoken ill of, abused, and threatened with swords or sticks on account of the *Lotus Sutra*? If I, Nichiren, were not here, this verse would be a false prediction.*

It also says: "Monks in this evil world will be cunning and ready to flatter others. They will preach the Dharma to laymen for worldly gain and be respected by the people just as the *arhat* who has the Six Superhuman Powers."* If there were no Pure Land* Buddhists or priests of the Zen* or Ritsu* school of Buddhism in this world, this prediction would also make the Buddha a great liar.

It says, "In order to slander us in the midst of a great crowd of people they will speak ill of us to kings, ministers, Brahmans, and men of influence." These would be empty words unless Buddhist priests in this world slandered me and had me exiled.

It is further stated, "We will be banished many times." If I, Nichiren, had not been exiled repeatedly on account of the *Lotus Sutra*, what could we do with these two words of "many times?" Even T'ien-t'ai* and Dengyō* did not read these two words from experience, much less other people. I, Nichiren, alone read them from experience. For I fit perfectly the Buddha's description of the person spreading the *Lotus Sutra* "in the dreadful and evil world" at the beginning of the Latter Age of Degeneration.

For example, the Buddha predicted in the *Fuhōzō-kyo, Sutra of Transmission of the Buddhist Teaching** that 100 years after His death there would be a great king named Aśoka. It is predicted in the *Māyā Sutra* that 600 years after the death of the Buddha, there would be a man named Nāgārjuna in South India, while the *Daihi-kyō, Sutra of the Great Compassion,* says: "Sixty years after the Buddha's death, there will be a man called Madhyāntika, who will build a base in the Palace of the Dragon King to spread Buddhism." These predictions of the Buddha all came true. Otherwise, who would have faith in Buddhism?

Nevertheless, in both the *Shō-hoke-kyō* [the Chinese translation of the *Lotus Sutra* by Dharmarakṣa] and *Myō-hoke-kyō* [Kumārajīva's Chinese translation of the *Lotus Sutra*], the Buddha has precisely defined the time for the spread of this sutra as when the "world is dreadful and evil," "the future Latter Age," "the Latter Age when the Dharma is about to be extinguished," or "the last [fifth] 500 year period* after the death of the Buddha."

Had there not been three kinds of strong enemies* against the one who practices the Lotus today, who would believe in the Buddha? Had there not been Nichiren, who would be the one who practices the *Lotus Sutra* to prove the Buddha's prediction? Even three Southern masters and seven Northern masters* in China as well as seven great temples of Nara in Japan were among the enemies of the *Lotus Sutra* during the Age of the Semblance Dharma. How can the schools of Zen, Ritsu, and Pure Land Buddhists today escape from being enemies of the sutra?

Since the words of the sutra correspond to me, the deeper I fall into disgrace with the Shogunate,* the greater my pleasure. This is like a Hinayana bodhisattva, who has not completely exterminated all delusions and evil passions, wishing to be reborn in this world. That is to say, as he sees his parents suffering greatly in hell, he would intentionally accumulate bad karma in order to go to hell himself, where he would be glad to share their sufferings. I, Nichiren, am in a similar situation. Though my sufferings today are difficult to bear, I am happy for the future when I will be free from the evil realms.

CHAPTER 8
Why Do Heavenly Beings Not Protect One Who Practices the Lotus Sutra?

Nevertheless, people doubt me, and I myself wonder why gods and deities have not come to help me. They made vows to the Buddha to protect one who practices the *Lotus Sutra*. I would think, therefore, that they should hurriedly come to his aid, calling him one who practices the *Lotus Sutra*, and carry out their promise to the Buddha, even if they have suspicions about him. Yet, none has come to help me. Does that mean that I am not one who practices the *Lotus Sutra*? Since this question is the basis of this writing and of cardinal importance in my life, I will take this up again and again in order to find a definite answer.

Passing through the state of Hsü, Chi-cha of Wu in ancient China is said to have seen the Lord of Hsü and sensed that the Lord was envious of his [Chi-cha's] treasured sword given by their king. Realizing that he had first to perform a royal mission, Chi-cha decided to present the sword to the Lord on his way back. However, the Lord was already dead when Chi-cha tried to see him again. Therefore, it is said, he placed the sword on the lord's tomb to carry out what he had promised in his heart. A man named Wang-shou is said to have paid for drinking water from a river by throwing coins in it, while Hung-yen followed his slain lord in death, by cutting open his stomach and inserting his lord's liver in it. These are examples of wise men repaying favors they had received.

How much more would great sages like Śāriputra* and Kāśyapa* repay favors? Upholding the 250 precepts and 3,000 rules of dignified conduct without fail, and free of delusions in view and desire,* they won freedom from the Six Realms of transmigration. They are leaders of the King of the Brahma Heaven,* Indra,* gods and deities and eyes of all the people.

Nevertheless, in those sutras preached 40 years or so* before the *Lotus Sutra*, they were discarded as being unable to obtain Buddhahood. By taking the pill of immortality, the *Lotus Sutra*, they were assured of obtaining Buddhahood as though a roasted seed would germinate, a broken rock would become whole again, and a dead tree would bear flowers and fruits. Not having formally become Buddhas by going through the eight stages in the life of the Buddha, how could they afford to forget what they owed to the sutra? If they did, they would be not only inferior to such wise men as Chi-cha and Hung-yen but also similar to those beasts that bite the hand that feeds them.

A turtle which had been saved by a man named Mao-pao in Chin China is said to have never forgotten his kindness and came to help him escape across a river when he was defeated in a battle. Han Emperor Wu-ti is said to have released a large fish he caught in Lake Kun-ming. In gratitude, it is said the fish at night presented him with a large gem. Even beasts repay the kindness they receive, not to mention those great saints.

Venerable Ānanda* was the second son of King Dronodana while Venerable Rāhula* was a grandson of King Śuddhodana. Born into families of high social standing and having attained the stage of *arhats*, they both had been considered as having no possibility of obtaining Buddhahood. During the eight-year preaching of the *Lotus Sutra* on Mt. Sacred Eagle,* however, they were granted the titles of Mountain Sea Wisdom Buddha and Stepping On Flowers of Seven Treasures Buddha respectively.

Had they not been assured of Buddhahood, thanks to the *Lotus Sutra*, who would respect them no matter how noble their family blood and how great their sainthood had been? King Chieh of the Hsia Dynasty and King Chou of the Yin [Shang] Dynasty were rulers of ancient China who were respected by their subjects. However, when they lost their kingdoms as a result of tyrannical governing, the term "Chieh-Chou" became a symbol of all that is wicked and cruel. Even men of humble origin or men with leprosy would feel offended today if they are called Chieh and Chou.

Had it not been for the *Lotus Sutra*, who would know the names of as many as 1,200 or even innumerable *śrāvaka*,* who were assured of obtaining Buddhahood in the sutra? Who would even listen to them? Even if 1,000 *śrāvaka* gathered together after the death of Śākyamuni Buddha and compiled all the Buddhist scriptures, nobody would read them, much less make their portraits, and statues of the Most Venerable One.* As they are, those *arhats* are respected and worshipped today simply because they were assured of Buddhahood in the *Lotus Sutra*. Without the *Lotus Sutra*, they would be like fish without water, monkeys without trees, infants without breasts, and subjects without a sovereign. How can they afford to discard one who practices the *Lotus Sutra*?

Listening to the pre-Lotus sutras,* those men of *śrāvaka* gained the Eyes of Heaven and Eyes of Wisdom in addition to human eyes. Additionally they gained the Eyes of the Dharma as well as the Eyes of the Buddha by listening to the *Lotus Sutra*. They should be able to see through all the worlds in the universe, not to mention being able to find one who practices the *Lotus Sutra* in this Sahā World.* Even if I, Nichiren, were so wicked a person to have abused those men of *śrāvaka* with a slanderous word or two, or abused and struck them with sticks or swords for one or two years, or one, two, 100, 1,000, 10,000 or 100 million *kalpa*, they would not abandon me so long as I am one who practices the *Lotus Sutra*. For instance, do any parents abandon children who abuse them? It is said that an owl, when grown up, eats its mother, but a mother owl does not give up its baby. A beast called *hakyō* is said to devour its father when grown up, but its father does not abandon its child. These are acts of beasts and birds. How could great saints of *śrāvaka* abandon one who practices the *Lotus Sutra*?

Therefore, the four great men of *śrāvaka* expressed their gratitude to the Buddha for assuring them of Buddhahood in the fourth chapter of the *Lotus Sutra,* Understanding by Faith, saying:

> Now we are men of *śrāvaka*
> In the true sense of the word,
> Who can cause everyone to listen
> To the way of the Buddha.
> Now we are *arhats*
> In the true sense of the word,
> Who deserve to receive offerings
> In various worlds
> Among various creatures,
> Gods, men, devils, and Brahmans.
> You, the World Honored One,
> Have done a great favor
> Out of Your deep compassion
> In expounding this rare teaching of the Lotus.
> Who would be able to repay Your favors
> Even in innumerable *kalpa?*
> No one will be able to repay Your favors
> Even if he tries to do so
> By serving You with his hands and feet,
> Respectfully bowing his head to You,
> And offering You all he has.
> No one will be able to repay Your favors
> Even if he tries to do so
> By carrying You on his head and shoulders,
> Showing respect from the bottom of his heart
> For *kalpa* as incalculable as sands of the Ganges River.
> No one will be able to repay Your favors
> Even if he tries to do so
> By offering You delicious food,
> Garments adorned with invaluable treasures,
> And various beddings and medicines;
> Or by erecting stupas
> Made of Malayagiri sandalwood
> Adorned with precious treasures;

Or by spreading garments of treasures
On the ground as offerings to You
For as incalculable *kalpa*
As many as sands of the Ganges River.

In the sutras preached before the *Lotus Sutra,* the men of *śrāvaka* were scolded and humiliated on numerous occasions in great assemblies of men and gods. Lamenting his lack of aspiration for enlightenment, for instance, Venerable Kāśyapa* cried out with a loud voice that resounded throughout the entire universe. Told by Vimalakīrti that anyone who gives alms to him will fall into the Three Evil Realms, dumbfounded Venerable Subhūti dropped his alms bowl. Having been told that *śrāvaka* men were not entitled to receive alms, Śāriputra* spit out the food he had in his mouth. Unable to see the intelligence of his audience, Pūrṇa* was scolded for being as stupid as putting manure in a beautifully decorated vase. The Buddha, who praised the Hinayana Āgama sutras and earnestly urged His disciples to uphold the 250 precepts earlier at the Deer Park, now suddenly changed His mind and scolded them as vehemently as this. It was a contradiction hard for them to swallow.

In another instance, when the Buddha scolded Devadatta* for being such a fool as to suck people's saliva, Devadatta, feeling a strong resentment against the Buddha as if he had been shot through the chest by a poisoned arrow, made a vow:

> Gautama is not a Buddha. I am the first son of King Dronodana, elder brother of Venerable Ānanda,* and a member of the Gautama clan. No matter how badly I behaved, He should have told me about it privately. How could He be a Buddha or a great man when He put me to such shame in the midst of a large crowd of men and gods? Formerly He was my enemy who robbed me of the woman I loved. Now He is my enemy who insulted me in front of a crowd. He will remain my sworn enemy generation after generation, life after life.

As I contemplate these instances, these great men of *śrāvaka* were originally from non-Buddhist* Brahman families or leaders of various non-Buddhist religions in India. Therefore, they were believed and respected by kings and lay followers. Some of them were originally of high social status and from rich families. Giving up rank and honor and suppressing their pride, they took off layman's clothes to put on shabby looking soil-colored robes, discarding their *hossu* brush of white long hair and bow and arrow, symbols of their high social standing. Like beggars, they followed Śākyamuni Buddha, each holding a beggar's bowl in hand, without a house to keep themselves alive. As all the people in the whole of India were disciples and followers of non-Buddhist religions, even the Buddha Himself encountered nine great difficulties,* including Devadatta's* attempt to kill Him by rolling a huge rock down a hill on Him, King Ajātaśatru's* attempt at killing Him by releasing a drunken elephant to attack Him, and King Agnidatta's attempt at the Buddha's life by giving Him only horse feed for 90 days.

When the Buddha went to a Brahman village to beg for food, He did not receive any offerings except for a bowlful of water in which rice had been washed. It is also said that the Buddha was once accused of breaking a Buddhist precept by a Brahman woman named Ciñcā who, placing a bowl on her stomach, claimed to have been made pregnant by the Buddha. Even the Buddha was confronted with difficulties such as these, not to mention His disciples, who had to go through numerous difficulties.

Countless people of the Śākya clan were murdered by King Virūḍhaka of Śrāvasti, and many more of them were trampled to death by drunken elephants. Nun Utpalavarṇā was beaten to death by Devadatta, and Venerable Kālodāyin was murdered and buried under horse manure, while Venerable Maudgalyāyana was beaten to death by a group of non-Buddhists armed with bamboo sticks.

Moreover, the six influential non-Buddhist masters joined forces in appealing to such powerful kings as Ajātaśatru and Prasenajit saying:

Śākyamuni is the most evil man in this world [Jambudvīpa*]. Wherever He goes, there are three calamities and seven disasters.* Just as many rivers flow into an ocean and many trees grow on a huge mountain, many evil men such as Kāśyapa,* Śāriputra,* Maudgalyāyana,* and Subhūti* gather around Śākyamuni. The primary duties of a man are to be a loyal subject and a filial child. However, they are fooled by Śākyamuni into renouncing their families against parental wishes. They hide themselves in the mountains, against the royal ordinance. As such they should not be allowed to stay in the country. It is due to their presence that we have frequent cosmic disorders and natural calamities in our lands these years.

These were difficult enough to bear, but there was more to come, making it hard for them to follow the Buddha. Not knowing what to do upon being scolded and shamed so often by the Buddha in front of the great crowd of men and gods, they only remained bewildered.

The heaviest blow of all hit them when the Buddha stated in the *Vimalakīrti Sutra:** "Those who offer alms to you, men of *śrāvaka*, cannot be called those who sow the seed in the 'fertile rice fields' where the seed of Buddhahood can germinate and grow. Those who give offerings to you will fall into the Three Evil Realms* of hell, hungry spirits and of beasts and birds."

This was when the Buddha was staying in the Āmrapali Garden, where an immeasurably large crowd gathered, including the King of the Brahma Heaven,* Indra,* the Sun God and the Moon God, the Four Heavenly Kings, and gods and dragon-gods in the heaven and earth. In the midst of them, the Buddha declared, "Those gods and men who give offerings to monks like Subhūti* will fall into the Three Evil Realms." How could they, those gods and men who heard Him say this, present offerings to such men of śrāvaka? After all, it even appeared that the Buddha was trying to kill off those men of the Two Vehicles.* Right-hearted men felt that He was too severe. Those Hinayana sages were barely able to sustain their lives with the offerings given to the Buddha.

As I contemplate this, if Śākyamuni Buddha had passed away after preaching only 40 years or so* without preaching the Lotus in the last eight years, who would have given offerings to these respectable people? They would certainly be in the realm of the hungry spirits alive.

However, just as the sun in spring melts away the ice and strong winds shake off all the dew, those sutras preached in some 40 years were discredited at once by one statement in the Preaching chapter of the *Sutra of Infinite Meaning*: "The truth has not been revealed yet."* Just as the strong wind disperses dark clouds revealing the full moon in the sky and the sun shines in the clear sky, it was made shiningly clear that "the Buddha reveals the truth after preaching the provisional Dharma for a long time." It was stated in the *Lotus Sutra*, the spotless mirror, in the indisputable words of the Buddha as clear as the sun and the moon in the sky that men like Śāriputra and Kāśyapa could obtain Buddhahood and that they would be Flower Light Buddha and Light Buddha respectively in the future. That was the very reason why lay followers among gods and men after the death of the Buddha continued to look up to those Hinayana sages as if they were Buddhas.

When the water is clear, the moon is bound to be reflected in it. When the wind blows, trees and grasses are bound to bend. So, when there is one who practices the *Lotus Sutra*, those sages such as Śāriputra* and Kāśyapa* should come to see him even if it means that they have to overcome such obstacles as great fires or huge rocks. Kāśyapa is said to have begun meditation to wait for the Buddha Maitreya, but this is not the time for him to do so. I wonder why they have not rushed to rescue the one who practices the *Lotus Sutra* when his life is at stake. Are we not in the last 500-year period,* at the beginning of the Latter Age of Degeneration?

Are these "widely propagated" scriptural words false? Am I, Nichiren, not one who practices the *Lotus Sutra*? Are they protecting those great liars of the Zen school, who insist that the truth cannot be expressed in writing and, therefore, the *Lotus Sutra* is not the truth? Are they defending the Pure Land sect which, deciding to "abandon, close, put aside and cast away"* everything except Pure Land doctrine, published the *Collection of Passages on the Nembutsu* on wood-block prints urging that the gate to the *Lotus Sutra* be closed, the sutra be thrown away, and the Lotus temples be closed down? Or is it that gods and deities, shying away from the great difficulties in the decadent world, do not descend to help the one who practices the *Lotus Sutra* in spite of their vow before the Buddha to do so? Both the sun and moon are still in the sky, Mt. Sumeru* still exists, the tides of the sea still rise and ebb, and four seasons come and go in order. Why is it then that no one comes to help the one who practices the *Lotus Sutra*? This doubt of mine grows greater and greater.

CHAPTER 9

The "3,000 Existences Contained in One Thought" Doctrine Preached in the Theoretical Section

Again, it appears that in the pre-Lotus sutras* great bodhisattvas,* gods, and men were guaranteed* to obtain Buddhahood in the future. However, that guarantee is merely one of color and shape without substance, just like trying to grab the moon's reflection in the water or taking the shadow for reality. We might say that in those pre-Lotus sutras they do not owe the Buddha as much as they seemed.

Upon reaching enlightenment under the bodhi tree, Śākyamuni Buddha did not preach. Instead some 60 great bodhisattvas such as Dharma Wisdom, Forest of Merit, Diamond Banner and Diamond Storehouse appeared before Lord Śākyamuni from all over the universe, in response to the request of such bodhisattvas as Dharmākara and Moon of Emancipation, to preach the doctrine concerning the 52 steps to Buddhahood such as *jūjū*, *jūgyō*, *jūekō* and *jūji*. This 52 step doctrine was not what they learned from Śākyamuni. The Kings of the Brahma Heaven* of all the worlds in the universe and others also came to preach, but what they preached was not what they learned from Śākyamuni. All the great bodhisattvas, gods, dragon-gods, and others in the Flower Garland* assembly who were great bodhisattvas and who had won Wonderful Emancipation before Śākyamuni Buddha, all of them preached. They might have been Śākyamuni's disciples in the past when He was still practicing the way of the bodhisattva. Or, they might have been disciples of those Buddhas in the universe who had won Buddhahood before Śākyamuni. At any rate they were not disciples of Lord Śākyamuni, who preached the Buddhist teachings for 50 years in India after attaining enlightenment under the bodhi tree.

It was only when Śākyamuni Buddha began preaching the Four Teachings* [piṭaka, common, distinct and perfect] in the Āgama sutras, Hōdō sutras and *Wisdom Sutra* that He began to have disciples. These sutras were preached by Śākyamuni, but His preachings in them were not really His own. Why is that so? It is because the distinct and perfect teachings in the Hōdō sutras and *Wisdom Sutra* were not any different from those in the *Flower Garland Sutra*, which were not of Śākyamuni Himself but of such great bodhisattvas as Dharma Wisdom. Those bodhisattvas appeared at first glance to have been the Buddha's disciples, but it is more proper to say they were His teachers. Having listened to them preach distinct and perfect teachings in the *Flower Garland Sutra*, the Buddha learned from them and repeated the teachings when He preached the Hōdō sutras and *Wisdom Sutra* later. Therefore, the distinct and perfect teachings of the Hōdō sutras and *Wisdom Sutra* are exactly like those in the *Flower Garland Sutra*, and those great bodhisattvas are teachers of Śākyamuni Buddha. This is the reason why in the *Flower Garland Sutra* these bodhisattvas were called "good friends,"* meaning not exactly teachers or disciples. The two teachings of *piṭaka* and common are merely branches of the distinct and the perfect. Those bodhisattvas such as Dharma Wisdom, who knew the latter, should have known the former as well.

The teacher reveals to disciples what they do not know. For instance, all followers of non-Buddhist religions in India* among men and gods before the time of Śākyamuni Buddha were disciples of Śiva, Viṣṇu and the Three Hermits. Although they split into 95 schools, their teachings did not go beyond those of the Three Hermits. Lord Śākyamuni had also been a student of those non-Buddhist schools, but while practicing ascetic and non-ascetic practices for twelve years, He perceived the principles of suffering, emptiness, impermanence, and egolessness in all phenomena. Thus, He was able to remove Himself as a student of non-Buddhist religions and claim to have won His wisdom without the guidance of teachers. So men and gods respected Him as a great teacher.

Therefore, during the time when the pre-Lotus sutras were preached, Lord Śākyamuni was not the teacher who revealed what others did not know, but He was rather a student of such bodhisattvas as Dharma Wisdom. Likewise, it is said in the first chapter of the *Lotus Sutra*, Introduction, that Bodhisattva Mañjuśrī* was a teacher of Śākyamuni Buddha for nine generations. In various sutras preached before the *Lotus Sutra* the Buddha is quoted as having said that He "never preached even one word." It means that His preachings did not go beyond what was preached by such bodhisattvas as Dharma Wisdom.

When the Buddha at the age of 72 preached the *Sutra of Infinite Meaning*derer* on Mt. Sacred Eagle in Magadha, India, He discredited all the sutras, major as well as minor sutras, expounded in the preceding 40 years or so* by declaring, "No truth has been revealed for some 40 years." Upon hearing this, great bodhisattvas as well as gods and people were all shocked and wished to know the true teaching. Although a shred of truth seems to have been revealed in the *Sutra of Infinite Meaning,* the truth itself was not yet revealed. It was as though the moon was about to appear over the mountains in the east. Its rays shone through the mountains in the west, but nobody could see the moon yet.

In revealing the single path to enlightenment replacing the three kinds of teaching for bodhisattvas, *śrāvaka* and *pratyekabuddha (kaisan kenitsu)** in the second chapter of the *Lotus Sutra,* Expedients, the Buddha briefly expressed the "3,000 existences contained in one thought"* doctrine held in His bosom. Since it was the first time for the Buddha to reveal the truth, it sounded to His disciples as faint as the voice of a nightingale heard by the half-asleep or the moon rising half way over a mountain covered by a thin cloud. Surprised by the words of the Buddha, Śāriputra* and other disciples called on the gods, dragon-gods, and great bodhisattvas, and together they petitioned the Buddha: "Gods and dragon-gods as numerous as sands of the Ganges River, 80,000 bodhisattvas trying to attain Buddhahood, and Wheel-turning Noble Kings* in 10 thousands, 100 millions of lands all respectfully hold hands together in *gasshō* and wish to hear the perfect teaching." In other words they requested Him to preach the doctrine that they had never heard during His preaching in more than 40 years of the pre-Lotus sutras, expounding four of the Five Flavors* and three of the Four Teachings.*

As for the "perfect teaching" which they wished to hear, it is said in the *Nirvana Sutra,* "The prefix *sad* of *saddharma* means perfect." It is said in the *Wu-i Wu-tê Ta-chêng Ssu-lun Hsüan-i Chi, Annotations on the Four Mahayana Treatises,* by Chun-cheng of T'ang China, "The prefix *sad* in *saddharma* is a Sanskrit word meaning six, which is a perfect number in India." Chi-tsang* [Grand Master Chia-hsiang] of Sui China says in *Fa-hua I-shu, Annotations on the Meaning of the Lotus Sutra,* "The word *sad* means perfect," while T'ien-t'ai* says in his *Fa-hua Hsüan-i, Profound Meaning of the Lotus Sutra,** fascicle eight, "The word *sad* is Sanskrit, translated here as *miao* in Chinese." Bodhisattva Nāgārjuna, the 13th patriarch in the succession of Buddhism, the primogenitor of schools of Buddhism such as the Flower Garland sect* and the Shingon sect,* a reincarnation of Hōunjizaiō Buddha, a great sage who attained the first stage of bodhisattvahood, says in his 1,000 fascicled work of *Dai-chido-ron, Great Wisdom Discourse,** that *sad* means six.

The *Miao-fa Lien-hua-ching* is a Chinese designation for the *Lotus Sutra,* which is called the *Saddharma-puṇḍarīka-sūtra* in India. Tripiṭaka Master Śubhākarasiṃha's* mantra representing the gist of the *Lotus Sutra* are as follows: "I put my faith in the everywhere-penetrating Buddha, the three-bodied Buddha.* When one attains Buddha Wisdom, which is opened and revealed to all people, he will, like the crisp clear sky, be able to get rid of all delusions and evil passions, accept the teaching of the *Sutra of the Wonderful Dharma* and live with joy, firmly upholding the teaching."

These mantra representing the gist of the *Lotus Sutra* came from an iron stupa in Southern India. The *Satsuri-daruma* contained in them means the True Dharma, while *"satsu"* means *shō* (true) or *myō* (wonderful). Therefore, the *Lotus Sutra* is called either the *Sutra of the Lotus Flower of the True Dharma* or the *Sutra of the Lotus Flower of the Wonderful Dharma*. Placing the two characters of *na* and *mu* in front of the latter, we get *Namu Myōhō Renge-kyō:** I put my faith in the *Sutra of the Lotus Flower of the Wonderful Dharma*.

The word *myō* means *gusoku* (to be equipped with perfect teaching). The word "six" means all kinds of practices collectively designated as six *pāramitā*[13] or six kinds of practices required for the attainment of Buddhahood. Śāriputra and others wished to know the way in which a bodhisattva* could fulfill the six *pāramitā* to obtain Buddhahood. *Gu* in *gusoku* means "mutually-possessed characteristics of the Ten Realms,"* and *soku* means to be satisfactory, that is to say, it is satisfactory for each of the Ten Realms to contain in itself characteristics of the other Nine Realms. Altogether of the 69,384 characters of the *Lotus Sutra*, in the 28 chapters in eight fascicles, each contains the character *myō*. Each of them represents the Buddha with 32 or 80 marks of physical excellence. As each of the Ten Realms contains in it characteristics of the realm of the Buddha, Grand Master Miao-lê* states in his *Annotations on the Great Concentration and Insight*, "Each realm contains characteristics of the realm of the Buddha, not to mention those of the other Nine Realms."

In response to the request by Śāriputra* and others to know how to fulfill the six *pāramitā*, Śākyamuni Buddha declares in the second chapter of the *Lotus Sutra*, Expedients, that all Buddhas hope to open the gate to the wisdom of the Buddha for the people. The people here refer to the men of the Two Vehicles such as Śāriputra, who had been considered unable to obtain Buddhahood, men of *icchantika** lacking Buddha-nature and all those in the Nine Realms [except the realm of the Buddha]. Therefore, His vow to save all the multitudes of people was at last fulfilled in preaching the *Lotus Sutra*. That is what He meant in declaring in the same second chapter of the *Lotus Sutra*: "I had vowed to make everyone exactly like Myself. The original vow of Mine has already been fulfilled."

Upon hearing this, great bodhisattvas and gods expressed their understanding in the third chapter of the *Lotus Sutra*, A Parable, "We have often listened to the Buddha preach, but have never heard of the Dharma as deeply as this." Grand Master Dengyō,* Founder of the Tendai sect in Japan, interprets this as follows: "That they had often listened to the Buddha preach means that they had listened in the past to such great Dharmas as the *Flower Garland Sutra* before they listened to the *Lotus Sutra*. And that they have never heard of the Dharma as deeply as this means that they have never heard of the teaching of the *Lotus Sutra*, in which all are assured of obtaining Buddhahood." That is to say, they said that while listening to various Mahayana sutras as numerous as the grains of sand in the Ganges River such as the *Flower Garland Sutra*, Hōdō sutras, *Wisdom Sutra, Revealing the Profound and Secret Sutra* and *Great Sun Buddha Sutra*, they had never heard of the attainment of Buddhahood by men of the Two Vehicles or the eternal life of the Buddha, the two doctrines which constitute the basis of Buddhism and the backbone of the "3,000 existences contained in one thought" doctrine.

CHAPTER 10
The "3,000 Existences Contained in One Thought" Doctrine Preached in the Essential Section

Having listened to Lord Śākyamuni preach the *Lotus Sutra*, various great bodhisattvas,* the King of the Brahma Heaven,* Indra, Sun God, Moon God, Four Heavenly Kings,* and others truly became His disciples. Since the Buddha considered them His own disciples, He sternly advised and commanded them as stated in the Beholding the Stupa of Treasures* chapter of the *Lotus Sutra*: "The Buddha told the great crowd, 'Anyone who would strive to uphold, read, and recite the sutra after My death should make sworn statements in front of Me.'" And so those great bodhisattvas and others followed the Buddha just as a gale blows twigs of small trees, as "good fortune" grass is swayed by a gale, or rivers flow into an ocean.

However, since it had not been long since the preaching of the *Lotus Sutra* had begun on Mt. Sacred Eagle,* it seemed to them dream-like and unreal. Then there appeared a stupa of treasures, which not only verified the first half of the preaching of the *Lotus Sutra* to be true but also prepared the way for the preaching of the latter half. Referring to all the Buddhas who appeared from all the worlds in the universe, the Buddha declared that they were all His own manifestations *(funjin)*.* Śākyamuni Buddha and the Buddha of Many Treasures* took seats side by side in the stupa that hung in the sky, appearing like the sun and the moon rising together up in the blue sky. A large crowd of men and gods appeared in the sky like constellations, while *funjin* Buddhas took lion-shaped thrones under jeweled trees.

Compared to this, when the Lotus-Repository World appeared in the *Flower Garland Sutra*,* Buddhas with Reward Body in this world and other worlds in the universe stayed in their respective worlds. Buddhas of other worlds did not come to this world to proclaim themselves to be manifestations *(funjin)* of Śākyamuni, nor did Śākyamuni visit them in other worlds in the universe. Only such great bodhisattvas as Dharma Wisdom came from the other worlds in the universe to see Śākyamuni Buddha in this world.

The eight venerable ones on eight lotus petals surrounding the Great Sun Buddha who appeared upon the preaching of the *Great Sun Buddha Sutra,* and the 37 venerable ones who appeared upon the preaching of the *Diamond Peak Sutra* seemed to be avatars of the Great Sun Buddha. However, unlike those Buddhas who appeared upon preaching of the *Lotus Sutra,* they were not Buddhas from the past completely provided with threefold bodies. The 1,000 Buddhas of the *Wisdom Sutra** and various Buddhas who appeared in six directions upon the preaching of the *Pure Land Sutra,** unlike those *funjin* Buddhas who came to this world to listen to the *Lotus Sutra,* did not bother to make long trips to visit this world from their respective lands. Those Buddhas who gathered together from the worlds in the universe when the *Sutra of the Great Assembly* was preached were also not *funjin* Buddhas. The four Buddhas appearing in four directions when the *Sutra of the Golden Splendor** was preached were merely Buddhas in transformed bodies [avatars], not in manifestation *(funjin).* In no sutra except for the *Lotus Sutra,* are those Buddhas who had obtained Buddhahood after years of practice and who completely possessed the threefold bodies referred to by Śākyamuni Buddha as "My manifestations."

Now in the 11th chapter of the *Lotus Sutra,* Beholding the Stupa of Treasures, a step was taken in preparation for revealing the Eternal Buddha in the 16th chapter, The Duration of the Life of the Tathāgata. It is stated in the Beholding the Stupa of Treasures chapter that Śākyamuni Buddha, who had attained enlightenment for the first time* only 40 years or so before under the bodhi tree at Buddhagayā, India, called the crowd of Buddhas, who had obtained Buddhahood as far earlier as one *kalpa* or ten, "My manifestations." This was against the principle of equality among Buddhas and greatly surprised everyone. If Śākyamuni Buddha had attained enlightenment only 40 years or so before, large crowds of people all over the universe would not be waiting for His guidance. Even if He was capable of appearing in manifestation to guide them in various worlds, it would have been of no use. Grand Master T'ien-t'ai* said in his *Profound Meaning of the Lotus Sutra,* fascicle nine, "Since there are so many of His manifestations, we should know that He has been the Buddha for a long time." It represents the consternation of the great assembly, men and gods who were surprised at the great number of Buddhas in manifestation *(funjin).*

To add to their surprise, the numerous great bodhisattvas, who had been guided by the Original Buddha in the past, sprang out of the earth* all over the whole world, according to the 15th chapter of the *Lotus Sutra,* Appearance of Bodhisattvas from Underground. They looked incomparably superior to Bodhisattvas Fugen (Universal-Sage)* and Monju (Mañjuśrī),* who had been regarded as ranking disciples of Śākyamuni Buddha. Compared to these bodhisattvas coming from underground, those great bodhisattvas, who had gathered upon the preaching of the *Flower Garland Sutra*,* Hōdō sutras,* and *Wisdom Sutra** and of the Beholding the Stupa of Treasures* chapter of the *Lotus Sutra*,* or the 16 bodhisattvas such as Bodhisattva Vajrasattva* in the *Great Sun Buddha Sutra** and other sutras, looked like monkeys waiting on Indra or woodcutters associating with court nobles. Even Bodhisattva Maitreya,* successor to Śākyamuni Buddha, did not know who they were, and neither did the gods and men below him.

Among those great bodhisattvas, appearing from out of the earth* of the whole world, the four great sages Jōgyō (Superior-Practice),* Muhengyō (Limitless-Practice), Jōgyō (Pure-Practice), and Anryūgyō (Steadily-Established-Practice) were outstanding in appearance. Awe stricken by these four, those great bodhisattvas and others who had come to listen to the preaching of the *Lotus Sutra* on Mt. Sacred Eagle* and up in the sky could not even gaze upon them nor understand who they were. Standing in front of these four who had come from underground, four bodhisattvas in the *Flower Garland Sutra*,* four bodhisattvas in the *Great Sun Buddha Sutra*,* and 16 bodhisattvas in the *Diamond Peak Sutra** seemed to be men squinting at the sun or fishermen facing the emperor. These four bodhisattvas from underground were like the four sages such as T'ai-kung-wang living with the people, or four elder statesmen of Shang-shan waiting on Emperor Hui, the second emperor of the Former Han dynasty. Indeed, the four bodhisattvas from underground appeared commanding and awe-inspiring. With the exception of Śākyamuni, the Buddha of Many Treasures, and Buddhas in manifestation, they would have been looked up to by everyone as "good friends."

Wondering who they were, Bodhisattva Maitreya said to himself:

I know all bodhisattvas in this world as well as those great bodhisattvas coming from all over the universe since the time Śākyamuni was still crown prince, through 42 years of preaching after His enlightenment at the age of 30, until His preaching of the *Lotus Sutra* on Mt. Sacred Eagle today. I know also every great bodhisattva in all pure and evil lands in the universe where I was sent on errands or visited on my own, but have never seen bodhisattvas like these. I wonder what kind of Buddha taught them? He must have been incomparably superior to Śākyamuni, the Buddha of Many Treasures, or Buddhas in manifestation in the universe. When we see the rain pouring, we can tell the size of the dragon who causes it. When we see large lotus flowers blooming, we can tell the depth of the lotus pond. I wonder what land they come from and what Buddha they were lucky enough to meet and what kinds of great Dharmas they learned and practiced.

Bodhisattva Maitreya was speechless, but perhaps with the Buddha's assistance, he was able to put his questions to Śākyamuni:

> We have never seen these innumerable numbers of bodhisattvas. Who expounded the Dharma for these bodhisattvas of great virtue, power, and energy? Who taught and guided them? Under whom did they begin to aspire for enlightenment and what teaching of the Buddha did they praise?... Buddha, the World Honored One! I have never seen them before. Please let us know the name of the world they come from. I know none of them. They appeared suddenly from underground. Please let us know why they emerged.

Grand Master T'ien-t'ai explains this in his *Words and Phrases of the Lotus Sutra* as follows:

> From the Buddha's first preaching under the bodhi tree after obtaining enlightenment, until the preaching of the *Lotus Sutra* today, there has always been an inflow of great bodhisattvas coming from various worlds in the universe to listen to Him preach. Their number is limitless, but I, Maitreya, saw them and remember them all with my wisdom as the successor of the Buddha. I also made trips to various worlds in the universe to see Buddhas in person and became acquainted with the beings there. Nevertheless, there is not even one whom I know among these bodhisattvas.

Grand Master Miao-lê further explained in his *Annotations on the Words and Phrases of the Lotus Sutra,* "Wise men know things in advance as a snake knows that it is a snake." The meaning of these words in the *Lotus Sutra* and annotations by T'ien-t'ai and Miao-lê are clear. That is to say, nobody had ever seen or heard of those bodhisattvas from the earth after Śākyamuni's enlightenment under the bodhi tree until that day, either in this world or in any of the worlds in the universe.

So the Buddha answered the question of Bodhisattva Maitreya: "Maitreya! It was I who taught and guided those great bodhisattvas whom you said you had never seen. After I attained perfect enlightenment in this Sahā World, I taught, guided, and controlled them, and encouraged them to aspire for enlightenment." He continued, "After I sat in meditation under the bodhi tree near the town of Gayā and was able to attain perfect enlightenment, I taught and guided them while preaching the supreme Dharma and caused them to aspire for enlightenment. Now they have all been proceeding to the highest enlightenment without falling back.... I have taught and guided them since the eternal past."

Then Bodhisattva Maitreya and other great bodhisattvas began to doubt the Buddha. At the time the *Flower Garland Sutra* was preached, numerous great bodhisattvas such as Dharma Wisdom gathered. While wondering who they were, Maitreya and others were told by Śākyamuni Buddha, apparently to their satisfaction, that Dharma Wisdom and other great bodhisattvas were Śākyamuni's "good friends."* The same thing happened to those great bodhisattvas who gathered together at Daihōbō where the *Sutra of the Great Assembly* was preached, and to those who gathered at Lake White Heron upon the preaching of the *Wisdom Sutra*. The great bodhisattvas appearing from underground now, however, seemed incomparably superior to them, and it appeared probable that they were teachers of Śākyamuni Buddha. Nevertheless, the Buddha declared that it was He who caused them to aspire for enlightenment, as if the Buddha taught and guided immature people as His disciples. It was only natural, therefore, that Bodhisattva Maitreya and others had serious doubts about Śākyamuni Buddha.

Prince Shōtoku* of Japan was a son of Emperor Yōmei, the 32nd sovereign of Japan. When he was six years old, elderly men coming from Paekche, Koguryô, and T'ang China paid homage to the Emperor. The six-year old crown prince declared that they were his disciples, and these elderly men holding hands in reverence said that the crown prince was their teacher. It was indeed a wonder. It is also said in a non-Buddhist work that a certain man, while walking on a street, came across a young man about 30 years old beating an old man of about 80 years old on the street. Asked what was the matter, the story says, the young man answered that this elderly man he was beating was his son. The relationship between Śākyamuni and great bodhisattvas from underground is similar to these stories.

Therefore, Bodhisattva Maitreya and others asked a question, "World Honored One! When You were the crown prince, You left the palace of the Śākya clan and sat in meditation under the bodhi tree not far from the town of Gayā until You attained perfect enlightenment. It has only been 40 years or so. How could You, World Honored One, achieve so much in so short a time?"

For 40 years or so starting with the *Flower Garland Sutra*, bodhisattvas have asked questions in every assembly to dispel the doubts all beings might have had. This, however, is the most serious question of all. In the *Sutra of Infinite Meaning*,* for instance, 80,000 bodhisattvas such as Great Adornment put forth a serious question concerning the apparent discrepancy in time required for attaining Buddhahood. While it has been said in the sutras preached in the first

40 years or so that it would take many *kalpa,* now it was preached that one could obtain Buddhahood quickly through the teaching of the *Sutra of Infinite Meaning.* However serious the question of Great Adornment Bodhisattva was, that of Maitreya was more crucial.

In another instance, cited in the *Sutra of Meditation on the Buddha of Infinite Life,* it is said that King Ajātaśatru,* incited by Devadatta, imprisoned his own father, King Bimbisāra, and tried to murder his own mother, Vaidehī. But two loyal subjects, Jīvaka* and Candraprabha, talked him into releasing his mother. Inviting the Buddha, Vaidehī first of all asked this question: "For what crime I might have committed in past lives did I give birth to such an evil son like this? What causes You, World Honored One, to be born as a cousin of such a wicked man as Devadatta?"

Of these two questions, "What causes You, World Honored One…" is a very serious doubt. "Wheel-turning Noble Kings* are not born together with enemies. Indra* does not live together with a demon. The Buddha has been a man of compassion from the time of innumerable *kalpa* in the past. Why was he born related to Devadatta, the great enemy? Isn't it because He was not really the Buddha?" Vaidehī might have well wondered. The Buddha did not answer this question. Therefore, those who read the *Sutra of Meditation on the Buddha of Infinite Life* do not understand the real relationship between Śākyamuni and Devadatta unless they read the 12th chapter of the *Lotus Sutra,* Devadatta.* This serious question from Vaidehī was not as serious a question as the one asked by Maitreya.

The 36 questions asked by Kāśyapa* in the *Nirvana Sutra** were also not as serious as the one asked by Maitreya. If the Buddha had not squarely answered the question to dispel this doubt, all the holy teachings of the Buddha's lifetime* would have appeared to be as worthless as bubbles, and the questions of everyone would have remained unanswered. Here lies the importance of the 16th chapter of the *Lotus Sutra,* The Duration of the Life of the Tathāgata.*

Thereafter, preaching the 16th chapter of the *Lotus Sutra,* the Buddha declared, "All the gods, men, and *asura* demons believe that this Śākyamuni Buddha was the one who had left the palace of the Śākya clan and sat in meditation under the bodhi tree not far from the town of Gayā and attained perfect enlightenment." This declaration in the *Lotus Sutra* represents what all the great bodhisattvas had in mind while listening to the sutras from the *Flower Garland* at the Hall of Enlightenment* to the 14th chapter of the *Lotus Sutra,* Peaceful Practices. "To speak the truth, good men," continued the Buddha, "it has been countless aeons [numerous hundreds, 10 thousands, 100 millions, *nayuta* of *kalpa*] since I obtained Buddhahood."

Thus with one stroke He denied as untrue all His previous statements such as "obtaining the first enlightenment"* said three times in the *Flower Garland Sutra,**

"the first enlightenment" in the Āgama sutras,* "the first meditation under the bodhi tree" in the *Vimalakīrti Sutra*,* "16 years after the first enlightenment" in the *Sutra of the Great Assembly*,* "I once sat in meditation at the place of practice in Buddhagayā" in the *Great Sun Buddha Sutra*,* "for 29 years since His enlightenment" in the *Sutra of the Benevolent King*,* "I once meditated under the bodhi tree in the place of enlightenment for six years" stated in the *Sutra of Infinite Meaning*,* and "At first I sat at the place of enlightenment, gazed on the tree, and walked around it meditating" in the second chapter of the *Lotus Sutra*, Expedients.*

Thus it was revealed that Śākyamuni had been the Buddha long since the eternal past, and it became clear that various Buddhas were all manifestations *(funjin)** of Śākyamuni Buddha.* In the pre-Lotus sutras,* as well as in the theoretical section* of the *Lotus Sutra*, various Buddhas and Śākyamuni Buddha were on the same level. Each practiced Buddhism on their own. Therefore, those who considered various Buddhas to be their Most Venerable One* did not worship Śākyamuni. Now, however, as Śākyamuni proved to be the Eternal Buddha, those Buddhas on the lotus petals in the *Flower Garland Sutra*,* or Buddhas in the Hōdō sutras,* *Wisdom** and *Great Sun Buddha Sutras** all became attendants of Śākyamuni Buddha.

Obtaining enlightenment at the age of 30, Śākyamuni Buddha took charge of this Sahā World,* which had been domains of the King of the Brahma Heaven,* the King of Devils in the Sixth Heaven, and others. But, now the Buddha reversed what had been said in the pre-Lotus sutras and in the theoretical section of the *Lotus Sutra* that this world is the defiled land whereas other worlds in the universe are pure lands. He now declared that this world is the land of the Original Buddha and what had been said to be pure lands throughout the universe were defiled lands of manifestations.

Since Śākyamuni Buddha is eternal and all other Buddhas in the universe are His manifestations, then those great bodhisattvas who were taught by manifested Buddhas* and who are from other worlds are all disciples of Lord Śākyamuni Buddha. If the Duration of the Life of the Tathāgata chapter* had not been expounded, it would be like the sky without the sun and moon, a country without a king, mountains and rivers without gems, or a man without a soul. Nevertheless, seemingly knowledgeable men of such provisional sects of Buddhism as Ch'eng-kuan* of the Kegon,* Chia-hsiang* of the Sanron, Tz'ŭ-ên* of the Hossō, and Kōbō* of the Shingon* tried to extol their own canons by stating: "The lord of the *Flower Garland Sutra* represents the Reward Body *(hōjin)** of the Buddha whereas that of the *Lotus Sutra* the Accommodative Body *(ōjin)*,"* or "the Buddha in the Duration of the Life of the Tathāgata chapter of the *Lotus* is an illusion. It is the Great Sun Buddha who is enlightened."

Clouds cover the moon and slanderers hide wise men. When people slander, ordinary yellow rocks appear to be gold and slanderers seem to be wise. Scholars in this age of decay, blinded by slanderous words, do not see the value of the gold in the Duration of the Life of the Tathāgata chapter. Even among men of the Tendai sect some are fooled into taking a yellow rock for gold. They should know that if Śākyamuni had not been the Eternal Buddha, there could not have been so many who received guidance from Him.

The moon does not shy away from its own reflection, but it cannot be reflected without water. Even though the Buddha hopes to convert the populace, He cannot show the eight major events in His life unless the causative relationship is ripe. It is like Hinayana sages of *śrāvaka*, who have listened to the Mahayana teaching and ascended the ladder of the bodhisattva way leading to Buddhahood, until they have reached the step of *shoji* in the distinct teaching or *shojū* in the perfect teaching. In the end, however, they have to wait for the future for their Buddhahood. It is because they have listened only to the pre-Lotus sutras and striven for self-control and self-salvation.

If Lord Śākyamuni had attained Buddhahood for the first time in this world, the King of the Brahma Heaven,* Indra,* Sun God, Moon God, the Four Heavenly Kings,* and others who owned this world as their domain from its beginning would have been the Buddha's disciples only for 40 years or so. And those who listened to the preaching of the *Lotus Sutra* for eight years on Mt. Sacred Eagle could hardly think that the new master, who had attained Buddhahood only 40 years or so ago, had actually been the Buddha from time immemorial. It seemed to them that Śākyamuni was behind those who had been in this world such as the King of the Brahma Heaven, Indra, and the Four Heavenly Kings.

But now since it has been revealed that Śākyamuni attained enlightenment in the eternal past,* Bodhisattvas Nikkō (Sunlight) and Gakkō (Moonlight), disciples of Medicine Master Buddha* in the world to the east, Bodhisattvas Kannon (Avalokiteśvara)* and Seishi (Mahāsthāmaprāpta),* disciples of the Buddha of Infinite Life in a land to the west, various disciples of Buddhas in various lands throughout the universe as well as disciples of the Great Sun Buddha* depicted in both the Diamond Realm Mandala and the Matrix-store Realm Mandala of the *Great Sun Buddha Sutra** and the *Diamond Peak Sutra** now are all disciples of Śākyamuni. Since Buddhas in the worlds throughout the universe are all manifestations *(funjin)** of Śākyamuni Buddha, their disciples are of course Śākyamuni's disciples. Even the sun, the moon, and stars, which have been in this world from its beginning, are disciples of Śākyamuni Buddha.

CHAPTER 11
Various Sects Confused about the Most Venerable One

Nevertheless, all Buddhist sects except for Tendai* are confused about their Most Venerable One.* The Kusha (Chu-she), Jōjitsu (Completion of Truth),* and Ritsu (Precept)* sects make the Most Venerable One Śākyamuni Buddha, who attained Buddhahood by going through the 34 steps of fighting against delusions and evil passions. This is like a crown prince of a world-honored sovereign, who, confused, thinks of himself as a son of an ordinary subject.

The four sects of Kegon (Flower Garland),* Shingon (True Word),* Sanron (ThreeTreatises),* and Hossō (Dharma Characteristics)* are of Mahayana* Buddhism, among which the Hossō and Sanron sects worship as their Most Venerable One a Buddha similar to the superior Accommodative Body of Mahayana Buddha (shōjin). It is just like a crown prince of a Heavenly King thinking of himself as the son of a warrior. The Kegon and Shingon sects establish Vairocana and the Great Sun Buddha instead of Śākyamuni Buddha as the Most Venerable One respectively. It is like a king's son despising his father while respecting a nameless person who acts as though he were the King of the Dharma.

The Pure Land sect considers the Buddha of Infinite Life,* who is merely a manifestation of Śākyamuni in the Pure Land to the West, to be the lord of this world and abandons Śākyamuni, who is the real lord of this world. The Zen sect, just like a lowly man with a little virtue despising his parents, despises the Buddha and His sutras.

They are all confused about the Most Venerable One. It is analogous to the situation before the time of the Three Emperors,* when people did not know who their fathers were and behaved like beasts and birds. Those Buddhist schools that do not know of The Duration of the Life of the Tathāgata* chapter in the *Lotus Sutra* are the same as beasts and birds. They do not know the debt they owe to the Eternal Buddha. Grand Master Miao-lê declared in his *Hokke Gohyaku Monron, 500 Inquiries into the Lotus Sutra:* "Eternity in the life of the Buddha, who is our parent, has not been revealed in the pre-Lotus sutras.... If one does not know the eternity of the life of his father, the Buddha, he is also confused about the Buddha land his father governs. Such a man, no matter how capable he may be, is not at all worthy of being a human."

Grand Master Miao-lê was a man of the T'ien-pao Period toward the end of T'ang China. Having widely read and deeply contemplated the canons of the Three Treatises, Flower Garland, Dharma Characteristics and True Word sects, he concluded that those who do not know the Original Buddha revealed in The Duration of the Life of the Tathāgata chapter are like "beasts and birds," who may be talented but do not know the land governed by the father. "No matter how capable he may be" refers to men like Fa-tsang* and Ch'eng-kuan* of the Flower Garland sect and Venerable Śubhākarasiṃha (Shan-wu-wei)* of the True Word sect, who were men of talent but, like children who do not know their father, did not know the true and eternal Śākyamuni Buddha.

CHAPTER 12
The "3,000 Existences Contained in One Thought" Doctrine as the Seed of Buddhahood

Grand Master Dengyō, the primogenitor of exoteric and esoteric Buddhism in Japan, has said in his *Hokke Shūku, Outstanding Principles of the Lotus Sutra:* "The canons of other sects, also preach some ultimate reality, which is the mother of Buddhahood. However, those scriptures have motherly love but no strictness of the father. Only the Tendai-Lotus sect, with both its strictness and love, is the parent of all sages, wise men, those who have much to learn and nothing to learn, as well as of those who aspire for enlightenment."

As for the three steps for obtaining Buddhahood, its seeding, nurturing and harvest, even those terms are not mentioned in the canons of the Shingon or Kegon sect, much less its true meaning. They maintain that one is able to reach the first of the 10 stages of bodhisattvahood and obtain Buddhahood within the present lifetime. However, as provisional sutras they do not preach the planting of seeds in the past. Thus they talk about attaining Buddhahood without planting seeds, which is like Chiao-kao of Ch'in China or Yuge no Dōkyō of Japan trying to usurp the throne without any right.

These schools of Buddhism fight one another for superiority, but I, Nichiren, do not jump in the scramble, leaving the matter to sutras. Based on the concept of the seed of Buddhahood preached in the *Lotus Sutra,* Bodhisattva Vasubandhu* insisted on the "supremacy of the seed" in his *Discourse on the Lotus Sutra.* This later became the "3,000 existences contained in one thought"* doctrine of Grand Master T'ien'-t'ai. The seed of the various venerable ones appearing in such Mahayana sutras as the *Flower Garland* and the *Great Sun Buddha Sutras** is without exception this "3,000 existences contained in one thought" doctrine. It was Grand Master T'ien-t'ai alone who perceived this in the history of Buddhism.

Ch'eng-kuan of the Flower Garland sect plagiarized this doctrine to interpret a saying in the *Flower Garland Sutra:* "Mind is like a skillful painter." The canons of the True Word sect such as the *Great Sun Buddha Sutra* do not contain any of the doctrines of "attainment of Buddhahood by men of the Two Vehicles,"* "Śākyamuni's attainment of enlightenment in the eternal past"* or "3,000 existences contained in one thought."* Having come to China and read the

Mo-ho Chih-kuan, Great Concentration and Insight, of T'ien-t'ai, Śubhākarasiṃha* thought of reading the T'ien-t'ai concept of "3,000 existences contained in one thought" into such expressions in the *Great Sun Buddha Sutra* as "reality of mind" and "the Buddha as the origin of all things" in order to lay the foundation for the Chen-yen (True Word) sect. He further adopted the finger signs* and mantra words and created a theology of "equality in doctrine but superior in ritualism,"* maintaining that the *Lotus Sutra* and the *Great Sun Buddha Sutra* were equal in doctrine [because both have the "3,000 existences contained in one thought" doctrine], but in ritualism the latter is superior [because it has finger signs and mantra].

Where in the *Great Sun Buddha Sutra* can we find doctrines of the "attainment of Buddhahood by men of the Two Vehicles" and "mutually-possessed characteristics of Ten Realms" represented in the Diamond Realm and the Matrix-store Realm Mandalas? This is the most serious falsification of all. Grand Master Dengyō declared in the *Ebyō Tendai-shū, T'ien-t'ai as the Fountainhead of Buddhist Sects:* "The newly transmitted Shingon (True Word) sect has hidden the fact that its proud transmission of doctrine was in fact smeared by the former T'ien-t'ai monk I-hsing, who, fooled by Śubhākarasiṃha, wrote the '3,000 existences contained in one thought' doctrine into it. The Kegon (Flower Garland) sect, which had been introduced to Japan earlier, has hidden the influence of T'ien-t'ai upon its theology as Fa-tsang's Five Teachings based on the Four Teachings of T'ien-t'ai."

If one had gone to Hokkaidō, he might be able to claim this well-known Japanese poem by Hitomaro to be his own:

At the first light of dawn
A boat leaves the foggy beach of Akashi,
Disappearing behind an island.

Perhaps islanders would be fooled by such a man. So are scholars of China and Japan by Śubhākarasiṃha and Fa-tsang.

Liang-hsü of the T'ien-t'ai school in China had this to say: "Compared to the *Lotus Sutra,* teachings of such schools as Chen-yen (Shingon), Ch'an (Zen), Hua-yen (Kegon), and San-lun (Sanron) are expedient gates leading to the true teaching of the *Lotus.*" It was because of his false preaching, stolen from the T'ien-t'ai doctrine, that Venerable Śubhākarasiṃha* was punished by Emma, the Lord of the Law. It must have been due to his change of mind and submission to the *Lotus Sutra* that he was later released. It was to show their submission to the *Lotus Sutra* that Śubhākarasiṃha and Amoghavajra (Pu-k'ung)* thereafter placed the *Lotus Sutra* in the center between the Diamond Realm Mandala and the Matrix-store Realm Mandala as if it were the great king served at left and right by two subordinates: the *Great Sun Buddha Sutra** of the Matrix-store Realm and the *Diamond Peak Sutra* of the Diamond Realm. In assessing the doctrines of various sutras, Kōbō of Japan regarded the *Flower Garland* higher than the *Lotus Sutra*, the latter being placed on the eighth stage in the development of mind behind the *Great Sun Buddha* and the *Flower Garland*. However, he, too, in transmitting ritualism to his own disciples such as Jitsue and Shinga and to disciples of Grand Master Dengyō such as Enchō and Kōjō, placed the *Lotus Sutra* in the center between the two mandalas as mentioned above.

In another instance, when Grand Master Chia-hsiang (Chi-tsang)* of the San-lun sect wrote the *Fa-hua Hsüan-lun, Treatise on the Profundity of the Lotus Sutra*, in 10 fascicles, he maintained, in contradiction to T'ien-t'ai, that the *Lotus Sutra* was preached during the fourth, not fifth, period of Śākyamuni's lifetime, because it was meant to lead the Two Vehicles of *śrāvaka* and *pratyekabuddha* into bodhisattvahood or to destroy men of the Two Vehicles so as to establish bodhisattvas. However, he later submitted to T'ien-t'ai and served him seven years, discontinuing his own lectures, dispersing his disciples, and even making himself a stool for T'ien-t'ai to climb up into a pulpit.

Grand Master T'zŭ-ên* of the Fa-hsiang (Dharma Characteristics)* sect expressed many false concepts in his *Fa-yüan I-lin-chang* in seven fascicles [or 12 fascicles]. Looking down on the *Lotus Sutra* he wrote: "The One Vehicle teaching* for all people is merely expedient, while the three separate teachings for bodhisattvas, *śrāvaka* and *pratyekabuddha* are the true teaching." However, one of his disciples, Hsi-fu, later wrote the *Fa-hua Hsüan-tsan Yao-chi*, in the fourth fascicle of which he maintained that the One Vehicle teaching in the *Lotus* is also true. Although his written statements were ambiguous, his heart was with T'ien-t'ai.

Ch'eng-kuan* of the Flower Garland sect wrote a commentary on the *Flower Garland Sutra*, in which he compared it with the *Lotus Sutra* and seemed to have concluded that the *Lotus Sutra* was expedient. However, he later wrote that the T'ien-t'ai sect considered the "3,000 existences contained in one thought" doctrine to be true, as did his own sect. Is it not that Ch'eng-kuan regretted what he had just written earlier? So did Grand Master Kōbō.* Without a mirror, one cannot see one's own face. Without enemies, one cannot see one's own faults. Scholars of the Shingon and other schools did not realize their own faults until they met Grand Master Dengyō.*

Therefore we say that, although Buddhas, bodhisattvas, men, and gods appearing in various sutras seem to have obtained Buddhahood through their respective sutras, in reality they were truly enlightened because of the *Lotus Sutra*. The four great vows* of Śākyamuni and other Buddhas, such as saving a countless number of people, were fulfilled in this sutra of the *Lotus*. In the second chapter, it is stated, "My (Buddha's) wishes are all fully satisfied."

CHAPTER 13
Five Holy Proclamations*

As I contemplate, it is doubtless that Buddhas, bodhisattvas, and gods appearing in such sutras as the *Flower Garland,* Sutra of Meditation on the Buddha of Infinite Life** and *Great Sun Buddha Sutra** would protect those who read and practice them. However, if those who read and practice those sutras should become antagonistic to those who practice the *Lotus Sutra,** those deities would abandon those who practice the *Flower Garland* and other sutras for those who practice the *Lotus Sutra*.

It is, for instance, like a filial son who would abandon his own father for royal service if his compassionate father should become an enemy of the king. This is a most filial act, and the same could be said of Buddhism. I believe that the Buddhas, bodhisattvas and 10 female *rākṣasa* demons mentioned in the Lotus will protect me. In addition, numerous Buddhas in the six directions and the 25 bodhisattvas mentioned in the canons of the Pure Land sect,* the 1,200 deities appearing in the two mandalas of the Shingon (True Word) sect,* as well as all Buddhas and guardian deities* of the seven sects of Buddhism will protect Nichiren. I believe it was in this way that guardian deities of the seven sects of Buddhism protected Grand Master Dengyō.*

I, Nichiren, believe that as soon as the one who practices* the *Lotus Sutra* appears, all those gods such as the Sun God and the Moon God, who heard the preaching of the Lotus in the "three meetings at two places"* [on Mt. Sacred Eagle and in the stupa appearing high in the sky] will hurry to his aid just as a magnet attracts pieces of iron and the moon reflects itself on the water. They will bear his difficulties and carry out the vows they made before the Buddha at those meetings. Nevertheless, they have not come to rescue me, Nichiren. Is it because I am not one who practices the *Lotus Sutra*? I must reconsider the sutra in the light of my own background in order to see what is wrong with me.

Some might ask how do I know that the Pure Land* and Zen* sects today are enemies of the *Lotus Sutra* and "evil friends"* of all people. To this I would not answer in my own words. Instead, I would show them the ugly faces of slanderers* of the True Dharma reflected in the mirror of sutras and commentaries, although I can't help those who were born blind.

In the 11th chapter of the *Lotus Sutra*, fascicle four, The Beholding the Stupa of Treasures, it is written:

Then the Buddha of Many Treasures in the stupa of treasures offered half of his seat to Śākyamuni Buddha.... The great crowd saw the two Buddhas sit cross-legged on the lion-shaped throne in the stupa of the seven treasures.... Śākyamuni Buddha... spoke out resoundingly to monks, nuns, laymen, and laywomen: "Who will expound the *Lotus Sutra* widely in this Sahā World?* Now is the time. I shall enter Nirvana* before long, and therefore hope to transmit this *Lotus Sutra* to someone so that it may be preserved after My death."

This was the first proclamation of the Buddha. "Then Śākyamuni Buddha, wishing to repeat what He had said, declared in verse" of the same chapter:

> The Saintly Master, the Buddha of Many Treasures,
> Who had passed away a long time ago,
> Came riding in the stupa of treasures
> For the sake of the Dharma.
> Why don't you, everyone,
> Strive to preserve the Dharma?
> ....
> Just as a strong wind
> Sways the twigs of a tree
> Those Buddhas employ these expedients
> To have the Dharma forever preserved.
> Listen, everyone!
> Who will uphold this sutra,
> And read and recite it
> After My death?
> Now is the time for you
> To make your vows before Me.

This was His second proclamation. Śākyamuni Buddha continued on:

> The Buddha of Many Treasures
> And the Buddhas of My manifestation
> Whom I have assembled here
> Wish to know who will do all this.
> ....
> Good men! Consider thoroughly
> Before making a great vow
> To preach this sutra.

For it is difficult to do so.
It is not so difficult
To preach all other sutras,
Which are as numerous
As the sands in the Ganges River;
It is not as difficult
To take Mt. Sumeru
And throw it over to
Countless Buddha lands;

....

As it is difficult
To preach this sutra
In the evil world
After My death.

....

It is not as difficult
To carry a stack of hay
And remain unburnt in the conflagration
Burning down the whole world
As it is difficult
To uphold this sutra
And preach it even to one person
After My death.

....

Good men!
Who will uphold this sutra
And read and recite it
After My death?
Now is the time for you
To make a vow before the Buddha.

This was the third proclamation of Śākyamuni Buddha. The fourth and fifth, which appear in the Devadatta chapter,* will be considered later.

The meaning of these words in the Beholding the Stupa of Treasures chapter is clear. It is as clear as the great sun shining in the sky or a mole on a white face. Nevertheless, those who were born blind, those who have slanted eyes, who are one-eyed, who believe that only their own teachers are wise men, or those who are stuck to false teachings will not be able to see. Despite all the difficulties, however, I will try to write here for those who aspire for Buddhism.

It is difficult to have the chance of hearing the *Lotus Sutra*, harder than to see the once-in-3,000-years peach flowers at Hsi Wang-mu's orchard or the *uḍumbara* flowers, which are said to bloom once in 3,000 years to foretell the coming of the Wheel-turning Noble King.* You should also know that even the eight-year war between Han Kao-tsu and Hsiang Yü for the control of China, the seven-year war in Japan between Minamoto no Yoritomo and Taira no Munemori, the struggle for power between the *asura* demons and Indra, or the battle between the gold-wing bird and the dragon king at Lake Anavatapta, do not exceed in importance and intensity the war between the *Lotus Sutra* and all other sutras. The truth of the *Lotus Sutra* was revealed in Japan twice. You should know that it was due to Grand Master Dengyō* and me, Nichiren. Blind persons will not believe this. It can't be helped. These words in the *Lotus Sutra* regarding the Three Pronouncements are an assessment through the meeting of Śākyamuni Buddha, the Buddha of Many Treasures,* and other Buddhas in manifestation* from all over the universe of all the Buddhist scriptures that exist in Japan, China, India, the Dragon Palace, heaven and all the worlds in the universe.

Question: Are those sutras such as the *Flower Garland Sutra,* Hōdō sutras, *Wisdom Sutra, Revealing the Profound and Secret Sutra,* *Ryōga Sutra (Entering Laṅkā Sutra),* *Great Sun Buddha Sutra* and *Nirvana Sutra* among what the *Lotus Sutra* calls the nine easier or the six difficult actions* to spread [the *Lotus Sutra*] after the death of Śākyamuni Buddha?

Answer: Tripiṭaka masters of the Flower Garland sect such as Tu-shun, Chih-yen, Fa-tsang, and Ch'eng-kuan say, "Both the *Flower Garland* and *Lotus Sutras* are among the six difficult actions. In name they are separate sutras, but they are one in principle in what they preach, just as it is stated in T'ien-t'ai's *Great Concentration and Insight,* 'In practicing Hinayana, there are four separate gates leading to the one truth.'"

Tripiṭaka Master Hsüan-chuang, Grand Master Tz'ŭ-ên and other Dharma Characteristic scholars maintain, "Both the *Revealing the Profound and Secret Sutra* and *Lotus Sutra* are among the six difficult actions because they preach the most sophisticated of the 'consciousness-only' doctrine expounded as the third or final stage, according to the Dharma Characteristics theology."

Chi-ts'ang (Grand Master Chia-hsiang) and others of the Three Treatises sect maintain: "The *Wisdom* and *Lotus Sutras* are different in name but identical in body. They preach the same Dharma."

Tripiṭaka Masters Śubhākarasiṃha, Vajrabodhi, Amoghavajra and other Indian-Chinese Chen-yen (Shingon) scholars say, "The *Great Sun Buddha Sutra* and the *Lotus Sutra* are the same in principle. They both are among the six difficult actions." However, Grand Master Kōbō in Japan states, "The *Great Sun Buddha Sutra* is not among the scriptures preached by Śākyamuni. It was preached by the Dharma Body* of the Great Sun Buddha." Some say, "As the *Flower Garland Sutra* was preached by the Reward Body* of the Buddha, it does not belong to either the six difficult actions nor the nine easier ones." Founders and scholars of these four schools maintain this. Several thousand later scholars repeat the same.

It is regrettable to say that if I, Nichiren, spoke up against them without reservation, people today would not even look at me. They would heap further injustice upon me even to the point of slandering me to the king and endangering my life. Nevertheless, in the *Nirvana Sutra* preached under the twin *śāla* trees, the will of our compassionate Father Śākyamuni Buddha, it is said that we should rely upon the Dharma [preached by the Buddha], not upon [interpretations by] a person."* It means that Four Reliances,* bodhisattvas who are to lead people after the death of the Buddha, are divided into four groups. In the fourth group are the highest ranking bodhisattvas such as Universal-Sage (Fugen) and Mañjuśrī (Monju), and even they should not be trusted unless they preach the sutras in hand.

It is also said in the *Nirvana Sutra* that we should rely only upon sutras that completely reveal the truth, not upon sutras that do not completely reveal the truth. This means that we must distinguish the true sutra from provisional ones before relying upon it. In the *Commentary on the Ten Stages by Bodhisattva Nāgārjuna*derson* it is also said that we should rely upon the honest commentaries on sutras and not upon evil ones. Grand Master T'ien-t'ai* says, "Adopt whatever agrees with the sutra, and do not believe in that which is not found in the sutra in word or in meaning," while Grand Master Dengyō* states, "Rely upon the words of the Buddha in sutras. Do not believe what has been transmitted orally." Enchin, the Grand Master Chishō,* states that we should transmit the Buddha's teaching only from sutras.

Now, as for the assessments of the sutras by the founders of the four Buddhist sects mentioned above, their judgements seem more or less to conform to sutras and their commentaries. However, they all seem to stick to the teaching of their own sects without correcting the errors of their own teachers. Their opinions are formed from egotism and distorted interpretations of sutras. It is self-decorated egocentricity! After the death of the Buddha, Vātsīputra and Vaipulya strengthened their theologies by adopting Buddhist doctrines. Likewise, Chinese thinking since the Later Han, when Buddhism was introduced, became more intricate than non-Buddhist thought in India before the time of Śākyamuni Buddha or Confucianism in the time of the Three Emperors and Five Rulers, when Buddhism was unknown. Misusing Buddhist doctrines, they skillfully established their evil teachings.

In the same way, teachers of such sects as Flower Garland (Kegon), Dharma Characteristics (Hossō), and True Word (Shingon), envious of T'ien-t'ai's true teaching, tend to resort to distorted interpretations of the true *Lotus Sutra* in order to fit it into their provisional teachings. Surely, those who aspire to enlightenment should be unbiased, distance themselves from sectarian quarrels, and not despise other people.

It is said in the 10th chapter of the *Lotus Sutra,* Teacher of the Dharma, that among the sutras that had already been preached, are now being preached, and will be preached,* the *Lotus Sutra* is supreme. Commenting on this, Grand Master Miao-lê* states in his *Annotations on the Words and Phrases of the Lotus Sutra:* "Besides the *Lotus Sutra,* some sutras claim to be the king of sutras, but they are not really the first among sutras as they do not claim to be first among those which have already been preached, are being preached, and will be preached." He also asserts in his *Commentary on the Profound Meaning of the Lotus Sutra:* "Although the *Lotus Sutra* is an incomparable Dharma above all the scriptures preached in the past, present, and future, many are confused about this, and they will suffer forever by slandering the True Dharma."

Surprised by this statement in the *Lotus Sutra* and Grand Master Miao-lê's commentaries on it, I have read all the Buddhist scriptures and commentaries by later teachers. As a result all my doubts have melted away. It is not even worth mentioning that ignorant men of the Shingon (True Word) today believe that theirs is superior to the *Lotus Sutra* because they have finger signs and mantra* or simply because Grand Master Jikaku* said so.

Likewise, it is said in the *Mitsugon-kyō, Sutra of Mystic Glorification:** "Such sutras as the *Jūji-kyō, Ten Stages Sutra, Daiju Kinnara-kyō, Kimnara Great Tree Sutra, Jinzū-kyō, Supernatural Powers Sutra* and *Shōman-gyō,* Srimala Sutra,* are all begotten from this *Mitsugon-kyō.* As such, this sutra is superior to all the Buddhist scriptures."

The *Daiun-gyō, Great Cloud Sutra* says: "This *Daiun-gyō* is the Wheel-turning Noble King among sutras because it preaches the real nature of people and everlasting Buddha-nature."

The *Six Pāramitā Sutra* states:

> All the true Dharmas preached by numerous Buddhas in the past and all the 84,000 wonderful Dharmas I am preaching in this world can be grouped in five categories: (1) sutras, the Buddha's teachings; (2) precepts; (3) commentaries on sutras; (4) the wisdom of the Buddha; and (5) mystic spells. With these five, I shall preach and convert all the people. Even if the people are incapable of upholding the sutras, precepts, commentaries, and

the wisdom of the Buddha, I can still enable them to obtain enlightenment. Even if they have committed such sins as the "four major sins," or "five rebellious sins," or even if those issendai *(icchantika),** who slander the Mahayana sutras, have committed serious sins, I can enable them to purge themselves of their sins and obtain emancipation and Nirvana* (enlightenment) at once. It is to such people that I preach the teachings of the mystic spells. These five categories of teachings are analogous to the "five tastes" of milk and four milk products, the most refined of which is the wonderful taste of "clarified butter" *(daigo).*[14] The teaching of the mystic spells is like the taste of *daigo*, which is the most exquisite of the five. It can cure various sicknesses and keep both body and mind healthy. So is the teaching of the mystic spells, the most admirable aspect of Buddhism that extinguishes serious sins of the people.

Next, in the *Gejimmitsu-kyō, Revealing the Profound and Secret Sutra,** it is stated:

The Bodhisattva Shōgishō again said to the Buddha that the World Honored One was at first in the Deer Park in Bārāṇasī, where He preached the true teaching of the Four Noble Truths* to those who aspired to the Hinayana sage of *śrāvaka.** It was such a rare teaching never preached before by gods or people. Nevertheless, the teaching preached then was imperfect, not without room for improvement and criticism. It was the source of endless controversy.

In the second period of preaching, for those who aspired to practice Mahayana* Buddhism, the Buddha preached that all phenomena are void without substance, without life and death, originally constant, unchanging and in the state of Nirvana. This was the preaching of the True Dharma without revealing the true intention of the Buddha. It was more rare than the one preached in the first period, but still there was room for further improvement. It was not yet a perfect teaching and was a source of constant squabbling.

And now in the third period, the Buddha preaches, for those who seek the teaching for all to obtain Buddhahood, that all phenomena are void without substance, without life and death, originally constant, unchanging, in the state of Nirvana, and of no substance. This is the preaching of the True Dharma with the Buddha's intention clearly revealed. It is the most wonderful and rarest of all the sutras. What the Buddha preaches now is the supreme teaching with no room for improvement or criticism. It is the perfect teaching, which would not cause any controversy.

The *Daihannya-kyō, Great Wisdom Sutra** states: "By following whatever teaching one listens to as an expedient, either within Buddhism or without, one can grasp the exquisite principle of the wisdom in this sutra. All worldly matters and actions can lead to ultimate truth by this wisdom. Nothing exists outside the realm of ultimate truth."

It is said in the *Great Sun Buddha Sutra,** fascicle one: "Vajrasattva! Practicing Mahayana Buddhism means to aspire to the teaching of the void and know that in all phenomena there is no self. Why is that so? It is because those who practiced Mahayana Buddhism in the past, observing the *arayashiki, ālaya-consciousness,* the substance of all phenomena, knew that all phenomena are illusory." It is stated also, "Vajrasattva thus abandoned the teaching of egolessness, realizing that his own mind was originally free, without birth or death." It preaches also, "The so-called emptiness is beyond the realm of six sensory organs and is without form or boundary, beyond futile squabbles and is analogous to space. A phenomenon is not an entity in itself." It states further, "The Great Sun Buddha said to Vajrasattva that Buddhahood is to know one's mind as it is."

Then it is asserted in the *Flower Garland Sutra:**

> Among the people in all worlds, there are few who aspire to the *śrāvaka** way. Even fewer people seek the *pratyekabuddha** way. Those who seek the Mahayana* teaching are extremely rare. Even then, it is easier to seek the Mahayana teaching as compared to having faith in this *Flower Garland Sutra*, which is extremely difficult to do. How much more difficult it is to uphold it, remember it correctly, practice as it teaches, and understand it truly! It is not as difficult to carry all the worlds in the universe on the head for as along as one *kalpa* without moving a centimeter as it is to have faith in this Dharma. It is not as meritorious to offer various things of joy to people as numerous as the dust of all the worlds in the universe for as long as one *kalpa* as it is to believe this Dharma. It is not as difficult to sustain 10 Buddha lands in the palm of your hand and float in the air for as long as one *kalpa* as it is to believe this Dharma. It is not as meritorious to offer things of joy to people as innumerable as the dust of 10 Buddha lands for as long as one *kalpa* as it is to uphold this sutra.

Finally it is said in the *Nirvana Sutra:**

> Although these Mahayana scriptures have immeasurable merits, one cannot even compare them with this *Nirvana Sutra*. The latter is a hundred, a thousand, a hundred thousand trillion times, or infinite number of times

more meritorious than the former. Good men! It is analogous to a cow producing milk, which in turn produces cream, which in turn produces clarified butter called *daigo*. This *daigo* is the supreme elixir. It cures all sicknesses of the people who take it as if it contained all medicines. Good men! The Buddha is the same. He preached the 12 kinds of scriptures* which in turn produced the Āgama sutras, which in turn produced Hōdō sutras,* from which stemmed the Wisdom Sutra,* from which was produced the *Nirvana Sutra*.* The *Nirvana Sutra* is like the taste of *daigo*, an allegory of the Buddha-nature* expounded in the *Nirvana Sutra*.

Each of the eight sutras cited above thus claims to be the supreme one. However, when compared to the references in the *Lotus Sutra* to "the sutras preached in the past, being preached at present, and to be preached in the future"* and "six difficult and nine easier actions,"* those statements look like stars compared to the moon and are like the nine mountains surrounding Mt. Sumeru compared to Mt. Sumeru.

Nevertheless, even such master teachers as Ch'eng-kuan* of the Hua-yen (Flower Garland),* Tz'ŭ-ên* of the Fa-hsiang (Dharma Characteristics),* Chia-hsiang* of the San-lun (Three Treatises)* and Kōbō of the Shingon (True Word),* who appeared to have the eye of a Buddha, were confused by those sutras. How much more confused are those blind present-day scholars! How can they see the comparative merits of those sutras? They are unable to perceive even a clear distinction between black and white or between Mt. Sumeru and a poppy-seed, much less a principle as abstract as the sky. Since they do not know the depth of the teaching, no one knows the depth of the principle preached in the teaching. As the citations from eight sutras above are in separate fascicles and are out of sequence, it may be difficult for the ignorant to differentiate the doctrine contained in them. Therefore, let me explain them in order to help ignorant people.

In considering kings, we must know the difference between the great ones and the minor ones. The *Great Cloud Sutra*, which claims to be the king of sutras, cited above, is merely a minor king. In considering "all" we must know the difference between all of a portion and all of a total. When the *Sutra of Mystic Glorification* says that it is the most superior of all scriptures, it does not mean all the Buddhist scriptures. In considering the "five flavors," we must know whether they are applicable to all of Buddhism or only to a portion of Buddhism. The *Six Pāramitā Sutra* cited above talks of the attainment of Buddhahood by all the people with grave sins but not by those without Buddha-nature.* How much less do they reveal the attainment of enlightenment by Śākyamuni in the eternal past!* The doctrine of the "five flavors" in this sutra is not equal to that of the *Nirvana*

Sutra. How can it face up to the *Lotus Sutra*, the attainment of Buddhahood by men of the Two Vehicles preached in the theoretical section* or the attainment of enlightenment by Śākyamuni Buddha in the eternal past expounded in the essential section?* Confused with this sutra, however, Grand Master Kōbō* of Japan classified the *Lotus Sutra* as the fourth or the second from the top among the "five flavors." Even the fifth and most refined *daigo* flavor of the *Six Pāramitā Sutra* cannot equal that of the *Nirvana Sutra*. How can it face up to that of the *Lotus Sutra*, which is superior to the *Nirvana Sutra*? What happened to Grand Master Kōbō? Nevertheless, he called Grand Master T'ien-t'ai* and other teachers thieves when he claimed in the *Kemmitsu Nikyō-ron, Discourse on Exoteric and Esoteric Teachings*, that Chinese teachers competed against one another in stealing the *daigo* flavor of the *Six Pāramitā Sutra*. Praising his own school, he further stated in it that wise men in the past had regrettably not tasted *daigo*.

Leaving aside this question, I will write this for my followers. Others will not believe in me and go to hell for slandering the True Dharma, which would in turn cause them to obtain Buddhahood. It is possible to know the salinity of the ocean by tasting one drop of water, and the advent of spring by seeing a flower bloom. In the same way without sailing thousands of kilometers over to Sung China, without spending as long as three years as Fa-hsien did to visit Mt. Sacred Eagle,* without entering the Dragon Palace as Nāgārjuna* did, without visiting Bodhisattva Maitreya as Asanga* did, or without attending the "three meetings at two places"* for lectures on the *Lotus Sutra* [two on Mt. Sacred Eagle and one up in the sky] you will be able to perceive the relative merits of all the sutras preached by the Buddha during His lifetime by reading this writing of mine.

As snakes are relatives of dragons, they can foretell a flood seven days before its coming. As crows had been fortune-tellers in past lives, they can foretell the fortune of the year. Birds are superior to human beings in their ability to fly. In knowing the comparative merits of sutras, I, Nichiren, am superior to Ch'eng-kuan of Hua-yen (Flower Garland), Chia-hsiang of San-lun (Three Treatises), Tz'ŭ-ên of Fa-hsiang (Dharma Characteristics) and Kōbō of Shingon (True Word). It is because I follow the tradition of T'ien-t'ai and Dengyō. How could they avoid committing the crime of slandering the True Dharma?*

It is I, Nichiren, who is the richest in Japan today, because I sacrifice my life for the sake of the *Lotus Sutra* and leave my name for posterity. Gods of rivers take orders from the master of a great ocean, and gods of mountains follow the king of Mt. Sumeru.* Likewise, when one knows the meaning of the "six difficult and nine easier actions"* and "scriptures preached in the past, are preached at present, and will be preached in the future" in the *Lotus Sutra*, one will automatically know the comparative merits of all the Buddhist scriptures without reading them.

Besides the Three Pronouncements* made in the 11th chapter* of the *Lotus Sutra,* Beholding the Stupa of Treasures, the Buddha issued two more proclamations* in the following 12th chapter of the same sutra, Devadatta, with the intention of having it spread after His death. Devadatta* had been regarded as a man of *icchantika** who had no possibility of attaining Buddhahood. Nevertheless, he was assured by the Buddha of becoming Tennō (Heavenly King) Buddha in the future. The 40-fascicled *Nirvana Sutra** has stated the existence of Buddha-nature in all, which is realized in this Devadatta chapter. Numerous offenders such as Zenshōbiku (Sunakṣatra)* and King Ajātaśatru* committed the Five Rebellious Sins* or slandered the True Dharma. Since the worst of them, Devadatta, was assured of becoming a Buddha in the future, all others would naturally be assured just as people follow a leader and twigs and leaves join a tree. That is to say the example of Devadatta assured of being the future Heavenly King Buddha has made it unmistakable that all offenders of the Five Rebellious Sins or Seven Rebellious Sins, slanderers of the True Dharma, and men of *icchantika,* all of them will attain Buddhahood someday. This is somewhat like deadly poison turning into nectar, the best of all flavors.

Also, the example of the dragon girl becoming a Buddha* does not mean only her. It means the attainment of Buddhahood by all women. In the Hinayana* sutras preached before the *Lotus Sutra* a woman is not thought of in terms of attaining Buddhahood. Various Mahayana* sutras appear to recognize women attaining Buddhahood or going to the Buddha land, but only after they changed themselves to the good by giving up the evil. This is not an immediate attainment of Buddhahood in this world, which can only be possible through the "3,000 existences contained in one thought"* doctrine. Therefore what the Buddha promised in those Mahayana sutras is in name only. On the other hand, the attainment of Buddhahood by the dragon girl in the *Lotus Sutra* is meant as an example for many, opening the way for women of the Latter Age to attain Buddhahood or reach the Buddha land.

Filial devotion preached in Confucianism is limited to this life. Confucian sages and wise men exist in name only because they do not help parents in their future lives. Non-Buddhist religions* in India know of the past as well as the future, but they do not know how to help parents. Only Buddhism is worthy of being the way of sages and wise men, as it helps parents in their future lives. However, both the Mahayana and Hinayana sutras expounded before the *Lotus Sutra* preach Buddhahood in name only, without substance. Therefore those who practice such sutras will not be able to obtain Buddhahood even for themselves, much less helping parents obtain Buddhahood. Now coming to the *Lotus Sutra,* when the enlightenment of women* was revealed, the enlightenment of mothers was realized. When a man as wicked as Devadatta could attain Buddhahood, the enlightenment of fathers was realized. These are the two proclamations of the Buddha in the Devadatta chapter, and this is the reason why the *Lotus Sutra* is the sutra of the filial way among all the Buddhist scriptures.

CHAPTER 14
The Bright Mirror Reflecting the Holy Predictions

Surprised at these Five Holy Proclamations* of the Buddha, three of which were revealed in the 11th chapter and two in the 12th chapter of the *Lotus Sutra*, bodhisattvas of the theoretical teachings swore to live up to His expectations in the 13th chapter, Encouragement for Keeping This Sutra.* Citing sutras as a mirror reflecting the truth, I now let you know how men of the Zen, Ritsu (Precept), and Pure Land sects and their followers today slander* the True Dharma.

A man called Nichiren was beheaded at one o'clock during the night of the 12th day in the ninth month last year. His soul has come to the province of Sado and is writing this in the midst of snow in the second month of the following year to be sent to his closely related disciples from past lives. As such this writing of mine may sound frightening to you but it should not be. How fearful others will be when they read this writing! This is the bright mirror in which Śākyamuni Buddha, the Buddha of Many Treasures,* and other Buddhas in manifestation* all over the universe reflect the state of Japan in the future, namely through the conditions of Japan today. Consider this as my memento in case I die.

Vowing to spread the *Lotus Sutra* in the Latter Age, uncountable bodhisattvas said to the Buddha in the 13th chapter, Encouragement for Keeping This Sutra, in verse form:

> We beseech You not to worry.
> We will expound this sutra
> In the frightful world
> After Your death.
> Ignorant people may
> Speak ill of us and slander us,
> Or abuse us with swords or sticks.
> We will endure all of them.
> Monks in the evil world
> Cunning, crooked, flattering, and arrogant,
> Boast themselves enlightened
> While they are not.
> Some monks will stay in a monastery,

Wearing robes, sitting quietly,
Claiming to be practicing the true way
Despising others staying among the people.
Attached to profit making
They will preach the Dharma for lay people
And will be revered by the people
As though they were *arhats* with Six Superhuman Powers.*
They will have evil thoughts.
Always thinking of worldly matters,
Taking advantage of being in a monastery,
They will be happy to find our faults.
....
Among the large crowd
In order to slander us
They will always speak ill of us
To the king, ministers, Brahmans,
Lay believers, and other monks
Saying that we are crooked in opinion
And preach non-Buddhist teachings.*
....
In the evil world in the *kalpa* of defilement are
Many dreadful matters
Such as evil spirits abusing and shaming us,
As we spread the True Dharma.
....
Evil monks of the defiled world,
Without knowledge of the Buddha
Using the expedient and provisional teachings,
Will slander us and frown at us;
Often we will be chased out of monasteries.

Grand Master Miao-lê explains this citation in the eighth fascicle of his *Annotations on the Words and Phrases of the Lotus Sutra, Hokke Mongu-ki:*

This citation from the 13th chapter of the *Lotus Sutra* could be divided into three parts. The first line [four phrases] refers to the evil people as a whole, that is, the so-called self-conceited lay people. The next line refers to self-conceited monks, while the following seven lines refer to those arrogant monks who consider themselves sages. Of the three, persecution by the first group of arrogant people is endurable. That of the second group is harder to endure, while that of the third group, self-styled sages, is most difficult to endure. The second and third groups are more cunning and less likely to reveal their faults.

Monk Chih-tu of Tung-ch'un* states in his *T'ien-t'ai Fa-hua-shu-i-tsuan, Tendai Interpretation of the Meaning of the Lotus Sutra:*

> First, in the five lines starting with "ignorant people" in the Encouragement for Keeping This Sutra chapter, the first line [verse] refers to those who commit "three kinds of evil acts," physical, verbal, and psychological acts, which are visible. The next line [verse] beginning with "monks in the evil world" refers to self-conceited arrogant monks. Third, the three lines [verses] following "some monks will stay in a monastery" refer to the acts of evil monks representing those of all the wicked people.

He also writes: "Two lines following 'among the large crowd' refer to reporting false charges to the authorities against the True Dharma and against those who spread it."

It is said in the *Nirvana Sutra,** fascicle nine: "Good men! Suppose a man of *icchantika** pretending to be an *arhat* stays in a remote corner in tranquility, slandering Mahayana sutras. Ordinary men who see him may think him to be an *arhat* or a great bodhisattva." The sutra says also:

> At the time this *Nirvana Sutra* spreads all over the world [Jambudvīpa],* evil monks will steal it and forcibly divide it up into many parts destroying the excellent color, fragrance, and taste of the True Dharma. Although these evil monks may recite such sutras, they will miss the true teaching of the Buddha replacing it with meaningless words of flowery rhetoric. They will rearrange the sutra taking the beginning part of the sutra and putting it at the end or vice versa, or they will move the beginning and ending parts to the mid-section, or the mid-part to the beginning or ending part. You must know that such evil monks are the demons' companions.

The six-fascicled *Nirvana Sutra, Hatsunaion-gyō** states:

> There will be a man of *icchantika** who acts like an *arhat* but commits evil acts, and there will be an *arhat* who acts like a man of *icchantika* but has compassion. An *arhat*-like man of *icchantika* refers to the people who slander Mahayana Buddhism. An *arhat* who acts like the man of *icchantika* refers to a man who despises the Hinayana sages of *śrāvaka* and widely

preaches Mahayana Buddhism, assuring the people that both he and they are bodhisattvas* because everybody has Buddha-nature in themself. Nevertheless, those people would consider him a man of *icchantika*.

It is said also in the *Nirvana Sutra:*

After the death of the Buddha, and after the Age of the True Dharma is over, monks in the Age of the Semblance Dharma will no longer be sages. On the surface, they will appear to keep precepts and recite sutras a little, but they will devour rich food and enjoy a prosperous life.... Although they will wear robes of Buddhist monks they will act for selfish gain just like hunters walking slowly aiming at game with narrow eyes, or cats stalking a rat. They will always utter this: "I have attained the stage of *arhat*."... They will appear to be wise men and virtuous people, but in heart they will harbor greed and jealousy just like Brahmans practicing the exercise of keeping silence. They will appear to be Buddhist monks but actually are not. With their rampant evil thoughts they will slander the True Dharma.

Now, in the light of the *Lotus Sutra* preached on Mt. Sacred Eagle and the *Nirvana Sutra* preached under the twin *śāla* trees, as bright as the sun and moon, and commentaries by Miao-lê of P'i-chan and Chih-tu of Tung-ch'un* as brilliant as a clear mirror, sectarian schools today and the ugly faces of Zen, Ritsu (Precept), and Pure Land followers in all of Japan are seen without a trace of a cloud.

It is said in [Chapter 13 of] the *Myōhōrenge-kyō, Sutra of the Lotus Flower of the Wonderful Dharma,* [Encouragement for Keeping This Sutra,] that it would be spread "in the dreadful and evil world after the death of the Buddha." [In Chapter 14, Peaceful Practices:*] "in the latter evil day," " in the latter days," "during the latter days when the Dharma is about to disappear." [In Chapter 17, Variety of Merits:*] "in the evil world during the Latter Age of Degeneration." And [in Chapter 23, Previous Life of Medicine-King Bodhisattva:*] "during the fifth 500-year period after the death of the Buddha." Likewise, it is said in the *Shōhoke-kyō, Lotus Sutra of the True Dharma,* Kanzeppon chapter, that the sutra would be spread "in the latter days" and "in the coming latter days." The *Tempon Hokekyō, Lotus Sutra with Additions* says the same.

It is true that Grand Master T'ien-t'ai* has written: "The three Southern masters and seven Northern masters* of Buddhism in China during the Age of the Semblance Dharma* have become the enemies of the *Lotus Sutra.*"* Grand Master Dengyō, too, has this to say: "Toward the end of the Age of the Semblance Dharma, scholars of the six sects in Nara [the Southern Capital*] were the enemies of the *Lotus Sutra*." During the time of these two grand masters, however, the enemies of the *Lotus Sutra* had not yet become apparent.

Nevertheless, statements cited above from the *Lotus Sutra* were made in the presence of Śākyamuni* Buddha and the Buddha of Many Treasures* sitting side by side in the stupa of seven treasures like the sun and moon, as well as Buddhas in manifestation* *(funjin)* from all over the universe sitting under bodhi trees like stars in the sky. Innumerable bodhisattvas, 80 trillion *nayuta* in number, consulted one another and decided that there would be three kinds of enemies of the *Lotus Sutra* at the beginning of the Latter Age of Degeneration* following the 1,000-year Age of the True Dharma* and another 1,000-year Age of the Semblance Dharma after the death of the Buddha. How could this be false?

It has been some 2,200 years since the death of Śākyamuni Buddha. Even if a finger pointing to the earth misses it, or flowers fail to bloom in spring, the three kinds of enemies of the *Lotus Sutra* are bound to appear in Japan. If so, who will be among the three kinds of enemies? Or, who will be considered to be one who practices the *Lotus Sutra*? We are not sure. Are we among the so-called three kinds of enemies? Or are we among those who practice the *Lotus Sutra*? We are not sure.

It was during the night of the eighth day of the fourth month in the 24th year (1029 BCE) of King Chao, the fourth sovereign of the Chou dynasty in ancient China, that rays of light in five colors flashed in the sky from north to south, brightening it as though it were daytime. The earth trembled six ways, rivers, ponds, and wells rose without rain, and all grasses and trees bloomed and bore fruit. It was miraculous! Greatly alarmed, King Chao consulted historian Su-yu about this and was told that this was an omen of the birth of a sage in the land to the west. The historian continued: "Nothing will happen for now, but in 1,000 years the teaching of that sage, who was just born in the western land will come to this land to save the people." Su-yu was a petty Confucianist who had not yet eliminated delusions and evil passions. Yet he was able to foretell 1,000 years in advance. As he predicted, Buddhism was introduced to China 1,015 years after the death of the Buddha, in the 10th year of the Yung-p'ing Era (67 CE) during the reign of Ming-ti, the second emperor of the Later Han.

The prediction of the *Lotus Sutra* is incomparably superior to that of Su-yu, as it was presented by bodhisattvas in the presence of Śākyamuni Buddha, the Buddha of Many Treasures, and the Buddhas in manifestation who had come from all over the universe. As such, how could there not be three kinds of enemies of the *Lotus Sutra* in Japan today? Śākyamuni Buddha has predicted in the *Fuhōzō-kyō, Sutra of Transmission of the Buddhist Teaching:** "During the 1,000-year Age of the True Dharma after My death, 24 will come in succession to spread My True Dharma." Besides such direct disciples as Kāśyapa* and Ānanda,* Monk Pārśva and Bodhisattvas Aśvaghoṣa and Nāgārjuna* had already appeared exactly as predicted 100, 600, and 700 years after the death of the Buddha respectively. Why is it that only this prediction of three kinds of enemies of the *Lotus Sutra* has not come true? If this prediction has not come true, the whole teaching of the *Lotus Sutra* will be false, and the assurance that Śāriputra* and Kāśyapa would be the future Kekō (Flower Light) and Kōmyō (Light) Buddhas respectively would come to naught. This would mean that the pre-Lotus sutras* would in turn become true and final with the result that Śāriputra and other *śrāvaka* would never obtain Buddhahood. It would mean that we should not offer any alms to such *śrāvaka* as Ānanda even if we should do so to dogs and foxes. What should we do then? What should we do?

The "ignorant people," the first of the three kinds of enemies of the *Lotus Sutra*, seem to be influential followers of the second and third enemies referred to as "monks in the evil world" and "monks in robes" in the Sutra. Therefore as cited earlier, Grand Master Miao-lê* in his *Annotations on the Words and Phrases of the Lotus Sutra* referred to this first kind of enemy as "self-conceited lay people," while Monk Chih-tu of Tung-ch'un* said in his *Tendai Interpretation of the Meaning of the Lotus Sutra* that they would "raise false charges to the authorities."

As for the second group of the three enemies of the *Lotus Sutra*, it is said in the Encouragement for Keeping This Sutra chapter of the *Lotus Sutra*: "Monks in the evil world will be cunning, crooked, flattering, arrogant, and boast of themselves as enlightened while they have not understood anything." The *Nirvana Sutra** states: "There will be evil monks then.... Although these evil monks recite this sutra, they will lose sight of the profound teaching of the Buddha."

Grand Master T'ien-t'ai interprets in his *Mo-ho Chih-kuan, Great Concentration and Insight:** "Those without faith in the *Lotus Sutra* consider it to be only for sages and to be too difficult for ignorant people like themselves. Those without wisdom become self-conceited considering themselves equal to the Buddha."

For instance, Grand Master Tao-ch'o, second patriarch of Chinese Pure Land Buddhism, stated in his *An-lê-chi, Collection of Passages Concerning Rebirth in the Pure Land,* that the second reason why the *Lotus Sutra* should be given up was that its teaching was too exquisite *(rijin mige)** for ignorant people to understand. Likewise, Hōnen, founder of the Pure Land sect in Japan, states in *Senchaku-shū, Collection of Passages on the Nembutsu:* "All religious practices except for the *nembutsu* do not suit the intelligence of the people nor the time."

Grand Master Miao-lê in his *Annotations on the Words and Phrases of the Lotus Sutra,* fascicle 10, warned against such misconceptions by saying: "Those who would misunderstand the *Lotus Sutra* perhaps do not know how meritorious the acts of beginners can be. They give credit to those of high rank and despise the beginners. It is shown in the *Lotus Sutra* that even the acts of beginners can be meritorious in the strength of the sutra."

Grand Master Dengyō, founder of the Tendai sect in Japan, also claims in his *Shugo Kokkai-shō, Treatise on the Protection of the Nation:* "The Ages of the True Dharma and the Semblance Dharma are about to pass with the Latter Age of Degeneration* just around the corner. It is exactly the time now for all people to be saved by the One Vehicle teaching* of the *Lotus Sutra.* How do I know this? It is said in the 14th chapter of the *Lotus Sutra,* Peaceful Practices, that the sutra will spread in the Latter Age when the Dharma is about to disappear." Venerable Eshin* says, "The whole of Japan is ready to believe the perfect teaching of the *Lotus Sutra.*"

Whom should we believe, Tao-ch'o or Dengyō, or Hōnen or Eshin? Tao-ch'o and Hōnen do not have any basis in the Buddhist scriptures, while Dengyō and Eshin base their assertions firmly upon the *Lotus Sutra.* Moreover, to all Buddhist monks in Japan, Grand Master Dengyō of Mt. Hiei is the master presiding over their initiation ceremony. How could they lean toward Hōnen, who is haunted by a heavenly devil, and abandon the master who performed their own initiation ceremony?

If Hōnen is a wise man, why did he not mention in his *Senchaku-shū, Collection of Passages on the Nembutsu,** those interpretations of Dengyō and Eshin to compare with his own? Since he did not do so, he should be blamed for having concealed them. It is towards Hōnen and other monks without any precepts and with evil views that the *Lotus Sutra* points as "the monks in the evil world," the second of the three kinds of enemies of the *Lotus.*

It is said in the *Nirvana Sutra:* "Before listening to this *Nirvana Sutra,* we all had evil views." Grand Master Miao-lê explains this in his *Fa-hua Hsüan-i Shih-ch'ien, Commentary on the Profound Meaning of the Lotus Sutra:* "The Buddha Himself called His pre-Lotus three teachings [*zōkyō, tsūgyō,* and *bekkyō*][15] evil." T'ien-t'ai, citing the words of the *Nirvana Sutra* just mentioned, says in his *Mo-ho Chih-kuan, Great Concentration and Insight:* "They called themselves evil. Isn't evil bad?" Miao-lê explains this in his *Annotations on the Great Concentration and Insight:*

> "Evil" means "wicked." Therefore we must know that only the *engyō* (perfect teaching) among the Four Teachings* is correct. But it has two meanings. First, it means that following the "perfect teaching" is correct while rejecting it is erroneous. This is a relative point of view [relative subtlety]. Secondly, it means that attachment is considered erroneous while detachment is correct. This is an absolute point of view [absolute subtlety].* Either way, we have to stay away from error. It is bad to attach ourselves to the "perfect teaching." How much worse it is to attach ourselves to the Three Teachings!

Compared to Hinayana Buddhism, all non-Buddhist schools in India are in error. Compared to the *Lotus Sutra,* the correct way of Hinayana Buddhism,* the first four of the so-called "five flavors" and the first three of the Four Teachings are all evil and erroneous. The *Lotus Sutra* alone is true and correct. The "perfect teaching" preached in pre-Lotus sutras* is called perfect but its perfection is only from a relative point of view. It is still inferior to the absolute exquisiteness of the *Lotus Sutra.*

Also the "perfect teaching" of the pre-Lotus sutras is erroneous because it still remains in the first three categories of the Four Teachings. Therefore, we are still treading the way of error even if we practice the ultimate teaching of the pre-Lotus sutras such as the *Flower Garland** and *Wisdom.** How much more should Hōnen and his disciples and followers be in error! They depended on such petty sutras as the *Kammuryōju-kyō, Sutra of Meditation on the Buddha of Infinite Life,* which are inferior to such pre-Lotus sutras as the *Flower Garland** and *Wisdom,** taking the *Lotus* in the *Kammuryōju-kyō* and urging Pure Land believers to put aside, throw away, close the gate to, and discard the *Lotus Sutra.* Aren't they the so-called slanderers of the True Dharma? Śākyamuni, Tahō (Many Treasures), and numerous other Buddhas from all over the universe came to this world in order to have the *Lotus Sutra* remain here forever. Hōnen and Pure Land believers in Japan claim that the *Lotus Sutra* in the Latter Age of Degeneration will perish before the Pure Land sect. Aren't they the enemies of those Buddhas?

As for the last of the three kinds of enemies of the *Lotus Sutra,* it is said in the [13th chapter of the] sutra: "Some monks will stay in a monastery, wearing robes, and sitting quietly.... They will preach the Dharma for lay people and will be revered by the people as though they were *arhats* with Six Superhuman Powers."* The six-fascicled *Nirvana Sutra, Hatsunaion-gyō** asserts: "Men of *icchantika** will act like *arhats* but commit evil acts, and *arhats* will act like men of *icchantika* but have compassion. An *arhat*-like man of *icchantika* refers to the people slandering Mahayana Buddhism. An *arhat* acting like a man of *icchantika* refers to a man despising the Hinayana sage of *śrāvaka** and widely preaching Mahayana Buddhism, saying to the people that both he and they are bodhisattvas* because everybody has Buddha-nature in themself. Nevertheless, those people would consider him a man of *icchantika.*"

The *Nirvana Sutra* states:

> After the death of the Buddha,... monks in the Age of the Semblance Dharma* will not be sages. On the surface, they will appear to keep the precepts and recite sutras a little, but they will devour rich food and enjoy a prosperous life. ...Although they wear robes of Buddhist monks, they will

act for selfish gain just like hunters walking slowly aiming at game and squinting eyes, or cats stalking a rat. They will always claim to be *arhats*.... Outwardly, they will appear to be wise and virtuous, but at heart they will harbor greed and jealousy just like Brahmans practicing the ascetic exercise of silence. They will appear to be Buddhist monks, but not actually be so. With their rampant evil thoughts they will slander the True Dharma.

Grand Master Miao-lê* says in his *Annotations on the Words and Phrases of the Lotus Sutra:* "The third group is most difficult to endure. It is because the latter group are more cunning and less likely to reveal their faults." Monk Chih-tu of Tung-ch'un states in his *Fa-hua Shu-i-tsuan, Tendai Interpretation of the Meaning of the Lotus Sutra:* "In the third place, three verses following 'some monks will stay in a monastery' refers to the acts of evil monks representing those of all the wicked people."

Where are what monk Chih-tu of Tung-ch'un* calls "acts of evil monks representing those of all the wicked people" in Japan today? Are they on Mt. Hiei,* in the Onjōji Temple,* Tōji Temple,* temples in Nara [Southern Capital],* Kenninji Temple, Jufukuji Temple, or in the Kenchōji Temple? We must find them. Are they those monks of the Enryakuji Temple on Mt. Hiei who put on helmets and wear armor? Or, are they those monks of the Onjōji Temple who arm themselves with armor and sticks in order to protect their Dharma Bodies of fivefold merit,[16] bodies of the enlightened? However, they do not look like those referred to in the Encouragement for Keeping This Sutra chapter: "monks who wear robes and stay in tranquility." People do not suppose that they are "revered by the people as though they were *arhats* with Six Superhuman Powers." Or, should I say that they are those who are "more cunning and less likely to reveal their faults?" Thus it seems that the third enemies of the *Lotus Sutra* refer to such monks as State Master Shōichi of Kyoto and Ryōkan* of Kamakura. Do not blame me for saying this. If you have eyes, look at yourselves in the light of the sutras.

It is stated in the *Mo-ho Chih-kuan, Great Concentration and Insight,** fascicle one, that nobody has ever heard of any work as clear and profound as the method of meditation expounded in it. While Grand Master Miao-lê says in his *Annotations on the Great Concentration and Insight,* fascicle one: "Ever since the Later Han Emperor Ming-ti introduced Buddhism into China, after he had dreamed of a golden man, until the Ch'en dynasty, many have learned and transmitted Zen Buddhism." According to *Ts'ung-i's Pu-chu, Additional Annotations to Three Major Works of T'ien-t'ai,** Bodhidharma transmitted Zen. Concerning this Zen Buddhism, it is said in the *Great Concentration and Insight,* fascicle five, that both those blind monks who do not study, practicing only meditation, and those crippled ones who do not practice meditation but only study are bound to fail.

After listing 10 ways of practicing Buddhism, Grand Master T'ien-t'ai states in the same *Great Concentration and Insight,* fascicle seven: "Except for translation, in nine out of 10 ways, I am vastly different from those monks in the world who study only the writings, or those Zen monks who are concerned with formality. Some Zen monks concentrate on meditation, but their meditation is either shallow or false. They practice none of the remaining nine except for meditation. This is not idle talk. Wise men in the future who have eyes should consider this seriously."

Grand Master Miao-lê explains this in his *Annotations on the Great Concentration and Insight, Chih-kuan Fu-hsing-ch'uan Hung-chüeh,* fascicle seven:

> Monks who study only the writings refer to those who are concerned only with scholastic aspects without understanding the true meaning of the scriptures through wisdom. Zen monks who are concerned only with formality refer to those who are concerned with the conventions of meditation without experiencing the true state of meditation. This is the same as the meditation of Brahmans, who will never gain complete freedom from delusions and passions. T'ien-t'ai's statement that some Zen monks concentrate only on meditation is an understatement sympathetic to them. In actuality, they lack both practice in meditation as well as wisdom to understand the doctrine. Those who practice Zen consider only meditation important and pay little attention to the study of doctrines. They interpret sutras from the viewpoint of meditation in such an absurd way as to say that the Eightfold Evil Path[17] and the Eight Winds[18] make the five meter tall Buddha,[19] and the Five Elements* of all existence and the Three Poisons of greed, anger, and stupidity make the Eightfold Evil Path. They confuse the six sensory organs with the Six Superhuman Powers,* or confuse the four basic elements of the material world [earth, water, fire, and wind] with the Four Noble Truths.* That such interpretations of the sutras are the worst of all is beyond question, an absurdity not worthy of discussion.

It is also stated in the *Great Concentration and Insight,* fascicle seven: "Once there lived a Zen master, Bodhidharma, in Yeh-lo, whose name was known all over the land. Wherever he stayed, people gathered in crowds gazing at him, and whenever he left, hundreds and thousands of people swarmed around him to bid farewell. Such was his fame, but no benefits were gained. So, at his last moment, he regretted his life."

Miao-lê again explains this in his *Annotations on the Great Concentration and Insight, Chih-kuan Fu-hsing-ch'uan Hung-chüeh,* fascicle seven: "Yeh is in Hsiang-chou, and it was called Yeh when it was the capital of Northern Chi, but Lo-yang when Northern Wei had its capital there. Bodhidharma is the primogenitor of Zen Buddhism in China and he contributed greatly to the rise of Buddhism. He converted the royal capital to Buddhism, but hid his own name out of deference to the wishes of the people. Lo refers to Lo-yang."

The six-fascicled *Nirvana Sutra, Hatsunaion-gyō*,* states: "Not seeing the ultimate destination means that no one can know how evil those men of *icchantika** can be." Grand Master Miao-lê asserts: "The last of the three groups of the enemies of the *Lotus Sutra* is the hardest to endure because it is the group most cunning and less likely to reveal faults."

Don't these citations clarify who the "three kinds of enemies"* at the beginning of the Latter Age* are? Those who are blind or one-eyed, or those who have wrong views may not see, but those who have a shred of the Buddha-eye should be able to see this. It is said in the Encouragement for Keeping This Sutra chapter of the *Lotus Sutra*: "They slander the one who practices the *Lotus Sutra* to the king, his ministers, Brahmans, and influential lay believers." Chih-tu of Tung-ch'un* explained: "They make reports to the authorities, slandering the True Dharma and the one who practices the *Lotus Sutra*." So in the past toward the end of the Age of the Semblance Dharma, such monks as Gomyō and Shūen petitioned the Imperial Court, slandering Grand Master Dengyō. Now, at the beginning of the Latter Age, such monks as Ryōkan* and Nen'a (Ryōchū)* have written letters to the Shogunate falsely slandering Nichiren. How can they not be of the "three kinds of enemies" of the *Lotus Sutra*?

Those of the Pure Land sect today say to the king, his ministers, Brahmans, and influential lay believers, who are followers of the Tendai-Lotus sect, that the *Lotus Sutra* is too profound in principle for us to understand, or its doctrine is too profound for our shallow intelligence. Are not they, who try to dissuade us from believing in the *Lotus Sutra*, what is referred in the *Great Concentration and Insight* to as "those monks who consider the *Lotus Sutra* to be only for sages and too difficult for ignorant people like themselves?"

The Zen sect maintains:

> The *Lotus Sutra* is a finger pointing to the moon while the Zen sect is the moon itself. After grasping the moon there is no need for the finger to point at it. Zen is the heart of the Buddha while the *Lotus Sutra* is merely His words. Having finished preaching all the sutras, including the Lotus, the Buddha picked up a bunch of flowers and gave it to Kāśyapa* because he alone understood what the Buddha meant. As proof, the Buddha entrusted him with His *kesa*, vestment, which has been handed down through 28 patriarchs of Buddhism in India to six patriarchs of Buddhism in China.

It has been a long time since such nonsense as this has fooled and confused the people of Japan.

High monks of the Tendai and Shingon sects enjoy high reputation within their respective sects without knowing what their own sects are. Being greedy and afraid of court nobles and warriors in power, they approve and even praise what the Pure Land and Zen schools claim. When Śākyamuni Buddha preached the *Lotus Sutra,* the Buddha of Many Treasures and numerous Buddhas in manifestation coming from all the worlds in the universe verified having it spread forever. Now the high monks of the Tendai sect seem to agree with the false claims of the Zen and Pure Land monks that the *Lotus Sutra* is "too exquisite for people to understand."* As a result, the *Lotus Sutra* exists in name only in Japan, without anyone attaining Buddhahood. Now whom should we consider one who practices the *Lotus Sutra*? Numerous monks were exiled for burning temples and stupas. Many high priests are frowned at for catering to the whims of court nobles and warriors in power. Should we call them those who practice the *Lotus Sutra*?

Exactly as the Buddha predicted, there are "three kinds of enemies of the *Lotus Sutra*"* all over Japan. Nevertheless, we don't see any of those who practice the *Lotus Sutra*. Does this mean that the words of the Buddha have been proved untrue? Could this be? After all, who has been abused and despised by the ignorant people for the sake of the *Lotus Sutra*? Which monk has been brought to the attention of court nobles and warriors in power? Which monk has often been exiled as predicted in the sutra? No such man exists in Japan, except for Nichiren. However, as Nichiren has been abandoned by the gods, he probably is not one who practices the *Lotus Sutra*. Then, who would be one who practices the *Lotus Sutra* to realize the Buddha's prediction?

Śākyamuni Buddha and His sworn enemy Devadatta* remained together, life after life, just as a shadow follows a body. Prince Shōtoku* and his political enemy Mononobe no Moriya were always together just as the flowers and fruits of the lotus appear at the same time. By the same token, when there is one who practices the *Lotus Sutra,* there must be the "three kinds of enemies of the *Lotus Sutra.*" As "three kinds of enemies of the *Lotus Sutra*" already exist, who is one who practices the *Lotus Sutra*? We must seek him out to make him our teacher. To meet such a man is as rare an occasion as a one-eyed turtle finding a piece of wood with the right size hole floating in an ocean.

Some raise the question:

> Although there seem to be the three kinds of enemies of the *Lotus Sutra* in this world today, those who practice the *Lotus Sutra* are not found

anywhere. It is difficult for us to call you one who practices the *Lotus Sutra* because there is a great deal of discrepancy. Affirming divine intervention in favor of one who practices, the Peaceful Practices chapter of the *Lotus Sutra* says: "Heavenly servants will come to serve the man who upholds the *Lotus Sutra* so that swords and sticks will not injure him, and poisons will not harm him;" in the fifth chapter, The Simile of Herbs, "His life in this world will be peaceful and he will be reborn in a better place in the future;" in the 26th chapter, Dhāraṇīs, "Should anyone hate and speak ill of the man who upholds the *Lotus Sutra,* his mouth will be sealed…anyone who does harm to him will have his head split into seven pieces like a twig of an *arjaka* tree;" and in the 28th chapter, Encouragement of Universal-Sage Bodhisattva, "He will be rewarded with happiness in this present life;" and "If anyone, upon seeing a man upholding this sutra, exposes his faults, justifiably or not, such a man will be afflicted with white leprosy."

They have good reason to doubt me. So I will answer their questions to dispel their doubt. It is said in the 20th chapter of the *Lotus Sutra*, Never-Despising Bodhisattva, that the one who practices the *Lotus Sutra* will be spoken ill of, despised, or struck with sticks, tiles, and stones. While it is said in the *Nirvana Sutra* that such a man will be killed or hurt. The *Lotus Sutra* also states in the 10th chapter, Teacher of the Dharma, that those who spread it will be the target of much hatred and jealousy even during the lifetime of the Buddha.

The Buddha Himself had His finger injured by Devadatta, and He met serious crises like this nine times* during His lifetime. Wasn't He one who practices the *Lotus Sutra?* Can't we call Bodhisattva Fukyō (Never-Despising)* one who practices the One Vehicle teaching* of the *Lotus Sutra* because he was despised and beaten? Venerable Maudgalyāyana* was murdered by Brahmans armed with bamboo sticks. This occurred after he was assured that he would be a future Buddha in the *Lotus Sutra*. Bodhisattva Kāṇadeva and Venerable Siṃha (Shishi Sonja), 14th and 25th patriarchs of Buddhism who transmitted the Buddha's teaching, were both murdered. Were they not those who practice the *Lotus Sutra?* In China, Chu Tao-sheng insisted that even an *icchantika* could attain Buddhahood and was banished to a temple in Su-chou, and Fa-tao was exiled to the south of the Yangtze River with his face branded with a hot iron rod when he admonished the emperor for persecuting Buddhists. Were these monks not those who practice the *Lotus Sutra?* Both Sugawara Michizane of Japan and Po Chü-i of China were banished because of their admonishment. Were they not worthy of being among those who practice the *Lotus Sutra?*

CHAPTER 15
The Three Great Vows

I wonder, why were these men persecuted? Suppose there is a person who never slandered the *Lotus Sutra* in his previous lives and is upholding it in this present life. Whoever accused him of a trivial worldly offense, or for no offense at all, will immediately receive punishment. *Asura* demons who attacked Indra* were immediately repulsed and the monster bird *konji-chō* who invaded Lake Anokuda to devour a dragon king was killed on the spot. Grand Master T'ien-t'ai in his *Profound Meaning of the Lotus Sutra,* fascicle six, asserts: "Our troubles and sufferings in this world are all due to our sins in our past lives, and rewards for our meritorious acts in this life will be received in our future lives." It is also said in the *Shinjikan-gyō, Sutra of Meditation on the Ground of the Mind:* "Our virtues or vices in our past can be seen in our present fortune. Our future fortune can be seen in our present acts," and in the Never-Despising Bodhisattva chapter* of the *Lotus Sutra:* "Thus the bodhisattva made amends for the past." It seems that Never-Despising (Fukyō) Bodhisattva* was attacked with rocks and tiles because of his past sins. It seems also that those who are destined for hell in the next life do not receive punishment even for serious sins in this life. For instance, some *icchantika** do not even receive punishment.

As for such people, it is stated in the *Nirvana Sutra* that Bodhisattva Kāśyapa told the Buddha, "Just as rays of sunlight reach the hearts of all through pores of their skin, the teaching of the Buddha reaches all, planting in them the seed of Buddhahood." The bodhisattva then asked the Buddha: "World Honored One! How can we plant the seed of Buddhahood in a person who does not aspire to Buddhahood?" The Buddha replied: "Suppose there is a person who, after listening to the *Nirvana Sutra,* does not aspire to Buddhahood and slanders the True Dharma instead. Such a man will dream a frightening dream of a *rākṣasa* devil at night, in which the devil will threaten to kill him unless he immediately aspires for Buddhahood. Suppose he, frightened, awoke, changed his mind and began aspiring to enlightenment, such a man is a great bodhisattva." Thus, except for extremely wicked men, when people slander the True Dharma, they will immediately dream like this and repent their folly.

The *Nirvana Sutra* also states that men of *icchantika* will never aspire for enlightenment. It is as certain as water not being found in dead trees and rocky mountains, as toasted seeds not germinating even in rain, as gems purifying dirty water but not the soil, as poison entering the human body when handled by a wounded hand, and as a great rain not remaining in the sky. A number of these similes are cited in the sutra to show that men of *icchantika* are not punished in this world, because it is certain that they will go to the Hell of Incessant Suffering* in the next life. It is just like the notorious reigns of King Chieh of Hsia and King Chou of Yin (Shang) in ancient China. Natural calamities did not occur during their reigns as their rule was to be destroyed for their great sins.

It could also be that because the True Dharma has been slandered* guardian gods have abandoned this land of Japan. As a result, slanderers of the True Dharma are not punished while those upholding it are left without divine assistance and are subjected to great difficulties. What is said in the *Konkōmyō-kyō, Sutra of the Golden Splendor:** "The number of those who practice the True Dharma grows less by the day" refers to this land today, when the True Dharma is being slandered. I have explained this in detail in my *Risshō Ankoku-ron, Treatise on Spreading Peace Throughout the Country by Establishing the True Dharma.**

In the final analysis, no matter how I am abandoned by gods and how much difficulty I encounter, I will uphold the *Lotus Sutra* at the cost of my own life. Śāriputra could not attain Buddhahood after having practiced the way of the bodhisattva for as long as 60 *kalpa* because he could not endure the difficulty presented by a Brahman who asked him for his eyes. Those who had received the seed of Buddhahood from the Eternal Buddha and Daitsūchishō (Great Universal Wisdom)* Buddha an incalculable number of *kalpa* ago could not obtain Buddhahood for as long as 500 or 3,000 dust-particle *kalpa* (*gohyaku jindengō* or *sanzen jindengō*)[20] until they listened to the preaching of the *Lotus Sutra* on Mt. Sacred Eagle in this world. It was because they had been misled by these "evil friends"* to abandon the *Lotus Sutra*. No matter what happens, abandoning the *Lotus Sutra* will cause us to be plunged into hell.

I have made a vow. Even if someone says that he would make me the ruler of Japan on the condition that I give up the *Lotus Sutra* and rely upon the *Kammuryō-ju-kyō, Sutra of Meditation on the Buddha of Infinite Life,** for my salvation in the next life, or even if someone threatens me saying that he will execute my parents if I do not say *Namu Amida-butsu*, and no matter how many great difficulties fall upon me, I will not submit to them until a man of wisdom defeats me by reason. Other difficulties are like dust in the wind. I will never break my vow to become the pillar of Japan, to become the eyes of Japan, and to become a great vessel for Japan.

CHAPTER 16
In Order to Attain Buddhahood One Must Compensate for All One's Sins

Some might wonder: "How do you know that your banishment and death sentence are results of sins in your past lives?" To them I would answer that copper mirrors reflect only colors and shapes, and the mirror the First Emperor of Ch'in used to test his subjects showed only present sins, but the mirror of Buddhism shows one's virtues or vices from the past. Therefore, it is said in the six-fascicled *Nirvana Sutra, Hatsunaion-gyō:** "Good men! Since you have committed numerous evil deeds and accumulated bad karma, you have to suffer in compensation for them…. You may be slighted, may look ugly, may suffer from lack of clothing or from insufficient food, unable to make a fortune, born to a poor family or to a heretic family, or suffer from royal persecutions, and many other difficulties. The reason you receive relatively light punishments like these in this world is due to your merit of upholding the Dharma. Otherwise you might have been punished much more severely."

This matches me, Nichiren, as perfectly as two halves of a tally. It explains why I have been persecuted, and thus all of my numerous doubts have faded away. Let us tally this sutra, phrase by phrase against me. As for "being slighted," which is phrased in the *Lotus Sutra*, A Parable chapter, as "being slighted, despised, hated with jealousy," I, Nichiren, have been despised for more than 20 years. "Being ugly-looking," and "suffering from lack of food and clothing," "unable to make a fortune," "being born to a poor family," "suffering from royal persecutions," and so on are all about me. Who can doubt it?

It is stated in the chapter of the *Lotus Sutra*, Encouragement for Keeping This Sutra, that such men will "be exiled many times" and this is restated in this *Hatsunaion-gyō*, as such men will "have many difficulties." The *Hatsunaion-gyō* also says, "Due to your merit of upholding the Dharma, you will receive relatively light punishment in this world;" and this is explained in the *Mo-ho Chih-kuan, Great Concentration and Insight,** fascicle five, as follows: "The merit of trivial acts of practicing Buddhism without tranquility of mind and meditation on truth is not strong enough to bring out our past sins hidden in ourselves. Only when we practice tranquility of mind and meditation on truth under any circumstances, can we bring our past sins out to the surface." It also warns us: "We will then be confronted at once by the Three Hindrances and Four Devils."*

In the past, beyond memory, I must have been born a wicked king and deprived those who practice the *Lotus Sutra* of their food, clothing and possessions on numerous occasions just as some people today in Japan have been destroying the Lotus temples. I must have also cut off the heads of numerous people who practice the *Lotus Sutra*. I may have purged myself of some of these grave sins but not all of them. Even if I have, there are the residuals. In order to attain Buddhahood, I must completely compensate for all those serious sins. My merits in spreading the *Lotus Sutra* are still shallow while my sins in the past are still deep. If I had preached only provisional sutras, grave sins in my past lives would not have been revealed. It is like a forging iron, for instance. Unless you hit it and forge it hard, hidden scars will not be seen. They appear only when the iron is hit hard many times on an anvil. Or it is analogous to squeezing hemp seeds. Unless squeezed hard, there is little oil. Ever since I, Nichiren, strongly condemned those who slander the True Dharma in Japan, I have been persecuted. It must be that grave sins in my past lives are revealed through my merits in defending the Dharma in this life. It is just as a piece of iron remains black unless heated by fire, and becomes red when placed in fire. Even calm water makes great waves when quickly stirred by a log. A sleeping lion roars loudly when awakened by the touch of a hand.

There is an analogy cited in the *Nirvana Sutra*:

> A sickly poor woman did not have a house to live in nor anyone to support her. She wandered around begging for food. While staying in an inn she gave birth to a child. The innkeeper chased her out. Carrying the infant born only a short while ago, she tried to go to some other place. On the way, she was overtaken by a bad storm, suffered from hunger and cold and was attacked by mosquitoes, horseflies, bees, and other poisonous insects. Coming to the Ganges River, she tried to wade through it carrying her baby. She was carried away by the flowing river, but she clung to her infant until both of them drowned. Such a woman will be reborn in the Brahma Heaven due to her merits of compassion. Mañjuśrī!* If a good man wishes to uphold the True Dharma,... he must do the same as the poor woman in sacrificing her own life in the Ganges because of her love for her child. Good man! Bodhisattvas upholding the Dharma should also be ready to sacrifice their lives.... Such people will be able to attain Buddhahood without seeking it, just as the poor woman will be reborn in the Brahma Heaven* without seeking it.

Grand Master Chang-an* has interpreted this citation with the concepts of the Three Hindrances [evil passion, evil karma, and painful retributions]. You should read it.

As I examine this passage comparing it to a person who spreads the *Lotus Sutra* in the Latter Age of Degeneration, "a poor person" refers to a man with little treasure of Buddhism, and "a woman" refers to a person with a little compassion. The "inn" means this world of defilement. "A child" refers to faith in the *Lotus Sutra*, which is the seed of Buddhahood. "Being chased out of the inn" refers to the banishment of Nichiren, and the "infant born only a short while ago" stands for the short period of time since the person began spreading the *Lotus Sutra*. The "bad storm" by which she was overtaken refers to the shogunal order of banishment, while "bees and horseflies" mean the three kinds of enemies of the *Lotus Sutra* who spoke ill of and abused Nichiren. The drowning of the mother and her baby refers to Nichiren being almost beheaded at Tatsunokuchi for his unwavering faith in the *Lotus Sutra*. Rebirth in the Brahma Heaven means his attainment of Buddhahood.

The principle of karmic law, which decides our fate in our future lives, is the same from hell to the Buddha land. As for the retribution of hell, only those who have committed the Five Rebellious Sins,* and slanderers* of the True Dharma will fall into the Hell of Incessant Suffering *(mugen jigoku)*.* Those who commit other crimes, even a murderer of all the people in China and Japan, will not fall in the Hell of Incessant Suffering. Instead, they would go to other hells and suffer many years there. Similarly it would be impossible for us in the world of desire to be reborn in the world of no desire *(shikikai)*[21] even if we should uphold all the precepts and practice all the virtuous acts without tranquility of mind and meditation on truth.

To be reborn the King of the Brahma Heaven in the world of no desire, we have to accumulate the merit of compassion in addition to practicing the meditation for beginners. The rebirth of this poor woman in the Brahma Heaven because of her compassion for her child does not follow ordinary karmic law. Chang-an* has two interpretations on this, but after all it is nothing but motherly compassion for a child that made the difference. Concentration of mind on a child looks like meditation. Thinking of a child from the bottom of one's heart looks like compassion. This is probably the reason why the mother was reborn in the Brahma Heaven although she had not accumulated any other favorable karma.

Also, many ways are claimed to lead to Buddhahood, such as the "mind-only" doctrine[22] of the Kegon sect, the Sanron doctrine of "the middle path of the eightfold negation,"[23] the "consciousness only" doctrine[24] of the Hossō sect, and the Shingon doctrine of the "five wheels,"[25] but none of these seem to work in actuality. The only way seemingly that leads to Buddhahood is the "3,000 existences contained in one thought"* doctrine of T'ien-t'ai.* However, we in the Latter Age of Degeneration do not possess the intelligence to understand it. Nevertheless, among all the sutras preached by Śākyamuni during His lifetime, only the *Lotus Sutra* embodies the gem of the "3,000 existences contained in one thought" doctrine. Doctrines of other sutras may look like gems, but in actuality they are merely yellow rocks. Just as, no matter how hard you squeeze sand, you will not get oil, or barren women will never have children, even wise men will not be able to attain Buddhahood by means of other sutras. As for the *Lotus Sutra*, even ignorant persons will be able to plant the seed of Buddhahood. The above citation from the *Nirvana Sutra* stating "Such people would be able to obtain Buddhahood without seeking it" must have meant this attainment of Buddhahood by means of the *Lotus Sutra*.

Not only I, Nichiren, but also my disciples will reach the land of Buddha unfailingly so long as we all hold on to unwavering faith no matter what difficulty confronts us. I have always told my disciples not to have a doubt from lack of heavenly protection and not to lament the lack of tranquility in this world. I am afraid, however, that they might all have doubts about these and no longer listen to me. It seems only natural that ordinary people, in the face of reality, will forget their promises. Having pity on their families, my lay followers must lament being separated from wives and children in this world. However, had they ever been truly separated from their beloved families throughout many lives in the past? Had they ever been separated for the sake of Buddhism? Theirs must have been the same sad separation. I, Nichiren, should continue upholding the *Lotus Sutra* and go to the Pure Land of Mt. Sacred Eagle,* so that I will be able to return to this world to guide its people.

Chapter 17
Persuasive and Aggressive Means of Propagation

Some might say that Nichiren, who claims that followers of the Buddha of Infinite Life and Zen Buddhism will fall in the Hell of Incessant Suffering, is belligerent and therefore, will fall into the realm of *asura*. Moreover, it is said in the 14th chapter of the *Lotus Sutra,* Peaceful Practices:* "Do not try to expose the faults of other people or of other sutras and do not despise other monks." Therefore, they might wonder whether or not Nichiren has been abandoned by the gods because he has not been following these words of the *Lotus Sutra*.

In response, I would cite the following words of the *Mo-ho Chih-kuan, Great Concentration and Insight,** fascicle 10: "There are two opposing ways of spreading Buddhism: the aggressive and persuasive. Such statements in the Peaceful Practices chapter as 'Do not be critical of others' represent the persuasive way, while such words of the *Nirvana Sutra* as 'Arm yourselves with swords and sticks, and behead those who break the teaching of the Buddha' stand for the aggressive way. Though these two ways are opposite in nature, they both benefit people."

Grand Master Miao-lê explains this in his *Chih-kuan Fu-hsing-ch'uan Hung-chüeh, Annotations on the Great Concentration and Insight,** fascicle 10, as follows:

> Regarding the two ways of spreading Buddhism and such words of the *Nirvana Sutra* as "Arm yourselves with swords and sticks," it is stated in the third fascicle of the *Nirvana Sutra* that those who uphold the True Dharma should arm themselves with swords and bows and arrows even if they will

not be able to uphold the Five Precepts and maintain integrity. Further, it speaks about the ancient king called Sen'yo the Great, who is said to have beheaded a Brahman on the spot when the Brahman slandered Buddhism. The sutra, in the second fascicle, also cites as an example, an order issued by a new doctor who found that the milk-medicine prescribed by his predecessor was doing harm to the people. To prevent people from taking the bad medicine, the order said, "Anyone who uses it will be beheaded." These are two examples of an aggressive means of spreading Buddhism. Although various scriptures preach many ways of spreading Buddhism, they all come down to these two ways in the end: the aggressive and persuasive.

In his *Words and Phrases of the Lotus Sutra, Fa-hua Wên-chü,** fascicle eight, Grand Master T'ien-t'ai explains the difference between the aggressive means of the *Nirvana Sutra* and the persuasive means of the Peaceful Practices chapter:

> Someone asked: "The *Nirvana Sutra* says that those who wish to uphold the True Dharma should befriend themselves with the king, arm themselves with bows and arrows, and crush the enemies of the True Dharma. The Peaceful Practices chapter of the *Lotus Sutra*, however, says that they should keep distance from those in power, humble themselves, and be kind to enemies. Is there not quite a difference between the two, the harsh way of the *Nirvana Sutra* and the gentle way of the *Lotus Sutra*?"
>
> I say in response, "Although the *Nirvana Sutra* preaches mostly the aggressive means of propagation, it also preaches the benevolence of the bodhisattva who loves all the people just as one loves an only child. So, it is not that it does not recognize 'persuasion' as a means of propagation. Although the Peaceful Practices chapter mainly preaches the gentle means of propagation, another chapter of the *Lotus Sutra* says that anyone who does harm to the one who practices the Lotus would have his head split into seven pieces. Thus this sutra also endorses the aggressive means. In other words, each of them preaches one or the other as the situation demands."

Grand Master Chang-an in his *Nieh-p'an-ching-su, Annotations on the Nirvana Sutra,** explains this:

> Regardless of whether they are monks or laymen, those who uphold the Dharma should not lose sight of the fundamental aim of spreading the *Nirvana Sutra* even at the cost of phenomenal aspects such as Buddhist precepts. Upholders of the True Dharma cannot be concerned with trivial

matters, as it is said in the sutra that they may not maintain dignity....
In the past when the world was at peace and the True Dharma could be
spread, it was only necessary for them to keep Buddhist precepts, not arms.
Today, however, when the world is full of danger and the True Dharma is
hidden, they have to keep arms, not Buddhist precepts. Regardless of the
past or present, if the time is full of danger, they should arm themselves.
If at peace, they should observe the Buddhist precepts. Thus, the means
of propagation should be chosen according to the condition of the time. It
cannot be said to be only one way or another.

As for your criticism that I, Nichiren, am belligerent, I am afraid that scholars today probably agree with you. Even my own disciples cannot get rid of the same doubts as yours and act just like men of *icchantika** despite my repeated admonishments.* So I have cited interpretations of T'ien-t'ai and Miao-lê above to guard against such criticism.

Now, two ways of propagation, the persuasive and aggressive,* are incompatible with each other just as are water and fire. The fire dislikes the water, and the water hates the fire. Those who prefer the persuasive tend to laugh at those who practice the aggressive and vice versa. So, when the land is full of evil and ignorant people, the persuasive means should take precedence as preached in the 14th chapter of the *Lotus Sutra*, Peaceful Practices.* However, when there are many cunning slanderers of the True Dharma,* the aggressive means should take precedence as preached in the 20th chapter, Never-Despising Bodhisattva.

It is the same as using cold water when it is hot and fire when it is cold. Plants and trees are followers of the sun, so they dislike the cold moon. Bodies of water are followers of the moon, so they lose their true nature when it is hot. As there are lands of evil men as well as those of slanderers of the True Dhama in this Latter Age of Degeneration,* there should be both aggressive and persuasive means of spreading the True Dharma. Therefore, to decide which of the two ways we should use, we have to know whether Japan today is a land of evil men or that of slanderers.

Suppose someone asks whether or not it would be effective to carry out the aggressive means of propagation when the time requires the persuasive means and vice versa. To this question, I would say, it would not be effective. It is said in the *Nirvana Sutra:**

Bodhisattva Kāśyapa inquired of the Buddha how His body become as indestructible as a diamond. He responded to Kāśyapa: "Kāśyapa! The Buddha has an indestructible body by virtue of upholding the True Dharma. Kāśyapa! I have this eternally indestructible body by virtue of upholding the True Dharma in My past lives. Good Men! In order to uphold the True Dharma, you must arm yourselves with swords and bows and arrows even if you cannot observe the Five Precepts and maintain your dignity.... Even if a Buddhist monk who upholds the precepts tries hard to preach, unless he is able to preach as forcefully as a lion... and defeats the evil opponents of Buddhism, he would not be able to save himself and others. You should know that such a monk is an idle man. Even if you observe precepts and practice pure conduct, you should know, you will not be able to do anything for the protection of Buddhism.... On the other hand, should a monk upholding the True Dharma aggressively defeat violators of the Buddhist precepts, they would probably all become angry and try to harm him. Even if he were killed, he is worth being called observant of the precepts and savior of himself and others."

Grand Master Chang-an* says in his *Annotations on the Nirvana Sutra*, fascicle eight, that whether we should adopt the aggressive means of propagation or the persuasive means must be decided according to the condition of the time, and therefore, we cannot say one way or the other. Grand Master T'ien-t'ai* says of this in the *Words and Phrases of the Lotus Sutra*, fascicle eight: "It all depends on the time. Sometimes resort to the aggressive means, other times use the persuasive means." For instance, we cannot harvest rice by cultivating rice paddies and planting rice seeds at the end of autumn.

During the era of Kennin (1201-03) two monks named Hōnen* and Dainichi* emerged to establish the schools of Pure Land and Zen respectively. Hōnen declared that in the Latter Age of Degeneration* not even one out of one thousand* could obtain Buddhahood by means of the *Lotus Sutra*, whereas Dainichi maintained that Zen is the essence of Buddhism transmitted distinctively outside written scriptures and verbal preachings. These two false teachings have spread all over Japan.

Scholars of Tendai and Shingon Buddhism are afraid of the Pure Land and Zen followers and try to cater to their whims just like a dog wagging its tail in front of its master and mice terrified by a cat. Preaching in the service of kings and generals, they themselves speak of what would lead to the destruction of Buddhism and the country. Such scholars of Tendai and Shingon Buddhism will fall into the realm of hungry spirits in this life and the Hell of Incessant Suffering* in future lives. Even if Tendai scholars reside in mountain forests and meditate on the "3,000 existences contained in one thought"* doctrine, or Shingon scholars stay in remote tranquility to concentrate on the three mystic practices [finger signs, spell words, and meditation], how can they attain Buddhahood without knowing whether the time calls for the aggressive means or the persuasive means of propagation?

Some people might wonder what is good about accusing those followers of Pure Land and Zen Buddhism, making enemies of them. In response, I will cite the *Nirvana Sutra:* "Suppose there is a virtuous monk who does not accuse anyone of harming Buddhism, does not try to purge or punish him. You should know that such a monk is an enemy of Buddhism. In case the monk accuses such a man, purges, and punishes him, such a monk is a disciple of the Buddha who truly follows Him.

Grand Master Chang-an explains this in his *Annotations on the Nirvana Sutra:**

> Those who destroy Buddhism are those within Buddhism working against Buddhism. Those heartless people who keep friendly relationships with such evil doers by overlooking their sins are their enemies. Those who are kind enough to try to correct them are the upholders of the True Dharma and true disciples of the Buddha. To prevent a friend from committing evil is really a friendly act. Therefore, one who accuses those of harming Buddhism is the Buddha's disciple, and one who does not purge those who do evil is an enemy of Buddhism.

CHAPTER 18
Be Aware of the Original Vows of Buddhas

Why did Śākyamuni Buddha, the Buddha of Many Treasures,* and many Buddhas in manifestation* coming from all over the universe gather together in the 11th chapter of the *Lotus Sutra,* Beholding the Stupa of Treasures? The chapter states that it was to make sure that the *Lotus Sutra* would spread forever. As we think of the intention of those Buddhas who wished to spread the *Lotus Sutra* for the benefit of all the children of the Buddha in the future, their compassion seems greater than that of parents who see their only child faced with great suffering. Having no sympathy with those Buddhas, however, Hōnen tightly shut the gate to the *Lotus Sutra* so that no one in the Latter Age of Degeneration* could enter it. It is a pity that Hōnen made them cast away the *Lotus Sutra.* It was just like fooling an idiotic child into throwing away his treasure.

Why shouldn't we warn our parents if we know that someone is trying to kill them? Shouldn't we prevent an evil drunken child from killing his parents? Shouldn't we prevent an evil man from setting a temple tower on fire? Should we leave our only child untreated when he is seriously sick? Those who do not discourage followers of Zen and Pure Land Buddhism in Japan are the same as those who do nothing to prevent evil acts. They are what Chang-an referred to when he said, "Those heartless people who keep friendly relationships with evil doers by overlooking their sins are their enemies." I, Nichiren, am like a compassionate parent of everyone in Japan, whereas everyone in the Tendai sect is their worst enemy. Hasn't Chang-an stated, "To prevent a friend from committing an evil act is really an act of friendship?"

Those who do not aspire to Buddhahood will never attain it. Lord Śākyamuni Buddha was abused by all non-Buddhist teachers in India as an evil man. Grand Master T'ien-t'ai* was spoken ill of as "a man who destroys his own two meter body by slandering the Buddha with an eight centimeter tongue" by the three Southern masters and seven Northern masters of Buddhism in China and Monk Tokuitsu* of Japan. Grand Master Dengyō* was laughed at by scholar-monks of Nara for not having seen the capital of T'ang China. However, these masters had nothing to be ashamed of because they were abused just for the sake of the *Lotus Sutra*. Praise by the ignorant should be regarded as most dishonorable. Perhaps Tendai and Shingon monks would be happy to see me, Nichiren, disgraced* by the Kamakura Shogunate, though it is pitiful and strange of them.

Śākyamuni Buddha gave up his land of eternal tranquility for this Sahā World.* Venerable Kumārajīva* traveled all the way from India to China. Grand Master Dengyō risked his life by going to China to study Buddhism. Bodhisattva Deva was killed by non-Buddhist heretics. Venerable Siṃha was beheaded by the king. Bodhisattva Medicine-King* burned his elbow to offer it as a light in gratitude for the preaching of the *Lotus Sutra* in past lives. Prince Shōtoku peeled off the skin on his finger to write in blood the title of the Brahma-net Sutra which he copied. When Śākyamuni was a Bodhisattva in a past life, he sold his own flesh to make an offering to a Buddha. Gyōbō Bonji (Aspiration for the Dharma) used one of his own bones to write down the true teaching. These are examples of those who spread Buddhism "in the way best suited to the situation," as Grand Master T'ien-t'ai put it. Keep in mind that Buddhism must be spread according to the times. My exile is merely a trifle in this present life, which is not lamentable at all. Instead, I feel it is a great joy as I am sure I will be rewarded with great happiness in my future lives.

Notes

1. *Kalpa*: a Sanskrit term meaning an immeasurably long period of time, said to be the period required to empty a city full of poppy seeds by taking away one every three years, or for an angel to wear away a 40 cubic kilometer stone by touching it with her robe once every three years.
2. *Rokkudō* or *rokkai*: hell, the realms of hungry spirits, beasts, *asura* demons, and human beings, and finally heaven, where souls of living beings transmigrate from one realm to another until they enter the world of Nirvana.
3. Ten Realms: according to T'ien-t'ai, the world of living beings consists of, in ascending order: hell, realms of hungry spirits, beasts, *asura* demons, and humans, heaven, realms of *śrāvaka* (*shōmon*), *pratyekabuddha* (*engaku*), bodhisattvas, and Buddhas.
4. *Yojana*: a unit of measurement of length in ancient India. The exact length is unknown, but it is said to be the distance of a day's journey by a royal chariot.
5. Chinese characters for filial piety, height and depth (thickness) can all be pronounced the same, "*kō*" in Japanese.
6. *Sanzen sekai*: the domain of a Buddha consists of 1 billion (1,000 x 1,000 x 1,000) worlds.
7. It is believed that the world goes through four *kalpa* (periods) of construction, continuance, destruction, and emptiness, each of which consists of 20 small *kalpa*. The average human lifespan in a small *kalpa* increases by a year per century from 10 years until it reaches the maximum human lifespan of 84,000 years. After it reaches the maximum human lifespan, the human lifespan grows shorter by a year per century until it reaches the minimum average human lifespan of 10 years. This is repeated 20 times within a *kalpa*.
8. *Jūgen rokusō-hōkai en'yū*: Kegon doctrine that all phenomena have six characteristics: the whole and parts, unity and variety, and growth and decline. Also that they are interdependent and that there are 10 mysterious gates through which this interdependency can be perceived.
9. *Yuishin hōkai*: phenomena are manifestation of mind, and mind represents phenomena.
10. *Kaiin sammai*: meditation that causes all truths to appear within the Buddha's wisdom, just as all things are reflected in the quiet ocean.
11. *Kondō muni*: everything is a total sum of karma, therefore, each thing is indistinguishable from one another.
12. Probably refers to the Mo-ho tribes in Manchuria.
13. Six *pāramitā*: charity, observing precepts, perseverance, efforts, meditation, and wisdom.
14. *Daigo*: see "Five Flavors" in the glossary.
15. Three teachings: part of the so-called Four Teachings. See the glossary.
16. Fivefold merit: five kinds of merit gained by those who have attained enlightenment: (1) freedom from any offenses against Buddhist precepts; (2) freedom from all illusions; (3) wisdom; (4) freedom from all bonds; and (5) awareness of the attainment of emancipation.

17. Eightfold Evil Path: contrasted with the Eightfold Noble Path leading to Nirvana: right views, right thoughts, right speech, right acts, right living, right effort, right mindfulness, and right meditation.
18. Eight Winds refer to the eight elements which arouse one's love and hate: profit, loss, slander, fame, praise, censure, pain, and pleasure.
19. The Buddha is said to have been five meters tall, twice as tall as normal human beings.
20. 3,000 dust-particle *kalpa (sanzen jindengō)* is the immeasurably long period of time described in the seventh [Kejōyu] chapter of the *Lotus Sutra*, A Parable, indicating how much time has passed since Śākyamuni preached the *Lotus Sutra* as the 16th son of Daitsūchishō Buddha: "Suppose someone smashed a major world system, consisting of 1,000 x 1,000 x 1,000 worlds, into ink-powder. Then he traveled eastward making a dot as large as a particle of dust with that ink-powder as he passed 1,000 worlds until the ink-powder was exhausted. Then all the worlds he went through were smashed into dust. The number of *kalpa* which has elapsed since Daitsūchishō Buddha passed away is infinitely larger than the number of particles of the dust thus produced."
21. *Shikikai:* see "Triple world" *(sangai)* in the glossary.
22. *Yuishin hōkai-kan:* doctrine of the *Flower Garland (Kegon) Sutra* claiming that mind is the ultimate existence and all phenomena are its manifestations.
23. *Happu chūdō-kan:* the middle path shown through the negation of eight false views of reality: neither birth nor extinction, neither cessation nor permanence, neither uniformity nor diversity, and neither coming nor going.
24. "Consciousness only" doctrine: claims that all phenomena are manifestations of one's consciousness.
25. "Five wheels": refer to the five elements (earth, water, fire, wind, and space) that constitute all things in the world.

Toki-dono Gohenji (ST 101)

Introduction

"Toki-dono Gohenji" was written at Ichinosawa on Sado Island on the 10th day of the fourth month in the ninth year of the Bun'ei Period (1272). The original manuscript on two pieces of paper is still kept at the Hokekyōji Temple, Nakayama, Chiba Prefecture. This was Nichiren's first letter written at Ichinosawa after moving from the Meditation Hall at Tsukahara, where he was originally exiled.

At the beginning of this letter, Nichiren expresses his gratitude for the donation from Toki Jōnin. He then asks the lord to read carefully the essay which he had sent to Shijō Kingo: the *Kaimoku-shō, Open Your Eyes to the Lotus Teaching*, because he had described the teaching fully in it.

Firmly convinced that he was truly one who practices the *Lotus Sutra*, Nichiren Shōnin answers the question of why he does not get any support from deities. He lists three reasons. First, deities had abandoned this awful country. Secondly, deities no longer had any power. And thirdly, powerful devils had gotten into the minds of the three kinds of strong enemies and controlled them. So deities such as the King of the Brahma Heaven* and Indra* could not do anything. Finally, he expresses his determination to live truly as one who practices the *Lotus Sutra* to the end of his life.

A Response to Lord Toki

I have received your monetary donation as mentioned in your letter. I do not know how to express my gratitude to you.

I wrote a little about the teaching of the Buddha and gave it to the messenger of Lord Shijō Kingo* the other day. Please read it carefully. Having studied most sutras of Buddhism, I have no doubt that I, Nichiren, am one who practices the *Lotus Sutra*.* However, it seems that there are three reasons why I have not had any heavenly support. First, the deities may have abandoned this awful country because it is filled with people without faith in the *Lotus Sutra*. Secondly, as the deities have not heard the sound of the *Lotus Sutra* for a long time, they grew powerless. Thirdly, powerful devils have gotten into the minds of the three kinds of strong enemies of the *Lotus Sutra* and controlled them, so deities such as the King of the Brahma Heaven* and Indra* cannot do much. I shall write more details about each reason and scriptural supports later.

Regarding my life, I have given it up. No matter what persecution overtakes me, I will never change my mind, nor have I any grudge at all. Many evil people are "good friends."* The use of a persuasive way or an aggressive way,* of propagating Buddhism depends on the time and situation. This is the Buddha's teaching, not my own idea. I shall see you in the Pure Land on Mt. Sacred Eagle.*

Yours sincerely,
Nichiren (signature)

On the 10th day of the fourth month

A Response to Lord Toki

P.S. I have no doubt that I am at the brink of death. I hope you will be very pleased in case I am beheaded, [consecrating myself to the *Lotus Sutra*]. It is like being robbed of a strong poison by a bandit in exchange for a precious treasure.

Shingon Shoshū Imoku (ST 106)

Introduction

This letter to Toki Jōnin and other followers of Nichiren was written at Ichinosawa, Sado, where Nichiren had been exiled, in the fifth month of the ninth year in the Bun'ei Era (1272). The original manuscript is kept at the Nakayama Hokekyōji Temple, Chiba Prefecture. It tells the differences between the Lotus school and other schools such as Shingon (True Word), Kegon (Flower Garland), Hossō (Dharma Characteristics), Zen and Jōdo (Pure Land).

At first Nichiren Shōnin explains the doctrines of other schools such as Shingon and points out the misunderstandings of their founders, claiming that he is the only person who has criticized them, although according to the *Nirvana Sutra* Buddha's disciples should rectify any wrong interpretation of Buddhist scriptures. Citing from the *Lotus Sutra* and the *Sutra on the Extinction of the Dharma*, Nichiren points out the prediction made in them that those who practice the *Lotus Sutra* would be spoken ill of, abused, threatened with swords and sticks, exiled or even executed if they tried to spread the teachings of the *Lotus Sutra*. He claims that he is the very person who fits this prediction.

In response to his critics who claim that he commits the sin of boasting and slandering others, for which he will fall into the Hell of Incessant Suffering, Nichiren maintains that according to the *Lotus Sutra* one who upholds the sutra is supreme among all living beings. Answering the question why Nichiren does not have heavenly protection if he is really one who practices the *Lotus Sutra*, Nichiren insists that an *asura*-king, who is strong enough to fight against the great King of the Brahma Heaven, Indra, and the Four Heavenly Kings, has entered the minds of the leaders of the Zen, Pure Land and Precept schools, taken over the mind of the king, and caused wise men of the country to disappear. Even the great King of the Brahma Heaven and Indra cannot defend the land against such a powerful *asura*-king, not to mention minor deities who protect Japan. Nichiren concluded this letter saying that only bodhisattvas from underground, Śākyamuni Buddha, the Buddha of Many Treasures, and other Buddhas would be able to face the task, and that is why Nichiren survived the near deadly danger at Tatsunokuchi at midnight on the 12th day of the ninth month in the previous year.

Following the *Kaimoku-shō, Open Your Eyes to the Lotus Teaching*, this letter preaches to his followers about the difficulties those who practice the *Lotus Sutra* will encounter, ,and how they should accept and endure those difficulties. It advises Lord Toki to let other followers of Nichiren be fully aware of them.

Differences between the Lotus Sect and Other Sects Such as the True Word Sect

To Lord Toki* and Others:

The Shingon (True Word) sect* of Buddhism did not originally exist in India. At the beginning of the K'ai-yüan Period during the reign of Emperor Hsüan-tsung in T'ang China, such Tripiṭaka masters as Śubhākarasiṃha,* Vajrabodhi* and Pu-k'ung* (Amoghavajra) stole the doctrine of "3,000 existences contained in one thought,"* which Grand Master T'ien-t'ai had found in the *Lotus Sutra,* and put it into the *Great Sun Buddha Sutra** to establish the Shingon school.

The Kegon (Flower Garland) school* was established during the reign of Empress Wu in T'ang China. Ch'eng-kuan,* the fourth patriarch in the lineage of the Kegon school, and others stole the doctrine of the 10 ways of meditation established by Grand Master T'ien-t'ai in his *Great Concentration and Insight,* and put this into the *Flower Garland Sutra.** That is how the Kegon school was established. It's not worth commenting on the Hossō (Dharma Characteristics)* and Sanron (Three Treatises)* schools.

The Zen school* was established by Grand Master Bodhidharma* in Liang China based on the *Entering Laṅkā Sutra* which explains only a part of the Mahayana doctrine of emptiness. However, Zen scholars claim with deep arrogance and insolence that there is no true enlightenment in the sutras [special transmission without scriptures or preachings*]. I must say that their behavior of ignoring Buddhist sutras is an act of demons in the heavens.

Opposing the scholars of the San-lun and Ti-lun schools in ancient China, such monks as Shan-tao* established out of their compassion the Pure Land school* based on such as the *Sutra of Meditation on the Buddha of Infinite Life,** insisting on the sole practice of chanting the *nembutsu* [invocation of the name of the Buddha of Infinite Life]. Hōnen* of Japan misunderstood this, taking the Tendai (T'ien-t'ai) and Shingon (True Word) schools for miscellaneous practices unsuitable for those in the Latter Age of Degeneration. Thus, he misled all the people in Japan, confusing them all in the darkness of a long night. It is I, Nichiren alone, who can rectify the false views of other schools and lead the people in the right direction.

The *Nirvana Sutra** states that if a good monk sees others destroying Buddhism and ignores them without denouncing them for their sins and chasing them out of their residences, he is an enemy of Buddhism. Grand Master Chang-an* explains this passage in the *Nirvana Sutra*: "A man who destroys Buddhism is an enemy of Buddhism. One who does not have compassion does not blame such a man, and instead pretends to be friendly to him. Such a man is his enemy. One who blames a destroyer of Buddhism and removes his evil mind is a man of kindness."

If the advocacy of Hōnen to abandon, close, set aside and cast away* the *Lotus Sutra* in order to cherish the *nembutsu*,* and if Zen monks' claim that the true teaching of the Buddha does not exist in Buddhist sutras* because it is directly transmitted without scriptures or preachings,* if these are against the intention of the Buddha, I, Nichiren, would be a wise father, a noble teacher or a holy master for the people in Japan. However, if I do not speak up, I would not be able to avoid the serious sin of being the enemy of all the people who does not have compassion, does not blame enemies of Buddhism and pretends to befriend them. However, I, Nichiren, have already tried to remove the evil minds of all the people in Japan, rulers as well as subjects. That is why I can say that I am their father. The country of Japan has already committed the three rebellious sins.* How can she escape a heavenly punishment?

The *Nirvana Sutra* also states:

> Śākyamuni Buddha then took a bit of soil, put it on a fingernail, and asked Bodhisattva Kāśyapa which had more soil: the fingernail or the all the worlds throughout the universe? Bodhisattva Kāśyapa answered that it was clear that the soil on a fingernail could not compare in amount with that in all the worlds all over the universe. The Buddha then preached: "People who commit the four major sins or the five rebellious sins,* and those who cut off the root of merit to become an *icchantika*,* and who do not believe in this sutra are as vast in amount as the soil in the entire worlds in the whole universe. On the contrary, those who do not commit the five rebellious sins, do not become an *icchantika*, do not cut off the root of merit, and uphold this *Nirvana Sutra* are as scarce as the amount of soil on a fingernail.

According to this passage in the *Nirvana Sutra*, which is supplementary to the *Lotus Sutra*, those who do not believe the *Lotus Sutra* are as plentiful as the amount of soil in all the worlds throughout the universe while those who believe it, like Nichiren in Japan today, are as rare as the amount of soil on a fingernail.

The *Lotus Sutra*,* Chapter 13, predicts, "There will be many ignorant people who speak ill of us and abuse us in the dreadful and evil world." *The Sutra on the Extinction of the Dharma* states: "After the death of the Buddha, there will be an age of corruption, when the five rebellious sins are daily occurrences and devilish ways are rampant. Devils in ministerial robes will destroy Buddhism and the number of wicked people will be as numerous as the particles of sand in the sea. When the world is about to end, the duration of sunlight and moonlight will gradually be shortened and virtuous people will disappear, except one or two." The sutra also states that when those devilish monks die, their spirits will fall into the Hell of Incessant Suffering. Dōryū* of the Kenchōji Temple and his followers, Ryōkan* of the Gokurakuji Temple and his followers, Shōichi of the Jufukuji Temple and his followers, and the rest of monks in Japan today will all fall into the Hell of Incessant Suffering as stated in this sutra.

It is stated in the *Lotus Sutra,* Chapter 11, that it is not as difficult to shoulder a load of hay and stay unburned in the fire of the *kalpa* of destruction at the end of the world as it is difficult to uphold this sutra and expound it to even one person after the Buddha's extinction. What I, Nichiren, have done, and consequent persecutions of me, fit perfectly in this scriptural statement. It is stated also in the sutra, Chapter 13, that ignorant people will speak ill of us, abuse us, and threaten us with swords or sticks. The Buddha predicts in the 13th and 23rd chapters of the sutra that one who practices the *Lotus Sutra*ature* will appear in the fifth 500-year period after the Buddha's extinction, and he will be spoken ill of, abused, threatened with swords and sticks, exiled or executed by ignorant people. If I were not here, the prediction made by Śākyamuni Buddha,* the Buddha of Many Treasures* and other Buddhas in all the worlds throughout the universe* would be groundless.

Question: You, Nichiren, may have a reason for claiming yourself to be superior to others, but are you not self-conceited to claim that you are superior to the founders of such Buddhist schools as Shingon (True Word),* Flower Garland,* Sanron (Three Treatises),* and Hossō (Dharma Characteristics)?* The Buddha preaches to us not to lie and that one is bound to fall into the Hell of Incessant Suffering* if he boasts, slandering others. You must be the one who will fall into the Hell of Incessant Suffering. That's why the *Heroic Valor Sutra* states, "It is like a poor man asking the king to kill him by claiming himself to be the king. Moreover, a man who wants to be the King of the Dharma, the Buddha, will never win a resulting reward if he claims to be equal to the Buddha without the right practices as a bodhisattva." The *Nirvana Sutra** states, "Talking about which monks will commit the sin of violating the ban on a serious lie, he who tells a lie causes others to think of him as an *arhat* while actually he is not." Does it not coincide with your case?

Answer: It is stated in the *Lotus Sutra,* Chapter 23: "Just as the great King of the Brahma Heaven* is the father of all living beings, this sutra is the wise father of all living beings." The chapter also states: "This *Lotus Sutra* is supreme among all sutras. He who upholds this sutra is supreme among all living beings."

Moreover, Grand Master Dengyō* declares in his *Outstanding Principles of the Lotus Sutra:** "The reason the Tendai-Lotus school is superior to others is the *Lotus Sutra* on which the school is based. This is not slandering others and boasting. I pray that a man of wisdom should find out which sutra is supreme in establishing a school of Buddhism."

The most beautiful and brightest star is the moon. What is brighter than stars and the moon is the sun. A man without a cabinet post in a large country ranks higher than a minister of a small country. Likewise, it is as clear as heaven is different from earth that one who practices Hinayana Buddhism who has not attained enlightenment or even one superhuman power is superior to a man who practices non-Buddhist religion* in India attaining five supernatural powers. Even a great bodhisattva* who practices sutras other than the *Lotus Sutra* is inferior to an ordinary person* who is in the beginner's stage of Notional Understanding* in practicing the *Lotus Sutra* and is moved upon hearing just its title. You must be surprised to hear this. We must decide the superiority of a man through the sutra he practices. How can we discuss the superiority of a man without knowing the superiority of the sutra he practices?

Question: Why do you not receive any protection of heavenly beings if you are really one who practices the *Lotus Sutra?**

Answer: It is stated in the *Lotus Sutra,* Chapter 13, that devils will enter their bodies and cause them to abuse and insult the one who practices the *Lotus Sutra.* The *Heroic Valor Sutra* preaches: "An *asura*-king will wage a war against the great King of the Brahma Heaven,* Indra and the Four Heavenly Kings* in order to conquer the worlds. He is originally an incarnation of gods and is still a kind of heavenly being."

This *asura*-king, who is strong enough to fight against the great King of the Brahma Heaven, Indra and the Four Heavenly Kings,* enters the minds of leaders of the Zen,* Pure Land* and Precept* schools. Then, gradually the king as well as his subjects all become dominated by him while wise men all disappear from the country. As I said, the *asura*-king is so powerful that even the great King of the Brahma Heaven and Indra cannot fight back effectively, not to mention minor gods who protect Japan. Only those great bodhisattvas, appearing from underground* as preached in the 15th chapter of the *Lotus Sutra,* Śākyamuni Buddha,* the Buddha of Many Treasures* and other Buddhas can protect Japan against him.

The sun and moon are clear mirrors shining on all the worlds in the universe, but do they know about Nichiren? I am sure that they know me. So, we should not doubt or worry about the protection of various heavenly beings. Nevertheless, I, Nichiren, have been persecuted because the sins which I committed in my past lives have not been completely eradicated. As I have been exiled because of my faith in the *Lotus Sutra,* some of my sins may have been atoned so the Buddha may protect me under His robe. It was the protection of the Buddha that saved me from near death at Tatsunokuchi at midnight on the 12th day of the ninth month last year. Grand Master Miao-lê said in his *Annotations on the Great Concentration and Insight* that the stronger our faith is, the greater the divine protection will be. Do not doubt this. You should firmly believe in and have no doubt that there is always divine protection.

Yours truly,

On the fifth day of the fifth month

Nichiren (signature)

Please pass around this letter and leave nothing to regret later.

To Lord Toki:
Please read this letter many times until you memorize it, and let other people listen to you while you read it. Have no regrets if I am not pardoned. Probably heavenly beings keep things as they are. As you can see from the case of Lay Priest Fujikawa, he would not have met such a tragic death this year if he had been banished last year. Contemplating this, I believe that it is the wish of the gods that I am not released yet, but probably ignorant people cannot believe this. It is an unfilial act of my disciples to show facial expressions indicating that Nichiren is desirous of being released. I cannot help such disciples to fare better in the next life. You folks had better keep this in mind.

Kanjin Honzon-shō (ST 118)

Introduction

The full title of this writing is *Nyorai Metsugo Go-gohyaku-sai Shi Kanjin Honzon-shō, A Treatise Revealing the Spiritual Contemplation and the Most Venerable One for the First Time in the Fifth 500-year Period after the Death of Śākyamuni Buddha*. It was completed in the Ichinosawa section of Sado Island on the 25th day of the fourth month in the 10th year of the Bun'ei Period (1273), a year following the completion of the *Kaimoku-shō*. It was sent to Toki Jōnin of Shimōsa Province together with the accompanying letter dated the following day, the 26th day of the fourth month.

Writing to Toki Jōnin from the port of Teradomari in Echigo Province (present-day Niigata Prefecture) on the way to banishment on Sado Island, Nichiren Shōnin mentions the four criticisms lodged against him. The last of the four was that Nichiren preaches only the doctrine without speaking of meditative practices. Responding to such criticism, Nichiren clarifies his ideological and religious foundation revealing the true meditative practices and the Most Venerable One while annotating Grand Master T'ien-t'ai's *Great Concentration and Insight* as the source of the "3,000 existences contained in one thought" doctrine. The title of this treatise means that this writing was the first revelation in the beginning of the Latter Age of Degeneration of the true teaching of the Buddha which had not been revealed for more than 2,220 years since His passing away.

Consisting of 30 sets of questions and answers, this writing can be divided into three sections: section one, the sacred title, *Odaimoku*; section two, the *honzon* of the essential section; and section three, the propagation of the True Dharma. Section one, from the first question to halfway through the 20th answer, discusses the doctrine of the "3,000 existences contained in in one thought" with regards to spiritual contemplation *(kanjin)*. Starting with the 18th answer, which is preceded by a reminder not to reveal what is said to the public, Nichiren develops his own interpretation of "3,000 existences contained in one thought" *(jigu no ichinen sanzen)* and the true meaning of the *Odaimoku*. In the second section, the last half of the 20th question, Nichiren preaches the Most Venerable One based on the essential section of the *Lotus Sutra*. Finally in the third section, Nichiren proves the truth of the *Lotus Sutra* through his own personal experiences, pointing out that the five characters of *Myō, Hō, Ren, Ge,* and *Kyō* are the panacea for the salvation of the people in the Latter Age and that Nichiren is the very person who should spread them. Although he does not use the term *kaidan*, precept platform, it is generally accepted that he implicitly revealed it in this section. The original manuscript in Nichiren's own handwriting is kept as a treasure in the Hokekyōji Temple in the Nakayama section of Ichikawa City, Chiba Prefecture.

A Treatise Revealing the Spiritual Contemplation and the Most Venerable One

By Nichiren, a Buddhist Monk

SECTION I
THE SACRED TITLE (ODAIMOKU)

The "3,000 existences contained in one thought" *(ichinen sanzen)* doctrine was first expounded by Grand Master T'ien-t'ai in his *Great Concentration and Insight, Mo-ho Chih-kuan,** fascicle five, [Chapter Seven]. According to him:

> A mind by nature contains 10 realms of living beings [realms of hells, hungry spirits, beasts, *asura* demons, men, gods, *śrāvaka, pratyekabuddha,* bodhisattvas, and Buddhas]. Since these 10 realms contain one another, there exist 100 realms in one mind. Each of these 100 realms, furthermore, consists of "three factors," that is to say, living beings, the land on which they live, and the five elements of living beings [matter, perception, conception, volition, and consciousness]. It also possesses "10 aspects" [form, nature, substance, function, action, cause, condition, effect, reward, and ultimate equality of these aspects]. Thus, 30 modes of existence are in one realm and 3,000 modes of existence in 100 realms. In short, 3,000 modes of existence are contained in a mind at any given moment. When there is mind, even for a momentary flash, 3,000 existences are in it.... Thus a mind is unfathomable.

Note: To say that 30 modes of existence are in a realm is another way of saying that a realm contains three factors and 10 aspects. Both are the same in effect.

The difference is merely in how they are described. Another version of the *Great Concentration and Insight* says that there exist three factors in a realm.

CHAPTER I
The "3,000 Existences Contained in One Thought," the Ultimate Doctrine of Grand Master T'ien-t'ai

Question (1): Grand Master T'ien-t'ai's three major works include the *Profound Meaning of the Lotus Sutra, Fa-hua Hsüan-i,** *Words and Phrases of the Lotus Sutra, Fa-hua wên-chü,* in addition to *Great Concentration and Insight*. Does he explain the term of "3,000 existences contained in one thought" *(ichinen sanzen)** in the *Profound Meaning*?

Answer: As Grand Master Miao-lê* points out, it is not explained therein.

Question (2): How about in the *Words and Phrases*?*

Answer: Miao-lê says this work does not explain it either.

Question (3): Where does he say so?

Answer: In his *Annotations on the Great Concentration and Insight, Mo-ho Chih-kuan Fu-hsing-chüan Hung-chüeh,* Miao-lê states that the term has not been revealed anywhere except in T'ien-t'ai's *Great Concentration and Insight*.

Question (4): Did T'ien-t'ai explain the term in the first four fascicles of the *Great Concentration and Insight*?

Answer: No, he did not.

Question (5): Do you have proof of that?

Answer: According to the fifth fascicle of Miao-lê's *Annotations,* Grand Master T'ien-t'ai for the first time applied the "3,000 existences contained in one thought" doctrine as a guide to explain the way of meditation in the fifth fascicle, [Chapter Seven,] of his *Great Concentration and Insight*.

Question (6): This is strange. The *Profound Meaning,* fascicle two, says:

"Each of the 10 realms contains characteristics of the other nine realms, making it altogether 100 realms. Since each realm contains 10 aspects *(jū-nyoze),** 1,000 aspects exist in 100 realms." Is it not stated in the *Words and Phrases*, fascicle one: "A mind contains 10 realms, each of which in turn contains 10 realms with 10 aspects in each realm, so there are altogether 1,000 aspects contained in a mind"? And surely Grand Master T'ien-t'ai declares in his *Profound Meaning of the Bodhisattva Avalokiteśvara Chapter, Kuan-yin Hsüan-i:** "10 realms possess one another, making 100 realms. Since each of the 100 realms contains 10 aspects, altogether 1,000 aspects are hidden in a mind. They do not reveal themselves before our eyes. Nevertheless, is there any doubt that they exist?"

Question (7): May I ask once more whether or not the "3,000 existences contained in one thought" doctrine is explained in the first four fascicles of the *Great Concentration and Insight?*

Answer: Miao-lê denies it.

Question (8): How does he deny it?

Answer: Fascicle five of Miao-lê's *Annotations on the Great Concentration and Insight* states:

> Compared to the seventh chapter, in [fascicles five through 10 of] the *Great Concentration and Insight*, Right Way of Meditation, the book's previous chapters do not preach the true way of practicing meditation at all. What is preached in the first six chapters are the 25 practical means, through which one will gradually deepen understanding of the true way of meditation. That is to say, they are preliminary steps toward the true way.... Explaining the true way of meditation in the seventh chapter of the *Great Concentration and Insight*, Grand Master T'ien-t'ai resorted to the "3,000 existences contained in one thought" doctrine. This is the ultimate and supreme teaching of T'ien-t'ai. Therefore, Grand Master Chang-an writes in the preface to T'ien-t'ai's *Great Concentration and Insight* that T'ien-t'ai reveals in it the truth of Buddhism as comprehended by his inner heart. How true it is! May those who try to read and understand this book never imagine that the truth of the T'ien-t'ai doctrine lies anywhere but here.

Actually, Grand Master T'ien-t'ai spread the teaching of the Buddha for 30 years, 29 of which he spent preaching his *Profound Meaning, Words and Phrases,* and other writings. He made it clear that the teaching of the Buddha in His lifetime can be divided into five periods* and eight teachings [four methods of teaching, as well as four doctrinal teachings.][1] He revealed also that a mind at any moment contains 10 realms [from the hells up to the realm of Buddhas], which contain one another, constituting 100 realms in a mind. Furthermore, each of those 100 realms possesses 10 aspects [form, nature, substance, function, action, cause, condition, effect, reward, and ultimate equality of these aspects]. Therefore, according to T'ien-t'ai a total of 1,000 aspects are contained in a mind at any given moment. He criticized false doctrines put forth by various masters in the past 500 years since the introduction of Buddhism to China. He also expounded a unique doctrine which even commentators in India had never put forth. Grand Master Chang-an,* a direct disciple of T'ien-t'ai, has stated: "Great discourses of commentators in India cannot compare with Grand Master T'ien-t'ai's doctrine, not to say opinions and comments of Chinese priest-scholars. This is not boasting. His doctrine is incomparably superior."

It is a pity, however, that T'ien-t'ai scholars of later generations, surrendering to the founders of the Kegon (Flower Garland) and Shingon (True Word) schools of Buddhism, were robbed of this valued treasure: the "3,000 existences contained in one thought" doctrine. Grand Master Chang-an foretold this when he lamented: "If these words of T'ien-t'ai should disappear, the future would be dark."

CHAPTER II
How "1,000 Aspects Contained in 100 Realms" and "3,000 Existences Contained in One Thought" Differ

Question (9): How does the term "1,000 aspects contained in 100 realms" *(hyakkai senyo)* differ from "3,000 existences contained in one thought" *(ichinen sanzen)?**

Answer: Speaking of a mind having "1,000 aspects contained in 100 realms," we consider sentient beings only. When we talk about "3,000 existences contained in one thought," we consider both sentient as well as non-sentient beings.

Question (10): If even non-sentient beings possess 10 aspects,* does this mean that even grass and trees possess senses so that they can obtain Buddhahood just like sentient beings?

Answer: This is difficult to understand and difficult to believe. In fact there are two aspects in which T'ien-t'ai is hard to understand and hard to believe: one is his theology, and the other his spiritual contemplation. What is difficult in his theology is the seemingly contradictory statements found in Buddhist scriptures preceding the *Lotus Sutra* and in the *Lotus Sutra* itself, which were preached by one person: the Buddha. The pre-Lotus sutras hold that the two groups of Hinayana sages called *śrāvaka* and *pratyekabuddha* [Two Vehicles*] and *icchantika* [those without Buddha-nature] will never reach Buddhahood, and that Lord Śākyamuni achieved Buddhahood for the first time in this life.* However, the *Lotus Sutra,* in both the essential *(hommon)* and theoretical *(shakumon)* sections, denies this, stating that even the Two Vehicles and *icchantika* can become Buddhas in the future, and that the Lord Śākyamuni is in fact the Eternal Buddha. Thus one Buddha claimed two views, as far apart as fire and water. How could anyone believe Him? This is the most difficult doctrine to understand and to put faith in.

The second difficulty in the T'ien-t'ai doctrine is his spiritual contemplation regarding his doctrine of "1,000 aspects contained in 100 realms" and "3,000 existences contained in one thought." It is founded on the concept of 10 aspects, maintaining that non-sentient beings such as grass, trees, and land possess 10 aspects, that is to say, even non-sentient beings have mind as well as body. This is hard to believe. However, worshipping wooden icons and portraits as *honzon** has been accepted in Buddhism as well as other religions. This is acceptable only through the T'ien-t'ai doctrine. Unless grass and trees possess both matter and spirit and the principle of cause and effect, it does not make sense at all to worship wooden icons and portraits.

Question (11): Where does it say that both grass and trees as well as the land, like sentient beings, possess 10 aspects and the principle of cause and effect?

Answer: Fascicle five of T'ien-tai's *Great Concentration and Insight** says: "The land on which sentient beings live, one of three factors of a realm, also possesses 10 aspects. Therefore, even in an evil land 10 aspects such as form, nature and substance exist." It is said also in Miao-lê's *Commentary on the Profound Meaning of the Lotus Sutra,* Fa-hua Hsüan-i Shih-ch'ien*, [fascicle six]: "Form, the first of 10 aspects, is contained in matter [those with form]. Nature is contained only in mind. Substance, function, action and condition are related to both matter and mind. Cause and effect are contained only in mind, while rewards are of matter only." Miao-lê preaches in his *Diamond Scalpel,* Chin-kang-pei-lun*: "Each blade of grass and each tree, even a particle of gravel or dust, possess three causes of Buddhahood: inborn Buddha-nature, wisdom for seizing it, and right actions which help develop this wisdom."

CHAPTER III
The Mutual Possession of the Ten Realms as Revealed in the Lotus Sutra

Question (12): I have learned that the "3,000 existences contained in one thought" doctrine was first expounded in the fifth fascicle of the *Great Concentration and Insight*, one of the three major works of Grand Master T'ien-t'ai. Now I would like to know the meaning of spiritual contemplation *(kanjin)** of the "3,000 existences contained in one thought."

Answer: Spiritual contemplation means for one to meditate on his own mind, observing through it 10 realms, from the hells up to the realm of Buddhas, all of which are by nature contained in every mind. For instance, one can see the six sense-organs [eyes, ears, nose, tongue, body, and mind] of other people, but one cannot see and know one's own six sense organs unless one sees one's reflection in a clear mirror. Despite the fact that various sutras often preach six realms of illusion [realms of hells, hungry spirits, beasts, *asura* demons, men, and gods] and four realms of holy beings [Buddhas, bodhisattvas, *pratyekabuddha* and *śrāvaka*], we do not see how our mind contains 10 realms, 100 realms, 1,000 aspects, and 3,000 modes of existence, unless we see our reflection in the clear mirror of the *Lotus Sutra* and writings of Grand Master T'ien-t'ai* such as *Great Concentration and Insight*.

Question (13): Which parts of the *Lotus Sutra* are you referring to? What does T'ien-t'ai's explanation of them mean?

Answer: The second chapter* of the *Lotus Sutra*, Expedients, [in fascicle one] states that the purpose of the Buddhas appearing in the worlds was "to cause all living beings to open the gate to the insight of the Buddha." This means that of the nine of the 10 realms of living beings [excepting the realm of Buddhas], each embraces the realm of Buddhas. In the 16th chapter, The Duration of the Life of the Tathāgata,* the sutra also declares: "As I said before, it is an immeasurably long time since I, Śākyamuni Buddha, obtained Buddhahood. My life spans an innumerably and incalculably long period of time. Nevertheless, I am always here and I shall never pass away. Good men! The duration of my life, which I obtained by practicing the way of bodhisattvas, has not yet expired. It will last twice as long as the length of time as stated above."[2] This passage also shows that the nine realms are included in the realm of Buddhas.

The following passages in the *Lotus Sutra* also show that the 10 realms of living beings embrace one another. It is said in the 12th chapter, Devadatta, that after an incalculably long period of time, Devadatta* will be a Buddha called "Heavenly King." This shows the realm of Buddhas included in the realms of hells as it says that even a man as wicked as Devadatta, who had tried to kill the Buddha and had gone to hell, will be able to become a Buddha.

In the 26th chapter, Dhāraṇīs, the Buddha praises the 10 female *rākṣasa* demons such as Lambā saying, "Your merits will be immeasurable even when you protect the person who keeps only the name of the *Lotus Sutra*." Since even these *rākṣasa* demons in the realm of hungry spirits protect the one who practices the *Lotus Sutra*, the 10 realms, from hells up to the realm of Buddhas, are comprised in the realm of hungry spirits.

The Devadatta chapter also states that a daughter of a dragon-king attained perfect enlightenment, proving the existence of the 10 realms in the realm of beasts.

The 10th chapter, The Teacher of the Dharma, says that even a demi-god like Asura King Balin, [a king of *asura* demons mentioned in the first chapter, Introduction,] will obtain Buddhahood if he rejoices for a moment at hearing a verse or a phrase of the *Lotus Sutra*. This shows that the 10 realms are contained in the realm of *asura* demons.

It is stated in the second chapter, Expedients: "Those who carve an image of the Buddha with proper physical characteristics in His honor have already attained the enlightenment of the Buddha," showing that the realm of humans includes the 10 realms.

Then in the first chapter, Introduction, and the third chapter, A Parable, various gods such as the great King of the Brahma Heaven declare, "we also shall be able to become Buddhas," proving that the 10 realms are contained in the realm of gods.

In the third chapter, the Buddha assures Śāriputra,* the wisest of His *śrāvaka* disciples, that he will also attain Buddhahood in future life and will be called "Kekō (Flower Light) Buddha." This confirms the existence of the 10 realms in the realm of *śrāvaka*.

The second chapter states that those monks and nuns who sought emancipation through the way of *pratyekabuddha* [without guidance of teachers by observing the principle of cause and effect] pressed their hands together in respect, wishing to hear the Perfect Way. This affirms the existence of the 10 realms in the realm of *pratyekabuddha*.

It is written in the 21st chapter, The Supernatural Powers of the Tathāgata, that bodhisattvas as numerous as particles of dust of 1,000 worlds, who had sprung up from underground, beseeched the Buddha for this true, pure, and great Dharma, namely the *Lotus Sutra*. This verifies the existence of the 10 realms in the realm of bodhisattvas.

Finally in the 16th chapter, the Buddha sometimes appears as a Buddha in the realm of Buddhas but at other times appears as some of the others who reside in the other nine realms. This indicates that the 10 realms are included in the realm of Buddhas.

Question (14): When we look at our own faces reflected in the mirror or faces of other people, we can see that our six sense-organs: eyes, ears, nose, tongue, body, and mind exist. However, we cannot see the existence of the 10 realms in our own mind and others'. How can we believe this?

Answer: Certainly, it is not easy to believe in their existence. It is said in the 10th chapter of the *Lotus Sutra,* The Teacher of the Dharma,* that the sutra is most difficult to put faith in and most difficult to comprehend. The 11th chapter, Beholding the Stupa of Treasures,* preaches the "six difficult and nine easier actions,"* maintaining that keeping faith in the *Lotus Sutra* after the death of Śākyamuni Buddha is harder than trying to grasp Mt. Sumeru and hurl it over countless Buddha lands.

According to Grand Master T'ien-t'ai,* "the *Lotus Sutra* is hard to have faith in and hard to understand because what is preached in both the essential and theoretical sections of the sutra is altogether different from what is preached in those sutras expounded before the *Lotus Sutra*." Grand Master Chang-an* states: "The doctrine of 'mutual possession of 10 realms' *(jikkai gogu)* is the very reason why the Buddha appeared in the world. How can we ordinary people be expected to put faith in the *Lotus Sutra* and comprehend it easily?" Grand Master Dengyō* maintains: "This *Lotus Sutra* is most difficult to believe and comprehend, because the sutra preaches the true intent of the Buddha."

After all, those with capacity to understand and have full faith in Buddhism who had the luck of listening to Śākyamuni Buddha preach the *Lotus Sutra* in India must have accumulated a great deal of merit in their past lives. Moreover, they were fortunate to have been assisted and guided by the Lord Śākyamuni Buddha, the Buddha of Many Treasures who had come to verify the truth of Śākyamuni's words, various Buddhas in manifestation* who had come from all over the universe, numerous bodhisattvas who had sprung up from underground,* and such distinguished disciples of Śākyamuni Buddha as Mañjuśrī and Maitreya. Nevertheless, there were some who were not converted to the *Lotus Sutra*. This is the reason why the self-conceited, as many as 5,000, walked out when the Buddha was about to start preaching [in Chapter Two, Expedients], and why some men and gods were transferred to other worlds [in Chapter 11, Beholding the Stupa of Treasures]. It was so even while Śākyamuni Buddha was alive. How much more difficult is it to believe in the *Lotus Sutra* in the Ages of the True Dharma and Semblance Dharma after the death of Śākyamuni Buddha, not to say in the beginning of the Latter Age of Degeneration![3] If you could easily believe the sutra, it would mean that the sutra is not the True Dharma.

Question (15): I do not dare question what the *Lotus Sutra* says and how T'ien-t'ai and his disciple Chang-an interpreted it regarding the "mutual possession of 10 realms." However, they sound as though they are saying that fire is water and black is white. It is difficult to understand although I believe this is what the Buddha preached. Now, no matter how many times we look at each other's faces, we see only a human being, not anything of other realms. It is the same with our own face. How is it possible to believe the "mutual possession of the 10 realms" doctrine?

Answer: As we often look at each other's faces, we notice our facial expression changes from time to time. It is full of delight, anger, or calm sometimes. But other times it changes to greed, ignorance, or flattery. Anger represents hells. Greed represents hungry spirits. Ignorance represents beasts. Flattery represents *asura* demons. Delight represents gods. And calm represents humans. Thus we see in the countenance of people six realms of illusion, from hells to the realm of gods. We cannot see four realms of holy ones [*śrāvaka, pratyekabuddha,* bodhisattvas, and Buddhas], which are hidden from our eyes. Nevertheless, we should be able to see them, too, if we look for them carefully.

Question (16): It is not entirely clear that the six realms of illusion exist in the realms of human beings, but I am beginning to think they seem to as I listen to you. Nevertheless, I cannot see the four realms of holy ones at all. What do you say about this?

Answer: You doubted the existence of six realms of illusion in the realm of men, but I tried hard to explain it until you said you seemed to understand it. The same might happen with four realms of holy ones. Therefore, I shall try to explain as much as possible what the sutras state, supplemented with reason. We see the so-called principle of impermanence everywhere in front of our eyes. We humans understand this principle, through which two groups of Hinayana sages [Two Vehicles*] called *śrāvaka* and *pratyekabuddha* try to obtain enlightenment [the stage of *arhats*]. How can we say then that the realms of two Hinayana sage groups are not included in the realm of men? A man, no matter how inconsiderate he may be, loves his wife and children. It shows that he is partly in the bodhisattva realm.

The only realm contained in the realm of men and yet hard to see is that of Buddhas. However, since we see nine other realms included in the realm of human beings, we can conjecture that the realm of Buddhas is also contained therein. You should firmly believe this and have no doubt about it. On the existence of the realm of Buddhas contained in the human realm, the *Lotus Sutra* states in the second chapter, Expedients, that the purpose of Buddhas appearing in the world was "to cause all living beings to open the gate to the insight of the Buddha." And in the *Nirvana Sutra,** we come across a passage which states: "Though having only a human eye, those who study Mahayana Buddhism are regarded the same as having the Buddha-eye because they see the truth of Buddhism." The reason why we, ordinary people,* born in the Latter Age, can put faith in the *Lotus Sutra* is that the realm of Buddhas is included in the realm of human beings.

Question (17): The Buddha's words on the "mutual possession of 10 realms"* (*jikkai gogu*) doctrine are all clear, but it is difficult to believe that the realm of Buddhas is contained in our vulgar minds. However, if we do not believe this now, there is no doubt that we will become *icchantika*,* men without Buddha-nature, and will never attain Buddhahood. We beseech you, please, to have great compassion and help us believe this and save us from falling into the Hell of Incessant Suffering.

Answer: You cannot believe even those words of the *Lotus Sutra* preaching the very reason why Buddhas appeared in the world. How can those who are ranked below the Buddha, such as the four ranks of bodhisattva-teachers to whom people turned for guidance after the death of the Buddha, and those of us in the Latter Age who are still at the stage of not being aware of Buddha-nature,[4] save you from being non-believers?

Nevertheless, I shall try because there were some who could not attain Buddhahood under the guidance of the Buddha but were enlightened by men like Ānanda. After all, man's capacity to understand and believe the teaching of the Buddha can be of two kinds. First, there are those who attain Buddhahood by seeing the Buddha in person and listening to Him preach the *Lotus Sutra*. Secondly, there are those who attain Buddhahood by means of the teaching of the *Lotus Sutra* without seeing the Buddha.

Moreover, some Taoist teachers in China before the introduction of Buddhism, and non-Buddhist masters in India before the rise of Buddhism grasped the right insight of Buddhism by means of Confucianism or the Four Vedas. Also, there are many bodhisattvas and ordinary people with superior capacities for comprehension and faith, whose good luck of having listened to such Mahayana sutras as the *Flower Garland Sutra*, Hōdō sutras, and the *Wisdom Sutra* caused sudden blooming of the seed of Buddhahood planted in them by Daitsūchishō (Great Universal Wisdom) Buddha 3,000 dust-particle *kalpa*[5] ago or by Śākyamuni Buddha 500 dust-particle *kalpa*[6] in the past. For example, Hinayana sages called *pratyekabuddha* suddenly realized the principle of emptiness by looking at flower petals flying in spring or tree leaves falling in autumn. This is how some attain enlightenment by means other than the teaching of the *Lotus Sutra*.

On the other hand, those who never had a chance of receiving the seed of Buddhahood in the past or those who attach themselves to the provisional or Hinayana sutras are unable to get rid of Hinayana and provisional views even if they came across the teaching of the *Lotus Sutra*. Insisting that their own views are right, they mistakenly consider the *Lotus Sutra* to be equal to the Hinayana sutras or equal or even inferior to such as the *Flower Garland Sutra** and *Great Sun Buddha Sutra*.* These masters themselves are inferior to Confucian and non-

Buddhist sages. I shall put this aside for now, however, because it has no direct connection to the "mutual possession of 10 realms"* *(jikkai gogu)* doctrine.

The "mutual possession of 10 realms" doctrine is as difficult to maintain as it is to see fire in a rock and flowers in wood. However, it is not totally impossible because rocks spark when struck together and a tree blooms in spring. It is most difficult to believe that the realm of Buddhas is contained in the realm of men because it is just like saying that fire is in water or water is in fire. However, it is said that dragon fire comes out of water and dragon water comes out of fire. This is difficult to believe, but we cannot help but believe it because of the evidence for this. You have come to believe that each of the eight realms is contained in the realm of men. Why can you not believe that the realm of Buddhas, too, is contained in it?

Ancient Chinese rulers, sages such as Yao and Shun, treated all people equally with compassion, proving the existence of the realm of Buddhas, at least a portion of it, within the realm of men. Never-Despising Bodhisattva, described in the 20th chapter of the *Lotus Sutra,* Never-Despising Bodhisattva, pressed his hands together in respect and bowed to anyone he met because whenever the bodhisattva saw a man, he saw a Buddha in him. Born to the human world, Prince Siddhārtha, young Śākyamuni, became the Buddha. This evidence should be enough to convince you to believe that the realm of Buddhas exists in the realm of men.

CHAPTER IV
Upholding the Lotus Sutra and Attaining Buddhahood

Keep what is said hereafter confidential and do not reveal it to others.

Question (18): Lord Śākyamuni is the Buddha, free of all delusions and evil passions. He is the lord of all the worlds in the universe and the master of all bodhisattvas,* two groups of Hinayana sages [Two Vehicles:* *śrāvaka* and *pratyekabuddha*], men and gods. Accompanied by the great King of the Brahma Heaven to the left and Indra to the right, followed by four categories of Buddhists [monks, nuns, laymen, and laywomen] and eight kinds of gods and demi-gods who protect Buddhism, and guided by a pair of Kongō gods, protectors of Buddhism, Śākyamuni goes out to preach as many as 84,000 doctrines in order to save all sentient beings. How could it be possible that the Buddha, as great as this, resides in the minds of us, ordinary men?

Part 1: According to the theoretical section* [first half] of the *Lotus Sutra,* and pre-Lotus sutras,* Lord Śākyamuni is the Buddha who obtained Perfect

Enlightenment for the first time under a bodhi tree at Buddhagayā in India. Looking for His acts of merit in His previous lives as a bodhisattva seeking Buddhahood, we find that He was once a prince so charitable to all the poor that He was called Prince Alms-giver. In one of His previous existences, He was Bodhisattva Judō who served Burning Light Buddha so respectfully as to cover a muddy road with his own hair to let the Buddha pass. He was once King Shibi, who sacrificed his own body to feed a hawk in order to save a pigeon, and at another time He was Prince Satta, who fed a hungry tiger his own body.

He persevered for an incalculably long period of time described variously in scriptures as three *asaṃkhya*[7] *kalpa,*[8] 100 major *kalpa,*[9] *kalpa* more in number than the number of dust-particles, innumerable number of *asaṃkhya kalpa*, the period between the first aspiration for Buddhahood and the attainment of it, or 3,000 dust-particle *kalpa*. All the while he served Buddhas as many as 75,000 or 76,000 or 77,000 in number fulfilling Bodhisattva practices to become the present Lord Śākyamuni Buddha. How can we believe that all the merit which the Buddha had accumulated as a bodhisattva striving for Buddhahood is inherent in the realm of bodhisattvas within our minds?

Speaking of the attainment of Buddhahood as the result of the practices of a bodhisattva, it is generally believed that Lord Śākyamuni Buddha attained Perfect Enlightenment for the first time under the bodhi tree at Buddhagayā. For some 40 years* afterwards, He manifested Himself as various Buddhas, preaching four doctrinal teachings [*tripiṭaka*, common, distinct and perfect teachings]. He thus preached the pre-Lotus sutras,* the theoretical section* of the *Lotus Sutra*, and the *Nirvana Sutra,** delivering salvation to all the people.

Namely, when preaching the *Flower Garland Sutra*, He appeared as Vairocana Buddha sitting on the lotus-platform in the center of the universe. In the Āgama sutras, He manifested Himself as a Buddha who had eliminated evil passions and attained Buddhahood by going through 34 stages of spiritual improvement. He showed the dignity of 1,000 Buddhas in sutras of the Hōdō period and *Wisdom Sutra*, and 1,200 Buddhas in such sutras as the *Great Sun Buddha Sutra* and the *Diamond Peak Sutra*. Moreover, in the theoretical section of the *Lotus Sutra*, the 11th chapter, Beholding the Stupa of Treasures,* He manifested four different Buddhas[10] in four lands: land cohabited by ordinary people and sages (*dōgo-do*), land temporarily established for those who have destroyed major evil passions (*hōben-do*), land without hindrance for bodhisattvas of higher stages (*jippō-do*), and the land of eternal tranquil light (*jakkō-do*) for the Dharma Bodied Buddha In the *Nirvana Sutra*, He exhibited four types of Buddha bodies: the inferior Accommodative Body as five meters tall, the superior Accommodative Body tall sometimes but short at other times, the Reward Body as Vairocana Buddha, and the everywhere-existing Dharma Body. Even after His death at the age of 80, He continues to save the people in the Ages of the True Dharma, Semblance Dharma and the Latter Age of Degeneration. Is such a great virtue of the Buddha inherent in the mind of us, ordinary men?

Part 2: Next let me examine this further on the basis of the essential section [last half] of the *Lotus Sutra*. Lord Śākyamuni Buddha is the Eternal Buddha who attained Perfect Enlightenment 500 dust-particle *kalpa** ago. His practice of the bodhisattva way also goes back to the eternal past. Ever since His attainment of Perfect Enlightenment, He has appeared in all the worlds in the universe as Buddhas in manifestation to expound Śākyamuni's lifetime preachings and save innumerable people.

The difference between those who were converted by this Eternal Buddha of the essential section of the *Lotus Sutra* and those converted by the Buddha of the theoretical first half of the *Lotus Sutra* is as far apart as a drop of water and a great ocean, or a particle of dust and a great mountain. When we compare one bodhisattva of the essential half to those of the theoretical section such as Mañjuśrī (Monjushiri) and Avalokiteśvara (Kannon) of all the worlds in the universe, the comparison of Indra [protector of Buddhism and its followers] to monkeys would not be sufficient. How can we believe that the virtue of the Eternal Buddha, as vast as this, is contained in the mind of us, ordinary people?

Part 3: Besides these Buddhas, there exist *śrāvaka* and *pratyekabuddha* of all the worlds in the universe who extinguished evil passions to attain the stage of *arhats,* the King of the Brahma Heaven, Indra, Sun God, Moon God, Four Heavenly Kings, and four Wheel-turning Noble Kings. Are all these and those of the realms below them, all the way down to the burning flame of the Hell of Incessant Suffering, are these supposed to be contained in the minds of us, ordinary men? Are they all a part of the 3,000 modes of existence supposedly contained in our own minds? It is impossible to believe this even if it is what the Buddha preached.

Part 4: Therefore, it seems that pre-Lotus sutras, which do not preach the "mutual possession of 10 realms" doctrine, are more correct than the *Lotus Sutra*. For instance, the Buddha is described in the *Flower Garland Sutra** as being "completely free from falsehood and pure as the empty sky." We read in the *Sutra of the Benevolent King, Ninnō-kyō:** "Having completely eliminated the root of evil passion, the Buddha possesses nothing but wonderful wisdom." It is said in the *Diamond Wisdom Sutra, Kongō Hannya-kyō:* "The Buddha has nothing but pure good."

We also come across a passage in Aśvaghoṣa's *Awakening of Faith in Mahayana, Daijōkishin-ron,* which says: "There is nothing but the virtue of purity in Buddha-nature." The *Discourse on the Theory of Consciousness-Only, Jō-yuishiki-ron,* a commentary on Vasubandhu's* *Thirty Verses on Consciousness-Only, Yuishiki*

Sanjū-shō, claims: "At the very moment when a bodhisattva is about to gain Buddhahood, he reaches the state of diamond meditation, the highest form of meditation, and the most perfect and purest of fundamental consciousness is induced. Then the minds of ordinary men and gods with evil passions as well as those of *śrāvaka* and *pratyekabuddha* are all eliminated as they are contrary to the fundamental consciousness."

These statements in pre-Lotus sutras differ much from the contentions of the *Lotus Sutra* in that the realm of Buddhas is a part of our minds. Comparing the two, we know that the pre-Lotus sutras are numerous and the period in which they were preached is longer. When we have to choose between the two uttered by one Buddha, the pre-Lotus appears more legitimate.

Besides, the Buddha predicted that Bodhisattva Aśvaghoṣa would be the 11th transmitter of Buddhism while Vasubandhu was a commentator who wrote as many as 1,000 works and was respected as one of the Four Reliances, leaders of the people after the death of the Buddha. Differing from them, Grand Master T'ien-t'ai, who expounded the "mutual possession of 10 realms," was a poor monk in China far away from India, the land of the Buddha, and he did not write even one commentary. Who would believe in such a man?

Part 5: Suppose we reject the vast amount of sutras preached over many years and side with one sutra, the *Lotus Sutra,* it would be beneficial for us if the doctrine of "mutual possession of 10 realms" is clearly defined in the sutra. However, where in the *Lotus Sutra* are there clear statements regarding the doctrines "mutual possession of 10 realms,"* "1,000 aspects contained in 100 realms,"* or "3,000 existences contained in one thought"?* Looking through the sutra, we cannot find any passage to this effect. Instead, we come across such contrary statements as the one in the second chapter, Expedients: "The Buddha has eliminated all that is evil." Does this not mean that no other realms except that of Buddhas exist in the mind of the Buddha, invalidating the "mutual possession of 10 realms" doctrine and that the *Lotus Sutra* preaches the same as the other sutras?

Part 6: No reference to the "mutual possession of 10 realms" doctrine can be found in Vasubandhu's *Commentary to the Lotus Sutra, Hokke-ron,* or Sāramati's *On the Treasure Vehicle of Buddha-nature, Kukyō Inchijō Hōshō-ron.* Neither the great scholars of Northern and Southern China nor the Japanese scholar-priests of the seven great temples in Nara have ever preached it.

Part 7: This is a slanted view of T'ien-t'ai alone, which has been misunderstood by Dengyō. T'ien-t'ai made so many mistakes that he was criticized by National Master Ch'eng-kuan,* who said, "It was T'ien-t'ai's error," and by Monk Hui-yüan [disciple of Fa-tsang], who stated, "T'ien-t'ai referred to Hinayana teachings as the 'three basket' teachings, confusing the meaning of the 'three baskets', which includes both Hinayana and Mahayana teachings." Monk Ryōkō of Nara criticized him: "T'ien-t'ai alone has not understood the essence of the *Flower Garland Sutra.*" Hossō Monk Tokuitsu of Japan spoke ill of him as well: "What is the matter with you, Monk T'ien-t'ai? Whose disciple are you? With a tongue less than eight centimeters long, you have slandered the teaching of the Buddha with a tongue huge enough to cover His face."[11] And Grand Master Kōbō, the founder of Shingon (True Word) Buddhism in Japan, said: "Chinese Buddhist masters have struggled to rob Shingon Buddhism of its term *daigo* (clarified butter) for the supreme teaching, by referring to their own schools as *daigo.*"

After all, the "3,000 existences contained in one thought" doctrine does not appear in any of the sutras preached by the Buddha during His lifetime, not even in name only. None of the Four Reliances who guided the people after the extinction of the Buddha have said a word about it. Scholar-monks of China and Japan have not accepted the doctrine, either. How can we believe it?

Answer [to Question (18)]: The seven parts of this question you have just asked are most difficult to answer. However, the differences between the *Lotus Sutra* and all the other sutras are clearly stated in those sutras. The former reveals the truth, while the latter do not. When the *Lotus Sutra* was preached, the Buddha of Many Treasures appeared to verify its truth, and numerous Buddhas in manifestation [*funjin* Buddhas] from all the worlds in 10 directions [all over the universe] came together to admire the preaching. Whereas, in the *Pure Land Sutra,* for instance, it is merely stated that Buddhas in the worlds of six directions showed their tongues in praise of the Buddha. The two groups of Hinayana sages called *śrāvaka* and *pratyekabuddha* [Two Vehicles],* who are guaranteed in the *Lotus Sutra* to attain Buddhahood, are condemned in other sutras to wander forever. According to the *Lotus Sutra* the Buddha has been the Eternal Buddha since 500 dust-particle *kalpa* ago, while according to other sutras, He attained Perfect Enlightenment for the first time under the bodhi tree at Buddhagayā.

Next, regarding your contention [in part 6] that commentators have not preached the doctrine of "mutual possession of 10 realms," Grand Master T'ien-t'ai* has this to say: "Vasubandhu and Nāgārjuna acknowledged it privately, but pretended not to have been aware of it, and they preached provisional teachings to suit the time. Nonetheless, the later scholar-masters understood them as they liked, held fast to their own opinions, and quarreled with one another in debate until they were all against the holy teachings of the Buddha."

Praising Grand Master T'ien-t'ai, Grand Master Chang-an* has stated: "Great discourses of commentators in India cannot compare with T'ien-t'ai's doctrine, not to say opinions and comments of Chinese priest-scholars. This is not excessive praise. His doctrine is incomparably superior." Such bodhisattvas as

Vasubandhu,* Nāgārjuna,* Aśvaghoṣa, and Sāramati* did not reveal it, because the time was not ripe.

As for the priest-scholars of China before T'ien-t'ai, some can be said to have been aware of the "jade" hidden in the Lotus, but others were not. Some of those who came after T'ien-t'ai surrendered to him in the end, though opposing at first, but others rejected T'ien-t'ai totally.

An explanation about the passage in the second chapter of the *Lotus Sutra* which you have cited [in part 5] is in order: "The Buddha has eliminated all that is evil." It is merely a citation in the *Lotus Sutra* from other sutras preached before it. It does not belong to the Lotus doctrine. Please read the sutra carefully, so that you may understand that the doctrine of "mutual possession of 10 realms"* is clearly preached in it. For instance, we read in the second chapter that the purpose of the Buddha appearing in the world was "to cause all living beings to open their gates to the insight of the Buddha."

Interpreting this passage in the *Lotus Sutra,* T'ien-t'ai said: "If the insight of the Buddha does not exist in all living beings, how can He open the gate to it? You should know from this that the insight of the Buddha is inherent in the minds of all living beings." And Chang-an declared: "If the insight of the Buddha is non-existent in living beings, how can anyone cause them to open the gate to or be aware of it? For instance, how can a poor woman without a treasure house show off treasure?"

It is still difficult to answer your question [in parts 1-3] regarding Lord Śākyamuni Buddha. This is what the Buddha warned us in the *Lotus Sutra* to be "most difficult of all that was preached, is being preached, and will be preached"* [in Chapter 10, The Teacher of the Dharma]. The "six difficult and nine easier actions"* referred to in the following 11th chapter, Beholding the Stupa of Treasures, also emphasize this.

Expounding this, Grand Master T'ien-t'ai* declared: "Because it is diametrically opposed to what was preached earlier in the pre-Lotus sutras, the Teaching of the *Lotus Sutra,* both the theoretical and essential sections, is difficult to comprehend and put faith in. It is as difficult as facing a spear." Grand Master Chang-an* stated: "The Buddha considers the preaching of the *Lotus Sutra* to be the very purpose for appearing in this world. How can the sutra be easily understood by us, ordinary men?" And Grand Master Dengyō* said: "This *Lotus Sutra* is most difficult to comprehend and believe in. It is because the Buddha's true intent is revealed in it."

Regarding your question [in part 7] of whether or not T'ien-t'ai had a biased view, I should say that during the period spanning the time the Buddha was still alive and some 1,800 years after His death, there appeared only three people throughout the three lands of India, China, and Japan who perceived the ultimate truth, that is, the *Lotus Sutra*. They are Śākyamuni Buddha of India, Grand Master T'ien-t'ai of China and Grand Master Dengyō of Japan, who are the three sages of Buddhism.

Question (19): What about such priest-scholars of India as Nāgārjuna and Vasubandhu?

Answer: These sages were also aware of the essence of the *Lotus Sutra*, but did not reveal it. Sometimes they would touch upon the theoretical section [first half] of the *Lotus Sutra*, but did not reveal the essential section [last half] of the *Lotus Sutra* or their spiritual contemplation at all. Perhaps it was because the time was not ripe although there were listeners with sufficient amount of comprehension, or perhaps both their time and listeners' capacity to understand were not ready.

Among those who followed T'ien-t'ai and Dengyō, there appeared many who knew the essence of the *Lotus Sutra* such as the truth of "3,000 existences contained in one thought." This was because they could take advantage of the wisdom of the two sages. Specifically, Chia-hsiang* of the San-lun school, more than 100 distant disciples of three Southern and seven Northern masters,* Fa-tsang* and Ch'eng-kuan* of the Flower Garland (Kegon) school, Tripiṭaka Master Hsüan-chuang* and Grand Master Tz'ŭ-ên* of the Fa-hsiang (Hossō) school, Tripiṭaka Masters Śubhākarasiṃha,* Vajrabodhi,* and Pu-k'ung* of the True Word (Shingon) school, Tao-hsüan* of the Lü (Ritsu) school, and others were at first opposed to the two sages but later surrendered to them completely.

Finally, let us try to answer your first question [in part 1 of Question (18)] whether the vast virtue of Lord Śākyamuni Buddha exists in our minds. The *Sutra of Infinite Meaning, Muryōgi-kyō,** which is regarded as an introductory teaching to the *Lotus Sutra*, explains how we attain Buddhahood:

> Suppose there was a prince just born to a king and his queen. Growing up day by day, month by month, year by year, the new prince has reached the age of seven. Though unable to attend the affairs of state, he is respected by his father's subjects and befriended by children of great kings. He is loved by his royal parents, who find it most enjoyable to chat with him constantly. Why is this? It is because the prince is still young. My good people, he who upholds this *Lotus Sutra* is just like this prince. His father is the Buddha, and his mother is this sutra. Just as the prince was born to the king and his queen, the Buddha and this sutra are united in one to give birth to the bodhisattva, upholder of this sutra. Suppose, having listened to the *Lotus Sutra*, he reads a phrase or a verse of it, or reads it once, twice, 10, 100, 1,000, 10,000 times, or 1,000,000,000,000 times the number of grains of sand of the Ganges River, unlimited and infinite number of times. Even if

he had not yet obtained the ultimate truth, he would be respected by all the four groups of Buddhists [monks, nuns, laymen, and laywomen] and the eight kinds of gods and demi-gods, protectors of Buddhism. Accompanied by great bodhisattvas, he would always be protected and cared for by Buddhas and completely surrounded by their benevolence. It is because he is a beginner on the way to Buddhahood.

Then, we come across the following passage in the *Sutra of Meditation on Universal-Sage Bodhisattva, Kan Fugen Bosatsu Gyōbō-kyō*,* considered to be the conclusion of the *Lotus Sutra*: "This Mahayana *Sutra of the Lotus Flower of the Wonderful Dharma* is the treasure house of all the Buddhas and the eyes of all the Buddhas in all the worlds in the universe in the past, present, and future. It is the seed of Buddhahood giving birth to all the Buddhas in the past, present and future. You must put the Mahayana teaching into practice lest the seed of Buddhahood be extinguished." And also: "This Mahayana sutra is the eyes of all the Buddhas. It is by means of this *Lotus Sutra* that all the Buddhas reach the stage of having Five Eyes.[12] The Buddha with three bodies [Dharma Body, Reward Body, and Accommodative Body] was born from this sutra. This sutra is the great seal of enlightenment impressed upon the sea of Nirvana, from which the Buddha with three pure bodies was born. The triple-bodied Buddha, therefore, is the source of happiness for men and gods alike."

Now, such a way of attaining Buddhahood has not been shown anywhere except in the *Lotus Sutra*. Looking closely at both exoteric and esoteric, or Mahayana and Hinayana sutras preached by Śākyamuni Buddha during His lifetime and the basic canons of various schools of Buddhism such as the Flower Garland (Kegon) and True Word (Shingon) schools, we find that Vairocana Buddha preached the *Flower Garland Sutra* on the lotus-platform in the center of the universe. We also see various Buddhas gather together from all the worlds in the universe to hear Śākyamuni Buddha preaching the *Sutra of the Great Assembly, Daijik-kyō*. 1,000 Buddhas came to hear the preaching of the *Wisdom Sutra, Hannya-kyō*, which expounds the teaching that both the defiled and pure are void and fused together. And some 1,200 Buddhas gathered for the preaching of the *Great Sun Buddha Sutra, Dainichi-kyō*, and *Diamond Peak Sutra, Kongōchō-kyō*.

These Buddhas, however, are those who attained Buddhahood for the first time in this life after a relatively short period of bodhisattvahood and have been Buddhas only a short while. They do not demonstrate the Buddha's attainment of Buddhahood in the eternal past after practicing the way of bodhisattvas for an immeasurably long period of time. Although they preach Śākyamuni's sudden attainment of Buddhahood, they have completely lost sight of the immeasurably long period of time in which He preached. In fact Śākyamuni began to preach, planting the seed of Buddhahood in the eternal past, 3,000 dust-particle *kalpa* ago, according to the theoretical section of the *Lotus Sutra,* and 500 dust-particle *kalpa* ago, according to the essential section of the *Lotus Sutra.* Śākyamuni Buddha continued to guide His disciples until they were all sure to attain Buddhahood during the preaching of the *Lotus Sutra* in His present life, completing the series of His preaching which began in the eternal past. The beginning and end of His preaching, which are clearly marked in the *Lotus Sutra,* however, are completely ignored by other sutras such as those just mentioned above.

Thus on the surface, such sutras as the *Flower Garland* and the *Great Sun Buddha* appear to be "distinct" and "perfect" teachings or to preach the ways of the Four Vehicles [Buddhas, bodhisattvas, *śrāvaka* and *pratyekabuddha*]. Thinking it over, however, we see that their teachings are still in the initial stages of *"piṭaka"* [Hinayana] and are "common" teachings, below those of "distinct" and "perfect" teachings.[13] They fail to preach the three causes of Buddhahood inherent in all living beings: Buddha-nature, the wisdom to see it, and right actions to develop the wisdom. How can they decide what the seed of Buddhahood is?

Upon coming to China after the time of Hsüan-chuang in the early T'ang dynasty, new translators of Buddhist scriptures encountered the T'ien-t'ai doctrine of "3,000 existences contained in one thought," and either wrote it into the sutras they had brought, or claimed that they had brought the doctrine from India. This gave rise to ignorant and evil hearts. T'ien-t'ai scholars were glad to find the same doctrine as their own in the newly transmitted scriptures, revered what had come from afar, looking down at what was near, or discarded the old preferring the new.

Nonetheless, without the seed of Buddhahood established on the basis of the "3,000 existences contained in one thought" doctrine, both attainment of Buddhahood by all sentient beings and the worship of wooden statues and portraits are empty names without reality.

Question (20): You have not responded to the serious question raised earlier regarding the realm of Buddhas in our minds, have you?

Answer: It is said in the *Sutra of Infinite Meaning, Muryōgi-kyō,* an introductory teaching to the *Lotus Sutra:* "Though unable to perform the six kinds of practice leading to Buddhahood, charity, observing precepts, perseverance, effort, meditation and wisdom, upholders of this sutra will inevitably receive merits from practicing them." The second chapter of the *Lotus Sutra* states: "We wish to hear the teaching equipped with the merit of Śākyamuni before and after His attaining Buddhahood;" and in the *Nirvana Sutra* it is said: *"Sad* in the *Sad-dharmapuṇḍarīka-sūtra, Lotus Sutra,* means 'to be equipped with.' "

Bodhisattva Nāgārjuna* says in his *Great Wisdom Discourse, Daichido-ron*, that *sad* means "six" while the *Annotations on the Four Mahayana Treatises, Wu-i Wu-tê Ta-chêng Ssŭ-lun Hsüan-i Chi*, by Hui-chün of T'ang China declares that *sad* should be translated as "six," which means "perfection" in India. The *Annotations on the Meaning of the Lotus Sutra, Fa-hua I-su, by Chi-tsang** states that *sad* is translated as "being equipped with." While Grand Master T'ien-t'ai states in his *Profound Meaning of the Lotus Sutra, Fa-hua Hsüan-i*, that *sad* is a Sanskrit term which is translated as *miao*, meaning "wonderful" in Chinese.

These should clarify that the *Lotus Sutra* is the way equipped with the merit of the Buddha accumulated before and after attaining Buddhahood. I fear that I may debase these passages if I try to interpret them, but I dare do so in order to answer your question. The gist of these passages is that Śākyamuni Buddha's merit of practicing the bodhisattva way leading to Buddhahood, as well as that of preaching and saving all living beings since His attainment of Buddhahood are altogether contained in the five characters of *Myō, Hō, Ren, Ge,* and *Kyō, Lotus Sutra of the Wonderful Dharma*, and that consequently, when we uphold the five characters, the merits which He accumulated before and after His attainment of Buddhahood are naturally transferred to us.

Thus, it is stated in Chapter Four of the *Lotus Sutra*, Understanding by Faith, that four great *śrāvaka* such as Kāśyapa rejoiced in their understanding of the teaching of the *Lotus Sutra* enabling *śrāvaka* to attain Buddhahood, and reported to the Buddha that they had been given invaluable jewels without asking for them. This represents the attainment of Buddhahood by the *śrāvaka* realm contained in our minds.

Not only the *śrāvaka* but also Śākyamuni Buddha is within us. For we encounter such a statement as this in the second chapter of the *Lotus Sutra:* "It was My [Śākyamuni's] original vow to let all beings become like Myself. My vow has now been fulfilled. I have helped them all enter the way of the Buddha." Does this not mean that Śākyamuni Buddha, who has attained Perfect Enlightenment, is our flesh and blood, and all the merits He has accumulated before and after attaining Buddhahood are our bones?

Moreover, the 11th chapter of the *Lotus Sutra,* Beholding the Stupa of Treasures,* states: "Those who uphold the teaching of this sutra are deemed to serve Me, Śākyamuni, and the Buddha of Many Treasures. They also serve Buddhas in manifestation here who adorn and glorify their respective worlds." This means that Śākyamuni Buddha, the Buddha of Many Treasures, and all the Buddhas in manifestation are in our minds, and that we, upholders of the *Lotus Sutra*, will follow their steps and inherit all the merits of those Buddhas.

This is the meaning of the passage in the 10th chapter of the *Lotus Sutra,* The Teacher of the Dharma, which reads: "Those who hear of this *Lotus Sutra* even for a moment, will instantly attain Perfect Enlightenment." A passage in the 16th chapter of the *Lotus Sutra,* The Duration of the Life of the Tathāgata, contends: "It has been many hundreds of thousands of billions of *nayuta*[14] of *kalpa* [an incalculably long period of time] since I have attained Buddhahood." It means that Śākyamuni Buddha, within our minds, is an ancient Buddha without beginning, manifesting Himself in three bodies, and attained Buddhahood in the eternal past described as 500 dust-particle *kalpa* ago.*

In the same chapter, another passage reads: "My life span, which I obtained through the practice of the way of bodhisattvas, has not yet expired. It is twice as long as the length of time stated above: 500 dust-particle *kalpa*." This reveals the bodhisattva-realm within our minds. The bodhisattvas described in the 15th chapter, Appearance of Bodhisattvas from Underground, who have sprung out of the great earth, as numerous as the number of dust-particles of 1,000 worlds,* are followers of the Original Buddha Śākyamuni who resides within our minds.

They are like T'ai-kung-wang and the Duke of Chou, retainers of King Wu of the Chou dynasty in ancient China, who at the same time served the King's young son, King Ch'eng. Or like Takeuchi no Sukune of ancient Japan, a leading minister to Empress Jingu, who concurrently served her son, Prince Nintoku. Just like them, Bodhisattvas Superior-Practice (Jōgyō), Limitless-Practice (Muhengyō), Pure-Practice (Jōgyō), and Steadily-Established-Practice (Anryūgyō), the four leaders of these bodhisattvas sprung from the earth, are simultaneously followers of the Original Buddha and bodhisattvas who reside in the minds of us, ordinary people.

Therefore, Grand Master Miao-lê* has declared in his *Annotations on the Great Concentration and Insight, Mo-ho Chih-kuan Fu-hsing-chüan Hung-chüeh:* "You should know that both our bodies and the land on which we live are a part of the 3,000 modes of existence which exist in our minds. Consequently, upon our attainment of Buddhahood, we are in complete agreement with the truth of '3,000 existences contained in one thought,' and our single body and single thought permeate through all the worlds in the universe."

SECTION II
THE MOST VENERABLE ONE (HONZON)

CHAPTER V
The Honzon of the Essential Section Representing the Eternally Imperishable Pure Land

During the 50 years or so since He attained perfect Enlightenment under the bodhi tree, and preached the *Flower Garland Sutra*, showing Himself in the Lotus Repository World, until His death in the *śāla* grove, Śākyamuni Buddha preached many sutras. In them, He revealed various pure lands such as the Lotus Repository World of the *Flower Garland Sutra, Kegon-kyo*, the Pure Land of Mystic Glorification in the *Mystic Glorification Sutra, Mitsugon-kyō*, the three pure lands revealed in the Beholding the Stupa of Treasures chapter of the *Lotus Sutra*, and the four lands in the *Sutra for Resolving Doubts Concerning the Age of the Semblance Dharma, Zōbō Ketsugi-kyō*.

These were all provisional lands shown in this world of impermanence, which goes through a cycle of four periods: the *kalpas* of construction, continuance, destruction, and emptiness.[15] They represent paradises such as that of the temporary land, the land of non-hindrance, and the land of tranquil light, [three of the "four lands" mentioned in the previous chapter,] or the Land of Bliss of the Buddha of Infinite Life, Land of the Emerald of Medicine Master Buddha in the east, or the Pure Land of Mystic Glorification of the Great Sun Buddha. The lords of these lands are transformations of Śākyamuni Buddha. Therefore, when Śākyamuni Buddha, the origin of these transformed Buddhas dies, they will all die. Likewise, their lands will all disappear.

Now, however, when the Eternal Buddha was revealed in the essential section of the *Lotus Sutra*, this world of endurance [Sahā World*] became the Eternal Pure Land, indestructible even by the three calamities of conflagration, flooding, and strong winds, which are said to destroy the world. It transcends the four periods of cosmic change: the *kalpas* of construction, continuance, destruction, and emptiness. Śākyamuni Buddha, the Lord-preacher of this Pure Land, has never died in the past, nor will He be born in the future. He exists forever throughout the past, present, and future. All those who receive His guidance are one with this Eternal Buddha. It is because each of our minds is equipped with the "3,000 modes of existence" and the "three factors," namely, all living beings, the land in which they live, and the five elements of living beings [matter, perception, conception, volition and consciousness].

This truth was not made clear in the first 14 chapters of the theoretical section of the *Lotus Sutra*. Perhaps, it was because the time was not ripe at this stage of preaching the *Lotus Sutra*, and the capacity of comprehension on the part of the listeners was not yet sufficient.

The heart of the essential section of the *Lotus Sutra, Namu Myō Hō Ren Ge Kyō*, [an absolute faith in the five-character title of the *Sutra of the Lotus Flower of the Wonderful Dharma*], was not transmitted even to the most trusted disciples such as Bodhisattvas Mañjuśrī or Medicine-King, and certainly not the lower-ranking bodhisattvas. Instead the Buddha called out numerous bodhisattvas from underground, for whom He expounded it during the preaching of eight chapters following the 15th chapter in the essential section of the *Lotus Sutra*, and entrusted them with the task of spreading it in the Latter Age of Degeneration.

The most venerable depiction of this transmission of *Namu Myō Hō Ren Ge Kyō* from the Eternal Buddha to His original disciples is:

Suspended in the sky above the Eternal Buddha Śākyamuni's Sahā World is a stupa of treasures, in which Śākyamuni Buddha and the Buddha of Many Treasures sit to the left and right of *Myō, Hō, Ren, Ge*, and *Kyō*. They are waited on by four bodhisattvas including Superior-Practice (Jōgyō) representing the original disciples of the Eternal Buddha called up from underground. Four more bodhisattvas including Mañjuśrī and Maitreya, take lower seats as followers, other great and minor bodhisattvas, those converted by the Buddha in the theoretical section and those who came from other lands, resemble numerous people sitting on the ground and looking up at court nobles. Also lined up on the ground are Buddhas in manifestation [*funjin* Buddhas] who gathered together from all the worlds in the universe in praise of the Buddha's preaching, representing provisional Buddhas in their respective lands.

No most venerable depiction such as this was revealed anywhere else by Śākyamuni Buddha during more than 50 years of His preaching in this life. Though He spent eight years preaching the *Lotus Sutra*, the scene was limited to the preaching in the sky above Mt. Sacred Eagle recounted in eight chapters. During the two millenniums after the death of Śākyamuni Buddha, the Ages of the True Dharma and the Semblance Dharma, some worshipped Śākyamuni Buddha accompanied by Kāśyapa and Ānanda as described in the Hinayana sutras. Others worshipped Him accompanied by such bodhisattvas as Mañjuśrī and Samantabhadra as He appeared in quasi-Mahayana sutras, the *Nirvana Sutra*, or the theoretical section of the *Lotus Sutra*. Many wooden statues and portraits were made of Śākyamuni Buddha as He preached Hinayana or quasi-Mahayana sutras, but statues and portraits of the Eternal Śākyamuni Buddha revealed in The Duration of the Life of the Tathāgata chapter of the *Lotus Sutra* were never made. Now in the beginning of the Latter Age of Degeneration, is it not the time that such statues and portraits are made for the first time?

SECTION III
PROPAGATING THE TRUE DHARMA

CHAPTER VI
The Lotus Sutra for the Latter Age

Question (21): You have said that for 2,000 years during the Ages of the True Dharma and the Semblance Dharma, scholar-monks and the so-called four ranks of bodhisattvas who guided the people after the death of Śākyamuni Buddha built temples and pagodas for various Buddhas such as the Buddha of Infinite Life, Great Sun Buddha, and Medicine Master Buddha. Some of them built temples and pagodas dedicated to Śākyamuni Buddha preaching the Hinayana, quasi-Mahayana, and pre-Lotus sutras* or the theoretical section* [first half] of the *Lotus Sutra*. None of them in the three lands of India, China, and Japan, neither a king nor his subjects, however, has ever revered the true *honzon* revealed in The Duration of the Life of the Tathāgata chapter of the *Lotus Sutra*, the Eternal Buddha with four bodhisattvas waiting on Him. It has startled me and I am just confused because it has never been said by anyone before. I ask you to explain it once more as I wish to hear it in detail.

Answer: The *Lotus Sutra* consists of eight fascicles and 28 chapters. Four steps of teaching [sutras of the first four tastes[16]] were preached before the *Lotus Sutra*, and the *Nirvana Sutra* after it. These lifetime preachings of the Buddha can be bound into one sutra. Those preached before the *Lotus Sutra*, from the *Flower Garland Sutra*, which was preached upon His attainment of Buddhahood at Buddhagayā, to the *Great Wisdom Sutra*, comprise the preface. The *Sutra of Infinite Meaning, Muryōgi-kyō,** the *Lotus Sutra*, and the *Sutra of Meditation on Universal-Sage Bodhisattva, Kan Fugen Bosatsu Gyōbō-kyō,** 10 fascicles in all, serve as the main discourse while the *Nirvana Sutra* constitutes the epilogue.

The 10 fascicles of the main discourse can further be divided into three parts. The *Sutra of Infinite Meaning* and the first Introduction chapter of the *Lotus Sutra* constitute the preface. The 15 and one-half chapters of the *Lotus Sutra* from the second chapter, Expedients,* to the 19-line verse in the 17th chapter, Variety of Merits,* mark the main discourse. The 11 and one-half chapters of the *Lotus Sutra* from the last half of the Variety of Merits chapter, where the four stages of faith during Śākyamuni's lifetime[17] are preached, to the 28th and final chapter of the sutra, plus the one fascicle of the *Sutra of Meditation on Universal-Sage Bodhisattva* make up the epilogue.

Furthermore, the 10 fascicles of the threefold *Lotus Sutra*, *Sutra of Infinite Meaning*, *Lotus Sutra*, and *Sutra of Meditation on Universal-Sage Bodhisattva*, can be divided into two sections, theoretical and essential, each of which contains a preface, main discourse, and epilogue. First, in the theoretical section, the *Sutra of Infinite Meaning* and the first Introduction chapter* of the *Lotus Sutra* compose the preface. The eight chapters of the *Lotus Sutra* from the second chapter, Expedients, to the ninth chapter, Assurance of Future Buddhahood* inclusive, represent the main discourse. And the five chapters from the 10th chapter, The Teacher of the Dharma,* to the 14th chapter, Peaceful Practices,* comprise the epilogue.

The Lord who preached this teaching is Śākyamuni Buddha, who had attained Buddhahood for the first time in this world* under the bodhi tree at Buddhagayā. He preached the truth of 1,000 aspects contained in 100 realms which had never been revealed before. It is the True Dharma which transcends all the sutras which had been preached [pre-Lotus sutras], are now being preached [*Sutra of Infinite Meaning*], and are to be preached [such as the *Nirvana Sutra*]. It is the innermost intention of the Buddha, which is difficult to have faith in and comprehend.

Inquiring into the past, we find a few who encountered this True Dharma. As stated in the seventh chapter, The Parable of a Magic City, when Great Universal Wisdom Buddha was a king, Śākyamuni Buddha, his 16th prince, sowed the seed of Buddhahood among the people. With the help of the pre-Lotus sutras, such as the *Flower Garland Sutra*, some were able to attain enlightenment afterwards by germinating the seed planted at the time of Great Universal Wisdom Buddha, cultivating it to maturity to bear fruit. This, however, was not the true intent of the Buddha. Just as a poison might show its effect on some people without their knowledge, only in certain people does the seed of Buddhahood have a chance to germinate and grow to maturity without the help of the *Lotus Sutra*. The aim of Śākyamuni Buddha to be born in this world was to gradually lead the two kinds of Hinayana sages called Two Vehicles* [*śrāvaka* and *pratyekabuddha*] and ordinary people* to the *Lotus Sutra*, by the way of the pre-Lotus sutras, whereby the seed may germinate and grow to bear the fruit of Buddhahood.

Also, of those men and gods who listened to Śākyamuni Buddha in His lifetime preach the eight chapters, the main discourse of the theoretical section of the *Lotus Sutra*, some received the seed of Buddhahood upon hearing a phrase or a verse and nurtured it until they attained Buddhahood. Others attained Buddhahood through the teachings of the *Lotus Sutra*, complemented by the Hinayana and provisional Mahayana sutras, upon arriving at the time when the *Sutra of Meditation on Universal-Sage Bodhisattva* and the *Nirvana Sutra* were preached. Or then after the death of Śākyamuni Buddha, during the Age of the True Dharma, that of the Semblance Dharma, or in the Latter Age of Degeneration. These men are like those of Śākyamuni's lifetime who were able to attain Buddhahood through the preaching of the pre-Lotus sutras.

Moreover, 14 chapters in the essential section can be regarded as one sutra with three parts: the preface, the main discourse, and the epilogue. The first half of the 15th chapter, Appearance of Bodhisattvas from Underground, is the prologue. The second half of the 15th chapter, the 16th chapter, The Duration of the Life of the Tathāgata,* and the first half of the following chapter, the Variety of Merits, a chapter and two-halves in all, make up the main discourse. The remainder constitutes the epilogue.

The Lord who preaches here is the Eternal Buddha, not Śākyamuni Buddha who attained Buddhahood for the first time in this world under the bodhi tree in Buddhagayā. Accordingly, what is preached here differs from what was preached previously as clearly as heaven and earth. That is to say, it is revealed here that all living beings in the 10 realms, as well as the world in which they live, manifest themselves to be eternal. It comes close to revealing the truth of the "3,000 existences contained in one thought," with only an extremely thin bamboo film separating them.

Compared to this Eternal Buddha and His teaching preached in the essential section, those teachings preached in the theoretical section, the pre-Lotus sutras, the *Sutra of Infinite Meaning*, and the *Nirvana Sutra*, namely, all the sutras preached prior to, at the same time as, and after the *Lotus Sutra*, are easy to believe and understand. It is because they are provisional teachings adjusted to meet the faith and comprehension of the unenlightened while what is preached in the essential section transcends them all and is difficult to believe and comprehend because it adheres to the true intent of Śākyamuni Buddha.

There is another triple division culminating in the essential section. Innumerable sutras beginning with the *Lotus Sutra* expounded during the time of the ancient Great Universal Wisdom Buddha, those preached by Śākyamuni Buddha during 50 some years of His lifetime, including the *Flower Garland Sutra*, 14 chapters of the theoretical section of the *Lotus Sutra*, and the *Nirvana Sutra*, as well as those preached by Buddhas in all the worlds in the universe in the past, at present, and in the future are the preface to the great Dharma of five characters hidden in the lines of the 16th chapter of the *Lotus Sutra*, The Duration of the Life of the Tathāgata.

Compared to the "one and two half-chapters"* of the *Lotus Sutra*, the 16th chapter, the second half of the preceding chapter and the first half of the following chapter, which comprise the main discourse according to this division, all other sutras may be called Hinayana teachings, false teachings, teachings that do not lead to Buddhahood, or teachings in which the truth is not revealed. Those who listen to these "expedient" teachings have little virtue and much illusion. They are immature in thinking, poor in heart, and solitary. Like birds and beasts, they do not know the existence of the Eternal Buddha, who is their father.

As stated above, even the perfect teachings of the pre-Lotus sutras and the theoretical section of the *Lotus Sutra* do not really lead to Buddhahood. How much less of a possibility do Hinayana-like sutras such as the *Great Sun Buddha Sutra* have! How much less chance of success do the seven schools such as Flower Garland (Kegon) and True Word (Shingon) established by commentators and masters have! Generally speaking, they are within the limit of *piṭaka*, common, and distinct teachings. Strictly speaking, they are the same as *piṭaka* and common teachings. Although they preach exquisite teachings, they do not discuss the sowing, nurturing, and cultivation of the seed of Buddhahood. As a result, the Buddhahood preached in them is equivalent to the annihilation of body and soul sought by Hinayana sages. This is what T'ien-t'ai meant when he pointed out the inconsistency of guidance in the pre-Lotus sutras. This is like a royal princess who is made pregnant by a beast. Her child is considered inferior even to the lowest caste. Let us put this aside for now.

The theoretical section of the *Lotus Sutra* consists of 14 chapters, of which eight chapters, two through nine, serve as the main discourse. At first glance, these eight chapters seem to be preached primarily for the two categories of Hinayana sages called *śrāvaka* and *pratyekabuddha* and only secondarily for bodhisattvas and ordinary people. On careful examination, they seem primarily reserved for ordinary people after the death of Śākyamuni Buddha, in the Age of the True Dharma, that of the Semblance Dharma, and the Latter Age of Degeneration.* These chapters are aimed especially at those people living in the beginning of the Latter Age of Degeneration.

Question (22): What is your proof for that?

Answer: It is stated in the 10th chapter of the *Lotus Sutra,* The Teacher of the Dharma:* "This sutra has aroused much hatred and jealousy even during the lifetime of the Buddha. How much more can this be expected after His death!" And in the 11th chapter, Beholding the Stupa of Treasures:* "The Buddha of Many Treasures and Buddhas in manifestation [*funjin* Buddhas] from all the worlds in the universe gathered together to make this Dharma live forever.... Buddhas in manifestation should remember My [Buddha's] intention to keep on spreading the Dharma forever." You may find similar statements in the 13th chapter, Encouragement for Keeping This Sutra,* and 14th chapter, Peaceful

Practices.* They show that the theoretical section of the *Lotus Sutra* is directed to those in the beginning of the Latter Age.

Speaking of the essential section of the *Lotus Sutra*, it is preached solely for those living in the beginning of the Latter Age. At first glance it appears that the seed of Buddhahood was planted in them by the Eternal Buddha in the eternal past or 500 dust-particle *kalpa* ago. The seed germinated and grew within them with the help of all the sutras from the *Lotus Sutra* preached by the 16th prince of Great Universal Wisdom Buddha 3,000 dust-particle *kalpa* in the past, to all those preached by Śākyamuni Buddha in this life before the *Lotus Sutra*, and the theoretical section of the *Lotus Sutra*. Finally the essential section of the *Lotus Sutra* enabled them to attain Buddhahood.

On closer examination, however, the essential section differs from the theoretical section. That is to say the essential section, all through the preface, the main discourse, and the epilogue, was preached for those people in the beginning of the Latter Age of Degeneration. The teaching of the essential section during the lifetime of Śākyamuni Buddha and that which would spread in the beginning of the Latter Age are likewise absolutely perfect. However, the former is for attaining enlightenment, whereas the latter is for sowing the seed of Buddhahood. While the former is crystallized in the 16th chapter, The Duration of the Life of the Tathāgata, with half a chapter each preceding and following it, the latter is solely embodied in the five characters of *Myō, Hō, Ren, Ge,* and *Kyō*, the title of the *Lotus Sutra*.

Question (23): Do you have a scriptural proof for that?

Answer: The 15th chapter, Appearance of Bodhisattvas from Underground,* states:

> Thereupon numerous bodhisattvas eight times the number of grains of sand in the Ganges River, who had come from other worlds, rose among the masses, pressed hands together in *gasshō*, bowed to the Buddha and said: "World Honored One! If you permit us to exert ourselves to uphold, read, recite, copy this sutra, and make offerings to it in this world of endurance [Sahā World] after Your death, we will expound it widely." Thereupon the Buddha said to the numerous bodhisattvas: "No, good men! I do not want you to uphold this sutra...."

This differs fundamentally, like water and fire, from what was stated in the 10th chapter, The Teacher of the Dharma,* and the following four chapters, which comprise the epilogue of the theoretical section. Towards the end of the 11th chapter, Beholding the Stupa of Treasures,* it states: "With a loud voice the Buddha addressed monks, nuns, laymen, and laywomen, asking who will preach the *Lotus Sutra* widely in this world." Even if this exhortation had been made by the Buddha alone, such great bodhisattvas as Medicine-King, the King of the Brahma Heaven, Indra, Sun God, Moon God, and Four Heavenly Kings would have taken it seriously. The Buddha of Many Treasures and various Buddhas from all the worlds in the universe joined in His exhortation. Having heard their courteous appeal, those bodhisattvas vowed, "We will not spare our lives in doing so." It was solely to comply with the will of the Buddha. Soon afterwards, however, the Buddha changed His intention and stopped those numerous bodhisattvas, eight times the number of grains of sand in the Ganges River, from propagating this sutra in this world. They were in a quandary. This is beyond the comprehension of an ordinary man.

Grand Master T'ien-t'ai explained it with six interpretations, three explaining why the Buddha dissuaded those numerous bodhisattvas from spreading this sutra in this world after His death, and three to explain why He waited for bodhisattvas to appear from underground. After all, Śākyamuni Buddha could not reveal His innermost enlightenment, or the great Dharma hidden in the lines of the Duration of the Life of the Tathāgata chapter, to those great bodhisattvas from other worlds who had been guided by the teaching of the theoretical section.

At the beginning of the Latter Age, there are lands where the True Dharma is slandered and those who live there have poor capacity for comprehension and faith in Buddhism. Therefore, instead of relying on bodhisattvas from other worlds, the Buddha called out great bodhisattvas from underground to entrust them with the task of transmitting the five characters of *Myō, Hō, Ren, Ge,* and *Kyō,* the essence of the Duration of the Life of the Tathāgata chapter, to the people in this world. It was also because those guided by the teaching of the theoretical section were not the original disciples of Śākyamuni Buddha.

As for entrusting the task to bodhisattvas from underground, Grand Master T'ien-t'ai states in his *Words and Phrases of the Lotus Sutra:* "These have been My [Śākyamuni's] disciples since time in the eternal past, and it is they who should propagate My Dharma." Grand Master Miao-lê says of this in his *Annotations on the Words and Phrases of the Lotus Sutra, Fa-hua Wên-chü-chi:* "It will be the joy of the world for a child to propagate his father's Dharma." And Tao-hsien's *Supplement to the Annotations on the Words and Phrases of the Lotus Sutra, Fu-chêng-chi,* says: "Because it was the Dharma preached by the Eternal Buddha in the eternal past, the task of spreading it was entrusted to those who received His guidance in the eternal past."

Moreover, it is said in the 15th chapter, Appearance of Bodhisattvas from Underground, that Bodhisattva Maitreya* begged the Buddha to clear his doubts about His original disciples from the eternal past saying:

> We have never doubted the truthfulness of Your auspicious sermons or the words uttered by You, and we believe that You know all things thoroughly. We are afraid, however, that those who have just begun to walk the bodhisattva way, if they hear these words of Yours after Your death, might not accept them in faith, causing the sin of destroying the Dharma. We beseech You, World Honored One, to explain this to remove our doubts. Good men in the future, too, will have no doubts when they hear it.

This passage shows that the preaching of the chapter, The Duration of the Life of the Tathāgata,* was requested for the sake of the people after the death of Śākyamuni Buddha.

The Duration of the Life of the Tathāgata chapter says: "Having taken poison, some had lost their senses while others had not.... Seeing this excellent medicine with good color and good scent, those who had not lost their senses took it and recovered from their illness." This refers to the capacity of all those who received the seed of Buddhahood in the eternal past as preached in the Duration of the Life of the Tathāgata chapter, those who had the opportunity to establish a connection with the Buddha Dharma at the time of Great Universal Wisdom Buddha as revealed in the seventh chapter, The Parable of a Magic City, and all those bodhisattvas, Two Vehicles, *śrāvaka* and *pratyekabuddha*, men and gods who received the teaching of the Buddha in the pre-Lotus sutras as well as the theoretical section of the *Lotus Sutra*, to attain Buddhahood in the preaching of the essential section. It is said in the same chapter:

> The remainder who had lost their senses were happy to see their father come back and requested him to cure their illness, but they refused to take the medicine their father offered them. Why did they not take it? It was because they had been affected by the poison, causing them to lose their senses and think that this excellent medicine, in both color and scent, was not good at all....
>
> "Now I have to devise an expedient means so that they may take this medicine," thought the father. "Now I will leave this excellent medicine here with you. You should take it without worrying about its effectiveness," instructed the father to his children and he again went abroad. Then he sent a messenger back to his children, telling them that their father had passed away.

The 17th chapter, Variety of Merits,* in the essential section of the *Lotus Sutra* states, "In the evil age of the latter Dharma...," indicating that the teaching was for the Latter Age of Degeneration.

CHAPTER VII
Propagators of the Lotus Sutra in the Latter Age

Question (24): What does "send a messenger back" mean in this sutra?

Answer: The messenger refers to the Four Reliances,* four ranks of bodhisattva-teachers whom people turned to for guidance after the death of Śākyamuni Buddha. There are four kinds of messengers. First, there are the bodhisattva-teachers of Hinayana Buddhism. They would mostly appear in the first 500 years of the Age of the True Dharma. On the other hand, the second kind, the bodhisattva-teachers of Mahayana, for the most part would appear in the latter 500 years of the Age of the True Dharma. The third kind, bodhisattva-teachers of the theoretical section, would appear mostly in the 1,000-year Age of the Semblance Dharma and partly in the beginning of the Latter Age of Degeneration. The fourth kind, bodhisattva-teachers of the essential section, namely those numerous bodhisattvas who had appeared from underground, would surely appear in the beginning of the Latter Age.

The phrase, "send a messenger back," in The Duration of the Life of the Tathāgata chapter, which I have just cited, refers to those bodhisattvas who were called out from underground. "This excellent medicine" refers to *Namu Myōhō Renge-kyō*, which is the essence of the chapter, The Duration of the Life of the Tathāgata, and which contains the five major principles: the name, entity, quality, function, and teaching of the *Lotus Sutra*.[18] The Buddha did not grant this excellent medicine to those bodhisattvas who had been guided by the teaching of the theoretical section, much less to bodhisattvas from other worlds.

The 21st chapter of the *Lotus Sutra,* The Supernatural Powers of the Tathāgata,* says: "Thereupon those bodhisattvas who had sprung up from underground, as numerous as the dust-particles of 1,000 worlds, all wholeheartedly pressed their hands together in reverence of the Buddha, looked up to the noble countenance of the Buddha and said to Him, 'World Honored One! We will propagate this sutra after Your death in the lands of Buddhas in manifestation [*funjin* Buddhas] and in this world from which You will pass away.' "

T'ien-t'ai offers an interpretation of this in his *Words and Phrases of the Lotus Sutra:* "No bodhisattvas other than those who had sprung up from underground made this vow to the Buddha." Tao-hsien* declared in his *Supplement to the Annotations on the Words and Phrases of the Lotus Sutra:* "The propagation of this sutra was entrusted only to those bodhisattvas who had sprung up from underground. Why was that? Because it was the Dharma preached by the Eternal Buddha in the eternal past, the task of preaching it was entrusted to those who received His guidance in the eternal past."

Still, Bodhisattva Mañjuśrī (Monjushiri) is a disciple of Immovable (Fudō) Buddha of the Golden World in the east. Avalokiteśvara (Kannon)* is that of the Buddha of Infinite Life in the west. Bodhisattva Medicine-King (Yakuō),* of Sun Moon Pure Bright Virtue (Nichigatsu Jōmyō-toku) Buddha. And Bodhisattva Samantabhadra (Fugen), of Treasure Power Virtue (Hōitoku) Buddha. These bodhisattvas have come to this world solely to assist Śākyamuni Buddha in carrying out the work of His ministry. They merely represent bodhisattvas who appeared in sutras preached before the *Lotus Sutra* or in its theoretical section, and who did not possess the great Dharma of the essential section. How can they qualify to propagate it in the Latter Age of Degeneration?

The Supernatural Powers of the Tathāgata chapter continues: "Thereupon the World Honored One... revealed His great divine powers before all the masses, stretching out His broad and long tongue until it reached upward to the Brahma Heaven.... Likewise all the Buddhas who were seated on the lion-shaped thrones under the jewel trees in all the worlds in the universe also stretched out their broad and long tongues."

To begin with, nowhere else in all the Buddhist scriptures, whether exoteric or esoteric, Mahayana or Hinayana, has it been recorded that Śākyamuni Buddha and many other Buddhas were sitting together and stretching out tongues that touched the Brahma Heaven. The broad, long tongues, which covered all the worlds mentioned in the *Pure Land Sutra*,* exist only in name without substance. The *Wisdom Sutra, Hannya-kyō*,* says that Śākyamuni Buddha's long and broad tongue covered the entire universe, emitted rays of light and preached the *Wisdom Sutra*. This, however, does not at all verify its truth. These pre-Lotus sutras are mixed or tinged with provisional teachings, not revealing eternity in the life and teaching of Śākyamuni Buddha. Having thus manifested the 10 divine powers, Śākyamuni Buddha transmitted the five characters of *Myō, Hō, Ren, Ge*, and *Kyō* to the original disciples of the Buddha from the eternal past, who had sprung up from underground. So it is stated in the Supernatural Powers of the Tathāgata chapter:

> Thereupon Śākyamuni Buddha proclaimed to the host of those bodhisattvas including Superior-Practice, who had sprung from underground: "The supernatural powers of the Tathāgatas are as immeasurable, boundless and unfathomable as shown above. Nevertheless, I shall not be able to reveal all the merits of this sutra even if I continue telling them, for the sake of

its transmission, with my divine powers for infinite myriads of *kalpa*. To sum up, all the Dharma of the Tathāgata, all the unrestricted supernatural powers of the Tathāgata, all the most secretly treasured teachings of the Tathāgata, and all the profundity of the Tathāgata are clearly revealed and explained in this *Lotus Sutra*."

T'ien-t'ai* comments on this in his *Words and Phrases of the Lotus Sutra*: "Following 'Thereupon Śākyamuni Buddha said to the host of bodhisattvas' is the third section of the chapter on Supernatural Powers, summarizing the essence of the *Lotus Sutra* and transmitting it to the bodhisattvas from underground." Dengyō* interpreted this in his *Outstanding Principle of the Lotus Sutra, Hokke Shūku*:

> Again, the Supernatural Powers of the Tathāgata chapter says: "To sum up, all the Dharmas of the Tathāgata... are clearly revealed in this *Lotus Sutra*." This makes it clear that the Dharmas embodying Perfect Enlightenment of the Buddha in the eternal past, all the unrestricted divine powers which the Buddha attained in the eternal past, all the teachings in which the Buddha's Perfect Enlightenment in the eternal past is most secretly treasured, and all the profundity which the Buddha attained in the eternal past, are all clearly revealed and explained in this sutra.

The manifestation of the 10 divine powers in the 21st chapter is for the sake of transmitting the five characters of *Myō, Hō, Ren, Ge,* and *Kyō* to the four bodhisattvas Superior-Practice,* Limitless-Practice, Pure-Practice, and Steadily-Established-Practice, representing the host of bodhisattvas who had sprung from underground. The first five powers are said to be for those during Śākyamuni's lifetime, and the last five for those after His death. Upon re-examination, however, we see them as all applicable for those after the death of Śākyamuni Buddha. Therefore, a passage of the same chapter following the one cited above reads: "Because bodhisattvas from underground vowed to uphold this sutra after the death of Śākyamuni Buddha, Buddhas with joy displayed immeasurable divine powers."

Furthermore, the following chapter, Transmission,* declares: "Thereupon Śākyamuni Buddha rose from His throne demonstrating His great divine powers. Placing His right hand on the heads of an immeasurably large number of bodhisattvas..., He said, 'Now I will transmit this Dharma to you.'" Thus Śākyamuni Buddha transmitted this sutra first to bodhisattvas from underground, then to bodhisattvas who had been guided by the teaching of the theoretical section, bodhisattvas who had come from other worlds, and finally to the King of the Brahma Heaven, Indra and the Four Heavenly Kings. Transmission completed, Śākyamuni instructed "all Buddhas in manifestation [*funjin* Buddhas], who had come from all the worlds in the universe, to go back to their respective worlds, and for the door to the Buddha of Many Treasures' stupa to be closed."

The remainder of the *Lotus Sutra,* starting with the 23rd chapter, Previous Life of Medicine-King Bodhisattva, and such sutras as the *Nirvana Sutra* represent a retransmission of this sutra, after bodhisattvas from underground had left, by the Buddha to bodhisattvas of the theoretical section and those from other worlds to be spread in the future. This is like gleaning.

CHAPTER VIII
Salvation for Those in the Latter Age

Question (25): Have those numerous bodhisattvas from underground ever appeared to propagate this sutra in this world during the 2,000-year span of the True Dharma and the Semblance Dharma?

Answer: No, they have not.

Question in surprise (26): The *Lotus Sutra,* especially its essential section, purports to be for those after the death of Śākyamuni Buddha. It was for this purpose that it was transmitted first to those bodhisattvas from underground. Why have they not appeared in this world to spread this *Lotus Sutra* in the Age of the True Dharma and of the Semblance Dharma?

Answer: I am afraid I cannot answer your question.

Repeating the Question (27): Why not?

Answer: I prefer not to speak of this.

Repeating the question once more (28): Why?

Answer: If I should speak of this, all the people in the world would be like those in the Latter Age of Degeneration after the death of Powerful Voice King (Ionnō) Buddha in the past. As described in the 20th chapter of the *Lotus Sutra,* Never-Despising Bodhisattva, they abused and disturbed Never-Despising (Jōfukyō) Bodhisattva, and ended up in hell for slandering the True Dharma. If I even mention a little of this among my own disciples, they would all slander it. I am afraid I have no choice but to keep my mouth shut.

Demanding an answer (29): If you conceal the answer despite your knowledge of it, you would violate the precept against meanness and greed.

Answer: I have been driven to the wall. Let me try to explain briefly. It is said in the 10th chapter, The Teacher of the Dharma,* "How much more hatred and jealousy will there be after the death of the Buddha!" The 16th chapter, The Duration of the Life of the Tathāgata,* states, "I now leave this excellent medicine here." References such as the following are made: "the evil world in the Latter Age of Degeneration," [in the 17th chapter, the Variety of Merits,]* and "propagate it throughout this world in the fifth 500-year period after the death of the Buddha," [in the 23rd chapter, Previous Life of Medicine-King Bodhisattva."*] The *Nirvana Sutra** maintains: "Suppose there are seven children. It is not that their parents love them unequally but it is natural to pay more attention to the one who is sick."

When we think of the Buddha's intent reflected upon the clear mirror of these passages, we see that His appearance in this world was not for the sake of those who heard Him preach the *Lotus Sutra* for eight years on Mt. Sacred Eagle. It was for those in the Ages of the True Dharma and the Semblance Dharma, and in the Latter Age of Degeneration. More precisely, it was not for the sake of those in the 2,000 years of the True Dharma and the Semblance Dharma, but for those like myself in the beginning of the Latter Age. The "sick ones" refer to the slanderers of the *Lotus Sutra* after the death of Śākyamuni Buddha. It was "for those who did not perceive and accept this medicine excellent both in color and flavor" that the Buddha said he would "leave this excellent medicine."

If we think of it this way, we can see why the bodhisattvas from underground did not appear during the Ages of the True Dharma and the Semblance Dharma. The 1,000-year Age of the True Dharma was appropriate for Hinayana and provisional Mahayana Buddhism, but not suitable for the preaching of the *Lotus Sutra* in terms of both the "capacity" of those to be taught and the "time" for it to be preached. Therefore, four ranks of Bodhisattva-teachers [Four Reliances] preached the Hinayana and provisional Mahayana teachings in order for the people to attain Buddhahood by nurturing the seed of Buddhahood that they had received during the lifetime of Śākyamuni Buddha. They did not preach the *Lotus Sutra* then because they knew that if they had preached it, many people would have slandered it rendering it impossible to nurture the seed of Buddhahood. The capacity of the people for comprehension then was like that of those who listened to the Buddha preach in the first four of the five periods during His lifetime.

Toward the end of the Age of the Semblance Dharma, Bodhisattvas Avalokiteśvara (Kannon) and Medicine-King (Yakuō) appeared in this world as Nan-yüeh* and T'ien-t'ai respectively, and they thoroughly explained the doctrines of "1,000 aspects contained in 100 realms"* and "3,000 existences contained in one thought,"* stressing the theoretical section as the central theme and the essential section as its supporting idea. They, however, merely reasoned in the abstract that 3,000 modes of existence are contained in the minds of the unenlightened. They did not practice and have others practice the actual way of realizing it, reciting and upholding the five characters of *Myō, Hō, Ren, Ge,* and *Kyō,* and revering the Most Venerable One as revealed in the essential section of the *Lotus Sutra (hommon no honzon).* A few people with the capacity to comprehend the True Dharma did exist, but nevertheless, the time was not ripe for the perfect teaching.

Now we are at the beginning of the Latter Age of Degeneration, when Hinayana teachings strike down Mahayana teachings, provisional teachings destroy true teachings, east is taken for west and west for east, and heaven and earth are upside down. Under these circumstances the four ranks of bodhisattva-teachers who preach the theoretical section of the *Lotus Sutra* remain in hiding. Gods desert the land which they are supposed to protect. Now for the first time those bodhisattvas from underground appear in this world attempting to encourage ignorant people to take the five characters of *Myō, Hō, Ren, Ge,* and *Kyō,* the excellent medicine of the Latter Age. Many ignorant people will fall into hell by slandering the five characters, but they will be saved eventually. This is what is Miao-lê meant in his *Annotations on the Words and Phrases of the Lotus Sutra:* "Slanderers of the True Dharma will fall into hell but they will inevitably be saved by virtue of having heard the True Dharma."

My disciples, think deeply! The countless bodhisattvas who had sprung up from underground were disciples of Lord Śākyamuni Buddha from the time He had first resolved to seek Buddhahood. Nevertheless, they neither came to see Him when He attained Buddhahood under the bodhi tree, nor visited Him when He passed away under the twin *śāla* trees. Thus they may very well be accused of not being filial.

Moreover, they did not attend the preaching of the 14-chapter theoretical section, and they were absent when the last six chapters of the essential section were preached. They came and left while the first eight chapters of the essential section were being preached. But these great high-ranking bodhisattvas made a vow in the presence of Śākyamuni Buddha, the Buddha of Many Treasures and numerous Buddhas in manifestation that they would propagate the Five Characters transmitted to them at the beginning of the Latter Age of Degeneration. How can they not appear right now?

You should know this! When these four great bodhisattvas, leaders of those who sprung up from underground, spread this sutra through aggressive means of propagation,* they would appear as wise kings reproaching ignorant kings. Practicing a persuasive means of propagation,* they would be monks upholding and spreading the True Dharma.

Question (30): Has the Buddha predicted this?

Answer: It is said in the 23rd chapter, Previous Life of Medicine-King Bodhisattva, that the *Lotus Sutra* will "spread throughout this world in the first 500-year period in the Latter Age of Degeneration." Grand Master T'ien-t'ai restated it in his *Words and Phrases of the Lotus Sutra:* "The benefit of the Wonderful Dharma will reach afar during the first half-millennium of the Latter Age." The *Annotations on the Words and Phrases of the Lotus Sutra* by Miao-lê interprets this: "It is not that there are no unseen merits of the *Lotus Sutra* at the beginning of the Latter Age." And Grand Master Dengyō in his *Treatise on the Protection of the Nation, Shugo Kokkai-shō,* declares: "Ages of the True Dharma and Semblance Dharma are almost over, and the Latter Age of Degeneration is just around the corner." Dengyō's interpretation that "the Latter Age of Degeneration is just around the corner" means that his time was not really ripe for the propagation of the essential section of the *Lotus Sutra.*

Predicting the beginning of the Latter Age in Japan, Grand Master Dengyō states in his *Outstanding Principles of the Lotus Sutra, Hokke Shūku:*

> As for the time, we are nearing the end of the Age of Semblance Dharma or we have reached the beginning of the Latter Age. As for the land, we are located to the east of T'ang China, and west of Chieh. As for the people, we live in defilement and corruption. We live in time of war and strife. It is said in the 10th chapter of the *Lotus Sutra,* The Teacher of the Dharma: "Many will hate this sutra, the *Lotus Sutra,* with jealousy even during His lifetime, not to mention after His death." There are good reasons for these words.

The "time of war and strife" in this citation refers to two current problems facing Japan: domestic disturbance *(jikai hongyaku-nan)** and the Mongol invasion of western Japan.

This is the very time when original disciples of the Buddha should spring up from underground, attend both sides of the Eternal Buddha revealed in the essential section of the *Lotus Sutra,* and establish in this land of Japan the supreme *honzon* in the world. The *honzon* such as this has never been established either in India, or in China.

As the time was not ripe when Prince Shōtoku of ancient Japan built the Shitennōji Temple, the Buddha of Infinite Life, the Lord Buddha of the Western Paradise, was enshrined there as the *honzon.* When Emperor Shōmu constructed the Tōdaiji Temple, with Vairocana Buddha, the Lord Buddha of the *Flower Garland Sutra,* as the Most Venerable One, he failed to reveal the true teaching of the *Lotus Sutra.* It was only later that Grand Master Dengyō slightly revealed the true teaching of the *Lotus Sutra*. However, since the time was not ripe, he established Medicine Master Buddha of the Land of the Emerald in the east as the Most Venerable One, without revealing the Buddha of the essential section, the one waited on by four bodhisattvas. This is because the task of establishing the true *honzon* was reserved for the bodhisattvas from underground who had been entrusted to propagate the *Lotus Sutra* in the Latter Age. These bodhisattvas who received the Buddha's mandate are nearby waiting underground. They have not emerged in either the Age of the True Dharma or in that of the Semblance Dharma. Should these great bodhisattvas fail to appear in the Latter Age of Degeneration, they would be terrible liars, and the predictions of Śākyamuni Buddha, the Buddha of Many Treasures, and all the Buddhas in manifestation would be just bubbles in the air!

Taking all of this into consideration, we are having earthquakes and comets more severe and longer than any that happened during the Ages of the True Dharma and Semblance Dharma. These cannot be disturbances caused by such protectors of Buddhism as *garuḍa* birds, *asura* demons, and dragon-gods. They can only be omens of the appearance of the four great bodhisattvas.

T'ien-t'ai has this to say in his *Words and Phrases of the Lotus Sutra*: "Looking at heavy rainfall, one can tell the size of the dragon which causes it. Looking at the abundance of lotus flowers, one can tell the depth of the pond." Miao-lê explains in his *Annotations on the Words and Phrases of the Lotus Sutra*: "Only wise men can foretell what is going to happen. Only snakes know the way of snakes." When the sky is blue, the land is bright, so those who know the *Lotus Sutra* can see the reasons for occurrences in the world.

CONCLUSION
Salvation through the Odaimoku

For those who are incapable of understanding the truth of the "3,000 existences contained in one thought," Lord Śākyamuni Buddha, with His great compassion, wraps this jewel with the five characters of *Myō, Hō, Ren, Ge,* and *Kyō* and hangs it around the neck of the ignorant in the Latter Age of Degeneration. The four great bodhisattvas will protect such people, just as T'ai-kung-wang and the Duke of Chou assisted the young ruler, King Chen, of the Chou dynasty, or the Four Elders of the Shang-shan attended child Emperor Hui of the Han dynasty in ancient China.

> On the 25th day of the fourth month
> in the 10th year of Bun'ei (1273)
> By Nichiren

Notes

1. *Hakkyō* refers to *kegi no shikyō*, four methods of teaching and *kehō no shikyō*, four doctrinal teachings of the Buddha classified by the Tendai doctrine. The former consists of (1) abrupt teaching, (2) gradual teaching, (3) secret teachings, and (4) indeterminate, that is non-fixed teaching. The latter consists of (1) *piṭaka* (Hinayana) teaching, (2) common teaching, applied to those who practice both Hinayana and Mahayana, (3) distinct, that is Mahayana teaching, and (4) perfect teaching.
2. "The length of time stated above" refers to *gohyaku jindengō:* literally 500 dust-particle *kalpa*. It means an inconceivably long period of time as described in the 16th chapter of the *Lotus Sutra* indicating how much time has elapsed since Śākyamuni's original enlightenment: "Suppose someone smashes 500 billion *nayuta, asaṃkhya* worlds into dust, and then takes it all toward the east, dropping one particle each time he passes 500 billion *nayuta, asaṃkhya* worlds. Suppose he continues traveling eastward in this way until he finishes dropping all the particles. Suppose all these worlds reduced to dust. Let one particle represent one *kalpa*. The time which has passed since I attained Buddhahood surpassed this by 100 billion *nayuta, asaṃkhya kalpa*."
3. See "Ages of the True, Semblance and Latter Dharmas" in the glossary. This refers to the three periods after the death of the Buddha. In the Age of the True Dharma, the first ten-century period, the Buddha's teaching is practiced and enlightenment can be attained. In the Age of the Semblance Dharma, the second 10-century period, the teaching is practiced but enlightenment is not possible. In the last period of 10,000 years, the Latter Age of Degeneration, the teaching exists but it is no longer practiced.
4. *Risoku* is the first, lowest. stage of bodhisattvahood according to T'ien-t'ai's classification, at which one is not aware of the truth that all human beings have Buddha-nature, and continues to wander in the six realms of illusions.
5. 3,000 dust-particle *kalpa (sanzen-jindengō)* is the immeasurably long period of time described in the seventh (Kejōyu) chapter of the *Lotus Sutra*, A Parable, indicating how much time has passed since Śākyamuni preached the *Lotus Sutra* as the 16th son of Daitsūchishō Buddha: "Suppose someone smashed a major world system, consisting of 1,000 x 1,000 x 1,000 worlds, into ink powder. Then he traveled eastward making a dot as small as a particle of dust with that ink powder as he passed 1,000 worlds until the ink powder was exhausted. Then all the worlds he went through were smashed into dust. The number of *kalpa* which has elapsed since Daitsūchishō Buddha passed away is infinitely larger than the number of particles of the dust thus produced."
6. See note 2.
7. An ancient Indian numerical unit, indicating an incalculably large number.
8. *Kalpa* is a Sanskrit term meaning an immeasurably long period of time, said to be the period required to empty a city full of poppy seeds by taking away one every three years, or for an angel to wear away a 40 cubic kilometer stone by touching it with her robe once every three years.

9. Major *kalpa*: period of time in which a world is said to be created, and then continues, declines, and disintegrates.
10. The Buddha is believed to have three bodies: Dharma Body *(hosshin)*, Reward Body *(hōjin)*, and Accommodative Body *(ōjin)*. These are sometimes divided into two groups of the inferior *(retsu-ōjin)* and the superior *(shō-ōjin)*. So it is possible to say that He has four bodies.
11. Having a long, wide tongue is one of the Buddha's physical excellences, considered a sign of words spoken truly.
12. Five kinds of eyes: (1) eyes of flesh, that is human; (2) divine eyes of gods; (3) eyes of wisdom of the Two Vehicles: *śrāvaka* and *pratyekabuddha*; (4) Dharma eyes of bodhisattvas; and (5) eyes of Buddhas which can see through all things covering past, present, and future. The eyes of Buddhas also possess all the other four.
13. See four doctrinal teachings *(kehō no shikyō)* in note 1.
14. A numerical unit in India: 100 billion, according to one source. Also spelled *niyuta* in Sanskrit.
15. It is believed that the world goes through four *kalpa*, that is periods of construction, continuance, destruction, and emptiness, each of which consists of 20 small *kalpa*. The average human lifespan in a small kalpa increases by a year per century from 10 years until it reaches the maximum human lifespan of 84,000 years. After it reaches the maximum human lifespan, human life grows shorter by a year per century until it reaches the minimum average human lifespan of 10 years. This is repeated 20 times within a *kalpa*.
16. First four of the five tastes: (1) *nyū*, milk, (2) *raku*, cream, (3) *shōso*, curdled milk, (4) *jukuso*, butter, and (5) *daigo*, clarified butter or ghee. Used in the Tendai school to describe the five periods of the teaching of the Buddha.,
17. The four stages of faith of those who uphold the *Lotus Sutra* during Śākyamuni's lifetime, formulated by T'ien-t'ai based on the 17th chapter of the *Lotus Sutra*. They are: (1) to produce even a single moment of faith in the sutra, (2) to understand the Buddha's teaching in the sutra, (3) to propagate this teaching, and (4) to realize the truth preached by the Buddha with deep faith.
18. *Gojū-gengi*, five major principles with which T'ien-t'ai interpreted the *Lotus Sutra*: *myō*, the title of the sutra; *tai*, entity of the sutra; *shū*, essential teachings of the sutra; *yū*, influence upon men; and *kyō*, evaluation of the sutra.

Kanjin Honzon-shō Soejō (ST 119)

Introduction

The *Kanjin Honzon-shō* completed by Nichiren Shōnin at Ichinosawa, Sado, on the 25th day of the fourth month in the 10th year of Bun'ei (1273) was sent to Toki Jōnin, together with this cover letter dated on the following 26th day. The original manuscript of the letter has been kept in the Nakayama Hokekyōji Temple in Ichikawa City, Chiba Prefecture.

Thanking Toki Jōnin for donating a summer kimono, three ink sticks and five writing brushes, Nichiren points out the significance of the *Kanjin Honzon-shō*, stating it is "of utmost importance" to him. Then he says that it was written for such followers as Ōta Jōmyō and Soya Kyōshin and that it should be read only by those with unshakable faith in the *Lotus Sutra*. He demands cautious handling of it because it contains the important doctrine which has never been heard of and which may cause many people to misunderstand. Having expressed his awareness of being a messenger of the Buddha who explained the doctrine for the first time in 2,220 years or so since the passing away of Śākyamuni Buddha, Nichiren Shōnin concludes the letter with his joy of seeing, together with his followers in the world of spiritual contemplation, Śākyamuni and the Buddha of Many Treasures as well as Buddhas in manifestation from all the worlds in the universe in the Pure Land of Mt. Sacred Eagle.

The Cover Letter to the Kanjin Honzon-shō

Thank you very much for the summer kimono, three ink sticks, and five writing brushes.

I have written a little on the doctrine of meditative practice, which I am sending to such people as Lord Ōta Jōmyō,* and Lay Priest Soya Kyōshin.*

This is of the utmost importance to me, Nichiren. You should keep this a secret unless you find someone with unshakeable faith in the *Lotus Sutra*, to whom you may show it. Concerning the ultimate teaching of the Buddha for those in the Latter Age, this writing contains many difficult questions with only short answers. Since this is a doctrine never heard of before, it may startle those who hear it. Should you decide to show it to others, you should not have several people read it together sitting side by side.

In more than 2,220 years after the death of Śākyamuni Buddha, nobody has ever explained the doctrine contained in this writing. Since we are now in the fifth 500-year period* after the death of the Buddha, the first 500-year period in the beginning of the Latter Age, when the True Dharma should be spread, I have expounded this in the face of public persecution.

I pray that all my followers who read this writing may feel the joy of visiting, together with me, Nichiren, the Pure Land of Mt. Sacred Eagle to look up at the faces of the Eternal Buddha Śākyamuni, the Buddha of Many Treasures, and countless Buddhas in manifestation from all the worlds in the universe.

Respectfully yours,
Nichiren (signature)

On the 26th day of the fourth month
in the 10th year of Bun'ei (1273)
Response to Lord Toki*

Kembutsu Mirai-ki (ST 125)

Introduction

The *Kembutsu Mirai-ki* was written by Nichiren Shōnin while in exile in the Ishida District of Sado Island on the 11th day of the fifth intercalary month in the 10th year of the Bun'ei Era (1273). Until 1875, 12 pages of the original manuscript were preserved at Kuonji Temple on Mt. Minobu, when they were destroyed in a fire. In this short essay, Nichiren gives "testimony to the truth of the Buddha's prediction" while stating his own prediction about the "future development" of Buddhism. It is an important essay of Nichiren Shōnin, in which he expressed his historic mission as he saw it.

In the second month of the ninth year in the Bun'ei Era (1272), Nichiren Shōnin wrote the *Kaimoku-shō. Open Your Eyes to the Lotus Teaching*, declaring himself to be an avatar of Jōgyō (Superior-Practice) Bodhisattva. A year later he published the *Hokke-shū Naishō Buppō Ketsumyaku, Successors of the Privately Transmitted Dharma of the Lotus Sect*, designating the successive transmitters of the teaching of the Buddha specially commissioned in the Stupa of Treasures. Two months later, in the fourth month of the 10th year of the Bun'ei Era, Nichiren Shōnin completed writing the *Kanjin Honzon-shō, Spiritual Contemplation and the Most Venerable One*, which he considered "of the utmost importance" to him, revealing the original Dharma teaching of the essential section *(hommon)* of the *Lotus Sutra*. It was followed within a month by another treatise, this *Kembutsu Mirai-ki*, to clarify who would be the leader to spread the True Dharma in the Latter Age of Degeneration. Revealing in this writing the four masters in three lands in the format of eight questions and answers, Nichiren Shōnin assigns himself as the fourth legitimate transmitter of the *Lotus Sutra* throughout India, China and Japan, who is in charge of propagating the Lotus teaching in the Latter Age of Degeneration.

Singling out the Buddha's words in the 23rd chapter, Medicine-King Bodhisattva, as His prophesy that the *Lotus Sutra* would spread widely in the world during the Latter Age, Nichiren Shōnin argues that the master-propagator of the true *honzon* and the *Odaimoku* based on the essential section *(hommon)* of the *Lotus Sutra* is none other than Nichiren himself, who has experienced the Buddha's prediction proving it to be true. He then states that it is natural that the True Dharma would spread westward from Japan through China and India to all over the world, and that natural calamities prevalent at the time foretell the worldwide spread of the Lotus teaching. Finally, Nichiren restates that he himself, who has verified the *Lotus Sutra* to be true, is the legitimate successor to Śākyamuni Buddha in India, T'ien-t'ai in China and Dengyō in Japan, and the true propagator of the *Lotus Sutra* in the Latter Age.

Testimony to the Prediction of the Buddha

The *Lotus Sutra*, fascicle seven, [Chapter 23, Previous Life of Medicine-King Bodhisattva",] reads: "Propagate this sutra throughout this world (Jambudvīpa)* in the last 500-year period,* namely at the beginning of the Latter Age of Degeneration, lest it should become extinct."

Coming across this passage, I once lamented saying: "It has already been more than 2,220 years since Śākyamuni Buddha passed away. For what sin of mine was I neither born during the Buddha's lifetime, nor fortunate enough to see the Four Reliances,* four ranks of bodhisattva-teachers whom people relied on after the death of the Buddha, in the Age of the True Dharma, or such great masters as T'ien-t'ai* and Dengyō in the Age of the Semblance Dharma?"

Thinking it over, however, I was elated and said to myself, "How lucky I am to have been born in the last 500-year period and encounter the true teaching of the *Lotus Sutra*!" Even during the lifetime of the Buddha, those who had been born during the time of the pre-Lotus sutras were unable to listen to the preaching of the *Lotus Sutra*. To have been born in the Ages of the True Dharma and the Semblance Dharma did not help much. Three Southern and seven Northern masters,* and scholars of Flower Garland (Kegon)* and True Word (Shingon)* Buddhism did not believe the *Lotus Sutra*.

Grand Master T'ien-t'ai stated in his *Words and Phrases of the Lotus Sutra*: "The benefit of the Wonderful Dharma will reach afar during the first half-millennium of the Latter Age of Degeneration."* He must have meant that now is the time for the *Lotus Sutra* to be propagated widely. Grand Master Dengyō said in his *Treatise on the Protection of the Nation, Shugo Kokkai-shō*: "The Ages of the True Dharma and the Semblance Dharma are almost over, and the Latter Age of Degeneration is just around the corner." These are the words of Grand Master Dengyō* wishing himself to have been born in the beginning of the Latter Age of Degeneration. Thus, my good luck of having been born in the Latter Age is superior to that of Nāgārjuna* and Vasubandhu* who came to the world in the Age of the True Dharma, or of T'ien-t'ai and Dengyō in the Age of the Semblance Dharma.

Question: You, Nichiren, are not the only one who was born in the first 500-year period in the Latter Age of Degeneration. Why do you feel particularly happy about this?

Answer: It is said in the *Lotus Sutra,* fascicle four, [Chapter 10, The Teacher of the Dharma:] "This sutra has aroused much hatred and jealousy even during the lifetime of the Buddha. How much more so after His death!" Grand Master T'ien-t'ai annotates this in his *Words and Phrases of the Lotus Sutra:* "Many hated this sutra with jealousy even during the lifetime of the Buddha. How much more so in the future! It is only natural that future propagation of this sutra will not be easy." In his *Annotations on the Words and Phrases of the Lotus Sutra,* Grand Master Miao-lê in turn explains this: "T'ien-t'ai said that it was only natural that future propagation of the *Lotus Sutra* would be not easy. He said this for the purpose of making us realize its difficulty."

Monk Chih-tu of Tung-ch'un also comments on this in his *Tendai Interpretation of the Meaning of the Lotus Sutra, T'ien-t'ai Fa-hua-su I-tsuan:* "Discarding five kinds of teaching, for men, gods, Hinayana sages of *śrāvaka* and *pratyekabuddha,* and bodhisattvas respectively, this *Lotus Sutra* established the one and supreme teaching leading all to Buddhahood. It rejects ordinary men, as well as sages, and discards all the pre-Lotus teachings, both Mahayana and Hinayana. Just as good medicine tastes bitter in the mouth, they all hate this sutra."

Moreover, Grand Master Dengyō has this to say in his *Outstanding Principles of the Lotus Sutra, Hokke Shūku:* "As for the time, it is toward the end of the Age of the Semblance Dharma or in the beginning of the Latter Age. As for the land, it is located to the east of T'ang China, and west of Chieh.[1] As for the people, they live in the evil world filled with five defilements.* They live in wars and strife. It is said in the *Lotus Sutra,* Chapter 10, The Teacher of the Dharma: 'Many will hate the *Lotus Sutra* with jealousy even during His lifetime, not to mention after His death.' There are good reasons for these words."

These words of Dengyō may seem to have described his own time, but in reality he was talking about today in the Latter Age of Degeneration. He says in his *Treatise on the Protection of the Nation, Shugo Kokkai-shō:* "The Ages of the True Dharma and Semblance Dharma are almost over and the Latter Age of Degeneration is just around the corner." These words are indeed meaningful.

It is said in the *Lotus Sutra,* [Chapter 23, Previous Life of Medicine-King Bodhisattva,] that during the first 500-year period in the Latter Age of Degeneration, the "King of Devils, his subjects, gods, dragons, *yakṣa* demons, *kumbhaṇḍa* [demons with bottle-shaped testicles], and others will take advantage of the time." Regarding "others," [in Chapter 26, Dhāraṇīs,] the sutra lists such devils and demi-gods as *yakṣa* demons, *rākṣasa* demons, hungry spirits, *pūtana* demons, *kṛtya* demons, red, yellow, black, or blue demons, or *yakṣa kṛtya* demons or human *kṛtya* demons who would take advantage of the shortcomings of those who spread the *Lotus Sutra*.

These passages of the *Lotus Sutra* preach that those, who had upheld in their past lives the "four tastes and three teachings" of the pre-Lotus sutras, non-Buddhist teachings or worldly teachings of the human realm and heaven, were reborn in this life as devils, evil gods or men, trying to harm those who practice the perfect and true teaching, the *Lotus Sutra*.

Question: In comparing the two Ages of the True Dharma and Semblance Dharma against the Latter Age of Degeneration, we find that the former two are far superior to the latter in terms of time as well as the capacity of the people to be taught. Why is it that the sutra rejects the superior time and superior capacity of the Ages of the True Dharma and Semblance Dharma, pointing to the Latter Age of Degeneration to be the time when the great Dharma should spread?

Answer: I do not know why. The Buddha's intention is unfathomable, but let me support one explanation. According to Hinayana sutras, during the 1,000-year Age of the True Dharma, immediately following the lifetime of the Buddha, all three, teaching, practice and Buddhahood, will exist. That is to say, there are those who put into practice the teaching of the Buddha and actually attain Buddhahood. During the 1,000-year Age of the Semblance Dharma, however, there remain only two, teaching and practice, such that there are some who practice the teaching of the Buddha, but nobody is able to attain Buddhahood. During the Latter Age of Degeneration, furthermore, only the teaching of the Buddha remains without anyone practicing it or attaining Buddhahood.

In contemplating this on the basis of the *Lotus Sutra*, we find that the existence of teaching, practice and Buddhahood during the 1,000-year Age of the True Dharma means that those who had heard the Buddha preach the *Lotus Sutra* during His lifetime were born to this world in the Age of the True Dharma to attain Hinayana Buddhahood by practicing the Hinayana teaching. Those who were born in the Age of the Semblance Dharma, however, had less chance of listening to the Buddha preach the *Lotus Sutra* during His lifetime. So none of them were able to attain Buddhahood by means of Hinayana sutras. They could only be reborn in the Pure Lands in the universe by means of provisional Mahayana sutras. In the Latter Age of Degeneration, neither Hinayana sutras nor provisional Mahayana sutras have any use. In Hinayana, only the teaching exists, nobody practices it or gains Buddhahood. In provisional Mahayana, both teaching and practice exist but nobody attains Buddhahood, esoteric or exoteric.

In the Latter Age of Degeneration, furthermore, the Hinayana and provisional Mahayana teachings established in the Ages of the True Dharma and Semblance Dharma steadily spread, each claiming to be supreme, the Hinayana attacking Mahayana Buddhism, the provisional* destroying the true and filling the land with slanderers of the True Dharma. The number of those who fall into the evil realms, such as hell or realms of hungry spirits and of *asura* demons, is more numerous than the particles of the great earth. Those who uphold the True Dharma and attain Buddhahood are less in number than grains of earth on fingernails.* Thereupon, all the gods who protect Buddhism abandon such a land, allowing evil gods and demons to enter the bodies of the king, his subjects, monks and nuns, and cause them to abuse and slander the one who practices the *Lotus Sutra*.

Nevertheless, if there is a man after the death of the Buddha who breaks the attachment to the false doctrines of the "four tastes and three teachings" of the pre-Lotus sutras and puts faith in the True Dharma of the *Lotus Sutra*, all the virtuous gods and numerous bodhisattvas who sprang up from underground* will protect such a one who practices the *Lotus Sutra*. Under such protection, this one who practices would be able to spread all over the world the *honzon* revealed in the essential section and the five character *Odaimoku* of *Myō, Hō, Ren, Ge,* and *Kyō*, the essence of the *Lotus Sutra*.

He is just like Never-Despising Bodhisattva, who in the Age of the Semblance Dharma after the death of Powerful Voice King Buddha spread in the land of that Buddha the 24 character passage in the *Lotus Sutra*, [Chapter 20,] saying: "I respect you deeply. I do not despise you. Why is this? It is because you all will practice the way of bodhisattvas and will be able to attain Buddhahood." With such propagation, the Bodhisattva was severely persecuted by all the people in the land, who beat him with sticks and threw stones at him.

Although the 24 characters of Never-Despising Bodhisattva differ in wording from the five characters which I, Nichiren, spread, they are the same in meaning. We both appeared in the world under the same conditions: he toward the end of the Age of the Semblance Dharma after the death of Powerful Voice King Buddha, and I at the beginning of the Latter Age after the death of Śākyamuni Buddha. Also Never-Despising Bodhisattva and I, Nichiren, are at the same stage of progress in the practice of the *Lotus Sutra*: he is in the initial "rejoicing upon hearing the *Lotus Sutra (sho-zuiki-hon)*" rank in the five-stage practice *(gohon)*,[2] while I am an ordinary man in the second stage of the "notional understanding *(myōji-soku)*" in the six-stage practice *(roku-soku)*.[3]

Question: How do you know that you are one who practices* the *Lotus Sutra* in the beginning of the Latter Age of Degeneration?

Answer: The following statements in the *Lotus Sutra* verify it to be the truth. "Many people hate this sutra with jealousy even in the lifetime of the Buddha, not to say after His death," [in Chapter 10, The Teacher of the Dharma]. "Ignorant people will speak ill of us [who propagate this sutra in the Latter Age of Degeneration], abuse us, and threaten us with swords and sticks.... We will be driven out of our monasteries from time to time," [in Chapter 13, Encouragement for Keeping This Sutra]. "Many people in the world will hate this sutra and few will believe it," [in Chapter 14, Peaceful Practices]. "People struck him [one who practices the *Lotus Sutra*] with sticks, pieces of wood, pieces of tile, and stones," [in Chapter 20, Never-Despising Bodhisattva]. "The King of Devils, his subjects, gods, dragons, *yakṣa* demons, and *kumbhaṇda* demons will take advantage of the time [the first 500-year period in the Latter Age of Degeneration]," [in Chapter 23, Previous Life of Medicine-King Bodhisattva].

To see that these words of the Buddha are not false, when we see the faces of all the people in Japan, the king and his subjects, monks and nuns, and laymen and laywomen, reflected upon these clear mirrors of the *Lotus Sutra*, there is nobody but I, Nichiren, who fits them perfectly. As for the time, we certainly are at the beginning of the Latter Age of Degeneration. Should there be no Nichiren today, these words of the Buddha would all be proved false.

Question closely: You are more self-conceited than Mahādeva of ancient India, who caused the first great schism in the community of Buddhist monks and nuns, or Shizen Biku, a disciple of the Buddha who believed himself to be an *arhat* and ended up in the Hell of Incessant Suffering. What do you have to say about this?

Answer: The grave sin you have committed in accusing me, Nichiren, is more serious than what was committed by Devadatta,* who fell in hell alive, or by Vimalamitra,* the Hinayana master who died a madman for slandering Mahayana Buddhism.

My words may sound self-conceited, but they were solely to show the infallibility of the Buddha's prediction. Suppose they were self-conceited, then whom can you name among all the people in Japan, except me, Nichiren, to be the one who practices the *Lotus Sutra*? In order to slander me, Nichiren, you are saying that the Buddha's prediction is false. Is it not you who are very wicked?

Question: You, Nichiren, seem to fit the prediction* by the Buddha, but I wonder whether or not there are others who practice the *Lotus Sutra* also in such lands as India and China. What do you think of this?

Answer: There will never be two suns in the world. How could there be two sovereigns in a country! There should be only one who practices the *Lotus Sutra* in the Latter Age of Degeneration.

Question: How do you know that?

Answer: The moon rises in the west and shines on the east. The sun rises in the east and sheds light on the west. Buddhism spreads the same way: In the Ages of the True Dharma and Semblance Dharma, it spreads from west to east. In the Latter Age of Degeneration, it spreads from east to west. When Venerable Amoghavajra (Pu-k'ung) and his disciple Han-kuang of the True Word (Shingon) school made a trip to India, a priest there said to Han-kuang: "I heard that T'ien-t'ai in China teaches superbly, differentiating true Buddhism from the false and judging the comparative superiority of Buddhist sutras. Is it not possible for you to translate his words and transmit them to India?" Hearing this from Han-kuang, Grand Master Miao-lê* wondered in his *Annotations on the Words and Phrases of the Lotus Sutra*: "Does this not mean that Buddhism has been lost in India and that the people in India are trying to find it in lands in four directions?" This seems to prove that Buddhism does not exist in India.

As for China, it has been some 150 years since barbarians from the north known as the Jürched conquered the Sung capital of Kaifeng during the reign of Emperor Kao-tsung. Meanwhile, both the Buddhist way as well as the royal way have been destroyed. Hinayana scriptures disappeared completely from collections of Buddhist scriptures in China, and Mahayana scriptures were mostly destroyed. A Tendai monk Jakushō took some Mahayana scriptures from Japan to China, where they remained like pieces of wood and stone wearing robes and holding alms bowls as there was nobody worthy of holding them. Therefore, Tsun-shih, a T'ien-t'ai (Tendai) monk of Sung China, has said in the *Special Collection on India, T'ien-chu Pieh-chi*: "Buddhism at first spread eastward to Japan from China just as the moon rises in the west shining on the east. Now it comes back from Japan to China just as the sun rises in the east and sheds light on the west." According to these statements there is no doubt that Buddhism has been lost in both India and China.

Question: Now I know that Buddhism has been lost in India as well as in China on the continent located to the south of Mt. Sumeru. However, how do you know that Buddhism does not exist on the three other continents to the east, west, and north of the mountain, either?[4]

Answer: Buddhism does not exist in those continents. Bodhisattva Universal-Sage said to the Buddha in the *Lotus Sutra*, fascicle eight, [Chapter 28, Encouragement of Universal-Sage Bodhisattva]: "I will protect this sutra with my divine powers so that it may be propagated and not be destroyed within the Jambudvīpa [the continent to the south of Mt. Sumeru] after Your death." The term "within" here makes it clear that the land of Buddhism does not include those three continents.

Question: The Buddha's prediction* must be as you say. Would you predict the future?

Answer: Contemplating the future on the basis of the prediction of the Buddha, we are in the beginning of the fifth 500-year period, that is, the first 500-year period in the Latter Age of Degeneration when Buddhism should rise in the land of Japan in the east. As omens, strange phenomena in the sky and natural calamities on earth* as were never seen in the Ages of the True Dharma and Semblance Dharma shall occur.

Great events are foreshadowed by great omens. The birth of the Buddha, His first preaching, and His death were paralleled by omens, good or bad, greater than any seen before or after. It was because the Buddha was the greatest sage of all. When the Buddha was born, according to various sutras, rays of light in five colors shone in four directions, so the night looked as bright as the day. When He passed away, it is said, twelve white rainbows spanned north and south and the sun stopped shining, so the day became as dark as night. For 2,000 years afterward, during the Ages of the True Dharma and the Semblance Dharma, although many sages were born and died, such great omens as those which preceded the birth and death of the Buddha never occurred.

Nevertheless, the great earthquake and strange phenomena in the sky which we have had since the Shōka Era (1257-59)* until this year, the 10th year of the Bun'ei Era (1273), are comparable to those great omens at the time of Śākyamuni Buddha's birth and death. You should know from these occurrences that a man as great as the Buddha is going to be born or is about to pass away. A great comet rose in the sky. Which great ruler or his subject does it foreshadow? An earthquake shook and tilted the great earth three times. Which sage or wise man does it foretell? You should know that these are not ordinary omens, good or bad, large in size. They solely foreshadow the rise or decline of this great Dharma!

T'ien-t'ai says in his *Words and Phrases of the Lotus Sutra:* "Looking at the heavy rainfall, one should know the size of the dragon which causes the rain to fall. Seeing the abundance of the lotus flowers, one can see the depth of the pond where the lotus grows." Miao-lê* interprets this in his *Annotations on the Words and Phrases of the Lotus Sutra:* "Men of knowledge know the cause of phenomena, and only snakes know the way of snakes." Only the one who practices the *Lotus Sutra* knows the rise of the great Dharma by looking at great omens.

Twenty-one years have already passed since I, Nichiren, became aware of the appearance of the one who practices the *Lotus Sutra* at the beginning of the Latter Age in the land of Japan. During these years, especially in the last few years, I have encountered a continuous series of calamities day by day and month by month. Surely I will be executed soon. It seems difficult for me to survive this month or this year. Who except me, Nichiren, is foreshadowed by those great omens? Those who have any doubt may ask my disciples to instruct them further.

How lucky I am to be able to extinguish within one life my sin of slandering the True Dharma* ever since the eternal past! How glad I feel to be able to wait on Lord Śākyamuni Buddha, whom I have yet never seen!

May I guide first of all those rulers of this land who have persecuted me. May I tell Śākyamuni Buddha about my disciples who have assisted me. May I present this great merit to my parents, who gave birth to me, before I die.

I now realize, though dimly, the heart of the 11th chapter of the *Lotus Sutra*, Beholding the Stupa of Treasures.* It is stated in this chapter: "Even a man as powerless as I can throw Mt. Sumeru* over to countless numbers of Buddha lands.... Even more so, it is not easy to uphold the *Lotus Sutra* in the evil world after the death of the Buddha." Grand Master Dengyō* interprets this in his *Outstanding Principles of the Lotus Sutra, Hokke Shūku*: "The Buddha has determined that it is easy to spread the sutras which are shallow in meaning, and difficult to spread those which are profound in meaning. A man should leave the shallow and take the deep. Therefore, Grand Master T'ien-t'ai, putting faith in Śākyamuni Buddha, spread the *Lotus Sutra* in China, and all the kinsfolk of Mt. Hiei,* receiving the teaching of the *Lotus Sutra* from T'ien-t'ai, spread it in Japan."

I, Nichiren, of Awa Province graciously received the teaching of the *Lotus Sutra* from three masters [Śākyamuni Buddha, T'ien-t'ai and Dengyō] and spread it in the Latter Age of Degeneration. Therefore, I dare add myself to the three masters, calling ourselves "four masters in three lands."*

Namu Myōhō Renge-kyō! *Namu Myōhō Renge-kyō!*

11th day of the fifth month (intercalary)
in the 10th year of the Bun'ei Era (1273)

by Monk Nichiren

Notes

1. Probably refers to the Mo-ho tribes of Manchuria.
2. Five progressive stages in the practice of the *Lotus Sutra* after the death of the Buddha, formulated by T'ien-t'ai in his *Hokke Mongu, Words and Phrases of the Lotus Sutra*: (1) to rejoice on hearing the *Lotus Sutra*, (2) to read and recite it, (3) to propagate it, (4) to uphold it and practice the six *pāramitā*, and (5) to perfect the six *pāramitā*.
3. Six stages in the practice of the *Lotus Sutra* formulated by T'ien-t'ai: (1) *ri-soku*, or the stage at which one had not heard the True Dharma and is ignorant of Buddhism; (2) *myōji-soku*, the stage at which one hears the name and reads the words of the *Lotus Sutra* and begins believing in it; (3) *kangyō-soku*, the stage at which one begins practicing what he learns; (4) *sōji-soku*, the stage at which one eliminates the first two of the three categories of illusion; (5) *bunshin-soku*, the stage at which one attains partial enlightenment; and (6) *kukyō-soku*, the highest stage of practice at which one eliminates all illusions and attains perfect enlightenment.
4. According to Buddhist cosmology, the world consists of four continents in the four directions from Mt. Sumeru.

Toki-dono Gohenji (ST 126)

Introduction

This letter was written on the sixth day of the seventh month in the 10th year of the Bun'ei Period (1273) at Ichinosawa on Sado Island. The original manuscript of this letter has been preserved at the Nakayama Hokekyōji Temple. Thanking Lord Toki for his donation, Nichiren Shōnin also explains why he has not been released from exile sooner, answering the question raised by Lord Toki. Comforting the lord, Nichiren Shōnin expresses his resolution to spread the teachings of the *Lotus Sutra* and its *Odaimoku* at the cost of his life. He has no doubt about his success and expresses his religious ecstasy as one who practices the *Lotus Sutra*.

A Response to Lord Toki

Thank you very much for your donation. I safely received two rolls of eyelet coins,* which I assume were sent by Lord Ōta* and you.

Nitchō, your son, is very talented, so I have decided to keep him here until the end of this year.

There is no need to grieve over me for not getting a release from exile. As I gave a warning in the *Risshō Ankoku-ron, Treatise on Spreading Peace Throughout the Country by Establishing the True Dharma,* some things will happen to this country and I suppose I am not getting released until that time.

Today, I am not sure of staying alive or dying here. However, at the same time I am sure that the five characters of *Myō, Hō, Ren, Ge,* and *Kyō* will spread widely in this Latter Age of Degeneration. Grand Master Dengyō tried to spread the perfect teachings of the *Lotus Sutra*. Of the three ways of learning, during his lifetime he was able to spread two: practicing meditation and cultivating wisdom. Regarding the third, his plan to establish the perfect and sudden precept platform was not allowed by the Imperial Court until after his death. To establish a platform is the "phenomenal aspect," which might have created greater difficulties than establishing the "noumenon" of meditation and wisdom.

Thus you may now know how difficult it is today, over 2,220 years after the death of the Buddha, to spread the teachings of the Eternal Buddha* revealed in the 16th chapter, The Duration of the Life of the Tathāgata, and the *Odaimoku*, the essence of the *Lotus Sutra*.

I am very fortunate indeed to live in the Latter Age of Degeneration spreading these teachings of truth, so I am getting much more reward than many of the past such as Dengyō, T'ien-t'ai,* Nāgārjuna,* and Vasubandhu. If not for the *Lotus Sutra*, which predicts the spread of the *Lotus Sutra* in the Latter Age, I would be nothing but the most self-conceited in the world. Praising T'ien-t'ai, Chang-an* said, "Tien-t'ai's interpretation of Buddhism is much more enriching than that of the Great Wisdom Discourse* of India. Why should we bother to compare him to Chinese masters? This is no exaggeration. This is the result of unbiased comparison of doctrines." The same could be said of my teaching founded on the *Lotus Sutra*, the great true teaching of the Lord Buddha. Without exaggeration it is much more enriching than those of great commentators such as Nāgārjuna and Vasubandhu. Therefore, T'ien-t'ai foretold, "In the last 500-year period* the wonderful way of the *Lotus Sutra* will spread widely." He was foretelling me. Lamenting for not having been born in the Latter Age of Degeneration, Dengyō stated, "The Latter Age of Degeneration* is around the corner."

How fortunate I am! I am spreading the teaching of the *Lotus Sutra*, confronting many persecutions and difficulties in this Latter Age of Degeneration just as it is foretold in the *Lotus Sutra*, Chapter 13, Encouragement for Keeping This Sutra: "Those who spread this *Lotus Sutra* after the death of the Buddha will be persecuted and chased out of monasteries often." I should be proud of myself. I am writing this as a response to everyone, so I believe I do not need to explain this in detail.

On the sixth day of the seventh month

Nichiren (signature)

Response to Lord Toki

Hakii Saburō-dono Gohenji (ST 127)

Introduction

This letter of Nichiren Shōnin was sent to Hakii Saburō Sanenaga from Ichinosawa on Sado on the third day of the eighth month in the 10th year of the Bun'ei Era (1273), when Nichiren Shōnin was 51 years old. The original manuscript of the letter has not been found, but a copy made by Nikkō Shōnin exists in the Kitayama Hommonji Temple.

This is in answer to the question of Sanenaga, who had sent a letter to Nichiren Shōnin in Sado, inquiring about Buddhism. He wanted to know why Nichiren Shōnin had been persecuted many times and not at all been at peace, since it is expected that those who practice Buddhism would be at peace in this world and be born into a good place in the future. Nichiren Shōnin quoted the Lotus and Nirvana Sutras in response.

Nichiren Shōnin had answered a similar question from his disciples in the *Kaimoku-shō, Open Your Eyes to the Lotus Teaching*. He restates that they should propagate the teaching of the *Lotus Sutra* without fear of persecution. In this sense, this letter and the *Kaimoku-shō* are two writings of Nichiren Shōnin revealing his belief as to why "those who practice the *Lotus Sutra* are confronted with persecutions and difficulties."

According to such chapters of the *Lotus Sutra* as Chapters 10, Teacher of the Dharma, Chapter 13, Encouragement for Keeping This Sutra, and Chapter 20, Never-Despising Bodhisattva, those who propagate the *Lotus Sutra* during the Latter Age of Degeneration are bound to encounter persecutions. The letter declares that in light of what is said in those chapters, Nichiren Shōnin has been persecuted exactly as the sutra says, and that in virtue of his merit of actually experiencing persecution, it is no doubt that he will attain Buddhahood in the future.

The letter also refers to the issue of national destruction, which Nichiren Shōnin foresaw in his *Risshō Ankoku-ron, Treatise on Spreading Peace Throughout the Nation by Establishing the True Dharma*. It also admires Sanenaga's unwavering faith, and explains that the five characters of the Wonderful Dharma are the True Dharma to spread throughout the Latter Age of Degeneration as the teaching leading all people to Buddhahood, the evil as well as *icchantika*, those without Buddha-nature.

A Response to Lord Hakii Saburō

Your letter reached me promptly. Upon reading my letter of response, I am sure, your doubts will disappear in a moment as when a gust of wind blows away a dark cloud and the beautiful moon appears in the sky. Nobody, regardless of whether they are high or low, believes that I, Nichiren, am one who practices the *Lotus Sutra*. People must be wondering why Nichiren, who claims to be one who practices the *Lotus Sutra*,* is confronted by many persecutions and difficulties while the sutra preaches that one who practices Buddhism is at peace in this world and will be reborn in a better place in future lives. They believe it must be that Nichiren is not aligned with the true intent of the Buddha.

Expecting such a vicious criticism from the beginning, I am not surprised even if I am exiled at the displeasure* of the ruler of Japan because it is clearly stated in the *Lotus Sutra* that one who practices the teachings of the *Lotus Sutra* in the Latter Age of Degeneration* will be confronted by many difficulties. Those who have eyes had better look at what the sutra says. It is said in the 10th chapter, Teacher of the Dharma: "Even during the lifetime of the Buddha many people hated this sutra with envy, not to mention the time after His death." The 14th chapter, Peaceful Practices, says, "This sutra is treated with hostility by so many people that it is difficult to believe it."

The 13th chapter, Encouragement for Keeping This Sutra, says: "Ignorant people will speak ill of us, abuse us, and threaten us with swords or sticks," "Some priests in the evil world will be cunning," "Some priests will live in a tranquil forest wearing patched clothing. Attached to worldly profits, they will expound the Dharma to men in white robes. They will be respected by people of the world as though they were *arhats* who have the six supernatural powers," "In order to speak ill of us and slander us in the midst of the great multitude, they will say to kings, ministers, Brahmans, householders and other priests, that our views are all wrong," "The devil will enter the bodies of these priests and cause them to abuse and insult us, who practice the *Lotus Sutra*," and "They will drive us out of our monasteries from time to time."

The *Nirvana Sutra** says, "Seeing an *icchantika** pretending to be an *arhat* who is living in a tranquil monastery and slandering Mahayana* Buddhism, ordinary people will take him for an *arhat* and a great Bodhisattva."* The sutra also says,

"In the Age of the Semblance Dharma after the Age of the True Dharma, priests pretend to keep Buddhist precepts chanting sutras a little bit, but they indulge in eating and drinking, thinking only of themselves. Even if they wear *kesa* robes for Buddhist monks, their minds are like those of hunters stalking game or cats trying to catch rats." The six-fascicled *Nirvana Sutra* states: "Some *icchantika* look like *arhats*."

Looking at current day Japan reflected in these clear mirrors of the true teachings of the Buddha, I can see the following clearly without a shred of doubt. To whom does the passage of "Some priests will live in tranquil forests wearing patched clothing" refer? Who is "respected by the people of the world like *arhats?*" Who are those whom "ordinary people will take for an *arhat* and a great Bodhisattva?" How about the "priests pretending to keep Buddhist precepts and chanting the sutras a little bit?" As the Buddha foresaw the state of Buddhism in the beginning of the Latter Age of Degeneration in these sutras through His Buddha-eye, if such evil persons do not exist today, it means that the Buddha predicted mistakenly, thereby disturbing the people. If that is the case, who would believe the precious doctrines preached in the first half and the latter half of the *Lotus Sutra* and the teaching of eternal Buddha-nature in the *Nirvana Sutra* preached in the *śāla* forest?

As I, Nichiren, try to prove the truth of the Buddha's words by applying these sutras to the state of Japan today, the statement that "Some priests will live in tranquil forests wearing patched clothing" refers to those in Zen, Ritsu and Pure Land temples such as Kenchōji, Jufukuji, Gokurakuji, Kenninji, and Tōfukuji. These devilish temples were built to destroy such Lotus-Tendai temples as the Enryakuji Temple on Mt. Hiei.* "Priests who pretend to keep Buddhist precepts" refer to those priests who wear gorgeous five-piece, seven-piece or nine-piece robes. "Those whom ordinary people regard as great Bodhisattvas" are Dōryū* of the Kenchōji Temple, Ryōkan* of the Gokurakuji Temple, and Shōichi* of the Tōfukuji Temple. "People of the world" means rulers of Japan, and "ignorant ordinary people" are all the people in Japan.

Because I am an unenlightened, ordinary man,* I, Nichiren, cannot simply assert what I believe to be true in the Buddha's teachings. But as for what I mentioned above, I can clearly ascertain it to be true just as when I put my hand into water and fire. The *Lotus Sutra* says that those who practice the *Lotus Sutra* will be spoken ill of, slandered, struck with swords or canes, and expelled. Observing the current state of Japan in the light of this scriptural statement, I see no one, except myself, who suffers from many persecutions and difficulties as the sutra predicts. Who is one who practices the *Lotus Sutra* if nobody who fits the description exists? Though there are enemies who persecute, as predicted in the sutra, one who practices the *Lotus Sutra* who suffers from persecutions does not exist. It is like east without west, or heaven without earth. If so, words of the Buddha prove to be false. What should we do? I may sound self-conceited, but I would like to contemplate this in order to find the true intent of the Buddha. I, Nichiren, am a messenger of the Buddha.

Furthermore, in the 20th chapter of the *Lotus Sutra*, Never-Despising Bodhisattva,* the Buddha describes Himself in His previous lives: "Once upon a time, there was a bodhisattva named Never-Despising.... He propagated the *Lotus Sutra* fervently despite persecutions." The sutra describes how evil people spoke ill of him, abused him or struck him with a stick or a piece of wood, and threw pieces of tile or stones at him. By showing such ascetic practices in His previous lives, the Buddha encouraged those who propagate in the beginning of the Latter Age of Degeneration.* Propagating the *Lotus Sutra*, Never-Despising Bodhisattva* was persecuted, and was struck with a stick or a piece of wood but attained the rank of the Buddha instantly. As I propagated the *Lotus Sutra*, my house was set on fire at Matsubagayatsu, and I was attacked by Tōjō Kagenobu at Komatsubara, exiled to Izu, and banished to Sado Island. Therefore, I will reach Buddhahood in the future without a doubt.

Even the Four Reliances [four ranks of bodhisattvas, whom Buddhists relied on for guidance after the death of the Buddha] during the Ages of the True Dharma and the Semblance Dharma encountered many misfortunes when they tried to propagate this sutra. For example, Deva Bodhisattva, the 20th lineal successor* of the Dharma, was killed by heretics, and the 25th successor, Venerable Siṃha was beheaded by an evil king. Buddhamitra, the eighth lineal successor of the Buddha Dharma, kept on preaching under a red flag flying in front of a royal palace for 12 years while Bodhisattva Nāgārjuna, the 13th successor, did it for seven years. In China, Tao-sheng was exiled to Su-shan because he insisted that all people can reach Buddhahood. Fa-tsu was exiled because he propagated energetically in Chang-an. Tripiṭaka Master Fa-tao was branded on his face and expelled because of his admonishment of Emperor Hui-tsung of the Sung Dynasty. And Hui-yüan* was severely punished for criticizing the anti-Buddhist policy of Emperor Wu of Northern Chou.

Grand Master T'ien-t'ai* had to engage in vigorous disputes against three Southern and seven Northern masters* while establishing his new theology, and Grand Master Dengyō* in Japan had to argue against the six schools of Buddhism in Nara during the reign of Emperor Kammu. Whether or not Buddhist masters encountered hardships depended on whether their opinions were adopted by a wise king or rejected by a foolish king. It did not depend on whether or not their ways of propagation were in accordance with the intent of the Buddha. The situations were like this even during the Ages of the True and Semblance Dharmas, not to mention the Latter Age of Degeneration! I, Nichiren, incurred the displeasure* of the Kamakura Shogunate for the sake of the *Lotus Sutra*. This is the greatest happiness that ever happened to me because it is like exchanging worthless pieces of tile and stones for pieces of gold and silver.

I, however, have one thing to deplore. The *Sutra of the Benevolent King* predicts: "Seven calamities will surely overtake a country when a saint leaves the country." The seven calamities include a severe drought, war and disorder among others. The *Sutra of the Golden Splendor* preaches: "When a king respects evil persons and foolishly punishes virtuous good persons, the movement of the sun, the moon and stars is disturbed, or unseasonable wind and rain will occur." Who are the evil persons whom a king respects in this scripture? They are priests such as Dōryū, Ryōkan, and Shōichi mentioned above. Who are the virtuous persons whom the king punishes? They are those who were expelled from their monasteries many times as stated in Chapter 13 of the *Lotus Sutra*, Encouragement for Keeping This Sutra. Irregularity in the movement of heavenly bodies refers to the strange phenomena in the sky and natural calamities on earth* frequently occurring in the last 20 years or so. If these passages in the *Sutra of the Benevolent King* and the *Sutra of the Golden Splendor* are true, banishment of me, Nichiren, who justly propagates the *Lotus Sutra*, is an omen of national destruction. Besides, having considered this before I was exiled, I submitted to the Shogunate the *Risshō Ankoku-ron, Treatise on Spreading Peace Throughout the Country by Establishing the True Dharma*. Therefore, there should be no doubt about it. It is truly deplorable that by tormenting the one who practices the *Lotus Sutra* this country will be overtaken by misfortunes leading to national destruction.

It has been 2,222 years since the Buddha entered Nirvana. The Dharma was spread by such bodhisattvas as Nāgārjuna and Vasubandhu as messengers of the Buddha in India during the 1,000-year Age of the True Dharma. The teachings they spread were not those of true Mahayana but of Hinayana and provisional Mahayana. Grand Master T'ien-t'ai appeared in China during the Age of the Semblance Dharma, overcoming evil doctrines of three Southern masters and seven Northern masters and clarifying the *Lotus Sutra* as supreme of all Buddhist sutras. In comparative superiority of sutras, T'ien-t'ai established a new theory of the five-period teaching, in which he made it clear that the *Lotus Sutra* was the complete and perfect teaching. In the practice of contemplation, he proved that 3,000 existences are contained in the momentary mind of an ordinary, unenlightened person. So the people in China called him a "Little Buddha" and respected him. However, of the threefold True Dharma of the *Lotus Sutra*, he spread the two perfect Dharmas of wisdom and meditation without teaching the perfect precepts.

Grand Master Dengyō appeared in Japan about 1,800 years after the death of the Buddha. He criticized the wrong interpretations of Buddhism by the six schools of Nara transmitted over 200 years from when Buddhism was introduced to Japan during the reign of Emperor Kimmei. Moreover, for the first time he spread the perfect precepts which T'ien-t'ai did not. These are the perfect and sudden grand precepts of the Enryakuji Temple on Mt. Hiei.

During more than 2,000 years after the death of the Buddha, Buddhism spread through India, China and Japan, establishing numerous temples in these countries. However, no temples have ever been built for Śākyamuni Buddha, who had attained Enlightenment in the eternal past as revealed in the essential section of the *Lotus Sutra*, and no one has ever spread the great Dharma consisting of the five characters of *Myō, Hō, Ren, Ge,* and *Kyō*, which was conferred on the bodhisattvas who had emerged from underground, disciples of the Eternal and Original Buddha Śākyamuni. Though the sutra says that it will be propagated in the beginning of the Latter Age of Degeneration, it has not been spread in any country. Does it mean that the right time* for its propagation has not come? Or, is it that the ability* of people to understand has not been ripe? The Buddha preaches in the 23rd chapter of the *Lotus Sutra*, Previous Life of Medicine-King Bodhisattva, "Propagate this sutra throughout the whole world in the last 500 year period after My extinction lest it be lost." Grand Master T'ien-t'ai explains this in his *Words and Phrases of the Lotus Sutra:* "The Wonderful Dharma will spread afar since the last 500 year period." Grand Master Dengyō says in his *Treatise on the Protection of the Nation:* "Ages of the True Dharma and Semblance Dharma are passing away progressively, and the Latter Age of Degeneration, when the One Vehicle teaching of the *Lotus Sutra* would be spread, is near at hand."

These passages in the sutra and commentaries point out the beginning of the Latter Age as the era in which the *Lotus Sutra* will be spread. A Brahman in India prophesied, "The Buddha will appear 100 years later" and a Confucian scholar in China predicted, "Buddhism will be introduced into China 1,000 years later." Even these prophecies made by ordinary persons proved to be true, how much more so with the holy prophecies of Grand Masters T'ien-t'ai and Dengyō? How much more so with the golden words of Śākyamuni Buddha and the Buddha of Many Treasures! There is absolutely no doubt that the time will come when the *Lotus Sutra* will spread, and Lord Śākyamuni Buddha and the five characters of the Wonderful Dharma will be received all over the world.

It may be, however, that even those who have often heard of such important teachings of Buddhism as this from me, Nichiren, abandon the faith when they see me encountering this severe persecution. I was thankful to hear that though you had only a few opportunities, a few hours each, to hear about these teachings, you have kept your faith in the *Lotus Sutra*. This must be your destiny from a previous life.

Grand Master Miao-lê states in his *Annotations on the Words and Phrases of the Lotus Sutra*: "If one in the Latter Age of Degeneration momentarily hears the *Lotus Sutra* and has faith in it, it is because he established a close relation to the sutra by listening to it in the past." He also says in the *Annotations on the Great Concentration and Insight*: "Without the wonderful relations established in the past, one who was born not in the lifetime of the Buddha or the Age of the True Dharma but toward the end of the Age of the Semblance Dharma cannot accept the *Lotus Sutra*, the supreme sutra of all sutras." The 18th chapter of the *Lotus Sutra*, Merits of a Person who Rejoices at Hearing This Sutra, preaches: "A person who served 10 trillion Buddhas in the past can be born as a human being and can have faith in the *Lotus Sutra*." The *Nirvana Sutra* also says that a person who was born in this evil world after the Buddha's extinction and can believe the *Nirvana Sutra* is the person who served Buddhas as numerous as the sands of the Hiraṇyavatī River in the past.

Ajātaśatru was an evil man who killed his father and imprisoned his own mother, but when the Buddha preached the *Nirvana Sutra*, the king attended His lecture and had a chance to hear Him preach the *Lotus Sutra*. Then not only was the malignant tumor that had developed in the body of the king due to the sin of killing his own father cured instantly, but also he, who was about to die, was able to live 40 more years. Eventually the king, who did not believe the Buddha Dharma, was converted by the Buddha reaching the stage of *shojū* in the bodhisattva way.

Devadatta, a cousin of the Buddha, and who injured the Buddha, was the worst man in the world. Devadatta, therefore, is abandoned as impossible to be saved in sutras preached before the *Lotus Sutra*. The 12th chapter of the *Lotus Sutra*, Devadatta, guarantees him to be Heavenly King Buddha in the future.

Contemplating these, I am convinced that ordinary people in the Latter Age of Degeneration commit sins more or less. Whether or not such a one can reach Buddhahood depends on not how serious their sin is but whether or not they believe in the *Lotus Sutra*. As a member of a warrior family you are always faced with killing people, which is firmly prohibited in Buddhism. It makes you an evil man. If you cannot leave your family and escape from society, how can you avoid falling into the three evil realms such as hell? You had best think about this carefully.

The *Lotus Sutra* preaches that ordinary people with sins and illusions can attain Buddhahood. Therefore you too can attain Buddhahood without changing yourself as an ordinary and evil person. T'ien-t'ai says in his *Words and Phrases of the Lotus Sutra*, "Sutras preached before the *Lotus Sutra* guarantee that virtuous persons obtain Buddhahood but not evil persons. However, both virtuous and evil persons are guaranteed to attain Buddhahood in the *Lotus Sutra*." Miao-lê states in his *Annotations on the Words and Phrases of the Lotus Sutra*, "The perfect teaching of the *Lotus Sutra* explains that the reverse can be the order as it is, but the other three teachings [*piṭaka*, common and distinct teachings] maintain that the reverse is the reverse, and the order is the order, clearly separating the virtuous from the evil." You should think hard of their meaning.

I would like to write about the question of whether or not anyone has ever attained enlightenment through sutras other than the *Lotus Sutra*, but I am afraid it should be told only to those who have basic knowledge of Buddhism such as names and numbers of doctrines. Nevertheless, there are some disciples of mine, whom I taught broadly about it. You may call them to inquire broadly about it. Then I will write to you again.

Yours truly,

Nichiren
(signature)

On the third day of the eighth month
in the 10th year of the Bun'ei Period

Response to Lord Nambu Rokurō Saburō
in the Province of Kai

My disciples such as Chikugo-bō, Ben-ajari, and Daishin-ajari are in Kamakura. Could you get in touch with them asking questions courteously? I already told them about the teachings of importance in my mind. They more or less understand the supreme doctrine of the *Lotus Sutra* that has not yet spread in Japan so they can explain what you want to learn.

Shōjō Daijō Fumbetsu-shō (ST 136)

Introduction

Pieces of the original manuscript of this letter, which Nichiren Shōnin sent to Toki Jōnin from Sado in 1273, still exist at the Tanjōji Temple and other places.

Since the last part of the letter is missing, there are a few differing opinions regarding the date the letter was written and to whom it was addressed.

In this letter Nichiren first explains the differences between the essential *(hommon)* teaching of the *Lotus Sutra* and teachings of all other sutras, Mahayana as well as Hinayana, declaring that all sutras are Hinayana in teaching except Chapter 16 of the *Lotus Sutra*, The Duration of the Life of the Tathāgata.

Secondly, he maintains that the doctrines of the attainment of Buddhahood by Two Vehicles, *śrāvaka* and *pratyekabuddha,* the Eternal Buddha and the "3,000 existences contained in one thought" are revealed only in the *Lotus Sutra,* and that therefore, the *hommon* section of the *Lotus Sutra* is the only true Mahayana teaching while all other sutras are Hinayana and not able to lead living beings to Enlightenment.

Thirdly, discussing the process of leading living beings to Enlightenment, which is the concrete reality of the seed of Buddhahood in "3,000 existences contained in one thought," Nichiren preaches that as the seeds planted in the past lose their chance to sprout in the Latter Age of Degeneration, bodhisattva disciples of the Original Buddha must appear in this world and plant the seed of Buddhahood for those who committed rebellious sins and slandered the True Dharma.

Lastly, Nichiren harshly criticizes the other sects for slandering the *Lotus Sutra,* causing themselves to fall into hell, destroying Buddhism and ruining the nation.

In this thesis, Nichiren concludes that only the doctrine expounded in the *hommon* chapters of the *Lotus Sutra* is Mahayana while others are all Hinayana, explaining in detail what is said in his *Kanjin Honzon-shō* regarding the differences between Hinayana and Mahayana sutras.

The Differences between Hinayana and Mahayana Teachings

The size of an object is not fixed. When a one centimeter object is compared to a one meter object, we say the former is smaller. Compared to a 1.5 meter man, a two or 2.5 meter man is taller. It is the same with Buddhism. Compared to non-Buddhist teachings,* all the teachings of the Hinayana and Mahayana schools can be called the Mahayana or Greater Vehicle. Grand Master Chang-an of China meant the same thing when he talked about the "gradual spread of the Great Dharma eastward" in his Introduction to the *Fa-hua Hsüan-i, Profound Meaning of the Lotus Sutra*. Grand Master Miao-lê of China interpreted the Great Dharma as Buddhism in general.

The four Āgama sutras* [Chinese translations of the Long, Medium, Additional and Miscellaneous Āgama Sutras] and all other Hinayana sutras preached at Deer Park for a period of 12 years are called the Hinayana or Lesser Vehicle sutras compared to all the successively revealed Mahayana or Greater Vehicle sutras. Of the Greater Vehicle sutras, those of inferior quality are considered Hinayana. There is a phrase in the Mahayana *Flower Garland Sutra** which reads, "Yearning for other Lesser Dharmas." Grand Master T'ien-t'ai interprets this in his *Fa-hua Wên-chü, Words and Phrases of the Lotus Sutra*, that "The Lesser Dharma here does not signify the ordinary Hinayana sutras. It refers to the lower of the 52 ranks of bodhisattvas [10 stages of security, 10 stages of profiting others and 10 stages of the transfer of merit to others] compared to the higher 10 stages of developing Buddha wisdom." Regarding the statement in the Expedients chapter* of the *Lotus Sutra,** fascicle one, "If I lead even a single person by the Lesser Vehicle, I shall be accused of stinginess," Grand Masters T'ien-t'ai and Miao-lê* definitely stated that the Lesser Vehicle sutras here include not only the Āgama sutras but also the *bekkyō,* distinct teachings, of the *Flower Garland Sutra* and the *tsūgyō,* common teachings, of both the Hōdō and Hannya sutras.* Moreover, T'ien-t'ai in his *Fa-hua Hsüan-i, Profound Meaning of the Lotus Sutra,** fascicle one, says that, "First expounding the Hinayana then merging them into the Mahayana" means to mix and merge the teachings of gradual and instantaneous enlightenment. Grand Master Chishō (Enchin) explains this: "Various provisional and true Mahayana sutras of the Buddha's Four Ways of Teaching, or Eight Teachings from the *Flower Garland Sutra* to the *Wisdom Sutra* are all *zengyō* and *tongyō,* teachings of gradual and instantaneous enlightenment, and the clarification of those Eight Teachings signifies merging them into the Great Perfect Teachings."

T'ien-t'ai explains the meaning of a small Dharma as seen in Chapter 16 of the *Lotus Sutra,* The Duration of the Life of the Tathāgata, "some people of small virtue and much defilement sought the teachings of a small Dharma." This does not indicate the Lesser Vehicle sutras such as Āgama sutras, T'ien-t'ai declares, nor the Great Vehicle sutras such as the *Flower Garland Sutra*. It does denote all sutras without the teachings of the Eternal Buddha including the first 14 chapters of the *Lotus Sutra*, the *Flower Garland Sutra*, the Hōdō sutras and the *Wisdom Sutra*. T'ien-t'ai further demonstrates that Lord Buddhas such as the Dharma-bodied Vairocana, Reward-bodied Vairocana and Great Sun Buddhas* of the *Flower Garland Sutra* and other sutras are all minor Buddhas [when compared to the Eternal Buddha].

According to this explanation by T'ien-t'ai, since the essential section of the *Lotus Sutra* is the essence of Buddhism, all other sutras, be they Mahayana or Hinayana, provisional or true, and exoteric or esoteric, such as the *Nirvana Sutra* and *Great Sun Buddha Sutra*, are Lesser Vehicle teachings. Of the eight Buddhist schools, not only are the Kusha,* Jōjitsu,* Ritsu* sects included in the Lesser Vehicle, but so are the Mahayana sects of Kegon,* Hossō,* Sanron* and Shingon.* Only the doctrines of the Tendai sect* comprise the Great Vehicle. It is because no sutras other than the *Lotus Sutra* reveal the great Dharmas of attaining enlightenment by persons of the Two Vehicles [*śrāvaka* and *pratyekabuddha*] and the concept of the Eternal Buddha. For instance, we do not call a person strong if he is merely able to hold on to a 30 or 60 kilogram rock. However, one who can carry a 300 kilogram rock is considered strong. The Greater Vehicle doctrines, such as the *Flower Garland Sutra,* which purports the perfect harmony of all existences in the Dharma realm and 41 stages of development in studying it; the *Wisdom Sutra,* which preaches the identity between the realm of Buddhahood and the nine other realms, 18 meanings of voidness and the 10 stages of the development [such as *kenne-ji*]; the *Bodhisattva Necklace Sutra,** which teaches the 52 Bodhisattva stages; the *Sutra of the Benevolent King,** which explains the 51 Bodhisattva stages; the *Medicine Master Sutra,** which illustrates the 12 great vows; the *Two-Fascicle Sutra,** which preaches the 48 vows; and the *Great Sun Buddha Sutra,* which teaches that mantra and *mudrā,** are all both great and secret Dharmas compared to Hinayana sutras. However, all of these sutras are still lesser Dharmas when compared to the *Lotus Sutra*, which reveals the attainment of enlightenment by the men of the Two Vehicles and the concept of the Eternal Buddha. It is the same as comparing one or two meters to 10 or 20 meters.

The concepts of attaining enlightenment by the Two Vehicles and the Eternal Buddha are vital to the *Lotus Sutra*. Although these concepts can scarcely be found in other sutras, they are not at all uncommon in the *Lotus Sutra*. The doctrine of *ichinen sanzen,** or the "3,000 existences contained in one thought," is the rarest and the most miraculous. This theory is revealed neither in the *Flower Garland* nor *Great Sun Buddha Sutras*. Moreover, the founders of the eight

Buddhist sects, except for Grand Master T'ien-t'ai, did not even know its name. The great philosophers Nāgārjuna* and Vasubandhu* of India knew it, but locked this important Dharma jewel of *ichinen sanzen* deep within their hearts instead of writing it down for others to see.

The Uzu school [of followers of Hermit Kapila in ancient India] stole the teaching of the Three Virtues from Buddhism, and Hermit Kaṇada formulated his Six Phrases based on Buddhist ideas. Likewise, Ch'eng-kuan* of the Kegon sect and Śubhākarasiṃha of the Shingon sect stole the "3,000 existences contained in one thought" doctrine and incorporated it into their own sects through reinterpretation of the key words of their basic canons: "identity of the mind, the Buddha and the people" in the *Flower Garland Sutra,* and "reality of the mind" in the *Great Sun Buddha Sutra.* Nevertheless, they criticized the Tendai sect, saying it was inferior to their own. These two masters are not thieves in the common sense, but thieves of the Buddha Dharma. We must clarify this point.

Recent scholars of the Tendai sect and many other schools hold that only the *Lotus Sutra* preaches attaining enlightenment by persons of the Two Vehicles of *śrāvaka* and *pratyekabuddha* and the doctrine of the Eternal Buddha. I ask them in return:

> If you concede that only the *Lotus Sutra* expounds the Dharma of attaining enlightenment by persons of the Two Vehicles and the concept of the Eternal Buddha, is not the *Lotus Sutra* the most wonderful? If the Dharma of attaining enlightenment by the Two Vehicles was not revealed in any sutras, then how could the Buddha's disciples attain Buddhahood, namely the 10 great disciples of the Buddha including Kāśyapa,* who excelled in the *dhuta* [way of frugal living], Śāriputra,* who was the wisest of all the Buddha's disciples, Maudgalyāyana,* who possessed supernatural powers, or the other disciples, the 1200 *arhats* [saints who have freed themselves from all craving and the cycle of rebirth], the twelve thousand *śrāvaka* or hearers of the Buddha's teachings and the countless people in the realms of the Two Vehicles [of *śrāvaka* and *pratyekabuddha*]? All these people, without encountering the *Lotus Sutra,* would not have been able to attain Buddhahood from the eternal past, nor would they ever be able to. For one who practices Buddhism, wouldn't this be an enormous defect? What would happen to those who supported such disciples of Buddha as Kāśyapa, the King of the Brahma Heaven,* Indra,* the four kinds of devotees, the eight kinds of beings who protect Buddhism besides monks and nuns, if the people of the Two Vehicles could not attain enlightenment?

If the concept of the Eternal Buddha [enlightened since the infinite past] had not been expounded in the *Lotus Sutra,* then all the Buddhas throughout the past, present and future would have been mere momentary Buddhas, due to the principle of impermanence. It would be as futile as having no sun or moon even though there are many stars in the sky, or as plants trying to grow in the ground without soil. This conclusion has been based on your recognition, however, of the supremacy of the *Lotus Sutra,* which teaches the concept of the Eternal Buddha and enlightenment of all people of the Two Vehicles [of *śrāvaka* and *pratyekabuddha*].

To say the truth, if attaining enlightenment by the people of Two Vehicles had not been revealed, then all beings in the nine realms would never be able to become Buddhas. The essence of the *Lotus Sutra,* as a reasonable Dharma, is that each sentient being in the 10 realms contains the 10 realms within itself. For example, each person is composed of the four elements of earth, water, heat and air. If one of these elements is missing, there will be no human being. It is true that not only human beings but also all other beings and non-beings such as grasses, plants and dust particles throughout the 10 realms each possesses the 10 realms. If the beings in the realms of Two Vehicles are not able to become Buddhas, then none of the eight realms can become Buddhas either. This is like nine siblings whose parents are still alive. If two of the nine are found to be inferior, the other seven will also be considered inferior. The Buddha and the *Lotus Sutra* are like parents and the people in the nine realms are like their real children. Therefore, if the people of the Two Vehicles of *śrāvaka* and *pratyekabuddha* will never be able to attain Buddhahood, how then could the bodhisattvas and six other ordinary children become Buddhas? There is no doubt about this because Śākyamuni Buddha preaches in the *Lotus Sutra,* "This triple world is My domain, in which all living beings are My children. There are many sufferings in this world…, and only I can save all beings."

All bodhisattvas make the Four Great Vows.* If a bodhisattva does not accomplish the first vow, how can he attain the fourth? All sutras preached prior to the *Lotus Sutra* state that bodhisattvas and ordinary people are able to attain Buddhahood, but never the people of the Two Vehicles. Thinking that they can become Buddhas while the people of the Two Vehicles cannot, wise bodhisattvas and ignorant people throughout the six realms felt happy. The people of the Two Vehicles plunged into grief and thought, "we should not have entered the Buddha way." Now in the *Lotus Sutra,* they are guaranteed to attain Buddhahood, so not only the people of the Two Vehicles, but also the people of the nine realms will all become Buddhas. Upon hearing this Dharma, bodhisattvas realized their misunderstanding. As stated in the pre-Lotus sutras, if the people of the Two Vehicles cannot attain Buddhahood, then the Four Great Vows cannot be accomplished. Consequently, bodhisattvas would also be unable to become Buddhas. When it was preached that people of the Two Vehicles were unable to attain Buddhahood, they should not have been left alone in sadness. Bodhisattvas should have joined them in grief.

Considering that the concept of the Eternal Buddha was first noted in the Duration of the Life of the Tathāgata* chapter, we realize not only that the concept was not revealed in the sutras prior to the *Lotus Sutra*, but also Śākyamuni Buddha proves Himself the greatest liar in the world [because of the contradiction between the *Lotus Sutra* and other sutras]. This is because the *Flower Garland Sutra* [considered peerless among the pre-Lotus sutras] declares, "After My ascetic practice, I finally attained enlightenment;" and in the *Great Sun Buddha Sutra*, it reads, "I sat under the bodhi tree and attained enlightenment in the past." In addition to this, the *Sutra of Infinite Meaning*, which "sincerely casts away all expedients and reveals the profoundest truth," states that "I sat at the place of enlightenment for the first time." Moreover, even chapter two in the first half [theoretical section] of the *Lotus Sutra* states, "I first sat at the place of enlightenment, then attained enlightenment." When comparing these words to the statement in The Duration of the Life of the Tathāgata chapter of the *Lotus Sutra*: "To tell the truth, it has been many hundreds of thousands of billions of *nayuta* of *kalpa* since I became the Buddha," there appears to be an immense discrepancy. There are huge differences in the sayings of the Buddha Himself, who seems to have been an enormous liar. How can the six senses contained in His eyes, ears, nose, tongue, body and mind be real? A house built on ice will surely melt away in spring. The reflection of the moon on the water's surface does not possess a true entity. Thus, attaining Buddhahood and rebirth in the Pure Land expounded during the pre-Lotus sutras are like the images of stars and the moon reflected on water. They are like the shadow that follows a body. From this viewpoint of the Eternal Buddha revealed in the Duration of the Life of the Tathāgata chapter, attaining enlightenment and becoming Buddhas preached in sutras prior to the *Lotus Sutra* are mere words without reality.

At the practice hall on Mt. Ta-su, Grand Master T'ien-t'ai* alone formulated the doctrines of attaining enlightenment by people of the Two Vehicles and the Eternal Buddha as well as the "3,000 existences contained in one thought." As a result, he authored 10 volumes each of *Fa-hua Hsüan-i, Profound Meaning of the Lotus Sutra,* *Fa-Hua Wên-chü, Words and Phrases of the Lotus Sutra,* and *Mo-ho Chih-kuan, Great Concentration and Insight.** He explained in these works that the doctrines of attaining enlightenment by people of the Two Vehicles and the Eternal Buddha are not expounded in any sutras other than the *Lotus Sutra*. In those days, 10 masters in Northern and Southern China, confused with the comparative superiority of various Buddhist doctrines, ended up establishing their own particular denominations such as the three-period teaching,* four-period or five-period, those of four sects, five sects, or six sects, single sound teaching, teachings of a half and a full, three teachings, and four teachings. In order to point out their mistakes, T'ien-t'ai clarified how the *Lotus Sutra* is superior through the doctrines of attaining enlightenment by people of the Two Vehicles and the Eternal Buddha. T'ien-t'ai did not mean, however, that people in the other seven realms will be allowed to become Buddhas.

Later, the Kegon sect classified Buddha's lifetime teachings in the Five Teachings* in the order of profundity. The Hossō sect divided the teachings into the Three-period Teaching.* Moreover, the Shingon sect classified the teaching by the doctrines of the Exoteric and Esoteric, the Five Divisions and the Ten Stages of Mind in addition to dividing the Buddha's teachings by the doctrine of the Four Phrases in the *Lecture and Explanation of the Great Sun Buddha Sutra*. However, these doctrines are all wrong, worse than the doctrines of the 10 masters of Northern and Southern China.* Since these doctrines are of the Shingon sect and not of the Tendai-Lotus sect, let me set them aside. More than a few scholars in our own school [of Tendai-Lotus] misunderstand the explanations of Grand Masters T'ien-t'ai, Miao-lê and Dengyō, insisting that although the doctrines of attaining enlightenment by men of the Two Vehicles [*śrāvaka* and *pratyekabuddha*] and the Eternal Buddha are not revealed in the sutras prior to the *Lotus Sutra*, people in the seven other realms are indeed able to attain Buddhahood. Those who embraced this view are increasing in number and spreading throughout Japan. This was taken advantage of by other sects, resulting in the decline of the Tendai-Lotus school. These Tendai scholars are as foolish as a dragonfly caught in a spider's web or a thirsty deer chasing heat waves taking them for water. Other examples of such idiocy are Minamoto no Yoritomo who had his own brother, Yoshitsune, killed in order to destroy Fujiwara no Yasuhira, Taira no Kiyomori who killed his own uncle, Heimanosuke Tadamasa, who tried to become the ruler of Japan by defeating the Minamoto Clan, or Minamoto Yoshitomo who was tricked into killing his own father, Tameyoshi. These are true examples of stupidity.

Scholars of the Tendai-Lotus sect today are as foolish as these people. In spite of T'ien-t'ai's explanation that no sutra except the *Lotus Sutra* revealed the doctrines of attaining enlightenment by people of the Two Vehicles and the Eternal Buddha, they believe that the other sutras reveal the enlightenment of bodhisattvas and ordinary men, and that since they do not belong to either of the Two Vehicles, they are able to attain Buddhahood through pre-Lotus sutras. Especially, as the doctrine of the Nine Grades of Rebirth in the Western Pure Land disclosed in the *Sutra of Meditation on the Buddha of Infinite Life* is easy to accomplish, they feel they can attain enlightenment if they cast away the *Lotus Sutra* and chant the name of the Buddha of Infinite Life* while wishing to be reborn in the Pure Land and see the Buddha of Infinite Life attended by Avalokiteśvara* and Mahāsthāmaprāpta* Bodhisattvas. Beginning with people in the Tendai sect today scholars of various Buddhist schools all are thinking this way.

To tell the truth, however, without the power of the *Lotus Sutra*, it is impossible for any living being to attain Buddhahood, break through the six lower realms and be reborn in any of the Pure Lands of Buddhas throughout the universe. It is the same as how a Japanese person who wishes to enter the Chinese Imperial Palace must first receive permission from the Japanese sovereign. You must rely on the power of the *Lotus Sutra* in order to leave this Sahā World to enter a Pure Land. For example, if a woman, whether she be an ordinary woman or a daughter of the Imperial Regent, bears a king's child, that child will someday become a king. On the other hand, if a daughter of a king bears a vassal's child, that child can never become a king. Accordingly all living beings including bodhisattvas, men of the Two Vehicles, human beings, heavenly beings and animals who will be reborn in Pure Lands throughout the universe do so as royal children of the *Lotus Sutra*. It is because children of the *Lotus Sutra* are all able to become Buddhas. The Āgama sutras* are like an ordinary woman bearing a child of an ordinary man. The Kegon, Hōdō and Hannya sutras are the same as a vassal woman married to a vassal. Bodhisattvas who belong to the perfect teachings of the *Flower Garland Sutra*, Hōdō sutras, the *Wisdom Sutra* and the *Great Sun Buddha Sutra* are the same as a noble woman married to a vassal. None of these are doctrines enabling one to be born in the Pure Land.

In the periods before the *Lotus Sutra* was expounded, some people were able to leave the cycle of the six realms upon listening to sutras such as the *Flower Garland Sutra*, Āgama sutras, Hōdō sutras, and *Wisdom Sutra*, but it was not due to the merit of those sutras. It was because in their previous lives they had planted the seeds of the *Lotus Sutra* in themselves, which sprouted upon listening to the pre-Lotus sutras before the *Lotus Sutra* was preached. It is like a *pratyekabuddha*, born into a world without the Buddha, realizing the law of impermanence by watching falling leaves, or a filial person being born in heaven. Watching the falling leaves and discharging filial duties are not the direct cause for attaining enlightenment or being born in the Brahma Heaven, but they are indirect causes which induce the seeds planted in the past to germinate, causing one to be born in heaven or attain the law of impermanence. For, if a person in his past lives had not reached the position of the Three Wise or the Four Virtuous of the Lesser Vehicle teachings, nor had he practiced filial duties, he cannot become a *pratyekabuddha* in this life by just watching the falling leaves, nor can he be born in heaven. Those who had not planted the seed of the *Lotus Sutra* in the past cannot even reach the initial steps toward enlightenment even if they attend the lectures on the *Flower Garland Sutra*. He cannot quench the illusions of thought and desire even though he listens to the Āgama sutras revealed at the Deer Park. He cannot be reborn in the Pure Land even if he listens to the *Sutra of Meditation on the Buddha of Infinite Life*. Furthermore, he may be able to ascend to the rank of a wise man of the Mahayana and Hinayana teachings, but not any higher. Listening to the *Lotus Sutra* and planting the seeds of Buddhahood in the fields of their minds for the first time, some of these people are able to ascend to the initial ranks of bodhisattvas in this lifetime, while others do not attain Buddhahood until they listen to the *Nirvana Sutra*,* or in future lives after the death of the Buddha.

Among people who heard the *Lotus Sutra* during their past lives, depending on the closeness of their relationship to it, some ascend to the initial steps toward enlightenment with the contributing cause of the *Flower Garland Sutra*, while others quench the illusions of thought and desire to become men of the Two Vehicles with the contributing cause of the Āgama sutras. Still others are born in the Pure Land with the contributing cause of practicing such sutras as the *Sutra of Meditation on the Buddha of Infinite Life*. You should also realize by now that it is the same with those who attain nirvana through the contributing cause of the Hōdō and Hannya sutras.

Their attaining nirvana, however, is not caused by the power of those sutras, but solely by the strength of the *Lotus Sutra*. Suppose there is a common or a noble woman who conceived a child by the king, people who do not know who the real father of the child is may consider the child to be a son of a commoner or a nobleman. They will all realize, however, that the baby is a child of the king when the king himself declares the truth. By the same token, when the *Lotus Sutra* informs you of those who are able to leave the triple world of birth and death or escape the cycle of the six realms and ascend the four realms through the pre-Lotus sutras, it is all because the seeds of the *Lotus Sutra* have been implanted within their lives throughout previous existences. Of the people who had planted the seed during their previous lives, those who are unresponsive and not able to attain nirvana through the pre-Lotus sutras are able to attain enlightenment through the *Lotus Sutra* during this lifetime. It is like a crown prince who was born by the queen but was raised by a wet nurse. The nurse is equivalent to the sutras prior to the *Lotus Sutra*.

During the Age of the True Dharma or one thousand years following the Buddha Śākyamuni's death, there were quite a number of people, though not quite as many as during the lifetime of the Buddha, who had planted the seeds of the *Lotus Sutra* during their previous lives but were unable to attain Buddhahood through the *Lotus* and *Nirvana Sutras*.* There were also those who planted the seed of the *Lotus Sutra* in this life. Even after the Buddha's demise, since the *Lotus Sutra* existed, there were countless people who changed faiths from non-Buddhist religions* to the Lesser Vehicle, then to Provisional Mahayana, and then to the True Mahayana: the *Lotus Sutra*. Bodhisattvas Nāgārjuna and Asaṅga* and Master Commentator Vasubandhu* are good examples of such people.

Throughout the 1,000-year Age of the Semblance Dharma, though not as many as in the Age of the True Dharma, there were a few people who had planted the seeds of the *Lotus Sutra* in their past lives. However, as the merit of Buddhism gradually decreased, sectarian prejudices grew as hard as a rock and their pompous attitudes became taller than mountains. Toward the end of the Age of the Semblance Dharma contentious engagements continued without pause. Consequently, countless people fell into the Hell of Incessant Suffering due to their slandering the True Dharma, not because of worldly crimes.

Today, over 200 years after entering the Latter Age of Degeneration, there exists not a single person who planted the seed of the *Lotus Sutra* in previous lives or at the time of the Buddha's preaching on Mt. Sacred Eagle. There may be a few who planted the seed, but this nation is full of consummated villains among the lay people and slanderers of the True Dharma among the priests and nuns. Those who have planted the seeds of Buddhahood are like a small amount of water trying to douse a great fire, a small fire in a great body of water, a drop of fresh water in the vast ocean or a small amount of gold in the earth. There are just too many slanderers of the True Dharma. These people did not possess virtue in either their past or present life.

The Pure Land sect makes people crazy by inciting them to chant the name of the Buddha of Infinite Life and casting away the *Lotus Sutra*, committing the crime of turning against the superior and slandering the subordinate. The Zen sect insists on the transmission of Buddhist doctrines without a sutra.* This school advocates that there is truth beyond the sutras and arrogantly despises the Buddha Dharma. Some people established the Hossō, Sanron and Kegon sects, regarding the *Lotus Sutra* as inferior. The Shingon or Great Sun sect considers the *Lotus Sutra* to be exoteric Buddhism revealed by the historical Buddha, which cannot be compared to the esoteric doctrines of Shingon preached by the Dharma-bodied Great Sun Buddha.

Therefore, people naturally become confused due to the vast array of doctrines while some become bewildered due to mistaken masters. Still, there are some who believe that the false teachings of the founders of denominations, commentators in India, or scholars in China and Japan are all true. Furthermore, possessed by evil and demons, some people take mistaken doctrines for the truth and propagate them. Some people who have merely a partial knowledge of Hinayana Buddhism arrogantly criticize the Great Dharma of Mahayana Buddhism. In order to practice their own meager doctrines, some tried to take over temples that propagate the great secret Dharma. Possessed by the so-called compassionate demons, some monks with three robes and an alms-bowl,* while practicing the doctrines of Hinayana Buddhism, consider the high priests of Mt. Hiei* to be heretics and evil, even though they themselves did not realize that their own teachings differed only slightly from theirs.

With this evil point of view, these priests deceive and confuse the ruler of the nation, causing the sovereign not to devote himself to the True Dharma, bringing about the destruction of the nation. It is similar to the case of foolish kings, Chou Hsin of Yin and King Yu of Chou, who destroyed their countries by being infatuated by their beautiful and elegant consorts, Chieh Chi and Pao Szŭ. Thus, Shōichi,* Dōryū,* Ryōkan,* Dōami* and Nen-ami,* who call themselves Zen masters, precept masters and those who practice Pure Land, are like pigeons who eat their own droppings or beautiful Hsi Shih who deceived King Fu-ch'a of Wu in China. They deceive the Kamakura Shogunate with the worthless precepts of Hinayana Buddhism.

Gochū Shujō Gosho (ST 139)

Introduction

Written in the 10th year of the Bun'ei Period (1273), when Nichiren Shōnin was 51 years old, neither details of the contents of this letter nor its recipient are clear, because the beginning and ending portions of the letter are missing. Nichiren quotes a sentence from the third chapter of the *Lotus Sutra,* A Parable: "All living beings therein are My children;" and annotations of T'ien-t'ai and Miao-lê to explain that only Śākyamuni Buddha is completely equipped with the three virtues of the master, teacher and father. Nichiren insists, therefore, that all human beings in this Sahā World should embrace Him because they are all His children while other Buddhas such as the Buddha of Infinite Life do not possess the three virtues and they have no relation to the Sahā World.

People in the World Letter

Śākyamuni Buddha* preaches in Chapter Three of the *Lotus Sutra,* A Parable, "All living beings in this world are My children. There are many sufferings in this world, and only I can save all living beings." This explains that only Śākyamuni Buddha possesses the three virtues of master, teacher and parent, and other Buddhas such as the Buddha of Infinite Life* are not equipped with them. I have already said this many times before. However, be sure that the words "only I can" are not found in Hinayana sutras nor in any of the pre-Lotus Mahayana sutras, which resort to expedient means or do not reveal the truth to those whose capacities to understand are not sufficient. They are the golden words of Śākyamuni Buddha in the *Lotus Sutra,* validated by the Buddha of Many Treasures* and all other Buddhas from all the worlds throughout the universe.* They are, the edict of a wise ruler, the instructions of a sage, and the words of the sole wise Father teaching all the people, including Pure Land believers today. It would be most regrettable for us not to comply with the words of Śākyamuni Buddha with these three virtues, commit 20 rebellious sins, and to fall into the Hell of Incessant Suffering. This teaching expounded in the first half of the *Lotus Sutra** is called the theoretical teaching *(shakumon)*. As we go into the latter half [essential section] of the *Lotus Sutra,* we find doctrines becoming increasingly deeper.

According to the *shakumon* section of the *Lotus Sutra,* the people in this Saha World* have been closely related to Śākyamuni Buddha since 3,000 dust-particle *kalpa* ago, without any relations to other Buddhas such as the Buddha of Infinite Life. Chapter Seven of the *Lotus Sutra,* The Parable of A Magic City, states: "Those who listened to the teachers then have always been beside those Buddhas.... Destiny has made them meet the preaching of the *Lotus Sutra* now." This statement tells us that we, the people in this Sahā World, have never been in Pure Lands of the universe of 15 other Buddhas such as the Buddha of Infinite Life. Grand Master T'ien-t'ai states in his *Words and Phrases of the Lotus Sutra:*

> An old interpretation considers the Buddha of Infinite Life as the rich father in the parable of the father and son. However, this is incorrect, and today we do not consider the Buddha of Infinite Life as the wealthy father. The Western Pure Land of the Buddha of Infinite Life and this Sahā World of Śākyamuni Buddha each have a different Buddha and karmic relations. The Buddha of Infinite Life is not the Lord Buddha of this Sahā World, so he was never born to and died in this world. He never guided us in this world. There are no relationships formed between the Buddha of Infinite Life and us like that of a father and son. There are no words in the *Lotus Sutra* which state that the Buddha of Infinite Life is our lord, teacher or parent. If you really want to encounter the Buddha, you need to contemplate this with your eyes closed.

Grand Master Miao-lê explains this in his *Annotations on the Words and Phrases of the Lotus Sutra:* "Śākyamuni Buddha and the Buddha of Infinite Life have completely different karmic relationships to the people in their past lives, and the worlds they guided are completely different. By birth and in growing up, the Buddha of Infinite Life and the people in this Sahā World have no father-son relationship." From these statements of T'ien-t'ai and Miao-lê, I would think the Buddha of Infinite Life and other Buddhas in the world all over the universe are like stepfathers whereas Śākyamuni Buddha is a compassionate, real father. T'ien-t'ai wrote many works interpreting the *Lotus Sutra*. However, we should know this interpretation of his to be fundamental, and consider Śākyamuni Buddha as the lord of this Sahā World. We find that T'ien-t'ai sometimes praises the Buddha of Infinite Life depending on sutras he relies on. It is like Vasubandhu, a famous scholar of Mahayana Buddhism, who used to praise Āgama sutras.

Considered from the point of view of the second half of the *Lotus Sutra*, *hommon*, that is essential teachings, we are the real children of Śākyamuni Buddha since the eternal past, 500 dust-particle *kalpa* ago. However, we attach ourselves to worldly affairs and lose sight of the *Lotus Sutra*, stick to old Hinayana and provisional Mahayana Buddhism and discard the *Lotus Sutra*, adhere to the first half of the *Lotus Sutra (shakumon)* and forget about the second half *(hommon)*, expect too much from the sutras which will be preached and abandon the *Lotus Sutra*, or are thinking only of the Pure Lands in other worlds in the universe or the Buddha of Infinite Life's Pure Land of Bliss. Confused by evil monks of seven or eight schools of Buddhism, we have abandoned the *Lotus Sutra* and have been unable to see Śākyamuni Buddha with three virtues for as long as 500 dust-particle *kalpa*. The 22nd fascicle of the *Nirvana Sutra** preaches, "An evil elephant hurts only our body, but an evil teacher or friend destroys both our body and heart." Grand Master T'ien-t'ai says, " If we keep improper company, we may lose the true purpose, falling into evil realms."

Question: In the 23rd chapter, The Previous Life of Medicine-King Bodhisattva,* in the epilogue section of the *Lotus Sutra*, women are encouraged to practice the sutra wholeheartedly, so that they may be reborn in the Pure Land of the Buddha of Infinite Life upon death. What do you think about this?

Answer: The Buddha of Infinite Life in the Previous Life of Medicine-King Bodhisattva chapter is not the same as the Buddha of Infinite Life in the pre-Lotus sutras and in the first half of the *Lotus Sutra*. They merely have the same name. The *Sutra of Infinite Meaning, Muryōgi-kyō,* says, "Even though they have the same name, their meanings are different." Miao-lê says in his *Annotations on the Words and Phrases of the Lotus Sutra*, "Even though you find the name of the Buddha of Infinite Life in the *hommon* section of the *Lotus Sutra*, it does not at all mean the Buddha of Infinite Life mentioned in the *Sutra of Meditation on the Buddha of Infinite Life*." These should dispel all your doubts. After all, Bodhisattvas* who are advanced in practice may easily come to this Sahā World from Pure Lands in the universe and can also easily go back there.

Hokke Shuyō-shō (ST 145)

Introduction

It is believed that Nichiren wrote this treatise at Mt. Minobu in Bun'ei 11 (1274). The original manuscript is kept as a treasure at the Hokkekyōji Temple in Chiba, Japan. In the second month of the year, Nichiren was released from Sado Island and returned to Kamakura. On the eighth day of the fourth month, he was summoned by the Shogunate and questioned about when the Mongolians were expected to invade Japan and about his faith. Realizing they would not accept his advice, Nichiren withdrew to Mt. Minobu, where he wrote this treatise revealing the essential teachings of the Original Buddha Śākyamuni, instructing his followers that salvation for people in the Latter Age of Degeneration would become a reality through these essential teachings. In it, Nichiren reveals that the *Lotus Sutra* is the essence of all sutras, and that the Lord Śākyamuni Buddha is in the center of all Buddhas.

Pointing out the sins of being unfilial and slandering the True Dharma committed in other sutras and schools, Nichiren criticizes them. He also explains the five character *Odaimoku, Myō Hō Ren Ge Kyō,* as the great Dharma to save people in the Latter Age of Degeneration, and reveals the Three Secret Dharmas of the essential section *(hommon)* of the *Lotus Sutra: Honzon, Kaidan* and *Odaimoku.* Maintaining that the widespread false teachings of Buddhism are the cause of strange phenomena in the sky and natural calamities on earth, three disasters and seven calamities, Nichiren decisively concludes that the continuing disasters and persecutions of Nichiren are omens of the *Odaimoku* spreading widely, and Superior-Practice Bodhisattva appearing. So he declares that there is no doubt about the establishment of the Three Secret Dharmas, and the spread of *Myōhō Renge-kyō* far and wide all over the world.

Treatise on the Essence of the Lotus Sutra

As I contemplate, the sutras and commentaries on them transmitted to Japan from India via China are said to be more than 5,000 fascicles according to the K'ai-yüan Era Catalog of Buddhist Scriptures, or 7,000 fascicles according to the Chen-yüan Era Catalog of Buddhist Scriptures. From those sutras and commentaries, it is difficult for one to form one's own opinion about which is superior or inferior in quality, shallow or profound in doctrine, easy or hard to practice, or the order in which they were preached. When one tries to learn from scholars and doctrines of various sects, there are so many different opinions that one can hardly make a right judgement.

The Kegon sect* maintains that the *Flower Garland Sutra* is the most excellent of all sutras.* The Hossō sect* holds that the *Revealing the Profound and Secret Sutra** is the best. The Sanron sect* insists that the *Wisdom Sutra** is supreme. And the Shingon sect* states that the three principal sutras of the Great Sun Buddha [consisting of the *Great Sun Buddha Sutra,* the *Diamond Peak Sutra,* and the *Sutra on the Act of Perfection*] are primary. The Zen sect* says that either the *Entering Laṅkā Sutra,* or the *Heroic Valor Sutra* is the best, but at other times they insist on a special transmission of Dharma without words and letters.* The Pure Land sect* holds that the triple Pure Land sutras* are the most suitable to the ability of people to understand in the Latter Age of Degeneration. The Kusha,* Jōitsu* and Ritsu* sects declare that the four Āgama sutras and their commentaries and precepts were expounded by the Buddha, but Mahayana sutras such as the *Flower Garland Sutra* and the *Lotus Sutra** were expounded not by the Buddha but some non-Buddhists.* Others have other opinions.

The founders of those sects are Tu-shun,* Chih-yen,* Fa-tsang,* and Ch'eng-kuan* [of the Kegon sect], Hsüan-chuang,* and Tz'ŭ-ên* [of the Hossō sect], Chia-hsiang* and Tao-lang* [of the Sanron sect], Śubhākarasiṃha*, Vajrabodhi* and Amoghavajra* [of the Shingon sect], Tao-hsüan* and Chien-chên* [of the Ritsu sect], T'an-luan,* Tao-ch'o* and Shan-tao* [of the Pure Land sect], and Bodhidharma* and Hui-k'o [of the Zen sect]. They are all saints and wise, and are well versed in three stores *(tripiṭaka)* of sutras, precepts, and commentaries. Their wisdom is as bright as the sun and moon, and their virtue sways all the world. In addition, as they founded respective sects based on three stores and with firm proof, the entire nation from kings and ministers to the people firmly believe them. Even if a man who is lacking in knowledge criticizes them in these latter days, nobody puts credence in him. It is very regrettable, however, if you pick up only rubble and rocks when you are on a mountain of treasures, or gather poisonous *eraṇḍa* in a forest of fragrant sandalwood. So, no matter how harshly people condemn me, I will scrutinize their assertions to adopt or reject their doctrines. My disciples should carefully study their teachings and doctrines.

Some of these founders of Buddhist schools themselves refer to sutras and commentaries in the Old Translation [translated before the T'ang Period], without consulting those in New Translation. Others, on the contrary, read them in the New Translation only, abandoning the Old Translation. Or, attached to their own sectarian prejudices, some add notes to sutras and commentaries to suit themselves and leave them for posterity. They are as foolish as a man who keeps on watching the tree stump into which a rabbit crashed and died. In contrast a wise man, reminded of the true shape of the moon by the apparent roundness of a paper fan, abandons the false idea of a paper fan and grasps the truth of the moon.

Now, ignoring false ideas of later commentators in India and mainstream interpreters and annotators in China and Japan, I devotedly open the fundamental sutras and commentaries, and see that of all sutras expounded by the Buddha in 50 years, the most important teaching is expounded in the Teacher of the Dharma chapter of the *Lotus Sutra*,* declaring that of all sutras preached in the past, being preached at present, and to be preached in the future, the *Lotus Sutra* is supreme.

Scholars of other sects must have seen this statement in the Teacher of the Dharma chapter. However, they do not correct their false ideas because they are perplexed with similar statements in sutras they rely on, being attached to their masters' false ideas, or afraid of losing the support of the king and his ministers. Similar sentences are, for example, "This is the king of the sutras" in the *Sutra of the Golden Splendor.** "This is the most excellent of all sutras" in the *Sutra of the Pure Land of Mystic Glorification.** "Dharaṇī-piṭaka [a collection of mystic spells] is the most important" in the *Six Pāramitā Sutra*. "Enlightenment is to know the true character of mind" in the *Great Sun Buddha Sutra.** "This sutra is the most difficult to believe but the truth lies in it" in the *Flower Garland Sutra.** "There is no truth but the ultimate reality of all phenomena expounded in this sutra" in the *Wisdom Sutra.** "Wisdom *pāramitā* is of prime importance" in the *Great Wisdom Discourse.** Or "This doctrine of the *Nirvana Sutra* is superior to the *Lotus Sutra*" in the *Nirvana Discourse*. These are similar in meaning to the statement in the Teacher of the Dharma chapter of the *Lotus Sutra*: "Of all the sutras preached in the past, present and future, the *Lotus Sutra* is supreme."

These sutras, however, are the king of sutras compared to sutras expounded by such as the King of the Brahma Heaven, Indra and the Four Heavenly Kings, or compared to Hinayana sutras. They are supreme of all sutras when compared to such as the *Flower Garland Sutra* and *Śrīmālā-Sutra*. However, they are not the great king of sutras compared to all the sutras of Mahayana and Hinayana, expedient and true,* and exoteric and esoteric* teachings expounded by the

Buddha for 50 some years of His lifetime. In other words, you should know how superior or inferior something is according to the object of comparison. It is the same as knowing how strong a man is by the strength of the enemy he defeats.

Besides, superiority of those sutras is decided solely by Śākyamuni Buddha, and is not supported by the Buddha of Many Treasures and Buddhas in manifestation in the worlds throughout the universe as the *Lotus Sutra* is. Do not confuse a personal opinion of one Buddha with the public announcements in the *Lotus Sutra* verified by the Buddha of Many Treasures and the Buddhas in manifestation all over the universe.

Those sutras are either Hinayana sutras expounded for men of Two Vehicles and ordinary men, or Mahayana sutras expounded to such Bodhisattvas as Mañjuśrī,* Vimukti-candra* (Moon of Emancipation) and Vajrasattva* (Diamond-being), who practiced the bodhisattva way for themselves and others. They are not expounded, as is the *Lotus Sutra*, to original disciples of the Eternal Buddha Śākyamuni, bodhisattvas who sprang up from underground* such as Superior-Practice.

Comparing the *Lotus Sutra* to all other sutras, we can list 20 points to prove that the *Lotus Sutra* exceeds all other sutras preached in the lifetime of the Buddha. Of the 20, two are most important. They are the "two doctrines of Three and Five." "Three" means the Buddha's act of teaching for over three thousand dust-particle *kalpa*, expounded in Chapter Seven of the *Lotus Sutra*, The Parable of a Magic City. Sutras expounded before the *Lotus Sutra* state that the length of the period when the Buddha practiced the Bodhisattva way was either three *asaṃkhya kalpa*, a long period exceeding a dust-particle *kalpa*, or innumerable *kalpa*. In those pre-Lotus sutras, the great King of the Brahma Heaven claims to have been the ruler of the Sahā World for 29 *kalpa*. So do other beings such as the King of Devils in the Sixth Heaven, Indra* and Four Heavenly Kings,* making it unclear who began ruling the Sahā World first, Śākyamuni Buddha or one of those heavenly beings. However, since Śākyamuni defeated devils by pointing His finger up toward the sky, the great King of the Brahma Heaven bowed to the Buddha, the King of Devils put his hands together in *gasshō*, and people of the triple world [realms of desire, form and non-form] all took refuge in the Buddha.

When we compare Śākyamuni Buddha in the *Lotus Sutra* to Buddhas in other sutras with respect to the period of practicing the Bodhisattva way and saving people, other Buddhas' length of practice is said to have been three *asaṃkhya kalpa* or five *kalpa*, while Śākyamuni Buddha has been a great Bodhisattva planting the seed of enlightenment in all living beings in the Sahā World since 3,000 dust-particle *kalpa* ago according to the Parable of a Magic City chapter of the *Lotus Sutra*. Therefore, none of the living beings in the six lower realms in this world have any relationship with any Bodhisattvas* in other worlds. It is said in the

Lotus Sutra, "Those who heard the Dharma from those *śrāmanera* (teachers) are now living under those Buddhas." T'ien-t'ai* stated [in the *Words and Phrases of the Lotus Sutra*], "The Buddha in the Western Pure Land is different from the Buddha in this Sahā World. Therefore, no relationship between parents and children exists between the Buddha of Infinite Life and us, ordinary beings in the Sahā World." Miao-lê explains this [in his *Annotations on the Words and Phrases of the Lotus Sutra*] that the Buddha of Infinite Life and Śākyamuni are different Buddhas. Their relationships to us from past lives are different. So are their ways of teaching. The Buddha sowing the seeds of Buddhahood in living beings is similar to parents giving birth to a child, and the Buddha guiding the people is similar to parents raising a child. If the parents who give birth to a child and parents who raise the child are different, the true relationship between parents and child does not exist.

In these days, people in Japan believe that the Buddha of Infinite Life* will come to save them. This is as nonsensical as feeding a baby cow on horse milk or trying to have the moon reflected on a roof tile.

When we compare Śākyamuni Buddha of the *Lotus Sutra* to Buddhas of other sutras as Enlightened Ones, with respect to their salvation of people, while other Buddhas attained Buddhahood tens, hundreds or thousands of *kalpa* ago, Lord Śākyamuni Buddha attained Wonderful Enlightenment in the remotest past 500 dust-particle *kalpa* ago.

Buddhas in worlds all over the universe such as the Great Sun Buddha* (Mahāvairocana Buddha), the Buddha of Infinite Life or Medicine Master Buddha* are all attendants of our Lord Original Buddha Śākyamuni. Śākyamuni Buddha is like the moon in the sky and other Buddhas are like its reflections on water. Vairocana Buddha, who is the lord-preacher of the *Flower Garland Sutra* and is seated on the center stage of Buddhas throughout the universe, and the Great Sun Buddha of the two mandalas of the Diamond Realm and Matrix-store Realm in the *Great Sun Buddha Sutra* and the *Diamond Peak Sutra* are attendants of the Buddha of Many Treasures* who appear in the Beholding the Stupa of Treasures* chapter of the *Lotus Sutra*. They are like retainers accompanying the King on both sides. Moreover, this Buddha of Many Treasures is also an attendant of the Eternal Lord Buddha Śākyamuni appearing in the Duration of the Life of the Tathāgata chapter* in the *Lotus Sutra*.

We, sentient beings in this Sahā World, have all been beloved children of the Lord Buddha Śākyamuni since 500 dust-particle *kalpa* ago. Because of our own faults, being undutiful to the Buddha, we had not been aware of being His children until today, but we are not the same as sentient beings in other worlds. The relationship between the Buddha and us, which was established in the remotest past, 500 dust-particle *kalpa* ago, is like the moon in the sky reflecting on clear water by itself. Our relationship to other Buddhas, which has never been established, is like deaf people unable to hear the peal of thunder or blind people unable to see the sun and moon.

Nevertheless, some Buddhist masters look down upon Śākyamuni Buddha and honor the Great Sun Buddha, while others say that Śākyamuni Buddha is not related to us but the Buddha of Infinite Life is. Still others revere Śākyamuni Buddha as He appears in Hinayana sutras, in the *Flower Garland Sutra* or in the theoretical section of the *Lotus Sutra*. These masters and their followers forget the Lord Śākyamuni Buddha, honoring various Buddhas of sutras other than the *Lotus Sutra*. They are like Prince Ajātaśatru who killed his father, King Bimbiśara, and followed Devadatta,* turning against Śākyamuni Buddha.

The 15th of the second month is the day of Śākyamuni Buddha's passing away and the 15th of the 12th month is also the day of commemoration for the compassionate father of the triple world, Śākyamuni Buddha. But such priests as Shan-tao,* Hōnen* and Yōkan,* deceived by masters like Devadatta, changed these days to the days of the Buddha of Infinite Life. Although the eighth of the fourth month is Śākyamuni Buddha's birthday, they changed it to Medicine Master Buddha's day. Is it an act of filial piety to change our compassionate father's memorial day to that of other Buddhas? It is expounded in Chapter 16 of the *Lotus Sutra*, Duration of the Life of the Tathāgata, "I, too, am the father of the world who wants to cure his deranged son." Grand Master T'ien-t'ai* explains this in his *Profound Meaning of the Lotus Sutra*, "At first our Bodhi-mind was awakened by this Buddha, and we attained enlightenment by following Him. As all rivers flow into the ocean, we are being led by our original relationship with this Buddha to our birth under this Buddha."

Question: For whom was the *Lotus Sutra* expounded?

Answer: There are two views about the eight chapters starting from Chapter Two of the *Lotus Sutra*, Expedients, to Chapter Nine,* Assurance of Future Buddhahood. If we read these chapters in the order of chapters from the beginning, we can see that the sutra was preached first of all for Bodhisattvas,* secondly for the men of Two Vehicles* such as *śrāvaka* and *pratyekabuddha*, and thirdly for ordinary people.* However, when we read the chapters in reverse order beginning with the 14th on Peaceful Practices [at the end of the theoretical section], followed by the 13th on Encouragement for Keeping This Sutra, the 12th on Devadatta, the 11th on the Beholding the Stupa of Treasures, and the 10th on the Teacher of the Dharma, we can see that these eight chapters were expounded for encouraging people after the Buddha's extinction. People during the lifetime of the Buddha are secondary. Of those after the Buddha's extinction, people in one thousand years of the Age of the True Dharma and one thousand years of the Age of the Semblance Dharma are secondary. The sutra was expounded mainly for the people in the Latter Age of Degeneration. Of those in the Latter Age of Degeneration, I, Nichiren, am the very person for whom it was expounded.

Question: Where is the proof for that?

Answer: The proof is in Chapter 10, The Teacher of the Dharma, saying, "Many people hate it [the *Lotus Sutra*] with jealousy even in My lifetime. Needless to say, more people will do so after My extinction."

Question: Where is a proper statement to prove that Nichiren is this person?

Answer: It is in Chapter 13, Encouragement for Keeping This Sutra, saying, "Ignorant people will speak ill of us, abuse us, and threaten us with swords or sticks."

Question: Is this not praising yourself?

Answer: I am overjoyed so much with the scriptural prediction fitting my life that I cannot help praising myself.

Question: For whom was the essential section of the *Lotus Sutra* expounded?

Answer: Two purposes are conceivable in preaching the essential section. First, the reason Śākyamuni Buddha reveals the eternity of His life in passing in Chapter 15,* Appearance of Bodhisattvas from Underground, [Concise Opening the Near and Revealing the Distant] is to enlighten His disciples who have been guided through teachings expounded for 40 years or so before the *Lotus Sutra* and in the first theoretical section of the *Lotus Sutra*. Secondly, one chapter and two half-chapters from the last part of the Appearance of Bodhisattvas from Underground chapter in which Maitreya raised a question, requesting the Buddha to preach for people after His extinction, through Chapter 16,* The Duration of the Life of the Tathāgata, to the first half of Chapter 17, Variety of Merits,* are exactly for clearly expounding the eternity of the Buddha [Expanded Opening the Near and Revealing the Distant]. This is solely for the sake of people after the death of the Buddha.

Question: Could you explain what is meant by "revealing the eternity of the life of the Buddha in passing"?

Answer: None of the great Bodhisattvas such as Mañjuśrī,* the King of the Brahma Heaven, Indra,* Sun God, Moon god, Star God, and the Dragon King were Śākyamuni Buddha's disciples while He was preaching the pre-Lotus sutras after attaining Buddhahood. Even before the Buddha began preaching upon attaining enlightenment, these Bodhisattvas and heavenly beings had already achieved the state of emancipation, and they preached by themselves distinct teachings and perfect teachings. After that, Śākyamuni Buddha expounded the Āgama sutras,* Hōdō sutras* and the *Wisdom Sutra.** However, these were not beneficial for those Bodhisattvas and heavenly beings because they already knew both distinct and perfect teachings, not to mention *piṭaka* and common teachings. It is said that the large serves also for the small. In detail, these Bodhisattvas and heavenly beings could have been Śākyamuni Buddha's masters or His "good friends" *(zen-chishiki),** not disciples. When eight chapters of the theoretical section proper of the *Lotus Sutra* were expounded, which they had never heard before, they became His disciples.

Men of the Two Vehicles such as Śāriputra* and Maudgalyāyana,* who had been the Buddha's disciples, awakened to their first aspiration for Buddhahood at the time of the Buddha's first sermon at Deer Park. The Buddha, however, expounded only expedient teachings to them for more than 40 years. Now in the *Lotus Sutra,** He expounded the True Dharma. And when the eternity of the life of the Buddha was suggested in Chapter 15, Appearance of Bodhisattvas from Underground, in the essential section of the *Lotus Sutra*, great Bodhisattvas, men of the Two Vehicles *(śrāvaka* and *pratyekabuddha)*, the King of the Brahma Heaven, Indra, Sun God, Moon God, Four Heavenly Kings, and the Dragon King, who had listened to the Buddha preach ever since the preaching of the *Flower Garland Sutra*, attained enlightenment, reaching the same rank as the Buddha or the one next to it. Therefore, when we look up to heaven today, we can see living Buddhas giving benefit to people while retaining their original ranks.

Question: For whom was the Duration of the Life of the Tathāgata chapter expounded, revealing the Buddha's enlightenment in the remotest past broadly and in detail?

Answer: The Duration of the Life of the Tathāgata chapter together with a half chapter each preceding and following it were expounded specially for the people living after the Buddha's extinction from beginning to end. It was expounded especially for those in this Latter Age of Degeneration such as Nichiren.

Question: Such a doctrine has never been heard of. Is it preached in any sutra?

Answer: My humble opinion can not match that of wise people in the past.

Even if I quote a proof from a sutra nobody would believe me. It is similar to the tragedies of Pien-ch'u and Wu Tzŭ-hsü of ancient China. Pien-ch'u of China obtained unpolished jewel stones, so he presented them to King Li and his successor, King Wu. But they did not realize the value of the stones and got angry with Pien-ch'u. Each King cut off one of Pien-ch'u's legs, so he lost both legs. Another successor, King Wen, polished the stones and finally realized that they were jewels. Wu-Tzŭ-hsü, a loyal minister of King Ho-lü of Wu, worried about the future of the country and admonished the successor on the throne many times in vain. Finally, he killed himself. Soon thereafter, it is said, his country was ruined. Likewise nobody will listen to me.

However, [if I may quote passages from the *Lotus Sutra* as proof,] it is stated in the Appearance of Bodhisattvas from Underground chapter that Maitreya Bodhisattva having wondered what the Buddha stated, said to Him, "If beginning bodhisattvas hear these words of Yours after Your extinction they may not believe them and commit the sin of slandering the Dharma." It means that had the Buddha not expounded the Duration of the Life of the Tathāgata chapter to reveal His eternity, ordinary people in the Latter Age would fall into evil realms such as hell by having doubts and slandering the Dharma. In the same chapter, the Buddha says, "I am leaving this excellent medicine here." Although this chapter seems to have been intended to benefit people in the past when the Buddha was alive, it is clear from this statement that the Buddha's true intention is to give benefit to people after His extinction. Benefiting those in the past is intended to show an example of the past for the people after His extinction.

The Buddha also declares in the *Lotus Sutra*: "For anyone who keeps this sutra in this evil world during the Latter Age of Degeneration" in the Variety of Merits chapter, "Buddhas joyfully display their immeasurable, supernatural powers in praise of those who will keep this sutra after My extinction" in the Supernatural Powers of the Tathāgata chapter, "Propagate* this chapter throughout this Sahā World in the latter 500 year period after My extinction lest it should be lost" in the Previous Life of Medicine-King Bodhisattva chapter, and "This sutra is a panacea for sick people in this Sahā World" in the same chapter. The Buddha also states in the *Nirvana Sutra*: "Suppose there are seven children, their parents love them all equally but care most for a sick child." *Icchantika* and slanderers of the True Dharma are like the first and second children of the seven whom parents care most about. Of many illnesses, slandering the *Lotus Sutra* is the most serious. Of many medicines, *Namu Myōhō Renge-kyō** is the most wonderful medicine.

This Sahā World is 7,000 *yojana* by 7,000 *yojana* in area, and it includes 80,000 countries. In 2,000 years of the Ages of the True Dharma *(shōbō)* and Semblance Dharma *(zōbō)*, the *Lotus Sutra* did not spread widely. If it does not spread during this Latter Age of Degeneration *(mappō)*, Śākyamuni Buddha would be a liar, validation of the truth of the *Lotus Sutra* by the Buddha of Many Treasures* would come to nothing, and broad, long tongues of Buddhas in manifestation throughout the universe to praise the preaching of Śākyamuni Buddha would become as fragile as banana leaves.

Question: For whom did the Buddha of Many Treasures verify the truth of Śākyamuni Buddha's preaching, Buddhas in manifestation all over the universe praise His preaching, and Bodhisattvas emerge from underground to prove the eternity of His life?

Answer: People understand that they were for those who were living during the Buddha's lifetime, but I, Nichiren, do not agree with them. Śāriputra and Maudgalyāyana are honored as the foremost in wisdom and in superhuman power respectively today. When we see the past, however, Śāriptura was Golden Dragon Buddha and Subhūti was Blue Dragon Buddha. As for the future, Śāriputra will become Flower Light Buddha. When the *Lotus Sutra* was expounded on Mt. Sacred Eagle,* Śāriputra was a great bodhisattva who instantly rid himself of three delusions of greed, anger and stupidity. In the original state, he was an old bodhisattva who had attained bodhisattvahood in heart but showed himself in the guise of a *śrāvaka*. Great bodhisattvas such as Mañjuśrī and Maitreya attained Buddhahood in the past but show themselves in the guise of bodhisattvas at present. The King of the Brahma Heaven, Indra, Sun God, Moon God and Four Heavenly Kings had been great saints even before Śākyamuni Buddha attained enlightenment under the bodhi tree.

Furthermore, they understood immediately all teachings of the four tastes and the four teachings expounded before the *Lotus Sutra*. There were no unwise men in the Buddha's lifetime. Whose doubts needed to be answered by proof of the Buddha of Many Treasures, the praise of many Buddhas all over the universe and the appearance of bodhisattvas from underground? There were no reasons for them to do so. Therefore, looking at the *Lotus Sutra,* we find that the Buddha says, "Many people hate it [the *Lotus Sutra*] with jealousy even in My lifetime. Needless to say, more people will do so after My extinction" in the Teacher of the Dharma chapter, and "In order to spread the *Lotus Sutra* for a long time in this world" in the Beholding the Stupa of Treasures chapter. Considering these statements, the *Lotus Sutra* is expounded for those of us living in the Latter Age of Degeneration. Therefore, referring to this period, Grand Master T'ien-t'ai* says, "Up to the fifth 500-year period after the Buddha's extinction, people received the merit of the Wonderful Dharma from afar." Grand Master Dengyō* also speaks of this period, "The Ages of the True Dharma and the Semblance Dharma have almost passed, and the Latter Age of Degeneration is shortly coming." The Latter

Age of Degeneration is coming shortly means that the time when he lived was not the time for the *Lotus Sutra* to spread, but the Latter Age of Degeneration is.

Question: What is the secret Dharma that Nāgārjuna,* Vasubandhu,* T'ien-t'ai and Dengyō did not spread during two thousand and some years after the Buddha's extinction?

Answer: They are the *Honzon** (Most Venerable One) and *Kaidan** (Precept platform) of the essential section, and the five-character *Odaimoku** of the *Lotus Sutra*.

Question: Why did they not spread them during the Ages of the True Dharma and Semblance Dharma?

Answer: If they had spread them during those times, the teachings of Hinayana, the expedient Mahayana and the theoretical section of the *Lotus Sutra* would have disappeared.

Question: Why do you try to spread them in the Latter Age of Degeneration if they could destroy Buddhism?

Answer: It is because in the Latter Age of Degeneration, all Buddhist teachings, both Hinayana and Mahayana, expedient and true Mahayana,* and exoteric and esoteric* teachings remain, but no one attains Buddhahood by practicing them. People in this Sahā World all commit the sin of slandering the True Dharma. In this adverse condition only the five characters of *Myō, Hō, Ren, Ge,* and *Kyō* should be forced on them in order to plant the seed of Buddhahood. For instance, Never-Despising Bodhisattva preached teachings of the *Lotus Sutra* for self-conceited priests and was persecuted. My disciples are in a favorable condition, able to put faith in the five characters to attain Buddhahood, but many others in Japan are not. Therefore, we have to forcibly spread the five characters of *Myō, Hō, Ren, Ge,* and *Kyō* among them to sow the seed of Buddhahood.

Question: Why do you disregard the whole of the *Lotus Sutra* or even its abridgment, emphasizing only its essence?

Answer: Hsüan-chuang* disregarded an abridgment and preferred the whole. He expanded the 40 fascicles of the *Great Wisdom Sutra* into 600 fascicles. Kumārajīva* preferred an abridgment to the whole. He condensed 1,000 fascicles of the *Great Wisdom Discourse** into 100 fascicles. I, Nichiren, disregard both an abridgment and the whole and prefer the essence. It is the five characters of *Myō, Hō, Ren, Ge,* and *Kyō* which Superior-Practice Bodhisattva (Jōgyō) transmitted from

Śākyamuni Buddha. It is said that Chiu Pao-yüan of Ch'in selected a fine horse by removing an unhealthy yellow horse, and that when Chih Tao-lin lectured on sutras, he disregarded details preferring an outline. The five characters of *Myō, Hō, Ren, Ge,* and *Kyō* are the precious doctrine preached by Śākyamuni Buddha when He entered the stupa of treasures sitting next to the Buddha of Many Treasures. Buddhas in Manifestation gathered together from all over the universe. The Buddha then invoked bodhisattvas from underground, chose the essence of the *Lotus Sutra* and expounded it for us people in the Latter Age of Degeneration. There should be no doubt about its merit in this world.

Question: Are there any omens for this Dharma to spread in this world?

Answer: The *Lotus Sutra* says, "Their true appearance..., such causes and effects of all things and phenomena are interrelated."* T'ien-t'ai says, "When a spider spins a web, there will be a happy event. When a magpie chatters, a visitor will come. As there is an omen for such a minor event, even more so will there be an omen for such a big event as spreading the Dharma."

Question: If so, are there any such omens now?

Answer: We had a severe earthquake in the first year of the Shōka* era, a huge comet in the first year of the Bun'ei era, and various strange phenomena in the sky and natural calamities on earth* following them. These are all omens for the *Lotus Sutra* to spread. Seven, 29 or innumerable calamities listed in the *Sutra of the Benevolent King,*ature* and various calamities mentioned in such sutras as the *Sutra of the Golden Splendor,* the *Sutra of the Great Assembly,* the *Guardian Sutra,* and the *Medicine Master Sutra** have already happened. Only the big disaster of the appearance of two, three, four, or five suns predicted in the *Sutra of the Benevolent King* has not actually taken place. However, according to residents on Sado Island two suns appeared to the west at around 4 p.m. on the 23rd day of the first month, or three suns according to others. It is also said that two Venuses appeared side by side only eight centimeters apart to the east on the fifth of the second month. Are they not most extraordinary phenomena that ever happened in Japan? The Ōbō Shōron chapter of the *Sutra of the Golden Splendor* predicts that when a strange meteor falls or two suns appear simultaneously, foreign enemies will attack the land, arousing panic among the people and ruining the country. It is said in the *Heroic Valor Sutra,** "Two suns and two moons will appear;" in the *Medicine Master Sutra,** "There will be an extraordinary eclipse of the sun and moon;" in the *Sutra of the Golden Splendor,** "A comet will appear often, two suns will appear at the same time, or an eclipse will happen often;" in the *Sutra of the Great Assembly,** "When Buddhism declines, the sun and moon will lose their brightness;" and in the *Sutra of the Benevolent King*,* "The sun and moon will lose their regular orbits. Seasons will be reversed. A red sun and a black sun will appear. Two, three, four or five suns will appear simultaneously. Darkness will prevail due to the eclipse of the sun. And one, two, three, four or five rings will surround the sun." These extraordinary phenomena of the sun and moon are the worst of seven, 29 or numerous calamities mentioned in the *Sutra of the Benevolent King*.

Question: What causes these major, medium and minor calamities?

Answer: The *Sutra of the Golden Splendor* says that it is because "People respect one who practices false teachings and torment and punish one who practices right teachings." The *Lotus Sutra, Nirvana Sutra*, and *Sutra of the Golden Splendor* preach, "Because people respect evil persons and punish virtuous ones, the movement of stars and seasons of wind and rain will lose their regularity." It is preached in the *Sutra of the Great Assembly*, "When Buddhism declines…, evil kings and evil monks will destroy the True Dharma." And in the *Sutra of the Benevolent King*: "When saints leave the land, seven calamities are bound to happen," "When monks are arrested and treated as prisoners regardless of laws and rules, Buddhism will be ruined soon," and "Seeking fame and wealth, many evil ministers will preach to the king, crown prince and princes about what will end up destroying Buddhism and their country. The king will believe them without discerning good from bad." Examining the state of current Japan reflected in the bright mirrors of these scriptural statements, we can see that natural disasters in heaven and on earth overtaking Japan today exactly match the sutras like two pieces of a tally. My insightful disciples shall see this fact for themselves. You should know that evil ministers today in Japan are trying to speak ill of the holy man to the emperor, princes and generals, causing him to leave the land.

Question: King Puṣyamitra ruined Buddhism in India, Emperor Wu-tsung of T'ang did the same in China, and Mononobe Moriya stood in the way of Buddhism in Japan. Deva Bodhisattva and Venerable Siṃha were killed while spreading the Dharma. Why did not major calamities happen then?

Answer: That's because the size of calamities depends on persons. For two thousand years of Ages of the True Dharma and the Semblance Dharma, evil kings and evil monks believed in heretic religions,* called themselves leaders or believed in wicked gods. Even though destroying Buddhism is a serious sin, their sin is less grave compared to evil beings and monks of today, who ruin Buddhism by breaking with Mahayana and putting faith in Hinayana or by breaking with the true teaching following the expedient. As they try to ruin

Buddhism internally and mentally without killing ministers or burning temples, their offense is more grave than that of previous generations. My disciples should see this fact and strengthen their faith in the *Lotus Sutra*. As you stare at a mirror with angry eyes, the mirror reflects your anger. Those strange phenomena in the sky are due to the human offense [of slandering the True Dharma]. Two suns appearing simultaneously is an omen of two kings standing side by side in one country. They will begin to fight. Stars disturbing the revolution of the sun and moon are omens of vassals infringing upon kings. Many suns competing against one another are omens of war in this world. Venuses appearing side by side are omens of fighting between princes. When the country has thus gone out of order, there is no doubt that holy men such as Superior-Practice Bodhisattva* will appear in this world, establishing the three doctrines of the essential section of the *Lotus Sutra,* and spreading the *Odaimoku* of *Namu Myōhō Renge-kyō** widely throughout the world.*

Risshō Kanjō (ST 158)

Introduction

Written in the 11th year of Bun'ei (1274), though some believe it was in the first or second year of Kenji (1275 or 76), this treatise was sent from Minobu to Sairen-bō Nichijō in Kyoto. It criticizes the doctrine then prevalent among Tendai monks on Mt. Hiei that the way of meditation expounded in the *Great Concentration and Insight* is superior to the teaching of the *Lotus Sutra*. Insisting that relying solely on meditation without theological studies is against the true intention of Grand Masters T'ien-t'ai and Dengyō, Nichiren Shōnin proves the superiority of the *Lotus Sutra* over the *Great Concentration and Insight* by pointing out that T'ien-t'ai's doctrine of "threefold contemplation in a single thought" or "3,000 existences contained in one thought" is the way of practice based on the *Lotus Sutra*. He further declares that the right way of practicing spiritual contemplation suitable to the Latter Age of Degeneration is chanting the *Odaimoku*.

A Treatise on Establishing the Right Way of Meditation

Similarities and Differences between the Lotus Sutra and the Great Concentration and Insight

Recently, priests of the Tendai school have been inclined to revere practicing spiritual contemplation,* ignoring the valuable teaching expounded in the first and second halves of the *Lotus Sutra,* namely the theoretical and the essential sections.

Now I ask you: Is their way of practicing spiritual contemplation based on the unique doctrine of "threefold contemplation in a single thought" or "3,000 existences contained in one thought,"* which Grand Master T'ien-t'ai* practiced and experienced in his mind and expounded in the *Great Concentration and*

Insight?* Or is it the way of contemplation of the Zen school propagated by Grand Master Bodhidharma?* If it is the Zen way of contemplation advocated by Grand Master Bodhidharma, I must say it is an unreliable and expedient way based on the *Entering Laṅkā Sutra* and the *Heroic Valor Sutra* expounded before the truth was revealed in the *Lotus Sutra*. When the wonderful Zen is expounded according to the *Lotus Sutra*,* that [previous] way of Zen should be discarded as expedient. For it is stated: "All expedients should be discarded and the truth will be revealed." If it is the Zen with Grand Master Bodhidharma as founder, it is based on the idea that there is a special teaching other than the teaching expounded by Śākyamuni Buddha [special transmission*], an idea as heretical as that conceived by a heavenly devil. Both are unreliable Zen by which one cannot accomplish the way of the Buddha. They should not be adopted.

If they claim that their spiritual contemplation is based on the "threefold contemplation in a single thought" expounded by Grand Master T'ien-t'ai in his *Great Concentration and Insight*, they should not be against his intention made clear in the writing regarding what should be discarded and what should be retained. If their way is based on the way stated in the *Great Concentration and Insight*, they should not be against the teaching of the *Lotus Sutra*. Since the *Great Concentration and Insight* preaches the way of practicing spiritual contemplation according to the doctrine of "3,000 existences contained in one thought" in the *Lotus Sutra*, the way to practice the "threefold contemplation in a single thought" is nothing but recognizing the Wonderful Dharma to be beyond conceptual understanding. Therefore, the priests who belittle the *Lotus Sutra* and make too much of spiritual contemplation commit the grave sin of slandering the True Dharma,* are men of false view, or are as wicked as a heavenly devil. This is because according to Grand Master T'ien-t'ai's "threefold contemplation in a single thought," "concentration and insight" means the unique state of mind in which one is enlightened with the truth of the One Buddha teaching through steadily maintaining the mind in tranquility with the *Lotus Sutra*.

Question: What authority verifies that Grand Master T'ien-t'ai's *Great Concentration and Insight* and the wonderful way of contemplation he attained in his mind, the doctrine of "3,000 existences contained in one thought" or "threefold contemplation in a single thought," are founded on the *Lotus Sutra*?

Answer: May I ask you in return whether there is proof that they are not founded on the *Lotus Sutra*? Those who believe that they are not founded on the *Lotus Sutra* present such verification as follows: It is said in the Introduction to the *Great Concentration and Insight* by Grand Master Chang-an, "In the *Great Concentration and Insight* Grand Master T'ien-t'ai expounded the teaching which he had practiced and attained in his mind." It is also stated [in the *Annotations on the Great Concentration and Insight*], "Grand Master T'ien-t'ai clearly expounded in the *Great Concentration and Insight* the spiritual contemplation from the practical viewpoint and made the '3,000 existences contained in one thought' doctrine the guide to the way of practice. Thus the *Great Concentration and Insight* is the perfect way of practicing the spiritual contemplation invented by Grand Master T'ien-t'ai. Therefore, it stands to reason that in this Introduction, Grand Master Chang-an appreciated the teaching of Grand Master T'ien-t'ai as an invaluable teaching practiced and experienced in his own mind."

These writings, however, do not in any way prove that Grand Master T'ien-t'ai did not depend on the *Lotus Sutra*. Instead, they show clearly that he depended on the sutra. For it is stated: "It is the teaching which Grand Master T'ien-t'ai practiced and attained in his mind," and the teaching which Grand Master T'ien-t'ai practiced is the way of practice according to the *Lotus Sutra*. Therefore, the Introduction written by Grand Master Chang-an presented as counter evidence proves that Grand Master T'ien-t'ai depended on the *Lotus Sutra*. Yet, the discussion with other Buddhist schools should be limited to the important issues.

If one insists that the *Great Concentration and Insight* of T'ien-t'ai is not based on the *Lotus Sutra*, you had better discard it right away. This is because it is stated in the regulations of Grand Master T'ien-t'ai: "The teaching consistent with the description of the sutra should be taken and the teaching without scriptural authority or with objectionable points should not be depended on." Grand Master Dengyō* states in his *Outstanding Principles of the Lotus Sutra*: "One should depend on the teaching of the Buddha, not on the teaching orally transmitted in later ages." Nāgārjuna* commented in his *Great Wisdom Discourse:** "The discussion based on the true sutra is correct and the discussion not based on the scripture is incorrect." Śākyamuni Buddha states in the *Nirvana Sutra*: "One should depend on the teaching of the Buddha rather than on the scholars who interpret the teaching." Grand Master T'ien-t'ai built upon the *Lotus Sutra* as the supreme teaching and respected Nāgārjuna as a patriarchal master. It is therefore unthinkable that Grand Master T'ien-t'ai misinterpreted the teaching of the scriptures or preached the *Great Concentration and Insight* according to the false views of non-Buddhist teachings, neglecting his own view that one should take the teaching consistent with the [teaching of the] scriptures.

Question: Then what are the writings which clearly show that the *Great Concentration and Insight* of Grand Master T'ien-t'ai is founded on the *Lotus Sutra*?

Answer: Since there are too many certain proofs, I will show here some of them. It is stated in the *Great Concentration and Insight*: "Among the gradual, indeterminate, and perfect and sudden concentration and insight, I will shed light on the perfect and sudden one according to the *Lotus Sutra* rather than speaking of the gradual and indeterminate ones." It is also stated in the *Annotations on the Great Concentration and Insight,** "The unfathomable system of practicing spiritual contemplation consisting of 10 stages, 10 objectives, relative extinction, and absolute extinction is established in the *Great Concentration and Insight* by collecting the gist of the *Lotus Sutra*." Grand Master Miao-lê states in his *Summary of the Great Concentration and Insight:*

> The theoretical study and the spiritual contemplation of the T'ien-t'ai school is founded on the thoughts of Nāgārjuna. Since Zen Master Hui-wên in the Northern Chi Dynasty merely presented the "three wisdoms and threefold contemplation," the correct wisdom has been attained by meditation on the *Lotus Sutra*, both theoretical study and spiritual contemplation have been widely discussed, and the content of spiritual contemplation has been well arranged since the time of Nan-yüeh* and T'ien-t'ai. If a person wants to practice spiritual contemplation according to the *Lotus Sutra*, he should decide the content of practice after establishing the clear answer to the issues on the provisional and true teachings,* and on the essential and theoretical sections. Since the *Lotus Sutra* is the sole scripture worthy of being called "Wonderful," the way of spiritual contemplation should be established according to this sutra. "Five expedients" as preparatory practice and the "ten-stage, ten-objective" way of observing mind are indeed the perfect and sudden [Tendai] meditation based entirely on the *Lotus Sutra*. Therefore, the perfect and sudden meditation is merely another name of meditation on the *Lotus Sutra* [since it is the way of practicing spiritual contemplation based on the truth of the *Lotus Sutra*].

The *Annotations on the Words and Phrases of the Lotus Sutra** says: "If the practice of spiritual contemplation is consistent with the teaching of the *Lotus Sutra*, it will become a wonderful way of practice different from such vain efforts as counting the treasures of other people. This shows that the *Great Concentration and Insight* is merely a means to attain the objective for knowing the Lotus meditation [like a coop which is unnecessary when the fish is caught]. If a person understands this meaning, he can truly obtain the essence of the *Lotus Sutra*."

It is also stated in the *Outline of the Teaching of the T'ien-t'ai School* by Hsing-man,* Grand Master Miao-lê's disciple who is said to have transmitted T'ien-t'ai Buddhism to Grand Master Dengyō: "The main purpose of the *Great Concentration and Insight* is to shed light on 'great concentration and insight,' an alternate term for the Lotus meditation, or to practice spiritual contemplation using the *Lotus*

Sutra." Such sources as cited above make it clear [that the *Great Concentration and Insight* is based on the *Lotus Sutra*], which no one can deny.

Question: Interpreting every word and phrase of the *Lotus Sutra*, Grand Master T'ien-t'ai devised four ways of interpretation according to karmic relations, the order of the teachings, the essential and theoretical, and spiritual contemplation. Interpreting them by way of spiritual contemplation, however, he seems to have abandoned the interpretations by way of the essential and theoretical. Also he says that while the *Lotus Sutra* is the teaching for those with inferior capacity who become enlightened gradually in the process of improving their capacity, the *Great Concentration and Insight* is expounded for those with superior capacity who can directly attain enlightenment. What do you think of this?

Answer: If it can be said that the *Lotus Sutra* is for those who have inferior capacity and gradually improve their capacity and is inferior to the *Great Concentration and Insight* expounded for those with superior capacity, are such sutras as those of the Flower Garland* and the True Word schools* superior to the *Lotus Sutra* according to the teaching of the present Tendai school? [That cannot be true absolutely.] It is shameful that people of the Tendai school in present-day Japan insist that Shingon (True Word) is superior to the *Lotus Sutra* because the former contains not only the phenomenal aspects such as finger signs and mantra but also the principle of the reality of all phenomena as the secret teaching of the Buddha. It is quite natural for them to think that the *Great Concentration and Insight* is superior to the *Lotus Sutra* [since they believe the *Lotus Sutra* is inferior to other sutras]. It is quite understandable.

You also insist that when interpreting spiritual contemplation, the way of thinking to divide the *Lotus Sutra* into the first half [theoretical section], and then the second half [essential section] should be discarded in order to show that the *Great Concentration and Insight* is superior to the *Lotus Sutra*. But in which part of the *Lotus Sutra* is it insisted that the interpretation by present-day scholars should be adopted and the basic teaching of the Buddha should be discarded? Even if it is the interpretation of Grand Master T'ien-t'ai, such thinking is inconsistent with the *Lotus Sutra*, the precious words of Śākyamuni Buddha and should never be adopted. The Nature of the Buddha chapter in the *Nirvana Sutra* says: "One should not depend on a person but on the Dharma." We should read and depend on the basic sutra rather than the thoughts of eminent scholars. Bodhisattva Nāgārjuna, Grand Masters T'ien-t'ai and Dengyō understood and practiced this admonition in the *Nirvana Sutra*. In addition, Grand Master T'ien-t'ai stated in his *Profound Meaning of the Lotus Sutra*:

The teachings from the period prior to the *Lotus Sutra* are extinguished when the great teaching [of the attainment of Buddhahood by the Two Vehicles] in the first half of the *Lotus Sutra* [the theoretical section] is expounded. [Though the teachings prior to the *Lotus Sutra* are indeed the excellent teachings of the Buddha, these expedient teachings complete their functions when the *Lotus Sutra* is expounded.] And the teaching in the first half of the *Lotus Sutra* is extinguished when the great teaching [of the attainment of Buddhahood by Śākyamuni Buddha in the eternal past] in the second half of the *Lotus Sutra* [the essential section] is expounded. [For the former is not the teaching of the Eternal Śākyamuni Buddha but of the historical and finite Śākyamuni Buddha.] Then, the teaching in the essential section of the *Lotus Sutra* is extinguished when the important teaching, spiritual contemplation, is revealed.

[Grand Master T'ien-t'ai attached such importance to spiritual contemplation although many less-than-learned monks misinterpret his real intention in making this statement, and insist that Grand Master T'ien-t'ai admitted the superiority of the *Great Concentration and Insight* over the *Lotus Sutra*.] What was the true intention of the Grand Master when he said this? During the Age of the Semblance Dharma, when Grand Master T'ien-t'ai was active, spiritual contemplation was the most important, if the content of spiritual contemplation was discussed by uniting all teachings of the first and second half of the *Lotus Sutra* into the mysterious teaching of the *Lotus Sutra*. However, [from the viewpoint of the *Lotus Sutra* as the basis of practice,] the teaching of the "reality of all phenomena" stated in the first half of the *Lotus Sutra* is too broad to understand and the doctrines of attaining Buddhahood by Śākyamuni Buddha in the eternal past and eternity of the Buddha stated in the second half are too profound to master. Therefore, thinking that the less-than-learned with their inferior capacity,* could never understand those teachings, Grand Master T'ien-t'ai insisted that the less-than-learned beginner should conceive the world of the Wonderful Dharma [or 3,000 existences contained in one thought] lurking in the mind of an ordinary person. Yet, he did not insist on discarding the *Lotus Sutra*. What does an ordinary person conceive in mind [other than the mysterious realm of the Wonderful Dharma] if he discards the *Lotus Sutra*? [Such a false way of thinking as discarding the *Lotus Sutra* as the basis for practice] seems like discarding a mysterious wish-fulfilling gem* that is thought to yield any asset one wants [and enable one to get rid of poverty at any time]. It is a pity that present-day scholars of the Tendai school assent to the assertion of other schools such as the Pure Land, Shingon and Zen, mistakenly interpret the thoughts of

Grand Master T'ien-t'ai, and fall into the great sin of slandering the *Lotus Sutra*, the True Dharma.

There are several provocative issues arising from the view that the *Great Concentration and Insight* is superior to the *Lotus Sutra*:

> 1. While the *Great Concentration and Insight* is merely what Grand Master T'ien-t'ai of Sui China attained at a hall for practicing the *Lotus Sutra* in Ta-su, the *Lotus Sutra* is the great teaching that Śākyamuni Buddha attained at the Place of Enlightenment in the eternal past.
>
> 2. It is needless to say that Śākyamuni Buddha is the World Honored One who obtained Perfect Enlightenment. On the other hand, Grand Master T'ien-t'ai did not reach the First Abode [the stage in which one can discard illusions in mind to recognize the truth correctly]. He is thought to be on the beginner's stages such as that of Notional Understanding,* Contemplation and Practice, or Semblance of Enlightenment. There is a great difference of 42 stages between Śākyamuni Buddha at the highest stage of Supreme Enlightenment and T'ien-t'ai at the beginning stage.
>
> 3. While the *Lotus Sutra* is the teaching that shows the real intention of Śākyamuni Buddha and all other Buddhas to appear in the world, the *Great Concentration and Insight* is merely the teaching which Grand Master T'ien-t'ai alone appeared in the world and mastered.
>
> 4. The *Lotus Sutra* is the great true teaching. The Buddha of Many Treasures* appeared in the stupa of seven treasures and verified the truth of the teaching of the *Lotus Sutra* [in the Beholding the Stupa of Treasures chapter]. The replica Buddhas coming from the worlds all over the universe admired it by stretching out their broad and long tongues [one of the marks of physical excellence of the Buddha] upwards until their tips reached the Brahma Heaven [in the Supernatural Powers of the Tathāgata chapter]. And the Buddha of Many Treasures declared that all descriptions [in the *Lotus Sutra*] are true. On the other hand, the *Great Concentration and Insight* is a teaching expounded solely by Grand Master T'ien-t'ai. [No Buddha has verified the truth of it.]

There are several other differences between the *Lotus Sutra* and the *Great Concentration and Insight* as above, but here I refrain from explaining further.

As for the other assertion, that if the teaching expounded for people with greater capacity is superior, it is better to discard the teaching of the truth and adopt the teaching of expedients [the provisional sutras]. [That is indefensible] because the interpretation in the *Great Concentration and Insight* by Grand Master T'ien-t'ai [as well as the *Annotations* on it by Grand Master Miao-lê] states: "The more expedients are included in the teaching, the higher is the stage of the person who receives the teaching." If one claims that the teaching is inferior because of the inferior capability of the audience, one had better adopt the expedient teaching and discard the true teaching. It is stated in the interpretation of Grand Master T'ien-t'ai: "The truer the teaching is, the lower the stage of those who receive it would be." If you insist that the *Great Concentration and Insight* is expounded for those with superior capacity to understand and that the *Lotus Sutra* is expounded for those with inferior capability, you seem to be saying that the *Great Concentration and Insight* was expounded for those with superior capacity because it is inferior to the *Lotus Sutra* [according to the interpretation of Grand Master T'ien-t'ai]. This should in fact be the case.

Since Grand Master T'ien-t'ai was among the audience who heard Śākyamuni Buddha expound the *Lotus Sutra* on Mt. Sacred Eagle, he propagated the teaching of the *Lotus Sutra*, which shows the sole purpose of the Buddha appearing in this world. However, as the time was not right for the spread of the sutra, he propagated the teaching of the *Odaimoku* of the *Lotus Sutra* in the name of the *Great Concentration and Insight*. Since Grand Master T'ien-t'ai was not a disciple of the Eternal Śākyamuni Buddha but of Śākyamuni as a manifestation of the Buddha, he did not propagate that which was entrusted directly to disciples of the Eternal Buddha such as Superior-Practice Bodhisattva, who had been trained ever since the eternal past. T'ien-t'ai propagated the teaching of the *Lotus Sutra*, which directly states the truth, by explaining it as the *Great Concentration and Insight*. In this sense, his teaching can be said to have been expedient rather than the Wonderful Dharma as unvarnished truth. Therefore, those who received the teaching of the *Great Concentration and Insight* from Grand Master T'ien-t'ai in the Age of the Semblance Dharma are, like those who heard the preaching of the pre-Lotus teaching in the lifetime of Śākyamuni Buddha, "people who received the perfect teaching taking on the expedients [provisional teaching]." People who receive the teaching from the Eternal Śākyamuni Buddha are those who receive the teaching of the Wonderful Dharma revealed in the essential section of the *Lotus Sutra* and go on their way correctly to enlightenment.

It is a great mistake to regard the *Great Concentration and Insight* in the same light as the *Lotus Sutra* because it equates the interpretation of Grand Master T'ien-t'ai, who inherited the teaching of Śākyamuni Buddha, and the fundamental sutra of Śākyamuni Buddha. It is even worse to insist on the evil view that the *Great Concentration and Insight* is superior to the *Lotus Sutra*. [The reason why Grand Master T'ien-t'ai emphasized the *Great Concentration and*

Insight and did not preach the importance of the *Odaimoku* of the *Lotus Sutra*] stems from whether he was a bodhisattva who emerged from underground entrusted by the Eternal Śākyamuni Buddha with propagation in the Latter Age of Degeneration* or a disciple of a manifestation Buddha, whether his time was the Age of the Semblance Dharma [as that of Grand Master T'ien-t'ai] or the Latter Age of Degeneration [as that of Superior-Practice Bodhisattva], or whether he was entrusted with propagation as one of many bodhisattvas described in the Transmission chapter of the *Lotus Sutra* or entrusted with special propagation as one of the bodhisattvas from underground in the Supernatural Powers of the Tathāgata chapter. It is the intention of the Buddha, who oversees the world, to let the one who practices the *Lotus Sutra* in the Latter Age of Degeneration shed light on such issues as these.

In this respect, it can be said that those scholars of the present Tendai school who insist on the superiority of the *Great Concentration and Insight* over the *Lotus Sutra* are ungrateful to their Founder T'ien-t'ai. How can they escape from that charge? Grand Master T'ien-t'ai was called Medicine-King Bodhisattva when he heard Śākyamuni Buddha preaching the *Lotus Sutra* on Mt. Sacred Eagle. He was at once Grand Master T'ien-t'ai in Sui China and Grand Master Dengyō in Japan. The teaching he propagated in his past, present and future lives is in its entirety the teaching of the Wonderful Dharma. There is no such person but Śākyamuni Buddha in India, China and Japan who has propagated the *Lotus Sutra* throughout the past, present and future. Being the noblest, Grand Master T'ien-t'ai was misunderstood by scholars of the Tendai school inheriting his teaching, who pinned the guilt of their mistake on the innocent Grand Master. Is this not a serious sin?

What then is the teaching that Grand Master T'ien-t'ai intended to maintain? Eminent scholars say that it is the "threefold contemplation in a single thought." But I, Nichiren, believe that though the perfect "threefold contemplation in a single thought" established on the basis of the true teaching of the *Lotus Sutra* seems to be a profound truth, it is merely a way of practice. For the way of meditation called "threefold contemplation" is a mere practice of cause [by which to attain the result: a state of enlightenment or the truth of the Wonderful Dharma.] A commentary by Grand Master Jikaku* states: "The threefold contemplation is the way of practicing contemplation to attain the substance of the Wonderful Dharma." Grand Master Dengyō has this to say: "The practice preached in the *Great Concentration and Insight* is for the accomplishment of the practice leading to the enlightenment of the Wonderful Dharma, the *Lotus Sutra*." In this sense, the threefold contemplation in a single thought is just a way to show the state of mind by which to attain the realm as the object of contemplation and virtue as a result of contemplation. And, since this way of contemplation of the "threefold contemplation in a single thought" was expressed by Grand Master T'ien-t'ai in his speeches and writings, it is the way of practice within one's consideration contrary to the Wonderful Dharma, which is the realm of Śākyamuni Buddha and His virtue. [On the other hand, the Wonderful Dharma is the teaching beyond conceptual understanding.]

Question: What is the teaching superior to the "threefold contemplation in a single thought"?

Answer: This is a very important teaching. Stated in the Expedients chapter as "only Buddhas," it is the realm that only the Buddha attained and cannot be expressed in our language. Therefore, the chapter states: "The Wonderful Dharma that the Buddha attained is too profound and elaborate to comprehend or express in words." Since even the Buddha, who has perfectly attained Supreme Enlightenment, said that the Dharma is beyond expression and comprehension, the bodhisattvas in the realm of Approximate Supreme Enlightenment, other inferior bodhisattvas,* *śrāvaka, pratyekabuddha* and ordinary people can never understand it.

Question: How can I recognize the existence of the superior teaching without hearing its name? [I would like to hear its name, at least.]

Answer: It is the teaching superior to the "threefold contemplation in a single thought" that Grand Master T'ien-t'ai attained in mind. Nevertheless, present-day scholars of the Tendai school in the lineage of the teaching of Grand Master T'ien-t'ai cannot understand it because they have not inherited its spirit correctly. Therefore, this is a very important teaching that certainly requires scrupulous attention. Though from the beginning it should not be talked about thoughtlessly, I will tell you its name because of your excellent determination. It is "A Word of the Dharma," namely a mysterious Dharma beyond discretion. It is what Grand Master Dengyō states in his Treatise Revealing the Precepts as "the threefold contemplation in a single thought stated in one word".

Question: What is its substance?

Answer: "A word" means the Wonderful Dharma.

Question: How do you know that the Wonderful Dharma is superior to the "threefold contemplation in a single thought"?

Answer: Because the Wonderful Dharma is the virtue or truth as the object of attainment while the threefold contemplation is merely a way of contemplation for one who practices to attain the virtue or truth. The Buddha speaks of this Wonderful Dharma in the Expedients chapter: "The Dharma attained in the place of enlightenment [is beyond question and comprehension]," "The Dharma I attained is wonderful and beyond comprehension," "This Dharma is beyond comprehension and discretion," and "The appearances of all things which are tranquil and extinguished are beyond description in words." [Interpreting these,] Grand Master T'ien-t'ai stated in the *Profound Meaning of the Lotus Sutra*: "*Myō* (Wonderful) means being beyond comprehension," "This Dharma transcends the world of description and is beyond the power of mind," and "The Dharma suggests that each of the 10 realms of living beings contains the 10 aspects* and that nine provisional realms and the real realm of the Buddha are one and inseparable. [It shows that an ordinary person and the Buddha are one.]" He also interpreted [the Wonderful Dharma] as the triple truth [of the void, impermanence and the middle], the threefold contemplation, the three thousand existences, or the inconceivable Dharma. It is possible to figure out the Dharma Grand Master T'ien-t'ai attained in mind because it is the Dharma Grand Master T'ien-t'ai considered. On the other hand, the Wonderful Dharma is the teacher of Buddhas. It is evident that the [inconceivable] Wonderful Dharma is superior to the conceivable threefold contemplation.

If the passage in the second chapter stating [that the Dharma attained in the place of enlightenment is wonderful and beyond comprehension and discretion] as cited above is true, the Wonderful Dharma is the very realm of the Buddha, who attained enlightenment in the eternal past* and is now at the Supreme Stage of Enlightenment. This realm of the Eternal Buddha cannot be attained by the lord teachers of pre-Lotus sutras, the theoretical section of the *Lotus Sutra*, or other Buddhas and bodhisattvas. The Expedients chapter states, "Only the Buddha has mastered this Dharma." This means that the Buddha, who was enlightened for the first time in this world under the bodhi tree, completely mastered from His viewpoint and within the realm which He could attain with His ability the teaching of the 10 realms and the 10 aspects, and the three thousand existences expounded in the theoretical section of the *Lotus Sutra*. The Wonderful Dharma of the objective reality that Śākyamuni Buddha in the realm of the eternal enlightenment has attained since the eternal past is beyond the consideration of the Buddha of the theoretical section, to say nothing of bodhisattvas and ordinary people.*

Grand Master T'ien-t'ai interprets the two characters of *chih* and *kuan* (concentration and insight) in the *Great Concentration and Insight*: "I call *kuan* the wisdom of the Buddha and *chih* the insight of the Buddha." This [interpretation], however, refers to the wisdom and insight of the Buddha in the theoretical section, not the ultimate wisdom and insight of the Buddha at the highest stage of Supreme Enlightenment. For the *Great Concentration and Insight* is based on the 10 realms, the 10 aspects, the 3,000 realms of existence, the triple truth and the threefold contemplation, which Grand Master T'ien-t'ai attained, and these thoughts are the real intention of the theoretical section in the first half of the *Lotus Sutra*. Therefore, we should remember that the *Great Concentration and Insight* is the wisdom and insight of the Buddha in the theoretical section. The reason why the *Great Concentration and Insight* states that "I will shed light on the wonderful insight absolutely beyond comprehension" is that T'ien-t'ai tentatively named the "wonderful insight of the 3,000 existences contained in one thought" expounded in it the "wonderful insight absolutely beyond comprehension."

Question: Hasn't Grand Master T'ien-t'ai truly attained the word of the Wonderful Dharma?

Answer: Though Grand Master T'ien-t'ai attained the Wonderful Dharma in mind, he did not propagate it outwardly. He kept the realm of profound enlightenment he attained to himself and outwardly did no more than call the Wonderful Dharma the threefold contemplation and show the way of practicing the doctrine of "3,000 existences contained in one thought."

Question: Why did Grand Master T'ien-t'ai not propagate the teaching of the Wonderful Dharma though he attained it?

Answer: First, [because Grand Master T'ien-t'ai lived in the Age of the Semblance Dharma while the *Lotus Sutra* should be spread in the Latter Age of Degeneration,] his days were not appropriate for the essence of the *Lotus Sutra* to be revealed. Secondly, [since propagation in the Latter Age of Degeneration was entrusted to bodhisattvas who had emerged from underground such as Superior-Practice Bodhisattva,] he did not take charge of the propagation. Thirdly, Grand Master T'ien-t'ai was a disciple of a manifestation Buddha [not of the Original Śākyamuni Buddha].

Question: Is there proof that Grand Master T'ien-t'ai attained the word of the Wonderful Dharma in mind?

Answer: This is the most important secret of the T'ien-t'ai school and unknown to most scholars in the world. There is a record of genealogy, called *The Profound Teaching Transmitted in the Sprinkling on the Head Ceremony*, which Grand Master T'ien-t'ai himself wrote. It had been kept in a stone tower since the Grand Master passed away. When Grand Master Dengyō went to T'ang China, that stone tower was opened by a key in the shape of eight tongues which appeared from underground, and the *Profound Teaching* was transmitted [to Grand Master Dengyō] from Venerable Tao-sui.* Written on this sheet of paper in transmission is "The Wonderful Intention of the Word, the Essential Meaning of the Teaching." [We are informed by this sentence that Grand Master T'ien-t'ai attained the word of the Wonderful Dharma.]

Transmitting the doctrine to his disciple, Grand Master Dengyō declared:

> The word of the Wonderful Dharma is the ultimate reality of Dharma Nature, and the realm of the five dusts consisting of form, sound, odor, taste and touch which a person perceives through the five sense-organs is a phenomenon in which the ultimate reality appears corresponding to each occasion. When a person attains the realm of no contemplation and no thought with his eyes closed, his appearance itself is the state of unchangeable ultimate reality. Therefore, upon hearing this "word of the Wonderful Dharma," a person can attain the realm which all teachings advocate and all the preachings of Śākyamuni Buddha in His lifetime are included in this word.

If what Grand Masters T'ien-t'ai and Dengyō said upon transmitting their teaching is true, we can see that the most essential teaching transmitted from Grand Master T'ien-t'ai is [not the threefold contemplation in a single thought but] the word of the Wonderful Dharma. The threefold contemplation in a single thought is merely a way of practice to attain the Wonderful Dharma. It is the practice as the cause and the Wonderful Dharma in the realm of enlightenment as the result. However, since the practice as the cause includes the result, and the enlightenment as the result includes the cause, the cause and the result are one and inseparable. Contemplating the Wonderful Dharma, which includes both the cause and result, a person can attain the merit of acquiring the Wonderful Principle of all [Buddhist] teachings [as mentioned in their transmission documents].

Thus, we should know that it is indeed a prejudice to insist on such a fallacy as, "The ultimate teaching of Grand Master T'ien-t'ai establishes a teaching of the 'concentration and insight of no thought' other than the distinction between the theoretical and essential sections, and this 'concentration and insight of no thought' is beyond description and thus the most important secret teaching." Great Bodhisattvas such as those called Four Reliances* respectfully interpreted the sutras expounded by the Buddha and developed their theories. Why should Grand Master T'ien-t'ai alone have established the "concentration and insight of no thought" against the thought of the Buddha? If this "concentration and insight" is not based on the *Lotus Sutra*, the *Great Concentration and Insight* of Grand Master T'ien-t'ai is the same as the [false] teaching of a heavenly devil teaching transmitted from heart to heart, without scriptures or preachings.* The *Great Concentration and Insight* by Grand Master T'ien-t'ai is not such a teaching. It is truly regrettable [that many people interpret the teaching incorrectly].

Grand Master Dengyō stated in the *Treatise Revealing the Precepts:* "Do not follow the law unless established by the lord. Do not believe the teaching unless it is of Śākyamuni Buddha, King of the Dharma." He also stated:

> When great bodhisattvas respected as Four Reliances* write commentaries on the sutras, they hold viewpoints either from the provisional sutras or the true sutras. Expounding the teaching for the Three Vehicles [of *śrāvaka, pratyekabuddha* and bodhisattvas], they distinguish among three [provisional] teachings [*piṭaka* teaching for *śrāvaka* and *pratyekabuddha,* common teaching for all and the distinct teaching for bodhisattvas] and one [true] teaching [perfect teaching for bodhisattvas]. Thus, Grand Master T'ien-t'ai set four steps in the pre-Lotus sutras to meet the needs of the Three Vehicles and established the teaching of the One Buddha Vehicle by the true teaching of the *Lotus Sutra.* There is also a distinction among the six ways of practice by bodhisattvas: charity, precepts, perseverance, endeavor, meditation and wisdom. The precepts themselves are separated into those of the Hinayana and the perfect precepts of the *Lotus Sutra.* As the precepts they observe are different from each other, their dignities are not the same. Therefore, the teaching Grand Master T'ien-t'ai maintained is firmly based on the thoughts of the great bodhisattvas and founded on the sutras which the Buddha expounded. [It is never from his own conjecture.]

The present-day Tendai school in Japan regards Grand Master Dengyō as its founder. Therefore, it would be betraying the Grand Patriarch Master Dengyō in Japan and Grand Master T'ien-t'ai in China for them to think that the *Great Concentration and Insight* of Grand Master T'ien-t'ai is not based on the *Lotus Sutra.* Since the teaching that Grand Masters T'ien-t'ai and Dengyō transmitted is based on the *Lotus Sutra,* their distant disciples should follow it. However, since in fact scholars of the present-day Tendai school betray its teaching, they should recognize that despite bearing the name of the Tendai school, the teaching they advocate is dependent on the prejudicial teaching of Bodhidharma and the false words of Tripiṭaka Master Śubhākarasiṃha.* According to the interpretations of Grand Masters T'ien-t'ai and Dengyō, the secret teaching T'ien-t'ai found deep in mind is nothing but the word of the Wonderful Dharma.

In this way, recent scholars of the Tendai school have lost the secret teaching inherited from Grand Master T'ien-t'ai and stored in the stone tower. And, based on their own ideas, they forged such writings as the transmission of the threefold contemplation in a single thought, put them in bags of brocade, hung them around their necks, and put them at the bottom of a box, claiming them to be invaluable. As a result, false teachings have spread throughout the nation, the real intention of Grand Master T'ien-t'ai's Buddha Dharma has been lost, and the Wonderful Dharma of Śākyamuni Buddha has been neglected. This is solely due to Bodhidharma's dogma of "special transmission without scriptures and preachings" and Śubhākarasiṃha's assertion that the *Lotus Sutra* is inferior to the *Great Sun Buddha Sutra*. Therefore, they do not know anything about doctrines of "the threefold contemplation in a single thought," "the triple truth in a single thought" and "3,000 existences contained in one thought," not to mention the *Great Concentration and Insight*. Moreover, they know nothing of [such fundamental aspects of the T'ien-t'ai teaching as] the essential and theoretical sections, relative subtleties and absolute subtleties, subtle contemplation of the *Lotus Sutra*, three kinds of doctrinal study,* provisional and true teachings,* four doctrinal teachings [*piṭaka*, common, distinct and perfect teachings], eight teachings [four methods of teaching and four doctrinal teachings], five periods* in the Buddha's lifetime preaching, and five flavors* [of milk, cream, curds, butter and ghee]. Needless to say, they do not know that they should propagate the Buddhist teaching in consideration of the content of teaching, capacity of people, time and nation [and that they should propagate the *Lotus Sutra* in the Latter Age of Degeneration]. It is natural that [owing to remote disciples, the teaching of the Tendai school] has become inconsistent, looking like neither the true teaching, nor the provisional teachings.

Since [scholars of the Tendai school] have been taught that the *Lotus Sutra* Grand Masters T'ien-t'ai and Dengyō transmitted is inferior to [the teachings of] the Zen and Shingon schools, they have become sympathetic to the false teachings of Bodhidharma and Shingon Buddhism, and their teaching has become ambiguous, like neither the provisional teaching nor the true teaching. As a result, the grave sin of slandering the True Dharma has fallen on them when they advocate the false assertion that the *Great Concentration and Insight* was superior to the *Lotus Sutra*, shifting responsibility to innocent T'ien-t'ai. Thus they have become the unfilial who disobeyed the venerable founder and committed the grave sin of slandering the *Lotus Sutra*, the True Dharma.

Regarding the way of contemplation preached by Grand Master T'ien-t'ai, ever since he attained the truth through the practice of meditation based on the *Lotus Sutra* at the place of practice on Mt. Ta-su of Kuang-chou, when he meditates on the Wonderful Dharma with his eyes open, all phenomena in the universe are workings of the ultimate reality functioning in accordance with environmental conditions. But when he contemplates the Wonderful Dharma with his eyes closed, they represent the permanently unchanging ultimate reality. These two, the ultimate reality functioning in accordance with conditions and the unchanging reality, are nothing but [the dynamic and static aspects of] the word of the Wonderful Dharma. Therefore, when a person recites the Wonderful Dharma, all existences will attain the realm of the Wonderful Dharma and all preachings of Śākyamuni Buddha during His lifetime will be included in this word [of the Wonderful Dharma]. In other words, Grand Master T'ien-t'ai believes that since the first half of the *Lotus Sutra*, the theoretical section, is too broad, and the second half, the essential section, is too profound [for ordinary people to understand], contemplation of the Wonderful Dharma is the most appropriate.

Unable to understand this, recent scholars failed to learn correctly the Wonderful Dharma Grand Master T'ien-t'ai had mastered, thought that the *Great Concentration and Insight* was superior to the *Lotus Sutra*, and that the Zen school was superior to the *Great Concentration and Insight*, discarded the *Lotus Sutra* while adopting the *Great Concentration and Insight*, and finally discarded the *Great Concentration and Insight* while adopting the Zen school. Monks in the Zen school hold to such views because they deeply believe such devilish words of Zen writings as: "A wisteria vine is hanging on a branch of a pine tree. What happens after the wisteria and pine are dead?" or "Break off a twig of a tree without climbing on it." Though they discuss it in various ways, the Buddha passed away as a pine tree is dead and the value of his teaching has disappeared as a wisteria is dead. Then, they insist that the sutras the Buddha expounded should be like a finger [the teaching] pointing to the moon [truth] and thus, there is no need to point to the moon if we know where the moon is. Conclusively, they believe they can say that only the teaching of Zen is surely the wonderful truth. This is a false assertion arising from a belief in Zen thought, which is as wicked as that of a heavenly devil, which slanders the True Dharma by insisting that one can attain Buddhahood when he sees the original nature of one's mind.

Śākyamuni Buddha, who attained enlightenment in the eternal past as described in the Duration of the Life of the Tathāgata chapter of the *Lotus Sutra*, has a permanent and imperishable life. Nevertheless, the Zen school considers this Eternal Buddha impermanent. This view is the same as the "prejudice of extinction" of the non-Buddhist teachings* in India, [the view that death marks the final end of the body and soul of a person and there is no possibility for him to come to life again]. It is a false view that goes against the invaluable teaching of Śākyamuni Buddha preached in the *Lotus Sutra* that all phenomena in the universe are at the stage of the ultimate reality and the changing state of the world is itself permanent. Since Zen, an expedient to the *Lotus Sutra,* is not the way leading to enlightenment, the assertion that it is permanent and true is a view as evil as the non-Buddhist "prejudice of eternity" [the view that both body and soul of a person are permanent and imperishable]. Politely speaking, the teaching of Zen is at the stage of expedient teaching of the Buddha. Frankly speaking, it is merely an evil teaching of the non-Buddhist religion.* The polite expression represents the viewpoint of general Buddhism while the frank remark is from the real viewpoint of the *Lotus Sutra.* From the viewpoint of the *Lotus Sutra* as the truth, I dare say that Zen is a non-Buddhist teaching of a heavenly devil.

Question: What is the proof that Zen is the teaching of a heavenly devil?

Answer: It is as mentioned above.

Risshō Kanjō Sōjō (ST 165)

Introduction

Written on the 28th day of the second month in the 12th year of the Bun'ei Era (1275), this letter was in response to Sairen-bō of Kyoto, who sent various gifts to Nichiren Shōnin at Minobu and asked him questions regarding the "new" doctrine among the Tendai scholars of the time claiming the superiority of the *Great Concentration and Insight* over the *Lotus Sutra*. Denying such allegations, Nichiren insists in the letter that the contrary is true. The title, "The Cover Letter...," is misleading because it is a letter outlining "A Treatise on Establishing the Right Way of Meditation" rather than a cover letter to it.

The Cover Letter to the Treatise on Establishing the Right Way of Meditation

May I express my sincere gratitude to you for sending a messenger to me all the way [from Kyoto to Mt. Minobu] recently. I have also received with deep appreciation the various gifts you so kindly sent me.

I understand that prevalent among scholars of the Tendai school* today are heretical doctrines that claim the superiority of the *Great Concentration and Insight** over the *Lotus Sutra,** and the superiority of the Zen school* over the *Great Concentration and Insight,* or claim that when the great teaching of "spiritual contemplation"* is revealed, both the theoretical and essential sections of the *Lotus Sutra* are useless.

Regarding your questions, there are various factions with different contentions within the Tendai school, but generally speaking they belong to either the Eshin or Danna faction.*

First, as for the claim of the Eshin faction, Tōyō-bō Chūjin says, "The *Great Concentration and Insight* explains the teaching of the essential and theoretical sections of the *Lotus Sutra.*" And it is stated in the *Great Concentration and Insight,* fascicle six:

Insight refers to the wisdom of the Buddha that perceives the interrelationship and perfect harmony of the triple truth [the truth of the void, impermanence and the middle] while concentration means the insight of the Buddha that observes this principle. When one practices [the way of meditation preached in] the *Great Concentration and Insight*, the wisdom and insight of the Buddha appear in one's mind as clearly as they were in front of one's own eyes.... It is the revelation of the wisdom and insight of the Buddha for those who practice the Three Vehicles [*śrāvaka, pratyekabuddha* and bodhisattva ways] to realize their misconception that the Buddha was a historical person enlightened under the bodhi tree at Buddhagayā.

The *Annotations on the Great Concentration and Insight** by Miao-lê, fascicle five, states:

The ten-stage method of practicing "spiritual contemplation" is based on the *Lotus Sutra*. Therefore, it was lauded by citing scriptural statements from the sutra. Speaking from the viewpoint of the theoretical section, the Buddha who had practiced this ten-stage meditation under the guidance of Great Universal Wisdom Buddha* in the remote past, 3,000 dust-particle *kalpa* ago, attained Buddhahood at the Hall of Enlightenment* in this world. This is enlightenment of the Wonderful Dharma. Speaking from the viewpoint of the essential section, while practicing the bodhisattva way in the remote past of 500 dust-particle *kalpa* ago, the Buddha attained the Enlightenment of the Wonderful Dharma by practicing the ten-stage meditation. Thus the Buddha attained enlightenment solely through this ten-stage method of meditation according to either the essential or theoretical section.

The first of the above two citations, the one from the *Great Concentration and Insight*, seems to claim that the *Great Concentration and Insight* covers only the essential section, but the second citation from the *Annotations* in fact appears to say that it covers both sections. Therefore, the Eshin faction contends that the *Great Concentration and Insight* explains both the essential and theoretical sections according to this statement.

Next, the Danna faction, which claims that the *Great Concentration and Insight* depends solely on the doctrine of all phenomena being the ultimate reality preached in the theoretical section of the *Lotus Sutra*, establishes its base on the third fascicle of the *Annotations on the Great Concentration and Insight*, which declares: "The *Great Concentration and Insight* is comprised of the 'four teachings and five tastes' borrowed [from various sutras] and is constructed by the wonderful and perfect principle of the *Lotus Sutra*. Therefore, the whole writing of the *Great Concentration and Insight* is nothing but the wonderful means of meditation based on the perfect and sudden One Vehicle teaching of the *Lotus Sutra*, which reveals the truth replacing the expedient." According to this passage, there is no doubt that the *Great Concentration and Insight* is founded upon the theoretical section of the *Lotus Sutra*.

Thus, although their contentions are not the same, they are the same in that neither of them can do without the essential or theoretical section or both.

Nevertheless, scholars of the Tendai school today insist on the superiority of the *Great Concentration and Insight* over the *Lotus Sutra*. From whom did they receive such a doctrine? To me, the comparative superiority between the *Great Concentration and Insight* and the *Lotus Sutra* is as clear as the difference between heaven and earth.

Politely speaking, the *Great Concentration and Insight* seems somewhat similar to the teaching of the theoretical section. Regarding the doctrine Grand Master T'ien-t'ai attained in mind, therefore, his disciple Chang-an admires him for having 10 virtues, the first of which is his attainment of the profound One Buddha Vehicle doctrine of the *Lotus Sutra* without a teacher. As the ninth virtue of Grand Master T'ien-t'ai, Chang-an praises him saying that T'ien-t'ai profoundly perceives the perfect and sudden teaching of the *Lotus Sutra*. The *Pictorial Biography of T'ien-t'ai*, part 4, states: "Upon practicing the *Lotus Sutra* for two weeks, his illusion completely disappeared and T'ien-t'ai entered the meditative concentration." Chang-an has this to say in the *Great Concentration and Insight*, fascicle one, "This *Great Concentration and Insight* expounds the doctrine which Grand Master T'ien-t'ai attained in his own mind." It is said in the *Annotations on the Great Concentration and Insight*, fascicle five: "In the paragraph explaining the ways of practicing spiritual contemplation in the *Great Concentration and Insight*, each sentence substantiates the wonderful doctrine of '3,000 existences contained in one thought' to be the guide for the way of observing the mind. Therefore, the Introduction to the *Great Concentration and Insight* refers to the 'doctrine attained in his own mind.'"

The doctrine which Grand Master T'ien-t'ai "attained in his own mind" refers to that of "3,000 existences contained in one thought," namely the "threefold contemplation in a single thought." The terms triple truth and threefold contemplation, mentioned in the *Bodhisattva Necklace Sutra** and the *Sutra of the Benevolent King*,* were reconstructed by T'ien-t'ai as "threefold contemplation in a single thought" and "3,000 existences contained in one thought" to represent what he had attained in his own mind. In so doing, T'ien-t'ai depended on the passage on the 10 aspects of reality and all phenomena representing the ultimate reality in the second chapter, Expedients, in the theoretical section of the *Lotus Sutra*. Thus we know that the whole work of the *Great Concentration and Insight* bases its foundation on the theoretical section.

To put it strongly, the T'ien-t'ai doctrine of "concentration and insight" is like the pre-Lotus sutras,* and the provisional Mahayana sutras preaching the distinct teaching, one of the four doctrinal teachings. It is what he attained while meditating at the Universal Wisdom Hall of Practice on Mt. Ta-su, and when T'ien-t'ai described it to his teacher-master, Grand Master Nan-yüeh, he was told that what he attained was nothing but mystic words and phrases of the pre-Lotus expedient sutras. Also, it is stated in the *Pictorial Biography of T'ien-t'ai*, part 4: "When T'ien-t'ai lectured on the *Great Wisdom Sutra*, written in golden ink, replacing his master Nan-yüeh, a doubt arose upon encountering the passage, 'a mind is equipped with 10,000 practices.' Grand Master Nan-yüeh explained this for T'ien-t'ai, saying that his question was concerned with a sequential doctrine of the *Great Wisdom Sutra*, which has not yet reached the level of the perfect and sudden wonderful doctrine of the *Lotus Sutra*."

Thus what T'ien-t'ai preached was the *Wisdom Sutra*, a pre-Lotus, quasi-Mahayana sutra. As it is said that what he preached was a sequential doctrine, it was a distinct teaching. And, as it is said that the mystic words and phrases he was able to attain were pre-Lotus expedients, we know that T'ien-t'ai's *Great Concentration and Insight* is similar to a pre-Lotus, expedient sutra, belonging to the category of the distinct teaching.

Since what T'ien-t'ai attained in mind, as stated above, is mystic words and phrases of the pre-Lotus sutras, which he explained in his *Great Concentration and Insight*, it is needless to say that it cannot be compared with the theoretical section of the *Lotus Sutra*, not to mention the essential section. In this sense, the contention of the Danna faction seems more reasonable. Armed with these points, you should argue against the evil contention that the *Great Concentration and Insight* is superior to the *Lotus Sutra*.

For details, I wrote another fascicle [*A Treatise on Establishing the Right Way of Meditation*] and sent it to you. [Please consult it as needed.] I have certainly written to relay to you the gist of the doctrine transmitted to me.

Respectfully yours,
Nichiren (signature)
28th day of the second month
in the 12th year of Bun'ei (1275)
In Response to Sairen-bō

Misawa-shō (ST 275)

Introduction

This letter was written in the fourth year of the Kenji Period (1278) by Nichiren from Minobu, addressed to Lord Misawa of Suruga Province (Shizuoka Prefecture today). It is a reply to a letter by Misawa containing questions about the teaching, sent together with a number of offerings. We know little about Lord Misawa except that he is known as a rather passive believer, unlike Shijō Kingo who is known to be an intensely ardent follower.

Nichiren begins by discussing the difficulty of Buddhist studies and the persecutions incurred by the Buddha and His disciples during His lifetime and after His death. Nichiren describes his own persecutions and explains how it is he and only he who has met with the sort of persecutions exactly as laid out in the stories about the future included in the Teacher of the Dharma chapter of the *Lotus Sutra*. Consequently, he claims that he is the foremost among those who practice the *Lotus Sutra* in the Latter Age of Degeneration, and as such, acknowledges his duty towards unselfish service, and explains that he entered Mt. Minobu without hesitation. Nichiren speaks of his own practice, differentiating that which he experienced up to his banishment to Sado Island from that which he realized after he was banished, clearly suggesting that the latter is the preferred model of thought and practice. Nichiren then touches upon obligations in faith, referring to his refusal to meet with the Lady Nun of Utsubusa, because she was only dropping by Minobu, and maintaining her original objective: to pay homage to her local Shinto deity. Finally, Nichiren emphasizes that the Shingon sect is the way of evil leading towards the destruction of the nation.

This letter represents a vital piece of evidence provided by Nichiren himself upon which many scholars rely in supporting the fact that there exists a difference in Nichiren's revelation of doctrines and intensity of teaching before and after his Sado exile.

A Letter to Lord Misawa of Suruga

I am very grateful for the many offerings that you have sent to us here in Minobu from so far away, such as the 100 *kōji* [a kind of orange, dark yellow in color and, flat and small in shape], seaweed, *nori* [processed seaweed], *ogo* [red seaweed], as well as the short-sleeved kimono from the Lady Nun of Utsubusa.

I have taken a close look at your letter. The Buddha in the *Nirvana Sutra** says: "People who study Buddhism number as many as the particles of dust upon the earth. However, those who go on to become Buddhas number as few as the particles of dust that can rest upon one's fingernail."* After contemplating the difficulty of attaining Buddhahood, I have observed something with some conviction. It is possible for one not to be able to learn Buddhism correctly despite one's study of Buddhism because of one's stupidity. Or, though one may be very intelligent, it is possible that one may go awry and not be able to learn Buddhism correctly as a result of studying under an incompetent teacher.

Inasmuch as one is able to find a worthy instructor and a genuine teaching, to rid oneself of fetters, and to approach the state of Buddhahood, one will inevitably be faced with seven imposing consequences called the three hindrances and four devils* [disturbances that stand in the way of Buddhist practices], just as sure as a shadow follows its source, and as clouds are present when it rains. Though one perseveres and succeeds in relieving oneself of six of the above, one would not be able to attain Buddhahood should one succumb to the seventh disturbance. I will refrain from discussing the six disturbances here. The seventh great disturbance is called the King of Devils in the Sixth Heaven.

When we, mere ordinary humans* of the latter period, have completely absorbed the spirit of all the holy teachings of the Buddha's lifetime,* understood the heart of the widely acclaimed work of the *Great Concentration and Insight** by Grand Master T'ien-t'ai and approach Buddhahood, we nonetheless realize how difficult a task this is to accomplish. Upon the sight of one within the reach of Buddhahood, the King of Devils in the Sixth Heaven would be stirred to say: "If one is an entity of this world, this one not only strives to depart from the illusion of life and death and become a Buddha but also tries to lead as many as possible into Buddhism, controls this world, and transforms this defiled world into a paradise. What ought to be done?" He then calls together all his henchmen in the triple world,* the three regions of desire, form and non-form, and commands them: "Put each of your specialties to good use, causing trouble for that one who practices [to escape the world of delusions]. If it is not possible, invade the hearts of his students and believers, or of the people of his nation, to admonish and coerce him into giving up his practice. And if that does not work, I will go down to earth myself, penetrate the body and soul of the leader of the state, through whom I can oppress the one who practices, and put an end to his or her acquisition of Buddhahood." So, in this manner, do the King of Devils and his henchmen discuss.

I, Nichiren, had always foreseen this kind of problem, that it would not be simple for a mere human of the Latter Age to become a Buddha. How Śākyamuni Buddha* attained enlightenment is explained copiously in various sutras, and they all maintain that the Buddha was bothered by the King of Devils of the Sixth Heaven who imposed persecutions which seemed unbearable. The crimes of Devadatta [who is said to have thrown a boulder from atop a mountain which drew blood from the small toe of Buddha's foot, which, as slight as it may seem, was still an act that caused injury], and King Ajātaśatru [who is thought to have let loose wild elephants in the attempt to trample Buddha to death] could all be attributed to the machinations of the King of Devils of the Sixth Heaven.

Moreover, the Teacher of the Dharma chapter of the *Lotus Sutra* claims, "Considering the numerous accounts of persecution even during Śākyamuni's lifetime, how much more can be expected after Śākyamuni's death." Whatever persecution occurs during Śākyamuni's lifetime, a mere human, as is Nichiren, would probably not be able to withstand such pressure for a day or even a moment. What would be more inconceivable would be to endure several major persecutions for 50 years or so. If that is not enough, it is said that the severity of the persecution would be 100, 1,000, 10,000, and 1,000,000 times greater for those of the latter period, which is why I have often wondered how we are to bear this.

They say that a sage knows the future. Of the three periods, past, present and future, being able to foresee the future defines the true worth of a sage. Not that Nichiren is a sage, but I have always known that Japan in this present day is on her way to destruction [unless she is converted to the true teaching of the *Lotus Sutra*]. Undoubtedly, this corresponds with the sutra that claims, "Problems are bound to increase after the death of the Buddha." For one to possess knowledge of this, and yet make admonishments, such a person is indeed the one who practices* the *Lotus Sutra* in the Latter Age of Degeneration whom the Buddha had predicted. Even if one is aware of the consequences, if one does not step forward, one will encounter problems within the cycle of life and death. Such a person, and not anyone else, would be made out to be a sworn enemy of Lord Śākyamuni Buddha, and a rival foe of the head of the Japanese state as well. Upon death, that person would fall to the Hell of Incessant Suffering, a hell much like a large castle to which the most vile of sinners are sent. The scene of people being tormented there is certainly indicative of this, so I have thought. We may be deprived of food and clothing, be admonished by our parents, brothers and sisters, and teachers, and be coerced by the head of the state and the masses. But let us protest without the slightest hesitation. These days, I am resolved that if one is to have reservations, then one should not protest at all.

From sometime in the remote past until this day, I must have had several occasions to have come into contact with the *Lotus Sutra,* and to have become a believer as well. As a consequence of this, I was probably able to withstand one or two instances of persecution. But since these tenacious obstacles have occurred in close succession, my faith may have been broken and weathered away. This time, regardless of what kind of difficulty I am to face, I proclaim that I am determined not to back down. Thus, I spoke up and have experienced this kind of persecution from time to time, just as is predicted by the sutra.

Presently, my singular concern is not to succumb to these great difficulties and not to abandon the *Lotus Sutra.* This has strengthened my faith. Through my experiences thus far, I have personally lived out the prophecies set forth in the sutra. I am confident that I can weather these ordeals, which is why I have come to live on this mountain. Whether or not each of you lose your faith in the *Lotus Sutra,* all of you have helped to save Nichiren's life at one time or another. How can I think of you as strangers? As before, I, Nichiren, do not care what happens to me. No matter what happens, if I am able to retain my faith and become a Buddha, I have pledged, without exception, to guide each and every one of you. That all of you are not as versed in Buddhism as is Nichiren, that you are secular, own property, have wives and children, as well as men in your employ, must make it difficult for you to persevere in maintaining faith. So being the case, I have long said that you may pretend not to be believers of the *Lotus Sutra.* As you all have come to Nichiren's aid, I will not disown you under any circumstance. I shall never neglect you.

Now, as far as my theology goes, I would like you to think that what I have expressed before being banished to Sado Island can be equated with the 40 or so years in which Śākyamuni had taught before revealing the *Lotus Sutra* [that is, the truth and true aims of the Buddha were not directly divulged in those years]. If the ruler of this country desires to govern the people under a proper political principle, then there will always be an opportunity for me to debate with the priests of the Shingon sect. I shall expound my precious teaching for the first time then. Even if I had discussed this only within the circle of my disciples, some of it would bound to have leaked out making it difficult to conduct a discussion [as a result of the scheming of the Shingon priests]. Such is why I have kept quiet about this with all of you. However, since the night of the 12th day of the ninth month in the eighth year of the Bun'ei Period (1271), when I was about to be beheaded at Tatsunokuchi [on the outskirts of Kamakura], I have come to think that it was unwise of me to have kept the truth from some of you who have stuck with me. There is a teaching I have disseminated quietly to my disciples from the island of Sado [where I had been banished].

This is a teaching which great commentators in India and great teachers in China and Japan who have come after the Buddha, such as Kāśyapa,* Ānanda,* Nāgārjuna,* Vasubandhu,* T'ien-t'ai,* Miao-lê,* Dengyō* and Gishin,* knew to be true in their hearts but never imparted. This is because the Buddha had strictly warned that, "this important teaching should not be passed on in the thousand years of the Age of the True Dharma and thousand years of the Age of the Semblance Dharma before entering the Latter Age of Degeneration." Nichiren is not a direct emissary of the Buddha. However, since I have come to be in this Latter Age of Degeneration and have, quite beyond expectations, attained this doctrine, I would like to transmit it in the capacity of a herald, until Bodhisattva Superior-Practice, a messenger of the Buddha, appears. Once this teaching is exposed, the teachings spread by the elders during the Ages of the True Dharma and Semblance Dharma would pale in comparison, just as the stars are obscured by the rising sun, or as if we see a dull performance after a skillful one. It is written in the sutras that when the Latter Age of Degeneration dawns, such things as the spiritual power of Buddhist sculptures and priests of the temples built in the Ages of the True and Semblance Dharmas would fade, and their only legacy would be the dissemination of this great teaching throughout the world (Jambudvīpa).* All of you should feel grateful that you are endowed with the opportunity to have come across such a wonderful teaching.

Now, my conscience is very stricken concerning the matter of the Lady Nun of Utsubusa because she, being quite elderly, came all the way here. However, I did not give her an audience because she came to see me here in Minobu after paying a visit to a local Shinto shrine. Had I met her, it would have instigated her to sin. A Shinto god is a follower, whereas the *Lotus Sutra* is the master. To visit the master after visiting their follower would also go against norms of society. Moreover, as long as one has become a nun, it goes without exception that one must first serve the Buddha. It was for the recurrence of these kinds of abhorrent gestures that I did not meet with her.

The Lady Nun is not the only one whom I have refused to meet. There are many who have dropped by after visiting Shimobe Spa. I have turned away these people as well. The Lady Nun of Utsubusa, from my stance, is as old as my parents. And because she came a long way without being able to meet me, she is apt to feel some discouragement. Nevertheless, I have acted with the intention that she may realize my underlying reasoning.

Aside from this, I have heard rumors that you have been ill after we last met about a year ago, prompting me to think of dispatching a messenger to inquire about your health. That may have been the best thing to do. But according to my disciples, sending someone would instead make you feel worse. Discerning this to be a lesson in decency, I decided not to pursue this. Always a solicitous man, I anticipated that you would send us a messenger if you were ill. But, since there was no intimation as such, I purposely kept my reserve. However it is a fact that I did contemplate this. Although transience is the way of the world, the fact that things appeared somewhat different this year from last, I was dispirited that I may not be able to hear from you again, until I received your correspondence, the utmost of delights. Please convey this to the Lady Nun as well.

I would prefer to explain the teaching in detail, however I will confine myself, as it would become too lengthy. Although I have already mentioned something about the Zen,* Pure Land,* and Ritsu sects,* it is primarily the Shingon sect that will devastate Japan and China. Not only did the six esoteric masters, Tripiṭaka Masters Śubhākarasiṃha,* Vajrabodhi,* Amoghavajra* and Grand Masters Kōbō,* Jikaku* and Chishō*, misinterpret the comparative superiority between the triple Shingon sutras [the *Great Sun Buddha Sutra*, the *Diamond Peak Sutra*, the *Sutra on the Act of Perfection*] and the *Lotus Sutra*, the three Grand Masters were completely misled in adopting and then disseminating to the head of Japan and her people, the creations of the three Tripiṭaka Masters, the two mandalas of the Diamond Realm and the Matrix Realm, which, to deceive people, were claimed to have come from India. Recall that the reason the Emperor Hsüan-tsung of China lost power was that he put faith in the teachings of the Shingon sect. Likewise, the country of Japan is slowly weakening. The agreement that the Great Bodhisattva Hachiman* would help to protect 100 generations of Japanese emperors was dismantled. That the 82nd ruler, Retired Emperor Gotoba, lost his reign to the military at Kamakura and was banished to the island of Oki, is another example of the fact that the three priests, including Grand Master Kōbō, offered prayers using a wrong scripture. It is just as is written in the 25th chapter of the *Lotus Sutra*: those who wish bad fortune upon others are the very ones who will suffer. As the Kamakura Bakufu purged the evil Shingon teaching along with evil Shingon masters, 18 more generations of emperors should succeed after the fall of Gotoba. By right, they should be able to rule for 100 generations, but alas, they have succumbed to the same mistaken teachings and their teachers, resulting in a vacuum of competent leadership. It is the will of the King of the Brahma Heaven,* Indra,* the Sun God and Moon God, and the Four Heavenly Kings* to have the country of Japan threatened by an outside power [the Mongols]. Despite the fact that one who practices the *Lotus Sutra* was sent to admonish them, these rulers have chosen to favor the messengers sent by the Shingon teachers, thus destabilizing society, politics, and the Buddhist teachings as well. In effect, they have become enemies of the *Lotus Sutra*, and with time, this country will be destroyed. The rash of epidemics forebodes the imminence of a large-scale war. Oh, how miserable, how miserable it is!

    23rd day of the second month
    Nichiren (signature)

To Lord Misawa:
    As always, please let it be known that the people of Suruga are all united in one.

Shimon Butsujō-gi (ST 277)

Introduction

Written to Lord Toki, in the fourth year of the Kenji Period (1278) at Mt. Minobu. The original letter is kept at the Hokekyōji Temple in Nakayama, Chiba Prefecture. It represents a letter of thanks to Lord Toki for sending a donation in memory of his late mother. It also includes a discussion of Buddhist concepts. The study of the *Lotus Sutra* includes two manners of practice involving the *jurui* seed and *sōtai* seed to attain Buddhahood. The letter clearly states that what we know as evil passions, karma, and suffering from pre-Lotus Sutra teachings, including the first half of the *Lotus Sutra,* can be transformed into the three merits: Dharma Body, wisdom, and emancipation. This is a concept that can only be found in the *Lotus Sutra,* says Nichiren, and by which one may become a Buddha with one's present body.

Listening to the One Buddha Vehicle Teachings for the First Time

Seven ties of coins have reached us here in Kai Province from Shimofusa Province. We have accepted this as a generous offering commemorating the third anniversary of your beloved mother's passing.

Question: At the beginning of the *Great Concentration and Insight,** Grand Master Chang-an praises it saying, "We have never heard of the teaching of the *Great Concentration and Insight* called tranquility and contemplation." What does this mean?

Answer: This is a word in praise of the perfect and sudden meditation, one of Grand Master T'ien-t'ai's three concepts of meditation: the gradual, mutable and perfect and sudden meditations.

Question: What is the perfect and sudden meditation?

Answer: It is another name for the Lotus Meditation.

Question: What then is the Lotus Meditation?

Answer: Regarding the practice of the *Lotus Sutra** for the ordinary and unenlightened people* in these latter days, there are two doctrines, that of *"jurui seed"** [opening and merging related concepts] and that of *"sōtai seed",** [opening and merging of opposite concepts] leading them into the one Buddha vehicle.

Question: What is the source of this information?

Answer: It originates from four characters, *shu* (seed), *sō* (appearance), *tai* (entity or body), and *shō* (nature), found in the fifth chapter of the *Lotus Sutra*, Simile of Herbs. *Jurui* seed and *sōtai* seed are based on the first of the above four characters, seed, specifically the seed of Buddhahood. The *Profound Meaning of the Lotus Sutra* comments on *jurui* seed, thus: "Anyone with a soul possesses the seed of Buddhahood. If one hears but a phrase of the sutra, one would realize that one has the seed of Buddhahood. Should one put one's hands together and bow in prayer towards the Buddha, then one is able to advance toward Buddhahood." *Sōtai* seed means opening and merging the three paths of evil passions, karma, and suffering, into three merits of *hosshin* (Dharma Body), *hannya* (wisdom) and *gedatsu* (salvation), respectively.

Of these two concepts, *jurui* seed has its basis in the *Lotus Sutra*, although some aspects of it can be related to various sutras occurring prior to the *Lotus Sutra*. Grand Master Miao-lê* has observed in his *Annotations to the Profound Meaning of the Lotus Sutra* that the *"jurui* seed but not *sōtai* seed can be found in distinct teachings." Distinct teachings, in this case, do not suggest the usual meaning referring to the four teachings, *zō (tripiṭaka), tsū* (common), *betsu* (distinct) and *en* (perfect), rather it points to the perfect teachings that have existed prior to the *Lotus Sutra* or the perfect teachings taught by those other than Grand Master T'ien-t'ai. Even within the theoretical section or the first half of the *Lotus Sutra*, verses of the Expedients chapter mention the opening and merging of *jurui* seed of human and heavenly beings. The teaching beginning with the verse "those who pay their respect to the ashes of the Buddha", followed by 20 or so lines claiming that even a small gesture of goodness would lead to enlightenment amounts to the opening and merging of *jurui* seed.

Question: What about the opening and merging of *sōtai* seed?

Answer: The *Great Concentration and Insight* states:

What does it mean to listen to a perfect teaching? It means that one's ephemeral body would be transformed instantly into that of the everlasting Dharma Body, one's evil passions into unsurpassed wisdom, and one's evil karma into emancipation. As it is observable, there are three names to this, but only one thing to which it refers. In short, three aspects have been connected with one phenomenon. In fact, since these three concepts all concern one entity, there should be no differences among them. Should one approach the epitome of the Dharma Body, then one also nears the utmost of wisdom and emancipation. Should one's wisdom be pure and just, then it follows that one's Dharma Body and emancipation would also be thus. Should one's emancipation be free and flowing, then it can be assumed that one's Dharma Body and wisdom would also be thus. In this way, parallels exist not only between the three bodies and the three evils, but in all phenomena. For this reason, all phenomena are intertwined with notions of Buddha Dharma, such that nothing is missing. This manner of viewing things is what is meant by "listening to a perfect teaching."

This interpretation represents a guide to the opening and merging of *sōtai* seed.

Question: What does this mean?

Answer: The citation above from the *Great Concentration and Insight* claims that "life and death" refers to our mind and bodies, which are the results of suffering from our past karmas, specifically those delineated by the five elements, the twelve sense fields [six sense-organs and their corresponding objects] and the 18 "worlds" [six sense organs and six corresponding objects plus six consciousnesses]. "Evil passions" can be categorized into three delusions:* delusions arising from incorrect views and thoughts, delusions as numerous as particles of dust, and delusions which hinder the knowledge of the ultimate reality. "Bad actions" refer to such serious sins as the five rebellious sins,* the 10 evil acts and the four major sins. Dharma Body stands for the Buddha with the Dharma Body, unsurpassed wisdom stands for the Buddha with the Reward Body, and emancipation refers to the Buddha with the Accommodative Body. From an indefinite past, we have been connected with the three paths: evil passions, karma and suffering. Fortunately, because of our association with the *Lotus Sutra*, we can be assured that the illusions of the three paths instantly convert to the three merits* of Dharma Body, unsurpassed wisdom, and emancipation.

Question: I ask with much hesitation whether it can be that fire can beget water, or that a rock may beget flowers. From the standpoint of Buddhism, it is understood that a bad effect would follow from a bad cause. Similarly, a good product would arise from something good. Nevertheless, when we look at our origins, it is clear that we are the products of the binding of our parent's red and white blood. In like manner, the root of evil can spawn impurity. While we could attempt to wash it with the waters of the ocean, it would still not be cleansed. When we examine our minds and bodies, that which receives this painful lot, we can say that they are composed of the three basic evil passions: greed, anger, and ignorance. When these two, evil passions and their painful results, come together to form various karma, they give rise to the paths of karma that chain us to the painful environment of the triple world* and six realms [lower six of the 10 realms]. It is like a bird trapped in a cage. How is it that the three ways, evil passions, karma, and suffering can turn into the three merits, Dharma Body, Reward Body and Accommodative Body of the Buddha? It is, for example, as difficult to expect an appealing fragrance to arise from feces made to look like sandalwood.

Answer: Your question is quite natural. It is difficult for me to provide a sufficient answer as well. In any case, Nāgārjuna,* the 13th transmitter* of the Buddhist teaching whom even Grand Master T'ien-t'ai respected as the Founder, comments on the single character *myō* in his *Great Wisdom Discourse:* "It is the same as a renowned doctor who prescribes a poison for medicine." What is meant here by poison? It refers to the three paths, that are our evil passions, karma, and suffering. Then what is meant by medicine? It refers to the three merits: Dharma Body, unsurpassed wisdom, and emancipation. What is meant by prescribing a poison for medicine? It means nothing but transforming the three evils to three merits. Grand Master T'ien-t'ai in his *Profound Meaning of the Lotus Sutra* states: " *Myō* of *Myōhō Renge-kyō* means unfathomable." And in the *Great Concentration and Insight,* he claims: "As one thought contains 10 realms, there should be no less than 3,000 modes of existence contained in one thought, making it impossible to separate one's thought from all existing things. This relationship is difficult to explain in words, such that this thought falls within the realm of incomprehension." Becoming a Buddha with one's present body* is not easily defined. These days, the Kegon* and Shingon* sects have stolen this profound concept of the *Lotus Sutra* and have made it their own. They are the most notorious burglars of the day.

Question: Is it possible for us, ordinary people* of this latter age of decadence, to grasp such a difficult teaching?

Answer: Since you may not be convinced by what I say, let me cite the 93rd section of Nāgārjuna's *Great Wisdom Discourse:** "Contrary to a general belief that an *arhat* who has attained control of all his evil passions cannot become a Buddha, that he does in fact attain Buddhahood can only be understood by the Buddha. It is well that Buddhist academics discuss this point. However, this is not something that can be proven through arguments. This fruitless discussion need not be necessary. This truth will make itself apparent if and when one attains Buddhahood. Those who have not attained enlightenment need not be pressed to debate a matter as whether or not one has attained Buddhahood and leave that to faith." This means that the deeper meanings of the *Lotus Sutra* [*sōtai* seed doctrine and immediate attainment of Buddhahood] are not understood even by those bodhisattvas of pre-Lotus sutras,* who believing in the distinct teaching have managed to rid themselves of the eleven forms of ignorance, and such great bodhisattvas of perfect teaching as Samantabhadra* and Mañjuśrī,* who have torn themselves away from the 41 types of ignorance. Needless to say, it is much more perplexing for the three vehicles [*śrāvaka, pratyekabuddha* and bodhisattvas] who are associated with the more rudimentary teachings of the *piṭaka* and common, or for the unenlightened of the latter age. Such is Nāgārjuna's thesis.

Pondering the *Great Wisdom Discourse*, we are reminded of the quotation in the second chapter of the *Lotus Sutra*, Expedients, which reads: "Only between Buddhas and Buddhas can this be understood." This quotation exists for the Two Vehicles* [*śrāvaka* and *pratyekabuddha*] who, through pre-Lotus teachings, have overcome the delusions arising from incorrect views and thoughts, have undertaken extreme austerities, turning the body to ashes and annihilating consciousness,* and are allowed to gain enlightenment by the grace of the *Lotus Sutra* which assures that the three ways of evil passions, karma, and suffering would immediately be transformed into the three merits of the Dharma Body, wisdom, and emancipation. Since what was believed to be beyond the reach of the Two Vehicles is attainable, it can be assumed that bodhisattvas and the untutored may also anticipate enlightenment. Grand Master T'ien-t'ai in his *Profound Meaning of the Lotus Sutra* claims: "Granted that the condition in which someone of the Two Vehicles reaches a state of extreme mental and physical exhaustion where desires, which were called poison, are thoroughly extinguished, then with the advent of enlightenment as guaranteed by the *Lotus Sutra* such a poison would be transformed into medicine. This summarizes Nāgārjuna's position. Nāgārjuna's *Great Wisdom Discourse* further claims, 'The *Lotus Sutra* is indeed truly representative of an esoteric teaching. Other teachings cannot be referred to as being so defined.' "

Question: What merits exist for us, the uneducated, in listening to such an important teaching?

Answer: With this we can say that we have truly heard the *Lotus Sutra* for the first time. Grand Master Miao-lê claims in his *Annotations on the Great Concentration and Insight*: "If indeed the three evil ways can readily become the three merits, then it becomes possible to cross both kinds of rivers separating life and death, that experienced by men who are lost in rebirth and that of bodhisattvas who have managed to free themselves from delusions, not to mention rebirth in the triple world and six lower realms. When we, the unenlightened of the latter age, hear this teaching, we are not the only ones to gain enlightenment, but our parents would so benefit as well. Without a doubt, this truly exemplifies filial piety. Forgive me for the lack of detail in my writing as I am not well, but I hope to touch upon it again when an opportunity permits.

28th day of the second month
in the fourth year of the Kenji Period

Nichiren (signature)

To Lord Toki*

Toki Nyūdō-dono Gohenji: Chibyō-shō (ST 294)

Introduction

Written on the 26th day of the sixth month in the first year of the Kōan Era (1278) at Minobu, the original manuscript of this letter, known also as *Chibyō-shō, Treatise on Healing Sickness*, has been kept as a treasure in the Nakayama Hokekyōji Temple in Chiba Prefecture. It was written in response to Toki Jōnin, who donated a summer fabric through Shijō Kingo when visiting Nichiren Shōnin on Mt. Minobu, and requested Nichiren to perform a prayer service to prevent widespread epidemics.

Stating that while physical sickness can be cured by medicine, mental sickness cannot be cured without right faith in the *Lotus Sutra*, Nichiren declares that only through the *Odaimoku*, the gist of the essential section of the *Lotus Sutra*, can we deal with the slanderers of the True Dharma who are prevalent in the world. Especially, he states, when we try to spread *Odaimoku* chanting in the Latter Age of Degeneration, we will encounter difficulties greater than those encountered by Grand Masters T'ien-t'ai and Dengyō. According to Nichiren, the greater difficulties he and his followers encounter show the appearance of the "actual" doctrine of "3,000 existences contained in one thought" in contrast to the "theoretical" doctrine advocated by T'ien-t'ai and Dengyō, and it represents the true doctrine of the essential section.

Here lies the uniqueness of Nichiren Buddhism. Nichiren Shōnin termed his own interpretation of the doctrine of "3,000 existences contained in one thought" "actual" and called that of T'ien-t'ai and Dengyō "theoretical." On the basis of this "actual" interpretation of the doctrine of "3,000 existences contained in one thought," Nichiren Shōnin found the way of saving people by having them put their faith in and chant the *Odaimoku*.

A Response to Lay Priest Lord Toki: Treatise on Healing Sickness

According to your letter, epidemics have been widespread recently. They say that human beings have two kinds of sickness. First, our bodies get sick. Our bodies consist of the four elements: earth, water, fire and wind. As each of the four elements has 101 sicknesses, our bodies have a total of 404 sicknesses. These physical sicknesses do not necessarily depend on the Buddha to be cured. There is no physical sickness that cannot be cured by the medicine prepared by such famed physicians as Jisui, Rusui, Jīvaka* and P'ien-ch'üeh.

In the second place, our minds get sick in a vast number of ways. Beginning with the three poisons of greed, anger and stupidity, sicknesses in our minds total as many as 84,000. Even the two heavenly beings and three hermits* or the six non-Buddhist masters* in India could not cure them, much less the medicines administered by such sage rulers of ancient China as Shen-nung and the Yellow Emperor.

Mental sickness can also be subdivided into various kinds such as shallow, deep, heavy and light. The 84,000 troubles in the mind of ordinary men* in the six lower realms of spiritual progress [hell, realms of hungry spirits, beasts and birds, fighting spirits, men, and gods] can all be cured by Hinayana Buddhas, commentators and masters of the Hinayana Āgama sutras* and Hinayana schools of Kusha (Higher Special Dharma),* Jōjitsu (Completion of Truth)* and Ritsu (Precept).* However, when such Hinayana people are shackled by Hinayana teachings and go against Mahayana principles or try to be equal to Mahayana countries, although they do not intend to go against Mahayana Buddhism, they [Hinayana Buddhists] and their countries will contract various sicknesses. When they try to cure their mental sickness by means of the teaching of Hinayana Buddhism, they only intensify their troubles instead of curing them. Only those who practice Mahayana sutras can cure them.

Likewise, when believers of such provisional Mahayana sutras as the *Flower Garland Sutra,* *Revealing the Profound and Secret Sutra,* *Wisdom Sutra,* and *Great Sun Buddha Sutra* adhere to their biased opinions, insisting that their inferior faith equals or is even superior to the *Lotus Sutra,* and when rulers of the land recognize them without discerning their prejudices, the 84,000 mental sicknesses such as the three poisons will result. The harder they try to heal the sickness by means of their respective canonical sutras, the worse their troubles will be. Even if they try to cure their troubles by the *Lotus Sutra,* it will not work. It is not because the sutra is not good enough but because the people who try to use it are prejudiced.

The *Lotus Sutra* consists of two parts: the theoretical section [first half] and the essential section [latter half]. The difference between them is as clear as water and fire or heaven and earth. It is greater than the difference between the pre-Lotus sutras* and the *Lotus Sutra.* Although there are differences between the pre-Lotus sutras and the theoretical section of the *Lotus Sutra,* there exist some similarities between them. The pre-Lotus sutras preach the eight teachings [four methods of teaching and four doctrinal teachings], of which the perfect teaching is somewhat similar to that expounded in the theoretical section. The concepts of the Buddha preached in the pre-Lotus sutras and the theoretical section are not exactly the same. They are Buddhas with the inferior Accommodative Body, the superior Accommodative Body, the Reward Body, and the Dharma Body. Nevertheless, they all talk about the same Buddha who attained Buddhahood under the bodhi tree at Buddhagayā at the age of 30.

Now, regarding the difference between the essential and theoretical sections, the lord-preacher of the former is the Eternal Buddha who has been the Buddha since the eternal past while that of the latter is the historical Buddha who attained Buddhahood in this life at Buddhagayā. The difference between the two is as clear as between a 100-year-old man and an infant. Not only the lord-preacher but also His disciples are as different as water and fire. How much more so is it the case with the Buddha land between the "four lands" preached in the theoretical section and the "land of eternal tranquil light" of the essential section! The difference is beyond expression. Those who mix up the two, the theoretical and essential sections, are like those who cannot differentiate fire from water.

The Buddha had made a clear distinction between the two sections, but during more than 2,000 years since He passed away no one in India, China, Japan and the entire world (Jambudvīpa)* has ever clearly differentiated them. Only T'ien-t'ai* of China and Dengyō* of Japan seemed to have almost made a distinction between them, but they did not clarify the Lotus Tendai (T'ien-t'ai) law of precepts among important doctrines of the essential and theoretical sections. After all, although Grand Masters T'ien-t'ai and Dengyō knew this well in mind, they did not explain it clearly because: (1) the time was not right, (2) the people's ability to understand was not ripe, and (3) they were not entrusted by the Buddha to propagate the doctrine.

Now, we have finally entered the Latter Age of Degeneration, when great bodhisattvas appearing from underground* such as Bodhisattva Superior-Practice should propagate the teaching of the essential section. As the Latter Age of Degeneration* is the time for the essential section to spread, even if people with faith in Hinayana Buddhism, quasi-Mahayana Buddhism, or the theoretical section of the *Lotus Sutra* spread their respective teachings without committing any mistakes, they will serve no useful purpose. It is like a medicine for spring that is not useful in fall. Even if it is still useful in autumn, its effectiveness is not as good as in spring and summer. How much less useful they would be when they, Hinayana and quasi-Mahayana Buddhists and believers of the theoretical section, become confused with the differences between Hinayana and Mahayana Buddhism and provisional and true teachings. Moreover, as rulers in the past had put faith in their scriptures, built temples for them and donated pieces of farm land, it not only is inexcusable but also destroys the basis of their faith for them to slight the teachings of their canons. Therefore, they are furious at the man who criticizes their canons, and they slander the True Dharma and persecute the one who practices the *Lotus Sutra*.

Rulers of Japan have various reasons for believing in those liars and persecuting the one who practices the True Dharma. They side with the majority, and are unable to change either the Dharma upheld by the past rulers, their own stupidity, or their contempt for the one who practices the True Dharma. As a result, protectors of the True Dharma such as the King of the Brahma Heaven*, Indra,* the Sun God and Moon God, and the Four Heavenly Kings* punish the country, causing three calamities and seven disasters* as severe as have never been seen before. This is how epidemics spread last year, this year, and in the Shōka Era (1257-59).

Question: You say that epidemics spread in Japan because this country persecutes the one who practices the *Lotus Sutra** causing the protective deities to leave the country. If so, why is it that not only non-believers of the *Lotus Sutra* but also your disciples suffer or even die from the disease?

Answer: Your question seems most reasonable, but it is like knowing only one side of a coin. Virtue and evil have originally been incompatible but inseparable.

Looking at it from this point of view, we see that provisional teachings of sutras other than the *Lotus Sutra,* and Buddhist sects based on them, maintain that bodhisattvas up to the second highest rank [*tōgaku:* equivalent to enlightenment] have merits as well as demerits. However, according to the doctrine of "3,000 existences contained in one thought"* based on the *Lotus Sutra,* each of our minds is equipped with virtue as well as evil. Even bodhisattvas of the highest rank [*myōgaku:* wonderful enlightenment] have evil in mind. The Dharma-nature originally existing in our mind appears as the protective deities of the *Lotus Sutra* such as the King of the Brahma Heaven* and Indra,* whereas the fundamental darkness of mind* innate in us becomes the King of Devils in the Sixth Heaven.

Virtuous deities dislike evil persons, and evil spirits hate virtuous people. In the Latter Age of Degeneration, demons naturally prevail over the land like useless pieces of tile and stone or weeds and bushes. Virtuous deities who protect the one who practices the True Dharma have grown scarce and sages and wise men can hardly be seen. Therefore, it seems reasonable to assume that more people among the disciples of Nichiren than those of Pure Land Buddhists, Shingon (True Word) masters, Zen and Ritsu (Precept) monks should fall ill or die from the recent spell of epidemics. However, I do not know why but fewer of my disciples than those of other sects have gotten sick or died. I wonder if it is because my followers are small in number or have strong faith.

Question: Has there been an epidemic in the past as widespread as the one today in Japan?

Answer: During the reign of Emperor Sujin, the 10th sovereign of Japan counting from Emperor Jimmu, an epidemic spread causing more than half of the population to suffer or die from it. The emperor for the first time ordered provinces to invoke such gods as Goddess Amaterasu,* successfully subduing it. Thus, he is called Emperor Sujin (Revering Gods). This incident took place before Buddhism was introduced to Japan. Three emperors, the 30th, 31st and 32nd, as well as their subjects died from smallpox and epidemics. Praying to the gods for help did not work those times.

In the past, during the reign of the 30th sovereign, Emperor Kimmei, the Korean nation of Paekche sent to the Japanese Court not only Buddhist sutras, commentaries and priests but also a gilt bronze statue of the Lord Śākyamuni Buddha.* Soga Iname and his party insisted on worshipping the Buddha, but imperial subjects such as Mononobe Okoshi and people in general objected, declaring that if they worshipped the Buddha, the gods of Japan would get angry and the country would crumble.

While the Emperor was unable to make up his mind, three calamities and seven disasters occurred, more severe than had been experienced in the past, causing many of the people to die from the epidemic. Taking advantage of this, the Mononobes appealed to the emperor to "abandon the statue of the Buddha in order to seek happiness." They not only disgraced the Buddhist monks and nuns but also burnt the gilt bronze statue of Śākyamuni Buddha in a charcoal fire. The temple for the Buddha built by Soga Iname was also burnt down. Soon thereafter, both the anti-Buddhist leader Mononobe Okoshi as well as the emperor who sided with him in persecuting Buddhism passed away. The pro-Buddhist leader, Iname, also died of sickness.

Thereafter, Buddhism began to revive under the patronage of Soga Umako and an imperial princess [a niece of Umako who later became Empress Suiko]. When an epidemic spread again, the anti-Buddhist leader Mononobe Moriya declared: "Three emperors have already passed away as they worshipped the Buddha. My father also died of sickness. You should know that Prince Shōtoku, Soga Umako, and other pro-Buddhists are enemies of my parent. They are public enemies." Several thousand people including Prince Anahobe and Prince Yasube banded together not only to destroy Buddhist temples and statues but also to fight a civil war. In the end Moriya lost his life. Thus for 35 years after Buddhism was introduced to Japan, three calamities and seven disasters befell year after year. After Mononobe Moriya was killed by Soga Umako and Shinto gods were defeated by Buddhas, calamities and disasters suddenly came to an end.

The three calamities and seven disasters which occurred thereafter from time to time mostly resulted from the confusion between the true and false Dharmas of Buddhism. As these later calamities and disasters were involved with merely a few people, few provinces, or few palaces, they stemmed from either divine wrath, slandering the True Dharma, or grievances of the populace. However, the three calamities and seven disasters during the last 30 years have not been caused at all by divine wrath and popular grievances but solely by the hatred of Nichiren by all the people in Japan. Therefore, all the people in every province, county, district and village bear the feeling of anger as fierce as never heard of in the past and persecute me, Nichiren. This is the first time for an ordinary man, who has not extinguished the illusions of thought and desire, to bear this fundamental darkness of mind.* When such ignorant people pray to gods, Buddhas and the *Lotus Sutra* for protection, their disasters will only increase. The five characters of the Wonderful Dharma, the gist of the essential section of the *Lotus Sutra*, can deal with calamities and disasters if only one puts faith in them, but this is what the Buddha especially entrusted to the one who practices the *Lotus Sutra*.* In the final analysis, therefore, the calamities and disasters since the Shōka Period (1257-59) will not cease unless the truth and falsehood of Buddhist Dharmas are decided in public discussions.

The ten-object, ten-stage meditation method preached in the *Great Concentration and Insight** by Grand Master T'ien-t'ai has never been practiced since then. At the time of Grand Masters Miao-lê* and Dengyō,* there were a few who practiced it. As nobody has opposed them, it has remained intact.

The *Great Concentration and Insight* states that the "three hindrances and four devils"* will disturb those who practice Buddhism, but they do not constitute the obstacles to those who practice provisional sutras. They have been happening one by one right now to me, Nichiren, the one who practices the *Lotus Sutra*, and the "three hindrances and four devils" are more powerful than at the time of Grand Masters T'ien-t'ai and Dengyō.

There are two ways of meditating on the doctrine of "3,000 existences contained in one thought." One is the "theoretical" way, and the other is the "actual" way. Grand Masters T'ien-t'ai and Dengyō practiced the former. I, Nichiren, now practice the latter. As my method of practicing meditation is superior, difficulties befalling me are harder to bear. What T'ien-t'ai and Dengyō propagated was based on the doctrine of "3,000 existences contained in one thought" expounded in the theoretical section, while what I, Nichiren, propagate is based on the doctrine of "3,000 existences contained in one thought" in the essential section.

The difference between the two is as great as the difference between heaven and earth. Remember this especially at the time of the last moment of life. Have an unwavering faith in the *Lotus Sutra* and continue chanting the *Odaimoku*, which is the right way of meditation based on the "actual" doctrine of "3,000 existences contained in one thought."

Respectfully yours,
26th day of the sixth month
Nichiren (signature)

P.S. I have received your donation of a summer fabric, which you entrusted to Lord Shijō Kingo* to deliver at his convenience. Please tell everyone that I have received their recent donation according to the list made by Lord Shijō Kingo. Articles donated by Lay Priest Lord Ōta* have also been gratefully accepted according to the list by Lord Toki. Regarding another aspect of the doctrine described in this letter, I wrote to Lord Shijō Kingo about it, so you may borrow and read it.

Honzon Mondō Shō (ST 307)

Introduction

Written on Mt. Minobu in the ninth month of the first year of Kōan (1278). The questions come from Jōken-bō, a priest of the Seichōji Temple in Awa (Awa County in Chiba Prefecture today). Jōken-bō had asked to receive a *honzon* and had posed several questions about it. Nichiren Shōnin inscribed a *honzon* for him and sent it along with this letter, which explained the significance of the *honzon* by employing a series of 13 questions and answers. Jōken-bō and Gijō-bō were the Dharma brothers of Nichiren Shōnin. Jōken-bō was in charge of tutoring Nichiren in his childhood. On the day that Nichiren first proclaimed the supremacy of the *Lotus Sutra* and inaugurated the practice of chanting *Namu Myōhō Renge Kyō*, these two priests helped Nichiren Shōnin flee Mt. Seichō to escape the wrath of the steward, Tōjō Kagenobu. They corresponded with Nichiren Shōnin, even after he retired to Mt. Minobu. At the time of Dōzen-bō's passing, Jōken-bō succeeded him as the head priest of Seichōji Temple. After that, Jōken-bō and Gijō-bō deepened their faith in Nichiren Shōnin's teaching but they did not convert due to local hostility to Nichiren.

At the beginning of this letter, it states that ordinary people of the Latter Age of Degeneration should regard the *Odaimoku* of the *Lotus Sutra* as the *honzon*. Nichiren quotes both The Teacher of the Dharma chapter of the *Lotus Sutra* and the Nature of the Buddha chapter of the *Nirvana Sutra* to prove this statement. He refutes the *honzon* of the other schools one by one. He states that Śākyamuni Buddha and Grand Master T'ien-t'ai regarded the *Lotus Sutra* as the *honzon*. Nichiren Shōnin followed their example, stating that because the teaching of the *Lotus Sutra* enables us to know the Buddha, he regarded the Dharma of the *Lotus Sutra* as the *honzon*. He especially criticizes the *honzon* of the Shingon sect. Critical of Kūkai, Ennin and Enchin, Nichiren describes the propagation of esotericism in China and Japan. He states that the all pervasive esoteric Buddhism in Japan after the death of Grand Master Dengyō (Saichō) had become an archenemy of the *Lotus Sutra*. He summarizes his own experience of propagating the *Lotus Sutra* and refuting the Shingon school. For Nichiren, refuting the Nembutsu and Zen teachings was only a beginning. He regarded the slandering of the True Dharma by the esoteric Buddhists as the gravest error. He points out that unfolding before their very eyes is the prophecy of national ruin due to slander of the True Dharma stated in the *Risshō Ankoku-ron, Treatise on Spreading Peace Throughout the Country by Establishing the True Dharma*. As an example of Shingon's destructive influence on Japan, he cites the failed attempt to restore the Imperial regime by the retired Emperor Gotoba during the Jōkyū Disturbance as well as the earlier destruction of the Heike clan. Nichiren Shōnin warned that an attempt to force the Mongols to surrender by using esoteric prayers would bring about a third and final proof of Shingon's ruinous influence. Nichiren Shōnin states that the *honzon* of the five characters of the Wonderful Dharma has never been revealed since the death of the historical Buddha. He proclaims that this is the *honzon* that is to be propagated in the Latter Age of Degeneration. Nichiren Shōnin concludes this letter with the determination to transfer the merit obtained by propagating the *Lotus Sutra* to his parents, to his teacher and to all people.

Questions and Answers on the Honzon

Question (1): As ordinary people* who live in the evil latter days what should we define as the *honzon*?*

Answer (1): We should regard the *Odaimoku** of the *Lotus Sutra** as the *honzon*.

Question (2): According to which sutra passages or which learned monk's interpretation?

Answer (2): The Teacher of the Dharma chapter* of the *Lotus Sutra*, fascicle four, says: "Medicine-King!* Erect a stupa of the seven treasures in any place where this sutra is expounded, read, recited or copied, or in any place where a copy of this sutra exists! The stupa should be tall, spacious and adorned. You need not enshrine My relics *(śarīra)* in the stupa. Why not? It is because this sutra contains My perfect body." In the Nature of the Buddha chapter of fascicle four of the *Nirvana Sutra** it is said: "Kāśyapa!* Each Buddha regards the Dharma as master. For that reason the Buddha reveres and makes offerings to the Dharma. Because the Dharma is eternal, each Buddha is also eternal." Grand Master T'ien-t'ai* declares in his *Lotus Meditation Repentance:* "Make a raised seat in the training hall and place the *Lotus Sutra* there. There is no need to place a statue of the Buddha or a relic or other sutras. Only the *Lotus Sutra* is needed."

Question (3): The *honzon* of the four kinds of meditation preached in the *Great Concentration and Insight,** fascicle two, by Grand Master T'ien-t'ai is the Buddha of Infinite Life.* The *Lotus Sutra Wisdom of Insight Manual* translated by Tripiṭaka Master Amoghavajra* regarded Śākyamuni Buddha* and the Buddha of Many Treasures* as the *honzon*. Why do you discard these interpretations and instead regard the *Odaimoku* of the *Lotus Sutra* as the *honzon*?

Answer (3): This is not my own idea. It is based on the scriptural statements cited above and the interpretations of Grand Master T'ien-t'ai. Regarding the accusation that the *honzon* of the four kinds of meditation in the *Great Concentration and Insight* is the Buddha of Infinite Life, the *honzon* at the time of continuous sitting meditation, continuous moving meditation and neither moving nor sitting meditation in the four kinds of meditation is indeed the Buddha of Infinite Life. This is based on the *Questions of Mañjuśrī Sutra*, the *Sutra of Meditation to Behold Buddhas* and the *Invocation of Avalokiteśvara Sutra* and so on. However, these sutras were preached before the *Lotus Sutra*.[1] They are not the sutras in which Śākyamuni Buddha revealed His true intentions.

There are two kinds of half-moving half-sitting meditation in the four kinds of meditation. One is the Hōdō Meditation in which the seven Buddhas and eight bodhisattvas in the Hōdō sutras* comprise the *honzon*. The other one is the Lotus Meditation wherein Śākyamuni Buddha and the Buddha of Many Treasures are the *honzon*. However, when we think about the content of the *Lotus Meditation Repentance* referred to before, we should in fact make the *Lotus Sutra* the *honzon*. The *Lotus Sutra Wisdom of Insight Manual* by Tripiṭaka Master Amoghavajra is based on the Beholding the Stupa of Treasures chapter* [of the *Lotus Sutra*], and it regards Śākyamuni Buddha and the Buddha of Many Treasures of the *Lotus Sutra* as the *honzon*, but this idea is not the true intention of the *Lotus Sutra*. The *Odaimoku* [sacred title] of the *Lotus Sutra* is the *honzon* of Śākyamuni Buddha, the Buddha of Many Treasures* and the Buddhas of the worlds throughout the universe.* This *Odaimoku* should be the *honzon* for the one who practices the *Lotus Sutra*.

Question (4): In Japan the 10 schools are the school of the Treasure Chamber of the Abhidharma (Kusha),* the school of the Perfection of Truth (Jōjitsu),* the Discipline school (Ritsu),* the school of Dharma Characteristics (Hossō),* the Three Treatises school (Sanron),* the Flower Garland school (Kegon),* the True Word school (Shingon),* the Pure Land school (Jōdo),* the Meditation school (Zen)* and the Lotus school (Hokke).* Each of these schools has a different *honzon*. The Kusha, Jōjitsu and Ritsu schools all regard the lesser Śākyamuni Buddha with an inferior Accommodative Body[2] as the *honzon*. The Hossō and the Sanron schools regard the greater Śākyamuni Buddha with a superior Accommodative Body,[3] the teacher of the common teachings, as the *honzon*. The

Kegon school regards Śākyamuni Buddha, who is the Reward-bodied Vairocana on the lotus platform as the *honzon*. The Shingon school regards the Great Sun Buddha* as the *honzon*. The Jōdo school regards the Buddha of Infinite Life as the *honzon*. The Zen school regards the historical Śākyamuni Buddha[4] as the *honzon*. Why does the Tendai school alone regard the *Lotus Sutra* as the *honzon*, while all the other schools regard the Buddha as the *honzon*?

Answer (4): Considering the fact that all of the other schools regard the Buddha as the *honzon*, the reason why the Tendai school alone regards the *Lotus Sutra* as the *honzon* must be very significant.

Question (5): What is that significant reason? Also, which is superior, the Buddha or the sutra?

Answer (5): The *honzon* is always that which is the ultimate concern. For instance, Confucius regards the Three Emperors and the Five Sovereigns as the Most Venerable *(honzon)*. As Buddhists, we should regard Śākyamuni Buddha as the *honzon*.

Question (6): If so, why do you regard the *Odaimoku* of the *Lotus Sutra* and not Sakyamuni Buddha as the *honzon*?

Answer (6): As we see from the sutra citations and their interpretations quoted above, even Śākyamuni Buddha and Grand Master T'ien-t'ai regarded the *Lotus Sutra* as the *honzon*. This is not my own biased view. That's why I, Nichiren, though I live in the latter age of the decadent Dharma, regard the *Lotus Sutra* as the *honzon*, just like Śākyamuni Buddha and Grand Master T'ien-t'ai did. This is because the *Lotus Sutra* is both father and mother to Śākyamuni Buddha and it is also the true intention of all Buddhas. Śākyamuni Buddha and the Great Sun Buddha and each and every Buddha in the worlds throughout the universe are all born from the *Lotus Sutra*. This is why we regard the *Lotus Sutra*, viewed as the father and mother of all Buddhas, as the *honzon*.

Question (7): What is the proof?

Answer (7): The *Sutra of Meditation on Universal-Sage Bodhisattva,** considered to be the epilogue to the *Lotus Sutra,* declares: "This Mahayana sutra is each Buddha's treasure store, the true intention of all the Buddhas in all the worlds in the universe of the past, present and future, and it is the seed that gives rise to all the Buddhas of the past, present and future;" and "This Mahayana sutra is the eye of each Buddha and each Buddha is provided with the five eyes[5] by this Mahayana sutra. The threefold body[6] of the Buddha is produced by this sutra.

This sutra contains all Dharmas just as the great ocean contains all water. The immaculate threefold body of the Buddha is produced by this ocean-like sutra. The three aspects of the Buddha's body are like a field where gods and human beings can plant merit, and they are the first among those who are worthy to receive offerings." According to these sutra passages, the Buddha is born to the *Lotus Sutra*, which is like a mother who gives birth. The Buddha is the body and the *Lotus Sutra* is the spirit. Therefore the eye-opening ceremony for portraits and wooden statues of the Buddha should be done with the *Lotus Sutra*. It is a grave mistake to do the eye-opening ceremony with the Buddha-eye finger signs and mantra* of the *Great Sun Buddha Sutra* as is generally done these days.

Question (8): Which is better, regarding the *Lotus Sutra* as the *honzon* or regarding the Great Sun Buddha as the *honzon*?

Answer (8): If we follow the insistence of Grand Masters Kōbō,* Jikaku* and Chishō,* then the Great Sun Buddha is superior to the *Lotus Sutra*.

Question (9): For what reason?

Answer (9): Summarizing the Ten Levels of Mind, Grand Master Kōbō declares in his *Precious Key to the Secret Treasury*: "The eighth is the *Lotus Sutra*, the ninth is the *Flower Garland Sutra* and the 10th is the *Great Sun Buddha Sutra*," in reference to the progression from the shallowest to the profoundest doctrines. In Grand Master Jikaku's *Annotations on the Diamond Peak Sutra* and *Annotations on the Sutra on the Act of Perfection* as well as Grand Master Chishō's *Guide to the Great Sun Buddha Sutra* it is taught that "The *Great Sun Buddha Sutra* is the first and the *Lotus Sutra* is the second."

Question (10): What do you think of them?

Answer (10): According to the judgment of Śākyamuni Buddha, the Buddha of Many Treasures and the Buddhas all over the universe, "the *Lotus Sutra* is the best of all the Buddhist scriptures* which have been preached,[7] are being preached[8] or will be preached."*[9]

Question (11): Priests of the Tendai, Shingon and other schools, as well as the ruler and subjects of Japan today, and all the people in the world think, "How can Priest Nichiren match such Grand Masters as Kōbō, Jikaku and Chishō?" What do you think of this?

Answer (11): I, Nichiren, would like to ask in response: First, do you think that Grand Masters Kōbō, Jikaku and Chishō are superior to Śākyamuni Buddha, the Buddha of Many Treasures and the Buddhas of the worlds throughout the universe? Second, all the people of Japan today, including the ruler of Japan and his subjects, are children of Lord Śākyamuni Buddha. The *Nirvana Sutra*, which is the last will and testament of the Buddha, says, "Rely on the Dharma and not on people." For us to say, "The *Lotus Sutra* is the foremost of all sutras" is to rely on the Dharma. Are not those priests, the ruler, and his subjects and all the people who think Nichiren is inferior to those three Grand Masters, and even their servants, horses and cattle, therefore, all disobedient towards Śākyamuni Buddha?

Question (12): So do you think that Grand Master Kōbō did not read the *Lotus Sutra?*

Answer (12): Grand Master Kōbō must have read all the sutras. However, in order to determine the relative profundity in doctrine among the Lotus, the *Flower Garland* and the *Great Sun Buddha Sutras* he misread the passages of the *Lotus Sutra* as, for instance, "This *Lotus Sutra* is the True Dharma of each Buddha. It is the lowest of all the sutras;" and "Medicine-King! There are so many sutras preached, and of these the *Lotus Sutra* is the third best." Furthermore, Grand Masters Jikaku and Chishō also misread it as saying, "Among sutras it is just in the middle;" and "It is the second." However, all of the Buddhas including Śākyamuni Buddha, the Buddha of Many Treasures and the Great Sun Buddha compare the *Lotus Sutra* with all the sutras, and preach, "the *Lotus Sutra* is the foremost,"[10] and "The *Lotus Sutra* is the very highest."[11] So, whom do you trust, Śākyamuni Buddha and the Buddhas throughout the universe, or the three Grand Masters Jikaku, Chishō and Kōbō? Because you look down on me, Nichiren, and instead trust in the opinions of the three Grand Masters, you have in effect disobeyed Śākyamuni Buddha and all the Buddhas throughout the universe.

Question (13): Grand Master Kōbō was from the province of Sanuki and was a disciple of Bishop Gonsō. He studied deeply the six schools [of Nara] including the Sanron and the Hossō,[12] and in the fifth month of Enryaku 23 (804) with the imperial commission of Emperor Kammu, he went to China. Obtaining an imperial permit from Emperor Shun-tsung, he inherited the Great Dharma of Chen-yen (Shingon) Buddhism from the Venerable Hui-kuo of the Ch'ing-lung Temple. Hui-kuo, the seventh patriarch of the Great Sun Buddha, passed on the Dharma of Chen-yen as if pouring water from one vessel to another. So, even though the people are not the same, the Dharma remained the same as if it were taught directly by the Great Sun Buddha himself. Although the vessels changed from the Great Sun Buddha to Vajrasattva,* followed by Nāgārjuna, Nāgābodhi, Vajrabodhi,* Amoghavajra,* Hui-kuo and finally Kōbō, the water which passed down remained the same Dharma of Chen-yen. Receiving the Dharma of Chen-yen from the Venerable Hui-kuo, Grand Master Kōbō returned to Japan by crossing the ocean of more than 3,000 *ri*, giving it to the three emperors Heijō, Saga and Junna. On the 19th of the fifth month of the 14th year of Kōnin (823), Kōbō received the imperial permit to build Tōji Temple, where he propagated the secret Dharma of Shingon. Because of this, everyone who uses a *vajra* [diamond-pounder] or rings the *vajra* bell of Shingon in the five provinces in the Capital District,[13] seven circuits,[14] 66 provinces,[15] and two islands,[16] that is, all over Japan, are all disciples of Grand Master Kōbō without exception.

Grand Master Jikaku was from Shimotsuke Province and was a disciple of Kōchi Bodhisattva.[17] In the third year of Daidō (808) at the age of 15, he climbed up Mt. Hiei,* where for 15 years he studied the six schools[18] as well as the Hokke (Tendai) and Shingon schools. Going over to T'ang China in the fifth year of Jōwa (838), during the reign of Emperor Wu-tsung, he met several revered T'ien-t'ai (Tendai) and Chen-yen (Shingon) priests of great renown such as Fa-ch'üan, Yüan-chêng, I-chên, Fa-yüeh, Tsung-jui, and Chih-yüan, in order to master the exoteric and esoteric teachings. Specifically, he spent 10 years studying Chen-yen to become the ninth patriarch after the Great Sun Buddha. Returning to Japan in the first year of Kajō (847), he became the teacher of Emperor Nimmyō, wrote commentaries on the *Diamond Peak Sutra** and the *Sutra on the Act of Perfection.** During the periods of Ninju and Saikō, he built the Sōji-in Temple on Mt. Hiei, and became the third Chief Priest of the Enryakuji Temple. The infusion of Shingon Buddhism into the Japanese Tendai school began with him.

Then Grand Master Chishō from Sanuki Province climbed up Mt. Hiei at the age of 14 in the fourth year of Tenchō (827), and became a disciple of Chief Priest Gishin.*[19] In Japan he studied the eight schools[20] under Chief Priest Gishin, Grand Masters Jikaku, Enchō,[21] and Kōjō.[22] In the first year of Ninju (853) with the imperial commission of Emperor Montoku, he went to China to study the exoteric and esoteric teachings under such masters as Āchārya Fa-ch'üan and Venerable Liang-hsü for several years during the reign of Emperor Hsüan-tsung (in the Ta-chung Era). In the second year of Ten'an (858) he returned to Japan and became the teacher of Emperors Montoku and Seiwa.

Successive rulers and their subjects have respected and revered these three Grand Masters and converted to their teachings as though they were the sun and moon for the sake of their present and future lives. Because of this, common people who have no understanding have no choice but to respect and believe these three Grand Masters and their teachings. Unless we disobey the admonition of Śākyamuni Buddha found in the *Nirvana Sutra:* "Rely on the Dharma and not on people," how can we depend on these teachers in China and Japan like Grand Masters Kōbō, Jikaku and Chishō instead of the Buddha? If we obey the admonition, then how can we gain a better understanding? In the end, what should we do?

Answer (13): In regard to the spread of Buddha Dharma in India during the first thousand years following the death of Śākyamuni Buddha, Hinayana teachings were propagated during the first 500 years and then Mahayana teachings during the second 500 years. During these years debates continued between Mahayana and Hinayana Buddhism, and between provisional and true teachings.* However a clear distinction did not develop yet between exoteric and esoteric teachings.* Buddha Dharma was transmitted to China for the first time 15 years after the beginning of the Age of the Semblance Dharma. At first, heated debates occurred between Confucianism and Buddhism, but no determination was reached as to which was superior. As Buddha Dharma gradually spread, quarrels began between Mahayana and Hinayana and between provisional and true teachings. However, no further differences developed between them until 600 years after the introduction of the Buddha Dharma into China, when the three Tripiṭaka Masters Śubhākarasiṃha,* Vajrabodhi* and Amoghavajra came from India to establish the Chen-yen school during the reign of Emperor Hsüan-tsung. As a result, other schools such as T'ien-t'ai and Flower Garland were looked down upon, and everyone from the Emperor down to the common people believed that the difference between the Chen-yen and the *Lotus Sutra* was as vast as that between heaven and earth. After that, at the time of Emperor Te-tsung, Grand Master Miao-lê* perceived that the Chen-yen could not compare to the *Lotus Sutra*, but since he didn't insist upon this strongly, there was no one who knew the comparative superiority between the Lotus and Chen-yen schools.

During the reign of the 30th Emperor Kimmei, the Buddha Dharma was transmitted to Japan for the first time through the Kingdom of Paekche. For more than 30 years after its introduction, there was a heated debate between the pro-Buddhists and the native Shintoists. During the reign of the 34th sovereign, Empress Suiko, Prince Shōtoku firmly established Buddha Dharma in Japan. Two high priests, Hyegwan from Koguryô and Kwallŭk of Paekche, came to Japan and established the Sanron school. At the time of Emperor Kōtoku, Priest Dōshō went to China, transmitting Zen Buddhism to Japan upon his return. During the reign of Emperor Temmu, Chihō brought the Hossō teachings from Silla. Then, during the reign of the 44th Emperor Genshō, Tripiṭaka Master Śubhākarasiṃha brought in the *Great Sun Buddha Sutra*,* but it did not spread widely. At the time of Emperor Shōmu, High Priest Shên-hsiang and Bishop Rōben brought over

Kegon teachings. At the time of the 46th Emperor Kōken, the revered priest Chien-chên* brought Ritsu teachings and the *Lotus Sutra*, but he only propagated the Ritsu school and not the *Lotus Sutra*.

In the seventh month of the 23rd year of Enryaku (804), during the reign of the 50th Emperor Kammu, Grand Master Dengyō went to China with an imperial commission and received the meditation methods and wisdom of the Lotus school from Tao-sui* and Hsing-man,* who were both disciples of Grand Master Miao-lê. Grand Master Dengyō also received the rules of conduct for bodhisattvas from Precept Master Tao-hsüan* through these two masters. Furthermore, he received the secret Dharma of Chen-yen from the Venerable Shun-hsiao before returning to Japan. It seemed to him that the comparative superiority between the Shingon and Hokke teachings could not be decided according to opinions of the Chinese scholars. Therefore, he compared interpretations of the *Great Sun Buddha Sutra* and those of the *Lotus Sutra* by himself, concluding that not only was the *Great Sun Buddha Sutra* inferior to the *Lotus Sutra*, but also its commentaries[23] had stolen the mind of T'ien-t'ai and put it into the Shingon school. Resentful of seeing the *Great Sun Buddha Sutra*, the basic sutra of the Shingon school, slighted, Grand Master Kōbō later tried to re-establish the reputation of the Shingon school by stating deceivingly, "The *Lotus Sutra* is inferior not only to the *Great Sun Buddha Sutra* but also to the *Flower Garland Sutra*." However, if Grand Masters Jikaku and Chishō had not propagated the doctrine of Grand Master Kōbō on Mt. Hiei* and at the Onjōji Temple,*[24] the mistaken views of Grand Master Kōbō would not have become widespread in Japan. Grand Masters Jikaku and Chishō did not agree that the *Flower Garland Sutra* was superior to the *Lotus Sutra*, but regarding the relative superiority between the *Lotus Sutra* and the *Great Sun Buddha Sutra* of Shingon, they agreed completely with Grand Master Kōbō. These two did not realize it, but unintentionally they became the archenemies of Grand Master Dengyō.[25]

Many high priests in Japan thereafter were both wise and virtuous, but they were not equal to the three Grand Masters Kōbō, Jikaku and Chishō. As a result, for more than 400 years until today, all the people in Japan have decided that Shingon [and its basis the *Great Sun Buddha Sutra*] is superior to the *Lotus Sutra*. Though there are some who happened to study Tendai Buddhism and realized that Shingon is not equal to the *Lotus Sutra*, they do not dare to speak up for fear of incurring the wrath of such nobles as the retired rulers at the Ninnaji Temple and the Chief Priests of Mt. Hiei. Others who studied Tendai Buddhism without understanding that Shingon is not equal to the *Lotus Sutra*, may say, "Shingon and the *Lotus Sutra* are on the same level." Shingon priests, however, simply sneer at them saying, "That is incredibly mistaken," and hardly take them seriously.

Consequently, hundreds of thousands of temples and shrines all over Japan belong to the Shingon school. Even if by chance there are temples where both Shingon and Hokke teachings are practiced, they treat Shingon as the lord and the *Lotus Sutra* as a retainer. Or although some study both Shingon and Hokke, they all privately believe that Shingon is superior. As heads of temples and supervising officials are all members of the Shingon school, and because it is natural that subordinates follow their superiors, people in Japan are all members of the Shingon school.

Even though people of Japan all pay lip service to the sutra saying that, "The *Lotus Sutra* is supreme," in their minds they hold that "The *Lotus Sutra* is second" or even "The *Lotus Sutra* is in third place." They do so not only in their minds but also in their words and deeds. After Grand Master Dengyō, there has been no one who practices the *Lotus Sutra* in more than 400 years who reads, "The *Lotus Sutra* is supreme" in body, mouth and mind. Furthermore, I doubt that the one who practices, who "properly keeps the *Lotus Sutra*" will ever appear. As Śākyamuni Buddha predicts in the Teacher of the Dharma chapter of the *Lotus Sutra*, "Many people hate it with jealousy even in My lifetime. Needless to say, more people will do so after My extinction." All the people in the Latter Age of Degeneration, from the Emperor down to the common people, are all archenemies of the *Lotus Sutra*.

I, Nichiren, am a child of a fisherman who lived at the edge of the sea in the Tōjō District of Nagasa, in Awa Province, which is the 12th of the 15 provinces in the circuit of Tōkaidō. At the age of 12, I went to the Kiyosumidera Temple in the same Tōjō District to study. However, since this was a remote place, even though it was called a temple, there were no scholars there. That is why I visited other provinces as a part of my training and study. Because I was a nobody and had no one who could teach me, it was difficult to learn about the origin of the 10 schools and the comparative superiority among them. So I earnestly prayed, beseeching Buddhas and the bodhisattvas for assistance, and pondered the teachings in all the sutras. As a result, when I examine the 10 schools, the Kusha school[26] seems to be a teaching of shallow principles that corresponds to the Hinayana teachings. The Jōjitsu school mingles Hinayana and Mahayana, so this is mistaken. The Ritsu school, originally a Hinayana school, later considered itself to be a provisional Mahayana school[27] and now a true Mahayana school. Besides, there are the Ritsu teachings that Grand Master Dengyō received from Tao-sui, which is different from the Ritsu school mentioned here. The Hossō school, originally a shallow teaching of provisional Mahayana, grew impudent claiming to be equal to true Mahayana, and in the end tried to overcome such true Mahayana schools as Tendai. It is like Taira Masakado and Fujiwara Sumitomo rebelling against the Emperor. The Sanron school, which preaches the provisional

Mahayana doctrine of emptiness, also believes itself to be true Mahayana. The Kegon school is said to be a provisional Mahayana school, but it is superior to the other schools like an Imperial Regent or Chancellor. However, it stands against the *Lotus Sutra* just like a subject rebelling against a great king. The Jōdo school is a provisional Mahayana school, but Shan-tao* and Hōnen* cleverly preached that all the sutras other than the Pure Land sutras were too advanced for people and that the triple Pure Land sutras were easy to understand. They also taught that although people's capacity to understand* is good[28] during the Ages of the True and Semblance Dharmas, it is poor during the Latter Age of Degeneration.* Thus they claimed that the *nembutsu* is the suitable teaching for the people of inferior capacity in the Latter Age of Degeneration. Based on the capacity of the people and not on the truth of the doctrine, they refuted all the holy teachings of the Buddha's lifetime* and established Pure Land Buddhism. For example, this is like a base but clever person deceitfully praising and paying respects to a man with a poor mind for the sake of some gain, thereby causing a truly wise man to leave him. The Zen school insists that there is a True Dharma aside from all the sacred sutras of Śākyamuni Buddha preached during His lifetime. This ridiculous notion of discarding the sacred sutras of Śākyamuni Buddha to follow one's own opinions is like killing a parent in order to employ his children or a subject killing his own lord and taking his place. The Shingon school is not only a great liar but they also hide their origins so that foolish people cannot see through them and are deceived. First of all, there was no school known as Shingon in India, as they say there was. Where is the evidence? In any case, because the *Great Sun Buddha Sutra*, the basic canon of the Shingon school, has been brought to Japan, we can compare it to the *Lotus Sutra* and see that it is seven grades below the *Lotus Sutra*. The proof is clear in both the *Great Sun Buddha Sutra* and the *Lotus Sutra*, but I will omit quoting passages here. Nevertheless, the Shingon school claims that the *Great Sun Buddha Sutra* is a lord who is two or three grades superior to the *Lotus Sutra*. This is absolutely wrong. It is like Liu-tsung of Han [one of the so-called 16 kingdoms] who destroyed the Western Chin Empire and made its last emperor, Min-ti serve as a groom, and Ch'ao-kao, the treacherous subject of the Ch'in Dynasty, devising a stratagem and willfully ascending to the imperial throne. It is like Great Arrogant Brahman of India making a statue of Śākyamuni Buddha as a leg for his pulpit. In China, no one understood these points, so in Japan no one has raised any doubts about the Shingon school since its introduction to Japan more than 400 years ago.

Because there has been confusion as to the correct discernment of Buddha Dharma, the political order has been degenerating until in the end this country will be invaded by foreign forces. This is how Japan is going to fall. Only I, Nichiren, have realized this. For the sake of Buddha Dharma and political order, I, Nichiren, compiled essential passages from various sutras in one fascicle of writing entitled the *Risshō Ankoku-ron, Treatise on Spreading Peace Throughout the Country by Establishing the True Dharma,* and submitted it to the late Lay Priest Saimyōji.* I explained all of this in detail in that writing, but because ignorant people found it too hard to understand, I will now directly explain it with evidence.

The 82nd sovereign of Japan, Emperor Gotoba, who was called "Dharma-King" after his retirement, tried to overthrow Hōjō Yoshitoki, the Shogunal Regent of the Kamakura Shogunate. At the outset, on the 15th day of the fifth month in the third year of Jōkyū (1221), the ex-emperor captured Hangan Iga Tarō Mitsusue,[29] Shogunal Deputy in Kyoto. He assembled soldiers in five provinces in the Capital District and seven circuits, trying in vain to vanquish Hōjō Yoshitoki of Kamakura in Sagami Province. He was defeated by Hōjō Yoshitoki, and in the end, the ex-emperor himself was exiled to Oki Island. Two of his princes were sent to Sado Island[30] and Awa Province[31] respectively, and his seven courtiers were beheaded. Why was he defeated so thoroughly? For a ruler like himself to conquer Yoshitoki, his own subject, would have been just like a hawk capturing a peacock or a cat grabbing a mouse, but the reality was as if the cat was eaten by the mouse or the hawk was caught by the peacock.

Besides that, the imperial court made efforts in prayer for the purpose of forcing the Kamakura Bakufu to surrender. Tendai chief priest Bishop Jien, an elder of the Shingon school, Omuro (head priest) of the Ninnaji Temple, the head of the Onjōji Temple, and the high priests of wisdom-observing-precepts who shone like the sun and moon in the seven and 15 great temples in Nara all prayed with blood, sweat and tears from the 19th day of the fifth month until the 14th day of the sixth month using the 15 altars for the secret Dharma of Shingon established by the three Grand Masters Kōbō, Jikaku and Chishō. Finally, Omuro of the Ninnaji Temple, who was an imperial prince, performed in the Main Hall of the Imperial Palace the great Dharma prayer beginning on the eighth day of the sixth month, a prayer that has never been repeated as many as three times. Then, on the 14th day of that month the Kamakura army broke through the defense line at Uji and Seta and raided Kyoto, capturing the three retired emperors. They at once set fire to the Imperial Palace and razed it. Then the army exiled the three retired emperors to the three provinces and beheaded the seven courtiers. On top of this, the army broke into the Omuro palace capturing and beheading Seitaka, beloved attendant of the prince, who could not bear the tragedy and died in agony. Thus, after Seitaka and his mother died, tens of millions of people who depended on this prayer service were either dead or wished that they were. All these things happened in only seven days, between the eighth day of the sixth month, when Omuro began his prayers, and the 14th day. The 15 altar secret Dharma ceremonies that were performed on this occasion were such great Dharma ceremonies as the One-Syllable Golden Wheel, the Four Heavenly Kings, Immovable Guardian King, Great Power and Virtue Guardian King, Wheel-turning Noble King, the Wish-fulfilling Gem, Guardian King of Love, the Buddha-eye, the Six Syllables (Mañjuśrī), Diamond Boy (Vajra-kumāra), Wonderful Sight Bodhisattva, Guardian King Āṭavaka (Taigensui Myōō), the National Protection Sutra and so on. The purpose of these Dharma ceremonies was to chastise the national enemies, kill them and send their spirits to the Pure Land of Mystic Glorification, where Great Sun Buddha resides. The performers of this prayer were actually high priests of great status, including 41 notable people such as the chief priest of Mt. Hiei, Bishop Jien,[32] the elder of Shingon at that time, Prince Omuro of the Ninnaji Temple, Bishop Ryōson of the Jōjūin Temple at Mii, and also more than 300 priests accompanied them. Although the Dharma prayers, the performers, and the age were perfect, why was the imperial court defeated in this conflict? Even though they did not win, nobody knows why they were so easily and shamefully defeated. For the ruler to conquer the subject, it is as easy as a hawk preying upon a lesser bird. It should have taken at least a year or two or a decade or two for the imperial forces to be defeated for any reason, but all of this began on the 15th day of the fifth month and they were defeated by the 14th day of the sixth month, taking only 30 days. In the meantime, Shogunal Regent Yoshitoki had not been aware of these ceremonies, so he did not use any prayers or countermeasures.

In my humble opinion, the reason this happened is because these people used the prayers of the false Dharma of Shingon. Even though only one person was at fault, it became a disaster for the whole country. Likewise the prayer of merely one person can lead to the destruction of one or even two countries. Furthermore, because 300 priests along with the ruler performed the Shingon prayers, becoming the great enemy of the *Lotus Sutra*, how could it not lead to destruction? The great evil Dharma that invited such a disaster moved to the Kantō area gradually with the passing of time, and Shingon priests were appointed head priests and officials of various temples, and they frequently performed this false prayer service. The people in the Kantō area were basically country warriors, who did not know whether this teaching was right or wrong, simply believing that they should worship the Three Treasures of the Buddha, Dharma and the Sangha. So naturally, they came to believe in Shingon. Due to the accumulated effects of the false Dharma of Shingon over the years, Japan is going to be invaded by foreign countries and is about to be destroyed. Not only the chief priests in the eight provinces in the Kantō area, but also those of Mt. Hiei, Tōji Temple, Onjōji Temple and the seven great temples of Nara that are all under the jurisdiction of the Kamakura Shogunate will be destroyed. Like the retired emperors in Oki, the Hōjōs have become believers of this great evil teaching of Shingon.

Regardless of the size of a nation, becoming the ruler depends upon the will of the King of the Brahma Heaven,* Indra, the Sun God, the Moon God and the Four Heavenly Kings.* Each of these heavenly beings have sworn to punish immediately those who have become the enemies of the *Lotus Sutra*. Because of this, the clan of Lay Priest Taira Kiyomori, acting on orders of the 81st sovereign Emperor Antoku, and in order to chastise Minamoto Yoritomo made Mt. Hiei their clan temple and made the deity of the Sannō Shrine their tutelary god.[33] Emperor Antoku, however, was drowned in the sea at Dan no Ura, and Bishop Myōun, the chief priest of Mt. Hiei, was killed by Kiso Yoshinaka, so the whole clan of Heike was destroyed at once. Presently, the first proof of bodily destruction due to belief in the wrong Dharma was the extinction of the Heike clan, and the second proof was the Jōkyū Disturbance.

The imminent Mongol invasion will be the third proof. Without heeding Nichiren's warning, if they use the false Dharma of Shingon to pray for the defeat of Mongol ambitions, the opposite will occur and Japan will be forced to surrender. In the 25th chapter of the *Lotus Sutra*, the Universal Gate of World-Voice-Perceiver Bodhisattva, it is said that "the curse will return to the originators." So, when we think about this, the *Lotus Sutra* is the great way which allows us to receive benefit through punishment. Minamoto Yoritomo was able to destroy the Heike through the virtue of his constant recitation of the *Lotus Sutra*, and that is definitely evidence that people will gain benefit in the present life.

The reason I, Nichiren, could discern this truth is due to the favors that I received from my parents and teachers. However, my parents have already died. The late Venerable Dōzen-bō was my teacher but, since I propagated the *Lotus Sutra*, he was afraid of Steward Tōjō Kagenobu, a Pure Land believer, and made a show of hating me as an enemy though in his heart he must have been sympathetic to me. Later, I heard that he seemed to have faith in the *Lotus Sutra* a little bit, but I do not know how he felt about it when he died. I am very much concerned about this. I hope that he has not fallen into hell, but I doubt that he could rid himself of the suffering of life and death. I am filled with regrets when I think of him wandering in the intermediate state between present and future lives. When Steward Tōjō Kagenobu tried to kill me in rage,[34] you and Gijō-bō* escorted me safely away from Seichōji Temple. So even though you did not do anything specifically for the sake of the *Lotus Sutra*, I regard this as a service to the *Lotus Sutra*, and I am sure that you both will cut the chain of life and death.

Nobody has ever propagated this *honzon**in the world (Jambudvīpa)* in more than 2,230 years since Śākyamuni Buddha expounded it. Grand Masters T'ien-t'ai in China and Dengyō in Japan roughly knew about it, but did not propagate it at all. Today, in the Latter Age of Degeneration, it should be widespread. The *Lotus Sutra* states that Bodhisattvas Superior-Practice* (Viśiṣṭacaritra) and Limitless-Practice (Anantacāritra) will appear in the world to spread it, but they have not yet done that. I, Nichiren, am not as great a man as those bodhisattvas, yet I have roughly understood it. So, as a forerunner, until those bodhisattvas appearing from underground* emerge, I have more or less propagated this sutra and became the spear point of the passage that foretells the "time after My extinction"[35] in the Teacher of the Dharma chapter of the *Lotus Sutra*. It is my hope to transfer my merits to my parents, my teacher and all the people in the world. In order to let you know these things in detail, I am sending you this writing answering your questions. Simply forsake other practices such as Shingon and *nembutsu* and single-mindedly pray before this *honzon* for your future life. I will write to you again, so please give my best regards to your fellow monks.

Notes

1. In the Sutra of Innumerable Meanings, the prologue to the *Lotus Sutra*, it states that in over 40 years of teaching the truth had not yet been revealed.
2. Inferior *Nirmāṇakāya*: The historical Buddha who expounds the *tripiṭaka* teachings.
3. Superior *Nirmāṇakāya*: The historical Buddha whose form is superior and can be discerned only by those of a higher capacity.
4. The Buddha who attained enlightenment for the first time beneath the bodhi tree.
5. The five eyes are the human eye, the heavenly eye, the wisdom eye, the Dharma eye and the Buddha eye.
6. The *trikāya* or threefold body of the Buddha consists of the *Dharmakāya* or Dharma Body, the *sambhogakāya* or Bliss Body, and the *nirmāṇakāya* or Transformation Body.
7. All the sutras expounded prior to the *Lotus Sutra*.
8. Referring to the *Sutra of Innumerable Meanings*, which is the prologue to the *Lotus Sutra*.
9. Referring to the *Sutra of Meditation on Universal-Sage Bodhisattva* which is the epilogue to the *Lotus Sutra*, and the *Mahayana Mahāparinirvāna Sutra*.
10. Cited from The Teacher of the Dharma chapter of the *Lotus Sutra*.
11. Cited from the Peaceful Practices chapter of the *Lotus Sutra*.
12. The other four being the Kusha, Jōjitsu, Ritsu and Kegon schools.
13. Yamashiro, Yamato, Kawachi, Izumi, and Settsu.
14. Tōkai, Tōsan, Hokuriku, San'in, Sanyō, Nankai, and Saikai.
15. The Five *Ki* and Seven *Dō* include the 66 provinces.
16. Iki and Tsushima.

Honzon Mondō Shō (ST 307)   271

17. Kōchi Bodhisattva was a priest of Onodera Temple in Shimotsuke, who first studied under a disciple of Ganjin named Dōchū, and then later, studied the Tendai doctrines directly under Saichō and propagated them in the Kantō area.
18. The six schools of Nara, consisting of the Kusha, Jōjitsu, Ritsu, Hossō, Sanron and Kegon schools.
19. The disciple of Saichō, from Sagami province, who accompanied Saichō to China as his translator.
20. The six older schools of Nara and in addition the newer Hokke and Shingon schools.
21. The second chief priest at Mt. Hiei and a disciple of Saichō.
22. Another disciple of Saichō.
23. Especially the *Guide to the Great Sun Buddha Sutra* by Āchārya I-hsing.
24. They both regarded the teaching of Shingon as essential.
25. The founder of the Japanese Tendai school to which they belonged.
26. A school which teaches from the perspective of the phenomenal world.
27. In other words an expedient Mahayana teaching.
28. In the Age of the True Dharma all the people have a high capacity to understand the Buddha Dharma.
29. Mitsusue was guarding Kyoto at Rokuhara.
30. Emperor Juntoku.
31. Retired Emperor Tsuchi Mikado.
32. The chief priest of Mt. Hiei.
33. A violation against the *Lotus Sutra*.
34. On the day of Rikkyō Kaishū in the fifth year of Kenchō (1253).
35. The prophecy states that the person who propagates the *Lotus Sutra* will definitely be persecuted after the passing of Śākyamuni Buddha.

Toki Nyūdō-dono Gohenji: Hongon Shukkai-shō (ST 310)

Introduction

Written on the first of the 10th month in the first year of the Kōan Era (1278) on Mt. Minobu. The original manuscript has been kept as a treasure in the Hokekyōji Temple in the Nakayama section of Ichikawa City, Chiba Prefecture. Also called *Hongon Shukkai-shō*, this letter was written in response to Toki Jōnin, who had reported about a debate he had with Ryōshō-bō, president of a Tendai Buddhist seminary, while asking some doctrinal questions. Jōnin, who had defeated Ryōshō-bō by citing from the *Annotations on the Words and Phrases of the Lotus Sutra*, reported this to Nichiren Shōnin. In response, Nichiren explains about overcoming illusions in the triple world by practicing provisional teachings, defines the sin of slandering the True Dharma as having no faith in the *Lotus Sutra*, and declares that Nichiren's doctrine for the Latter Age of Degeneration is the "third doctrine," which neither T'ien-t'ai nor Miao-lê preached. After further explanation of the meaning of observing precepts, Nichiren Shōnin advises Jōnin to refrain from having argumentative debates.

A Response to Lay Priest Lord Toki: Treatise on Overcoming Illusions of the Triple World by Provisional Teachings

I have skimmed through your letter reporting your debate against Ryōshō-bō, a Tendai scholar-priest.

According to your letter, you supported your point by citing from the *Annotations on the Words and Phrases of the Lotus Sutra*, fascicle nine: "Overcoming illusions of the triple world* [three realms of this world in which unenlightened beings transmigrate] by means of provisional teachings preached before the *Lotus Sutra* is merely provisional." Ryōshō-bō then declared, "Absolutely there exist no such interpretations."

The 16th chapter of the *Lotus Sutra*, The Duration of the Life of the Tathāgata,* states, "Various sutras preached by the Buddha ever since His attainment of

Buddhahood in the eternal past are nothing but the truth. None of them are provisional." This is interpreted by Grand Master T'ien-t'ai in his *Words and Phrases of the Lotus Sutra,** fascicle nine: "All those who overcame illusions of the triple world through provisional teachings inevitably attained enlightenment. From this we can see that provisional pre-Lotus sutras were expounded for the purpose of leading the people to the True Dharma of the *Lotus Sutra*."

Grand Master Miao-lê explains it further in his *Annotations on the Words and Phrases of the Lotus Sutra,** fascicle nine: "Overcoming illusions of the triple world through provisional teachings of pre-Lotus sutras is provisional extinction. It is not true extinction. Therefore, it is termed 'provisional extinction.' Those who engaged in three kinds of Buddhist practice [bodhisattvas, men of śrāvaka and pratyekabuddha] during the pre-Lotus periods all got rid of illusions of the triple world, and there exist no humans and heavenly beings who did not escape from the suffering of the three lowest realms [hell, realm of hungry spirits and that of beasts]. Compared to the complete extinction of illusions of the triple world through the teaching of the *Lotus Sutra*, however, theirs is merely a provisional extinction."

These interpretations of T'ien-t'ai* and Miao-lê* are based on the scriptural statements in the 16th chapter of the *Lotus Sutra*, The Duration of the Life of the Tathāgata: "Good men, seeing those with little virtue and much sin who desired to learn Hinayana teachings, the Buddha preached various Dharmas for them before preaching the *Lotus Sutra* in order to lead them into the One Vehicle True Dharma, and He has been preaching them ever since."

This scriptural statement slights the teachings of the Buddha, beginning with the distinct and perfect teachings of the *Flower Garland Sutra** that he expounded first upon attaining enlightenment to the first 14 chapters of the *Lotus Sutra* [theoretical section], by calling them Hinayana teachings preached for those with less virtue and much sin, or a provisional means of getting rid of illusions of the triple world. Thus, such schools of Buddhism as the Flower Garland (Kegon) sect* based on the *Flower Garland Sutra*, the Dharma Characteristics (Hossō) sect* based on the *Revealing the Profound and Secret Sutra,** the Three Treatises (Sanron) sect* based on the *Wisdom Sutra,** the True Word (Shingon) sect* based on the *Great Sun Buddha Sutra,** the Pure Land (Jōdo) sect* based on the *Sutra of Meditation on the Buddha of Infinite Life,** and the Zen sect* based on the *Entering Laṅkā Sutra,** none of these will ever enable their faithful followers to extinguish illusions of the triple world* or escape from the suffering of the three lowest realms even if they practice Buddhism as preached in their respective canons. How much less those who claim their basic sutras to be truer than or superior to the *Lotus Sutra*. They are as foolish as those who spit to heaven or grab the great earth in rage.

Regarding the idea that all sutras preached before the last half [essential section] of the *Lotus Sutra* are Hinayana, even the 24 venerable masters who transmitted the Dharma* including such great commentators as Nāgārjuna* and Vasubandhu* in India did not expound this for more than 1,500 years following the death of Śākyamuni Buddha, although they knew it. In China, it has been more than 1,000 years since Buddhism was introduced, but no one knew about this idea, except Grand Masters T'ien-t'ai and Miao-lê, who roughly talked about it. They, however, did not go so far as to reveal its truth. The same was true with Grand Master Dengyō* of Japan.

Contemplating this, I, Nichiren, see this idea restated in the Jumyō chapter of the *Nirvana Sutra:** "Suppose someone denies the eternity of the Three Treasures [the Buddha, Dharma and Sangha], such a man will lose his three refuges in the purity of Buddhism and all the merit of upholding the precepts. He will never gain the rewards for practicing the three kinds of teachings for *śrāvaka,** *pratyekabuddha** and bodhisattvas."* This scriptural statement in the *Nirvana Sutra* apparently expounds what is preached in The Duration of the Life of the Tathāgata chapter of the *Lotus Sutra*.

Following this statement, the *Nirvana Sutra* cites a parable saying that as a tree is necessarily accompanied by its shadow, the Buddha is believed in because of His eternal life. The teaching of The Duration of the Life of the Tathāgata chapter is likened to a tree, and pre-Lotus sutras as well as the first half of the *Lotus Sutra* are likened to the shadow of the tree. The *Nirvana Sutra* states also that benefits of understanding the teachings of the Buddha through such means as the "five periods,"* "eight teachings* [four doctrinal teachings and four methods of teaching]," provisional and true teachings, and Mahayana and Hinayana doctrines are like the shadow of the tree, which is the doctrine of The Duration of the Life of the Tathāgata chapter in the essential section of the *Lotus Sutra*. The sutra also declares that those who negate the eternal life of the Buddha are like a tree without a shadow in darkness. It means that benefits of those sutras expounded by Śākyamuni Buddha during His lifetime before The Duration of the Life of the Tathāgata chapter are likened to the shadow of a tree in darkness. They are of those who had listened to the teaching of The Duration of the Life of the Tathāgata chapter and been planted with the seed of Buddhahood in the distant past. Those who had not received the seed have neither a tree nor a shadow to speak about.

According to your letter, Ryōshō-bō also declared that not putting faith in the *Lotus Sutra* is not necessarily slandering the True Dharma,* and that he who has no faith in the *Lotus Sutra* does not necessarily go to hell. It is preached, however, in the *Lotus Sutra*, fascicle five [Chapter 15, Appearance of Bodhisattvas from Underground]: "Suppose there is someone who harbors a doubt about this sutra and does not believe it, he will instantly fall into hell." There is no doubt that one who has no faith in the *Lotus Sutra* commits the sin of slandering the True Dharma, for which one will fall into hell.

You should always keep in mind that in considering the comparative superiority and profundity between the *Lotus Sutra* and pre-Lotus sutras,* Grand Master T'ien-t'ai established three distinctions between the ultimate teaching of the *Lotus Sutra* and the provisional teachings in pre-Lotus sutras. Of the three, what I, Nichiren, expound is the third doctrine* regarding the question of whether or not the relationships between the Lord Buddha and His disciples are eternal.

Some scholars in China and Japan, beginning with Grand Master T'ien-t'ai, preached the first and second doctrines regarding the capacity of listeners and completeness in the Buddha's guidance as vaguely as a dream. Nobody, however, has ever preached the third doctrine. Grand Master T'ien-t'ai explained the differences among the three in his *Profound Meaning of the Lotus Sutra,* and Grand Master Miao-lê stated in his *Commentary on the Profound Meaning of the Lotus Sutra* that the first two were doctrines of the theoretical section while the third doctrine was of the essential section. Grand Master Dengyō held almost the same opinion. None of them, however, insisted on centering on the third doctrine. After all, they wanted to give us the merit of practicing this doctrine in the Latter Age of Degeneration.* It is stated in the 23rd chapter of the *Lotus Sutra,* Previous Life of Medicine-King Bodhisattva: "The teaching of the *Lotus Sutra* will be spread widely in the fifth 500-year period [beginning of the Latter Age]." It must have foretold the revelation of this doctrine today in the Latter Age of Degeneration.

As I was not a witness of this debate, I do not know how it was, but Ryōshō-bō is learned and well-informed. What would have happened if he and his men forcibly declared themselves winners saying: "Stop! Stop! We have certainly read the passage"? It was fortunate that they were unaware of Miao-lê's interpretation in the *Annotations on the Words and Phrases of the Lotus Sutra,* fascicle nine. It must have been a heavenly punishment for them to have said that there existed no such passage in the 60-fascicles of the major works of Grand Masters T'ien-t'ai and Miao-lê. Their sin of slandering the True Dharma must have been revealed when you, a messenger of the *Lotus Sutra,* accused them.

You also report in your letter that Daishin-bō has shown a sign of repentance as a result of this debate. He must have a reason for it. You had best find out in detail why Ōta Jirōhyōe of Kashima and Daishin-bō as well as Master of Hon'in have repented.

At any rate you won the debate, and as stated in the sutra, the King of Devils in the Sixth Heaven is bound to interfere with those who practice the

Lotus Sutra.* This is explained as the delusion of devils among the 10 objects of meditation listed by Grand Master T'ien-t'ai in his *Great Concentration and Insight*. Devils delight in obstructing the virtuous and helping spread evil. Unable to force virtuous people to do evil, however, devils cannot help but let them do meritorious deeds. Or, they will encourage those who practice the teachings for Two Vehicles* [men of *śrāvaka* and *pratyekabuddha*], such as doctrines of the "four noble truths" and the "twelve links of cause and effect," to switch to less meritorious practices like the "five precepts" and "10 good acts." Bodhisattvas practicing the "six *pāramitā* ways leading to Buddhahood" may be encouraged to downgrade to Two Vehicle teachings. Finally, those who single-heartedly practice the purely perfect teachings of the *Lotus Sutra* are induced to downgrade the practice to such as the "distinctive teaching." This is explained in detail in the *Great Concentration and Insight,** fascicle eight, so it would be good for you to consult it.

As I understand, Ryōshō-bō questioned you closely, asserting: "According to Grand Master T'ien-t'ai, those who practice concentration and insight [the system of meditation set forth by T'ien-t'ai] must observe Buddhist precepts to keep themselves pure." The *Words and Phrases of the Lotus Sutra** states that those in the first three of the five stages of practice for believers of the *Lotus Sutra* after the death of Śākyamuni Buddha are not required to keep the precepts. This is also clearly stated in the 17th chapter of the *Lotus Sutra,* Variety of Merits.

The discrepancy between the *Words and Phrases of the Lotus Sutra* and the *Great Concentration and Insight* is explained in Grand Master Miao-lê's *Annotations on the Words and Phrases of the Lotus Sutra,** fascicle nine: "The *Words and Phrases of the Lotus Sutra* advises those in the initial stages of practice to refrain from observing Buddhist precepts, while the *Great Concentration and Insight* allows those in the advanced stages to keep the precepts." Also, there are two groups in the first stage, who rejoice upon hearing the *Lotus Sutra:* those with a high caliber are allowed to observe precepts but those with a low caliber are disallowed.

Regarding the observance of Buddhist precepts, we must consider the differences between the Age of the True Dharma, the Age of the Semblance Dharma and the Latter Age of Degeneration as well as between the persuasive and aggressive means of propagation.* Grand Master Dengyō states in his *Treatise on the Light for the Latter Age of Degeneration* that one who keeps the precepts in the Latter Age of Degeneration is as rare as a tiger without a leash in a market place. We should take all these into account in practicing meditation while observing Buddhist precepts.

The debate this time turned out to be victorious for you. However, you should not engage in an argumentative debate in Shimofusa Province (northern Chiba Prefecture) again. By defeating such scholars as Ryōshō-bō and Shi'nen in a debate, I am afraid it would be beneath your dignity to meet with others in debate.

I hear that Ryōshō-bō and Shi'nen have been disparaging Nichiren. How foolish of them to criticize me, Nichiren, without even seeing or hearing me speak! It is like mosquitoes and horseflies abusing the king of lions. It is incomprehensible that followers of the Tendai-Lotus school neither chant *Namu Myōhō Renge-kyō** nor chastise those who chant the *nembutsu*, much less chastise those who both do not chant the *Odaimoku* themselves and abuse those who chant it.

Regarding Daishin-bō, as I have said to you earlier, please teach him to reason strictly. If he has really changed his mind, as you said, it seems that the 10 female *rākṣasa* demons,* guardian deities of the *Lotus Sutra*, have attached themselves to Daishin-bō, and they brought him back to be one who practices the True Dharma. Or is it that a messenger of the King of Devils who had haunted and distracted him decided to leave? "Devils enter their bodies," stated in the 13th chapter of the *Lotus Sutra*, Encouragement for Keeping This Sutra, is not at all an empty phrase.

Though I have many things to say, as this messenger is in a great hurry, I wrote this letter during the night.

Sincerely yours,

Nichiren (signature)

On the first day of the 10th month

Shokyō to Hokekyō to Nan'i no Koto (ST 367)

Introduction

The original manuscript of this letter to Toki Jōnin, written on the 26th day of the fifth month in the third year of the Kōan Era (1280) at Mt. Minobu, has been kept as a treasure in the Nakayama Hokekyōji Temple in Ichikawa, Chiba Prefecture. It answers a question asked by Lord Toki regarding a phrase in Chapter 10 of the *Lotus Sutra* saying that the sutra is *nanshin, nange*: difficult to believe and understand.

Citing interpretations of Nāgārjuna and T'ien-t'ai, Nichiren Shōnin states that various sutras other than the Lotus can be easily understood and believed because they were preached by the Buddha with expedient teachings in order to cater to the whim of listeners *(zuitai)*. On the contrary, he maintains, the *Lotus Sutra* is hard to understand and believe because the Buddha directly preached His true intention according to His own mind without compromising *(zuijii)*.

Nichiren laments that misconceptions of such masters as Kōbō, Jikaku and Chishō toppled Buddhism, causing the disappearance of the True Dharma, which in turn resulted in confusion and corruption in Japan. He insists that as Buddhism is a body and the world is its shadow, the *Lotus Sutra*, which leads all the people to Buddhahood, must be established as the basis of Buddhism as well as the world.

The Difficulty and Ease of Understanding the Lotus Sutra and Other Sutras

Question: It is preached in the 10th chapter of the *Lotus Sutra*,* The Teacher of the Dharma,* fascicle four, that the *Lotus Sutra* is difficult to believe and understand. What does this mean?

Answer: It has been more than 2,000 years since the Buddha preached the *Lotus Sutra*. Having existed in India 1,200 years or so and about 200 years in China, the *Lotus Sutra* was transmitted to Japan more than 700 years ago. During these years after the death of Śākyamuni Buddha, no one, except for three people, has ever truly read this phrase in the *Lotus Sutra*. They are Bodhisattva Nāgārjuna, and Grand Masters T'ien-t'ai and Dengyō. First of all Bodhisattva Nāgārjuna* in India declared in his *Great Wisdom Discourse:** "The teaching of the *Lotus Sutra* enabled the men of Two Vehicles, *śrāvaka* and *pratyekabuddha*, who had been considered as having no chance of attaining Buddhahood, to attain Buddhahood. It is like a great physician who knows how to use poison as medicine." Indeed this shows that Bodhisattva Nāgārjuna truly read and clarified the meaning of the four-character phrase of being difficult to believe and understand.

In China, Grand Master T'ien-t'ai,* the wisest, explains this phrase in his *Profound Meaning of the Lotus Sutra:* "Of all sutras which had been preached, are now being preached and will be preached* in the future, the *Lotus Sutra* is the most difficult to believe and comprehend."

Grand Master Dengyō* of Japan further expounds this in his *Outstanding Principles of the Lotus Sutra:* "Sutras that were preached during the four [pre-Lotus] periods of Śākyamuni's lifetime preaching, the *Sutra of Infinite Meaning,** which is now being preached, as well as the *Nirvana Sutra,** which will be preached, are easy to believe and understand. It is because they are preached with expedient means according to people's capacity to understand.* On the contrary, the *Lotus Sutra* is the most difficult to believe and comprehend because it is the true teaching preached according to the Buddha's own mind,* directly revealing the Buddha's enlightenment."

Question: Why is the *Lotus Sutra* difficult to believe and understand while other sutras are easy to believe and understand?

Answer: Various sutras other than the *Lotus Sutra* are easy to believe and understand because Śākyamuni preached them to suit the capacity of the people to understand, without revealing His true intention. On the other hand in the *Lotus Sutra*, Śākyamuni directly revealed His state of mind without compromising with people's ability for comprehension. Clearly it is the true teaching, which is not easily understood and believed by ordinary people. Nevertheless, Grand Master Kōbō* and followers of Shingon Buddhism of the Tōji Temple in Japan mistook the *Lotus Sutra* to represent the difficult doctrine among exoteric teachings but the easy one compared to esoteric teachings. According to Grand Masters Jikaku (Ennin)* and Chishō (Enchin)* and their followers, both the *Lotus* and the *Great Sun Buddha Sutras** are difficult, but a comparison between the two shows that although the former, too, is difficult, the latter is the most difficult. These two opinions of Tōji esotericism and Tendai esotericism prevailed throughout Japan.

Having read these sutras, I, Nichiren, conclude that when we compare non-

Buddhist scriptures* with sutras of Hinayana Buddhism, the former are easier to understand and believe than the latter. Compared to the *Great Sun Buddha Sutra*, however, Hinayana sutras are easier to understand and believe than the *Great Sun Buddha Sutra*. Compared to the *Wisdom Sutra*,* the *Great Sun Buddha Sutra* is easier to understand and believe, while the *Wisdom Sutra* is difficult. Likewise, when we compare the *Wisdom Sutra* to the *Flower Garland Sutra*,* the *Flower Garland Sutra* to the *Nirvana Sutra*, the *Nirvana Sutra* to the *Lotus Sutra*, the first half [theoretical section] to the second half [essential section] of the *Lotus Sutra*, we see that the former of the respective pair is easier to understand and believe than the latter, which proved that the *Lotus Sutra* is the most difficult of all sutras, that is to say, it is the True Teaching.

Question: What is the sense of knowing which sutras were preached according to the Buddha's own mind or not, and which sutras are easy or difficult to understand and believe?

Answer: This doctrine proving the *Lotus Sutra* to be the ultimate teaching of all sutras is the lamp that shines in the darkness of the long night in the world of illusions through life and death, and it is the sharp sword that cuts off the root of spiritual ignorance. The teachings of such Buddhist schools as the True Word sect* and the Flower Garland sect* were preached with expedients according to the ability of the people to understand, so it is easy to understand and believe. However, they do not really represent the true intention of the Buddha. As their canons were expounded by the Buddha catering to the whims of those in the nine realms [of hell, hungry spirits, beasts and birds, fighting spirits, human beings, gods, śrāvaka , pratyekabuddha, and bodhisattvas], they are called *zuitai* [according to other people's minds]. It is like a wise father following the wish of his ignorant children. The sutra in which the Buddha clearly speaks of His enlightenment is called *zuijii* [according to His own mind]. It is like a sage father guiding his ignorant children. Examining such sutras as the *Great Sun Buddha Sutra*, the *Flower Garland Sutra* and the *Wisdom Sutra*, I can say that they are all doctrines of *zuitai*.

Question: What proves that sutras other than the Lotus were preached according to other people's minds?

Answer: The *Śrīmālā Sutra** preaches: "Those whose capacity to understand is too low to distinguish causes from effects and the virtuous from the evil are taught the five precepts and 10 good acts, which are the root of goodness for human and heavenly beings, in order to nourish their capacity. For those who want to become *śrāvaka*,* the *śrāvaka* teaching [the four noble truths] is preached, and for those wishing to be *pratyekabuddha*,* the *pratyekabuddha* teaching [12 links of cause and effect] is preached. Those wanting to become Mahayana bodhisattvas are assigned to practice the bodhisattva way of six *pāramitā*." This is exactly the way of preaching the "easy" sutras. The same can be said of such sutras as the *Flower Garland Sutra*, the *Great Sun Buddha Sutra*, the *Wisdom Sutra*, and the *Nirvana Sutra*.

On the contrary, it is stated in the *Lotus Sutra*, Chapter 10, The Teacher of the Dharma:

> The World Honored One then said to the 80,000 bodhisattvas through Medicine-King Bodhisattva:* "Medicine-King! Do you see in this great mass innumerable gods, dragon kings, *yakṣa, gandharva, asura, garuḍa, kiṃnara, mahoraga,* human, and non-human beings, as well as four kinds of devotees seeking the *śrāvaka* teaching, the *pratyekabuddha* teaching or the way to Buddhahood? If any of them rejoices even momentarily on hearing even a verse or a phrase of the *Lotus Sutra* in front of the Buddha, I will bestow to all of them a guarantee of attaining Buddhahood."

Many sutras other than the *Lotus* preach variously according to the caliber of listeners. For instance the five precepts are preached for those in the human realm, the 10 good acts for those in the realm of heaven, compassion and charity for the King of the Brahma Heaven, equal alms-giving among priests for the King of Devils, 250 precepts for monks, 500 precepts for nuns, the four noble truths for men of *śrāvaka*, the 12 links of cause and effect for men of *pratyekabuddha*, and the six *pāramitā* for bodhisattvas. It is like water taking its shape according to the container or an elephant exerting its strength according to the enemy.

This is not the case with the *Lotus Sutra*, in which the same *Lotus Sutra* is preached for all the eight kinds of protectors of the *Lotus Sutra* and four kinds of devotees. It is as if a ruler straightening a curved line or a lion exerting his full power regardless of the strength of its prey. When we examine various sutras reflected in the bright mirror of the *Lotus Sutra*, there is no doubt that both the triple Shingon sutras and the triple Pure Land sutras are expedient teachings preached according to the mind of other people.

Nevertheless, whatever happened to Buddhism in Japan? Because people are swayed by the opinions of Grand Masters Kōbō, Jikaku and Chishō, the truth of the *Lotus Sutra* expressing the true intent of the Buddha has been hidden for the past 400 years in Japan. This is like trading a gem for a piece of stone, and sandalwood for an ordinary tree. As the truth of the Buddha Dharma eclipses, the world gets out of order. Buddhism is a body and the world its shadow. When a body is not straight, its shadow also is slanted.

It is fortunate, however, that at least my followers, who believe the *Lotus Sutra*, the true intent of Śākyamuni Buddha, will automatically flow into the sea of Nirvana to attain Buddhahood. On the contrary, Buddhist scholars in the world today, who believe the provisional teachings preached according to other people's minds, will be drowned in the sea of sufferings. I will explain this again in detail.

Sincerely,
On the 26th day of the fifth month

Nichiren (signature)

To Lord Toki,* in response

Sandai Hihō Honjō-ji (ST 403)

Introduction

This letter to Ōta Jōmyō is said to have been written on the eighth day of the fourth month in the fourth year of the Kōan Era (1281) at Minobu. The authenticity of this letter, whether or not it was really written by Nichiren Shōnin, has been hotly debated from olden times. The purpose of writing this letter was to explain for his followers the Three Great Secret Dharmas* lying at the foundation of Nichiren Buddhism.

Regarding the Three Great Secret Dharmas, Nichiren Shōnin referred to them for the first time when he talked about the "three doctrines of the essential section" in his *Treatise on the Essence of the Lotus Sutra* written soon after retreating to Mt. Minobu. In the second place, his *Essay on Gratitude* mentions the "True Dharma which was not propagated by T'ien-t'ai and Dengyō" and three doctrines which "the Buddha bequeathed to those in the Latter Age of Degeneration": the *honzon, kaidan* and *Odaimoku* based on the doctrine preached in the essential section. Although he explains the first and the third Dharmas, he just mentions the name of the term *hommon no kaidan* in the *Essay on Gratitude*.

The term "Three Great Secret Dharmas" is not used by Nichiren in any of his writings except this treatise, which is also the sole source of information about the form of the *kaidan* Nichiren had in mind. In this sense this document is unique among Nichiren's writings, and this is the very reason why its authenticity has been hotly debated.

The Transmission of the Three Great Secret Dharmas

It is preached in the 21st chapter of the *Lotus Sutra*, The Supernatural Powers of the Tathāgata, fascicle seven: "In short, all the teachings of the Buddha, all the unhindered, supernatural powers of the Tathāgata, all the stores of the secret lore of the Tathāgata, and all the profundities of the Tathāgata are revealed and explained in this sutra." Grand Master T'ien-t'ai explains this in his *Words and Phrases of the Lotus Sutra* saying, "These four are the gist of the *Lotus Sutra*."

Question: What are the indispensable Dharmas summed up by the four phrases?

Answer: They are the *honzon* (most venerable one),* *kaidan* (precept platform)* and the five-character *Odaimoku*,* which Śākyamuni Buddha had practiced in the eternal past upon attaining enlightenment with the true aspect of all phenomena, and which is now preached in the 16th chapter of the *Lotus Sutra*, The Duration of the Life of the Tathāgata. They had been kept in secret during the years Śākyamuni preached the pre-Lotus sutras since He attained Buddhahood for the first time in this world under the bodhi tree, through the preaching of the theoretical section of the *Lotus Sutra*, until He began revealing the eternal life of the Buddha in the 15th chapter, Appearance of Bodhisattvas from Underground, in the essential section of the sutra.

Lord Śākyamuni Buddha did not teach these great secret Dharmas to such great bodhisattvas as Samantabhadra and Mañjuśrī, attendants of the Buddha throughout the past, present and future, much less other disciples below them. Therefore, the formality of preaching these secret Dharmas was quite different from that of preaching the pre-Lotus sutras and the 14 chapters in the theoretical section of the *Lotus Sutra*. It took place in the land of eternal, tranquil light, with the Eternal Buddha as the lord preacher completely equipped with the three bodies [Dharma, Reward and Accommodative] of a Buddha, and the listeners were of one body with the Buddha.

Appropriate for such an occasion, in order to reinforce the attainment of Buddhahood in the eternal past, the Buddha especially called out from the bottom of the land of eternal tranquil light the four bodhisattvas such as Superior-Practice* who had been disciples of the Original Śākyamuni Buddha since the eternal past, and He entrusted them with these Three Great Secret Dharmas.* Precept Master Tao-hsien* stated, "As the doctrines to be transmitted were those which had been attained in the eternal past, they were entrusted to the disciples of the Eternal Buddha from the eternal past."

Question: In what age will be spread the secret Dharmas entrusted to Superior-Practice and other bodhisattvas called up from underground?

Answer: The 23rd chapter of the *Lotus Sutra*, The Previous Life of Medicine-King Bodhisattva, fascicle seven, preaches: "Propagate this chapter throughout this world during the last 500-year period after My extinction lest it should be lost." Reading this passage in the sutra respectfully, I see that the time for the secret Dharmas to spread will be after the passage of the 2,000-year periods of the Ages of the True Dharma and the Semblance Dharma, namely during the fifth 500-year period after the death of the Buddha, which coincides with the beginning of the Latter Age of Degeneration, when it is believed that strife becomes rampant, and Buddhism progressively declines to extinction.

Question: The compassion of the Buddhas is like the moon in heaven. As the moon reflects its shadow on water whenever it is calm, Buddhas should grant favors wherever the capacity of the people for comprehension is clear. Nevertheless, it seems unfair for the Buddha to say that His secret Dharmas will be revealed only in the Latter Age of Degeneration among the three ages following His death. What do you think of this?

Answer: Although the moonlight of Buddhas' compassion brightens the darkness of the people in the nine realms of spiritual development, from hell at the bottom up to the realm of bodhisattvas, it does not reflect upon the muddy water of slanderers of the True Dharma* and of those who have no goodness in mind *(icchantika).**

Hinayana and expedient Mahayana teachings are suited to the capacity* of those in the 1,000-year Age of the True Dharma. The teaching of the theoretical section in the first half of the *Lotus Sutra* is suitable for those in the 1,000-year Age of the Semblance Dharma. The first 500-years in the Latter Age of Degeneration, however, is the time when The Duration of the Life of the Tathāgata chapter in the essential section of the *Lotus Sutra* should be taught solely, and the other 13 chapters should be set aside. It is because the doctrine in the chapter matches the capacity of the people.

The doctrine preached in The Duration of the Life of the Tathāgata chapter is not suitable for the capacity of those in the second 500-year period of the Age of the Semblance Dharma, much less the first 500-year period. Those in the Age of the True Dharma were not ready for the theoretical section of the *Lotus Sutra*, much less the essential section. In the Latter Age of Degeneration, the pre-Lotus sutras and the teaching of the theoretical section of the *Lotus Sutra*, which were suitable in the Ages of the True Dharma and the Semblance Dharma, no longer enable the people to shed delusions of life and death and attain Buddhahood. The 16th chapter of the essential section preaches the single, indispensable teaching for extinguishing delusions and attaining Buddhahood.

Looking at it this way, I am sure that in providing guidance the Buddha acts impartially. He just preaches the Dharma suitable to the time and capacity of the people.

Question: Regarding the propagation of Buddhist Dharmas after the death of the Buddha, during the Ages of the True Dharma and Semblance Dharma and the Latter Age of Degeneration, it has become clear that the original bodhisattva disciples of the Eternal Buddha and other bodhisattvas were entrusted with different duties. It still remains unclear whether or not there is an unambiguous scriptural statement to prove that The Duration of the Life of the Tathāgata chapter represents the sole teaching for the salvation of people in the evil and corrupt world in the Latter Age of Degeneration.

Answer: You sound so pressing that I will answer your question. Hearing my answer, you must firmly believe it. What you ask for is the passage in The Duration of the Life of the Tathāgata chapter saying, "I will leave this excellent medicine here. You should take it. Do not worry that your sickness will not be cured."

Question: As it has been proved by a clear statement in this sutra that The Duration of the Life of the Tathāgata chapter is the single teaching for the salvation of the evil world in the Latter Age of Degeneration, there is no doubt about it. Nevertheless, what are the Three Great Secret Dharmas* preached in the chapter?

Answer: They are the most important doctrines cherished in my mind. As your aspiration is admirable, I will briefly explain them. The *honzon* (most venerable one) established in the 16th chapter of the *Lotus Sutra* is Lord Śākyamuni Buddha who has been closely tied with us in this Sahā World by the bond of cause and effect ever since attaining Buddhahood 500 dust-particle *kalpa** ago, and who is equipped with the eternal three bodies [Dharma, Reward, and Accommodative] of the Buddha. The Duration of the Life of the Tathāgata chapter refers to this as "the Buddha's secret lore and divine powers," which were explained by Grand Master T'ien-t'ai in his *Words and Phrases of the Lotus Sutra*: "It is mysterious *(pi)* of one body being identical to a triple-body and confidential *(mi)* of a triple-body being identical to one body. It is mysterious because it has never been explained, and confidential because only the Buddha knew it. The Buddha has always been equipped with the three bodies attained in the eternal past throughout the past, present and future, but He has kept it confidential without ever revealing it in other sutras."

The *Odaimoku* has two meanings: the *Odaimoku* which was practiced during the Ages of the True Dharma and Semblance Dharma, and that which is practiced in the Latter Age of Degeneration. During the Age of the True Dharma, Bodhisattvas Vasubandhu and Nāgārjuna chanted the *Odaimoku* solely for the sake of their own practice. During the Age of the Semblance Dharma, Grand Masters Nan-yüeh and T'ien-t'ai chanted only the *Odaimoku, Namu Myōhō Renge-kyō*. They, too, chanted it for their own practices, not to guide other people. Their

Odaimoku was a practice for attaining enlightenment based on the teaching of the theoretical section of the *Lotus Sutra*. The *Odaimoku* which I, Nichiren, recite today in the Latter Age of Degeneration is the *Odaimoku* of *Namu Myōhō Renge-kyō* which, unlike that of the previous ages, is not merely the practice for personal enlightenment but it is the practice for also benefitting others. This five-character *Odaimoku* is not just a title of the *Lotus Sutra*. It contains the five profound meanings* of the name, entity, quality, function and teaching.

Regarding the *kaidan*, center for the practice of the *Lotus Sutra*, should it not be established at the most outstanding place resembling the Pure Land of Mt. Sacred Eagle with the blessing of an imperial edict and a shogunal directive? Should it not be at such a time when the laws of the kingdom and Buddha Dharmas are in perfect accord, with both the king and his subjects all believing in the Three Great Secret Dharmas revealed in the essential section of the *Lotus Sutra*, and when the meritorious works of King Virtuous* and Monk Virtue Consciousness* in the past recur in the evil and corrupt world in the Latter Age of Degeneration? We have to wait for the opportune time for its realization. This is what we call the actual precept platform, *ji-no-kaidan*, where all the people of India, China and Japan as well as of the Sahā World should repent their sins. Furthermore such heavenly beings as the great King of the Brahma Heaven and Indra should come to assemble to practice the Lotus teaching.

After the establishment of this *kaidan* of the essential section of the *Lotus Sutra*, the one on Mt. Hiei based on the theoretical section of the sutra would be useless.

Nevertheless, Grand Masters Jikaku and Chishō, the third and fourth Head Priests of the Enryakuji Temple on Mt. Hiei, contradicted the Founder of the temple, Grand Master Dengyō, and the first Head Priest Gishin. Based on the false opinion that the *Great Sun Buddha Sutra* and the *Lotus Sutra* are equal in doctrine but the former is superior in ritualism because it preaches finger signs, that is *mudrā*, and mantra, Jikaku and Chishō slighted their own precept platform on Mt. Hiei as trivial and useless, transforming the pure, clean, and wonderful *kaidan* based on the principle of the Middle Way into that which is as worthless as mud. My sadness is beyond expression. I can't lament enough. It is more regrettable than Mt. Malaya in southern India, noted for its sandalwood trees, turning to a heap of rubble, and its grove of fragrant woods to bushes of thorns.

Now, how can we have those scholars who can justly tell which sutra of all the holy preachings of the Buddha during His lifetime* is the most wonderful step on the *kaidan* of the chaotic Enryakuji Temple today? We have to think through the comparative superiority between the *Lotus Sutra* and the *Great Sun Buddha Sutra* to give a full account.

These Three Great Secret Dharmas are certainly what I, Nichiren, at the head of the group of bodhisattvas who emerged from underground received from

Lord Śākyamuni Buddha orally more than 2,000 years ago. Therefore, what I practice today are the actual Three Great Secret Dharmas revealed in The Duration of the Life of the Tathāgata chapter, which are exactly the same as what were transmitted on Mt. Sacred Eagle without a shred of difference.

Question: What is the scriptural proof for the "3,000 existences contained in one thought" doctrine?

Answer: I should say there are two kinds. First, it is preached in the second chapter, Expedients: "Reality of all phenomena consists of their appearances, natures, bodies.... The Buddhas, the World Honored Ones, wish to open the gate to Buddha wisdom." These are scriptural proofs showing the existence of 3,000 Dharma worlds even in the moment of thought of unenlightened beings suffering at the bottom of delusions and evil passions.

Secondly, The Duration of the Life of the Tathāgata chapter preaches, "Nevertheless, it has been numerous and limitless aeons since I actually attained Buddhahood...." This represents the "3,000 existences contained in one thought" doctrine attained by Śākyamuni Buddha in the eternal past. Now in the Latter Age of Degeneration I, Nichiren, exert myself to disseminate this "actual 3,000 existences contained in one thought" (*ji no ichinen sanzen*) doctrine shown in The Duration of the Life of the Tathāgata chapter. I have kept this doctrine of the Three Great Secret Dharmas secret in my heart. However, if I do not leave it in writing for the future, I am sure, my disciples would be sorry for my lack of compassion after my death. It is useless to regret then, so I am writing this to be sent to you. After reading it once, please keep it confidential. Do not show it to others or talk about it indiscriminately.

The second chapter of the *Lotus Sutra,* Expedients, preaches that the one great purpose* of the Buddhas appearing in the world was to preach the *Lotus Sutra.* This is because the sutra treasures the Three Great Secret Dharmas, which should be kept confidential. Do not reveal them to others.

> On the eighth day of the fourth month
> in the fourth year of the Kōan Era
>
> Nichiren (signature)
>
> To Lord Ōta Kingo, in Response

Glossary

Note: Included in this glossary are words and phrases marked with asterisks in the text. They were chosen by the authors of the modern Japanese translations of the original writings of Nichiren for the purpose of clarifying the characteristics of his doctrine. Most entries are in English as they appear in the text, except proper nouns (which appear in the language of the country of their origin), and a few special terms for which appropriate English terms are not readily available. Words and phrases within parentheses following each entry are the Japanese terms used by Nichiren which are alphabetically rearranged and attached to the end of the glossary for the convenience of those who are well versed in Japanese.

A bit of soil on a fingernail (*sōjō no tsuchi*)
A phrase taken from the *Nirvana Sutra,* meaning as small as the amount of soil caught under a fingernail. It is likened to a slight chance of being born into the human world. Nichiren likened it to a small number of people who put faith in the *Lotus Sutra.*

Abandon, close, set aside and cast away (*sha, hei, kaku, hō*)
The term *shahei kakuhō* was coined by Nichiren to represent the doctrine of Hōnen, who insisted that only the nembutsu is the appropriate teaching for the people in the Latter Age of Degeneration, negating all other doctrines and practices. The four characters are taken from the *Collection of Passages on the Nembutsu* by Hōnen advising the people to put aside the Holy Way teachings, namely all teachings other than those of the Pure Land.

Accommodative Body (*ōjin*)
See "Threefold body of a Buddha."

Additional Annotations to Three Major Works of T'ien-t'ai (*Fuchū*)
Written in 14 fascicles by Ts'ung-i, 1042–1091 CE, of Sung China. In this work, Ts'ung-i tried to explain what has been left unexplained by T'ien-t'ai in his three major works and by Miao-lê in his commentaries on T'ien-t'ai's works.

Admonition *(kangyō)*
Śākyamuni Buddha urged those who listened to Him to spread the *Lotus Sutra* in the Latter Age of Degeneration at the cost of their lives. Nichiren Shōnin referred to this as the Buddha's admonition and tried to carry this out as His messenger by submitting the *Risshō Ankoku-ron, Treatise on Spreading Peace Throughout the Country by Establishing the True Dharma*, to the Kamakura military government, urging the shogunate as well as the people to put faith in the *Lotus Sutra*. This *Rissho Ankoku* campaign of Nichiren Shōnin is designated as his national admonition.

Ages of the True, Semblance and Latter Dharmas *(shō-zō-matsu)*
Refers to the three ages after the Buddha's death constituting: (1) the Age of the True Dharma, lasting 1,000, or some say 500 years, in which the Buddha's teaching is properly practiced and Buddhahood can be attained; (2) the Age of the Semblance Dharma lasting 1,000, or some say 500 years, in which the teaching is practiced but Buddhahood is no longer attainable; and (3) the Age of the Latter Dharma, that is the Latter Age of Degeneration, lasting 10,000 years, in which only the teaching exists. Accepting the 1,000 year theory for the Ages of the True and Semblance Dharmas each, Nichiren Shōnin held that the Latter Age began 2,000 years after the death of the Buddha.

Āgama sutras *(Agon-gyō)*
Original Buddhist scriptures. As they contain many words which are believed to have been preached by the historical Śākyamuni Buddha, it is believed that they were written earlier than *Kegon-kyō*, the *Flower Garland Sutra*. There are four groups of Chinese Āgama sutras: (1) *Jō-agongyō*, Long Āgama sutras; (2) *Chū-agon-gyō*, Middle-length Āgama sutras; (3) *Zōitsu-agon-gyō*, Increasing-by-One Āgama sutras; and (4) *Zō-agon-gyō*, Miscellaneous Āgama sutras. According to T'ien-t'ai's classification of the Five Periods and Eight Teachings, Nichiren considers the Āgama sutras to be Hinayana teachings preached in the second period, which are several steps below the *Lotus Sutra*.

Ajātaśatru, King *(Ajase-ō)*
A king of Magadha in Central India during Śākyamuni's lifetime, who is said to have been incited by Devadatta to have his father Bimbisāra killed and his mother Vaidehī imprisoned. He also tried to kill Śākyamuni with a drunken elephant. Later however, he converted to Buddhism and supported the first Buddhist Council for the compilation of Śākyamuni's teachings. To Nichiren the salvation of King Ajātaśatru, who had committed the Five Rebellious Sins, represented an example of salvation of evil persons by virtue of the Lotus teaching. Nichiren thus cited the story of the king in his attempt to convert people in the Latter Age of Degeneration.

All the holy teachings of the Buddha's lifetime *(ichidai shōgyō)*
Teachings of Śākyamuni Buddha preached to save people during His lifetime, from His attainment of enlightenment under the Bodhi tree to His death at the age of 80. Systematizing them all in the "five periods" and "eight teachings," Grand Master T'ien-t'ai maintained that the *Lotus Sutra* represented the true intent of the Buddha. Following the T'ien-t'ai doctrines of the "five periods" and "eight teachings," Nichiren Shōnin insisted on the supremacy of the *Lotus Sutra* over all other Buddhist scriptures.

All the scriptures of Buddhism *(Issaikyō)*
In a narrow sense, this refers to all the sutras which Śākyamuni Buddha preached. In a broader sense it refers to all the Buddhist scriptures including the sutras, *vinaya* or precepts, and *abhidarma* or discourses on Buddhism written by later scholars or propagators after the passing of the Buddha. They are also called the Great Pitaka sutras, *Daizōkyō*, All Pitaka sutras, *Issaizōkyō*, or All sutras, *Issaikyō*. Nichiren considered them all as "The Buddha's Golden Words," and held fast to the affirmative viewpoint of scriptures. Nevertheless, he insisted that the *Lotus Sutra* is supreme of all Buddhist scriptures, and that it alone reveals the true intent of the Buddha.

Amoghavajra *(Fukū)*
See "Pu-k'ung, Tripiṭaka Master."

Ānanda *(Anan)*
One of Śākyamuni's 10 great disciples, Ānanda was a cousin of Śākyamuni and also younger brother of Devadatta. As a personal attendant, Ānanda accompanied Śākyamuni for many years, and is known as the foremost in hearing and remembering the Buddha's teachings. He played a central role in compiling the Buddha's teachings at the First Buddhist Council after the death of the Buddha. Describing the history of the *Lotus Sutra*, Nichiren considers him along with Kāśyapa as two pioneering leaders of Buddhism during the Age of the True Dharma after the death of Śākyamuni.

Annotation on the Great Concentration and Insight *(Maka Shikan Fugyō-den Guketsu)*
Abbreviated as *Guketsu* or *Gu* in Nichiren's writings. In this writing of 10 fascicles, Grand Master Miao-lê annotates on T'ien-t'ai's *Great Concentration and Insight, Mo-ho Chih-kuan*, revealing the profound practices expounded by T'ien-t'ai and refuting misunderstandings which arose after T'ien-t'ai's death. Along with T'ien-t'ai's *Great Concentration and Insight*, this writing of Miao-lê had great influence on the theology of Nichiren Shōnin, who often cited it to prove his points.

Annotations on the Nirvana Sutra *(Nehangyō-sho)*
This work of Grand Master Chang-an, 561–632 CE, the second patriarch of the T'ien-t'ai sect in China, annotated the southern version of the *Nirvana Sutra*. It is believed that Nichiren often relied on these annotations when he read the *Nirvana Sutra*.

Annotations on the Words and Phrases of the Lotus Sutra *(Hokke Mongu-ki)*
This work by Miao-lê is sometimes abbreviated by Nichiren simply as *Ki*. Claiming the supremacy of the *Lotus Sutra*, Nichiren often cited both T'ien-t'ai's *Words and Phrases of the Lotus Sutra*, and Miao-lê's annotations of it to strengthen his points.

Appearance of Bodhisattvas from Underground Chapter *(Yūjutsu-hon)*
The 15th chapter of the *Lotus Sutra*. Bodhisattvas from other worlds requested permission to preach in the Sahā World, but Śākyamuni Buddha refused to allow them. Then numerous great bodhisattvas emerged from underground, headed by the Four Great Bodhisattvas. On behalf of bodhisattvas as many as 80,000 times the sands of the Ganges River, Bodhisattva Maitreya inquired what kind of training these great bodhisattvas had gone through. The Buddha explained that those bodhisattvas appearing from underground had been His disciples in the Sahā World in the past. Thus the Buddha began to reveal His eternal life, which is expounded in the following 16th chapter.

Asaṅga Bodhisattva *(Mujaku Bosatsu)*
Native of north India and a great exponent of the consciousness-only doctrine of Mahayana Buddhism in the fourth–fifth century CE. Traditionally it is said that he often visited Bodhisattva Maitreya in the Tuṣita Heaven to receive the ultimate teaching of the consciousness-only doctrine.

Assurance of Future Buddhahood Chapter *("Ninki-hon")*
An abbreviation of the full title of the ninth chapter of the *Lotus Sutra, Ju-gaku Mugaku Ninki-hon,* The Assurance of Future Buddhahood of the Śrāvakas Who Have Something More to Learn and the Śrāvakas Who Have Nothing More to Learn. In this chapter, Śākyamuni Buddha assures Ānanda, His personal servant, of his future existence as Mountain Sea Wisdom Superhuman Power King Buddha, *Sengai-e Jizaitsūō*. He also assures Rāhula, His own son, of his future existence as Stepping on Seven Treasure Flowers Buddha *Toshippōke*. The Buddha also predicted His 2,000 *śrāvaka* disciples to be future Buddhas called Treasure Form, *Hōsō*.

Attaining enlightenment in the eternal past *(kuon jitsujō)*

Central theme of the *hommon*, the essential section of the *Lotus Sutra*, especially of the 16th chapter. It insists that Śākyamuni Buddha did not attain Enlightenment for the first time at Buddhagayā in India, but that He has been enlightened since the eternal past. Attainment of Buddhahood by Śākyamuni at Buddhagayā is merely a temporal appearance of the Original True Buddha who has been guiding and saving all the people ever since. Nichiren's claim of the *Lotus Sutra* as the ultimate True Teaching of the Buddha based on the two doctrines: "attaining Enlightenment in the eternal past (by Śākyamuni Buddha)" and "obtaining Buddhahood by Two Vehicles (two groups of Hinayana sages — *śrāvaka* and *pratyekabuddha*)."

Attainment of Buddhahood by women *(nyonin jōbutsu)*

Attainment of Buddhahood by women had long been denied by Buddhism in Japan, India, and China. This was so not only among Buddhists but also among those in the secular world. Discrimination against women gradually disappeared from Buddhist scriptures such as the *Lotus Sutra*, in which attainment of Buddhahood by women is clearly recognized. The 12th chapter of the *Lotus Sutra* preaches that women, who have been regarded incapable of becoming kings or Buddhas because of their inherent five hindrances, can attain Buddhahood. The chapter speaks of a dragon king's daughter, eight years old, becoming a Buddha. Stressing the importance of attainment of Buddhahood by a dragon daughter, Nichiren said, "The example of a dragon girl becoming a Buddha does not mean only her. It means the attainment of Buddhahood by all women." Living in the feudal period in Japan over 700 years ago, Nichiren asserted his conviction for sexual equality.

Avalokiteśvara Bodhisattva *(Kannon Bosatsu)*

Kanzeon or *Kannon* in Japanese, meaning "One Who Sees the Voices of the World." He made an original vow to pay close attention to people to save them, out of profound compassion. The 25th chapter of the *Lotus Sutra* preaches that he assumes 33 different forms and appears anywhere to save people from suffering. In Pure Land Buddhism, he is an attendant of the Buddha of Infinite Life representing compassion. Nichiren considered him as a bodhisattva disciple of Buddhas in manifestation, *shakke*, appearing in the pre-Lotus sutras and in the first half, or theoretical section, of the *Lotus Sutra*. He also said that Kannon appeared as Grand Master Nan-yüeh to spread the Lotus in the Age of the Semblance Dharma.

Avīci Hell *(abigoku)*
Also called *abijigoku* or *abidaijō* in Japanese. See "Hell of Incessant Suffering."

Becoming a Buddha with one's present body *(sokushin jōbutsu)*
Attainment of Buddhahood by ordinary people with their present body in this world. The Japanese term *genshin jōbutsu* is also used to mean an ordinary, that is ignorant person becoming a Buddha with his present body. This doctrine is preached by the Tendai and Shingon Sects, in contrast to the doctrine of rebirth in the Pure Land of Utmost Bliss, where people can practice Buddhism to become Buddhas. Nichiren Shōnin preaches that Buddhahood is attainable for one who upholds and chants the Odaimoku: Namu Myōhō Renge-kyō.

Beholding the Stupa of Treasures Chapter *(Hōtō-hon)*
In the 11th chapter of the *Lotus Sutra*, the Buddha of Many Treasures appeared within a stupa that emerged from the earth and was decorated with seven treasures. This Buddha verified the truth of the Buddha Śākyamuni's preaching. The replica Buddhas, *funjin*, were called from 10 directions, meaning from all over the universe. The doors of the stupa tower were opened and both Buddhas, Śākyamuni and Many Treasures, sitting side by side, called for those who would propagate the *Lotus Sutra* after the Buddha's demise. At this point the expounding assembly was moved to the sky. Nichiren in his writings designated the 12 chapters from this chapter to the 22nd chapter, Transmission, as the preaching to the assembly in the sky.

Bodhidharma, Grand Master *(Daruma Daishi)*
The founder of Zen Buddhism in China popularly known as Ta-mo, or Daruma. He was an Indian who came to China, introducing the teaching of meditation. Details of his life are not known for sure. According to one tradition, he was the third son of the king of a state in South India and he came to China on the invitation extended by Emperor Wu of Liang. He went to Liang's capital to preach Zen meditation but soon left for the Shao-lin-ssŭ, or Shōrinji, of Mt. Sung-shan, or Sūzan, where he is said to have sat against a wall for nine years.

Bodhisattva *(bosatsu)*
The Japanese term *bosatsu* is a transliteration of the original Sanskrit. Those who practice Buddhism not only for themselves but also for others without discrimination are called bodhisattvas. Like the lotus in a muddy pond having graceful flowers, bodhisattvas stay in the ugly world, helping others in suffering without thinking of their own happiness. In Mahayana Buddhism many bodhisattvas assist not only the Buddha Śākyamuni but also many

other Buddhas such as Amida, the Buddha of Infinite Life, Great Sun Buddha, Medicine Master Buddha, and Vairocana Buddha. Among the well-known bodhisattvas are Kannon Bosatsu, or *Avalokiteśvara*, and Jizō Bosatsu, or *Kṣitigarbha*.

Bodhisattva Necklace Sutra *(Yōraku-kyō)*
This two-fascicle sutra was translated by Chu Fo-nien of China, and it expounds the original karma of a bodhisattva. Nichiren Shōnin regarded this sutra together with the *Brahma-Net Sutra* as revealing the precepts of the expedient Mahayana doctrines.

Bodhisattvas appearing from underground *(jiyu no bosatsu)*
The term *jiyu no bosatsu* refers to the numerous bodhisattvas who emerged from the earth as described in the 15th chapter of the *Lotus Sutra*. They are also called *honge no bosatsu* meaning bodhisattvas guided by the Original Buddha in the eternal past. Their emergence revealed that the attainment of enlightenment by Śākyamuni was in the eternal past, and provided Him with the occasion of preaching the True Dharma of the last half of the *Lotus Sutra*. Headed by Bodhisattvas such as Superior-Practice, Jōgyō, they were entrusted in the 21st chapter of the *Lotus Sutra* to spread the sutra after the death of Śākyamuni. Realizing himself to be an avatar of Jōgyō Bodhisattva, Nichiren strived to spread the *Lotus Sutra*.

Brahma Heaven *(Bonten, Daibonten)*
The first of the four meditation heavens, *shozen-ten*, in the Realm of Form, *shikkai*. Also called Daibonten, after Daibon, the King of the Brahma Heaven above Mt. Sumeru. In Indian mythology Daibon is regarded as the supreme god and creator of the universe. In Buddhism he and Indra are the two supreme protective deities of Buddhism. Daibon requested Śākyamuni Buddha to preach upon His enlightenment, and he also attended the preaching assemblies of the *Lotus Sutra*. Nichiren worshipped him and invoked him in his mandala honzon.

Buddha-nature *(busshō)*
It refers to the inborn nature of a Buddha or possibility to be a Buddha. In Tendai doctrine it consists of three types: (1) inborn nature to become a Buddha, *shōin busshō*; (2) the wisdom to realize inborn Buddha-nature, *ryōin busshō*; and (3) meritorious deeds which make wisdom grow, *en'in busshō*. Nichiren insists that the *Lotus Sutra* alone preaches that all three elements of Buddha-nature are thoroughly present in any living being.

Buddhas in manifestation *(funjin)*

Funjin Buddhas are various forms the Buddha uses as means of saving different beings. They preach to guide beings in the worlds all over the universe. In the 11th chapter of the *Lotus Sutra*, Beholding the Stupa of Treasures, they gathered to listen to the Lotus assembly in front of the Stupa of Many Treasures; and in the 21st chapter of the sutra, The Supernatural Powers of the Tathāgata, they proved the truth of Śākyamuni's preaching by touching the Brahma Heaven with their long, wide tongues.

Buddhas in 10 directions *(jippō no shobutsu)*

Refers to Buddhas who preach in the worlds all over the universe. See "Buddhas in manifestation."

Capacity of people to understand *(kikon)*

Refers to the mental capacity of people to react to the dharma, or to understand and accept a religious teaching. Kikon is sometimes abbreviated as *ki*.

Chang-an, Grand Master *(Shōan Daishi)*

561–632 CE. His name was Kuan-ting, but he was known as Grand Master Chang-an after his birthplace. He was a disciple and the successor to Grand Master T'ien-t'ai, founder of the T'ien-t'ai school in China. Chang-an recorded and compiled most of his master's lectures including the three major works: *Profound Meaning of the Lotus Sutra, Words and Phrases of the Lotus Sutra,* and *Great Concentration and Insight*. He deserves credit for making T'ien-t'ai's lectures available today. He himself wrote the *Profound Meaning of Nirvana*, and the *Annotations on the Nirvana Sutra*. Nichiren recognized his relationship to T'ien-t'ai as analogous to that of Ānanda to Śākyamuni, and often quoted from his *Annotations on the Nirvana Sutra*, though comparably less than from T'ien-t'ai and Miao-lê.

Ch'êng-kuan *(Chōkan)*

738–839 CE. Fourth patriarch of the Hua-yen or Kegon school in China. He is credited for the revival of Flower Garland or Kegon theology. Also known as National Master Ch'ing-liang, *Seiryō Kokushi*. Ch'eng-kuan studied various Mahayana schools of Buddhism, including Tendai meditation under Miao-lê. He later concentrated on the study of Flower Garland Buddhism, producing many books such as *Kegon-gyō-sho, Commentary on the Flower Garland Sutra*, in 60 fascicles. Believing firmly in the supremacy of the *Lotus Sutra*, Nichiren harshly criticized Ch'eng-kuan for claiming superiority of the *Flower Garland Sutra* and for "stealing" the "3,000 existences in one thought" doctrine of T'ien-t'ai.

Chi-ts'ang *(Kichizō)*
549–623 CE. Also called Grand Master Chia-hsiang after the temple where he resided. He systematized the *San-lun,* or Three Discourses theology and is sometimes regarded as the founder of the San-lun sect in China. He lectured not only on the San-lun but also the *Lotus* and *Flower Garland Sutras,* and wrote such commentaries as the *Profound Meaning of the Three Treatises* and *Profound Meaning of the Lotus Sutra.* Nichiren maintained that Chia-hsiang misinterpreted the *Lotus Sutra,* but later repented, becoming a disciple of T'ien-t'ai. Chi-ts'ang is said to have been impressed by T'ien-t'ai so deeply that he offered himself to T'ien-t'ai to use as a stepladder whenever T'ien-t'ai went up to the platform on the stage to preach.

Chien-chên *(Ganjin)*
668–763 CE. Chinese monk who founded the Japanese Ritsu sect. Chien-chên studied the T'ien-t'ai, *Tendai,* and Lü, *Ritsu,* teachings, eventually becoming a famous lecturer on Lü Buddhism. In response to the invitation of the Japanese monks, Yōei and Fushō, he came to Japan in 753 after five unsuccessful attempts. He built the precept-platform, *kaidan,* in the Tōdaiji Temple, making it the center for granting Buddhist precepts. Afterward, he built the Tōshōdaiji Temple in Nara, where he spread the Ritsu teachings. Nichiren Shōnin stated that Chien-chên transmitted the Ritsu and Tendai teachings but propagated only the Ritsu as an expedient means of spreading the *Lotus Sutra.*

Chih-yen *(Chigon)*
602–668 CE. The second patriarch of the Chinese Hua-yen, *Kegon* or Flower Garland sect. He was generally called Grand Master Chih-hsiang. He entered the priesthood at 14, and studied the Kegon teaching under Tu-shun. Living at the Chih-hsiang-ssǔ Temple on Mt. Chung-nan, he spread Kegon Buddhism vigorously.

Chishō, Grand Master *(Chishō Daishi)*
814–891 CE Also called Enchin, he was a disciple of Gishin, first *zasu,* Chief Minister of the Enryakuji Temple, and became the fifth *zasu.* He studied both Tendai and Shingon teachings in China for six years, and vigorously spread Tendai esotericism in Japan. Nichiren severely criticized him for following the example of Ennin, Grand Master Jikaku, in betraying their founder, Grand Master Dengyō, and slandering the true Dharma.

Clarification of the Precepts *(Kenkai-ron)*
Written by Grand Master Dengyō, who wanted to establish a Mahayana ordination center on Mt. Hiei. In the previous year, 818 CE, his petition submitted to the Imperial Court to permit him to do so was strongly opposed by the six sects of Nara. Dengyō wrote *Kenkai-ron* to rebuff their arguments and to explain the Mahayana precepts.

Collection of Passages on the Nembutsu and the Original Vow *(Senjaku-shū)*
Abbreviation of *Senjaku Hongan Nembutsu-shū, Collection of Passages on the Nembutsu and the Original Vow*, by Hōnen, founder of the Jōdo or Pure Land sect. Citing from the triple Pure Land sutras and Shan-tao's interpretation of them, Hōnen advocates the Pure Land doctrine concentrating on the nembutsu for rebirth in the Pure Land. In *Risshō Ankoku-ron, Shugo Kokka-ron*, and other writings, Nichiren harshly criticized Hōnen and his *Senjaku-shu* for insisting on single-minded devotion to the nembutsu.

Commentary on the Profound Meaning of the Lotus Sutra *(Hokke Gengi Shakusen)*
A commentary by Grand Master Miao-lê on T'ien-t'ai's *Hokke Gengi, Profound Meaning of the Lotus Sutra*.

Commentator *(ronji)*
Literally commentators on sutras, but Nichiren uses it to refer to high Buddhist priests in India.

Comparative study of Buddhist doctrines *(kyōsō)*
Abbreviation of the *Kyōsō Hanjaku*, classification of Buddhist scriptures from some sectarian points of view such as T'ien-t'ai's "five periods and eight teachings" and "three standards of doctrinal comparison" and Nichiren's "five-fold comparison" and "four sets of the three divisions in teaching." It also refers to the doctrinal aspect as opposed to *kanjin*, practice of meditation or *jisō*, ritual.

Dainichi *(Dainichi)*
?–? CE. Dainichi Nōnin was a self-educated Zen priest in the early Kamakura Period. He founded the Sambōji Temple in Settsu Province, Hyōgo Prefecture, and spread Zen Buddhism of the Southern Sung tradition, which he named the Nihon Daruma-shū, insisting that the essence of Buddhism, Zen, is transmitted by non-literal and non-verbal means. Nichiren was critical of Dainichi for relying on the *Ryōga-kyō*, a provisional sutra preached in the third period, and for insisting on *kyōge betsu-den*, non-literary, non-verbal transmission. Nichiren referred to Dainichi's teachings as "an act of heavenly demons."

Delusions arising from incorrect views and thoughts *(kenji no waku)*
Literally thoughts and views of worldly desires and passions. See "Three delusions."

Dengyō, Grand Master *(Dengyō Daishi)*
767–822 CE. Founder of the Tendai sect in Japan, he is also known as Saichō. He was ordained at the Tōdaiji Temple, but later entered Mt. Hiei and studied the teaching of T'ien-t'ai, the patriarch of the T'ien-t'ai school in China. Entering T'ang China in 804, Dengyō mastered the teachings of T'ien-t'ai, Zen, esoteric Buddhism and precepts before returning to Japan. He engaged in heated debates against the Hossō priest Tokuitsu on Buddha-nature and also against the superintendent of Buddhist priests in Nara on the establishment of the Mahayana Precept Platform on Mt. Hiei. His major works include the *Shugo Kokkai-shō, Defense of the Country, Hokke Shūku, Passages of the Lotus Sutra,* and *Kenkai-ron, Treatise on Precepts.* Regarding Saichō as one who practices the *Lotus Sutra,* Nichiren respected him as an indispensable transmitter of the teaching of the *Lotus Sutra.*

Depend on the dharma, not on people *(ehō fu-enin)*
This commandment of the Buddha to rely on what was preached by the Buddha in sutras rather than opinions of the *ninshi,* Buddhist masters in China and Japan, is expounded in the *Nirvana Sutra* as one of the four standards which Buddhists must follow. Nichiren considered it as fundamental for us to grasp correctly the true intent of the Buddha and quoted it often in his writings. Firmly upholding this standard as the Buddha's golden words, Nichiren concluded that when one honestly believes and accepts the words of the Buddha as stated in the sutras, it is clear that the *Lotus Sutra* is nothing but the True Dharma of the Buddha. Thus according to Nichiren "depend on the dharma" means "depend on the *Lotus Sutra.* "He insisted that we should rely on the *Lotus Sutra,* rather than opinions of various masters of various schools of Buddhism. See "Four Reliances."

Devadatta *(Daibadatta)*
Daibadatta, also called Daiba or Chōdatsu in Japanese, was an elder brother of Ānanda, a cousin and a follower of Śākyamuni. He was extremely intelligent and is said to have memorized all 80,000 scriptures of Buddhism. Nevertheless, attached to worldly gains and fame, he tried to take over the leadership of the Buddhist order and even tried to kill the Buddha. He is said to have fallen into the Hell of Incessant Suffering while yet alive for committing three of the Five Rebellious Sins. Based on the 12th chapter of the *Lotus Sutra,* in which he is guaranteed to be a future Buddha, Nichiren maintained that all evil-doers, even slanderers of the True Dharma, can be saved by the *Lotus Sutra.*

Devadatta Chapter (*Daiba[datta]-hon*)
The 12th chapter of the *Lotus Sutra*. The first half of the chapter preaches that Devadatta, the archenemy of Śākyamuni Buddha, had been His teacher in a past life, and assures Devadatta of his future existence as a Buddha. It shows the strength of the *Lotus Sutra* enabling even evil persons to attain Buddhahood. The second half proved the attainment of Buddhahood by women through the example of a dragon girl attaining Buddhahood immediately with her present body.

Dharma Body (*hosshin*)
See "Threefold body of a Buddha."

Diamond Peak Sutra (*Kongōchō-kyō*)
Two Chinese versions exist. One translated by Amoghavajra in three fascicles. The other by Vajrabodhi in four fascicles. This and the *Dainichi-kyō, Great Sun Buddha Sutra*, are the two basic scriptures of esoteric Buddhism. While the *Great Sun Buddha Sutra* reveals the Womb World, this sutra expounds the teaching of the Diamond World, on which the Diamond World Mandala is based. According to T'ien-t'ai's five-period doctrine, Nichiren Shōnin relegates this sutra as expedient and provisional preached during the third Hōdō period.

Diamond Scalpel (*Kongōbei-ron*)
Abbreviated as *Kombei-ron* or *Kompei-ron*. A work in question and answer form by Grand Master Miao-lê, sixth patriarch of T'ien-t'ai Buddhism, refuting Ch'eng-kuan of the Flower Garland school, who denied that non-living beings have Buddha-nature. Miao-lê insisted in this writing that Buddha-nature is possessed by all beings, both living and non-living.

Disciples of Buddhas in manifestation (*shakke*)
The Japanese term *shakke* refers to followers taught and guided by Buddhas of the pre-Lotus sutras and the first half, or *shakumon,* of the *Lotus Sutra*. These Buddhas are manifestations of the Eternal, Original Buddha. They are differentiated from those bodhisattvas who emerged from the earth in the 15th chapter of the *Lotus Sutra*, who are disciples of the Original Buddha and are called *honge*. Disciples of manifestation Buddhas consist of two groups of bodhisattvas: those who had been in this Sahā World and those who came from other worlds in the universe. Nichiren maintained that the duty of *shakke* was to spread the dharma in the Buddha's lifetime, the Age of the True Dharma and that of the Semblance Dharma. It was the duty of the *honge* to spread the teaching of the Buddha in the Latter Age of Degeneration. He believed himself

to have been an avatar of Jōgyō, Superior-Practice Bodhisattva, and strived to spread the message of the *Lotus Sutra*.

Disgrace with the shogunate *(kanki)*
The Japanese term *kanki* means falling into disgrace with the government, master, or father. It also refers to official punishments such as banishment and death. Nichiren described his exiles to Izu and Sado by the Kamakura military regime as "twice falling into disgrace."

Dōami *(Dōami)*
See "Dōamidabutsu."

Dōamidabutsu *(Dōamidabutsu)*
?–1287 CE. Refers to Dōkyō-bō Nenkū. Born in Yamato Province, Nara Prefecture, he became a disciple of Kakumyō-bō Chōsai, a grand disciple of Hōnen. He spread the nembutsu while residing in the Shinzenkōji Temple in Nagoe, Kamakura. Together with Nen-a Ryōchū, he represented the Pure Land school in Kamakura during that time.

Doctrinal study *(kyōsō)*
See "Comparative study of Buddhist doctrines."

Domestic Disturbance *(jikai hongyaku-nan)*
Refers to domestic power struggles or fighting among comrades, as mentioned in the *Medicine Master Sutra,* as one of the seven disasters predicted to occur if the True Dharma is slandered. Nichiren pointed out in his *Risshō Ankoku-ron* that the troubles of domestic disturbance and invasion of Japan by foreign forces were inevitable so long as Japan stood against the True Dharma of the *Lotus Sutra*. The prediction of civil war became a reality when a power struggle erupted among the Hōjōs in the second month of the ninth year of the Bun'ei Era, 1272 CE, and Hōjō Tokisuke attempted a coup d'etat. Nichiren then likened his *Risshō Ankoku-ron* to the prediction of Śākyamuni Buddha.

Duration of the Life of the Tathāgata Chapter *(Juryō-hon)*
It is commonly believed that Śākyamuni Buddha achieved enlightenment at the age of 30 or 35 under the pipal tree at Gayā, India. However this 16th chapter of the *Lotus Sutra* declares that in truth He achieved enlightenment an inconceivably long time ago and that the Pure Land is nothing but this Sahā World where we live, revealing the true substance of historical Śākyamuni Buddha and the true *honzon*. The theology of Nichiren Shōnin is based on this Original Śākyamuni Buddha, who controls all other Buddhas and their Pure Lands.

Encouragement for Keeping This Sutra Chapter *(Kanji-hon)*
The 13th chapter of the *Lotus Sutra*. In the 11th chapter, Beholding the Stūpa of Treasures, the Buddha asked who would spread the teaching of this sutra after the Buddha's demise. In this chapter, both bodhisattvas, such as Medicine-King, and *śrāvaka* responded swearing that they would propagate it. Then in the 20-line verse at the end of the chapter, 800,000, 100,000,000 *nayuta* of bodhisattvas made a vow to spread the teaching at the risk of their lives. This verse states that propagators will encounter three kinds of strong enemies: (1) lay followers who persecute them; (2) evil-minded men of religion; and (3) outwardly holy, self-conceited priests of high rank. Nichiren regarded this verse as a prediction of the Buddha Śākyamuni. As his experiences matched this forecast of the Buddha, it strengthened his belief that he was truly practicing the *Lotus Sutra*.

Entering Laṅka Sutra *(Ryōga-kyō)*
A later Mahayana sutra written near the fifth century A.D. It preaches the ālaya-consciousness, *arayashiki* and Buddhahood in a living being, *nyorai-zō*. Bodhidharma, the first patriarch of Zen Buddhism in China, is credited with bringing it to China. This underpins the claim of Zen Buddhists that the truth has not been transmitted through word or language.

Epilogue *(rutsū)*
See "Preface, main discourse and epilogue."

Equal in Doctrine but Superior in Ritualism *(ridō jishō)*
Tendai esotericism claimed, in comparing the *Lotus Sutra* to the *Great Sun Buddha Sutra*, that they were equal in doctrine, but the *Great Sun Buddha Sutra* was superior in ritualism because of its finger signs, *mudrā*, and mantras. This doctrine was initiated by En'nin, Grand Master Jikaku, on the basis of the *Annotations on the Great Sun Buddha Sutra* by I-hsing and was transmitted to Enchin, Grand Master Chishō, An'nen and others. Classifying the *Lotus Sutra* below the *Great Sun Buddha Sutra*, it clearly showed the shift of Tendai theology toward esoteric Buddhism, which Nichiren vehemently criticized as against the true intent of the Buddha. From the standpoint of pure Lotus Buddhism, Nichiren protested against the disappearance of the orthodox Lotus teaching established by T'ien-t'ai and Dengyō, stating that the *Lotus Sutra* with its "3,000 existences contained in one thought" doctrine is supreme both in doctrine and ritualism.

Eshin and Danna factions *(Eshin-ryū, Danna-ryū)*
The Eshin faction within the Tendai sect in Japan was founded by Genshin, who is popularly known as Eshin Sōzu after his residence, the Eshin-in Temple at Yokawa on Mt. Hiei. A group centering around Kakuun, Genshin's "brother" with the same teacher-master, is called Danna faction after Kakuun's alternate name, Danna Sōjō.

Eshin, Venerable *(Eshin Sōzu)*
Also named Genshin, 942–1017 CE. A priest of the Tendai sect who studied both exoteric and esoteric teachings on Mt. Hiei under Ryōgen, 18th head of the Enryakuji Temple. He wrote the *Ōjō Yōshū, Essentials of Salvation*, which had a tremendous influence on Pure Land Buddhism in Japan. He later wrote the *Ichijō Yōketsu, Essentials of the One Vehicle Teaching*, stressing the universal existence of Buddha-nature and One Vehicle teaching of the *Lotus Sutra* as opposed to the Hossō doctrine of "five distinctive natures of living beings." Nichiren at first considered Eshin as an outstanding priest of the Tendai sect, but later criticized him harshly as a parasite within the Lotus school.

Essential section *(hommon)*
The second half, 14 chapters of the *Lotus Sutra* from the 15th chapter, Appearance of Bodhisattvas from Underground, to the last chapter, Encouragement of Universal-Sage Bodhisattva, is referred to as the essential section, meaning the teaching of the original Buddha: Buddha in substance in contrast to a Buddha in manifestation. The main theme of this section is replacing the teaching of the Buddha attaining Buddhahood in this world for the first time with the doctrine of Śākyamuni attaining Enlightenment in the eternal past. In the theoretical section the world of the Buddha's Enlightenment is expounded to guide the people, whereas in the essential section the Original Buddha was revealed to show that the Buddha's guidance of the people continues from the eternal past into the infinite future. While T'ien-t'ai established his theology based on the theoretical section, Nichiren tried to apply the teaching of the Buddha based on the essential section as the means of saving people in society.

Evil friend *(aku-chishiki)*
Meaning literally "bad knowledge." The term *aku-chishiki* refers to an evil friend or teacher who preaches the evil dharma to lead people astray blocking the right way leading to Buddhahood. It is used as an antonym of *zen-chishiki*, good friend. The third chapter of the *Lotus Sutra*, A Parable, uses it as an antonym of a good friend, *zen'yū*. Nichiren considered Devadatta, who incited King Ajātaśatru, a typical "evil friend." Nichiren also uses the term to mean an "evil teacher" like Hōnen who destroys the virtuous minds of people while leading them by slandering the True Dharma.

Exoteric and esoteric teachings *(kengyō-mikkyō)*
Exoteric teachings are those preached clearly in words and writings according to the ability of listeners. These are contrasted with esoteric teachings preached by the Great Sun Buddha secretly and beyond the understanding of ordinary people. The Shingon sect maintains that exoteric teachings were preached by the Accommodative-bodied Śākyamuni Buddha while the esoteric teachings by the Dharma-bodied Great Sun Buddha, and that therefore the latter is superior. However, Nichiren insists that Shingon sutras, which preach neither the "attainment of Buddhahood by *śrāvaka* and *pratyekabuddha*" nor the "attainment of Buddhahood by Śākyamuni Buddha in the eternal past," are inferior to the *Lotus Sutra*, which is the true esoteric teaching.

Expedients Chapter *(Hōben-pon)*
The second chapter of the *Lotus Sutra*. At the beginning of this chapter, Śākyamuni arises from meditation and tells Śāriputra that only Buddhas can realize the true aspect of all phenomena consisting of 10 factors. This is the doctrine of *shohō jissō*, all phenomena as the reality of existence, and *jūnyoze*, 10 suchnesses. Upon repeated requests by Śāriputra to explain why only Buddhas can understand it, the Buddha revealed the truth: that Buddhas appear in this world in order to lead all people to attain Buddha wisdom, and that teachings for Three Vehicles, *śrāvaka*, *pratyekabuddha* and bodhisattvas, are merely expedients to lead the people to the One Buddha Vehicle.

Eyelet coins *(gamoku)*
This term stems from the shape of the coin that looks like the eye of a bird. Usually these coins were laced together with a piece of string. Nichiren Shōnin sometimes received these coins as donations for a memorial service or to support his propagation.

Fa-ts'ang *(Hōzō)*
643–712 CE. The third patriarch of the Chinese Hua-yen, Flower Garland sect. He is considered the systematizer of the Flower Garland doctrines. After studying Buddhism on Mt. Tai-po, he became a disciple of Chih-yen. After the death of his master, Fa-ts'ang entered the priesthood, writing many books and spreading the Flower Garland teachings. He was patronized by Empress Wu, *Sokuten Bugō*, and was given the title of Grand Master Hsien-shou, *Genju Daishi*.

Finger signs and mantras *(in-shingon)*
Finger signs in esoteric Buddhism symbolizing the enlightenment attained by Buddhas and bodhisattvas. Fingers represent the five elements of earth, water, fire, wind, and space. Those on the left hand are for meditation and those on

the right hand, wisdom. These signs are one of the three secrets of body, mouth, and mind, through which one can attain Buddhahood in this corporal life. The secret of the mouth involves speaking mantras, called *shingon*, true word, or *darani*. spells. The secret of the mind includes meditation upon their *honzon* or object of reverence: the Great Sun Buddha.

Five aggregates of all existences *(go'on)*
Known also as *go'un* in Japanese. Buddhist philosophy considers all physical and mental things and phenomena in this world consist of five aggregates or five elements: (1) form or matter; (2) perception; (3) mental conception and ideas; (4) volition; and (5) consciousness.

Five defilements *(gojoku)*
Five spiritual, physical and social evils which characterize the Latter Age: (1) defilement of the age including famines, plagues, and wars; (2) defilement of views meaning wrong views; (3) defilement by evil passions of greed, anger and stupidity; (4) defilement of people through their physical and spiritual decline; and (5) defilement of life through shortening life span. In Japanese literature the term "evil world with five defilements" means corruption and pollution of the world.

Five Flavors *(gomi)*
Many teachings were preached during the lifetime of Śākyamuni Buddha. Grand Master T'ien-t'ai divided these into five categories by the periods in which they were preached. He named these periods Flower Garland or *Kegon*, Āgama or *Agon*, Expanded Teachings or *Hōdō*, Wisdom Teachings or *Hannya*, and *Lotus* and *Nirvana Sutras* or *Hokke-Nehan*. The *Kegon* period is the first three weeks after the Buddha attained enlightenment. The *Agon* period covered 12 years of preaching Hinayana sutras. The *Hōdō* Period is the following eight years of preaching Mahayana sutras. The *Hannya* period is 22 years of preaching the *Wisdom Sutra*. The *Hokke-Nehan* period is the last eight years preaching the *Lotus* and *Nirvana Sutras*. These five periods of preaching are likened to the five tastes of milk and milk products: *Kegon* to milk, *Agon* to cream, *Hōdō* to curdled milk, *Hannya* to butter, and *Hokke-Nehan* to ghee, a finished product, proclaiming that the *Lotus* and *Nirvana Sutras* reveal the true teaching of the Buddha.

Five Holy Proclamations *(goka no hōshō)*
Refers to the "Three Holy Proclamations." These include the Buddha's words in Chapter 11 of the *Lotus Sutra* exhorting people to spread the *Lotus Sutra*, plus guarantees in the 12th chapter of future Buddhahood for Devadatta and

a female dragon. The last two are also interpreted as the Buddha's exhortation for evil persons and women to spread the sutra.

Five hundred (million) dust-particle kalpa (*gohyaku jinden-gō*)
An inconceivably long period of time described in Chapter 16 of the *Lotus Sutra*. It indicates how much time has elapsed since Śākyamuni's original enlightenment. The term is an abbreviation of *gohyaku-senman-oku nayuta asogi-ko:* 500 — 1,000 — 10,000 — 100 million — *nayuta-asamkya-kalpa* meaning a limitless and incalculable length of time.

Five periods (*goji*)
The Tendai doctrine classifying the Buddha's lifetime teaching according to the following five periods: (1) *Kegon* period, first three weeks after His enlightenment; (2) *Agon* period, 12 years preaching Hinayana sutras; (3) *Hōdō* period, eight years preaching Mahayana sutras; (4) *Hannya* period, 22 years preaching the Hannya-kyō; and (5) *Hokke-Nehan* period, last eight years preaching the *Lotus* and *Nirvana Sutras*. T'ien-t'ai also systematized what was preached during these five periods by the Buddha in Eight Teachings: four methods of teaching and four doctrinal teachings. He insisted that the Buddha's ultimate intent was expressed in the *Lotus Sutra*. Following this T'ien-t'ai doctrine, Nichiren emphasized the supremacy of the Lotus teaching.

Five Profound Meanings (*gojū-gen*)
The five viewpoints from which T'ien-t'ai interpreted the *Lotus Sutra* in his *Profound Meaning of the Lotus Sutra*. They are name, entity, quality, function and teaching. "Name" means the interpretation of the title of the sutra explaining the Wonderful Dharma that unify the provisional and true teachings. "Entity" explains the ultimate principle expounded in the sutra: true entity of all phenomena. "Quality" explains the principle doctrines of the One Vehicle teaching. "Function" discusses the benefit and power of the sutra: elimination of doubts and giving birth to devotion. "Teaching" discusses the comparative study of Buddhist doctrines, defining the *Lotus Sutra* as the supreme teaching. Nichiren states in his *Kanjin honzon-shō, Spiritual Contemplation and the Most Venerable One:* "'This 'excellent medicine' signifies nothing but 'Namu Myōhō Renge-kyō' of the name, entity, quality, function and teaching." He thus maintained that the five or seven Chinese characters of *"Namu Myōhō Renge-kyō"* are equipped with the "Five Profound Meanings."

Five rebellious sins (*gogyaku*)
Those who committed any of the five rebellious sins are said to fall into the Hell of Incessant Suffering. They are: (1) killing one's own father; (2) killing

one's own mother; (3) killing an arhat; (4) injuring the Buddha; and (5) causing disunity in the Buddhist order. Nichiren Shōnin explains that the "five rebellious sins" do not exist because neither the Buddha nor an arhat are in the Latter Age of Degeneration, and he emphasizes the seriousness of the sin of slandering the True Dharma rather than that of the five rebellious sins in the Latter Age. Three of the five, killing an arhat, injuring the Buddha, causing disunity in the Buddhist order, are called the "three rebellious sins."

Five Rulers *(gotei)*
The five model rulers of ancient China who are credited to have contributed to the development of the Chinese civilization and system of government.

Five Teachings *(gokyō)*
The Kegon sect classifies Buddhist scriptures into five categories: (1) the Hinayana teachings such as the Āgama sutras; (2) the initial Mahayana teachings such as the *Hannya* and *Gejimmitsu* sutras; (3) the later teachings of Mahayana such as *Kishin Ron,* or *Awakening of Faith in Mahayana;* (4) the Sudden-Enlightenment Teachings of Mahayana such as the *Yuima Sutra;* and (5) Perfect One Vehicle Teachings such as the *Flower Garland Sutra* and *Lotus Sutra.* The Perfect Teachings are further divided into two teachings of the distinct and common, considering the *Flower Garland Sutra* as being the unsurpassed doctrine of the One Vehicle teachings with the *Lotus Sutra* being placed in an inferior position, the same as the Three Vehicle teachings.

Fixed nature *(ketsujō-shō)*
This term refers to those whose nature is predetermined to become *śrāvaka, pratyekabuddha,* or Buddhas. This is according to the Hossō doctrine of *goshō kakubetsu,* five mutually distinctive natures. This doctrine states that the first two of these, *śrāvaka* and *pratyekabuddha,* also called those of the Two Vehicles, have no chance of becoming Buddhas. However in the *Lotus Sutra,* it is guaranteed that they will become Buddhas in the future.

Flower Garland school *(Kegon-shū)*
Also known as the Kegon sect. One of the thirteen Buddhist schools in China and also one of the six Buddhist schools in Nara, based on the *Kegon-kyō, Flower Garland Sutra.* This school classifies the Buddha's lifetime teachings into five teachings and 10 doctrines to show the superiority of the *Flower Garland Sutra.* The school preaches that all phenomena are one and interpenetrate without obstruction: one penetrates all and all are contained in one. This school was introduced to Japan by the Chinese monk Tao-hsüan during the Nara period in 736 CE. Nichiren considered the Kegon school to be one of the better

Mahayana schools but still inferior to the *Lotus Sutra*. This is because it does not preach the two important doctrines of the attainment of Buddhahood by the Hinayana sages called the Two Vehicles, and the attainment of Buddhahood by Śākyamuni Buddha in the eternal past. When Nichiren criticized the Flower Garland school, he always spoke of Ch'êng-kuan, who in his view stole the "3,000 existences contained in one thought" doctrine of T'ien-t'ai and put it into the theology of his own school while criticizing the T'ien-t'ai (Tendai) school.

Flower Garland Sutra *(Kegon-kyō)*
This sutra is said to have been preached by the Buddha upon attaining enlightenment under the bodhi tree in Buddhagayā. Saying that the whole world is a manisfestation of Vairocana Buddha, the sutra maintains that one is the whole and the whole is one, insisting that a particle of dust contains the whole world and a moment includes eternity. Based on the T'ien-t'ai concepts of the five periods of preaching and eight kinds of teaching of the Buddha, Nichiren Shōnin insisted that the *Flower Garland Sutra* is inferior to the *Lotus Sutra* because it preaches neither the attainment of Buddhahood by Hinayana sages called the Two Vehicles, *śrāvaka* and *pratyekabuddha*, nor the attainment of Buddhahood by Śākyamuni Buddha in the eternal past.

Forty years or so *(shijū yonen)*
The *Seppō-hon*, Expounding the Dharma chapter of the *Muryōgi-kyō*, *Sutra of Infinite Meaning*, states, "The truth has not been revealed during forty years or so." It states in Chapter 15 of the *Lotus Sutra*, *Yūjuppon*, Appearance of Bodhisattvas from Underground, "For the first time in about 40 years since attaining enlightenment." It means that the *Lotus Sutra*, revealing the true intent of the Lord Śākyamuni Buddha, was preached during the last eight years of His preaching after having preached expedient sutras in the Kegon, Agon, Hōdō, and Hannya periods. The phrase, forty years or so, is used to divide the expedient teachings and the true teaching of the Buddha's lifetime preachings. See "Truth has not been revealed."

Four Great Vows *(shigu seigan)*
The Four Great Vows, which all bodhisattvas pledge to fulfill, are also referred to as the General Vows. They are: (1) Sentient beings are innumerable, I vow to save them all. This is a pledge to lead all sentient beings throughout the vast ocean of suffering to the other shore of Nirvana; (2) Our evil desires are inexhaustible, I vow to quench them all. This is a pledge to free all sentient beings from all illusions; (3) The Buddha's teachings are immeasurable, I vow to study them all. This is a pledge to learn and understand all the Buddha's

teachings; and (4) The way of the Buddha is unexcelled, I vow to attain the path sublime. This is a pledge to attain Nirvana.

Four Heavenly Kings (*Shiten-nō*)

Also called the Four Great Heavenly Kings, *Shidaiten-nō*. They are kings of the four-king heavens, *shiō-ten*, around Mt. Sumeru. While serving Indra, they control the eight kinds of gods and demi-gods to protect Buddhism and those who put faith in it. As they vowed to protect this world and Buddhism in it, they are also called the Four Heavenly Kings Who Protect the World, *Gose Shiten-nō*. They consist of four guardian kings: *Jikoku-ten*, Sanskrit *Dhṛtarāṣṭra* in the east, *Zōchō-ten*, Sanskrit *Virūḍhaka* in the south, *Kōmoku-ten*, Sanskrit *Virūpākṣa* in the west, and *Tamon-ten*, Sanskrit *Vaiśravaṇa* in the north. Nichiren Shōnin highly esteemed the Four Heavenly Kings as protectors of the *Lotus Sutra,* placing large signs for them at the four corners of the great mandala honzon.

Four masters in three lands (*sangoku shishi*)

Three lands mean India, China and Japan. Four masters refer to Śākyamuni Buddha, initiator of the Lotus teaching, and those who transmitted it: Grand Masters T'ien-t'ai and Dengyō, and Nichiren Shōnin. The term stems from the *Kembutsu Mirai-ki, On the Buddha's Prophecy*, which states, "I, Nichiren of Awa Province graciously received the teaching of the *Lotus Sutra* from three masters and spread it in the Latter Age of Degeneration. Therefore, I dare add myself to the three masters, calling ourselves 'four masters in three lands'." This statement of Nichiren shows how he believed the faith in the *Lotus Sutra* has been transmitted to him while also professing his conviction that he is the master propagator of the *Lotus Sutra* in the Latter Age of Degeneration.

Four Noble Truths (*shitai or shishōtai*)

Teaching for *śrāvaka*, revealing the truth from four aspects. These were *kutai*, the truth of suffering; *jittai*, the truth regarding the cause of suffering; *mettai*, the truth regarding the extinction of suffering; and *dōtai*, the truth regarding the path to Nirvana. *Kutai* reveals that the world of delusion in the cycle of life and death is full of suffering. *Jittai* shows that suffering is caused by evil passions and karma. *Mettai* tells that exclusion of evil passions and karma leads to the extinction of suffering. *Dōtai* is the Eightfold Noble Path to extinguish the suffering. *Kutai* is the result of *jittai*, which is the cause of *kutai*. *Mettai* is the result of *dōtai*, and *dōtai* is the cause of *mettai*. Causal relationship between *kutai* and *jittai* is in the world of suffering, and that between *mettai* and *dōtai* is in the world of Nirvana.

Four Reliances *(shie)*
According to the *Nirvana Sutra*, four standards which Buddhists must follow: (1) to rely on the dharma, not upon persons; (2) to rely on the meaning, not upon words; (3) to rely on wisdom, not upon knowledge; and (4) to rely on the sutra completely revealing the truth, not upon sutras that do not reveal the whole truth. This term also refers to four ranks of Buddhist leaders whom people can rely upon after the death of the Buddha, classified by those leaders' achievements. Nichiren claimed that the dharma on which people should rely is the *Lotus Sutra*. He identified the four ranks of leaders with the Hinayana, Mahayana, theoretical section, and essential section of the *Lotus Sutra*, claiming that those whom people in the Latter Age should depend on are bodhisattvas who emerged from the earth and that he himself was the leader of that bodhisattva group.

Four teachings *(shikyō)*
These are *kegi no shikyō*, four methods of teaching and *kehō no shikyō*, four doctrinal teachings in the T'ien-t'ai doctrine of the Five Periods and the Eight Teachings. The four methods of teaching classify the ways of preaching of the Buddha into four categories: *tongyō*, abrupt teaching; *zenkyō*, gradual teaching; *himitsukyō*, secret teaching; and *fujōkyō*, indeterminate teaching. Abrupt teaching means the profound teaching beyond the understanding of the people. This corresponds to preaching the *Flower Garland Sutra*. Gradual teaching is a way of preaching in which the people are taught gradually with expedients in accordance to their capacities. This refers to the Āgama sutras, the Hōdō sutras, and the *Wisdom Sutra*. Secret teaching is the teaching whereby the listeners benefit differently without being aware of how they are benefitting. This refers to the preaching of the *Flower Garland Sutra*, the Āgama sutras, the Hōdō sutras and the *Wisdom Sutra*. Indeterminate teaching is the teaching whereby the listeners each gain different merit while being aware of this. This also refers to the *Flower Garland Sutra*, along with the Āgama sutras, the Hōdō sutras and the *Wisdom Sutra*.

The four doctrinal teachings classify the preaching of the Buddha into four categories: *zōkyō*, *piṭaka* teaching; *tsūgyō*, common teaching; *bekkyō*, distinct teaching; and *engyō*, perfect teaching. *Piṭaka* teaching corresponds to the Hinayana teaching and common teaching refers to the teachings for the Three Vehicles: *śrāvaka*, *pratyekabuddha*, and bodhisattvas. Distinct teaching is the teaching for bodhisattvas. Perfect teaching is the teaching that contains everything perfectly. With various sutras classified according to the four doctrinal teachings, the *Flower Garland Sutra* contains both perfect and distinct teachings; the Āgama sutras consist only of the *piṭaka* teaching; the Hōdō sutras are the teaching whereby the *piṭaka* teaching is compared to common, distinct, and perfect teachings. The *Wisdom Sutra* contains distinct and perfect teachings along with the common teaching. The *Lotus Sutra* purely expounds the perfect teaching. The *Nirvana Sutra* restates the four teachings and unites them into the perfect teaching.

The following diagram shows relations between the five-period teaching classified by T'ien-t'ai and the four doctrinal teachings.

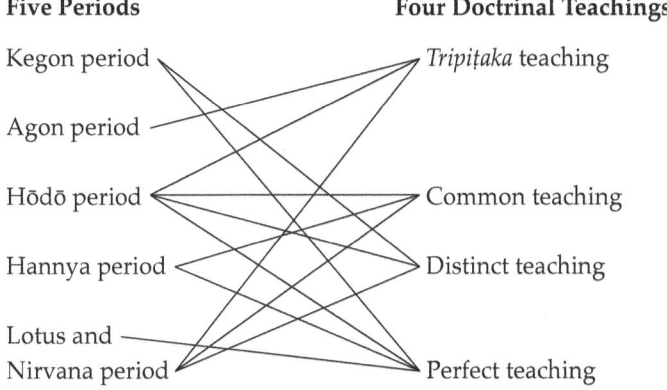

Four ways of meditation (*shishu zammai*)
Four kinds of meditation described in the first chapter of the *Great Concentration and Insight* by T'ien-t'ai: (1) sitting meditation; (2) walking meditation; (3) half-walking, half-sitting meditation; and (4) neither walking nor sitting meditation.

Fundamental darkness of mind (*gampon no mumyō*)
Refers to the most fundamental of all illusions and evil passions innate in people. This cannot be extinguished easily but it must occur to advance toward Buddhahood. Nichiren Shōnin preached that fundamental darkness had to be cut off by the sharp sword of the Buddha's secret divine power, namely the *Lotus Sutra*, in order for one to attain Buddhahood.

Gijō-bō (*Gijō-bō*)
A priest of Seichōji Temple, also called Kiyosumi-dera, in Awa Province, the southern part of present-day Chiba Prefecture. It is not known either when he was born or when he died. He was a disciple of Dōzen-bō, and senior to Nichiren Shōnin. Nichiren Shōnin received his elementary education from Gijō-bō and Jōken-bō. On April 28th of the fifth year of the Kenchō Era, 1253 CE, Nichiren Shōnin expressed his conviction of faith in the *Lotus Sutra* and was persecuted by the steward Tōjō Kagenobu and other nembutsu believers. Gijō-bō and Jōken-bō escorted him away from Seichōji Temple to safety.

Gishin *(Gishin)*

781–833 CE. The first Chief Minister, *zasu*, of Enryakuji Temple on Mt. Hiei. Well versed in Chinese, Gishin accompanied Grand Master Dengyō to T'ang China in 804 as his interpreter. According to the will of Dengyō, he succeeded the Grand Master as the head of the Tendai sect in Japan and established the Mahayana ordination platform, precept platform, on Mt. Hiei, performing ordination ceremonies. His work, *Anthology of the Tendai-Lotus Theology*, does not show all the effects of esotericism. Nichiren Shōnin maintained that the Tendai-Lotus school established by Dengyō in Japan based on the *Lotus Sutra* did not outlast Gishin.

Goddess Amaterasu *(Tenshō Daijin)*

Nichiren often cited Goddess Amaterasu and Great Bodhisattva Hachiman as native deities of Japan.

Good friend *(zen-chishiki)*

Meaning literally "good knowledge," the term refers to a reliable friend or teacher who leads one to the Buddha Dharma. Chapter 23 of the *Lotus Sutra* uses it to describe one who causes people to aspire for bodhi-mind, meaning enlightenment. Nichiren said that in the Latter Age of Degeneration we have to take the *Lotus Sutra* as *zen-chishiki* because there is no person worthy of being a "good friend." When Nichiren called Hōjō Tokimune, Shogunal Regent, who persecuted him a "good friend," he meant that Tokimune gave him a chance to prove himself to be one who practices the *Lotus Sutra*.

Great Concentration and Insight *(Maka Shikan)*

A series of lectures, consisting of ten fascicles, given by Grand Master T'ien-t'ai and recorded by his disciple Grand Master Chang-an. It preaches ten-object, ten-stage meditation to attain the truth of the *Lotus Sutra* expounded in T'ien-t'ai's *Profound Meaning of the Lotus Sutra* and *Words and Phrases of the Lotus Sutra*. Nichiren Shōnin considered the doctrine of "3,000 existences contained in one thought" preached in the seventh chapter, Right Meditation, the ultimate essence of T'ien-t'ai Buddhism and the fundamental truth of the *Lotus Sutra*. Considering the practice of meditation on "3,000 existences contained in one thought" not fully appropriate for the Latter Age of Degeneration, Nichiren maintained that upholding the five-character Odaimoku, *Namu Myōhō Renge-kyō* is the "actual" "3,000 existences contained in one thought" and chanting the Odaimoku the suitable practice in the Latter Age of Degeneration.

Great earthquake of the Shōka Era *(Shōka no dai-jishin)*

On the 23rd of the eighth month in the first year of the Shōka Era, 1257 CE, a severe earthquake shook the Kamakura area. This motivated Nichiren Shōnin to write the *Rissho Ankoku-ron*. Living in Kamakura and experiencing this severe temblor and calamities that followed it, Nichiren studied a collection of all the sacred writings of Buddhism to see what caused these disasters. He then wrote a series of treatises beginning with the *Shugo Kokka-ron, Treatise on National Protection,* followed by the *Sainan Taiji-shō, Eliminating Calamities* and finally *Rissho Ankoku-ron*.

Great Sun Buddha *(Dainichi Nyorai)*
The indispensable object of worship according to esoteric Buddhism. It is defined as the Buddha in Dharma Body, in which the truth of the whole universe is contained. Esoteric Buddhism claims that this Buddha is the fundamental Buddha from which all other Buddhas emerge. In Tendai esoteric theology, the Great Sun Buddha and Śākyamuni Buddha are identical, while in Shingon esotericism, they are regarded as different Buddhas, Dharma-bodied Great Sun Buddha being superior to Accommodative-bodied Śākyamuni Buddha. Nichiren, from the viewpoint of supremacy of the *Lotus Sutra*, regarded the Shingon doctrine as false, insisting that the Great Sun Buddha is a subordinate of the Original and Eternal Buddha Śākyamuni revealed in the 16th chapter of the *Lotus Sutra*.

Great Sun Buddha Sutra *(Dainichi-kyō)*
Translated in seven fascicles by Śubhākarasiṃha from Sanskrit into Chinese, this is one of the three canons of Shingon Buddhism. The Great Sun Buddha in the Dharma Body preached to Vajrasattva the doctrine of "becoming a Buddha immediately in the present body" through cooperative practices of, body, mouth and mind, of *mudrā* finger signs, mantra and *samādhi*, meditation. On the basis of the "five periods and eight teachings" classification, Nichiren criticized it as being a provisional sutra preached in the Hōdō period. In addition, Nichiren claimed, it is as inferior as Hinayana sutras because it does not reveal the Original and Eternal Buddha.

Great Universal Wisdom Buddha *(Daitsūchi-shō-butsu)*
The story of this Buddha, called *Daitsūchi-shō* or *Daitsū* appears in the seventh chapter of the *Lotus Sutra*, A Parable. According to this chapter, the Buddha preached the *Lotus Sutra* 3,000 dust-particle kalpa ago for a period of 8,000 kalpa. His 16 sons all became Buddhas. The youngest of them was Śākyamuni Buddha, who preached the *Lotus Sutra* in this Sahā World in order to save those who received the seed of Buddhahood by listening to Daitsū Buddha preach the *Lotus Sutra*. Based on this story, T'ien-t'ai divided the process of attaining Buddhahood into three stages: sowing the seed, *shu*; its germination and growing, *juku*, and harvest or enlightenment, *datsu*.

Great Wisdom Discourse *(Daichido-ron)*
This commentary on the *Wisdom Sutra* by Nagarjuna is one of his major writings. He not only annotates each sentence of the sutra, but also discusses numerous theories on various doctrines, especially concerning those of the *Lotus Sutra* and the *Flower Garland Sutra* including the theory of emptiness, Middle path, and ultimate reality.

Guarantee of the Buddha *(kibetsu or ki)*
Guarantee of attaining Buddhahood in the future granted by the Buddha.

Guardian deities *(shugo no zenjin)*
Nichiren referred to some of the so-called *hachibushū*, eight kinds of gods and demi-gods as *shugo no zenjin*, literally good gods for protection. These are: *ten* or gods; *ryū* or dragons; *yasha* or yakṣa; *kendatsuba* or gandharva; *ashura* or asura; *karura* or garuḍa; *kinnara* or kiṃnara; and *magoraga* or mahoraga. He claims in the *Risshō Ankoku-ron* that fed by the taste of the True Dharma, these virtuous deities gain strength. But when the True Dharma is lost in a land, they will abandon that land and return to heaven, leaving the land overtaken by disasters and calamities.

Guardian Sutra *(Shugo-kyō)*
Abbreviation of the *Shugo Kokkai-kyō, Sutra of Guarding the National Boundaries*. Consisting of 10 fascicles in Chinese, it taught that guarding the sovereign of a nation means protecting all the people in the land. Kūkai adopted it as a sutra of praying for national protection. Nichiren Shōnin often cites it and the *Sutra of the Benevolent King* to support his description of why calamities befall on lands after the death of the Buddha.

Hachiman, Great Bodhisattva *(Hachiman Daibosatsu)*
Originally a Shinto god of agriculture worshipped by the Usa clan of Kyushu in southern Japan, Hachiman in association with Buddhism began to be worshipped in the Capital Region during the Nara Period in the eighth century. In the early Heian Period, 894–1185 CE, the Imperial Court granted the title of Great Bodhisattva to Hachiman. In 860, Buddhist Priest Gyōkyō invoked the Shinto god of Hachiman at the Iwashimizu section of Kyoto and worshipped him as the protector of the Imperial Capital. It was around this time that Hachiman began to be regarded as being Emperor Ōjin, 15th Emperor of Japan, in a previous life. The Hachiman Shrine at Iwashimizu was greatly venerated by the Imperial Court as second only to the Ise Shrine for Goddess Amaterasu. In the late 12th century CE, Minamoto Yoritomo, the founder of the first military regime, established the Hachiman Shrine at Kamakura. With the spread of the

military government, the worship of Hachiman became nationwide as the guardian deity of local communities. Nichiren Shōnin regarded Hachiman as a manifested trace of the original substance that is Śākyamuni Buddha. Claiming that Hachiman was a guardian deity of the state of Japan as well as those who practice the *Lotus Sutra*, Nichiren included Hachiman in his mandala honzon.

Hall of Enlightenment *(Jakumetsu Dōjō)*
This refers to two places: (1) where Śākyamuni attained enlightenment located in the vicinity of the Nairañjanā River in Magadha, India; and (2) where Śākyamuni preached the *Flower Garland Sutra* at the foot of a large pipal tree to the south of Gayā in Magadha.

Hei no Saemonnojō *(Hei no Saemonnojō)*
Taira Yoritsuna, ?–1293 CE, a ranking vassal of the Hōjō family, held important positions such as second in command of the Board of Warriors of the Kamakura Shogunate. He was in charge of arresting Nichiren in 1271 CE and was one of the moving forces within the Bakufu when it persecuted followers of Nichiren in 1279 CE. Nichiren Shōnin appealed to him several times in vain to accept Nichiren's proposal made in the *Risshō Ankoku-ron*.

Hell of Incessant Suffering *(mugen jigoku)*
One of the eight hells. The adjectival phrase *mugen* is *avīci* in Sanskrit, meaning to be subjected to incessant suffering. This hell, the worst of all hells, is said to exist under the ground of the *Jambudvīpa*: the world in which we live. Those who have committed the five rebellious sins and slandered the True Dharma will fall into this hell. Those who are in this hell constantly cry out for help from their eternal anguish, so it is also called the Avīci Crying Hell. The hell is also called Avīci Castle because the area is so vast that no one can find the way out easily.

Heroic Valor Sutra *(Shuryōgon-kyō or Shuryōgon zammai-kyō)*
One of the early Mahayana sutras referred to in the *Kegon-kyō*, *Flower Garland Sutra*, and often cited in the *Daichido-ron*, *Great Wisdom Discourse*. In response to the question put forth by Bodhisattva *Ken'i*, Firm Will, about what kind of meditation would enable him to quickly attain Buddhahood, Śākyamuni Buddha taught him to practice the Heroic Valor Meditation and explained this meditation. He also explained that the compassion of Mahayana teachings would cover all, including people of impurity, in their future lives.

Hinayana *(shōjō)*
See "Mahayana-Hinayana."

Hōdō period *(Hōdō-bu)*
See "Hōdō sutras."

Hōdō sutras *(Hōdō-kyō)*
A general term used to mean all Mahayana sutras as a whole. It is also used to mean Mahayana sutras preached during the Hōdō period according to the five period classification of T'ien-t'ai. In the latter use, such sutras as the *Great Sun Buddha Sutra* and the *Pure Land Sutra* are included in the category. Nichiren used the term in the latter sense. Holy teachings preached in Śākyamuni Buddha's lifetime: *ichidai shōgyō*. This included what the Buddha preached between His attainment of enlightenment under the Bodhi tree and His death at the age of 80. Systematizing these teachings into the "five periods" and "eight teachings," Grand Master T'ien-t'ai maintained that the *Lotus Sutra* represented the true intent of the Buddha. Following the T'ien-t'ai doctrines of "five periods" and "eight teachings." Nichiren Shōnin insisted on the supremacy of the *Lotus Sutra* over all Buddhist scriptures.

Hōnen Shōnin *(Hōnen Shōnin)*
1133–1212 CE. Founder of the *Jōdo-shu*, Pure Land sect, in Japan. At the age of 13, he went to Mt. Hiei to become a Buddhist priest. At the age of 43, he was converted to Pure Land Buddhism by Shan-tao's *Commentary on the Sutra of Meditation on the Buddha of Infinite Life*. Soon thereafter he left Mt. Hiei to preach the teaching of the *nembutsu*, chanting devotion to Amida Buddha. As the teaching of the nembutsu spread, Buddhists on Mt. Hiei and in Nara appealed to the authorities for suppression and Hōnen was banished to Tosa Province. In writing such essays as the *Shugo Kokka-ron, Treatise on National Protection*, and *Risshō Ankoku-ron, Treatise on Spreading Peace Throughout the Country by Establishing the True Dharma*, Nichiren Shōnin harshly criticized the nembutsu practice and called Hōnen a slanderer of the True Dharma.

Hossō sect *(Hossō-shū)*
One of the six Buddhist schools in the Nara period, the *Hossō*, or Dharma Characteristics school is based on six sutras and eleven treatises such as the *Revealing the Profound and Secret Sutra* and the *Treatise on the Theory of Consciousness-Only*. Transmitted by Hsüan-chuang during the T'ang Dynasty, Grand Master Tz'ŭ-ên established this sect in China. Analyzing and studying the reality of all things from the viewpoint of the Consciousness-Only doctrine, the school is called *Hossō*, meaning "the reality of all things." This school declined in China but flourished in Japan especially at the Gangōji and Kōfukuji Temples as the core of the six schools in Nara. It insisted on the Three Vehicle doctrine and criticized the One Vehicle doctrine of the T'ien-t'ai or Tendai and

San-lun or Sanron schools. Nichiren Shōnin criticized the Three Vehicle doctrine of the Hossō sect from the viewpoint of the supremacy of the *Lotus Sutra*.

Hsing-man *(Gyōman)*
738(?)–823(?) CE. According to Nichiren Shōnin, Hsing-man was a disciple of Grand Master Miao-lê, the sixth patriarch of the T'ien-t'ai school in China, and he transmitted T'ien-t'ai teaching to Grand Master Dengyō, who had come from Japan to study Buddhism.

Hsüan-chuang, Tripiṭaka Master *(Genjō Sanzō)*
600–664 CE. Also written Hsüan-tsang. Founder of the Chinese *Fa-hsiang,* or Dharma Characteristics school. To master the Consciousness-Only doctrine in the original Sanskrit, he traveled to India by way of Central Asia. He spent 17 years, 629–645 CE, traveling and studying Buddhism chiefly at Nālanda in Magadha, India. He returned to Ch'ang-an with many volumes of Buddhist scriptures and translated them. His description of his trip to and through India is called the *Record of Western Regions of the Great T'ang.*

Hui-yüan *(Eon)*
523–592 CE. Scholar-monk who systematized the Ti-lun or Jiron theology during the Northern and Southern Dynasties and Sui era in China. He is said to have admonished Emperor Wu of the Northern Chou when the emperor tried to abolish Buddhism.

I-hsing *(Ichigyō)*
683–727 CE. Chinese Shingon priest popularly called I-hsing A-she-li or Zen Master I-hsing. He studied Zen and T'ien-t'ai teachings and also precepts of Buddhism. He was an expert in mathematics, astronomy, and calendars. He studied esoteric Buddhism under Shan-wu-wei, in Sanskrit. *Śubhākarasiṃha*, assisted him in translating the *Great Sun Buddha Sutra,* and wrote the *Commentary on the Great Sun Buddha Sutra.* Because I-hsing adopted the T'ien-t'ai doctrine of *ichinen-sanzen,* 3,000 Existences in One Thought, in writing this commentary, Nichiren criticized him for "stealing" the T'ien-t'ai doctrine.

Icchantika *(issendai)*
Those who are inherently unreceptive to the teaching of the Buddha, and therefore have no possibility of attaining Buddhahood no matter how hard they try. The *Lotus* and *Nirvana Sutras,* however, preach that *icchantika,* too, can attain Buddhahood. Nichiren maintains that even those *icchantika* who slandered the True Dharma, the *Lotus Sutra,* can become Buddhas due to the great compassion of the Original Śākyamuni Buddha. He thus stresses the great power of the *Lotus Sutra* to save all beings.

Indra *(Taishaku or Shakudaikannin)*
Originally a Hindu god of thunder, he was later incorporated into Buddhism as one of the two main protective deities of Buddhism, together with Bonten, King of the Brahma Heaven. Living in a palace called *Kiken-jō*, Joyful Sight, in the *Tōriten*, Trāyastriṃśa Heaven atop Mt. Sumeru, Indra is the Lord of this heaven who controls the Four Heavenly Kings and 32 other gods of that heaven. While Śākyamuni was practicing the bodhisattva way, Indra is said to have assumed various forms to test His resolution, but protected Him after He attained Buddhahood.

Infinite Life, Buddha of *(Amida-butsu)*
Lord Preacher of the Western Pure Land. According to the *Sutra of Meditation on the Buddha of Infinite Life*, this Buddha originally was a king in the eternal past who entered the priesthood under Sejizaiō Buddha, Sanskrit *Lokeśvararāja*. He was then called Hōzō Biku, Sanskrit *Dharmākara*. Making 48 vows to save people, Hōzō Biku performed bodhisattva practices for aeons of time, finally becoming a Buddha. Since then he has been preaching in the Pure Land of Utmost Bliss in the West. From the viewpoint of the *Lotus Sutra* as the supreme teaching, Nichiren Shōnin claimed that this Buddha is a mere manifestation of the Eternal, Original Buddha Śākyamuni and does not have any relation to us in the Sahā World.

Introductory Chapter *(Johon)*
The first chapter of the *Lotus Sutra*. Those who gathered on Mt. Sacred Eagle to hear Śākyamuni preach witnessed the six kinds of auspicious omens. They learned, through the conversation between Bodhisattvas Maitreya and Mañjuśrī, that the all-important *Lotus Sutra* was about to be preached.

Jambudvīpa *(Embudai)*
Jambu is the name of a tree, and *dvīpa* stands for a continent. According to Buddhist cosmology, four continents exist on four sides of Mt. Sumeru. The one on the south is called *Jambudvīpa*, also *Embudai* or *Nan-embudai*, because it is abundant with jambu trees. It is the world where we people live. It is also called the Sahā World.

Jikaku, Grand Master *(Jikaku Daishi)*
794–864 CE. Also called Ennin. He was the third *zasu*, Chief Minister of Enryakuji Temple. At the age of 15, he entered the priesthood as a disciple of Grand Master Dengyō on Mt. Hiei and studied the Tendai-Shingon teachings in China for more than 10 years, 835–847 CE. The record of his travels to China is the *Nittō Guhō Junrei-ki, Record of a Pilgrimage to China in Search of the Dharma*. He

wrote many works including the *Kongōchō-kyō-shō*, *Commentary on the Diamond Peak Sutra*, and the *Soshitsuji-kyō-shō*, *Commentary on the Act of Perfection Sutra*. He did much to make the Tendai teaching esoteric. For this, Nichiren was harshly critical of Jikaku, branding him a slanderer of the True Dharma.

Jīvaka *(Giba)*
A great physician in India during the lifetime of the Buddha. While serving King Ajātaśatru of Magadha in Central India, he urged the king, who had been trembling with fear of falling into hell for his sin of killing his own father, to see the Buddha and embrace Buddhism. Nichiren enumerates Jīvaka together with Ch'ih Shui and Liu Shui, who are mentioned in Buddhist sutras, as well as Pien Ch'üeh of ancient China as typical of great physicians in the past world.

Jōjitsu sect *(Jōjitsu-shū)*
One of the thirteen sects in China and six schools in Nara. This school focused on the *Treatise on the Establishment of the Truth*. It was studied by many in China until it was judged by Chi-ts'ang as a Hinayana doctrine. This school was introduced to Japan during the Nara period as incidental to the *Sanron*, or Three Discourses school.

Jurui seed and sōtai seed *(jurui-shu, sōtai-shu)*
Two sorts of *kaie*, opening and merging into Buddha vehicle doctrines, in Nichiren Buddhism. The first is *jurui* seed: such acts as listening to sutras and worshipping Buddhas can become a seed of Buddhahood. The second is *sōtai* seed. This claims that three paths of evil: passions, karma and suffering, immediately become three merits of Dharma Body, unsurpassed wisdom and emancipation respectively. With these two doctrines, the *Lotus Sutra* can save both the evil and the virtuous. Nichiren Shōnin preached the *sōtai* seed as the immediate attainment of Buddhahood with our present body through upholding the *Lotus Sutra*.

Kāśyapa *(Kashō)*
More precisely called Mahā-kāśyapa or *Dai-kashō*. One of the 10 senior disciples of the Buddha Śākyamuni, Kāśyapa was known as the most excellent in practicing asceticism. In the *Lotus Sutra* he was assured of enlightenment by Śākyamuni. After the Buddha's demise, Kāśyapa led the Buddhist order and carried out the compilation of Buddhist sutras. For 20 years he propagated the Hinayana teaching as the first of the 24 successors to Śākyamuni. Nichiren pointed out Kāśyapa's future Buddhahood as an example of *nijō sabutsu*, attaining Buddhahood by a person belonging to the Two Vehicle group, stressing the superiority of the *Lotus Sutra* to all other sutras.

Kātyāyana *(Kasennen)*

One of Śākyamuni Buddha's 10 major disciples, respected as the greatest debator. In the sixth chapter of the *Lotus Sutra*, it is predicted that in the future he will be a Buddha named *Embunadai-konkō*, Jāmbūnada Golden Light Buddha.

King of the Brahma Heaven *(Bonten-nō)*

Also called *Daibonten-nō, Bonnō,* or simply *Bonten*. In Indian mythology he was regarded as the supreme god and creator of the universe. In Buddhism, this god is regarded as the lord of the *Shozen-ten*, the first of the four meditation heavens in the realm of *shikikai*. Together with Indra, they are the most supreme protective deities of Buddhism. He requested Śākyamuni Buddha to preach upon His enlightenment, and he also attended preaching assemblies of the *Lotus Sutra*. Nichiren worshipped him and invoked him in his mandala honzon.

Kōbō, Grand Master *(Kōbō Daishi)*

774–835 CE. Founder of the Shingon sect in Japan, he is also known as Kūkai. Entering the priesthood under Gonzō, he went to T'ang China in 804, transmitting Shingon esoteric Buddhism from Hui-kuo or Keika, a disciple of Pu-k'ung. He wrote such treatises as *Jūjūshin-ron, Treatise on Ten Stages of the Mind*, and *Ben-kemmitsu Nikyō-ron, Treatise on Esoteric and Exoteric Teachings*, advocating superiority of the Shingon teaching, insisting attainment of Buddhahood with one's present body, and spreading esoteric teaching. Nichiren harshly criticized him for despising both Śākyamuni Buddha and the *Lotus Sutra*.

Kumārajīva, Tripiṭaka Master *(Kumarajū)*

344–413 CE. Also known as *Rajū* in a Japanese abbreviation. Coming from Kucha, or Kiji, during the early period of the Northern and Southern dynasties in China, he translated 35 volumes of sutras and commentaries in more than 300 fascicles from Sanskrit to Chinese. These included the *Lotus Sutra, Wisdom Sutra* and *Great Wisdom Discourse*. His disciples are said to have numbered more than 3,000. Nichiren thought of him very highly and respected him for laying the foundation for Lotus Buddhism.

Kusha sect *(Kusha-shū)*

One of the six schools of Buddhism during the Nara Period in Japan. Founded on the teaching of the *Abhidharma-kośa, Kusha-ron, Discourse on the Repository of Abhidharma Discussions*, by Vasubandhu or *Seshin*. It was transmitted into Japan in the seventh century CE and studied by many scholar-monks in the

Nara Period as a branch of the Hossō sect, without establishing itself as an independent sect. Nichiren enumerates it, as well as the Ritsu and Jojitsu schools, as a Hinayana school.

Last (fifth) 500-year period *(go-gohyakusai)*
According to *Daijik-kyō*, the *Sutra of the Great Assembly*, the history of Buddhism after the death of the Buddha is divided into five 500-year periods, each with a characteristic feature: (1) attainment of emancipation; (2) practice of meditation; (3) reading and listening to many Buddhist teachings; (4) building many temples; and (5) doctrinal disputes. Applying these five periods to the theory of gradual decline of Buddhism through three periods, they fit into the 1000 years of the Age of the True Dharma, 1000 years of the Age of the Semblance Dharma, and the beginning of the Latter Age of Degeneration, which Nichiren regarded as the time for the spread of the *Lotus Sutra*. See Nichiren's treatise *Senji-shō, Selecting the Right Time*, for details.

Latter Age of Degeneration *(mappō)*
One of the three periods after the Buddha Śākyamuni's demise: *shōbō, zōbō* and *mappō*. This is the period of degeneration which starts two thousand years after the Buddha Śākyamuni's demise. During this period, it was believed, although the teaching of the Buddha still existed, nobody could achieve enlightenment no matter how hard one studied and practiced it. The period is also called *matsudai* or *masse* in Japanese. The *mappō* idea appeared around the sixth century in India. In China, it appeared during the Sui and T'ang dynasties, 589–907 CE, and in Japan, during the Heian and Kamakura Periods, 794–1333 CE. Hōnen, Shinran, Dōgen and Nichiren were all influenced by this concept. Nichiren tried to save the people in the Latter Age by putting faith in the *Lotus Sutra* and chanting the Odaimoku: *Namu Myōhō Renge-kyō*.

Lives in the past, present and future *(sanze)*
In Buddhism every existence in this world is conceived not as static but as always changing throughout the past, present and future. Applying it to our life, it may be our past life, present life or future life; in reference to Buddhas, they may be Buddhas in the past, present or future. These three are, however, never in separation; they, like the current of a large river flowing into the ocean, are fused in the eternal future. This is why we may call all the Buddhas "the Buddhas from the 10 directions throughout the past, present and future lives." The 16th chapter of the *Lotus Sutra* preaches that the Eternal, Original Śākyamuni Buddha continues to save all living beings throughout their past, present and future lives.

Long, wide tongue *(kōchō-zetsu or chōzetsu)*
One of the 32 characteristics of excellence in a Buddha. The Buddha is said to have a long and wide tongue that could cover His whole face. By extending His huge tongue, the Buddha proved some things to be true. In Chapter 21 of the *Lotus Sutra, Supernatural Powers of the Tathāgata, Jinriki-hon*, various Buddhas in manifestation extended their tongues to attest to the truth of the *Lotus Sutra.*

Lord Toki *(Toki-dono)*
See "Toki Jōnin."

Lotus Sutra *(Hokke-kyō)*
Abbreviation of the *Sutra of the Lotus Flower of the Wonderful Dharma*, translated into Chinese by Kumārajīva in eight fascicles, originally seven fascicles. There exist two more Chinese versions: *Shō Hoke-kyō* translated by Dharmarakṣa in 10 fascicles and *Tembon Hoke-kyō* by Jñānagupta and Dharmagupta in seven fascicles. According to Grand Master T'ien-t'ai, the first half, 14 chapters, of the *Lotus Sutra*, Kumārajīva version, is called the theoretical section and the latter half, 14 chapters, the essential section. The theoretical section with the second chapter, Expedients, preaches at its core that the Three Vehicle teachings are expedient and that the true intention of the Buddha is to lead all living beings to Buddhahood by the One Vehicle teaching. The essential section, especially the 16th chapter, Duration of the Life of the Tathāgata, preaches that Śākyamuni Buddha has been enlightened since the eternal past saving all living beings ever since. It reveals also that this Saha World is the eternal, imperishable Pure Land. While Grand Master T'ien-t'ai formulated his doctrine based on the theoretical section, Nichiren formulated his doctrine and faith based on the essential section, and promulgated the Odaimoku, *Namu Myōhō Renge-kyō.*

Mahā Prajāpatī *(Makahajahadai Bikuni)*
Younger sister of Princess Māyā, Śākyamuni's mother, who raised Him after Princess Māyā passed away seven days after giving birth to Him. Mahā Prajāpatī, married the young Siddhartha's father, King Śuddhodana of Kapilavastu, and raised Him. She gave birth to Ānanda, half-brother of the Buddha, who later became one of the 10 great disciples of the Buddha. After the passing of King Śuddhodana, Mahā Prajāpatī together with Yaśodharā, the mother of Rāhula, entered the Buddhist order, becoming the first nuns. The 13th chapter of the *Lotus Sutra* predicts that Nun Mahā Prajāpatī as well as 6,000 nuns will become *Issai Shujō Kiken,* Gladly Seen by All Buddhas.

Mahāsthāmaprāpta Bodhisattva *(Seishi Bosatsu)*
The Japanese name *Seishi* means Great Strength. In Pure Land Buddhism, Seishi is one of the two attendants of the Buddha of Infinite Life and represents wisdom, while Avalokiteśvara, *Kannon*, represents compassion. He appears among 80,000 bodhisattvas in the first chapter of the *Lotus Sutra*, and the Buddha preached the 20th chapter of the *Lotus Sutra* to him.

Mahayana-Hinayana *(daijō-shōjō)*
Meaning literally a great vehicle and a lesser vehicle, the terms were used to designate two major streams of Buddhism. Vehicles were likened to doctrines leading people to enlightenment. Great Vehicles are large and superior means of transportation in which not only those who themselves practice Buddhism, but many others are also carried to salvation, while lesser vehicles are smaller and inferior in which only self-salvation is attainable. Following T'ien-t'ai's interpretation, Nichiren regarded the Āgama sutras as Hinayana and sutras preached in the Kegon, Hōdō, Hannya, and Hokke-Nehan periods as Mahayana. He also declared that the true Mahayana is the hommon section of the *Lotus Sutra* alone, considering the sutras preached before the *Lotus Sutra* all Hinayana.

Main discourse *(shōshū-bun)*
See "Preface, main discourse and epilogue."

Maitreya Bodhisattva *(Miroku Bosatsu)*
A bodhisattva who is said to be a Buddha in the future replacing Śākyamuni. It is believed that upon death he was reborn in the Tuṣita Heaven, where he will reside for 5,670,000,000 years before being reborn in this Sahā World to save those who had not been saved by Śākyamuni Buddha. In the *Lotus Sutra*, he is a bodhisattva disciple of Buddhas in manifestation, *shakke*, who request the Buddha to preach, *hokki-shū*.

Mañjuśrī Bodhisattva *(Monjushiri Bosatsu)*
Left-hand attendant of Śākyamuni, mounted on a lion, Bodhisattva Mañjuśrī represents the virtue of wisdom and enlightenment. In the first chapter of the *Lotus Sutra* he foretells the preaching of the Lotus by Śākyamuni Buddha, and in Chapter 12 he reveals the attainment of Buddhahood by a dragon girl. Nichiren lists this bodhisattva's name in his mandala honzon as a representative of bodhisattvas in the theoretical section, *shakumon*, of the *Lotus Sutra*.

Many Treasures, the Buddha of *(Tahō-butsu)*

Also known as *Tahō-nyorai*. The Lord of the Treasure Purity World to the east, who vowed to appear wherever the *Lotus Sutra* is preached after death to verify the truthfulness of the sutra. In Chapter 12 of the *Lotus Sutra*, Beholding the Stūpa of Treasures, *Hōtō-hon*, it is preached that this Buddha in the stupa adorned with seven treasures emerged from the great earth attesting to the truth of what was preached by Śākyamuni Buddha. Nichiren Shōnin claims this as one of the reasons the *Lotus Sutra* is considered supreme of all Buddhist scriptures.

Maudgalyāyana *(Mokuren)*

Also known as *Mokkenren* in Japanese, he was one of the Buddha Śākyamuni's 10 senior disciples. He is said to have been foremost in mastering superhuman power. He became a disciple of the Buddha together with Śāriputra, mastering this power and becoming an *arhat* or *arakan*, a holy man. In the *Lotus Sutra* he was assured of becoming a Buddha in the future, but was killed by a non-Buddhist while the Buddha was still alive. Nichiren cites his death as an example of persecutions against Buddhists during the Buddha's lifetime compared to those after His death. It is well known that he saved his mother who was suffering among hungry spirits after her death. Nichiren advocated that it was the teaching of the *Lotus Sutra* that saved Maudgalyāyana's mother from the realm of hungry spirits.

Medicine-King Bodhisattva *(Yakuō Bosatsu)*

One of the 25 bodhisattvas described in the *Lotus Sutra*. The 23rd chapter of the sutra relates that in previous lives he had been a bodhisattva called *Issaishujōkiken*, Gladly Seen by All Beings, who burned his own body as an offering to the Buddha. Because of this, he was reborn in the land of *Nichigatsujōmyōtoku*, Sun Moon Pure Bright Virtue Buddha, and when this Buddha passed away, the bodhisattva burned his elbow as an offering to Him. He appears in the 10th, 13th, and 26th chapters of the *Lotus Sutra* as a man who listened to the preaching, swore to propagate it after the death of the Buddha, and to protect those who uphold it. Nichiren regarded the bodhisattva's burning himself as an exemplary act of upholding the True Dharma. Nichiren also considered both Medicine-King Bodhisattva and Grand Master T'ien-t'ai, regarded an avatar of Medicine-King Bodhisattva, as foretelling the appearance of bodhisattvas from underground, depicted in Chapter 15 of the *Lotus Sutra*. These bodhisattvas were disciples of the of the Original Śākyamuni Buddha. Nichiren considers himself as an avatar of Bodhisattva Superior-Practice, head of the group entrusted to spread the Lotus teaching in the Latter Age of Degeneration.

Medicine Master Buddha *(Yakushi Nyorai)*
Lord of the Pure Emerald World to the east, who is believed to have made 12 vows to heal all illnesses of the people and bring happiness to them. Belief in this Buddha is popular in both China and Japan.

Medicine Master Sutra *(Yakushi-kyō)*
Revealing the 12 great vows of the Medicine Master Buddha, the lord and teacher of the Pure Emerald World to the East, this sutra teaches the virtues of a person who upholds the name of this Buddha. Nichiren Shōnin quotes phrases from this sutra and also from the *Sutra of the Golden Splendor* concerning the causes of the three calamities and seven disasters that beset the world during the period of mappō, or the Latter Age of Degeneration.

Miao-lê, Grand Master *(Myōraku Daishi)*
(711–782). Known also as Chan-jan or Venerable Ching-shi, Miao-lê is the sixth, or possibly ninth, patriarch of the T'ien-t'ai sect in China. Regarded as the restorer of the T'ien-t'ai sect, he wrote many books including commentaries on T'ien-t'ai's three major works: *Annotations on the Great Concentration and Insight, Annotations on the Words and Phrases of the Lotus Sutra,* and *Commentary on the Profound Meaning of the Lotus Sutra.* Nichiren esteemed him highly as the legitimate successor to T'ien-t'ai and quotes him often.

Most Venerable One *(honzon)*
At first, such symbols as footprints of the Buddha and the dharma-wheel were regarded as *honzon*: objects of veneration. Later images of the Buddha Śākyamuni began to appear in the late first century CE. Many images of the Buddha, bodhisattvas, and disciples of the Buddha were built in Tibet, China, Korea and Japan, but in the southern countries in Asia *honzon* were mostly images of the Buddha Śākyamuni. In Nichiren Buddhism the *honzon* is the Buddha Śākyamuni revealed in the essential section of the *Lotus Sutra* who has three characteristics: (1) command of fundamental reverence; (2) being the most revered since the eternal past; and (3) possession of constant, unchanging form since the eternal past. It rests on the "3,000 existences contained in one thought" doctrine, and represents the symbolic world where the Buddha Śākyamuni in the essential section of the *Lotus Sutra* saved, is saving and will be saving all living beings without discrimination. There are several ways to show this *honzon* in concrete form: (1) the Sacred Title, *Odaimoku* of the *Lotus Sutra, Namu Myōhō Renge-kyō,* written in Chinese characters; (2) a statue of Śākyamuni Buddha; (3) mandala, drawn on a sheet of paper with the Odaimoku, in the center, accompanied by bodhisattvas and others appearing in the *Lotus Sutra;*

(4) the Sacred Title accompanied by Śākyamuni Buddha and the Buddha of Many Treasures; or (5) Śākyamuni Buddha accompanied by the four great bodhisattvas: Jōgyō, Muhengyō, Jōgyō and Anryūgyō. In essence, however, these are one, that is to say they all represent Lord Śākyamuni Buddha who preached the essential section of the *Lotus Sutra*.

Mt. Hiei *(Eizan)*
Refers to Enryakuji Temple on Mt. Hiei, which is the head temple of the Tendai sect located at Sakamoto-cho in Ōtsu-shi, Shiga Prefecture. It was founded by Grand Master Dengyō, or Saichō, in the seventh year of the Enryaku Era, 788 CE. Many founders of the new Buddhist schools in Kamakura Period studied at this temple. It is believed that Nichiren spent most of his study period in the Kyoto area at the Enryakuji Temple. However, Nichiren later regarded this temple as an esoteric Buddhist temple that had abandoned the *Lotus Sutra* since the time of Chief Priest Ennin.

Mutual possession of 10 realms *(jikkai gogu)*
According to T'ien-t'ai the world consists of 10 realms: hell, realms of hungry spirits, beasts, asura demons, human beings, heavenly beings, *śrāvaka, pratyekabuddha,* bodhisattvas and Buddhas. Each of these realms mutually contains characteristics of the nine other realms in itself. This means that human beings have characteristics of the nine other realms from beings in hell up to Buddhas; asura demons have those of the rest of the 10 realms; Buddhas also have characteristics of the nine other realms. This idea was set up by Grand Master T'ien-t'ai based on some passages in the *Lotus Sutra* such as "The Buddhas appear in the worlds in order to cause all living beings to open the insight of the Buddha." It meant to him that those beings in the nine realms other than the realm of Buddhas also possessed characteristics of Buddhas. This idea of "Mutual possession" provided the basis for another important T'ien-t'ai doctrine, "3,000 existences contained in one thought." Nichiren Shōnin founded and spread the practice of chanting *Namu Myōhō Renge-kyō* on the foundation of these two inseparable ideas as the ultimate means of attaining Buddhahood by ordinary, meaning unenlightened people.

Nāgārjuna Bodhisattva *(Ryūju Bosatsu)*
Circa 150–250 CE. A great exponent of early Mahayana Buddhism, he was born in southern India. After completely mastering Brahmanism, he moved to northern India, studying Theravada and Mahayana Buddhism. Having achieved thorough knowledge of Buddhism, Nāgārjuna is regarded as the founder of the eight Buddhist schools in China and Japan. He wrote many important books such as the *Great Wisdom Discourse*.

Nambu Rokurō *(Nambu Rokurō)*
1223–1279 CE. Also known as Nambu Sanenaga or Hakii Sanenaga of Kai Province, present-day Yamanashi Prefecture. Converted by Nikkō around 1269 CE, Nambu Rokurō became one of the most prominent followers of Nichiren in the province. He donated Mt. Minobu to Nichiren Shōnin, who lived in the mountain from 1274 CE to 1282 CE.

Namu Myōhō Renge-kyō *(Namu Myōhō Renge-kyō)*
Namu Myōhō Renge-kyō refers to the "Odaimoku of the essential section," one of the Three Great Secret Dharmas of Nichiren Shōnin. Namu means putting absolute faith in or seeking refuge in, so this phrase means to have faith in the teaching of the *Lotus Sutra*. According to Nichiren, the Odaimoku of the *Lotus Sutra* is not a mere title of a sutra but it is charged with all the merits of the *Lotus Sutra* preached by Śākyamuni Buddha. Therefore, by putting faith in it and chanting it we will be given all the merits of the sutra. Thus, he considered chanting the Odaimoku as the basis of practicing the *Lotus Sutra* and the only way leading to Buddhahood for us in the Latter Age of Degeneration.

Nan-yüeh, Grand Master *(Nangaku Daishi)*
Grand Master T'ien-t'ai's teacher Hui-ssŭ 514 or 515–577 CE, who lived in Mt. Nan-yüeh. A man of purity who detached himself from the six sense organs, he is said to have been an avatar of Bodhisattva Avalokiteśvara and to be the first who tried to preach in a way suitable to the Latter Age of Degeneration.

Nen'a Ryōchū *(Nen'a Ryōchū)*
1199–1287 CE. Also called Nen Amidabutsu. Third patriarch of the Chinzei school of the Pure Land sect, who systematized the Pure Land theology and founded many temples in the Kantō area of eastern Japan. Nichiren considered him and Dō Amidabutsu the two pillars of Pure Land Buddhism in Kamakura.

Never-Despising Bodhisattva *(Fukyō Bosatsu)*
As described in the 20th chapter of the *Lotus Sutra*, this bodhisattva, also called *Jōfukyō Bosatsu* in Japanese, believed that everyone had Buddha nature, and bowed to everyone he met saying, "I respect you deeply because you surely will become a Buddha." Some of those to whom he said these words became angry and threw stones and pebbles at him, but he never stopped bowing and uttering those words to them. The chapter tells us that what Never-Despising Bodhisattva did was identical to what Buddha Śākyamuni had done in his past lives. The chapter also states that those who persecuted this bodhisattva had to endure the Hell of Incessant Suffering. But upon hearing Śākyamuni Buddha's lectures on the *Lotus Sutra*, they were guaranteed to become Buddhas

in the future. Nichiren Shōnin exerted himself to follow the example of Never-Despising Bodhisattva as one who practices the *Lotus Sutra* in the Latter Age of Degeneration. Nichiren interpreted the aggressive means of propagation, *shakubuku*, practiced by this bodhisattva as well as by himself, as the way to sow the seed of the *Lotus Sutra* in the heart of those who persecuted them.

Never-Despising Bodhisattva Chapter *(Fukyō-hon)*
The 20th chapter of the *Lotus Sutra*, the full title of which in Japanese is *Jōfukyō Bosatsu-hon*. See "Never-Despising Bodhisattva."

Nine great difficulties *(kuō no dainan)*
The nine major hardships that Śākyamuni encountered during His lifetime: (1) a beautiful but evil woman named Sundarī spread rumors that she was having an affair with Śākyamuni; (2) a maid servant gave Him an offering of stinking rice gruel in a Brahman city; (3) the Buddha was forced by King Ajita to feed Himself and 500 disciples nothing but horse fodder for three months; (4) many of the members of the Śākya clan were slaughtered by King Virūdhaka of Kosala; (5) Śākyamuni was unable to receive alms in a Brahman city; (6) a Brahman woman called Chinclāmānavika claimed that she was made pregnant by the Buddha; (7) Devadatta injured the Buddha in his attempt at His life; (8) once the Buddha suffered from an icy wind that continued to blow for eight days; and (9) Śākyamuni went through ascetic practices for six years before attaining enlightenment. The term *kuō no dainan* was coined by Nichiren, stressing the difficulty of spreading the Lotus teaching during the Latter Age of Degeneration, which he claimed to be harder than the nine ordeals the Buddha had to endure during His lifetime.

Nirvana *(nehan)*
The ultimate goal of Buddhist practice, enlightenment or Buddhahood, in which evil passions are all extinguished; the state of mind completely free from the illusions of the three poisons: greed, anger, and stupidity.

Nirvana Sutra *(Nehan-gyō)*
Nehan-gyō, Nirvana Sutra, is an abbreviation of *Daihatsunehan-gyō, Great Nirvana Sutra*. Two versions of the Chinese translation exist: (1) the so-called Northern version translated by Dharmakṣema in 40 fascicles; and (2) the Southern version revised and reorganized by Hui-kuan, Hui-yen and Hsieh Ling-yün of the six-fascicled *Daihatsunaion-gyō* translated by Fa-hsien in 36 fascicles. The sutra preaches that the death of Śākyamuni Buddha is an expedient, and that actually His life is eternal and imperishable. It preaches also the "existence of Buddha-nature in all living beings." Grand Master T'ien-t'ai regarded this

sutra, together with the *Lotus Sutra,* supreme of all the sutras preached by the Buddha during the five periods of His preaching. Following T'ien-t'ai, Nichiren Shōnin considered it to be the teaching to save those who were missed by the *Lotus Sutra.* Nichiren also placed great importance on such doctrines preached in the *Nirvana Sutra* as "Depend on the Dharma, not on people" and "Ruthless chastisement of evil monks is the duty of a Buddhist."

Non-Buddhist scriptures *(geten)*
Literally "outer" scriptures, meaning those of non-Buddhist teachings. See "Non-Buddhist Teaching."

Non-Buddhist teaching *(gedō)*
Meaning literally "an outside way," in contrast to *naidō*, "inner way," meaning Buddhism. The term is used by Buddhists to designate a non-Buddhist teaching or its followers, sometimes as a derogative term to mean an evil or false opinion. In writings of Nichiren the outer scriptures generally refer to writings of Confucianism or Brahmanism. Nichiren Shōnin considered these and such non-Buddhists as "two heavenly beings and three hermits" of India as initial steps leading to Buddhism.

Not even one out of 1,000 *(senchū muitsu)*
A phrase associated with Shan-tao, who established the theological foundation of the Pure Land school of China. He stated in his *Hymns of Praise Concerning Rebirth in the Pure Land* that even if a man wishes to be reborn into the Pure Land of Utmost Bliss by practicing any of the ways other than the five kinds of right practice, not even one out of one thousand people can attain it. He thus denied the merit of practicing the Holy Way Gate such as the *Lotus Sutra.*

Notional understanding, perception and practicing *(myōji, kangyō)*
The second and third of the six stages, *rokusoku*, in the practice of the *Lotus Sutra* formulated by T'ien-t'ai. The former refers to the stage at which one hears the name and reads the words of the *Lotus Sutra* and begins to believe in it while the latter is the stage at which one practices what he perceives. Nichiren Shōnin, however, insists that one can attain Buddhahood, without going through the six stages, immediately upon believing in the Odaimoku, *Namu Myōhō Renge-kyō,* and chanting it.

Obtaining Buddhahood by Two Vehicles *(nijō sabutsu)*
One of the two great doctrines of the *Lotus Sutra*. Expounded in the theoretical section, *shakumon*, of the *Lotus Sutra*, this doctrine maintains that even the two groups of Hinayana sages called *śrāvaka* and *pratyekabuddha*, Two Vehicles, who

are declared incapable of becoming Buddhas in such Mahayana sutras as *Kegon* and *Yuima Sutras,* can attain Buddhahood through the One Vehicle teaching of the *Lotus Sutra*. It shows that salvation through the *Lotus Sutra* is available to all. Along with the *kuon jitsujō* doctrine, attainment of Buddhahood by the Original Buddha in the eternal past, it provided Nichiren with a theoretical foundation when he claimed the superiority of the *Lotus Sutra* of all the teachings preached by the Buddha.

Odaimoku *(odaimoku)*
See "Namu Myōhō Renge-kyō."

One chapter and two half-chapters *(ippon nihan)*
The term refers to the 16th chapter, the last-half of the 15th and the first half of the 17th chapters of the *Lotus Sutra*. The last half of the 15th chapter briefly reveals the attainment of Buddhahood by Śākyamuni in the eternal past by revealing the relationship between the Buddha and the bodhisattvas who emerged from underground. The 16th chapter concentrates on the eternity of the Buddha while the first of the 17th chapter expounds the merit of bodhisattvas having deep faith in the *Lotus Sutra* with great joy upon hearing the eternality of the Buddha. So, Nichiren considered these "one chapter and two half-chapters" to be the main discourse of the essential section of the *Lotus Sutra*.

One great purpose *(ichidaiji innen)*
The second chapter of the *Lotus Sutra* declares: "Buddhas appeared in the world for the sole great purpose...," revealing that not only Śākyamuni Buddha but also other Buddhas appeared, appear, and will appear in order to have all living beings grasp, see, awaken in, and enter the wisdom of the Buddha.

100 realms and 1,000 aspects *(hyakkai sen'nyo)*
T'ien-t'ai doctrine based on the *Lotus Sutra* saying an individual mind has 10 realms, from hell up to the Buddha realm, each of which includes in itself characteristics of the other nine realms, making 100 realms. Each of these 100 realms has 10 factors, such as form, nature, etc., so there are 1,000 aspects of existence. As these 1,000 aspects have three modes, there are 3,000 modes of existence within a mind at any moment.

One Vehicle teaching *(ichijō-kyō)*
The One Vehicle means the only teaching which leads people to Buddhahood. It is stressed in the *Lotus Sutra* which states: "In all the Buddha lands

throughout the universe, there exists but the One Vehicle dharma; there is neither a Two Vehicle teaching nor a Three Vehicle teaching." The One Vehicle also means unification, both unification of the teaching and the unification of those who practice the teaching. Thus the *Lotus Sutra* preaches attainment of Buddhahood by those of the Two Vehicles, *śrāvaka* and *pratyekabuddha*. While the Tendai doctrine stresses unification with the term *Kaisan ken'itsu*, outgrowing the Three Vehicles and revealing the One Vehicle, Nichiren maintained that the One Vehicle doctrine shows the superiority of the *Lotus Sutra* over other sutras.

One who practices the Lotus Sutra *(Hokke-kyō no gyōja)*
As it is preached in the *Lotus Sutra* that those who practice the sutra after the death of the Buddha will encounter great difficulties, Nichiren Shōnin believed that he was one who practiced the *Lotus Sutra* because he experienced various persecutions and difficulties as predicted in it.

Onjōji Temple *(Onjōji)*
Also called Miidera, it is located at Onjōji-machi, Ōtsu-shi, present-day Shiga Prefecture, which was formerly called Ōmi Province. This is the Grand Head Temple of the Jimon Group of the Tendai sect. Founded by Otomoyota-ō, it was restored by Enchin, Grand Master Chishō, in the first year of the Jōgan Era 859 CE. Nichiren Shōnin stayed there while studying in Kyoto and Nara.

Ordinary man *(bombu or bompu)*
In contrast to a sage, an ignorant and ordinary man; an unenlightened man. Nichiren considered that the people in the Latter Age of Degeneration are all ignorant and slanderers of the True Dharma, stressing that the boundless compassion of the Original Śākyamuni Buddha is to save these ignorant and ordinary people in the Latter Age.

Ōta Jōmyō *(Ōta Jōmyō)*
1222–1283 CE. Also known as Ōta Kingo, Lay Priest Ōta, Ōta Saemonnojō, Jōmyō Shōnin, etc. Together with Lay Priest Soya, Kanahara Hōkyō, and Toki Jōnin, Ōta Jōmyō was a pillar among the followers of Nichiren in Shimofusa, present-day northern Chiba Prefecture. Nichiren wrote him letters in Chinese with the contents of profound doctrine. Nichiren encouraged Lord Ōta, who was sickly, to have firm faith in the *Lotus Sutra* by pointing out how his sickness in this life was lessening the heavy retribution of the serious sin in his past life of slandering the True Dharma.

Outgrowing the provisional and revealing the essential *(hosshaku kempon)*
Outgrowing the teaching of the theoretical section, *shakumon*, of the *Lotus Sutra* and revealing the concept of the Eternal Buddha. It is stated in Nichiren's *Kaimoku-shō, Open Your Eyes to the Lotus Teaching*: "The second chapter, Expedients, in the theoretical section of *Lotus Sutra* makes up for one of the two faults of the pre-Lotus sutras by revealing the teaching of '3,000 existences in one thought' and 'obtaining Buddhahood by Two Vehicles.' As the chapter has not yet revealed the Original and Eternal Buddha by outgrowing the provisional and revealing the essential, it does not show the real concept of '3,000 existences in one thought.' Nor does it establish the true meaning of 'obtaining Buddhahood by Two Vehicles.'" This means that as the theoretical section of the *Lotus Sutra* does not reveal the eternity of the Buddha, true Buddhahood is not available. In the essential section, in which the Enlightenment of the Buddha in the eternal past is preached, the "mutually-possessed characteristics of the 10 Realms" and "3,000 existences in one thought" doctrines are truly established, through which all beings are saved.

Outstanding Principles of the Lotus Sutra *(Hokke Shūku)*
Written by Grand Master Dengyō in order to refute the argument of Hossō priest Tokuitsu. Dengyō argued to prove the superiority of the *Lotus Sutra* in 10 chapters.

A Parable Chapter *(Kejōyu-hon)*
The seventh chapter of the *Lotus Sutra*. After preaching a parable for disciples with intermediate capability, the Buddha revealed His relationship to disciples with inferior capacity. In the remotest past, 3,000 dust-particle kalpa ago, He was the 16th and youngest son of the Buddha called *Daitsūchishō*, Great Universal Wisdom. Śākyamuni Buddha and His 15 brothers each taught the *Lotus Sutra*, declaring that those who received the seed of Buddhahood, the *Lotus Sutra*, even in such a remote past are bound to attain Buddhahood.

Peaceful Practices Chapter *(Anrakugyō-hon)*
The 14th chapter of the *Lotus Sutra*. In the 13th chapter, the Buddha did not allow bodhisattvas, *śrāvaka* and others to spread the sutra in this or other worlds. In this chapter, in response to Bodhisattva Mañjuśrī's question about how bodhisattvas in the initial stages of practice should spread the sutra in the evil age after the death of Śākyamuni, the Buddha preached four ways: by peaceful deeds, words, thoughts and vows. The chapter also contains the parable of the priceless gem in the topknot, showing how difficult it is to encounter and listen to the *Lotus Sutra*.

Persuasive and aggressive means of propagation *(shōju-shakubuku)*
Shōju refers to the means of spreading a religion by converting non-believers through gentle persuasion, while *shakubuku* pursues the means by aggressive and harsh criticism. Nichiren considered the beginning of the Latter Age of Degeneration filled with slanderers of the True Dharma as the time for *shakubuku*. So he practiced *shakubuku* to plant the seed of Buddhahood in the heart of those slanderers.

Practicing the Pure Dharma Sutra *(Shōjō hōgyō-kyō)*
The text of this one-fascicled sutra, which has been cited as the source of the contention that three Chinese sages, Lao-tzu, Confucius and Yen-hui, were dispatched by the Buddha, has never been found. Scholars today consider it to be fabricated.

Pre-Lotus period *(nizen)*
Meaning literally "prior to," the term is used by Nichiren to mean the teachings and sutras preached by the Buddha before the *Lotus Sutra* was expounded. According to Grand Master T'ien-t'ai's five period classification, sutras preached before the *Lotus Sutra* are provisional and expedient. Following T'ien-t'ai's idea, Nichiren Shōnin maintains that no one can attain Buddhahood through the teachings of the pre-Lotus sutras.

Preaching according to own mind *(zuijii)*
Describes preachings by Śākyamuni Buddha, when He preaches His enlightenment as it is, is termed in Japanese *zuijii*: literally, according to own mind. When He preaches variously, using expedient means, according to the ability and wishes of the people listening to Him, it is called *zuitai*: according to the mind of others.

Preaching according to the mind of others *(zuitai)*
See "Preaching according to own mind."

Preaching of the Buddha *(tem-bōrin)*
Meaning literally to turn the wheel of the dharma, *tem-bōrin* refers to the preaching of the Buddha. The Buddha's teaching, which eliminates all evil passions of the people, is likened to the wheel treasure, *rinbō*, of the Wheel-Turning Noble King, *Tenrinjōō*, which crushes all the evils of living beings. *Sho tem-bōrin*, the first preaching of the Buddha, refers to His first preaching for the five monks, His former attendants, at Bārāṇasī.

Precept platform *(kaidan)*
See the "Three Great Secret Dharmas."

Precept sect *(Risshū)*
See "Ritsu sect."

Prediction *(mirai-ki)*
Refers to sutras or other writings foretelling something to occur in the future. Nichiren considered the *Lotus Sutra*, and others such as the *Sutra of the Great Assembly* and *Sutra of the Benevolent King*, which describe the state of the Latter Age of Degeneration, as well as writings of such masters in the past as T'ien-t'ai, Miao-lê and Dengyō as "predictions." The 20-line verse in the 13th chapter and Śākyamuni's wish to spread the Lotus teaching in the Latter Age stated in the 23rd chapter of the *Lotus Sutra* are the "predictions" that supported Nichiren's missionary zeal. In a sense the *Risshō Ankoku-ron* was a "prediction" by Nichiren.

Preface, main discourse and transmission *(jo, shō, rutsū)*
It is customary to explain scriptures in three steps: preface or introductory remarks, main discourse or central theme, and transmission or amplifying the virtue of the sutra for the purpose of dissemination. Likewise, Nichiren organizes the teachings of the Buddha's lifetime into three stages, claiming that the core teaching of the Buddha's 50 years of teaching lies in the 16th chapter of the *Lotus Sutra*, and that the *Nirvana Sutra* is its transmission.

Previous Life of Medicine-King Bodhisattva Chapter *(Yakuō-bon)*
The 23rd chapter of the *Lotus Sutra*. In this chapter, the Buddha told Bodhisattva *Shukuōke*, Star-King-Flower, that Medicine-King Bodhisattva twice in previous lives burned his own body for thousands of years as an offering of light to the *Lotus Sutra* and the Buddha who then preached it. After relating this story, the Buddha states that the merit of upholding even one verse of the *Lotus Sutra* is far superior than this offering, and that Star-King-Flower should strive to propagate this "Medicine-King" chapter during the last 500-year period after the death of Śākyamuni Buddha.

Prince Shōtoku *(Shōtoku Taishi)*
574–622 CE. The third prince of Emperor Yōmei, who served Empress Suiko as her Imperial Regent. He carried out reform programs such as promulgation of the 17 Article Constitution and the adoption of the 12-cap rank system. He was a devout Buddhist who greatly contributed to the rise of Buddhism

in Japan by writing commentaries on three Buddhist sutras: *Hokke* or *Lotus*, *Yuima* or *Vimalakīrti*, and *Shōman* or *Lion's Roar of Queen Shrimala*. He also built the Shitennōji Temple. Nichiren stressed the relationship between the prince and the *Lotus Sutra* by claiming that the prince was an avatar of Kannon Bodhisattva.

Profound Meaning of the Bodhisattva Avalokiteśvara Chapter *(Kannon-gen)*
Abbreviation of the lecture *Kannon Gengi*, *Kuan-yin Hsüan-i* in Chinese, by T'ien-t'ai recorded by his disciple Chang-an. T'ien-t'ai comments on the 25th chapter of the *Lotus Sutra* in the light of five major principles, *gojū gengi*, of name, entity, quality, function and teaching.

Profound Meaning of the Lotus Sutra *(Hokke Gengi)*
Fa-hua-hsüan-i in Chinese, consisting of 10 fascicles. What T'ien-t'ai lectured on the title of the *Lotus Sutra* was recorded and compiled by his disciple Chang-an. It explains the title in detail and expounds the profound doctrine of this sutra through the five major principles: *ming*, name; *t'i*, entity; *tsung*, quality; *yung*, function; and *chiao*, teaching.

Provisional and true teachings *(gonjitsu)*
See "Provisional teachings."

Provisional teachings *(gongyō)*
The term *gon* means provisional as against what is "true" and "ultimate." Provisional teachings were used by the Buddha or His assistants as the most effective means of helping the people who lacked the capacity to understand the true teachings. Nichiren Shōnin considers that all Buddhist teachings, except the *Lotus Sutra*, are provisional.

Pu-k'ung, Tripiṭaka Master *(Fukū)*
Also known as Amoghavajra, 705–774 CE. The sixth patriarch of the Shingon sect. Born in northern India, Pu-k'ung came to China at the age of thirteen and entered the Buddhist order under the guidance of Vajrabodhi studying esoteric Buddhism. After Vajrabodhi's death, he visited India and returned with 1,200 fascicles of sutras and discourses. He was trusted by the three reigning Emperors: Hsüan-tsung of the T'ang dynasty and two successors, who established esoteric Buddhism as the state religion. He translated sutras such as *Hannyarishu-kyō*, *Heart and Perfection of Naya Wisdom Sutra* and *Bodaishin-ron*, *Treatise on Bhodi-Mind*. Pointing out his mistakes in the *Bodaishin-ron* and failure in praying for rain, Nichiren condemned him for slandering the True Dharma.

Pure Land school *(Jōdo-shū)*
Also called the Nembutsu school, it was founded in Japan by Hōnen, or Genkū Shōnin, who preached that one should put faith in the original vow of the Buddha of Infinite Life, Amida Buddha, and chant the name of this Buddha, *nembutsu*, to be reborn in the Pure Land of Utmost Bliss. The school was founded on the basis of the triple Pure Land sutras, regarded the Buddha of Infinite Life the *honzon*, and divided all of the teachings of Śākyamuni Buddha into pairs: Holy Way and Pure Land, hard and easy practices, or right and miscellaneous practices. According to this classification, this school negates all other Buddhas and sutras and insists on chanting the nembutsu single-mindedly. Nichiren Shōnin harshly criticized this school for neglecting the Original, Eternal Śākyamuni Buddha, and the true teaching of the Buddha, the *Lotus Sutra*, according to the provisional sutras. He said that for this believers of the Pure Land teaching would all fall into the Hell of Incessant Suffering.

Pure Land Sutra *(Amida-kyō)*
One fascicle, translated by Kumārajīva. One of the triple Pure Land sutras, this sutra describes the Pure Land of Utmost Bliss to the West of the Buddha of Infinite Life. It mentions that numerous Buddhas of the six directions appeared to praise the virtue of the Buddha and testify to the truth of this sutra. It then states that one can be reborn in this Pure Land by chanting the name of this Buddha. Based on T'ien-t'ai's "five period teaching" doctrine, Nichiren maintains that the *Pure Land Sutra* is a provisional teaching preached in the third period and that the Buddha of Infinite Life has nothing to do with and is useless to the people in this world, the Sahā World.

Pūrṇa *(Furuna)*
One of Śākyamuni's 10 major disciples, noted as the foremost in preaching the dharma. Originally a non-Buddhist, Pūrṇa was converted to Buddhism, actively assisting the Buddha in propagating the dharma. The eighth chapter of the *Lotus Sutra* predicts him to be a Buddha called *Hōmyō*, Dharma Brightness. Nichiren often cites him as an example of the Two Vehicles obtaining Buddhahood.

Rāhula *(Ragora)*
Son of Śākyamuni Buddha and Princess Yaśodharā before He left the family. Rāhula later became one of Śākyamuni's 10 major disciples, respected as foremost in the inconspicuous observance of precepts. In Chapter Nine of the *Lotus Sutra* he is predicted to be a Buddha called *Tōshippōke*, Stepping on Seven Treasure Flowers.

Relative and absolute subtleties *(sōdaimyō-zetsudaimyō)*
In the *Hokke Gengi, Profound Meaning of the Lotus Sutra,* T'ien-t'ai interpreted the subtlety, *myō,* of the Myōhō Renge-kyō from two viewpoints to show the profundity of the *Lotus Sutra:* (1) relative subtlety, *sōdaimyō,* meaning that the *Lotus Sutra* is superior to all other sutras; and (2) absolute or all encompassing subtlety, *zetsudaimyō,* meaning that the *Lotus Sutra* cannot be compared to any other sutra because it includes and integrates all other sutras. In other words, no sutra can exist outside the *Lotus Sutra,* claiming to be superior or inferior to it.

Revealing the Profound and Secret Sutra *(Gejimmitsu-kyō)*
This five-fascicled sutra translated into Chinese by Hsüan-chuang is the basic canon of the *Fa-hsiang,* Dharma Characteristics sect. It is regarded as the first Buddhist scripture to preach the consciousness-only doctrine which insists that all things and phenomena represent the mind. According to the T'ien-t'ai doctrine of the five periods, Nichiren considered it to be a provisional sutra preached in the third period, Hōdō.

Revealing the single path replacing the three teachings *(kaisan ken'itsu)*
Discarding the three teachings for *śrāvaka, pratyekabuddha* and bodhisattvas and revealing the single path to Enlightenment is the central theme preached in the first half, *shakumon* or theoretical section, of the *Lotus Sutra.*

Revelation of eternal life of the Buddha *(kempon)*
Revealing the eternal life of the Buddha in the essential section of the *Lotus Sutra,* replacing what is preached in the theoretical section. According to the theoretical teaching, Śākyamuni Buddha attained Enlightenment under the pipal tree at Gayā, India, about 3,000 years ago, but in the essential section it is expounded that Śākyamuni had attained Buddhahood in the eternal past, extending His helping hand to those of us who live in this Latter Age. Nichiren Shōnin emphasizes this in his *Kaimoku-shō, Open Your Eyes to the Lotus Teaching,* and other writings.

Reward Body *(hōjin)*
See "Threefold body of a Buddha."

Right time *(toki)*
At the outset of his *Senji-shō, Selecting the Right Time,* Nichiren states, "To study Buddhism, first of all we must know the right time, *toki.*" The right time in this context means proper time to spread the teaching of the *Lotus Sutra* as it does in the second chapter of the *Lotus Sutra,* when the Buddha declares, "The reason

why I did not tell this to you is that the right time, *toki*, had not come yet. Now is the very time, *toki*, to say this. I will definitely preach the Great Vehicle." According to Nichiren, the proper time to preach the *Lotus Sutra* was the last eight years of the Buddha's lifetime and during 10,000 years of the Latter Age.

Ritsu sect *(Ritsu-shū)*
One of the six sects of the Nara period in Japan that preached the observance of the Mahayana precepts as the way to attain Buddhahood. It was transmitted to Japan by Chien-chên, in Japanese *Ganjin*, who arrived in 754 CE. Nichiren regarded it as one of the three Hinayana sects, calling it "Ritsu, the national enemy." Especially critical of Ritsu Masters Eison and Ninshō, also called Ryōkan, contemporaries of Nichiren, he insisted that in the Latter Age of Degeneration the observance of the Hinayana precepts was useless and that upholding the *Lotus Sutra* is the true observance of the precepts.

Roundabout way to Buddhahood *(ryakkō shugyō)*
The term *ryakkō shugyō* literally means practicing various preachings for many *kalpa*, or aeons, in order to attain Buddhahood. Nichiren maintains that the teachings expounded in the pre-Lotus Mahayana sutras are ways requiring inconceivably long periods of time to reach Buddhahood and that only the *Lotus Sutra* preaches the way to attain it with this corporal body.

Ruler, teacher, and parents *(shu, shi, shin)*
Nichiren Shōnin maintained that Śākyamuni Buddha, who has the three virtues of a ruler, a teacher and a parent, is the sole savior of the people in the Latter Age of Degeneration. The possession of these three virtues by one person is a prerequisite of the Savior-Buddha, and only the Lord Śākyamuni Buddha has this qualification, according to Nichiren.

Ryōkan *(Ryōkan)*
1217–1303 CE. Refers to Ryōkan-bō Ninshō, leading figure of the Precept school, *Ritsu-shū*, in Kamakura. He was a disciple of Eison of the Saidaiji Temple in Nara but came to Kamakura to spread Buddhist precepts. Patronized by Hōjō Tokiyori and Nagatoki among others, he founded the Gokurakuji Temple in Kamakura. Nichiren regarded the Buddhist precepts, both Hinayana and Mahayana, as evil teachings that confused people, leading them to the evil realms.

Sacred Eagle, Mt. *(Ryōjusen)*
See "Pure Land of Mt. Sacred Eagle."

Sahā World *(shaba sekai)*
This world in which we live. The Sanskrit term *sahā* means endurance. Unlike the world of Bliss to the west, this world is conceived as being polluted by three poisons and the people in it must endure sufferings. Based on the 16th chapter of the *Lotus Sutra,* Nichiren insists that this Sahā World is the Land of Eternal Tranquil Light, where the Original Śākyamuni Buddha resides, and that we should uphold the *Odaimoku,* sacred title of the *Lotus Sutra,* to purify this Sahā World, polluted with evil passions, in the Latter Age of Degeneration.

Saimyōji, Lay Priest *(Saimyōji Nyūdō)*
Refers to the fifth Shogunal Regent Hōjō Tokiyori, 1227–1263 CE, after he entered the priesthood. Son of Tokiuji, he became the Shogunal Regent at the age of 20, consolidating the power of the Hōjō family and the shogunate. At the age of 30, he resigned as Regent and built the Saimyōji Temple. Thereafter, he was called *Saimyōji Nyūdō,* Lay Priest of the Saimyoji Temple. Even after resigning, he remained the most powerful man in the government. This is why Nichiren Shōnin submitted his *Risshō Ankoku-ron* admonition to the shogunate, to Saimyōji Nyūdō in the first year of the Bunnō Era, 1260 CE. Nichiren thought that Tokiyori understood him and then took proper measures for releasing Nichiren from the exile to Izu Province when Tokiyori found out that Nichiren had been exiled on a false charge.

Śākyamuni Buddha *(Shakuson)*
Founder of Buddhism. Śākyamuni literally means the "Sage of the Śākya clan." Born to King Śuddhodana and Queen Māyā, He was named Siddhārtha Gautama. On her way to her parents' home, Queen Māyā gave birth to Siddhārtha at the Lumbini Park. It is said upon birth the infant Buddha declared: "Above and under heaven, I alone am revered." Feeling the agony of life, Siddhārtha abandoned His family at the age of 19, another version says 29, to seek the way of enlightenment in asceticism. Unable to attain liberation from the sufferings of life, He gave up ascetic practices, sat in meditation under the bodhi tree, and finally gained Enlightenment at dawn of the eighth day of the 12th month. He became the Buddha, Enlightened One, at the age of 30 or 35. For 50 long years after that, the Buddha went around many places in India preaching both the Mahayana and Hinayana teachings until He passed away under the twin śāla trees in Kuśinagara at the age of 80 in 485 BCE. Other sources say 386 or 383 BCE. The Buddha's teachings preached during His 50 year missionary life were collected and compiled as sutras and precepts by disciples after His death. They were systematized by Grand Master T'ien-t'ai of China in the Five Periods of preaching and Eight Teachings. According to

this system, Nichiren Shōnin regarded the *Lotus Sutra* to be the conclusion of Śākyamuni Buddha's lifetime preaching. Nichiren paid much attention to the persecutions the Buddha had encountered while preaching. Feeling that he experienced the same persecutions as those of the Buddha, Nichiren Shōnin preached that those of us in the Latter Age of Degeneration could attain Buddhahood due to the compassion of the Eternal Buddha Śākyamuni.

Sanron sect *(Sanron-shū)*
See "Three Discourse school."

Śāriputra *(Sharihotsu)*
One of the Buddha's ten senior disciples, he is known as the foremost in wisdom. He had practiced Brahmanism before joining the Buddhist Order together with Maudgalyāyana. He was an *arhat, arakan* or holy monk in Hinayana teachings until he was enlightened by the "Revealing the single path replacing the Three Vehicle teaching" doctrine in the second chapter of the *Lotus Sutra*. The Buddha assured him of becoming a Buddha in the future. He assiduously assisted the Buddha in spreading Buddhism but died before Him. Nichiren took him as an example of attaining Buddhahood by men of the Two Vehicles: *śrāvaka* and *pratyekabuddha*.

Semblance Dharma, the Age of *(zōbō)*
This refers to the second of the three periods after the death of the Buddha. These are: (1) the Age of the True Dharma; (2) The Age of the Semblance Dharma; and (3) the Latter Age of Degeneration. The first lasts 500 or 1,000 years. Here the teaching of the Buddha is properly practiced and enlightenment is attainable. The second also lasts 500 or 1,000 years. In this period, some practice Buddhism but enlightenment is no longer attainable. The final period lasts 10,000 years. Nobody can practice the teaching and attain enlightenment. Nichiren believed that both the first two lasted 1,000 years, and that the last would begin 2,000 years after the death of the Buddha.

Seven Disasters *(shichinan)*
See "Three calamities and seven disasters."

Shan-tao, Venerable *(Zendō Oshō)*
618–681 CE. Third patriarch of the Pure Land school in China. He was popularly known as 'the Master of the Kuang-ming-ssŭ' after the temple where he lived and was also called Grand Master Chungnan. He learned Pure Land Buddhism from Tao-ch'o and wrote such works as the *Commentary on the Sutra of Meditation on the Buddha of Infinite Life*, establishing the theological foundation of Pure

Land Buddhism. He considered nembutsu chanting to be the right practice and rejected all other practices as miscellaneous. Hōnen, the founder of the Pure Land sect in Japan, especially respected Shan-tao and depended on him. However, Nichiren Shōnin criticized Shan-tao for not knowing the profundity of the teaching. He said Shan-tao fell into hell alive for slandering the *Lotus Sutra* by saying "not even one out of one thousand" can attain Buddhahood by the teaching of the *Lotus Sutra*. He is said to have committed suicide by jumping from a willow tree at the Kuan-ming-ssŭ Temple.

Shijō Kingo *(Shijō Saburōzaemonnojō)*
1229–1296 CE. More fully called Shijō Saburōzaemonnojō Yorimoto or Shijō Nakatsukasanojō Yorimoto. Kingo was a Kamakura warrior who served the Ema family of the Hōjō clan. He is said to have converted to Nichiren Buddhism shortly after Nichiren began missionary activities in Kamakura, and had been a leading member of the Nichiren Order. When Nichiren was about to be beheaded at Tatsunokuchi in 1271 CE, Kingo expressed his determination to follow Nichiren in death. In 1277 CE, he became involved in the debate between Nichiren's disciple Sammi-bō and Priest Ryōkan's protege Ryūzō-bō. It developed into a religious conflict between Kingo and Lord Ema, who threatened to confiscate Kingo's fief. At this point Nichiren advised Kingo never to give up his faith in the *Lotus Sutra* even if he has to go against the wishes of his parents or lord because that is the true way of repaying kindness. Nichiren also wrote the *Yorimoto Chinjō, Yorimoto's Letter of Explanation in the name of Kingo*. Soon the situation improved for Kingo, his confiscated fief was restored, a new fief was granted, and the bond between him and the lord was stronger than ever. Yorimoto was also an expert in medicine and often prescribed medicine for Nichiren on Mt. Minobu.

Shōichi *(Shōichi)*
1202–1280 CE. Zen priest in the Kamakura period, who was also known as Ennibō, Enni, and Ben'en. After studying Tendai Buddhism, he studied Zen from Masters Eichō and Shin'yū before going to Sung China in 1235 CE for further study. Having learned Rinzai Zen from Master Wu-chun, he returned to Japan and established the Shōtenji Temple at Hakata. He was posthumously given the title of State Master Shōichi by Emperor Hanazono in 1311 CE. He was the first Zen monk in Japan to have received this honor.

Six difficult and nine easier actions *(rokunan kui)*
Chapter 11 of the *Lotus Sutra*, Beholding the Stūpa of Treasures, mentions nine things considered relatively easy compared to the six difficult things relating to the work of spreading the *Lotus Sutra* after the death of Śākyamuni Buddha.

Each of the nine "easy" things seems impossible to do, but it means that they are easier than: (1) preaching; (2) copying; (3) reading; (4) upholding; (5) listening to; and (6) revering the *Lotus Sutra*. Nine easier actions are: (1) preaching sutras other than the Lotus; (2) hauling Mt. Sumeru to other Buddha Worlds; (3) lifting the whole universe with a toe; (4) preaching sutras on top of the Highest Heaven; (5) grabbing the sky with the hands and walking around the world; (6) carrying the great earth on the foot to the Brahma Heaven; (7) walking through fire with hay on the back; (8) preaching 84,000 sutras for people and giving them superhuman powers; and (9) leading the masses to arhatship and giving them superhuman powers. Nichiren took this passage for the Buddha's prediction regarding the difficulty in spreading this sutra in the Latter Age of Degeneration after the death of the Buddha, and he sacrificed his life for the propagation of the *Lotus Sutra*, actually experiencing what is preached in it.

Six-fascicled Nirvana Sutra *(Hatsunaion-gyō)*
Refers to the *Nirvana Sutra* translated into Chinese by Fa-hsien in six fascicles. These correspond to the first 10 of the 40 fascicles of the sutra translated into Chinese by Dharmakṣema.

Six non-Buddhist masters *(rokushi gedō)*
Six influential thinkers in Central India during the Buddha's lifetime who openly challenged the traditional Brahman authority.

Six superhuman powers *(rokutsū or rokujinzū)*
Refers to transcendental faculties of a Buddha, bodhisattva, or arhat: (1) heavenly eyes; (2) heavenly ears; (3) ability to read other people's minds; (4) ability to know former lives; (5) ability to go anywhere; and (6) ability to destroy all evil passions. The first five faculties are referred to as five superhuman powers, *gotsū* or *gojinzū*.

Slandering the True Dharma *(hōbō)*
In general, *hōbō* or *hihō shōbō* means abusing or speaking ill of Buddhism, but Nichiren specifically stated that abusing or condemning the *Lotus Sutra*, the true teachings of the Buddha Śākyamuni, was an act of *hōbō*, the most serious sin of all. He insisted that those who knew the true intent of Śākyamuni and did not try to spread it were committing the sin of *hōbō*. Nichiren tried to secure the tranquility of the country by stopping people from slandering the True Dharma. For this purpose, Nichiren tried to spread the teaching of the *Lotus Sutra* throughout his lifetime at the risk of his own existence.

Southern Capital *(Nanto)*
Alternate name for Nara, located south of Kyoto, the Northern capital. Nara was the Imperial Capital for 75 years, 710–784 CE, during the reigns of seven Emperors from Gemmyō to Kammu. During these years the seven great Buddhist temples, Tōdaiji, Kōfukuji, Gankōji, Daianji, Yakushiji, Saidaiji, and Hōryūji, adorned the skyline of Nara, and scholar-monks of the six sects of Buddhism, Sanron, Hossō, Kegon, Ritsu, Jōjitsu and Kusha, competed in scholarship.

Soya Kyōshin *(Soya Kyōshin)*
1224–1291 CE. A leading follower of Nichiren Shōnin who lived in Soya District of Shimōsa Province, northern Chiba Prefecture today. Together with Toki Jōnin and Ōta Jōmyō of Shimōsa, he was one of Nichiren's early converts.

Special transmission without scriptures or preaching *(kyōge betsuden)*
The Zen school insists that Śākyamuni Buddha's enlightenment cannot be transmitted with teachings in words or characters but only from heart to heart. This claim of Zen Buddhists was unacceptable to Nichiren because it slights Buddhist scriptures, especially the *Lotus Sutra*.

Spiritual contemplation *(kanjin)*
A way of practicing Buddhism by observing one's own mind. The Tendai school advocates attaining the unfathomable world of the Buddha by observing one's own mind according to "threefold contemplation in a single thought," whereas Nichiren Shōnin preached putting faith in the Eternal Śākyamuni Buddha, revealed in the essential section, as the Most Revered One, *honzon*, and upholding by body, mouth and heart the five-character Sacred Title, *Odaimoku*, of the *Lotus Sutra*, representing both His practice of Buddha Dharma leading to Buddhahood and His great virtue as the Enlightened One. This is chanting of the Odaimoku, *Namu Myōhō Renge-kyō*, which is the sole and absolute way of practicing Buddhism in the Latter Age of Degeneration. The difference in the ways of practicing Buddhism, between T'ien-t'ai and Nichiren stems from the difference in time. As T'ien-t'ai lived in the Age of the Semblance Dharma. His doctrine placed emphasis on the theoretical section regarding the essential section as secondary, whereas Nichiren, a man of the Latter Age of Degeneration, placed primary stress on the essential section. Accordingly while T'ien-t'ai advocated the observation of mind by the "threefold contemplation in a single thought" based on the doctrinal teaching of the theoretical section, Nichiren called for the chanting of the Odaimoku based on what he referred to as the "actual" teaching of the essential section.

Śrāvaka and pratyekabuddha *(shōmon and engaku)*
See "Two Vehicles."

Śrīmalā Sutra *(Shōman-gyō)*
The one-fascicled sutra expounded by Queen Śrīmalā, *Shōman*, and translated into Chinese by Guṇabhadra in 436 CE. It preaches the One Vehicle doctrine and the inherent existence of Buddha-nature in all living beings.

Strange phenomena in the sky, natural calamities on earth *(tempen chiyō)*
The Japanese term *tempen* refers to abnormal phenomena due to unusual conditions in the sky such as severe rains and winds, eclipse of the sun and moon, and droughts. The term *chiyō* means calamities on earth such as earthquakes and floods. These cause such disasters as famines and epidemics. Holding that these disasters were caused by the people who abandoned the True Dharma and put faith in evil dharmas, Nichiren Shōnin insisted that they should promptly eliminate the evil dharmas and seek refuge in the True Dharma.

Śubhākarasiṃha, Tripiṭaka Master *(Zemmui Sanzō)*
637–735 CE. Śubhakarasiṃha left the throne of Udayana in Central India and learned esoteric Buddhism at Nalanda Monastery. Entering China under the patronage of Emperor Hsüan-tsung of T'ang, he translated sutras and wrote discourses, laying the foundation for Chinese esoteric Buddhism. Nichiren claimed, however, that Śubhakarasiṃha fell into hell upon death due to his slandering of the True Dharma.

Subhūti *(Shubodai)*
One of the 10 major disciples of the Buddha. Originally a merchant in Śrāvastī, the capital of the kingdom of Kosala, Subhūti was converted by Śākyamuni when he listened to Him speak at the dedication of the Jetavana Monastery, *Gion Shōja*. Gentle in nature, he did not quarrel even against non-Buddhists who attacked and persecuted him. He was respected by many and received great offerings. Thus he is known as the foremost in receiving alms among the Buddha's disciples.

Sumeru, Mt. *(Shumisen)*
According to Buddhist cosmology, this is the mountain in the center of the universe. It stands 80,000 yojana high above as well as below sea level. At the top is the palace of Indra. The Four Heavenly Kings dwell half way up the mountain. On the four sides are the Four Continents, the southern of which is the Sahā World of human beings. Nichiren likens the *Lotus Sutra*

to this mountain as the prime of all the sutras. The 10th chapter of the *Lotus Sutra* states that of the numerous sutras which had already been preached, Hinayana and Mahayana sutras preached before the *Lotus Sutra*, are now being preached, the triple Lotus sutras, and will be preached, the *Nirvana Sutra*, the *Lotus Sutra* is supreme and most difficult to believe and comprehend. Nichiren considered this statement as proof of the supremacy of the *Lotus Sutra* among all the scriptures.

Sunakṣatra *(Zenshō Biku)*
Sunakṣatra is said to have kept the 250 precepts of Hinayana and was wise enough to memorize all the holy teachings of the Buddha. However, he later was induced by his "evil friend" to have faith in a heretical teaching, and acted against Buddhism. As a result, he fell into hell.

Superior-Practice Bodhisattva *(Jōgyō Bosatsu)*
One of the four leaders of those who emerged from the earth described in the 15th chapter of the *Lotus Sutra*. They are the *honge no bosatsu*, bodhisattvas guided by the Original Buddha in the eternal past, and entrusted with the task of spreading the *Lotus Sutra* in the Latter Age of Degeneration. After being exiled to Sado, Nichiren was firmly convinced that he was Jōgyō Bodhisattva who was entrusted by the Eternal True Buddha with the task of saving the world of Defilement and evils in the Latter Age of Degeneration.

Supernatural Powers of the Tathāgata Chapter *(Jinriki-hon)*
The 21st chapter of the *Lotus Sutra*, *Nyorai Jinriki-hon* is abbreviated as *Jinriki-hon*. In this chapter, the Buddha displays His superhuman powers, transmitting the essence of the sutra, the five-character Odaimoku, *Namu Myōhō Renge-kyō*, to the bodhisattvas from underground, and entrusting them with the duty of saving the people in the Latter Age of Degeneration. It was based on this chapter that Nichiren Shōnin realized himself to be the avatar of Bodhisattva Superior-Practice, head of the bodhisattvas from underground, who was entrusted by the Buddha to save all the people in the Latter Age.

Sutra of Infinite Meaning *(Muryōgi-kyō)*
Translated into Chinese by Dharmajātayaśas in 481 CE, it consists of three chapters: Virtuous Practices, Preaching, and Ten Blessings. From its content, the sutra is regarded as an introductory teaching to the *Lotus Sutra*, or as a part of the *Threefold Lotus Sutra*. It is stated in the Preaching chapter: "The truth has not been revealed for 40 years or so," differentiating the *Lotus Sutra* from all the sutras preached before it. Based on this statement, Nichiren claims all the pre-Lotus sutras to be provisional and considers the *Lotus Sutra* the True Dharma.

Sutra of Meditation on the Buddha of Infinite Life *(Kan-muryōju-kyō, Kangyō)*
One of the triple Pure Land sutras, basic scriptures of the Pure Land sect. According to its content, Śākyamuni expounded the Buddha of Infinite Life and His Pure Land of Bliss for the imprisoned Vaidehī at Rājagṛha in Magadha. Shan-tao of T'ang China wrote a commentary on it claiming the nembutsu, chanting the name of the Buddha of Infinite Life, to be the only way of salvation. Based on this, Hōnen Shōnin founded the Pure Land sect of Japan. Based on T'ien-t'ai's "five periods and eight teachings" classification, Nichiren Shōnin relegated the sutra to a provisional teaching preached in the third Hōdō period. Also abbreviated as Kangyō.

Sutra of Meditation on Universal-Sage Bodhisattva *(Kan Fugen Bosatsu Gyōbō-kyō)*
One fascicle sutra translated into Chinese in 442 CE by Dharmamitra, also called *T'en-mo-mi-to* or *Dommamitta*. It is abbreviated as the *Kan Fugen-gyō* in Japanese. Preached shortly before the Buddha passed away, the sutra declares the death of the Buddha in three months and teaches how to repent the evils resulting from six sense organs. Since this sutra is a continuation of the last chapter of the *Lotus Sutra*, T'ien-t'ai considered it as the conclusion of the *Lotus Sutra*.

Sutra of Mystic Glorification *(Mitsugon-gyō)*
The *Daijō Mitsugon-Kyō* or simply *Mitsugon-kyō* in Japanese. It preaches the consciousness-only doctrine, and is one of the basic canons of the *Hossō*, Dharma Characteristics Sect. Nichiren refused to accept its claims that it was supreme of all Buddhist scriptures.

Sutra of the Benevolent King *(Ninnō-kyō)*
There are two Chinese versions, both in two fascicles, translated by Kumārajīva and by Amoghavajra, Pu-k'ung. Preached to King Prasenajit of Kosala regarding the way to protect the nation, it has been revered both in China and Japan as one of the three state-protecting sutras. Nichiren cites from the Kumārajīva version in explaining "three calamities and seven disasters." The Shingon sect uses the Amoghavajra version.

Sutra of the Golden Splendor *(Konkōmyō-kyō)*
Two Chinese translations of this sutra exist. One translated by Dharmakṣema, *Dommushin*, in four fascicles and another by I-ching, *Gijō*, in 10 fascicles. Together with the *Lotus Sutra* and the *Ninnō-kyō, Sutra of the Benevolent King*, it has been worshipped as one of the three state-protecting sutras. I-ching's version has been recited and preached in Japan in state-temples and in the Imperial Court since the Nara Period. Nichiren cited a chapter of the sutra

translated by I-ching, *Shitennō Gokoku-bon, Protection of the Country by the Four Heavenly Deities,* when he gave his account of the reasons for disasters and calamities in the Latter Age.

Sutra of the Great Assembly *(Daijik-kyō or Daishū-kyō)*
Consisting of 60 fascicles, it was translated into Chinese by T'an Wu-chien of Northern Liang and others separately. Nichiren's concept of the Latter Age of Degeneration stems from the descriptions in this and three other sutras about the causes of calamities and the gradual decline of Buddhism through five "500-year periods." Nichiren insists that the Latter Age of Degeneration, when the *Sutra of the Great Assembly* predicts the disappearance of the "pure dharma," virtuous teaching, is the very period when the virtuous teaching of the Lotus would widely spread.

Sutra of Transmission of the Buddhist Teaching *(Fuhōzō-kyō)*
Also known as *Fuhōzō Innen-Den,* it is a record of the 24 successors of the Buddha. The Chinese translation by Chih-ch'ieh-yeh and T'an-yao is in six fascicles. According to it, the first transmitter of Buddhism after the Buddha was Kāśyapa. The 24th and last, Āryasimha, *Shishi Sonja,* was killed by King Dammira. Nichiren considered this sutra as a prediction of the Buddha, maintaining that those transmitters of Buddhism appeared exactly as predicted by the Buddha.

Sutra on the Act of Perfection *(Soshitsuji-kyō)*
Translated by Śubhākarasiṃha in three fascicles. One of the three mystic sutras of esoteric Buddhism, the other two being the *Great Sun Buddha Sutra* and the *Diamond Peak Sutra.* It preaches the way to attain perfect results in all works in both the mundane world and the dharma world. It is regarded specially important by Tendai esotericism, but Nichiren Shōnin slights it as a provisional teaching preached in the Hōdō period according to T'ien-t'ai's five period doctrine.

Sutra on the Decline of the Dharma *(Hō-metsujin-kyō)*
One-fascicled sutra explaining the extinction of Buddhism after the death of the Buddha. The translator of the Chinese version is unknown and it is suspected to be a fabrication. As its content is somewhat similar to such Mahayana sutras as the *Nirvana Sutra* and *Sutra of the Great Assembly,* it is believed to have been written in the fourth century CE. It is a short sutra reflecting the decline of the Buddhist world.

Sutras which have been preached, are being preached, and will be preached *(i-kon-tō)*

The 10th chapter of the *Lotus Sutra,* The Teacher of the Dharma, states that of the numerous sutras which had already been preached, are now being preached, and will be preached, the *Lotus Sutra* is supreme and most difficult to believe and comprehend. Interpreting this, Grand Master T'ien-t'ai states in his *Words and Phrases of the Lotus Sutra* that the sutras which had already been preached refer to the pre-Lotus sutras; those which are now being preached mean the *Sutra of Infinite Meaning,* which is the introduction to the *Lotus Sutra,* and that which will be preached is the *Nirvana Sutra.* The *Lotus Sutra* is superior to all these sutras. According to Nichiren, these three categories of sutras are easy to believe and understand because they were provisional teachings preached according to the capacity of the people while the *Lotus Sutra* is difficult to believe and comprehend because it is the true teaching expounding the true intent of the Buddha without compromising. Thus the term *i-kon-tō* is often used by Nichiren to prove the superiority of the *Lotus Sutra,* in the same way as he quotes "The truth has not been revealed during the pre-Lotus period of 40 years or so" from the *Sutra of Infinite Meaning* and the Buddha of Many Treasures verifying the words of Śākyamuni Buddha in the 11th chapter of the *Lotus Sutra,* Beholding the Stūpa of Treasures.

T'an-luan *(Donran)*

476–542 CE. Founder of the Chinese Pure Land sect. Ordained on Mt. Wut'ai, he at first studied the four-discourse teaching, but later was converted to Pure Land Buddhism when he met Bodhiruci and received the *Sutra of Meditation on the Buddha of Infinite Life.* Nichiren Shōnin criticized T'an-luan for not knowing the difference in profundity of doctrines and also for slandering the Buddha by defining the Pure Land teaching to be supreme according to his two-way classification: the easy and difficult ways to practice.

Tao-ch'o *(Dōshaku)*

562–645 CE. The second patriarch of Chinese Pure Land Buddhism. He entered the priesthood at the age of 14, studying the *Nirvana Sutra.* At 48, however, he was converted to the Pure Land teaching by T'an-luan. He wrote the two-fascicled *An-lo-chi, Collection of Passages Concerning Rebirth in the Pure Land.* At the beginning of the *Senjaku-shū, Collection of Passages on the Nembutsu,* Hōnen cited from *An-lo-chi,* proclaiming the establishment of the Pure Land sect in Japan by dividing the holy teaching of the Buddha into the Holy Way and the Pure Land. Nichiren criticized the Pure Land masters for disregarding both the profundity of doctrines and the difference between true and provisional dharmas.

Tao-hsien *(Dōsen)*
A Buddhist monk in China during the T'ang dynasty, who entered Chang-an during the Ta-li Period, 766–779 CE, to spread T'ien-t'ai Buddhism. He wrote many books.

Tao-hsüan *(Dōsen)*
596–667 CE. As the Founder of the Nan-shan Lü or Precept Sect, Tao-hsüan is also called Precept Master Nan-shan or Grand Master Nan-shan. Nichiren criticized the precepts advocated by Tao-hsüan and Chien-chên, *Ganjin*, describing the precepts as being Hinayana.

Tao-lang *(Dōrō)*
?–? CE. A transmitter of San-lun, Three-Treatises Buddhism in China who appeared before Chi-tsang. The San-lun Sect in China was founded by Kumārajīva, and was transmitted through Tao-lang to Chi-tsang in several generations. A priest living in the Northern Liang period, he participated in the translation of the *Nirvana Sutra* by Dharmakṣema. Tao-lang was esteemed highly for his study and practice of Buddhism, and he was called "Tao-lang in the West of the Yellow River" as he was a man of the Kansu region.

Tao-lung *(Dōryū)*
1213–1278 CE. Zen priest of the Lin-chi Sect in China, known as *Rinzai* in Japanese. He came to Japan in the fourth year of the Kangen Era, 1246 CE, to become the founder of the Kenchōji Temple in Kamakura at the request of Hōjō Tokiyori. He spread Exclusive-training Zen in place of then prevalent Side-practicing Zen and laid the foundation for the *Rinzai* Zen Sect in Japan. Nichiren considered him as representative of all Zen Buddhism, but criticized him as an evil monk who slandered the *Lotus Sutra*.

Tao-sui *(Dōzui)*
?–? CE. Seventh patriarch of the T'ien-t'ai school in China. He taught the precepts for bodhisattvas to Grand Master Dengyō who had come from Japan. However, Nichiren Shōnin mistakenly states in his *Questions and Answers on the Honzon* that Dengyō received the precepts for bodhisattvas from Precept Master Tao-hsüan instead of Tao-sui.

Teacher of the Dharma Chapter *(Hosshi-hon)*
The 10th chapter of the *Lotus Sutra*, in which Śākyamuni Buddha preaches to Medicine-King Bodhisattva and 80,000 bodhisattvas, praising the great merit of having faith in the *Lotus Sutra*. Based on this chapter are such important Nichiren doctrines as *i-kon-tō*, sutras which have already been preached, and

now being preached and will be preached; prediction of great difficulties for those who spread the teaching of the *Lotus Sutra;* the propagator of the *Lotus Sutra* as the messenger of the Buddha; and the "three rules of preaching" or *sanki:* wearing the robe of the Buddha, meaning to have a gentle and forbearing heart; sitting on the throne of the Buddha, meaning to know the principle of non-substantiality; and entering the room of the Buddha, meaning to have profound compassion.

Teachers in China and Japan *(ninshi)*
Nichiren used the term *ninshi* to mean Buddhist priests in China and Japan who spread Buddhism guided by commentators and translators.

Ten aspects *(jūnyoze)*
Ten aspects of existence are shown in the Chapter Two of the *Lotus Sutra,* Expedients. These are: (1) appearances; (2) natures; (3) entities; (4) powers; (5) activities; (6) primary causes; (7) environmental causes; (8) effects; (9) rewards and retributions; and (10) the equality of the above nine factors. Combining this with another concept of the 10 realms of living beings, Grand Master T'ien-t'ai formulated the doctrines of "3,000 existences contained in one thought" doctrine, *ichinen-sanzen,* and "Mutual possession of 10 realms": each of the 10 realms containing the characteristics of nine other realms.

Ten female rākṣasa demons *(jūrasetsu [nyo])*
In the 26th chapter of the *Lotus Sutra,* these demons together with other deities vowed before the Buddha that they would protect those who practice the sutra. They are Lambā, Vilambā, Kūta. Dantī, Puṣpadantī, Makuṭadantī, Keśinī, Acalā, Mālādharī, Kuntī, and Sarvattvojohārī. Nichiren Shōnin revered them as the protectors of the *Lotus Sutra,* including them in his Great Mandala Honzon.

Tendai sect *(Tendai-shū)*
The T'ien-t'ai or Tendai sect in China was founded by Grand Master T'ien-t'ai with the *Lotus Sutra* as its basic canon. T'ien-t'ai classified Buddhist scriptures with the doctrines of five periods of preaching and eight teachings. He also preached the practice of the "threefold contemplation in a single thought" and "10-stage meditation." The T'ien-t'ai sect was transmitted to Japan by Grand Master Dengyō, who founded the Tendai Hokke school. As Dengyō also transmitted teachings of precepts, Zen and esoteric Buddhism, Tendai-shū in Japan accepted them as well. Esoteric Buddhism was popularized by later Tendai school leaders such as Ennin and Enchin, and Tendai Buddhism became both esoteric and exoteric. Nichiren Shōnin, originally a Tendai monk, through experience as one practicing the *Lotus Sutra,* established his unique theology

based on the essential section of the *Lotus Sutra*. Realizing himself to be a transmitter of the true teaching of the Buddha, namely the *Lotus Sutra*, Nichiren harshly criticized Ennin, Enchin and others who made the Tendai-Lotus sect strongly esoteric.

Theoretical section *(shakumon)*
The first half of the *Lotus Sutra,* from the first chapter, Introductory, to the 14th chapter, Peaceful Practices, is called the *shakumon,* meaning literally the teaching of the Buddhas in manifestion. The main theme of this section is replacing the provisional teaching for the Three Vehicles, *śrāvaka, pratyekabuddha* and bodhisattvas, with that of the One Buddha Vehicle leading all people to Buddhahood. T'ien-t'ai classified all the Buddha's teachings on the basis of the theoretical section, but Nichiren reinterpreted it from the standpoint of the essential section, the last half of the *Lotus Sutra* to save people in the Latter Age of Degeneration.

Third doctrine *(Daisan no hōmon)*
Used in *Hongon shukkai-shō,* the *Response to Lay Priest Lord Toki,* the term refers to the third of T'ien-t'ai's "three doctrinal differences" between the *Lotus Sutra* and pre-Lotus sutras, regarding (1) capacity of listeners to understand; (2) complete course of guidance: seeding, nurture, and emancipation; and (3) eternity in the relationship between the Buddha and His disciples. Of the three, Nichiren Shōnin placed emphasis on the third doctrine, claiming that the Eternal Buddha has been guiding us from the eternal past.

Those without Buddha-nature *(mushō)*
The Japanese term *mushō* refers to those who do not have Buddha-nature. According to the Hossō doctrine such people will never become Buddhas. However, the *Lotus* and *Nirvana Sutras* preach that even the *icchantika,* who have no Buddha-nature, can attain Buddhahood. Nichiren stresses the attainment of Buddhahood by *icchantika* without Buddha-nature through the great compassion of the Eternal True Buddha.

Three calamities *(sansai)*
See "Three calamities and seven disasters."

Three calamities and seven disasters *(sansai shichinan)*
According to Buddhist cosmology, the world goes through four periods: kalpa of construction, kalpa of continuance, kalpa of destruction, and kalpa of emptiness. The three calamities of warfare, epidemic, and famine that occur in the kalpa of continuance are called the three minor calamities while fires,

floods, and severe winds in the kalpa of destruction constitute the three major calamities. Seven disasters refer to those caused by slandering the True Dharma. According to the *Sutra of the Benevolent King* these are: (1) loss of brilliance of the sun and the moon; (2) loss of brilliance of constellations; (3) fire; (4) flood; (5) strong winds; (6) drought; and (7) bandits. According to the *Medicine Master Sutra* these are: (1) epidemics; (2) foreign invasions; (3) civil wars; (4) changes in constellations; (5) eclipses of the sun and the moon; (6) unusual storms; and (7) unseasonable storms. According to Chapter 25 of the *Lotus Sutra* these are: (1) fire; (2) flood; (3) *rakṣasa* or *rasetsu* demons; (4) the ruler; (5) other demons; (6) imprisonment; and (7) bandits.

Three delusions *(sanwaku)*
This is a Tendai doctrine that classifies the delusions and evil passions that exist in the minds of all people. These consist of (1) delusions of view and desire, *kenji no waku* which arise from incorrect views and thoughts; (2) delusions as innumerable as particles of dust and sand, *jinja no waku* which hinder knowledge of salvation methods; and (3) delusions about the principle of the Middle Way or the ultimate reality, *mumyō no waku* which hinder knowledge of the ultimate reality. The last mentioned, *mumyō* is especially regarded as fundamental.

Three Discourse school *(Sanron-shū)*
One of the thirteen Buddhist schools in China and also one of the six schools in Nara. It is based on the *Fundamental Verses on the Middle Way* and the *Treatise on the Twelve Gates* by Nāgārjuna, and the *One-hundred Verse Treatise* by Āryadeva, a disciple of Nāgārjuna. The theology of the Sanron school in China was established by Grand Master Chia-hsiang, or Chi-ts'ang, and transmitted to Japan in 625 CE.

Three Emperors *(sankō)*
Three legendary rulers of ancient China who are credited with creating Chinese civilization: Fu-hsi taught divination and fishing, invented the writing system, and instituted the marriage system; Shen-nung taught agriculture, medicine and trade; and the Yellow Emperor was the inventor of clothing, boats, carts, bows and arrows.

Three evil realms *(san'aku-dō)*
Also referred to as *sannakudō, san'aku, sannaku,* or *san'akushu* in Japanese. Hell, realm of hungry souls or *gaki,* and realm of beasts and birds or *chikushō,* where living beings would fall into after death due to their sins, are the bottom three of the 10 stages of spiritual development within each individual. Adding the realm of fighting spirits, *shura,* they are called the four evil realms: *shiakushu* or *shiakudō.*

Glossary

Three Great Secret Dharmas (*Sandai hihō*)
The three important doctrines Nichiren Shōnin established as the goal for those in the Latter Age of Degeneration to practice: *hommon no honzon,* the most revered one; *kaidan,* the place for practicing the *Lotus Sutra;* and *Odaimoku,* chanting based on the teaching of the essential section of the *Lotus Sutra.* From when he proclaimed the establishment of Nichiren Buddhism, Nichiren claimed to have been one who practiced the *Lotus Sutra,* trying to convey the Buddha's predictions in the sutra to those in the Latter Age of Degeneration. The narrow escape at Tatsunokuchi marked the turning point in his religious life. Realizing that he was the avatar of the Bodhisattva Superior-Practice, Nichiren taught the three great secret dharmas as the model for practicing Buddhism in the Latter Age of Degeneration, fulfilling the duty of the Buddha's messenger.

Three Great Vows of Nichiren (*sandai seigan*)
Toward the end of the *Kaimoku-shō, Open Your Eyes to the Lotus Teaching,* Nichiren declared that he would never break his vows to become a pillar of Japan, the eyes of Japan, and a great vessel for Japan. They are referred to as the Three Great Vows of Nichiren, which lay at the base of his religious activities from when he proclaimed Nichiren Buddhism for the purpose of saving all the people in Japan.

Three hindrances and four devils (*sanshō shima*)
The hindrances and devils that block the way to Buddhahood. The three hindrances refer to evil passions, evil karmas, and painful retributions such as going to hell. The four devils refer to evil passions, physical pain, death, and the king of devils. Grand Master T'ien-t'ai states in his *Great Concentration and Insight,* fascicle five, that as practicing and understanding of "tranquility and contemplation" proceed, "three hindrances and four devils" compete to interfere with those who practice, proving the doctrine to be true. Following T'ien-t'ai's concept of "three hindrances and four devils," Nichiren maintains that those who spread the teaching of the *Lotus Sutra* in the Latter Age of Degeneration are bound to be persecuted by the "three hindrances and four devils" and that only those who endured such difficulty would prove to be those who practice the *Lotus Sutra.*

Three kinds of enemies (*sanrui no tekinin*)
Also called *sanrui no gōteki* or *sanrui no onteki,* the term refers to three kinds of enemies who try to persecute propagators of the *Lotus Sutra* in various ways. The first group is lay followers who believe in and support the second and third groups. The second group is self-conceited priests and priestesses who mislead suffering people. The third group is those priests, male or female, who

are highly respected by people but are strongly attached to worldly matters. Encountering all these enemies as predicted in the 13th chapter of the *Lotus Sutra*, Nichiren strengthened his belief that he was one who practiced the *Lotus Sutra*.

Three Kings *(sannō)*
This term can refer to three different groups of monarchs. First is the three sage-kings of ancient China: (1) King Yü of Hsia; (2) King T'ang of Yin; and (3) King Wen or Wu of Chou. It can also refer to three evil rulers who lost their kingdoms in ancient China: (1) King Chieh of Hsia; (2) Chou-hsin of Yin; and (3) King Yu of Chou. Lastly, it could mean three emperors of ancient Japan who opposed the introduction of Buddhism: (1) Kimmei; (2) Bidatsu; and (3) Yōmei.

Three meetings at two places *(nisho san'e)*
Refers to where Śākyamuni Buddha preached the *Lotus Sutra*. The *Lotus Sutra* was expounded on Mt. Sacred Eagle and up in the sky above it in three lecture meetings. From Chapter One to the first half of Chapter 11 the *Lotus Sutra* was expounded on Mt. Sacred Eagle. From the last half of Chapter 11 through Chapter 22 it was expounded up in the sky. Then from Chapters 23 to 28 it was expounded on the mountain again.

Three merits *(santoku)*
See "Ruler, teacher and parents."

Three-period teaching *(sanji-kyō)*
Classification of the Buddhist scriptures by the *Hossō* or Dharma Characteristics sect into three categories: (1) the teaching of existence, *ukyō*, preached first in sutras such as the Āgama sutras; (2) the teaching of the void, *kūkyō*, expounded next in sutras such as the *Wisdom Sutra;* and finally (3) the teaching of the Middle Way preached in sutras such as the *Flower Garland Sutra* and the *Revealing the Profound and Secret Sutra*. The teaching of the Middle Way insists that reality lies beyond existence and non-existence and is considered supreme.

Three Pronouncements *(sanga no chokusen)*
In the 11th chapter of the *Lotus Sutra*, Beholding the Stupa of Treasures, the Buddha Śākyamuni urged participants in the assembly three times to propagate the *Lotus Sutra* after His demise. The first exhortation was accompanied by His desire to transmit the sutra. At the next exhortation He expressed His desire to perpetuate the dharma. Finally He preached how difficult it will be to spread the dharma after His death. Together with His guarantee of future Buddhahood for Devadatta and for a female dragon in the 12th chapter, they are called the Five Holy Proclamations of the Buddha.

Three Rebellious Sins *(sangyaku-zai)*
Refer to three of the Five Rebellious Sins, but the scriptures do not agree exactly what constitutes the three rebellious sins. During the lifetime of the Buddha, both Ajita, who killed his father, mother, and an arhat, and Devadatta, who killed an arhat, injured the Buddha, and caused disunity in the Buddhist order, were accused of committing the Three Rebellious Sins.

Three robes and one alms-bowl *(sanne ippatsu)*
Three robes and one alms-bowl were what priests were allowed to own. They wore one big robe and two kinds of kesa made of nine or five pieces of cloth. They also used a bowl for begging for food. Besides these, ordained monks were also allowed to have a cushion to sit on and a water filter. Nichiren Shōnin criticized Zen and Ritsu priests as deceivers who broke the "three robes and one bowl" rule as they approached those in power in order to curry favor and special treatment.

Three Southern and seven Northern masters *(Nansan Hokushichi)*
This term was first used by T'ien-t'ai in his *Profound Meaning of the Lotus Sutra* to describe the state of Buddhist studies in China during the Period of Northern and Southern Dynasties centering to the south of the Yangtze River and north of the Yellow River. Though their systems of comparative studies of Buddhist doctrines varied, they all held that either the *Nirvana Sutra* or the *Flower Garland Sutra* to be supreme of all sutras. T'ien-t'ai rearranged and integrated them into his Five Period and Eight Teaching classification asserting the supremacy of the *Lotus Sutra*. Highly esteeming this classification, Nichiren praised T'ien-t'ai in the highest terms for completely refuting the false doctrines of the three Southern and seven Northern masters and establishing the new classification centering on the *Lotus Sutra* for the first time in the history of Buddhism.

3,000 existences contained in one thought *(ichinen sanzen)*
The doctrine preached in the *Great Concentration and Insight* by Grand Master T'ien-t'ai maintaining that 3,000 modes of existence are contained in the mind of an ordinary person at any given moment. It is based on the teaching of the 10 aspects of all phenomena preached in the second chapter of the *Lotus Sutra*. 3,000 modes of existence, conditions under which all things exist and phenomena take place, are arrived at by multiplying 10 realms, stages of spiritual development, by 10 because each of the 10 realms is said to be equipped also with characteristics of the other nine realms. The resulting 100 realms are further multiplied by the 10 aspects of all phenomena and also by the three factors of existence: living beings, environment, and the five constituent elements of living beings. As it is proved that 3,000 modes of

existence are included in an individual's mind, it is logically possible that those who practice Buddhism known as the Two Vehicles, *śrāvaka* and *pratyekabuddha*, who have been denied attaining Buddhahood in the pre-Lotus sutras, as well as we, ordinary persons, enter the world of enlightenment attained by the Buddha. Based on the T'ien-t'ai doctrine of "3,000 existences contained in one thought," Nichiren advocated that chanting the Odaimoku of Namu Myōhō Renge-kyō is the only practical way for ordinary people in the Latter Age of Degeneration to attain Buddhahood. A related concept is "3,000 existences in 100 realms," *hyakkai sanzen*. This refers to all things in the universe expressed in terms of 10 realms, 10 reality aspects and the three categories of realm. The 100 realms are the world in which each of the 10 realms: hell, hungry spirits, animals, asura, men, heavenly beings, *śrāvaka, pratyekabuddha*, bodhisattvas, and Buddhas, contains the characteristics of the other nine realms. Each of the 100 realms contains 10 reality aspects: form, nature, substance, function, action, cause, condition, effect, reward, and ultimate non-differentiation of the above nine aspects, and each of these 1,000 reality aspects contains the three categories of realm: realms of sentient beings, non-sentient beings and the five elements of all existences. The resulting figure 3,000 refers to the whole universe. The doctrine that the 3,000 existences are contained in the thought of a person, "3,000 existences contained in one thought," is the ultimate teaching which Grand Master T'ien-t'ai expounded in the fifth fascicle of the *Great Concentration and Insight*.

Threefold body of a Buddha *(sanjin)*

A Buddha is supposed to have three bodies: (1) *hosshin*, Dharma Body, representing the ultimate truth to which He was enlightened; (2) *hōjin*, Reward Body attained by religious practices; and (3) *ōjin*, Accommodative Body, the body of a Buddha who manifests to save the unenlightened in this world. The Eternal Śākyamuni Buddha revealed in the 16th chapter of the *Lotus Sutra* is equipped with all of these three bodies.

Throughout the World *(isshiten shikai)*

Literally one set of four continents and four seas. In Buddhist cosmology a set of four continents, *shiten*, with Mt. Sumeru in the center, the sun, the moon, the King of the Brahma Heaven, Indra, Four Heavenly Kings and four oceans surrounding them constituting the world. This is also called *itten shikai*, four seas under the heaven, or *isshi tenge*, one set of four continents.

T'ien-t'ai, Grand Master *(Tendai Daishi)*

Also named Chih-i, 538–597 CE, he founded the T'ien-t'ai sect of China, which presided over most of the Buddhist orders during the dynasties of

Liang, Ch'ên and Sui in China. With the *Lotus Sutra* as his basis, T'ien-t'ai wrote *Fa-hua hsüan-i, Profound Meaning of the Lotus Sutra, Fa-hua wên-chü, Words and Phrases of the Lotus Sutra,* and *Mo-ho chih-kuan, Great Concentation and Insight,* which are known as the three major works constituting the core of his theology. Nichiren's theology was much influenced by that of T'ien-t'ai. Nichiren developed and expanded T'ien-t'ai's concept of "3,000 existences in one thought" making it applicable to the Latter Age of Degeneration. In his writings, Nichiren depended heavily on the three major works of T'ien-t'ai as well as the *Lotus* and *Nirvana Sutras.*

Tōji Temple *(Tōji)*
Located at Kujō-machi, Minamiku, Kyoto, Tōji Temple refers to Kyō'ō-Gokokuji Temple, Grand Temple of the Tōji Group within the Shingon sect. Founded in the 15th year of the Enryaku Era, 796 CE, it was given to Kūkai by Emperor Saga in the 14th year of the Kōnin Era, 823 CE, as a practice center of the Shingon school. Together with the Kongobuji Temple on Mt. Kōya in Wakayama Prefecture, it is one of the two basic centers of the Shingon sect in Japan.

Toki Jōnin *(Toki-dono; Jōnin Shōnin)*
1216–1299 CE. One of the earliest lay followers of Nichiren Shōnin. A vassal of the Chiba family, Protector of Shimofusa Province, Jōnin lived in Wakamiya in Shimofusa Province, present-day Nakayama section of Ichikawa City in Chiba Prefecture. He was highly esteemed by Nichiren Shōnin, who entrusted him with a number of important works written in classic Chinese such as *Kanjin Honzon-shō, Spiritual Contemplation and the Most Venerable One.* He understood Nichiren's doctrine and spread the words of Nichiren among Nichiren's lay followers. After the death of Nichiren, Jōnin entered the priesthood calling himself Nichijō, converted his family temple Hokke-dō, Lotus Hall, into the Hokkeji Temple, which is regarded as the origin of the present-day Nakayama Hokekyōji Temple.

Tokuitsu *(Tokuitsu)*
A priest of the Hossō sect in Nara during the Nara period. At the age of 33 or thereabout in 782 CE, he moved to the northern Kantō and northeastern Honshu areas building many temples including the E'nichiji Temple in Aizu, Fukushima Prefecture, where he died and was buried. Priest Tokuitsu was critical of Tendai doctrine and engaged in a heated dispute with Dengyō regarding the validity of One Vehicle doctrine and the Three Vehicle doctrine.

Too exquisite *(rijin gemi)*
Criticizing the Holy Way teachings such as the *Lotus* and *Nirvana Sutras*, Hōnen in his *Senjaku-shū*, Collection of Passages on the Nembutsu, says that they are too profound in doctrine for inferior people in the Latter Age to understand and too difficult to put into practice.

Transmission Chapter *(Zokurui-hon)*
22nd chapter of the *Lotus Sutra* translated by Kumārajīva. In contrast to transmitting the sutra specifically to the bodhisattvas from underground in the 21st chapter, in this chapter Śākyamuni Buddha asked all the bodhisattvas to spread it widely. Then the door of the stupa of Many-Treasures was closed and Buddhas gathered from various worlds all over the universe returned to their respective lands, ending the ceremony in the air.

Treatise on Spreading Peace Throughout the Country *(Risshō Ankoku-ron)*
One-fascicle essay written by Nichiren in 1260 CE and submitted to Hōjō Tokiyori, former shogunal regent of the Kamakura Bakufu. Motivated by successive calamities overtaking Japan for several years, Nichiren claimed that the heavenly calamities and disasters on earth resulted from the lack of the True Dharma and the spread of evil dharmas, and that unless the rulers of the land established the True Dharma, Japan soon would be troubled by domestic disturbance and foreign invasion. This prediction of Nichiren proved to be true when the Mongol envoy arrived in Japan in 1268 CE, the so-called "uprising of Hōjō Tokisuke" occurred in 1272 CE, and the first invasion of Japan by Mongols took place in 1274 CE. The essay was copied by Nichiren himself several times during his lifetime as it was the central principle underlying the religious activities of Nichiren throughout his life.

Triple Pure Land sutras *(Jōdo sambu-kyō)*
Refers to the three canons of Pure Land Buddhism: *Muryōju-kyō*, the *Sutra of the Buddha of Infinite Life*; *Kammuryōju-kyō*, the *Sutra of Meditation on the Buddhia of Infinite Life*; and *Amida-kyō*, the *Pure Land Sutra*. Each of these preaches rebirth in the Pure Land of Utmost Bliss, *gokuraku jōdo*, the land of the Buddha of Infinite Life, Amida Buddha.

Triple thousand worlds *(sanzen [daisen] sekai)*
According to Buddhist cosmology, a world consists of four continents surrounding Mt. Sumeru. A set of 1,000 of these worlds is called the small thousand-world, 1,000 of which make the middle thousand-world, 1,000 of which in turn become the great thousand-world. The great thousand-world

is called the triple thousand-world because this group includes 1,000 x 1,000 x 1,000 worlds. The term is often used in the sense of the whole world or universe.

Triple world *(sangai)*
The triple world refers to the three regions of the world of illusion: (1) the region of desires, *yoku-kai,* consisting of hell, realms of hungry spirits, beasts and birds, fighting spirits, men, and part of heaven; beings of which have sexual desire and other appetites; (2) the region of form, *shiki-kai,* consisting of part of heaven, where inhabitants have material form but no desires; and (3) region of non-form, *mushiki-kai,* consisting of part of heaven where inhabitants are free from both desires and restrictions of material existence. Unenlightened beings transmigrate between these three regions. The third chapter of the *Lotus Sutra*, A Parable, likens this world of illusion and suffering to a house on fire.

True cause and true result *(hon'in-honga)*
Causal conduct of the Eternal Buddha revealed in the *hommon,* essential section of the *Lotus Sutra* and His resulting virtue. That is to say, it means the great merit of Śākyamuni Buddha's practice since the eternal past and the great virtue He gained as the result of His great conduct.

True Word school *(Shingon-shū)*
One of the esoteric schools of Buddhism in Japan founded by Grand Master Kōbō, also named Kūkai. The Great Sun Buddha is worshipped as the Most Venerable One: *honzon.* Its basic scriptures are the *Great Sun Buddha Sutra, Diamond Peak Sutra,* and *Sutra on the Act of Perfection.* It insists on the supremacy of esotericism to exotericism and attainment of Buddhahood in one's present body. Entering China, Grand Master Kōbō received the teaching of esoteric Buddhism from Master Hui-kuo, or *Keika.* Returning to Japan in the first year of the Daidō Era, 806 CE, he propagated its teaching at the Kongōbuji Temple on Mt. Kōya and the Tōji Temple in Kyoto. Nichiren called both the esotericism of the Tōji Temple and Tendai esotericism the "Shingon sect," severely criticizing them for their insisting on the superiority of the Shingon teaching over the *Lotus Sutra* by their doctrines of the "10 stages of mind" and "superiority of esotericism to exotericism."

Tu-shun *(Tojun)*
558–640 CE. The first patriarch of the Chinese Hua-yen, *Kegon* or Flower Garland sect. He is also known as Zen Master Tu-shun or Honorable Ti-hsin. He entered the priesthood at 18 and practiced Zen under Seng-chen of the Yin-sheng-ssŭ Temple. He lived on Mt. Chung-nan, propagating Hua-yen

Buddhism. He is said to have worked miracles and was worshipped as an avatar of Bodhisattva Mañjuśrī. He died at 84 and was succeeded by his disciple Chih-yen.

Tung-ch'un *(Tōjun)*
Chih-tu (Chido) of Tung-ch'un, who wrote a commentary on the *Lotus Sutra*, He is sometimes referred to as Tung-ch'un.

Turning the body to ashes and annihilating consciousness *(keshin metchi)*
Having completely gotten rid of evil passions and attachments, one is left with physiological functions such as sickness and fatigue so long as one is alive. The state of Nirvana in which one does not have even physiological functions is referred to the Nirvana without residue, *muyo nehan*. This was conceived by Hinayana sages, *śrāvaka* and *pratyekabuddha*, as the goal to be reached by turning the body to ashes and annihilating consciousness. The Nirvana with physiological functions, *uyo nehan*, was not considered the true Nirvana even if all evil passions were eliminated.

Tuṣita Heaven *(Tōsotsu-ten)*
The fourth of the six heavens in the realm of desire, in which a future Buddha spends their last life as a bodhisattva before coming down to the Sahā World. It is believed that Śākyamuni Buddha riding on a white elephant came down from this heaven to the womb of Queen Māyā. At present Bodhisattva Maitreya dwells there until 5,670,000,000 years from now, when he will descend to earth.

Twelve kinds of scriptures *(Jūnibu-kyō)*
Scriptures divided into 12 groups according to the style of exposition such as sutras (prose), verses, allegories, and narratives of past lives.

Twenty-eight constellations *(nijūhasshuku)*
Astronomy in ancient India divides the stars into 28 groups. Fortune telling using stars and constellations spread to China and Japan, where it is still in use.

Two Heavenly Beings and Three Hermits *(niten sansen)*
The two Heavenly Beings refer to Maheśvara, *Daijizaiten,* and Viṣṇu, *Bichūten,* two of the most important deities in Brahmanism and Hinduism in India. Maheśvara is the supreme deity and Viṣṇu takes care of the whole universe. Hermits Kapila, Ulūka, and Ṛṣabha are upheld as the legendary founders of ancient Indian philosophy.

Two Vehicles *(nijō)*
Two kinds of Hinayana sages called *śrāvaka* and *pratyekabuddha* are referred to as the Two Vehicles. They are arhats who are completely rid of evil passions, but Mahayana Buddhists consider them as selfish because they are concerned with self-salvation, neglecting to help others. Most Mahayana sutras regard them as unable to attain Buddhahood, but the *Lotus Sutra* preaches the possibility of attaining Buddhahood by the Two Vehicles. Nichiren Shōnin placed great importance on the doctrine of Buddhahood by the Two Vehicles, considering it one of the two reasons for the superiority of the *Lotus Sutra* to all other sutras.

Two-fascicle Sutra *(Sōkan-gyō)*
Refers to the *Sutra of the Buddha of Infinite Life*, which consists of two fascicles.

Tz'ŭ-ên, Grand Master *(Jion Daishi)*
632–682 CE. Also known as K'uei-chi, he founded the Fa-hsing, or *Hossō* school in China. He was one of the disciples of Hsüan-chuang, or Hsüantsang, and translated Buddhist scriptures including the *Cheng-wei-shih-lun*, in Japanese *Jōyuishikiron*, and in English *Perfection of Consciousness-Only*. He also wrote commentaries such as the *Fa-hua-hsüan-lun*, in Japanese *Hokke-genron*, and in English *Treatise on the Profundity of the Lotus Sutra*, and *Fa-yüan-i-lin*, in Japanese *Hō'on-girin*, and in English *Forest of Meanings in the Garden of the Law*. Nichiren criticized him for admiring the *Lotus Sutra* superficially by insisting that the One Vehicle teaching was expedient. Nichiren also said that T'zŭ-ên subjected himself to T'ien-t'ai in mind though not outwardly.

Universal-Sage Bodhisattva *(Fugen Bosatsu)*
Right-hand attendant of Śākyamuni Buddha, representing the virtue of principle, *ri*, meditation, *jō*, and practice, *gyō*. Universal-Sage Bodhisattva leads other bodhisattvas to assist the Buddha's missionary endeavor. In Chapter 28 of the *Lotus Sutra*, he appears riding on a white elephant to protect those who practice the *Lotus Sutra*. Nichiren's Great Mandala Honzon includes the name of Fugen representing bodhisattva disciples of Lord Śākyamuni in the theoretical section of the *Lotus Sutra*.

Vajrabodhi *(Kongōchi)*
671–741 CE. Regarded as the fifth patriarch of the Shingon sect. Born in Central India as a prince, he studied esoteric Buddhism from Nāgābodhi, a disciple of Nāgārjuna, in the Nālanda Monastery. Entering China by sea in 720 CE, Vajrabodhi founded a temple in China, where Buddhist ordination ceremonies for transmitting teachings were performed. In criticizing Shingon Buddhism, Nichiren pointed out Vajrabodhi's failure in prayers for rain-making.

Vajrasattva Bodhisattva *(Kongō Satta)*
The second of the eight patriarchs of the Shingon sect, who is said to have received the esoteric teachings directly from the Great Sun Buddha, which were written down in the form of the *Great Sun Buddha Sutra* and sealed in an iron tower in southern India. It is said that this tower was opened by Nāgārjuna several centuries later, when Vajrasattva transmitted the esoteric teachings to Nāgārjuna.

Variety of Merits Chapter *(Funbetsu kudoku-hon)*
Refers to the 17th chapter of the *Lotus Sutra*. In this chapter Śākyamuni Buddha told Bodhisattva Maitreya that those who have even a single moment of faith upon listening to the eternal life of the Buddha, preached in the 16th chapter, will gain unfathomable merit. In the latter half of the chapter the Buddha elaborates the way to have faith in and practice the Lotus teaching after the death of the Buddha. These are the four stages of faith and five stages of practice.

Vasubandhu Bodhisattva *(Tenjin Bosatsu)*
A Buddhist scholar known also as *Seshin* in Japanese, he is believed to have lived around the fifth century CE in Gandhara in northern India. At first he studied Hinayana Buddhism, but was converted to Mahayana by his older brother, Asaṅga, becoming a great promoter of the Consciousness-Only school of Mahayana Buddhism. He wrote many works such as *Kusha-ron*, the *Discourse on the Repository of Abhidharma Discussion*, and *Hokke-ron*, the *Discourse on the Lotus Sutra*. Nichiren says of him that living in the Age of the True Dharma, Vasubandhu spread the provisional Mahayana teachings although he grasped the true meaning of the *Lotus Sutra* in his heart because he knew that neither the time nor the capacity of the people to understand were ripe for the True Dharma.

Vimalakīrti Sutra *(Jōmyō-kyō)*
Also known as *Yuima-kyō* in Japanese. One of the typical early Mahayana sutras. Vimalakīrti, the central figure of the sutra, was a wealthy lay believer of Buddhism. Through discussions and debates between him and the disciples of the Buddha and bodhisattvas, the sutra explains the core of the Mahayana doctrines in a beautiful literary style.

Vimalamitra *(Muku Ronji)*
Buddhist commentator of Kashmir, who is said to have fallen into the Hell of Incessant Suffering with his tongue split into five pieces as he strongly believed in Hinayana and vehemently slandered Mahayana Buddhism. Nichiren cites him as an example of slandering the True Dharma.

Vimukti-candra Bodhisattva *(Gedatsugatsu Bosatsu)*
A bodhisattva mentioned in the *Jūji-hon*, Ten Stages chapter of the *Flower Garland Sutra*. Representing the mass of people, this bodhisattva, *Gedatsugatsu*, Moon of Emancipation, requests Bodhisattva Kongōzō to preach the 10 stage doctrine. Emancipation represents the highest of the 10 stages and the moon stands for a bodhisattva practicing the 10 stage doctrine.

Virtue Consciousness, Monk *(Kakutoku Biku)*
As preached in the second chapter of the *Nirvana Sutra*, Monk *Kakutoku*, Virtue Consciousness, in a past life strove to uphold the True Dharma and was attacked by heretics. He was rescued by King *Utoku*, Virtuous, who died from a wound he sustained. Nichiren often cites this tradition of Monk Virtue Consciousness and King Virtuous who helped him, likening himself to the monk. Nichiren also uses this story to justify his own aggressiveness in propagation.

Virtuous, King *(Utoku-ō)*
The name of Śākyamuni in a previous lifetime preached in the *Kongoshin*, Unbreakable Body chapter of the *Nirvana Sutra*. He sacrificed his life in defending Monk Virtue Consciousness, *Kakutoku*, who spread the True Dharma. Nichiren Shōnin highly esteemed the king as a model of upholding the True Dharma and chastising those who slandered it.

Wheel-turning Noble King *(Tenrinjōō)*
Cakravartin in Sanskrit, and *Tenrinjōō, Tenrinnō* or *Rinnō* in Japanese. The term refers to an ideal king who rules by the True Dharma, not by force, and is believed to have the 32 physical excellences of a Buddha and seven treasures including a wheel, or *cakra*. There are four kinds of kings according to the qualities of the wheel: One with a golden wheel, *konrin-ō*, rules all the four continents of the world; one with a silver wheel, *ginrin-ō*, rules three continents; one with a copper wheel, *dōrin-ō*, rules two; and one with an iron wheel, *tetsurin-ō*, rules only one.

Wide propagation *(kōsen rufu)*
The term *kōsen rufu* comes from the 23rd chapter of the *Lotus Sutra*: "Propagate this chapter widely throughout the Jūmbudvīpa in the last 500-year period after My death." It means the widespread dissemination of the *Lotus Sutra* during the last or fifth 500-year period, which is the beginning of the Latter Age of Degeneration. Nichiren took this statement of the Buddha as proof that the *Lotus Sutra* is destined to be widely spread during the Latter Age.

Wisdom Sutra *(Hannya-kyō)*

Abbreviation of the *Hannya haramitta-kyō, Mahāprajñapāramitā-sutra*, a general term covering various sutras which claim to have the power of leading upholders to enlightenment through the power of wisdom or prājñā. There are many Chinese translations of the *Wisdom Sutra* including those by Kumārajīva and Hsüan-chuang. According to Grand Master T'ien-t'ai's classification, Nichiren Shōnin criticized the *Wisdom Sutra* as provisional, stressing the supremacy of the *Lotus Sutra* of all Buddhist scriptures.

Wish-fulfilling gem *(nyoi hōju)*

A gem which is said to have supernatural powers of fulfilling all wishes. It is likened to the virtue and teaching of the Buddha. Nichiren Shōnin likened the doctrine of "3,000 existences contained in one thought" to this wonderful gem when he said, "A wish-fulfilling gem of 3,000 existences contained in one thought."

Words and Phrases of the Lotus Sutra *(Hokke Mongu)*

Abbreviated by Nichiren as *Mongu*, this treatise was preached by Grand Master T'ien-t'ai and recorded by his disciple Chang-an in 10 fascicles. Dividing the *Lotus Sutra* into three divisions and also into two parts and six divisions, T'ien-t'ai interpreted the words and phrases of the *Lotus Sutra* through four guidelines: (1) causes and circumstantial causes; (2) four doctrinal teachings; (3) essential and theoretical teachings; and (4) introspection into mind. While transmitting the interpretations of the *Lotus Sutra* expounded in this thesis, Nichiren preached his own understanding of the *Lotus Sutra* through his own experiences. It must be mentioned here also that Nichiren regarded the essential teaching the first, while T'ien-t'ai laid stress on the theoretical teaching.

Yaśodharā *(Yashutara Bikuni)*

Wife of Śākyamuni before He left home to be a monk seeking the way. She had a son, Rāhula, by Him. It is predicted in the 13th chapter of the *Lotus Sutra* that she will be a Buddha called *Gusoku Semman Kōsō Nyorai*, Emitting Ten Million Rays Buddha.

Yōkan *(Yōkan)*

1032–1111 CE. Also called *Eikan*, he was a minister of the *Sanron*, or Three Treatises sect in the last years of the Heian Period. He was ordained at the age of 11 and began his studies of Sanron. He also studied with other sects such as *Kegon*, Flower Garland, and *Hossō*. He practiced nembutsu and devoted himself to the spread of the Pure Land teaching by writing the *Ōjō-jūin* and

Ōjō-kōshiki, etc. Nichiren Shōnin recognized him, along with Genshin and Hōnen, as an important figure in the history of Pure Land Buddhism and criticized him severely.

Young Ascetic in the Snow Mountains *(Sessen Dōji)*
The name of Śākyamuni Buddha in a previous life expounded in the *Shōgyō* or Holy Practice chapter of the *Nirvana Sutra*. When Śākyamuni Buddha was practicing austerities in the Snow Mountains in pursuit of enlightenment, a hungry demon appeared reciting half of a verse from a Buddhist teaching: "All things and phenomena are changeable, this is the law of life and death." The Young Ascetic begged the demon to tell him the second half, and was told that the demon was too hungry to tell. Promising his own flesh and blood, Young Ascetic was able to hear the last half of the verse: "Extinguishing the cycle of birth and death, one enters the joy of nirvana." Following the example of Young Ascetic's willingness to give his life to the True Dharma, Nichiren Shōnin risked his life for the spread of the *Lotus Sutra*.

Zen school *(Zen-shū)*
School of Buddhism which claims to attain Buddhahood by way of sitting meditation, *zazen*. In Japan the term generally refers to three schools of Zen: Rinzai, Sōtō and Ōbaku. They maintain that the True Dharma is transmitted directly from a master to disciples without writing or preaching. Therefore, it can be attained not through studies of doctrines but by meditation. Nichiren Shōnin criticized them saying that abandoning all Buddhist scriptures is an act of heavenly devils.

Japanese Equivalents

Japanese Entry	English Entry
abigoku	Avīci Hell
Agon-gyō	Āgama sutras
Ajase-ō	Ajātaśatru, King
aku-chishiki	Evil friend
Amida-butsu	Infinite Life, Buddha of
Amida-kyō	Pure Land Sutra
Anan	Ānanda
Anrakugyō-hon	Peaceful Practices chapter
bombu	Ordinary man
bompu	Ordinary man
Bonten	Brahma Heaven
Bonten-nō	King of the Brahma Heaven
bosatsu	Bodhisattva
busshō	Buddha-nature
Chigon	Chih-yen
Chishō Daishi	Chishō, Grand Master
Chōkan	Ch'êng-kuan
Daibadatta	Devadatta
Daiba[datta]-hon	Devadatta chapter
Daibonten	Mahābrahman Heaven
Daichido-ron	Great Wisdom Discourse
Daijik-kyō or Daishū-kyō	Sutra of the Great Assembly
daijō-shojō	Mahayana-Hinayana
Dainichi	Dainichi
Dainichi Nyorai	Great Sun Buddha
Dainichi-kyō	Great Sun Buddha Sutra
Daisan no hōmon	Third doctrine
Daitsūchi-shō-butsu	Great Universal Wisdom Buddha
Dengyō Daishi	Dengyō, Grand Master
Dōami	Dōami
Dōamidabutsu	Dōamidabutsu

Japanese Equivalents 367

Donran	T'an-luan
Dōryū	Tao-lung
Dōrō	Tao-lang
Dōsen	Tao-hsüan
Dōsen	Tao-hsien
Dōshaku	Tao-ch'o
Dōzui	Tao-sui
ehō fu-enin	Depend on the dharma, not on people
Eizan	Mt. Hiei
Embudai	Jambudvīpa
Eon	Hui-yüan
Eshin Sōzu	Eshin, Venerable
Eshin-ryū, Danna-ryū	Eshin and Danna factions
Fuchū	Additional Annotations to Three Major Works of T'ien-t'ai
Fugen Bosatsu	Universal-Sage Bodhisattva
Fuhōzō-kyō	Sutra of Transmission of the Buddhist Teaching
Fukū	Pu-k'ung, Tripiṭaka Master, Amoghavajra
Fukyō Bosatsu	Never Despising Bodhisattva
Fukyō-hon	Never-Despising Bodhisattva chapter
Funbetsu kudoku-hon	Variety of Merits chapter
funjin	Buddhas in manifestation
Furuna	Pūrṇa
gamoku	Eyelet coins
gampon no mumyō	Fundamental darkness of mind
Ganjin	Chien-chên
Gedatsugatsu Bosatsu	Vimukti-candra, Bodhisattva
gedō	Non-Buddhist teaching
Gejimmitsu-kyō	Revealing the Profound and Secret Sutra
Genjō Sanzō	Hsüan-chuang, Tripiṭaka Master
geten	Non-Buddhist scriptures
Giba	Jīvaka
Gijō-bō	Gijō-bō
Gishin	Gishin
go-gohyakusai	Last (fifth) 500-year period
gogyaku	Five rebellious sins
gohyaku jinden-gō	500 (million) dust-particle kalpa
goji	Five periods
gojoku	Five defilements

gojū-gen	Five Profound Meanings
goka no hōshō	Five Holy Proclamations
gokyō	Five Teachings
gomi	Five Flavors
gongyō	Provisional teachings
gonjitsu	Provisional and true teachings
goshō kakubetsu	Five mutually distinctive natures
gotei	Five Rulers
go'on	Five aggregates of all existences
Gyōman	Hsing-man
Hachiman Daibosatsu	Hachiman, Great Bodhisattva
Hannya-kyō	Wisdom Sutra
Hatsunaion-gyō	Six-fascicled Nirvana Sutra
Hei no Saemonnojō	Hei no Saemonnojō
Hō-metsujin-kyō	Sutra on the Decline of the Dharma
Hōben-pon	Expedients chapter
hōbō	Slandering the True Dharma
Hōdō-bu	Hōdō period
Hōdō-kyō	Hōdō sutras
hōjin	Reward Body
Hokke Gengi	Profound Meaning of the Lotus Sutra
Hokke Gengi Shakusen	Commentary on the Profound Meaning of the Lotus Sutra
Hokke-kyō	Lotus Sutra
Hokke-kyō no gyōja	One who practices the Lotus Sutra
Hokke Mongu	Words and Phrases of the Lotus Sutra
Hokke Mongu-ki	Annotations on the Words and Phrases of the Lotus Sutra
Hokke Shūku	Outstanding Principles of the Lotus Sutra
hommon	Essential section
Hōnen Shōnin	Hōnen Shōnin
hon'in-honga	True cause and true result
honzon	Most Venerable One
hosshaku kempon	Outgrowing the provisional and revealing the essential
Hosshi-hon	Teacher of the Dharma chapter
hosshin	Dharma Body
Hossō-shū	Hossō sect
Hōtō-hon	Beholding the Stupa of Treasures chapter
Hōzō	Fa-ts'ang

hyakkai sen'nyo	One hundred realms and 1,000 aspects
i-kon-tō	Sutras which have been preached, are being preached, and will be preached
ichidai shōgyō	All the holy teachings of the Buddha's lifetime
ichidaiji innen	One great purpose
Ichigyō	I-hsing
ichijō-kyō	One Vehicle teaching
ichinen sanzen	Three thousand existences contained in one thought
in-shingon	Finger signs and mantras
ippon nihan	One chapter and two half-chapters
Issaikyō	All the scriptures of Buddhism
issendai	Icchantika
isshiten shikai	Throughout the World
Jakumetsu Dōjō	Hall of Enlightenment
jikai hongyaku-nan	Domestic Disturbance
Jikaku Daishi	Jikaku, Grand Master
jikkai gogu	Mutual possession of 10 realms
Jinriki-hon	Divine Powers of the Buddha chapter
Jion Daishi	Tz'ŭ-ên, Grand Master
jippō no shobutsu	Buddhas in 10 directions
jiyu no bosatsu	Bodhisattvas appearing from underground
jo, shō, rutsū	Preface, main discourse and transmission
Jōdo sambu-kyō	Triple Pure Land sutras
Jōdo-shū	Pure Land school
Jōgyō Bosatsu	Superior-Practice, Bodhisattva
Johon	Introductory chapter
Jōjitsu-shū	Jōjitsu sect
Jōkyū no kassen	Jōkyū Incident
Jōmyō-kyō	Vimalakīrti Sutra
Jōnin Shōnin	Toki Jōnin
jūnyoze	Ten aspects
jūrasetsu [nyo]	Ten female rākṣasa demons
jurui-shu, sōtai-shu	Jurui seed and sōtai seed
Juryō-hon	Life Span of the Buddha chapter
kaidan	Precept platform
kaiji gonyū	Open, show, perceive and enter

kaisan ken'itsu	Revealing the single path replacing the three teachings
Kakutoku Biku	Virtue Consciousness, Monk
Kan Fugen Bosatsu Gyōbō-kyō	Sutra of Meditation on Universal-Sage Bodhisattva
Kan-muryōju-kyō, Kangyō	Sutra of Meditation on the Buddha of Infinite Life
kangyō	Admonition
Kanji-hon	Encouragement for Upholding This Sutra chapter
kanjin	Spiritual contemplation
kanki	Disgrace with the shogunate
Kannon Bosatsu	Avalokiteśvara Bodhisattva
Kannon-gen	Profound Meaning of the Bodhisattva Avalokiteśvara chapter
Kasennen	Kātyāyana
Kashō	Kāśyapa
Kegon-kyō	Flower Garland Sutra
Kegon-shū	Flower Garland school
Kejōyu-hon	A Parable of a Magic City chapter
kempon	Revelation of eternal life of the Buddha
kengyō-mikkyō	Exoteric and esoteric teachings
kenji no waku	Delusions of views and thoughts
Kenkai-ron	Clarification of the Precepts
keshin metchi	Turning the body to ashes and annihilating consciousness
ketsujō-shō	Fixed nature
kibetsu or ki	Guarantee of the Buddha
Kichizō	Chi-ts'ang
kikon	Capacity of people to understand
Kōbō Daishi	Kōbō, Grand Master
kōchō-zetsu or chōzetsu	Long, wide tongue
Kongō Satta	Vajrasattva Bodhisattva
Kongōbei-ron	Diamond Scalpel
Kongōchi	Vajrabodhi
Kongōchō-kyō	Diamond Peak Sutra
Konkōmyō-kyō	Sutra of the Golden Splendor
kōsen rufu	Wide propagation
Kumarajū	Kumārajīva, Tripiṭaka Master
kuō no dainan	Nine great difficulties

kuon jitsujō	Attaining Enlightenment in the eternal past
Kusha-shū	Kusha sect
kyōge betsuden	Special transmission without scriptures or preaching
kyōsō	Comparative study of Buddhist doctrines
Maka Shikan	Great Concentration and Insight
Maka Shikan Fugyō-den Guketsu	Annotation on the Great Concentration and Insight
Makahajahadai Bikuni	Mahā Prajāpatī
mappō	Latter Age of Degeneration
mirai-ki	Prediction
Miroku Bosatsu	Maitreya, Bodhisattva
Mitsugon-gyō	Sutra of Mystic Glorification
Mokuren	Maudgalyāyana
Monjushiri Bosatsu	Mañjuśrī Bodhisattva
mugen jigoku	Hell of Incessant Suffering
Mujaku Bosatsu	Asaṅga Bodhisattva
Muku Ronji	Vimalamitra
Muryōgi-kyō	Sutra of Infinite Meaning
mushō	Those without Buddha-nature
myōji, kangyō	Notional understanding, perception and practicing
Myōraku Daishi	Miao-lê, Grand Master
Myōshōgon-ō-hon	King Wonderful-Adornment chapter
Nambu Rokurō	Nambu Rokurō
Namu Myōhō Renge-kyō	Namu Myōhō Renge-kyō
Nangaku Daishi	Nan-yüeh, Grand Master
Nansan Hokushichi	Three Southern and seven Northern masters
Nanto	Southern Capital
nehan	Nirvana
Nehan-gyō	Nirvana Sutra
Nehangyō-sho	Annotations on the Nirvana Sutra
Nen'a Ryōchū	Nen'a Ryōchū
nijō	Two Vehicles
nijō sabutsu	Obtaining Buddhahood by Two Vehicles
nijūhasshuku	Twenty-eight constellations
Ninki-hon	Assurance of Future Buddhahood chapter
Ninnō-kyō	Sutra of the Benevolent King

ninshi	Teachers in China and Japan
nisho san'e	Three meetings at two places
niten sansen	Two Heavenly Beings and Three Hermits
nizen	Pre-Lotus period
nyoi hōju	Wish-fulfilling gem
nyonin jōbutsu	Attainment of Buddhahood by Women
Odaimoku	Odaimoku
ōjin	Accommodative Body
Onjōji	Onjōji Temple
Ōta Jōmyō	Ōta Jōmyō
Ragora	Rāhula
ridō jishō	Equal in Doctrine but Superior in Ritualism
rijin gemi	Too exquisite
Risshō Ankoku-ron	Treatise on Spreading Peace Throughout the Country
Risshū	Precept sect
Ritsu-shū	Ritsu sect
rokujinzū	Six superhuman powers
rokunan kui	Six difficulties and nine easier actions
rokushi gedō	Six non-Buddhist masters
rokutsū	Six superhuman powers
ronji	Commentator
rutsū	Epilogue
ryakkō shugyō	Roundabout way to Buddhahood
Ryōga-kyō	Entering Lanka Sutra
Ryōjusen	Sacred Eagle, Mt.
Ryōkan	Ryōkan
Ryūju Bosatsu	Nagarjuna, Bodhisattva
Saimyōji Nyūdō	Saimyōji, Lay Priest
san'aku-dō	Three evil realms
sandai hihō	Three Great Secret Dharmas
sandai seigan	Three Great Vows of Nichiren
sanga no chokusen	Three Pronouncements
sangai	Triple world
sangoku shishi	Four masters in three lands
sangyaku-zai	Three Rebellious Sins
sanji-kyō	Three-period teaching
sanjin	Threefold body of a Buddha
sankō	Three Emperors

Japanese Equivalents

sanne ippatsu	Three robes and one alms-bowl
sannō	Three Kings
Sanron-shū	Three Discourse school
sanrui no tekinin	Three kinds of enemies
sansai shichinan	Three calamities and seven disasters
sanshō shima	Three hindrances and four devils
santoku	Three merits
sanwaku	Three delusions
sanze	Lives in the past, present and future
sanzen [daisen] sekai	Triple thousand worlds
Seishi Bosatsu	Mahāsthāmaprāpta Bodhisattva
senchū muitsu	Not even one out of 1,000
Senjaku-shū	Collection of Passages on the Nembutsu and the Original Vow
Sessen Dōji	Young Ascetic in the Snow Mountains
sha, hei, kaku, hō	Abandon, close, set aside and cast away
shaba sekai	Sahā World
shakke	Disciples of Buddhas in manifestation
shakumon	Theoretical section
Shakuson	Śākyamuni Buddha
Sharihotsu	Śāriputra
shichinan	Seven disasters
shie	Four Reliances
shigu seigan	Four Great Vows
Shijō Saburōzaemonnojō	Shijō Kingo
shijū yonen	Forty years or so
shikyō	Four teachings
Shingon-shū	True Word school
shishu zammai	Four ways of meditation
shishōtai	Four Noble Truths
shitai	Four Noble Truths
Shiten-nō	Four Heavenly Kings
shō-zō-matsu	Ages of the True, Semblance and Latter Dharmas
Shōan Daishi	Chang-an, Grand Master
shōju-shakubuku	Persuasive and aggressive means of propagation
shōjō	Hinayana
Shōjō hōgyō-kyō	Practicing the Pure Dharma Sutra
Shōka no dai-jishin	Great earthquake of the Shōka Era

Shōman-gyō	Śrīmalā Sutra
shōmon to engaku	Śrāvaka and pratyekabuddha
shōshū-bun	Main discourse
Shōtoku Taishi	Prince Shōtoku
shu, shi, shin	Ruler, teacher, and parents
Shubodai	Subhūti
Shugo-kyō	Guardian Sutra
shugo no zenjin	Guardian deities
Shumisen	Sumeru, Mt.
Shuryōgon-kyō	Heroic Valor Sutra
Shuryōgon zammai-kyō	Heroic Valor Sutra
sōdaimyō-zetsudaimyō	Relative and absolute subtleties
sōjō no tsuchi	A bit of soil on a fingernail
Sōkan-gyō	Two-fascicle Sutra
sokushin jōbutsu	Becoming a Buddha with one's present body
Soshitsuji-kyō	Sutra on the Act of Perfection
Soya Kyōshin	Soya Kyōshin
Tahō-butsu	Many Treasures, the Buddha of
Taishaku or Shakudaikannin	Indra
tem-bōrin	Preaching of the Buddha
tempen chiyō	Strange phenomena in the sky, natural calamities on earth
Tendai Daishi	T'ien-t'ai, Grand Master
Tendai-shū	Tendai sect
Tenjin Bosatsu	Vasubandhu, Bodhisattva
Tenrinjōō	Wheel-turning Noble King
Tenshō Daijin	Goddess Amaterasu
Tōji	Tōji Temple
Tojun	Tu-shun
Tōjun	Tung-ch'un
toki	Right time
Toki-dono	Toki Jōnin
Tokuitsu	Tokuitsu
Tōsotsu-ten	Tuṣita Heaven
Utoku-ō	Virtuous, King
Yakuō-bon	Previous Life of Medicine-King Bodhisattva chapter
Yakuō Bosatsu	Medicine-King Bodhisattva
Yakushi-kyō	Medicine Master Sutra

Japanese Equivalents

Yakushi Nyorai	Medicine Master Buddha
Yashutara Bikuni	Yaśodharā
Yōkan	Yōkan
Yōraku-kyō	Bodhisattva Necklace Sutra
Yūjutsu-hon	Appearance of Bodhisattvas from Underground chapter
Zemmui Sanzō	Śubhākarasiṃha, Tripitaka Master
zen-chishiki	Good friend
Zen-shū	Zen school
Zendō Oshō	Shan-tao, Venerable
Zenshō Biku	Sunakṣatra
zōbō	Semblance Dharma, the Age of
Zokurui-hon	Transmission chapter
zuijii	Preaching according to own mind
zuitai	Preaching according to the mind of others